English G

access 3

Lehrerfassung

Vokabeltrainer-App

Verfügbar für: iOS, Android und Windows Phone

Dieses Buch gibt es auch auf
www.scook.de Es kann dort nach Bestätigung der Allgemeinen Geschäftsbedingungen genutzt werden.

Buchcode: **q4e2v-vm79o**

English G Access · Band 3
Lehrerfassung

Im Auftrag des Verlages herausgegeben von
Jörg Rademacher, Mannheim

Erarbeitet von
Laurence Harger, Wellington, Neuseeland
Cecile Niemitz-Rossant, Berlin

unter Mitarbeit von
Dr. Annette Leithner-Brauns, Dresden; Birgit Ohmsieder, Berlin; Mervyn Whittaker, Bad Dürkheim

in Zusammenarbeit mit der Englischredaktion
Dr. Philip Devlin (koordinierender Redakteur), Bonnie Glänzer (Lehrerfassung), Gareth Evans, Stefan Höhne, Dr. Christiane Kallenbach (Projektleitung), Uwe Tröger *und beratend* Filiz Bahsi, Christiane Bonk, Gwendolyn Düwel, Solveig Heinrich, Renata Jakovac *und* Lothar Teworte (digitales Schülerbuch)

Beratende Mitwirkung
Peter Brünker, Bad Kreuznach; Anette Fritsch, Dillenburg; Uli Imig, Wildeshausen; Thomas Neidhardt, Bielefeld; Wolfgang Neudecker, Mannheim; Dr. Andreas Sedlatschek, Esslingen; Sieglinde Spranger, Chemnitz; Marcel Sprunkel, Köln; Sabine Tudan, St. Georg; Friederike von Bremen, Hannover; Harald Weißling, Mannheim

Illustrationen
Tobias Dahmen, Utrecht/NL; Burkhard Schulz, Düsseldorf *sowie* Stefan Bachmann, Wiesbaden, Christian Bartz, Berlin und Roland Beier, Berlin

Fotos
Nigel Wilson Photography, Bristol

Umschlaggestaltung und Layoutkonzept
kleiner & bold, Berlin; hawemannundmosch, Berlin; klein & halm, Berlin

Layout und technische Umsetzung
Eric Gira, zweiband.media, Berlin

Soweit in diesem Buch Personen fotografisch abgebildet sind und ihnen von der Redaktion fiktive Namen, Berufe, Dialoge und Ähnliches zugeordnet oder diese Personen in bestimmte Kontexte gesetzt werden, dienen diese Zuordnungen und Darstellungen ausschließlich der Veranschaulichung und dem besseren Verständnis des Buchinhaltes.

Legende zur Lehrerfassung

1 ⊙ 12	CD- und Tracknummern
school	Lernwortschatz (produktiv)
°spy	Situativer Wortschatz (nicht produktiv)
Box "when", Voc, S. 197	Verweis auf Wortschatzbox im *Vocabulary*
+(to) groan	Hinweis auf zusätzl. Wortschatz im *Vocabulary*
were used by them	Grammatische Strukturen
YT	Übungen, die zur Lernaufgabe hinführen
KV 1 · FöFo 1.1 · …	Verweise auf Begleitmedien
[kaɪəˈdiːð]	Aussprachehinweis
Lernfeld: Die S …	Hinweis auf Lernfelder, die abgedeckt werden
Alternative: …	Didaktische Hinweise, Alternativen oder Zusätze
learned · sat	Lösungen (geschlossene Aufgaben)

www.cornelsen.de

Die Internetadressen und -dateien, die in diesem Lehrwerk angegeben sind, wurden vor Drucklegung geprüft. Der Verlag übernimmt keine Gewähr für die Aktualität und den Inhalt dieser Adressen und Dateien oder solcher, die mit ihnen verlinkt sind.

Dieses Werk berücksichtigt die Regeln der reformierten Rechtschreibung und Zeichensetzung.

1. Auflage, 1. Druck 2015

Alle Drucke dieser Auflage sind inhaltlich unverändert und können im Unterricht nebeneinander verwendet werden.

© 2015 Cornelsen Schulverlag GmbH, Berlin

Das Werk und seine Teile sind urheberrechtlich geschützt. Jede Nutzung in anderen als den gesetzlich zugelassenen Fällen bedarf der vorherigen schriftlichen Einwilligung des Verlages.

Hinweis zu den §§ 46, 52 a UrhG: Weder das Werk noch seine Teile dürfen ohne eine solche Einwilligung eingescannt und in ein Netzwerk eingestellt werden. Dies gilt auch für Intranets von Schulen und sonstigen Bildungseinrichtungen.

Druck: Mohn Media Mohndruck, Gütersloh

ISBN 978-3-06-033072-0

PEFC zertifiziert
Dieses Produkt stammt aus nachhaltig bewirtschafteten Wäldern und kontrollierten Quellen.
www.pefc.de

English G Access 3 enthält folgende Teile:

Units	die fünf Kapitel des Buches
Text File (TF)	eine Sammlung englischer Gedichte, Geschichten und Sachtexte
Skills File (SF)	eine Beschreibung wichtiger Lern- und Arbeitstechniken
Grammar File (GF)	eine Zusammenfassung der Grammatik jeder Unit
Vocabulary	das Wörterverzeichnis zum Lernen der neuen Wörter jeder Unit
Dictionary	alphabetisches Wörterverzeichnis zum Nachschlagen (Englisch-Deutsch und Deutsch-Englisch)

In den Units findest du diese Überschriften:

Background file	Informationen über Land und Leute
Looking at language	Beispiele sammeln und sprachliche Regeln entdecken
Language help	Hilfe in Form von sprachlichen Regeln
Practice	Aufgaben und Übungen
Writing course	englische Texte besser schreiben
The world behind the picture	vom Bild in den Film – Videoclips mit Aufgaben
Text	eine spannende Geschichte oder ein informativer Text

Du findest auch diese Symbole:

Symbol	Beschreibung
🔊	Texte, die du dir anhören kannst: www.englishg.de/access
www	zusätzliche Materalien, die du unter www.englishg.de/access finden kannst
🌐	Landeskundliche Informationen zu Großbritannien und Irland
🚩	deinen Alltag mit der Alltagskultur anderer Länder vergleichen
■■□□□	Übungssequenz: neue Grammatik intensiv üben und dann anwenden
Early finisher	zusätzliche Aktivitäten und Übungen für Schüler/innen, die früher fertig sind
More help	zusätzliche Hilfen für eine Aufgabe
You choose	eine Aufgabe auswählen
EXTRA	zusätzliche Aktivitäten und Übungen für alle
My Book	schöne und wichtige Arbeiten sammeln
Study skills	Einführung in Lern- und Arbeitstechniken
Your task	Was du in einer Unit gelernt hast, kannst du in einer Lernaufgabe zeigen.
🎧 💬 📖 ✏️ ▶️	Hören Sprechen Lesen Schreiben Hör-Seh-Verstehen
🇬🇧	Mediation (zwischen zwei Sprachen vermitteln)
👥 👥 👥 🧩	Partnerarbeit Partnercheck Gruppenarbeit Kooperative Lernform

Inhalt

	You learn about …	Your task (Lernaufgabe)	Texts
Unit 1 This is London	• Sending messages and holiday postcards • Talking about sights • Making plans • Reading a street map • Reading a tube map *Mo's London films* *Find out about cricket (p. 11)*	 Mo	A Up on the roof B London attractions C Watching the cricket **Background file** London for free (p. 23) **Text** The Notting Hill Carnival Parade (p. 24)

 Kaleidoscope · The British Isles

Unit 2 Welcome to Snowdonia	• Town and country • Moving house • Planning a trip • Volunteer work • Sports *Find out more about Cardiff's attractions (p. 33)*	Imagine you're moving to Wales. Write about how your life would change. (p. 43) Emily	A Everything is wrong B Climbing Mount Snowdon **Background file** Wales (p. 33) Viewing: Facts about Wales (p. 33) **Text** Snowdonia at night (p. 40)
Unit 3 A weekend in Liverpool	• Visiting a museum • Talking about famous people • Talking about buildings and their history • Football in a stadium • Football on the radio • Sport *Find out more about Liverpool (p. 44)*	Write about the person behind the name of a street or building near your home. (p. 60)	A Morgan's plan B At the Slavery Museum C At Anfield Road **Background file** The Beatles (p. 50) **Song** You'll never walk alone (p. 57) **Text** A Liverpool hero (p. 60)

Inhalt

Skills	Language		
Writing course Good sentences (p. 16) **Study skills** Giving feedback (p. 17) **MyBook** Final draft of a text (p. 17) **Viewing** A bus tour of London Making the film: Time (p. 22) **Access to cultures** Small talk (p. 13)	**Vocabulary** holidays, German *gehen* **Grammar** simple past / present perfect (Revision); present perfect progressive with for and since **Pronunciation** different stress in German and English words (p. 13)	**8** Part A 10 Part B 14 Part C 20	Skill in focus: Speaking
		26	
Study skills Using an English-German dictionary (p. 32) **Access to cultures** Similar words (p. 35) **Writing course** Paragraphs and topic sentences (p. 38) **MyBook** A text about a city or the countryside or text about a film (p. 38) **Viewing** Adam's video blog Making a video (p. 39)	**Vocabulary** jobs **Grammar** will-future (Revision); conditional 1 (Revision); conditional 2	**28** Part A 30 Part B 34	Skill in focus: Reading
	Dylan		
MyBook An info box about a Beatles song (p. 50) **Writing course** Structuring a text (p. 51) **Study skills** Ordering and structuring topic vocabulary (p. 58) **Viewing** *There's only one Jimmy Grimble* – feature film The language of film (p. 59) **Access to cultures** Free national museums (p. 53)	**Vocabulary** describing actions, sport **Grammar** relative pronouns, relative clauses (Revision); contact clauses; the passive	**44** Part A 46 Part B 52 Part C 56	Skill in focus: Listening
	Gwen, Morgan, Gareth		

Inhalt

	You learn about …	Your task (Lernaufgabe)	Texts
Unit 4 My trip to Ireland 	• Legends • Natural wonders • Discovering a country's history • Crossing borders • Life on a farm *Find out more about …* • *the Giant's Causeway (p. 66)* • *Irish history (p. 67)*	In a team, make a brochure with practical tips for Irish students who want to visit Germany. (p. 80) Lewis	A Belfast and the northern coast B Lewis's travel posts C Arrival in the Burren Background file Moments in Irish history (p. 67) Text The horse ride (p. 78)
Unit 5 Extraordinary Scotland 	• Festivals • A scientific project • Helping friends in trouble *Find out more about Scottish traditions (p. 86)*	Interview someone with an unusual hobby. Make a poster with the interview and present it to the class. (p. 97)	A Extraordinary west coast B Star performers Background file This is Scotland (p. 86) Text Missing (p. 94)

Text File	Text 1 Underground etiquette Cautionary verse	Text 2 London shapes Poems	Text 3 Jerry Excerpt from novel	Text 4 A Liverpool street Song

116 More help	136 Sports words	172 Vocabulary
126 Early finisher	138 Skills File	198 Dictionary English – German
134 Partner pages	154 Grammar File	221 Dictionary German – English

> Die hier und auf den Folgeseiten aufgeführten Angebote sind nicht obligatorisch abzuarbeiten. Die Auswahl der Übungen und Übungsteile richtet sich nach den Schwerpunkten des schulinternen Curriculums.

Inhalt

Skills	**Language**	
Study skills Teamwork (p. 69) **Writing course** Using time markers in a story (p. 77) **MyBook** A story **Viewing** Yu Ming is ainm dom Making the film: Feelings (p. 73) **Access to cultures** The Irish language (p. 73) Accents (p. 75)	**Vocabulary** countries, travelling **Grammar** modals (Revision); modal substitutes; simple past (Revision); past perfect **Pronunciation** consonants	**64** Part A 66 Part B 70 Part C 74 *Skill in focus: Writing*
Viewing Escape to … Scotland Making the film: Split screen and music (p. 87) **Study skills** A good presentation (p. 92) **MyBook** **Writing course** The elements of writing (p. 93) **Access to cultures** Sheepdog trials (p. 96)	**Vocabulary** music and entertainment **Grammar** reflexive pronouns / each other; indirect speech	**82** Part A 84 Part B 90 *Skill in focus: Mediation*

Lauren

Text 5	**Text 6**	**Text 7**	**Text 8**	**98**
Juggling with Gerbils	*Finn McCool*	*The Titanic*	*The Off-side Trap*	
Poems	Irish legend	Non-fictional text	Play	

243 List of names	248 True and false friends	253 Instructions
244 Countries & continents	250 Early finisher – answers	254 Quellenverzeichnis
246 Irregular verbs	252 Classroom English	256 How to give feedback

1 Unit

Leistungsmessung Unit 1

This is London

Lernfeld S. 8–9: Die S können Orte, Dinge und Menschen in **London** in Bildern und Hörtexten wiedererkennen, sich dazu Notizen machen, diese benennen oder in einen Bericht über London einbeziehen.

Text File: zu Unit 1 passen **Text 1** und **2**.

London
8 million people
611 square miles
300 languages
Europe's biggest street festival
…

1 London pictures

Think: Do you recognize any of the places, people, signs … in the pictures?
Make notes on what you know. *Lösung: siehe Bilder*

Pair: Exchange information with a partner.
- I think that's …
- Do you know what that is?
- That must/could be … What do you think?

If you still have questions about any pictures, write them down.

Share: Join another pair and try to find answers to your open questions.

2 London sounds

Listen to these sounds of London.
Match as many as you can to the pictures.
1 N · 2 D · 3 F · 4 R · 5 C · 6 L · 7 G · 8 A ·
9 E · 10 M · 11 H · 12 R · 13 I · 14 J

F — The Shard
River Thames

I — Hyde Park

J — Notting Hill Carn…

3 London and you

Do you know London?
Yes? When were you there? What did you do?

- I went to London in …
- We visited … and I saw …
- The best thing about my trip was …

No? Tell your group what you would like to see and do there.

- I'd really like to see …
- I've always wanted to see …
- One thing that I'd really like to do is …

➡ **Workbook** 1 (p. 8)

Part A

> **Lernfeld S. 10:** Die S können sagen, worum es in einem Text über die Lehrwerksfiguren geht. Sie weisen das Leseverständnis nach, indem sie Rätselfragen zu den Figuren beantworten und entwerfen.

1 Up on the roof

The Shard

Emily Mo Luke

"Here we are," Mo said to his friend Luke and pointed to a huge glass building.
"You want to take photos of One New Change?" Luke asked. "But why? It's just a shopping centre."
5 "Oh – have you been here before?" Mo asked.
"Yeah, I came with Dad a few months ago. We bought Mum's birthday present here."
"So, have you been up on the roof too?"
"The roof? No. Why?"
10 "Well, you'll see. That's where I want to take some photos."

❖

"Just one more photo, Luke," Mo said. "As soon as these people move out of the way."
There were lots of tourists on the roof. Mo and
15 Luke could hear all the different languages.
"St Paul's Cathedral ist mehr als 350 Jahre alt," a man said.
"Hey, that's German!" Mo said to Luke.
"Buckingham Palace'ı görebiliyor musun?"
20 "And what language is that, Mo?" asked Luke.
Mo didn't know.
"Beth ydi enw yr adeilad yna?" said a woman, and pointed to the °Shard. [beθ ˈʌdi ˈenuː ɪə əˈdeɪlæd ˈʌnə]
"Please don't speak Welsh, Mum," a girl replied.
25 "You have to practise your Welsh for your new school, Emily. I'm only trying to help."
The girl was quiet. A man looked up from a map.
"The building is called the Shard, Emily. It's the tallest building in Europe."
30 "No, it isn't!" Mo whispered. Then he couldn't stay quiet. "Excuse me. The Shard is only the tallest building in western Europe. There are two taller buildings in Moscow."
"Oh, I see," said the man, and smiled at Mo.
35 "But," Mo went on, "the Shard is 306 metres high.
It has 87 floors, 44 lifts, and amazing views from the top."
"Oh, have you been up there?" the man asked. Mo shook his head. "It's much too expensive."
40 "So how do you know all about it?" Emily asked.
"I put a post about it on my blog last weekend," Mo explained. For a moment nobody said anything. Then Luke asked:
"Are you here on holiday?"
45 "Yes, we are," said the man. "But we only arrived yesterday evening, so we haven't seen much yet."
"But we have a lot of plans," the woman said.
"Mum wants to visit lots of museums," Emily said.
"But I'd really like to do something different."
50 "Well," said Luke. "Notting Hill Carnival is this weekend."
"And the England–Australia test match!" Mo went on.
"I'm not into cricket," Emily replied, "but the
55 carnival sounds fun."
"Yes, it is," said Mo. "Well, I hope you enjoy your holiday. And now I must take my photo."
"Er … wait a minute," said Emily. "Your blog – could you give me the address?"
60 "Sure," said Mo. "Just give me your number and I'll text you. Oh … and I'm Mo, by the way. And this is my friend Luke."

2 Who is this?

> **b/c) Alternative:** Durchführung als Ratespiel mit **KV 2: Appointment partners.** Die S verfassen Sätze, treffen sich mit Partnern und erraten abwechselnd die gesuchte Person.

a) 👥 Take turns to say who the people are.
This person …
1 has been to *One New Change* before.
2 wants to take photos.
3 can understand German.
4 says something in Welsh.

1 Luke • 2 Mo • 3 Mo • 4 Emily's mum

b) Write four more sentences like the ones in a).

c) 👥 Read your sentences to your partner.

This person doesn't want to speak Welsh.

I think that's …

➔ **Workbook** 2 *(p. 9)*

FöFo 1.1 Part A **1**

> **Lernfeld S. 11:** Die S können einfache Sachtexte mit Hilfe von Bildern und Grafiken im Großen und Ganzen verstehen *(skimming)*. Sie können einfachen Hörtexten über vertraute Themen konkrete Informationen entnehmen und dazu *true-false-statements* beantworten.

3 Mo's blog

Say what this page on Mo's blog is about. Which photo did he take at One New Change, and why? Which other pages on Mo's blog would you like to read? What information might you find there?

Zusatz: Die S überlegen sich einen Entwurf für einen eigenen Blog (Inhalt/Design).

Mo's blog is about him, London in film, cricket. He took a photo of St Paul's Cathedral because the view was good from there. • I'd like to read … • I might find the rules of cricket / pictures of the Harry Potter places in London / Mo's age, hobbies or nickname there.

4 Mo sends a link 🎧

Listen to a conversation between Emily Evans and her parents.

a) Listen. Then say which parts of Mo's blog they talk about. What else do you learn about Mo?

b) Read the statements below. Listen again. Are they true or false? Correct the false statements.

1. Mr Evans gets a text message.
   That's false. Emily gets a text message.
2. Mrs Evans explains why Mo took a photo of St Paul's Cathedral.
3. Emily knows all about the film *Notting Hill*.
4. Mr Evans wants to tell Emily about the film *Notting Hill*.
5. The *About me* page has lots of information about Mo.
6. Mr Evans wants to see Mo's cricket page.
7. Mo and Luke play cricket for a London team.
8. Emily wants to watch the England–Australia match.

2 False. Emily explains why Mo took the photo. • 3 False. Emily doesn't know anything about the film. • 4 True • 5 False. It doesn't say much about Mo. • 6 True. • 7 True. • 8 False. Mr Evans wants to watch the match.

🌐 Find out about London in Mo's other films. Find out about cricket.

Follow the link: die S recherchieren online weiter.

Language Awareness: Durch die Einführung von *false* kann hier die Unterscheidung zwischen *right/wrong* (strukturelle, grammatikalische Betrachtung) und *true/false* (inhaltliche Betrachtung) hervorgehoben werden.

1 Part A Practice

KV 3 • Folie 2, 3 • FöFö 1.1 • LAS 1.1, 1.2

Lernfeld S. 12–13: Die S können **Kollokationen** bilden und anwenden. Sie können von Erlebnissen erzählen, die zu bestimmten und unbestimmten Zeitpunkten in der Vergangenheit geschehen sind *(simple past* und *present perfect)*.

1 WORDS City holidays

Wörter mit einem + werden hier neu eingeführt.

TIP
When you practise vocabulary, it helps to learn verbs and nouns that go together.

a) Write down verb/noun combinations like this:
go by bus, take the bus, wait for the bus, get on …

go by	bus · the bus
go on	car
take	+Tube · the Tube
get on	+underground · the underground
wait for	a tour · a boat trip

go to	a hotel · a bed & breakfast
+stay at	a map · a website · a +timetable
have	a cathedral · a museum · a +gallery
look at	the theatre · the cinema
queue at	a café · a +restaurant · a carnival
visit	a park · a shopping centre
walk around	lunch · a cup of tea · a drink

b) What do you do on holiday in a big city? Correct the silly sentences.
You don't queue at a cup of tea. You queue at a …

1 You go to a drink.
2 You visit a map.
3 You wait for a park.
4 You stay at the bus.
5 You walk around a tour.
6 You take a gallery.
7 You go on a drink.
8 You look at lunch.
9 You have a café.
10 You go by a hotel.

Early finisher Make three more silly sentences.

More help ➔ p. 116   + new words   ➔ Workbook 3 (p. 9)

More help: Die S suchen die *verb/noun combinations* in einer Wortschlange.

2 REVISION Your holidays (Simple past)

a) Write questions like these for a partner:
Did you stay at home or go away?
Did you go to a city / to the coast / …?
Where did you stay? What …?

More help ➔ p. 116 **More help** bietet Ideen für Fragen.

When you're finished, go to a bus stop.

A bus stop is a place in the classroom where you meet a partner to work with.

Hier kann **KV 3: Bus stop** eingesetzt werden.

b) Take turns to ask and answer questions. Take notes on your partner's answers.
A: What did you do in Dresden?
B: We walked around the city centre and went on a boat trip.

c) Go to another bus stop. Tell your new partner about your last partner's holiday.
A: Jan went on a boat trip in Dresden. He …

➔ GF 1.1: Simple past (p. 155) ➔ Workbook 4 (p. 10)

3 REVISION Have you ever …? (Present perfect)

Find out if you have both done the same things in your lifetime.
Each make a window for the answers.

Have you ever been to London?   *Have you ever eaten shark?*   *Yes I have. / No, I haven't.*

| WE HAVE BOTH …
 eaten shark.
 … | ONLY I HAVE …
 visited another country.
 … |
| WE HAVEN'T …
 played cricket.
 … | ONLY MY PARTNER HAS …
 been to Darmstadt.
 … |

Early finisher ➔ p. 126

Early finisher: Worträtsel

➔ GF 1.2: Present perfect (p. 156)

Part A Practice 1

4 REVISION — A message from London (Simple past or present perfect?)

Complete Emily's message with the correct tenses: simple past or present perfect.

Hey Amelia,
Hi from London. I ¹... (arrive) on Friday evening (with Mum and Dad), so we ²... (already do) a few things. Yesterday morning we ³... (go) up to the roof of a building where we ⁴... (have) a great view. On the roof we ⁵... (meet) two boys – Luke and Mo. They ⁶... (give) us some tips. Luke ⁷... (tell) us about a carnival at a place called Notting Hill.
After lunch we ⁸... (visit) St Paul's Cathedral and then we ⁹... (take) a red London bus to Hyde Park. It ¹⁰... (be) beautiful there, and the park is really huge. ¹¹... you ¹²... (ever be) there?
There are lots of places that we ¹³... (not be) to yet – like Buckingham Palace, so I ¹⁴... (not have) tea with the Queen either (LOL). And we ¹⁵... (not visit) any museums yet, but Mum has plans! ¹⁶... you ¹⁷... (enjoy) your trip to France last week? What ¹⁸... (be) the weather like there? In London it ¹⁹... (not rain) yet! Hugs, Emily xxx

1 arrived
2 have already done
3 went
4 had
5 met
6 gave
7 told
8 visited
9 took
10 was
11 Have
12 ever been
13 haven't been
14 haven't had
15 haven't visited
16 Did
17 enjoy
18 was
19 hasn't rained

More help → p. 116 → GF 1.3 Present perfect or simple past? (pp. 156–157) → Workbook 5 (p. 10)

More help: Signalwörter für *simple past/present pefect* sind farblich markiert.

5 Pronunciation (Different stress in German and English words)

a) Write down the German and English words. Underline the stressed vowel in each word.

interessiert	interested
Familie	family
Kathedrale	cathedral
Moment	moment

Palast	palace
Programm	programme
Tourist	tourist
traditionell	traditional

TIP
Check the stress marks ['] in the Dictionary.
interested [ˈɪntrəstɪd]
cathedral [kəˈθiːdrəl]

05 b) Listen and check.

→ *True and false friends (p. 248)* → Workbook 6 (p. 11)

6 Everyday English Small talk

Lernfeld: Die S können nach einem Muster einen **Small talk** auf Englisch führen.

1 06

a) Two people meet at *One New Change*. Read their dialogue. Put the orange sentences in the right order. Then listen and check.

   A: It's a great view of the cathedral, isn't it?
5 B: Thanks. Have a nice day.
   A: Have you been here before?
3 B: I'm John. Nice to meet you, Sandy.
   A: Well, I work near here, so I come here often. By the way, my name is Sandy.
4 B: Just for a long weekend.
   A: How long are you staying in London?
2 B: No, this is my first time. I'm a tourist.
   A: Well, enjoy the rest of your visit. Bye.
1 B: Oh, yes, it's amazing.

b) Practise the dialogue.

c) Act out your own dialogue.
Partner A → *p. 132* Partner B → *p. 135*

Access to cultures

In Britain and in other English-speaking countries, people often have short, friendly conversations with people they don't know – for example, at a shopping centre or a bus stop. Then they say goodbye and don't expect to meet again.
What about your country? Is it the same there?

→ Workbook 7 (p. 11)

13

1 Part B 3 • KV 4 • FöFo 1.1

Lernfeld S. 14–15: Die S können Hör- und Lesetexte zu **Sehenswürdigkeiten in London** verstehen und mithilfe der Informationen daraus eigene Pläne für einen Tag in London erarbeiten und mit einem Partner diskutieren.

1 London attractions

Say what the headings and pictures tell you about each of the four attractions.

2 The Evans family's plans 🎧

1 ▶07 a) Listen to Emily and her parents. Which attraction would each of them like to visit?
Emily: London Eye • Mr E: Tower of London, Big Ben • Mrs E: Natural History Museum

b) Why do you think Emily and her parents have chosen "their" attractions?
Read texts A–D. Then say what their reasons could be. Mögliche Lösungen: siehe Unterstreichungen

I think Emily's mum wants to go to … because …

I'm sure Emily likes … because …

1 ▶08 c) Listen to Emily and her parents. What are their arguments *for* and *against* the attractions?
What do they decide to do today?
What are they going to do tomorrow?
today: Natural History Museum • tomorrow: Notting Hill Carnival

3 Your plans

👥 Make plans for a day in London. Talk about arguments for and against the four attractions. Then agree on two attractions you would like to visit.

London Eye: for: Emily can pay with her own money / against: expensive • NHM: for: free, great place for young people, can learn about our planet, can see very old animals there / against: boring, not interested in old animals
Tower: for: lots of history, tour with a Beefeater, see the ravens, Crown Jewels / against: enough history at school

A

● LOVELY PLANET **London** *and its treasures*

NATURAL HISTORY MUSEUM

This cathedral of science is <u>THE</u> place for everyone who is interested in the history of our planet.

Open every day – 10:00 – 17:50

<u>Entry</u> free

KV 4: Talking about plans for a day in London liefert Phrasen und Zwischenfragen zur Bearbeitung, die auch für eine Kommunikationsprüfung hilfreich sind.

37

B

Inside Big Ben Inside Big Ben

Everyone calls this famous clock tower 'Big Ben', but its real name is the Elizabeth Tower. Big Ben is **in fact** the name of the largest bell inside it. (+fact)
The bell rang for the first time on 11th July 1859. Today, not only Londoners hear the clock every hour; around the world millions of people also hear it on BBC radio. Most people who visit London see Big Ben from the outside. Why don't you climb the tower and see the inside too?

Tour times
December–May, Mon–Fri: 9:15, 11:15, 14:15
May–September, Mon–Fri: 9, 11, 14 and 16
Tours are only for people who live in the <u>UK</u>.
Tours are free, but please <mark>reserve</mark> your place early.

What will you see?
The tour will take you up 334 stone <mark>steps</mark> to hear Big Ben °<u>ring out the hour</u>. You'll have an amazing view over London – and a <u>chance</u> to walk behind the °<u>clock faces</u> and see the °<u>clock wheels</u> at work.

14

Part B 1

C THE LONDON EYE
FACTS AND FIGURES

1. The London Eye travels at less than 1 km an hour. That's as fast – or slow – as a tortoise. This means that a ride takes about 30 minutes and you have lots of time to enjoy the sights.
2. The London Eye is 135m high. That is like 64 red telephone boxes on top of each other.
3. From the top of the Eye you can see around 40 km on a clear day. There is a great view of famous sights like Buckingham Palace, the Houses of Parliament, the Shard and St Paul's Cathedral.
4. 800 people can travel in the Eye at one time, as many as in 11 big red London buses.

Opening times
The London Eye is open every day except Christmas Day.
The first ride starts at 10:00am, and the ticket office opens at 9:30am.
Check the website for more details.
www.londoneye.com

Tickets & Prices	on the day	online
Adult (16+)	£19.95	£17.96
Child (4–15 yrs)	£14.00	£12.60
Child (under 4)	FREE	FREE
Family of four	£67.91	£54.33

London Eye: Conceived and designed by Marks Barfield Architects

D TOWER OF LONDON — Over 900 years of history.
Box "German "während"", Voc, S. 175

During its long history, the Tower of London has been a palace, a prison, and even a zoo.
When you take the tour with one of the °Beefeaters who guard the Tower, you'll hear many stories and legends from the past. One legend is that six ravens must always live at the Tower. If they leave, the king will fall. The Beefeaters look after the ravens and feed them 'bird biscuits', full of blood!
The Tower is also home to the Crown Jewels. School classes which visit the Tower education centre can try on a copy of the Crown.

White Tower
Crown Jewels
Ravens

Opens	Closes	Adult	Child
9 am Tues to Sat 10 am Sun and Mon	17:30 (16:30 Nov to Feb)	£21.45	£10.75 (under 16)

1 Writing course — Good sentences

4 • KV 5 • FöFo 1.3

Lernfeld S. 16: Die S können einen Text schreiben und ihn mit **Adjektiven**, **Adverbien**, **time phrases** und **linking words** lebendiger gestalten.

Writing course und *Study skills* können als eine Einheit unterrichtet werden.

1 Learn how

Good sentences give your readers a clearer picture of what you want to say.

a) Read the tips on the right.
   Think of more examples for each tip.

> You can use *terrible* or *awful* instead of *bad*.

> *Five years ago* or *during the holidays* are examples of time phrases.

TIP
1. Use different adjectives (*bright, fantastic, dark, …*) to describe people, things and places – not just *good, bad* and *nice*.
   Use adverbs (*quietly, slowly, …*) for actions.
   Use *really, very, a bit* etc. (*really slowly, very quietly, a bit dark*) to be more exact.
2. Use time phrases (*last week, tomorrow, …*) to tell your reader when things happened.
3. Use linking words (*and, but, because, …*) and relative clauses to link short sentences.

b) Read the first draft of Leon's text. Then look at his corrections.
   Say how he has followed the tips.
   Suggest other ways to make his text better.

> Mit **KV 5: Writing course – Good sentences** können die S direkt im Text arbeiten.

My trip to London   Leon Schmidt

My family and I were in London from Friday night to Saturday. We stayed at a hotel. It was near London Bridge. I had a nice view of the River Thames from my window.
We visited the Natural History Museum. The exhibits were very good. There were also lots of people there. The queue for the dinosaurs was long. We waited over an hour. It was worth it! There was a big model of T. Rex. It moved and roared. We also went to the Tower of London. We went on a tour there. I didn't like it. The tour guide spoke too fast. His jokes weren't funny.
We had dinner at an Indian restaurant. I had vegetable curry. It was good. I ate too much. I felt sick.
London is a nice city. Two days aren't enough. There are so many places to visit.

My trip to London   Leon Schmidt

My family and I were in London ~~from Friday night to Saturday~~ **for the weekend**. We stayed at a hotel. It was near London Bridge. I had a ~~nice~~ **fantastic** view of the River Thames from my window.
On Saturday we visited the Natural History Museum. The ~~exhibits~~ were ~~very good~~ **really amazing**. It was also very crowded. ~~There were also lots of people there.~~ The queue for the dinosaurs was **really** long. We waited over an hour, **but** it was worth it! There was a ~~big~~ **huge** model of T. Rex, **which** moved and roared. We also went to the Tower of London. We went on a tour there. I didn't ~~like it~~ **enjoy it because** the tour guide spoke too fast **and** his jokes weren't funny.
On Sunday we had dinner at an Indian restaurant. I had vegetable curry. It was **great** good, **but** I ate too much. I felt **a bit** sick **in the evening**.
London is a **great** nice city, **but** two days aren't enough. There are so many **exciting** places to visit.

> **adjectives:**
> \+ beautiful
> great
> fantastic
> amazing
> \– silly
> boring

➡ SF 10: Good sentences (p. 144)   ➡ **Workbook** 8 (p. 12)

2 Now write …

You choose Choose a), b) or c).

a) Describe a place that you visited in the summer holidays.
b) Write a short story about a person that you met in London.
c) Describe the loudest / quietest / strangest / most dangerous / … place in your hometown.

➡ **Workbook** Wordbank 1–2, 5, 7

KV 6 • FöFo 1.3

Part B Practice

Lernfeld S. 17: Die S können ihrem Partner Rückmeldung zu ihren Texten geben und anhand von Rückmeldungen ihre eigenen Texte überarbeiten.

1 Study skills: Giving feedback on a text

Language awareness: L sollte darauf hinweisen, dass *feedback* nicht zählbar ist.

With good feedback, you can improve your writing. On this page you will learn to
- check another student's text.
- give good feedback to another student.
- react to the feedback that you get.

KV 6: Giving feedback on texts unterstützt die S beim Erstellen ihrer Rückmeldung.

a) Checking a text

Give your partner the text you wrote for 2 on p. 16.
Look back at the writing tips on p. 16.
Read your partner's text and enter your feedback in a copy of the checklist on p. 256.

Make notes on how your partner can improve his/her text. Check spelling and grammar too.

b) 👥 Giving feedback

Make comments, suggestions and corrections on your partner's text. Follow these steps:

1 Tell your partner what he/she did well:
 • I really liked what you wrote here because …
 • The details were interesting and …
 • I liked it when you used the word …
 • This was really fun to read because …
 • My favourite part was … because …

2 Say what you think your partner didn't do well. Say what he/she could do better.
 • Your sentences are really short. Maybe you could link these two sentences with …
 • It's hard to understand *when* something happens. Why don't you use …
 • You use the same adjective more than once. You could use a different adjective here.
 • Why don't you use an adverb with this verb?

3 Point out grammar and spelling mistakes.

c) Revising your text

Think about what your partner has said. Decide what to change.

 Write your final text.

➡ Workbook *9–10 (p. 13)*

Study skills

Giving feedback on a text

Wenn ich jemandem eine Rückmeldung zu einem Text gebe …
- sollte ich zuerst sagen, was …
- dann sollte ich erklären, was …
- …

Vergleiche deine Ideen mit dem Abschnitt im Skills File:

➡ *SF 14: Feedback – writing (p. 146)*

1 Part B Practice

 5 • FöFo 1.4

Lernfeld S. 18: Die S können nach dem Weg fragen und **Wegbeschreibungen** geben. Sie nutzen dazu auch den Plan der **Londoner U-Bahn**.

2 REVISION How can I get there?

a) Find these places on the map of London on the front inside cover of your book:
- the British Museum
- the Millennium Bridge
- the London Eye
- Piccadilly Circus

Then explain where they are. Take turns.

> It's in …. Street/Road ·
> It's near … <name of tube station> ·
> It's on the corner of … Street and … ·
> It's between … <names of tube stations/ roads/other places>

b) You're at Russell Square tube station. Ask the way to other places on the map.

> *How can I get to the British Museum, please?*

> *Walk along Southampton Row. Then turn right into …*

More help → p. 117 **More help** bietet Hilfe zur Wegbeschreibung.

Early finisher Find a partner. Give directions to places in your town.

a) British Museum: near Goodge Street and Russell Square stations, on the corner of Bloomsbury St and Great Russell St · Millennium Bridge: near Tate Modern, between Blackfriars and Cannon Street stations · London Eye: between Waterloo Station and Westminster Bridge · Piccadilly Circus: at Piccadilly Circus Tube station, between Haymarket and Regent St

→ **Workbook** 11 (p. 14)

3 Go by tube

Language awareness: L kann vorab auf die Aussprache von Leicester [ˈlestə], Gloucester [ˈɡlɒstə], Euston [ˈjuːstən] und Greenwich [ˈɡrenɪtʃ] hinweisen.

a) You're staying near Marble Arch. You want to go by tube to Big Ben.
Practise this dialogue. Take turns.

A: How do we get from here to Big Ben?
B: Big Ben? That's Westminster tube station. We take the Central line eastbound from Marble Arch to Bond Street. And then we change to the Jubilee line southbound.

> take the … line · change to the … line ·
> northbound · southbound ·
> eastbound · westbound

b) Choose other sights from the map on the inside cover.
Find the nearest tube station.
Act out more dialogues like the one in a).

→ **Text File 1** (p. 98) → **Workbook** 12 (p. 14)
Text File 1: Underground etiquette

4 WORDS German *gehen*

Lernfeld: Die S kennen verschiedene Bedeutungen im Englischen für das deutsche Wort „gehen".

Some German words like *gehen* have lots of different meanings in English.
Choose eight sentences that match the pictures. Translate them into German. Use a form of *gehen*.

1 They're going for a walk.
2 I don't feel well.
3 The clock is slow. (+ be fast)
4 How are you?
5 Can you answer the phone?
6 We've missed it! Let's walk.
7 I'm fine, thank you.
8 It's too cold to go swimmning.
9 This torch doesn't work.
10 You can't do that!
11 What's the book about?
12 Just head for the church.

A 12 Geh einfach zur Kirche.
B 5 Kannst du ans Telefon gehen?
C 10 So geht das nicht.
D 8 Es ist zu kalt, um schwimmen zu gehen.
E 9 Die Taschenlampe geht nicht.
F 3 Die Uhr geht nach.
G 6 Wir haben ihn verpasst. Lass uns zu Fuß gehen.
H 2 Mir geht's nicht gut.

Early finisher Look at the four sentences that didn't go with a picture. Translate them into German.
1 Sie gehen spazieren. · 4 Wie geht es dir? · 7 Mir geht's gut, danke. · 11 Worum geht es in dem Buch?

5 A station announcement

Lernfeld: Die S können deutsche (Bahnhofs-)durchsagen verstehen und auf Englisch zusammenfassend vermitteln.

TIP

a) You're at a train station on your way to Bonn. You hear an announcement. Listen carefully.

b) A British family doesn't understand. Act out a dialogue to answer their questions. Take turns at playing the British speaker.
1 We're going to Bonn.
  Was that announcement for our train? Yes, it was.
2 What's the problem? This is the wrong platform.
3 When and where does it leave now?
  The train leaves 20 minutes later, not at 15.25. And it doesn't leave from platform 7. You have to go to platform 23.

The most important thing about mediation is the *message*. You don't have to translate every word. If you don't know *Gleis* in English, try to explain it.

➜ **Workbook** 13–14 (pp. 14–15)

Das Wort *platform*, das für die Übung benötigt wird, kann über den Morph-Comic vorentlastet werden.

The adventures of Morph

Part C

Lernfeld S. 20: Die S können einer Geschichte, die sie gelesen/gehört haben, Informationen entnehmen und den Handlungsverlauf erklären.

1 🔊 Watching the cricket

On Sunday morning Luke rang Mo's doorbell. When Mo opened the door, Luke said, "It's 10:30, Mo. The cricket is on TV."
In the living room, Mo's big sister Mishal was on
5 the sofa. She was watching a music show. The music was so loud she didn't notice the two boys. "Can we watch the cricket, Mishal?" asked Mo, but Mishal didn't answer. So Mo shouted, "Mishal! The cricket **is on**. Can we watch the test match?" (+be off)
10 Mishal looked over at the two boys: "**No way!**"
"You've been watching TV **for hours**," Mo said.
"No, I haven't," his sister said. "I've been watching **since 10**, when Mum went out. Remember? **And anyway**, the cricket lasts all day. You can watch it
15 later."
"But we're going to Notting Hill Carnival later, Mishal," Luke said and smiled at her. "Please, can we watch the cricket before we go? Please?"
"Nice **try**, Luke," Mishal said, "but no."
20 Then she picked up the **remote** and **turned** the volume **up** even louder. [Box "(to) turn", Voc, S. 177]
Luke and Mo looked at **each other**. Mo made a face at his sister, then he said, "OK, Luke, let's just go to the carnival."
25 Five minutes later the two boys were walking towards the tube station when they passed a **pub**. Luke pointed through the door to a big TV screen. "Look, the cricket is on. Let's watch it **for a while**."
"But we can't go into a pub," Mo said. "We're not
30 old enough."
"But we *can* watch through the door."
The boys stood at the door of the pub and looked in. After a while, Mo felt a **tap** on his shoulder. He turned round. A man shook his head at them. "I've
35 been waiting here for five minutes, boys. Do you think I can go in now?"
"Sorry," Mo and Luke both said. They moved to the side and the man went in.
The match was getting very exciting and the boys
40 slowly moved a bit closer to the TV. In a few minutes, they were just inside the door of the pub. They could hear the TV now too: "**The English team has been playing much better since the break**," the °**commentator**'s voice said.
45 When England made a °**breakthrough**, Mo shouted "Yes!" and Luke clapped his hands and sang, "England! England!"
Suddenly they heard another voice.
"All right, you two," said the barman. "**I've been**
50 **watching you since you came in.** You're too young to be in here, you know that. **Off you go now.**" [Box "off", Voc, S. 177]
Luke and Mo turned round and left the pub.
"Notting Hill, here we come!" Mo shouted and they ran off together **towards** the tube station.

2 Follow the story

👥 Take turns to explain:
1 why Luke goes to Mo's house. — *1 He wants to watch cricket with him.*
2 what Mo and Luke's plans for they day are.
3 why they can't do what they want to at home.
4 where they go instead. — *2 First they want to watch a part of the cricket match and then they plan to go to Notting Hill Carnival.*
5 what happens there.

3 Mo's sister Mishal is watching a music show on TV.
4 They walk towards the Tube station and stop at a pub. They want to watch the match through the door because they are not allowed to go into the pub.
5 Luke shouts "England, England" and the barman tells them that they are not allowed to be there.

3 Have a go

Lernfeld: Die S sprechen **vorbewusst** darüber, wie lange sie bereits bestimmte Dinge tun **(present perfect progressive)**.

Say how long you have been doing these things:

sit on this chair		... minutes
I've been sitting on this chair for 25 minutes.		... hours
go to this school	for	... days
learn English		... weeks
use this book		... months
work on this page		... years

Zusatz: KV 7: Watching the cricket gibt 6 kommunikative Sprechanlässe vor. In 3er-Gruppen ziehen die S reihum eine Situation und erzählen „ihre" Geschichte. Sprechen sie länger als 30 Sekunden, erhalten sie 1 Punkt, sprechen sie länger als eine Minute,

7 • Folie 4 • FöFo 1.5 • LAS 1.4

Part C Practice 1

Lernfeld S. 21: Die S können sagen, seit wann sie oder andere eine bestimmte Sache bereits machen und einander dazu Fragen stellen *(present perfect progressive)*.

Looking at language

Look at these sentences from p. 20.
Then complete the explanation.
You've been watching TV for hours.
I've been waiting here for five minutes.
The English team has been playing much better since the break.

The **present perfect progressive** has three parts:
have/has + _been_ + _ing_ -form

We use this tense to say that something started in the past and is still going on now.
I've been watching TV since 3 o'clock.
= I started at 3:00 and I am still watching TV now.

3 o'clock   now

In German we use
1 the … tense in situations like this. *present*
2 … for the English *for* and *since*. *seit*

➜ GF 1.4: Present perfect progressive (pp. 157–158)

1 I've been waiting for the bus …
(Present perfect progressive)

Complete each sentence in two ways: with *for* and *since*.

1 I … (wait) for the bus …
   I've been waiting for the bus   *for 20 minutes.*
                                           since nine o'clock.
2 You … (watch) TV …   2 You've been watching TV for … / since …
3 It … (rain) …   3 It has been raining for … / since …
4 She … (feel) ill …   4 She has been feeling ill for … / since …
5 I … (learn) maths at school …   5 I've been learning … for … / since …
6 We … (have) lessons in this classroom …   6 We've been having … for … / since …

for	since
20/45/… minutes	8:30/nine o'clock/…
a few hours	yesterday evening
two/three/… days	last week/January/…
a year/two years/…	2010/2011/…
…	…

➜ Workbook 15 (p. 15)

2 I've been living here …
(Present perfect progressive)

Complete Mo's sentences.

*I'm a Londoner.
I've been living here …*

Use the verb in brackets and *for* and *since*.

1 I'm a Londoner. I … (live) here … I was three.
2 I like languages. I … (learn) German at school … three years.
3 My sister Mishal loves music. She … (sing) in a band … over a year.
4 I have a blog. I … (write) posts … last March.
5 My friend Luke and I love cricket. We … (play) in the same team … a long time.
6 Luke is a big fan of Notting Hill Carnival. He … (go) there … he was twelve.

More help ➜ p. 117   **More help:** In den Sätzen müssen nur *since* und *for* ergänzt werden.
➜ Workbook 16 (p. 16)
1 I've been living … since • 2 I've been learning … for • 3 She's been singing … for • 4 I've been writing … since • 5 We've been playing … for • 6 He's been going … since

3 How long …?

a) Make a profile like this about yourself.

Name:	Daniel		
Hometown:	Berlin	Languages:	English/…
Address:	…straße 14	Sports:	football/…
School:	… Gymnasium	Hobbies:	choir/…

b) Meet a partner at a bus stop.
Swap profiles. Then ask and answer like this:

How long have you been living in Berlin?

I've been living in Berlin for thirteen years.

How long have you been going to … Gymnasium?

More help ➜ p. 117   **More help** bietet einige Beispielfragen.

c) Go to another bus stop. Tell your new partner about your last partner.
Daniel has been singing in a choir since last May.

Early finisher ➜ p. 126 ➜ Workbook 17 (p. 16)
Early finisher: Logikfragen mit *present perfect progressive*.

1 The world behind the picture

1 A bus tour of London

The number 11 bus passes lots of famous sights. You can get on and off as often as you like and walk to sights near the route too.

a) Look at the London map on your inside cover.
   Make a list of sights like the one below.
   Put a star beside *your* five favourites.

On the bus route	Near the bus route
St Paul's Cathedral	The Tower of London ★
...	...

b) Watch the film.
   Tick (✓) the places on your list that you see.

c) Watch again and listen for information about your favourites.
   Write captions for each one that you see.
   1 The royal family lives here.
   2 ...

The royal family lives here.

That's easy! Buckingham Palace.

d) 👥 Read your captions to your partner.
   Can he/she say what your favourites are?

2 Making the film: Time

Lernfeld: Die S können über **erzählte Zeit** und **erzählende Zeit** sprechen sowie über **Montagen** als Zeitraffer (Filmsprache).

a) Watch the film again. Think about *time*.
   How long was the film?
   The film was about 5 minutes. I think the "real" tour took about 2.5 hours.
   How long do you think the tour really was?
   Give reasons for your opinion.
   You can check the distances on the map.

b) Think about speed.
   The film-maker often speeds up the film.
   Where in the film does he do this?
   What could his reasons be?
   Do you think it's a good idea?
   It's a good idea because the film would be very long without it.

He does this when he's walking a long distance or there aren't any sights sights near the route.

c) Say which statement you agree with.

   I liked the film because I had the feeling I was sitting on the bus.

   It was a pity that we didn't see the person who was speaking.

What else did you like/not like about the film?

➡ Text File 2 (p. 100)
Text File 2: London shapes

EXTRA FöFo 1.5 | **Background file** 1

Lernfeld S. 23: Die S können einfachen Sachtexten Informationen zu **Sehenswürdigkeiten in London** entnehmen und diese mit Sehenswürdigkeiten in ihrer Stadt/Region vergleichen.

London for free

Big cities can be very expensive, but in London there's lots that will cost you nothing at all!

1 Museums and galleries
Most of London's most famous museums and galleries are free! See Van Gogh's °*Sunflowers* at the °**National** Gallery. Or °**admire** the Rosetta Stone in the **British Museum** and find out how modern people learned to read °**Egyptian** °**hieroglyphics**.

2 Bridges over the Thames
If you have all the time in the world, you can walk across 27 of 34 bridges over the River Thames. They are great places to see life on the water or London's beautiful buildings.
With some bridges, like **Vauxhall Bridge** or Tower Bridge, the view *of* the bridge is at least as good as the view *from* it.

3 London's parks
London is one of the greenest cities in the world. °**Escape** from the °**noise** and °**traffic** and crowds at the Diana, Princess of Wales °**Memorial** °**Fountain** in Hyde Park. Or imagine you're really in the country and watch the deer in **Richmond Park**, the largest in London.

4 °Architecture and music
You have to pay to get into London's two most famous churches, St Paul's Cathedral and **Westminster** °**Abbey** – °**unless** you go to a °**service** there. Then you can admire the °**majestic** buildings and listen to their wonderful choirs.

5 °Fabulous views
So the Shard is too expensive? Don't worry! There are many great free views in London. If you're in the City, take the lift to the roof of *One New Change*. Or in North London take a walk on Hampstead °**Heath** and climb **Parliament Hill** with all of London °**below** you.

> 👥 Think of the five best free attractions in your town or °**region**.
> Which are similar to the free attractions in London? Which are different?

➡ **Workbook** *18 (p. 17)*

1 Text

🔊 The Notting Hill Carnival Parade

"Hurry," said Emily, "or I'll miss Mo and Luke."
"Don't be silly, Emily," her mum replied, "There'll be thousands of people at the carnival. There's no way you'll see those two boys there."
The platform at the tube station was full. When the train came in, everyone moved to the doors.
"Dad!" said Emily and pointed to two free seats. "You and Mum sit there. I can stand."
But more and more people got onto the train at each station, and they pushed Emily further and further away from her parents.
At Notting Hill Gate, everyone got off. Emily tried to wait for her parents, but the crowd pushed her along the platform and up the stairs. Out in the street, she held onto a lamppost. She scanned the sea of faces, but her parents didn't appear.

❖

Dancers in bright costumes moved along the street. Caribbean music filled the air. On the crowded pavement, Mo held his camera high and took as many photos as he could. Luke tried to move to the front of the crowd.
"Where are you going?" Mo shouted.
"I want to see my cousins. They're in the parade with my Uncle Ray. They're drummers!"

❖

Emily tried to call her parents.
"The number you are calling is not available at the moment. Please try again later."
All around Emily, it was getting louder. The sound of drums filled her ears. People were shouting wildly and blowing whistles. The crowd danced to the music and everyone was pushing against her. She started to panic. Then she took out her phone again. "Just do it!" she said to herself. A moment later she tapped 'Call Mo'.

❖

"Who?" said Mo. "Oh, right, Emily – I remember. … You're at Notting Hill Carnival? Cool, I'm here too, with Luke. … Oh! … Don't worry. Tell us where you are! We'll come and find you. … Well, can you see a street sign? … Westbourne Grove? Where exactly?
… Emily? Oh no, … I've lost her."
He called back, but Emily didn't answer.
"Maybe she's in trouble, Luke," he said. "We have to find her. She's in Westbourne Grove."

Emily

❖

Emily bent down between someone's dancing legs and picked up her phone.
"Oh no!" she cried. "It doesn't work." She decided to go back to the tube station but it was impossible to move on the crowded pavement.
"I'll have to walk with the parade," she thought.
She climbed under the rope onto the road. Suddenly she was in the middle of a group of dancers. On their backs were huge wings in all the colours of the rainbow. They turned in circles, faster and faster, and sang:
"Chiga-lee-a-chiga-lee-chiga-lee-bom!"
Emily started to feel dizzy. Suddenly she felt a pair of hands on her waist.
"Come and dance with me," said a voice. Emily turned and looked into a strange painted face.
"Aaaaaah," she screamed. "Don't touch me!"

❖

"It's too crowded here," said Mo. "If we want to find her quickly, we'll have to join the parade."
"But we're not wearing costumes." Luke replied.
"We just have to dance to the music – like this."
Mo started to move his hips in a little circle.
"That's not how you dance, Mo!" Luke laughed.
"You have to have rhythm, man. Watch me!"
And the two boys danced their way towards Westbourne Grove as fast as they could.

"Sorry if I scared you," said the man with the painted face. "When I saw you with the dancers, I thought you wanted to take part."
"No," said Emily. "I was looking for my parents. I've lost them. And …"
Suddenly, a loud voice filled the air.
"Hello, Notting Hill! How are you feeling?"
The crowds in the street clapped and roared. Emily looked up and saw a red bus. On the open roof was a man with a loudspeaker, and drummers and dancers in bright orange costumes.
"Come on," said the man with the painted face. "Let's take that bus. Ray won't mind. You can sit downstairs and rest for a bit. And then we'll look for your mum and dad." [Box "(to) mind", Voc, S. 178]

There was no sign of Emily in Westbourne Grove.
"Man, my eyes are tired," said Luke. "I can't look at any more faces!"
"And my legs are tired," Mo replied.
"Hello, Notting Hill! Do you want to dance?" said a voice over a loudspeaker.
"No, thanks," said Mo under his breath.
Luke looked up. "Mo! That's Uncle Ray's bus."
"Your uncle has a bus?" asked Mo.
"That's him with the loudspeaker. And my cousins are playing the drums."

Luke took Mo's arm and ran towards the bus.
"Come on," he said. "Let's go up to the top. I'm sure we'll see Emily from there."

"Are you feeling better now?" asked the man with the painted face.
"Yes," smiled Emily. "I'm sorry I screamed at you."
"Don't worry," said the man. "Let's go to Ray."
Upstairs, the dancers were dancing to the drums. Emily started tapping her foot to the rhythm. The man with the painted face went over to Ray and whispered in his ear. Then Ray took his loudspeaker and spoke:
"Hello, Notting Hill! Hello, Mr and Mrs Evans from Cardiff. Can you hear me? Your daughter Emily is waiting for you here, so please come up!"
"What?" said Mo. The two boys looked around. And there was Emily behind them.
"Mo! Luke!" she said. "How did you get here?"
"The question is: How did *you* get here?" Mo replied. "And who is that man?"

1 How did they feel?

Say how Emily, Mo and Luke felt at different points in the story. You can use these words:

angry · excited · lonely · happy · scared · shocked · surprised · unhappy · worried

I think Emily felt excited when she was on the train.

I think Mo was worried when …

2 The end of the story

How does Emily find her parents? What happens when they meet?

Neigungsdifferenzierung: Die S wählen aus drei kreativen Aufgaben – Text, Cartoon oder Dialog – um den Text fortzuführen.

You choose Choose a), b) or c).

a) Write an ending of about 10 to 15 lines.
b) 👥 Make a cartoon.
   One partner can draw pictures.
   The other can write the speech bubbles.
c) 👥 Write a dialogue and act it out.

➜ Workbook 19 (p. 17)

3 EXTRA A British Isles album

Each student will make one page for the album.

a) Choose your topic, e.g.
London museums, Big cities, Ireland north and south,
The rivers and lakes of the British Isles, ...

🌐 You can watch the video clips again to get ideas.
Agree with your teacher when your page should be ready.

b) Now follow these steps:
- Collect information and pictures.
- Write your text(s).
- Make your page for the class album.

➔ SF 22: Putting a page together (p. 152)

Kaleidoscope — The British Isles

1 A first look ▼ Länge: 1:28

a) Look at the map and the key. What do they tell you about the British Isles? Talk about countries, cities, mountains, water …

b) Watch the first video clip.
Say what you've learned about the British Isles.

2 Land and people ▼

a) Look at the eight captions.
Say what you already know about the topics.

1 London — Länge: 1:14

2 City highlights — Länge: 2:25

5 Sport — Länge: 2:15

6 Music — Länge: 1:59

- UK/Ireland border
- UK country border
- Belfast capital city
- cities by population:
  - ☐ over 5 million
  - ■ over 1 million
  - ● over 500,000
  - ● over 100,000
  - ● under 100,000
- railway lines
- important roads
- ferry links
- ▲ 1045 metres above sea level

→ Lewis McCray's trip around Ireland

3 Land and water — Länge: 1:34

4 Languages — Länge: 2:34

An Ghaeltacht

7 Food — Länge: 2:34

8 History — Länge: 3:33

b) Watch the other video clips.
Note down the three topics you liked most.
Which country would you like to know more about?
👥 Compare your ideas. Give reasons why you are interested in a topic or a country.

2 Unit Leistungsmessung Unit 2

Welcome to Snowdonia
[snəʊˈdəʊniə]

Falls nötig kann an dieser Stelle im Plenum noch einmal wichtiger Wortschatz zur **Bildbeschreibung** gesammelt werden.

1a–c) können auch als wechselnde Partnerarbeiten mithilfe von **KV 2: Appointment partners** durchgeführt werden.

1 Welsh countryside

a) Make a list of words to describe the picture.

b) Compare your lists and add words.

c) Take turns to describe the picture.

> *In the background, I see mountains with shadows on them.*

> *On the left, there's a …*

d) Imagine you're in the picture. Choose a place and describe what you can see, hear, smell or feel there. Can your partner guess where you are?

> *I can see some birds in a tree and hear a river behind it.*

> *OK … are you in the field in the middle of the photo?*

➡ Workbook 1 (p. 22)

YT 2 A long journey

a) ➡ pp. 26–27 Look at the map and find Cardiff and Caernarfon. Describe the route between them (mountains? big cities? …?) [kəˈnɑːvər]

b) Listen and find out who the people are and the reason for their journey.

c) Listen again. Say how the girl feels and how she shows her feelings.

More help ➡ p. 118   ➡ **Text File 3** (p. 101)

More help bietet Hilfe in Form von Satzhälften.   Text File 3: Jerry

YT EXTRA Imagine the family's arrival in Caernarfon.

 a) or b).

Neigungsdifferenzierung: Die S können die Fortsetzung entweder zeichnen oder in einem Text beschreiben.

a) Draw a picture story about it.

b) Write a mail from the girl to a friend in Cardiff.

2b) Who: Emily, her mum, her dad · Reason: Emily's mother has a great new job in Wales
2c) how she feels: angry, not happy about moving · how she shows it: not nice to her parents (doesn't want to stop for lunch, doesn't want to go on a trip Mount Snowdon, …)

Unit 2

Lernfeld S. 28–29: Die S können ein **Bild beschreiben** und dafür eine Wortsammlung anlegen. Sie können sich in das Bild hineinversetzen und beschreiben, was sie empfinden. Sie können sich **in andere Personen hineinversetzen**, wenn sich ihre Lebenssituation, z.B. durch einen Umzug, stark ändert. Sie können die **Gefühle dieser Person verstehen** und beschreiben, und ihre Geschichte in einer Art weiterentwickeln, die die vorherigen Erlebnisse berücksichtigt.

Text File: zu Unit 2 passt **Text 3**.

Your task

Your task for this unit:
Imagine you're moving to Wales. Write about how your life would change.

2 Part A

KV 8A/B • FöFo 2.1

Lernfeld S. 30: Die S können einer kurzen Geschichte über ein Gespräch zwischen Eltern und Kindern Informationen entnehmen und die Gefühle der Sprecher erkennen.

1 Everything is wrong

As Emily walked down the long path to her new home, her legs felt heavy and tired. The house was dark and empty. Then she remembered that her mum was out at sea. Mrs Evans was a scientist who
5 studied sea animals and plants.
Emily walked across the garden to her dad's workshop. There was music in the air – someone was singing a Welsh song. She walked through the workshop door and turned the radio off. "If I hear
10 one more word of Welsh, I'll scream!" she said.
Emily's dad was building a table. He was a carpenter and made all kinds of beautiful furniture. His workshop smelled of wood and special oils.
"Someone has had a bad day," he said.
15 "I just don't like that music – that's all," said Emily. She picked up a hammer from the table.
"What's happened?" Mr Evans asked.
"I don't want to talk about it." Emily started hitting an old piece of wood with the hammer.
20 "But if you talk about it, you'll feel better. And put that hammer down! It's making me nervous."
"Sorry!"
"So, tell me what's wrong?"
"What's wrong? Everything is wrong! Seven hours
25 of school and then Welsh lessons at the learning centre. I have to work harder than all the others! And my Welsh still sounds funny – kids laugh when I speak. *And* it's hard to understand the teachers – they speak so fast!"
30 "Which language do your classmates speak at the breaks: English or Welsh?"
"Breaks are the worst! Today at lunch, we were talking about the class trip to Snowdon. Then this boy came over. Dylan. He *never* stops telling jokes.
35 He said something in Welsh and everybody laughed except me. I asked a girl what was so funny, and she said, 'Oh forget it, you probably don't want to know.' Then the bell rang for the end of break. I know that boy was making fun of me."
40 "Well, if you laugh with the others, you won't feel so bad."
"That's silly, Dad. How can I laugh at their jokes if I don't understand them?"
"Give it more time. You'll soon speak Welsh as well
45 as the others … if you don't give up."

Mr Evans

Emily

"Yeah, right, Dad," said Emily. She picked up the hammer again. "When will Mum be back?"
"She won't be back till tomorrow. So I'll make my famous vegetable curry for dinner."
50 "Hmm… If you don't mind, Dad," said Emily, "I'll cook tonight. I'm *really* hungry, and …"
"You don't like my curry?" he said in a sad voice. Then he laughed. "Just a little joke. Let's have pizza instead then."

Die **KV 8A: Freeze frame** und **8B: Everything is wrong - Freeze frame** bieten Hilfe zu Erstellung und Auswertung des *freeze frame*.

2 Understanding the story

a) Look at lines 1–22 again. Describe Emily's feelings. How does she show them?

b) Read lines 24–47 again. Then describe Emily's relationship with her classmates.

c) Choose a part of the text and show it as a freeze frame.
Your partners describe the scene and guess which part of the text it is.

2 a) frustrated (ll. 1–3: the way she comes home) • angry (ll. 9–10: turns off the radio) • angry/sad (ll. 16–19: hits wood, doesn't want to talk)
2 b) she has problems at school • the kids laugh about her • a boy called Dylan says things in Welsh and everybody laughs

30

Part A Practice 2

2, 3 • Folie 5, 6 • KV 9 • FöFo 2.1 • LAS 2.1, 2.2

Lernfeld S. 31: Die S können über zukünftige Handlungen sprechen *(will-future)* und Bedingungen ausdrücken *(conditional sentences 1)*.

1 WORDS Jobs

Lernfeld: Die S können **Berufe** umschreiben.

a) Complete each sentence with the right word.

> actor • ⁺architect • artist • ⁺astronaut •
> carpenter • dentist • farmer • ⁺hairdresser •
> ⁺musician • ⁺painter • scientist

1 Astronauts travel to the moon or other planets.
2 … study plants, animals or other things in the natural world.
3 … paint pictures or people's houses.
4 … play an instrument.
5 … draw plans for new buildings.
6 … cut other people's hair.

2 Scientists • 3 Painters •
4 Musicians • 5 Architect •
6 Hairdressers

b) Write sentences for the other jobs in the box.
  1 … in films or plays or TV shows.

More help ➔ p. 118   **More help:** Berufe müssen nur vorgegebenen Sätzen zugeordnet werden.

c) Write down the jobs from a) in a list.
   Add other jobs that you know.

d) Act out a job from your list. The others say what you're doing and guess the job.

A: You're playing an instrument.
B: Yes, right!
C: You're a musician.

b) 1 Actors act … • 2 Artists draw or paint pictures. •
3 Carpenters make furniture. •
4 Dentists are doctors for people's teeth. • 5 Farmers work on a farm.

➔ **Workbook** 2 *(p. 22)*

2 REVISION Tom thinks he'll be an astronaut *(will-future)*

Zur Zeitersparnis kann **KV 9: Tom thinks he'll be an astronaut** verwendet werden.

a) What do you think you'll be or do in the future? Copy the table and add ideas.
Then make appointments with three classmates and interview them.

What we will be/do	Me	Partner A	Partner B	Partner C
in 5 years				
in 10 years				
in 20 years				

More help bietet einige Zukunftsideen.   **More help** ➔ p. 118

b) Report interesting ideas to the class.
  • Tom thinks he'll be an astronaut in 20 years.
  • Dilek thinks she'll work in Hollywood in …

c) Write sentences about what you *won't* do.
  I'm sure I won't be in Germany in 10 years.
  I'm sure I won't play for Chelsea in …

➔ GF 2: Future *(pp. 159–160)* ➔ **Workbook** 3 *(p. 23)*

3 REVISION If I don't go to bed … (Conditional 1)

a) CHAIN GAME Look at the sentences in the game. Think of endings for the last sentence.

A: If I don't go to bed, I won't get enough sleep.
B: If I don't get enough sleep, I'll be tired tomorrow.
C: If I'm tired tomorrow, I'll play badly in the match.
D: If I play badly in the match, our team won't win.
E: If our team doesn't win …

b) Play the if-sentence game. You can use these ideas:

If we work hard for the English test, …
If you eat too much, …
If the weather is nice tomorrow, …
If you don't wear warm gloves, …

Early finisher: Worträtsel.
Early finisher ➔ p. 127

➔ GF 3.1: Conditional 1 *(p. 161)*
➔ **Workbook** 4 *(p. 23)*

2 Part A Practice

Lernfeld S. 32: Die S benutzen verschiedene Strategien, um in einem zweisprachigen Wörterbuch die richtige Bedeutung eines Wortes zu erfassen und so ihren Wortschatz zu erweitern.

   4 • FöFo 2.2

4 Study skills: Using an English-German dictionary

When you read English texts, try first to understand a new word from the context.
Thinking about what kind of word it is (noun, verb, adjective, etc.) can help you to understand it.
If you really need to check the meaning, you can use a dictionary.

a) Write down what you think the underlined words mean. Check on the right.
👥 Compare your results.

1 That's not your pen, it's <u>mine</u>!
2 My grandfather worked in a <mark>coal</mark> <u>mine</u>.
3 They <u>mine</u> the gold deep <mark>underground</mark>.
4 The navy dropped <u>mines</u> in the enemy harbour.

1 meiner • 2 Bergwerk • 3 abbauen • 4 Minen (Militär)

---

headword → **part of speech** → **example**

mine¹ [maɪn] *Pronomen*
1 meine(r, -s): *Your bike is newer than mine.* Dein Rad ist neuer als meins. • ***It's mine.*** Es gehört mir. • ***some friends of mine*** ein paar Freunde von mir
2 at mine *umg* bei mir zu Hause

← **translation**

mine² [maɪn] *Substantiv*
1 ≈ *Zeche* Bergwerk, Mine
2 MILITÄR Mine

↑ **context**

mine³ [maɪn] *Verb* (**mining**): *auch* **mine for** *Bodenschätze* abbauen

---

b) Say what the <u>underlined</u> words below mean.
Use a dictionary if you need to.

1 He didn't want to sit on the <u>ground</u> because it was wet.
2 My parents will <mark>ground</mark> me if I'm late.
3 Welsh is one of the country's two <mark>official</mark> languages.
4 He works as a city <mark>official</mark>.

1 Boden • 2 Hausarrest geben • 3 amtlich, Amts- • 4 Beamter

c) Words like *for, on, up, away, …* can change the meaning of a verb. Say what the <u>underlined</u> verbs mean in German.
Use a dictionary if you need to.

1 Let's <u>look for</u> a good place to have lunch.
2 I <u>look after</u> my baby sister every Sunday.
3 He <u>looked around</u> the room to see if he knew anyone.
   1 suchen • 2 (auf jn.) aufpassen • 3 sich umsehen
4 Please <u>look up</u> the meaning of that word.
5 We're <u>looking forward</u> to your visit next week.
6 The <mark>police</mark> are <u>looking into</u> the fire at the hotel.

4 nachschlagen • 5 sich (auf etwas) freuen • 6 untersuchen

d) Translate these sentences into German.
Use a dictionary if you need to.

1 Nicholas <u>came up with</u> a new idea.
2 He <u>came down</u> the stairs at 9 am.
3 Her aunt <u>came down with</u> malaria.
4 Can you <u>come over</u> to my house tomorrow?
5 We <u>came across</u> an old church on the moor.
6 Chelsea <u>came back</u> well in the second half.

➡ **Workbook** 5 *(p. 24)*

1 Nicholas hatte eine neue Idee. • 2 Er kam um 9 Uhr die Treppe runter. • 3 Ihre Tante bekam Malaria. • 4 Kannst du morgen zu mir (nach Hause) kommen? • 5 Wir fanden zufällig eine alte Kirche im Moor. • 6 Chelsea holte in der zweiten Hälfte gut auf.

e) Find a partner and open a dictionary at any page. Each write down the answers to these questions.

1 What is the first headword on the page?
2 What is the longest headword on the page?
3 Which word has the most different meanings?
4 How many words do you already know?

👥 Compare your answers.

Box "(to) look after/around/for/…", Voc, S. 180
Box "(to) come across/down/over/…", Voc, S. 180

Study skills

Working with an English-German dictionary

Wenn ich ein Wort nicht verstehe, …
– sollte ich zuerst versuchen, …
– dann sollte ich überlegen, …
– …

Vergleiche deine Ideen mit dem Abschnitt im Skills File:

➡ *SF 5: English-German dictionaries (p. 141)*

EXTRA FöFo 2.2 — **Background file** 2

Lernfeld S. 33: Die S können einem landeskundlichen Text über Wales Informationen entnehmen, Fragen dazu stellen und die Informationen für einen Vergleich mit ihrem Bundesland nutzen.

Facts about Wales
- A country in the UK
- °Population (2011): 3.06 m
- Area: 20,779 square km
- °Capital: Cardiff (Caerdydd) [kaɪəˈdiːð]
- Languages: English, Welsh
- Highest point: Snowdon, 1085 m

The capital city
Cardiff, the capital, is Wales's largest city (346,000). With over 300,000 tourists a year, it is one of Britain's favourite cities. People go there to see its old castle or watch the Welsh Parliament at work.
Or they visit the Welsh °National Museum or the famous *Doctor Who* °Experience.

(www) **Find out more about Cardiff's attractions.**
Follow the link: die S recherchieren online weiter.

°Steel, coal and °rugby: the Valleys
Wales was °once a land of steel and coal. In 1945, 30 °per cent of all Welsh men worked in these °industries in the valleys of south Wales. But today, steel and coal are no longer important. The last coal mine closed in 2008.
One million people still live in the Valleys, but today they work in °manufacturing or °health and social services.

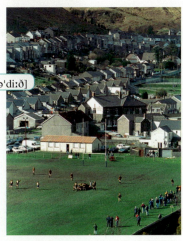

The Valleys are still a centre of Welsh culture, and rugby, the "national sport" of Wales, is very popular. There are rugby °grounds in most of the towns and villages.

[əˈsteðvɒd]

The National Eisteddfod (Eisteddfod Genedlaethol Cymru)
The Eisteddfod is the biggest festival in Wales and °takes place in a different town every year. 150,000 visitors come for a °mix of music, dance and theatre. There are competitions for everything from disco dancing to large choirs, many of them for young kids and teens.
The Eisteddfod goes back to 1176. It °promotes Welsh language and culture and all official events are in Welsh. But everyone is welcome, even if they can't speak Welsh.

Two languages
Welsh and English are official languages in Wales. That's why road signs are °bilingual. Everyone in Wales speaks English, but about 20 per cent of the population also speak Welsh, the country's °original °Celtic language. In the north-west, the number of Welsh speakers is higher. There, many people use Welsh in everyday life and at school.

a) Compare Wales with your *Bundesland*. Think about size, population, languages, sport, culture, festivals, the capital, …

b) Watch the video and find out more about Wales.

Länge: 4:58

c) Write six questions for a quiz on Wales.
👥 Ask your partner your questions.

➡ Workbook 6 (p. 24)

b) Wales is the smallest country in the UK · students can learn Welsh at school · street signs are in English and Welsh · the Welsh language comes from the Celts · many tourists visit Wales because of its beautiful nature, its culture and festivals · there are lots of sheep in Wales

2 Part B

Lernfeld S. 34–35: Die S verstehen Texte, die von Wales handeln, und können Fragen dazu beantworten.

1 🔊 Climbing Mount Snowdon 1 ▶ 22   [ˈsnəʊdn]

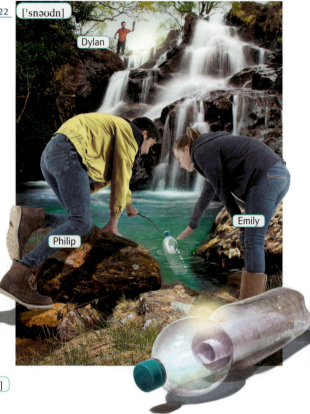

On Friday morning, Emily's class travelled by bus to Snowdonia National Park. When they arrived, their teacher, Mrs Grant, spoke to the group, first in Welsh, then in English. "Before we start, please
5 choose a partner. You should know where he or she is all the time. The walk to the top of Mount Snowdon isn't easy and I don't want any accidents or lost children." Mrs Grant scanned the students' faces to make sure they were listening. She went
10 on: "We'll stop for lunch in about two hours, when we get to the waterfalls. Altogether, the walk will take eight hours, so we won't be back here at the hostel till 6 pm. OK?"
"OK, Miss!" the students shouted, and hurried
15 around to find their partners.
"Will anyone choose me?" Emily wondered. She studied the ground and wished she could disappear into it. Then someone tapped her on the shoulder. It was Dylan. "He wants to make fun of me again,"
20 she thought.
"Wyt ti wedi dewis partner?" [wɪt ti wedi ˈdewɪs paːtnə]
Emily pretended not to understand.
"Sorry?" she asked.
"Have you chosen a partner, Emily?" he repeated.
25 "Not really," she answered.
"Good, me neither. Is this your first time here?"
Emily nodded.
"Well, I've been here lots of times."
"Really?" said Emily in a bored voice.
30 "Yes. If you gave me a pound for every trip, I would be rich." Dylan started talking about his last trip, but Emily wasn't listening any more.
"Why did it have to be him?" she thought.
They started walking. Everyone was excited. Some
35 of the boys climbed and jumped off the big rocks along the path, until Mrs Grant stopped them.
Time went by quickly, and they were soon at the waterfalls.
"See that waterfall?" Dylan said. "If I had a °kayak,
40 I'd °paddle right down from the top to this pool."
"That's a stupid idea, Dylan," said a boy called Philip. "If you did that, you would die. If I were you, I'd go down inside a great big beach ball. That way, you wouldn't hit the rocks!"
45 "Let's test your idea, then," said Dylan. "See this water bottle? I'm going to write a note and put it inside. Then I'm going to run to the top, and drop it into the water. Does anyone have a pen?"
Emily gave Dylan her pen. He wrote something on
50 a piece of paper and put it into the bottle.
"You wait here at the pool and catch the bottle before it goes downstream," Dylan said, and started to climb up the side of the waterfall. Emily looked around nervously. "I hope Mrs Grant
55 doesn't see," she whispered.
"Ready?" Dylan shouted down from the top of the waterfall. He held up the bottle with the note inside. Then he threw it into the waterfall. The bottle sailed down, crashed against a rock, flew up
60 in the air again, and then dropped back into the water. Emily and the others waited by the pool. As the bottle came nearer, Emily tried to fish it out, but it was too far from the edge. Mrs Grant blew her whistle. The break was over and it was time to
65 go on. Emily tried to reach the bottle with a stick, but she only pushed it towards Philip.
"I've got it!" he shouted. Dylan ran over to Philip, grabbed the bottle, and gave it to Emily.
"This is for you," he smiled. "If Philip read it, he
70 could get the wrong idea."

34

Then Mrs Grant blew her whistle again. The others were already on their way. "I'll read it later," she said under her breath, and put the bottle into her rucksack.
75 As they went on up the mountain, the path became steeper.
"How much further is it to the top?" asked Philip. "We've been walking for hours!"
"Let's sing a song," said Dylan. "An English one
80 that Emily knows." Emily went bright red. Dylan thought for a moment. "What about *If I had a hammer?*"
Emily knew the song. "If I had a hammer, I'd hammer in the morning ..." She and her dad often
85 sang it together. Dylan started singing and the others sang along with him. Then Emily joined in. They sang song after song. Before long, they were at the top of Mount Snowdon.
"Wow, what a view!" Philip shouted. "Amazing!"
90 Emily looked across the countryside. Yes, the view was amazing. But she was only thinking one thing: what was the message in the bottle?

2 On the walk

a) Choose the correct answer to each question: a, b or c.

1 Before the walk, Mrs Grant tells the students not to
   a) lose their partners
   b) be late for lunch
   c) get back to the hostel too early.

2 When Dylan asks Emily about her partner, she
   a) doesn't understand him
   b) says that she already has one
   c) doesn't give a clear answer.

3 Dylan tells Emily that
   a) he always gets money for climbing Snowdon
   b) she should give him some money
   c) he has climbed Snowdon many times before.

4 Dylan says he'd like to go down the waterfall in a
   a) kayak
   b) beach ball
   c) big water bottle.

5 The message in the bottle is for
   a) Mrs Grant
   b) Philip
   c) Emily.

6 Emily puts the bottle in her rucksack because
   a) there is no time to read the message
   b) she wants to join in the singing
   c) she isn't interested in the message.

b) What do you think Dylan's message in a bottle says? Write your idea down on a piece of paper. Collect all the ideas in class and read them out. Vote for your favourite.

3 Similar words

The word *partner* is the same in Welsh, English and German.

Think of a language that you speak at home or at school, or a language that you learn (Latin, German, Turkish, French, …).
Write down five words that are similar to English words and mean the same.
But be careful – similar words *can* have different meanings, e.g.
English: map – German: Landkarte (not Mappe!)
➡ *True and false friends (p. 248)*

4 Have a go

Lernfeld: Die S bilden **vorbewusst** Bedingungssätze *(conditional sentences 2)*.

Say what you would do if you were alone on a small island.
If I were alone on a small island, I would …

- collect wood
- make a fire
- talk to the fish
- climb a tree
- look for food
- …

2 Part B Practice

Lernfeld S. 36–37: Die S können **Bedingungssätze** bilden und verwenden *(conditional sentences 2)*.

Looking at language

a) Complete these sentences from pp. 34–35.

if-clause	main clause
If you … me a pound for every trip, *(gave)*	I'd be rich.
If I … a kayak, *(had)*	I'd paddle right down … *(from the top to this pool.)*
If I … you, *(were)*	I'd go down inside a … *(great big beach ball.)*
If Philip … it, *(read)*	he'd get the wrong idea.

b) Say how we form conditional 2 sentences.
- In the *if*-clause, the verb is in the … **past**. *simple*
  With the verb *be*, we often say *If I …* instead of *If I was*. *were*
- In the **main clause**, we use … or … + infinitive. *could · would*

c) Look at this German sentence.
Wenn der Bus schneller fahren würde, kämen wir früher an.

Which translation is correct?
If the bus would drive faster, we would arrive earlier.

If the bus drove faster, we would arrive earlier.

Now make a rule to help you to form *if*-clauses correctly. *Never use would in the if-clause.*

➡ GF 3.2: Conditional 2 (pp. 161–162)

1 If I had … (Conditional 2)

a) Finish five of the sentences with the best idea from the box. Use *would* or *could*.

> do more at weekends ·
> have more fun in breaks · not know the time ·
> often visit them · paddle across the lake

1 If I had a kayak …
   If I had a kayak, I could … paddle across the lake.
2 If we had a climbing wall at school … *I would have more fun in breaks.*
3 If I had friends in Wales … *I would often visit them.*
4 If we had a sofa in our classroom … *I would have more fun in breaks.*
5 If we didn't have clocks or watches … *I wouldn't know the time.*
6 If we didn't have school on Mondays … *I could do more at weekends.*
7 If I had eyes in the back of my head … *I would have more fun in breaks.*

Early finisher Think of as many endings as you can for the other two sentences.

b) Read the first verse of the song. Then listen. **1 ▶ 23**
What else do the singers say they would do?

If I had a hammer (Hays & Seeger)
If I had a hammer,
I'd **hammer** in the morning,
I'd hammer in the evening,
All over this land.
I'd hammer out danger,
I'd hammer out a **warning**,
I'd hammer out love between
my brothers and my sisters,
All over this land.

If he had a bell, he'd ring it.
If he had a song, he'd sing it.

EXTRA Use these ideas to write another verse.

> dance · **drum** · flag ·
> torch · pen · poem

> dance · fly · light ·
> **play** · say · write

If I had a drum, I'd play it in the morning.

2 If I were a police officer … (Conditional 2)

Think of six jobs. Write a sentence about what you could or would do in each job.

If I were a police officer, I'd catch lots of thieves.
If I became a cameraman, I could film action movies.

More help ➡ p. 119   **More help:** Berufe müssen nur vorgegebenen Tätigkeiten zugeordnet werden.

EXTRA Read your sentences.
Say which job would be best for you, and why.

➡ Workbook 7 (p. 25)

5, 6 • Folie 7 • FöFo 2.2, 2.3

Part B Practice 2

3 What would happen if …? (Conditional 2)

a) Emily doesn't feel at home in North Wales.
   Sometimes she wants to

- run away to London
- shout at Dylan
- walk alone in the hills
- invite classmates home
- stop speaking Welsh
- ask a teacher for help

b) Say what would happen.

If Emily ran away to London, she could see Mo and Luke.

Yes, but if she ran away, she wouldn't have a place to live. So that's not a good idea.

Are Emily's ideas good or bad? Make notes like this:

Idea	+	–
run away to London:	see Mo and Luke	no place to live
…		

More help ➜ p. 119 **More help** bietet einige Ideen.

➜ Workbook 9 (p. 25)

4 If I were the head teacher …

a) Which of these things would you do if you were the headteacher? Make a list. Then add more ideas.

- buy more whiteboards
- allow mobiles in class
- have a school uniform
- start dancing lessons
- send students that fight home
- give students free sweets

Yes	No
– more whiteboards	– …
– …	

- more whiteboards: students would learn better.
- mobile phones: …

b) On a different piece of paper, make notes about your reasons.
c) You're a reporter. Interview the headteacher. Use your partner's list from a) to ask questions. Then swap roles.

You say you would buy more whiteboards. Why?

Well, students would learn better if we had more whiteboards.

➜ Workbook 10 (p. 26)

5 A conservation project

a) You want to work for a project in Wales. But will your parents agree to take you there? Take notes about the project in German.

b) Use your notes to explain what the project is about and what you will need. Take turns.

Lernfeld: Die S können zu einem englischsprachigen Flyer Notizen anfertigen und wesentliche Informationen ins Deutsche übertragen.

TIP
Give only key information when you mediate. The Skills File can help you to take good notes.
➜ SF 16: Mediation (p. 148); SF 8: Taking notes (p. 143)

Volunteer for a conservation project in Wales!
The Snowdonia Project needs **you!**

"This was the best week in our whole college course. It was a real honour to work at the hostel and on the footpaths on Snowdon!"
Gemima, 16 [dʒəˈmeɪmə]

We are working so that future generations can enjoy Snowdonia's beautiful countryside and amazing wildlife. When we do practical conservation work, we invite local people and visitors to take part in our workdays. Join us. Remember: It's your Snowdonia.

Why volunteer?
You can see more of Snowdonia, meet new friends, keep fit and active, get training and experience and feel that you have done something special.

General information
You will need warm work clothes, waterproofs and strong boots or wellies. Trainers are not acceptable.
We provide tools, gloves, training, insurance, first-aid kit.
Travel expenses to/from work sites: 25p/mile, maximum £15
We do a full risk assessment before each activity and a First Aider is always present.
A responsible adult must accompany all under 18-s.

b) Beim Snowdonia Project arbeiten Freiwillige daran, die Natur und die Tiere Snowdonias zu schützen und für die Zukunft zu bewahren. Im Projekt engagieren sich Menschen, die dort leben, aber auch Besucher. Man kann viel von Snowdonia sehen und das Gefühl bekommen, etwas Besonderes getan zu haben. Man braucht warme Kleidung und feste Schuhe, die restliche Ausrüstung wird gestellt. Es ist immer ein Erwachsener dabei sowie jemand, der Erste Hilfe leisten kann.

➜ Workbook 11–13 (p. 26–28)

2 Writing course — Paragraphs and topic sentences

 7 • KV 10, 11 • Folie 8 • FöFo 2.4

Lernfeld S. 38: Die S können einen Text schreiben, in dem sie ihre Gedanken in **Absätzen** und *topic sentences* strukturieren. Sie können Rückmeldungen zu Texten geben und ihre eigenen durch Rückmeldungen verbessern.

YT 1 Learn how

People don't think in paragraphs.
When you write, ideas often come all at once.
But paragraphs and topic sentences help you to organize ideas more clearly for your reader.

> A paragraph is a group of sentences that are all connected to one main idea.

> A topic sentence tells your reader what the main idea of a paragraph is. Try to start each paragraph with a topic sentence.

KV 10: Writing course – Paragraphs and topic sentences stellt den Text zur Bearbeitung zur Verfügung.

A trip to the top of Snowdon
by Philip Nash

On Friday our class walked to the top of Mount Snowdon. It's 13 km and a 1,085 metre climb to the summit. It was a long, hard walk up and back down again, but all 24 kids in our class managed it.
At 10 am, we started walking on the Watkin Path. The first part of our walk was easy. We walked for two hours through a beautiful forest and stopped at some amazing waterfalls for lunch. We stayed there until it was time to continue our walk. The second part of our walk was hard. The path was rocky and steep. Sometimes we had to use our hands – like real mountain climbers. We reached the summit at 2 pm. At the top of Snowdon the sky was clear, so we had a great view of Snowdonia National Park. We saw a great big lake and mountain after mountain. The trip back was fun because it was all downhill. We even ran down some parts of the path. But we still needed energy: our class ate a total of 59 chocolate bars on the way down! We reached our hostel at 6 pm. We were really tired, but we all felt like heroes!

Box "Numbers", Voc, S. 181

+uphill, downstream, upstream

a) Read Philip's report. On a copy, mark where other paragraphs should start. Underline the topic sentence for each paragraph.

b) 👥 Compare *where* you marked paragraphs. Did you choose the same first sentences? Explain your reasons.
- I started the paragraph here because …
- I think this is the topic sentence and these sentences go with it.
- I think this sentence goes in the next paragraph.

2 Now write …

Neigungsdifferenzierung: die S wählen ihr Thema aus.

You choose a) or b).
Write at least four paragraphs about:
a) a walk through a big city, a forest, in the mountains, or by the sea.
b) a film you have seen

➔ Workbook *Wordbank 1, 5, 7*

KV 11: Checklist – Writing hilft bei der Erstellung des eigenen Textes.

TIP
1. Before you start writing, make a °mind map or table to collect and organize your memories and ideas.
2. The 5 **Ws** (When? Where? What? Who? Why?) can help you to find ideas.
3. Start a new paragraph for every new idea.
4. Use a topic sentence in each paragraph. In the other sentences add details or examples.

3 … and revise

a) 👥 Give feedback. Read your partner's text and make notes to answer these questions:
- Does it have clear paragraphs?
- What is the topic sentence in each paragraph?
- Do you get information about the 5 Ws?

Take turns to make comments, suggestions and corrections.

b) Think about what your partner has said. Decide what to change and write a second draft.

KV 6: Giving feedback on texts hilft bei der Erstellung des Rückmeldung.

➔ SF 12: Paragraphs (p. 145)
➔ SF 14: Feedback – writing (p. 146)
➔ SF 15: Revising texts (p. 147)

➔ Unit 1 (p. 17): Feedback   ➔ Workbook 14 (p. 28)

2 The world behind the picture

Lernfeld S. 39: Die S können einem *video blog* Informationen entnehmen und Fragen dazu beantworten. Sie planen einen eigenen Video-Blog-Beitrag und filmen ihn (EXTRA).

1 Adam's video blog

Watch the blog. Say what you learn about Adam.

Länge: 3:03

> One thing I've learned is that Adam speaks …

> Another thing is that he …

One thing I learned is that Adam speaks Welsh. Another thing is that he speaks very fast. He also uses his arms very often when he talks. Adam is very funny.

2 Adam and Welsh

Watch the video again. Choose the right answer for each question: a or b.

1. Adam says the number of Welsh speakers is
   a) 500,000   **b) 3,000,000**
2. He says his first school was
   a) English-speaking   **b) Welsh-speaking**
3. He says that, for him, changing from one language to the other is
   a) sometimes difficult   b) always easy
4. In English, the Welsh word for *goodbye* means
   a) big carrot   **b) big fun**

3 Making a video

a) Adam is a blogger who talks about his everyday life. Tell your partner about other bloggers you know. Say what you think about them.

> I've seen a blogger who talks about …

> I think he's really funny because …

b) Plan a video blog like Adam's. Complete the table with ideas from the box. Add more ideas of your own.

things I need	before I start	while I'm filming
a good place to film	think of a good topic	…
…	…	

> a good place to film · computer · look at the camera · look friendly/angry … · make notes · smile · speak clearly · think of a good topic · use captions · use music/sounds/… · wear something interesting

Early finisher ➔ *p. 127* **Early finisher:** Memory-Game.

EXTRA Choose a topic and make your blog.

The adventures of Morph

2 Text

Snowdonia at night

Look at the pictures in the story. Where are Dylan and Emily? Who are the other people in the pictures and what are they doing? Say in a few sentences what you think the story is about.

When the class got back to the hostel, Emily ran to the toilet and closed the door behind her. She pulled the bottle out of her rucksack and tried to shake out the note, but the neck of the bottle was
5 too narrow. With a pencil, she **pressed** hard against the note and tried again and again to pull it towards her. **Finally**, she had the note in her hand and **was able to** read the message:
Meet me at the last door on the 2nd floor at 8 pm.
10 *I want to show you something! Dylan.*
Emily put the note back into her rucksack and hurried downstairs. The kitchen and dining room were noisy and crowded. A large choir group from Bangor was staying at the hostel too. Emily
15 entered the kitchen, where the kids from her class were preparing the evening **meal**.
During dinner, Emily **kept checking** the time on the big clock over the dining room door. At five to eight, she looked across the table at Dylan. He
20 nodded, pointed to the stairs, pressed his finger against his chest, and **silently** said: "I'll go first." Then he left the table and disappeared up the stairs.
A few minutes later, Emily stood up to follow him.
25 "Where are you going, Emily?" said Mrs Grant. "We haven't had dessert yet."
"I'm really tired, Miss," replied Emily. "I think I'll go to bed early."
"All right. Good night, then."

❖

30 Emily ran up the stairs. It was dark on the first floor, but she didn't turn on the lights. She walked to the end of the **corridor** and almost screamed as a hand touched her shoulder.
"Shshsh ... it's only me!" said Dylan. "Come, it's
35 this way – Look! These stairs go to the roof!"
"The roof? Are you sure we can go up there? I mean, won't Mrs Grant be angry?"
"Don't worry, Emily. It's all right. I've done this before," said Dylan. "Come on!"
40 Emily followed him up. At the top of the stairs, there was another door. Dylan pushed it open. They walked out onto the roof and looked out. The trees were full of dark shadows, and behind the trees, a large lake °**shimmered** in the moonlight. The
45 night sky was clear and full of **stars**.
"Welcome to Snowdonia!" Dylan said.
"It's **magical**," whispered Emily.
"Come on," Dylan said. "We can **lie down** here and look up at the stars."
50 "Lie down?" she asked, "but ..."
"Don't worry. It's all right. No one will find us."

❖

Back downstairs it was as **busy** and noisy as before. Emily's classmates were **clearing** dishes from the table. In the living room area, the choir group were
55 sitting in a circle, laughing and talking. One of the girls whispered to her neighbour.
"Morgan, let's go upstairs and get our guitars."
"Good idea, Gwen. I want to play a new song for you. Gareth and I wrote it together."
60 At the top of the stairs, they felt a cool **breeze**.
"Brrr ... it's cold up here!" said Gwen.
"Of course it's cold! Someone has left the door to the roof open," said Morgan. "Look!"
"Hey, can you really go up to the roof?" Gwen
65 asked. "Let's go and **have a look**, then!"
"But what if someone finds out? We'll get into trouble, I'm sure," said Morgan.
"Oh, come on. We'll just say that we went through the wrong door," said Gwen, and pushed Morgan
70 up the stairs.

❖

"What was that sound?" Emily whispered to Dylan.
"What sound?"
"I heard something."
"It's probably just the trees. You always hear those
75 kinds of sounds in the country," said Dylan.
"Wow!" Emily whispered. "A °**shooting star**!"
"I think you *were* right," whispered Dylan.
"What do you mean?"
"Someone *is* coming up the stairs," he said.
80 Emily **sat up** like a **wooden** puppet, her eyes **wide** open in the dark. Two **figures** appeared on the roof. A girl spoke:
"Look, Morgan. We're not alone. Hey, can we join you?" she asked, and walked towards Emily and

Text 2

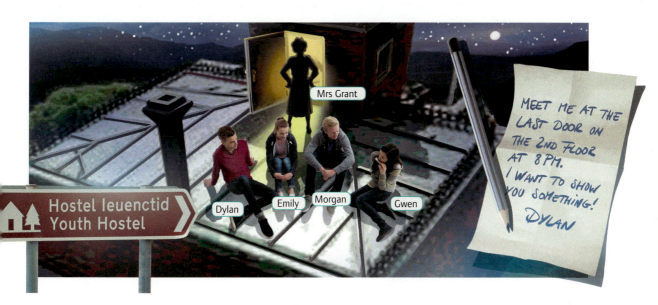

Dylan. "My name's Gwen, and this is Morgan."
"Hi! I'm Dylan and this is Emily."

❖

"What a great place," said Morgan. "So many stars! You can even see the °Milky Way."
Dylan pointed up at the sky. "See that bright light there?" he said. "That's the planet Venus. If you lie down and look up, the view is amazing."
"Right! Good idea," Gwen said, and they all lay on their backs.
"Wow! It's so beautiful!" said Gwen.
She took out her °harmonica and played a few notes. Morgan started to sing a song:

Cold star, you're such a cold star.
Why are you so far, cold star, cold star?
Why are you so far away-ay-ay-ay?
Never calling me, never touching me. Cold star.

Box "such a" + "so", Voc, S. 182

❖

"Wow, you sing really well! What's the name of that song?" Emily asked. "It's really nice."
"The name?" Morgan asked. "Oh, I don't know. I've just made it up. Let's try again. This time, all of us join in, OK? One, two, three: Cold star…"
The four kids sang the song again and again. They changed the words and sang louder each time. And then, as they looked up into the night, a shadow moved slowly over their heads. There was something behind them.

"What, may I ask, are you doing up here?" asked a voice that Emily and Dylan knew very well.
"We're looking at the stars, Mrs Grant," said Dylan. "We've learned a lot about stars this year in science and we thought …"
"That's enough, Dylan. The party is over. Go downstairs, please. It's very dangerous up here and it's against the rules."
"But, Mrs Grant …" started Dylan.
"Don't argue, Dylan," Mrs Grant said.
They stood up and walked back down the stairs. Nobody said another word.
"Please go to your rooms," said Mrs Grant.
"Are we going to be in trouble, Miss?" asked Emily.
"We'll talk about that tomorrow. It's been a long day and now it's time to get some sleep."

❖

Emily and Dylan didn't sit together at breakfast, but more than once their eyes met between °spoonfuls of cornflakes and bites of toast. Mrs Grant wasn't there yet.
"I hope she won't come," Emily thought. But Mrs Grant did come. "Follow me," she said, and went towards the hostel director's office.
"What you both did last night is not only against the rules, it's very dangerous!" Mrs Grant began. "We've given Mr Smart, the hostel director, a very bad picture of our school. He could send the whole class back home. Do you understand that?"
Emily and Dylan nodded.

2 Text

"He isn't going to do that," Mrs Grant went on.
145 "But we have to show him that our students know how to behave. It will be your job, Emily and Dylan, to wash the floors in the corridors, in the toilets and in the living room each day for the rest of our weekend. Mr Smart will show you where the
150 mops are. Any questions?"
"No, Mrs Grant," said Emily and Dylan.
"Good. Then you can start work now."

Box "Question word + to-infinitive", Voc, S. 183

1 ▶ 32 "Careful," laughed Emily as Dylan wildly mopped the corridor floor, "you're splashing me!"
155 "Oops!" said Dylan. Then he started to sing: "Have you seen the mopping man, the mopping man, the mopping man…?"
"Good song," said Emily, "but I know a better one." Quietly, she began to sing: "Cold star, you're such
160 a cold star …"
Dylan put his mop down and joined in: "Why are you so far, cold star … "

8 • VAS 2.1, 2.2

1 The story

a) Were your ideas about the story and the people in it correct?

b) Match these headings to the right part of the story.
   4 We aren't alone (ll. 71–86)
   3 Door to the roof (ll. 52–70)
   5 Looking up at the stars (ll. 87–100)
   1 The note in the bottle (ll. 1–29)
   6 The dark shadow (ll. 101–130)
   7 You've broken the rules (ll. 131–152)
   2 Welcome to Snowdonia (ll. 30–51)

c) Make groups of four.
   Each student chooses two parts of the story and sums up each part in one or two sentences.
   Then put all the sentences together to tell the story.

2 A fair punishment?

a) What do you think about Dylan and Emily's punishment? Make notes like this:

fair because	not fair because
roof dangerous	kids only wanted to see stars
…	

More help ➔ p. 119   **More help** bietet einige Aussagen zur Auswahl an.

b) Discuss your ideas in a double circle.

3 Points of view

Neigungsdifferenzierung: Die S wählen zwischen zwei kreativen Schreibaufträgen aus unterschiedlichen Perspektiven.

You choose   a) or b)

a) Imagine you're Emily or Dylan.
   In four or five sentences, write about what you think about the other.

b) Imagine you're Dylan or Mrs Grant.
   Write one part of the story again from that person's point of view.

EXTRA Find other classmates who chose the same task. Compare your ideas.

➔ Workbook 15–16 (p. 29)

Your task

Alle Schritte können im Unterricht bearbeitet werden. Steps 1 und 4/5 bieten sich aber auch für die Bearbeitung zu Hause an.

Imagine you had to move to Wales with your family.
Write a short text for an online magazine about how your life would change.

Step 1
Look through Unit 2 again and note down the important things that you have learned.
Think about topics, vocabulary, skills, …

Step 2
👥 Read the task again carefully.
Then discuss which things that you have learned in Unit 2 will help you with your text.
Present your group's ideas to the class.

Step 3
👥 Think about why you could have to move.

One student writes down *one* idea on a piece of paper. Then another student adds an idea.
Go on like this for two minutes.

Step 4
Decide where you would move to.

Step 5
Think about how your life would change. What would you miss about Germany?
Make notes. Then write your text.

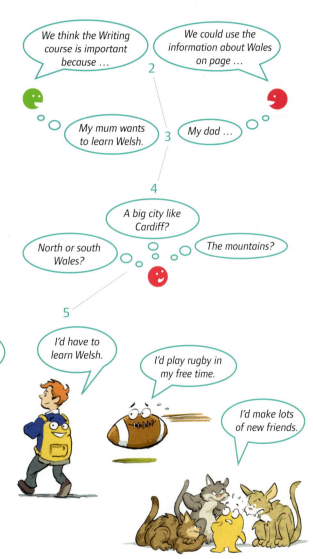

- We think the Writing course is important because …
- We could use the information about Wales on page …
- My mum wants to learn Welsh.
- My dad …
- A big city like Cardiff?
- North or south Wales?
- The mountains?
- I'd live in a cottage in …
- I'd have to learn Welsh.
- I'd play rugby in my free time.
- I'd make lots of new friends.
- If I moved to Wales …

KV 6: Giving feedback on texts hilft bei der Rückmeldung.

Step 6
👥 Swap texts. Your teacher will give you a checklist. Use it to give your partner feedback.

Step 7
Think about the feedback from your partner.
Then revise your text.

➡ SF 15: Revising texts (p. 147) ➡ **Workbook** Wordbank 7

3 Unit

Leistungsmessung Unit 3

A weekend in Liverpool

Text File: zu Unit 3 passen Text 4 und 5.

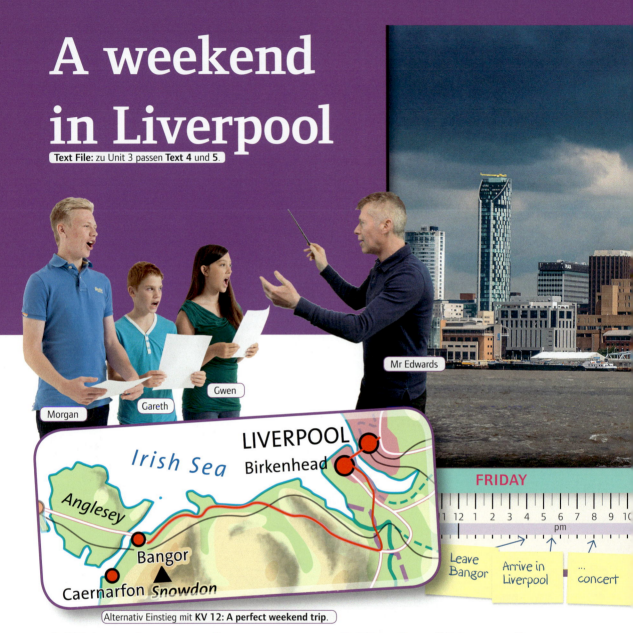

Alternativ Einstieg mit KV 12: A perfect weekend trip.

1 We're going on a trip

a) Say what the people are doing.
Who do you recognize from Unit 2?
Say what you remember about them.

b) Describe the route from Bangor to Liverpool.

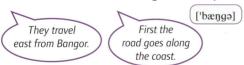

They travel east from Bangor. *First the road goes along the coast.* [ˈbæŋɡə]

a) Morgan and Gwen · they were on the roof of the youth hostel · Gwen plays the harmonica
b) First they travel east from Bangor. The road goes along the coast for a long time. Then the road goes slightly south-east through the countryside. Then they turn left and take the road north to Birkenhead. Liverpool is on the other side of the river.

2 The city of Liverpool

a) Imagine you are on the boat in the picture. Write a short message to a friend and describe what you see.

b) Compare the view of Liverpool with your hometown. What's different? What's similar?

c) ➡ pp. 26–27 Find Liverpool and name the nearby towns. How far away is London?

   Find out more about Liverpool.
   Follow the link: die S recherchieren online weiter.

2 c) Liverpool: is on the west coast of England, close to the Irish Sea and north of Wales. · Nearby towns: Birkenhead, Manchester, Bolton, Preston, Blackpool · Distance to London: 290 km (or 180 miles)

44

1 • KV 12, 13 • FöFo 3.1

Unit 3

Lernfeld S. 44–45: Die S können Hörtexten Informationen über einen unbekannten Ort entnehmen und Notizen zum zeitlichen Ablauf anfertigen. Sie können ihre Heimatstadt mit **Liverpool** vergleichen.

| SATURDAY | SUNDAY |

8 9 10 11 12 1 2 3 4 5 6 7 8 9 10 11   6 7 8 9 10 11 12 1 2 3 4 5 6 7 8 9 10 11
am   pm   am   pm

Zur Zeitersparnis kann **KV 13: The Liverpool programme** verwendet werden.

3 The Liverpool programme

a) Copy the timeline. Then listen to Mr Edwards, the choir leader, and take notes.
Complete the timeline with the times for everything in the box.

> arrive back in Bangor • **explore** Liverpool •
> Beatles show at the Cavern Club •
> free afternoon • River Mersey **cruise** •
> **International Slavery** Museum • concert • +slave
> leave Liverpool

Your task

At the end of this unit:
Write about the person behind the name of a street or building near your home.

b) Compare and check your timelines.

Friday: 8 pm: concert
Saturday: 9 am: explore Liverpool • 12 pm: International Slavery Museum • 5 pm: Beatles Show at the Cavern Club
Sunday: 10:30 am: River Mersey Cruise • afternoon: free • 5:30 pm: leave Liverpool • 7 pm: arrive back in Bangor

➡ **Workbook** 1 (p. 34)

45

3 Part A

Lernfeld S. 46–47: Die S können einen Text über die Lehrwerksfiguren verstehen und sagen, was sie vorhaben und ob sie ihren Plan einhalten.

If you visited a city for the first time, would you explore by yourself or go on a guided tour? Give reasons.

(Alternativer Einstieg über **KV 14: Map of Liverpool**.)

1 Morgan's plan   2 ▶ 02

Morgan: We have three hours. Let's go to the °waterfront at Albert °Dock.
Gareth: OK, we can go through Mathew Street on the way.
5 Gwen: Mathew Street? The street that's full of tourist shops?

(Picture 1 speech bubbles: "Please, not more Beatles!" / "Gareth … Remember the plan we made!" / "We could go to the Beatles Story too. It's on the way.")

Gwen / Morgan / Gareth

Gareth: For tourists who like the Beatles – like me!
Gwen: But I want to see the real Liverpool.
10 Morgan: OK, here's the plan. We walk to the waterfront and go along Mathew Street on the way. So you see all the Beatles stuff that you want to.
Gareth: Maybe I'll buy some John Lennon
15 sunglasses. He's the Beatle I like best.
Morgan: And *Gwen* decides what we do after that.   (+before that)
Gwen: I'd like to go to Greaty.
Morgan: Greaty?
Gwen: It's a market which sells food and clothes,
20 and things normal people buy.
Gareth: The real Liverpool!
Gwen: It's in *Great* Homer Street. Greaty. Get it?
Morgan: OK, that's what we'll do if no one protests.   (+protest (n.))

(Picture 4 speech bubbles: "Is this the right way for the market?" / "Well, that's the cathedral we went to for the concert yesterday. I'd love to sing there." / "Me too. But right now I'd like to know where we're going.")

2 A city walk   2 ▶ 03

Read the picture story.
Then take turns to describe the scenes.
Did the kids keep to Morgan's plan?

A: In the first picture, the kids are walking along Mathew Street.
B: Right. That's where Gareth wanted to go. And it's part of Morgan's plan.

Picture 2: waterfront - part of the plan • Picture 3: Chinatown - not part of the plan • Picture 4: Cathedral - not part of the plan • Picture 5: trying to find Great Homer Street/Greaty is their plan, but they're too far away • Picture 6: a shop - not part of the plan

3 The real Liverpool

a) Listen to the dialogue between the choir kids and two local kids, Grace and Charlie Hill. Say which of these topics they talk about.

Chinatown · drinks · a drumming workshop · football · James Clarke Street · Liverpool Cathedral · the real Liverpool

Write them in a list.

b) Listen again. Take notes about each of the topics in your list.

c) Take turns to say what you found out about the topics in your list.

drinks: Gareth and Gwen: banana-coconut drink · the three drinks are £ 3.30
a drumming workshop: Slavery Museum · Charlie and Grace did it on a class trip · about African drumming
football: everyone in Charlie's family is a Liverpool fan · next day: game at Anfield · kids couldn't get tickets · maybe they can use Charlie's family's tickets
James Clarke Street: Charlie and Grace live there · in Vauxhall · other side of the city centre
the real Liverpool: Gwen wants to see real Liverpool · Charlie and Grace are the real Liverpool

→ Text File 4 (p. 103)
Text File 4: A Liverpool street (Penny Lane)

3 Part A Practice

3 • FöFo 3.2 • LAS 3.1

1 Telephone information for tourists 2 05–06

Lernfeld: Die S können einer englischsprachigen automatischen Telefonansage Informationen entnehmen und diese auf deutsch weitergeben.

a) You're in Liverpool.
Partner A: You phone *The Beat Museum of Liverpool*.
Listen and take notes on Message 1.
Partner B: You phone *The Merseyside Football Museum*.
Listen and take notes on Message 2.

TIP
Before you listen, write down the main things that you want to find out.
You can use English or German for your list and for your notes.

b) Tell your partner in German what you have found out.

➜ Workbook 2 (p. 34)

Partner A: Öffnungszeiten: 10–17 Uhr, 7 Tage/Wo. • weitere Informationen: Webseite • man kann Nachricht hinterlassen, wenn man zurückgerufen werden möchte • Partner B: Öffnungszeiten: 10–18 Uhr, 7 Tage/Wo. (außer Weihnachten) • Öffnungszeiten während Schulferien: siehe Webseite • der Besuch dauert ca. 2 Stunden • die Audio-Tour dauert 1,5 Stunden, in 7 Sprachen

2 WORDS John Lennon was a famous musician

a) Use the ideas below to make six sentences like this:
John Lennon was a famous musician who wrote Imagine and other songs.

Cate Blanchett	brilliant	actor	build	*Imagine*
Gustave Eiffel	famous	architect	+design	the Boy Scouts
John Lennon	great	+engineer	+found	the Eiffel Tower
Norman Foster	well-known	musician	+invent	the thermometer
Steffi Graf	…	scientist	play (in)	*The Hobbit*
Galileo Galilei	Australian	+sportsperson	win	the *Reichstag* building
Robert Baden-Powell	British	+soldier	write	the Wimbledon Singles
…	French	…	…	
	Italian			
	…			

+design (n.)

More help ➜ p. 120
More help: Die S ordnen Satzhälften einander zu und verbinden sie mit *who*.

b) Use your own ideas to write three more sentences like the ones in a).

Early finisher ➜ p. 128 **Early finisher:** Strange answers.

Cate Blanchett is a famous Australian actor who played in *The Hobbit*. • Gustave Eiffel was a great French engineer who built the Eiffel Tower. • Norman Foster is a well-known British architect who designed the Reichstag building. • Steffi Graf is a famous German sportsperson who won the Wimbledon Singles. • Galileo Galilei was a brilliant Italian scientist who invented the thermometer. • Robert Baden-Powell was a British soldier who founded the Boy Scouts.

3 REVISION Crossword clues (Relative pronouns)

Write clues for the crossword.
Use relative pronouns, e.g.

1 A thing **which** you can see in the sky at night.
2 A person **who** works with you in class.

3 A black thing which people use to make fire.
4 A person who sings.
5 The things which people wear on the nose to see.
6 A thing which you use to clean the floor.
7 The Welsh boy who likes the Beatles.
8 Something which is at the end of your arm.
9 A thing which takes people upstairs.
10 An animal which swims in a river or the sea.
11 A white animal which you see in the countryside.

More help ➜ p. 120
More help: Ideen sind vorgegeben.

Early finisher ➜ Go to a bus stop and find a partner. Play this game.

The part of your body that has fingers. *That's easy! 8.*

Crossword:
1 down: SPARTAN... (S)
2 across: PARTNER
3 down: COAL → C
4 down: ...
5 across: SINGER
6 across: MOP
7 across: GARETH
8 down: HAND
9 down: LIFT
10 down: FISH (?)
11 across: SHEEP

➜ GF 4.1: Relative clauses (p. 162) ➜ Workbook 3 (p. 35)

Differenzierung/Alternative: Die S erstellen eigene Kreuzworträtsel, die dann die jeweiligen Partner lösen.

Part A Practice **3**

4 • Folie 9 • FöFo 3.2 • LAS 3.2

Lernfeld S. 49: Die S wiederholen **Relativsätze** und verwenden *contact clauses*.

> **Language help**
>
> When a relative pronoun is the **object**, you can leave it out.
>
> He's the Beatle who I like best.
> … der Beatle, den ich am liebsten mag.
> … the Beatle ~~who~~ I like best.
>
> Remember the plan that we made!
> … den Plan, den wir gemacht haben!
> … the plan ~~that~~ we made!
>
> When a relative pronoun is the **subject**, you cannot leave it out.
>
> He's the Beatle who wrote the best songs.
> … der Beatle, der die besten Songs schrieb.
>
> We need a plan that will work.
> … einen Plan, der funktioniert.
>
> Relative clauses without relative pronouns are called *contact clauses*. ➜ GF 4.2: Contact clauses (p. 163)

4 What was the name of that place …? (Contact clauses)

In the evening, Gareth tells other choir **members** about the walk, but he has forgotten lots of details.

I got these sunglasses in Mathew Street. And then … — Gareth

Gwen, what was the name of that place we went to after Mathew Street?

Albert Dock! — Gwen

a) Write down Gareth's other questions to Gwen. Use contact clauses.

What was the name of the …
1 town • see on the other side of the Mersey
   What was the name of the town we saw … ?
2 Chinese gate • see
3 church • would like to sing in
4 market • not find
5 green bananas • see outside that shop
6 girl and boy • meet at the shop

b) 👥 Find the answers to Gareth's questions. Then act out a dialogue.

What was the name of the town we saw … ?

Birkenhead!

a) 2 What was the name of the Chinese gate we saw? • 3 What was the name of the church we would like to sing in? • 4 What was the name of the market we didn't find? • 5 What was the name of the green bananas we saw outside that shop? • 6 What were the names of the girl and boy we met at the shop?

b) 2 Chinatown Arch • 3 the cathedral • 4 Greaty • 5 plantains • 6 Grace and Charlie

5 Gwen's photos (Contact clauses)

Gwen talks about the photos she took.

Make sentences with contact clauses if possible. If not, use a relative pronoun in the sentence.

1 shops • wanted to see.
   These are the shops Gareth wanted to see.
2 the shop • sells John Lennon sunglasses
   This is the shop that sells …John Lennon sunglasses.
3 the sunglasses • bought there
   These are the sunglasses Gareth bought there.
4 one of the ferries • crosses the Mersey
5 the Chinese gate • saw on our walk
6 the kids • gave us tickets for the match
7 the shop • work in
8 the fruit • looks like green bananas

4 This is one of the ferries which crosses the Mersey.
5 This is the Chinese gate we saw on our walk.
6 These are the kids who gave us tickets for the match.
7 This is the shop they work in.
8 This is the fruit that looks like green bananas.

➜ **Workbook** 4 (p. 35)

More help ➜ p. 120 **Early finisher** ➜ p. 128

More help: Die Sätze sind ausformuliert. Die S entscheiden, ob ein Relativpronomen nötig ist.

Early finisher: Rätsel.

49

3 Background file

Lernfeld S. 50: Die S können einen Text über die **Beatles** verstehen und eigene Informationen zu einem Song recherchieren. Sie können gut strukturierte Texte über Bands/Sänger schreiben.

YT
The Beatles – a Liverpool band

The band
The Beatles are the best-selling band in history, with over 600 million records sold. From their first meeting in 1957 to their 1970 album *Let It Be*, they changed the history of pop music.

The beginnings
The Beatles' success story started in 1960, when the young musicians (George was only 17!) played in clubs in Liverpool and Hamburg. They made their first record, *Love Me Do*, in London in 1962.

A new sound
The band from Liverpool was the first British group to take the world by storm with a new sound in rock music. Two guitars, a bass, drums and two or three singers may not seem new now, but in those days, it was a revolution. In the early 1960s, the "Fab Four" toured the world and "Beatlemania" was born.

Second revolution
In 1966, the Beatles gave their last concert. Because of their great success in the years before, they were able to experiment and change their style. On their later albums like *Sgt. Pepper's Lonely Hearts Club Band* or *Abbey Road*, they mixed many musical styles and created a whole new sound. These albums started another pop music revolution.

The solo careers
So far, the ex-Beatles have recorded 64 solo albums since they stopped recording together.

John Lennon – who some people have called **the "soul" of the Beatles** – became a fighter for freedom and peace, but he was murdered in 1980. His song *Imagine* is still well known all over the world:
Imagine all the people, living life in peace …
You may say I'm a dreamer, but I'm not the only one …

Paul McCartney – **the "heart" of the Beatles** – still attracts thousands to his concerts today. He sang *Hey Jude* at the opening of the 2012 London Olympics.

George Harrison – **the "spirit" of the Beatles** – was influenced by Indian culture and made music to raise money for people in poor countries. He died in 2001.

Ringo Starr – **the one "who played the drums"** – worked on musical projects and films and still performs with different artists.

a) Choose a Beatles song and find out more about it (who wrote it, when; which album it was on; what it is about; …)
Write a short info box about your song.

b) GALLERY WALK Hang up the info boxes, walk around and read them all.
Bring your Beatles song to class. Present it and play it to your classmates.

Text File 4: A Liverpool street (Penny Lane) kann auch hier eingesetzt werden.

3 Structuring a text — Writing course

Lernfeld S. 51: Die S können einen Text in **sinnvolle Abschnitte** gliedern *(introduction, body, conclusion)*. Sie können Feedback zu Texten von Partnern geben und aufgrund von Rückmeldungen Anderer ihre eigenen Texte verbessern.

YT 1 Learn how

A text is easier to follow when it has an **introduction**, a **body** and a **conclusion**.

- In the **introduction**, you tell your reader what your text is about.
- In the **body**, you go into detail about your topic. You usually use **several** paragraphs.
- In the **conclusion**, you can give your **opinion**, or **end** with an interesting or funny fact about the topic.

+in my opinion

a) Read these five paragraphs about the Beatles and Hamburg. On a copy, label the paragraphs *introduction, body* and *conclusion*. Decide on the right order.   Introduction: C · Body: E, A, B · Conclusion: D

A On their second trip they played in better clubs like the Kaiserkeller, the Top Ten and the Star Club, but the **schedule** was still very hard. Sometimes they started playing at 7pm and didn't finish until 7 am the next morning! In 1961 they played every night for 98 nights without **a day off**!

B They didn't **earn** much for their concerts, but their Hamburg **experience** was an important part of their training as musicians and as a band. **As** John Lennon said: "**I might have been born** in Liverpool – but I **grew up** in Hamburg."

C Many people say that the Beatles invented the **modern** rock band, but not everyone knows that their **success** began in Hamburg. Between August 1960 and December 1962, they made five trips to the city, and **performed** 281 times.

D If you go to Hamburg today, you can visit the Beatles Platz on the corner of the Reeperbahn and Große Freiheit streets. It's a **popular monument** to the famous band's experience in Germany.

E On their first trip, the Beatles performed in the Indra Club – a small and dirty place in the Reeperbahn area of Hamburg. They played four **one-hour concerts** each night.

b) Compare your labels. Did you label the text in the same way? Do you agree on the right order? Explain your reasons.

2 Now write …

Write about your favourite band or sports team.

TIP
1. Organize your ideas and plan your paragraphs. (See the TIPS on p. 38.)
2. Write your text. **Remember**:
   - say what the text is about (first paragraph)
   - use topic sentences in the body of the text
   - find a good way to end your text.
3. Read your text. Check your topic sentences and decide **if** the paragraphs are in a good order.
4. Change the order of the paragraphs if necessary.

3 … and revise

KV 6: Giving feedback on texts hilft bei der Rückmeldung.

a) 👥 Give feedback. Read your partner's text and make notes to answer these questions:
- Is there a good introduction to the topic?
- Do the paragraphs in the body of the text give more information about the topic? Are they in a good order?
- Does the conclusion end the text in a funny or interesting **way**?   Box "way", Voc, S. 185

Take turns to make comments and suggestions.

b) Think about your partner's feedback. Decide what to change and write a second draft.

➡ SF 10: Good sentences (p. 144);
   SF 14: Feedback – writing (p. 146)
➡ **Workbook** 5–6 (pp. 36–37), Wordbank 1, 7

Part B

> Lernfeld S. 52–53: Die S können Texten und Bildern, die eng mit der Geschichte einer Stadt verbunden sind (hier Liverpool), Informationen entnehmen und diese anderen weitergeben.

1 At the slavery museum

2 ▶ 07 (+leader) The guide **led** the choir group into the first gallery. "This museum <u>was founded</u> to tell the story of slavery," she began. "But it also tells us about life in West Africa before the slave **trade**. And that's what we'll learn about in the first gallery."

"We'd have much more fun at the Beatles Story!" said Gareth under his breath.

"Sssh!" said Gwen and Morgan together.

In the gallery, the guide pointed to a **mask**. Gareth jumped in front of Morgan and Gwen. He held his hands on his head like **horns** and rolled back his eyes to look like the mask. Gwen had to laugh, but Morgan didn't find it funny. "Come on, you two. Do you have to behave like little kids?" The guide smiled. "So you like the goat's face?"

"Sorry?" said Gareth.

"This mask is a goat's face. It <u>was made</u> in West Africa a long time ago. Similar masks <u>are worn</u> in Nigeria today, at the festivals of the Ogoni **people**." [oʊˈɡoʊni]

"Who wears them?" Morgan asked.

"Boys and young men wear masks with animal faces at festivals and parties."

[ˈuːduː]
[ˈiːbəʊ]

2 ▶ 08 "Is that a drum?" Gwen asked.

"Yes," said the guide. "It's an udu – an instrument of the Igbo people. Udus <u>are made</u> of **clay**, not wood. And they have a funny **shape**, like water **pots**. In fact, they <u>are also called</u> water pot drums because first they <u>were used</u> to **carry** water. And then one day someone found that they could also make music. It was probably a woman. Carrying water is a woman's job and, usually, udus <u>are played</u> by women."

"What about that drum there?" Morgan asked.

"That's a djembe, a drum of the Bamana people. It has a great sound, probably [ˈdʒembeɪ] [bæˈmɑːnə] because <u>it's played</u> with **bare** hands, not with sticks. <u>It's used</u> at special events, like family celebrations."

"My cousin has a drum like that," Gareth said. "Are they really from Africa?"

"Yes," said the guide, "but they're very popular in Britain now."

"I'd like to try it," Gareth said.

"Maybe you can in your workshop … Ah, here's your workshop leader now. So I'll leave you, and see you later for our tour of the second gallery."

A tall man with °**dreadlocks** walked towards them.

"My name is Gordon Skeefe," he said and shook hands with everyone.

2 In the first gallery

a) When Gareth made a face like the mask, Gwen, Morgan and the guide reacted differently. Describe their reactions.

b) Say what you think about how Gareth behaved.
- I think he didn't show enough **respect**.
- It was only a joke. He didn't want to hurt anyone.
- In my opinion, it's OK to have fun in a museum.
- I agree. / I don't agree.
- …

3 The drumming workshop **2 ▶ 09**

Listen to Mr Skeefe. Take notes on:
- what he says about Jamaica — in the West Indies; he was born there
- where his **ancestors** come from — Africa (probably Nigeria)
- why he has travelled to western Africa — to find out more about the music of his ancestors
- what he says about the drums
- why he says Gareth is like a baby

EXTRA Say how you think Gareth feels after the workshop. Is he still sorry that he couldn't go to the Beatles story?

<u>what he says about the drums:</u> the Udu is played by Igbo women at celebrations · the djembe can make three different sounds (pe, pa, pu) · you can make different rhythms with these three sounds · <u>why he says Gareth is like a baby:</u> babies copy the sounds of their mothers, so they learn how to speak · Gareth copied the sounds of the drum and has learned the language of the drums

6 • Folie 10 • FöFo 3.4   Part B   3

4 After the second gallery

Look at the picture of Morgan, Gareth and Gwen and say how they feel.
Why do you think they feel like this?

5 The slave trade

a) Make groups of four.
Each partner chooses one of the texts on pp. 133–134. Read your text and take notes.

> **TIP**
> The 5 **Ws** (When? Where? What? Who? Why?) can help you to find the important information when you take notes.

b) Use your notes to say what you have read. When everyone has spoken, say what was new to you, or what surprised or shocked you.

c) Tell the class how your group reacted.

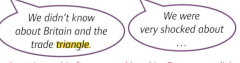

6 Have a go

> **Lernfeld:** Die S verwenden vorbewusst das **Passiv**.

The mask on p. 52 was made in West Africa. Say where other things were made. You could talk about your pencil, your computer, your mobile, your family car, your T-shirt …

Access to cultures

You can visit national museums everywhere in the UK for free.
What about museums in your country?
What are the advantages of free museums?

5a) Text 1: 17th/18th century: British sent goods to Africa; African rulers paid with people • British sold Africans in America for sugar, tobacco etc. and became rich
Text 2: journey Africa to America: ca. 8 weeks • bad conditions: tiny space, many died • in America: captives had to work as slaves
Text 3: plantations = big farms owned by white Europeans • living conditions = awful: long days, brutal punishments, little food, many died young
Text 4: slaves' protest: slow work, pretend to be sick, rebellions, traditional songs • 18th century: people in Britain changed their opinion about slavery • 1807: UK parliament bans slave trade; 1833: UK parliament bans slavery (but in many countries, slavery was still allowed)

3 Part B Practice

LAS 3.3

Lernfeld S. 54–55: Die S verwenden das **Passiv** (im **simple present**, **simple past** sowie das **Passiv mit** *by*).

Looking at language

a) Look at these sentences:
1. Similar masks are worn in Nigeria today.
2. Boys and young men wear masks with animal faces.

Which sentence tells us *who* wears the masks?
That sentence is *active*. The other sentence is *passive*.

How many of these sentences have a passive verb form?
This museum was founded to tell the story of slavery.
Udus are made of clay, not wood.
A tall man with dreadlocks walked towards them.

b) To make the passive, we use a form of *be* + the past participle.

Complete these sentences from p. 52.
This mask … made in West Africa.
In fact, they … also called water pot drums.
First they … used to carry water.
It … played with bare hands.

Say what tenses the sentences are in.

➡ GF 5: The passive (pp. 164–165)

1 Building an Igbo house (Passive sentences: simple present) ['iːbəʊ]

Complete the sentences with a verb in the passive.

1. First, a good place … (choose), usually on land that … (own) by the family.
2. Then the land … (clear) to make **room** for the building.
3. After that the building **materials** … (collect).
4. Different materials … (need): mud, wood and grass.
5. The mud … usually (make) with clay and water, but sometimes sand … (add) too.
6. The floors and walls … (build) with the mud.
7. Sometimes wood … (use) with the mud to make the walls stronger.
8. The finished walls … (paint) with special designs.
9. The roof … (**cover**) with grass.
10. Heavier work … (do) by men. Easier jobs … (do) by women and children.

1 is chosen, is owned · 2 is cleared · 3 are collected · 4 are needed · 5 is usually made, is added · 6 are built · 7 is used · 8 are painted · 9 is covered · 10 is done, are done

➡ Workbook 7 (p. 37)

2 They aren't worn at Igbo festivals (Passive: simple present)

Correct the wrong information in each sentence. You can check the facts on p. 52.

1. Goat face masks are worn at Igbo festivals.
   – No, they aren't worn at Igbo festivals.
   They're worn at Ogoni festivals. [əʊˈɡəʊni]
2. Goat face masks are worn by young women and girls.
   – No, they … *No, they aren't worn by young women and girls. They're worn by boys and young men.*
3. An udu is made of wood.
   – No, it … *No, it isn't made of wood. It's made of clay.*
4. Udus are played by men and older boys. [ˈuːduː]
5. Djembe drums are also called water pot drums.
6. The djembe is used every day. [ˈdʒembeɪ]
7. The djembe is played with sticks.

More help ➡ p. 121 | **More help:** Die S müssen nur die Passivformen verwenden.

4 No, they aren't played by men and older boys. They're played by women.
5 No, they aren't called water pot drums. Udus are called water pot drums.
6 No, the djembe isn't used every day. It's used at special events, like family celebrations.
7 No, the djembe isn't played with sticks. It's played with bare hands.

Early finisher Look at exercise 1 again. Make three wrong sentences about Igbo houses. Find a partner to correct your sentences.

7 • Folie 11 • KV 15 • FöFo 3.4

Part B Practice 3

3 Which is oldest? (Passive: simple past)

a) Look at the pictures and read the dialogue.
A: Which one was built first?
B: I think Chinatown Arch was built first.
A: Sorry, that's wrong. The Chinatown Gate was built in 2000. The Brandenburg Gate was built in the 18th century. OK, it's your turn.

b) Partner A: Continue on p. 132.
Partner B: Continue on p. 135.

Colone Cathedral: started 1248, finished 1880 / Liverpool Cathedral: started 1907, finished 1978 • Mona Lisa: painted 1503–1507 / portrait of Beethoven: painted 1820 • Berlin Underground: opened 1902 / London Underground: opened 1863 • Treasure Island: written 1881–1883 / Oliver Twist: written 1837–1839 • Lift: invented 1852 / Escalator: invented 1895

Chinatown Arch Liverpool
Brandenburg Gate Berlin

➜ Workbook 8 (p. 38)

4 Oliver Twist was written by … (Passive with by)

a) Make sentences like the ones in the examples.

Oliver Twist was written *by Charles Dickens*.

The 2014 World Cup was won *by Germany*.

	build	by …
Romeo and Juliet	paint	
Treasure Island	sing	
The 1966 World Cup	win	
The 2010 Eurovision Song Contest	write	
Imagine		
We Are the Champions		
Hadrian's Wall		
The Eiffel Tower		
The Mona Lisa		

TIP
With the passive, we use *by …* if we want to say who did something.

More help: Die Zuordnung von Personen und Handlungen ist farblich markiert.

More help ➜ p. 121

b) Compare your answers.

Romeo and Juliet was written by William Shakespeare. • *Treasure Island* war written by Robert Louis Stevenson. • The 1966 World Cup was won by England. • The 2010 Eurovision Song Context was won by Lena. • *Imagine* was written by John Lennon. • *We Are the Champions* was sung by Queen. • Hadrian's Wall was built by the Romans. • The Eiffel Tower was built by Gustave Eiffel. • The *Mona Lisa* was painted by Leonardo da Vinci.

5 Liverpool quiz

Liverpool football
- Liverpool has two famous football teams. Liverpool FC was founded in 1892. Everton was founded in 1878.
- The football goal net was invented by an Everton fan in 1889. This made it easier to see when a goal was scored.

Liverpool buildings
- Liverpool's Anglican cathedral is the UK's largest, and the fifth largest in the world. It was designed by Sir Giles G. Scott.
- The name of Liverpool's airport was changed to John Lennon International Airport in 2002.

Liverpool culture
- Liverpool is the city with most galleries and national museums in the UK outside London.
- John Lennon was born in Liverpool in 1940.
- Over 250 bands are invited to perform in the Liverpool International Music Festival every year.

Liverpool firsts
- Europe's first Chinese community was founded in Liverpool in the 1850s.
- Britain's first mosque opened here in 1889.
- The UK's first Nobel prize was won here in 1902 by Sir Ronald Ross for his work on malaria.

a) Make groups of four. Each student reads *one* fact sheet and makes questions.
When was … founded/born/… ?
Where is/was … ? • How many … ?
What was … in 1889? • …

b) Read the other three fact sheets.

c) Ask your questions to the group.

➜ Workbook 9–10 (pp. 38–39)

Zusatz: Die **KV 15: The goalkeeper was bitten by a mouse** dient der weiteren Einübung des Passivs und als inhaltliche Hinführung zu Part C.

55

3 Part C

Lernfeld S. 56–57: Die S können Hörtexten Informationen zu einem Sportereignis entnehmen und dem Text Bilder zuordnen. Sie können die Informationen aus dem Hörtext nutzen, um über eigene Erlebnisse zu berichten.

1 The match at Anfield 🎧 2 ▶11–15

a) Look at the scenes in pictures A–E and say what is happening.

b) You will hear the five scenes in the right order. Listen and match each scene to a picture.
1D · 2E · 3B · 4C · 5A

I think scene 1 is picture A.   *No, scene 1 is picture …*

c) Listen again. Take notes about each scene.
Scene 1: Choir kids wait, G + C arrive late.
Scene 2: …

d) 👥 Compare your notes.
Change or add information if necessary.
Scene 2: Chelsea fans are welcomed, fans sing a song
Scene 3: one nil for Chelsea, Gareth claps
Scene 4: Liverpool scores, 2:1 for Liverpool
Scene 5: kids leave the stadium, say goodbye to each other

2 The match on the radio 🎧 2 ▶16

Listen to a report about the match. Find out
- which of these players scored:
  Barnes · (Bates) · Beedle · Jezzard · (Oscar)
- the **score** at half-time   Chelsea lead 1:0
- the **final** score.   Liverpool win 2:1

Add the information to your notes.

TIP
We talk about football scores like this:
1:0	one nil	1:1	one all
2:1	two one	2:2	two all

Part C 3

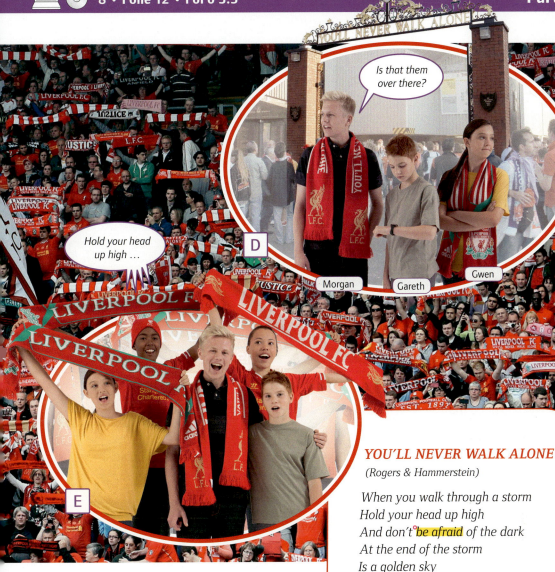

3 A great afternoon

Neigungsdifferenzierung: Die S wählen eine Perspektive ihrer Wahl.

a) **You choose** Imagine you are one of the five kids at the match. Use the notes you took in 1 and 2 to write about *your* afternoon there.

b) Swap texts.
Read your partner's text and give feedback. Say what is good about it:

- ✓ It has an introduction, a body and a conclusion.
- ✓ It has all the important information.
- ✓ The information is in a good order.
- ✓ The sentences are linked well.
- ○ …

➡ SF 14: Feedback – writing (p. 146)
➡ Inside back cover: Giving feedback

KV 6: Giving feedback on texts hilft bei der Rückmeldung.

YOU'LL NEVER WALK ALONE
(Rogers & Hammerstein)

When you walk through a storm
Hold your head up high
And don't °be afraid of the dark
At the end of the storm
Is a golden sky
And the sweet °silver song of the °lark
Walk on through the wind
Walk on through the rain
°Though your dreams be tossed and blown
Walk on walk on with hope in your heart
And you'll never walk alone

4 The fan song

Read the lyrics of the Liverpool fan song and choose what you think its message is:
1. Don't walk alone in bad weather.
2. (Never give up your dreams.)
3. Everyone needs sunshine after a rainy day.

EXTRA Listen to the song and sing along.

3 Part C Practice

9 • Folie 12 • KV 15, 18 • FöFo 3.5

1 WORDS Grace and Charlie's favourite sport

Match the words in the box to the picture of the football match.

Zusatz: Die S üben Passivsätze im thematischen Kontext von Fußball ein, indem sie die in **KV 15: The goalkeeper was bitten by a mouse** dargestellten Szenen in einem Fußballstadion beschreiben.

football¹ • football fan⁸ • player² • goal⁴ • shirt⁵ • ⁺referee⁷ • ⁺goalkeeper³
• socks⁹ • ⁺°shin guards¹⁰ • goalkeeper's glove⁶

➜ Workbook 11 (p. 39)

2 Study skills: Ordering and structuring topic vocabulary

Lernfeld: Die S können Wortschatz zu einem Thema ordnen und strukturieren.

Before you write a text, it helps to order and structure vocabulary for your topic.

a) What equipment do football players need?
   Add as many words as you can to the equipment umbrella.

   players' ⁺equipment
   socks
   shirt
   …

b) When you order topic words, you can use a tree diagram.
   Look at this diagram and say where you would add your equipment umbrella.

```
                        a football match
        ┌──────────────────┼──────────────────┐
    ⁺stadium             people           competitions
    ┌────┬─────┐      ┌────┬──────┬──────┐   ┌─────────┬──────────┐
  on ⁺pitch  off pitch team fans referee   national   international
                                           (England)
  corner    seat    players equipment ⁺manager  ⁺scarf  whistle  °Premier   …
    …        …     goalkeeper shirt              …     ⁺free kick  League
                      …        …                                     …
```

c) Add words from 1 and from the right to a copy of the diagram in b).

   More help ➜ p. 121
   KV: 16: Tree diagram – A football match spart Zeit.
   More help: Die Wörter sind bereits vorsortiert.

   flag watch
   midfielder foul penalty area
   °refreshment stalls substitute defender
   cards song fa cup ticket office
   °terrace striker penalty
   goal fifa world cup

d) Now make a tree diagram for one of these sports:
   basketball • hockey • tennis • volleyball
   ➜ Sports words (pp. 136–137)

Study skills

Ordering and structuring topic vocabulary
Wenn ich einen Text zu einem bestimmten Thema schreibe, sollte ich zuerst …

Vergleiche deine Ideen mit dem Abschnitt im Skills File.
➜ SF 1: Structuring vocabulary (p. 139)

➜ Workbook 12–13 (p. 40)

▶ **The world behind the picture** 3

Lernfeld S. 59: Die S können Vermutungen über einen Film anstellen und diese anhand des gesehenen Ausschnitts verifizieren, indem sie besonders die **Körpersprache** der Figur(en) und die **Musik im Film** zu Rate ziehen.

1 The story

There's only one Jimmy Grimble is a film about a boy who gets a pair of football boots from an old woman. The old woman says the boots are magic, but Jimmy throws them away.

Say why you think he doesn't want the boots.

2 The bullies

a) 👥 You can't see Jimmy's face in this still. But can you guess how he feels? Discuss your ideas.

b) Watch part 1. Then say
 • what happens to Jimmy's boots
 • why this is a problem
 • how Jimmy **solves** the problem.

c) Say what you think of the way the other boys behave.
 ➜ Text File 5 *(p. 104)*

Länge: 3:05

b) what happens to Jimmy's boots: his new boots are stolen by the boys and thrown away
why this is a problem: his football team has a match and he has no boots to play with now
how Jimmy solves the problem: he runs back and picks up the old "magic" boots again

3 The match

a) 👥 Look at the still. Discuss what you think has happened to Jimmy.

b) Watch part 2.
Then say how Jimmy's feelings change.

(At first he feels very …) (Then he is …) (At the end, he feels …)

Länge: 1:59

4 The language of film

a) Watch part 2 without sound.
Say how Jimmy's face and body language tell us about his feelings.

(The way he closes his eyes and looks down tells us …) (The way he jumps up and down shows that …)

b) Now watch with sound. Say what happens
 • when the music is playing
 • when the music stops
 • in the **slow motion** scenes.

EXTRA Say what effect the music and slow motion have.
I think the music makes the film more …

59

3 Text

Lernfeld S. 60–61: Die S können einem Text Informationen über einen *local hero* entnehmen und erkennen, was er/sie Großes geleistet hat. Sie können Ideen zusammentragen, welche Leistungen jemandem zu einem *hero* machen und darüber sprechen.

A Liverpool hero

Look at the the man in the pictures. Why do you think he is remembered?

[ˈvɒksɔːl]

On hot summer's days, kids like to be near the water, and it was no different over a hundred years ago in Liverpool. One hot summer's day in 1911, a group of children from Vauxhall, a poor area of the
5 city, walked from Scotland Road over to the Leeds & Liverpool Canal. The sun shone strongly from a blue sky and they wanted to cool off in the deep, cold water. The canal is still there today but no one swims in it now.
10 That afternoon, over 100 years ago, the children played happily next to the water. People who crossed the bridge on Eldonian Way could hear the children's screams and laughter as they passed. The swimmers jumped in and out of the canal; those
15 who couldn't swim sat on the edge with their legs in the water.
Little Willy was one of the boys who sat on the edge. The cool water felt good on his feet, but the sun was so hot on his face and arms. "If only I
20 could just put some cold water on my face," he thought. "Then I'd feel much better."
He started to bend down and moved his arms towards the water. His fingers touched the surface and disappeared and then, with a great big splash,
25 Willy's whole body followed and he fell in. He seemed to go down in the canal for ever. He didn't know where was up and where was down. The cold, dirty water burned his open eyes and he could see nothing in the dark canal. When his head
30 came up, he opened his mouth and screamed, but he couldn't reach the side. He screamed again and again and tried to hold his head out of the water but he kept going under. His mouth was full of water. He was so scared he couldn't really think
35 any more. His friends in the water were scared too. They didn't want to go near him and be pulled under. Those on the canal's edge were too far away to reach him. Like many others before him, Willy was going to drown.
40 Then, suddenly, out of nowhere, a man appeared. He was big and strong and he ran to the canal and dived in. He soon reached Willy and swam quickly back to the side with him. Willy was saved. The big, strong man who saved him was James Clarke.
45 Today, almost everyone in Liverpool, almost everyone in Britain, learns to swim when they're young, often at school. But it wasn't always like that, and James Clarke, a champion swimmer from Liverpool, was one of the people who helped to
50 change things.

60

JAMES CLARKE

- Born in 1886 in Georgetown, British Guyana, South America.
- He arrived in Liverpool as a °stowaway at the age of 14.
- He was found in the city and went to live with an Irish family in Vauxhall.
- In 1914 he married a young Irish woman. They had 13 children together.
- He worked in the docks.
- He loved swimming and started his career at Wavertree Swimming Club.
- He became a swimming champion there and later at other clubs in Liverpool.
- For 40 years he performed in swimming shows in many parts of Britain. His favourite trick was to put a bucket over his head and sit under water and sing "Oh my darling, Clementine".
- He saved many children, sailors and dock workers from drowning in the River Mersey and the Leeds & Liverpool Canal. He helped the police to find the bodies of people who had drowned.
- He believed that all children should be able to swim, so he started to give lessons at his local pool. His idea spread until there were swimming lessons in schools all over the city.
- He was a local hero. When he died in 1946, children °lined the streets from his home to the church where his funeral took place.
- In 1986, "James Clarke Street" became the first street in Liverpool that was named after a black man.

1 Did you get it?

Choose the right ending for each sentence: a, b or c.

1. Little Willy fell into the water because he wanted to …
   a) cool his face.   b) disappear.   c) swim.

2. James Clarke came to Liverpool in …
   a) 1886.   b) 1900.   c) 1914.

3. His swimming career started in the …
   a) Leeds and Liverpool Canal.
   b) River Mersey.
   c) Wavertree Swimming Club.

4. He often saved people from drowning …
   a) all over Britain.
   b) in the canal and in the River Mersey.
   c) in the Wavertree Swimming Club.

5. This gave him the idea to …
   a) call the police.
   b) start swimming lessons for children.
   c) work in swimming shows.

2 What do you think?

Name the thing about James Clarke that most makes him a hero in your eyes. Tell the class.

3 Local hero

a) Work in groups of four. Make a placemat on an A3 piece of paper. Think how someone could become a hero in your area. Write your ideas in your corner of the placemat.

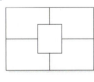

b) Turn the placemat and read the others' ideas. Discuss the ideas and agree on the best one. Write it in the middle of the placemat.

c) Present your idea to the class.

EXTRA Imagine you interviewed the local hero who carried out this idea.
Write the interview.

→ Workbook 14 (p. 41)

Text File 5: Juggling with gerbils (Gedichte von Brian Patten)

3 Unit

Your task

> **Steps 1–4** werden von den S als Hausaufgabe/Projekt bearbeitet. Dies kann in EA, aber auch als PA oder in kleinen Gruppen passieren.
> **Step 5** führt dann die Ergebnisse in der Klasse zusammen.

The story behind a name

📖 Imagine a British school has asked students from your school to write a text for its magazine. Like James Clarke Street in Liverpool, lots of German streets and buildings have a story behind them. Write a text about the person behind the name of a building or street in your area.

STEP 1
Choose a bridge, street, school, theatre … in your area.
Take a photo of the name sign and the building or street.

STEP 2
Get information from the internet or a library. Here are some ideas about what you could find out:
- a few important facts about the place you choose (e.g. when the bridge/school/… was built)
- some facts about the person and why he or she is famous
- when the building or street was named after the person
- why it is important to remember the person or event

Take notes and organize your information in a mindmap or table.

STEP 3
Write a first draft of your text. Organize your information in paragraphs.
Your text should have:
- an introduction, e.g.
  In Germany, lots of places are named after people. Not far from my house is a bridge which is called …
- a body: remember to start each paragraph with a topic sentence.
  - *The Carl-Schurz-Brücke was built in … /*
  - *Carl Schurz is famous because he was the first German who … Schurz was born in …*
- a conclusion
  It is important to remember people like Schurz because …

STEP 4
Go to p. 63 to check your first draft. Then revise it.

STEP 5
🧩 **GALLERY WALK** Hang up your text and photos in the classroom.
Walk around, read the other texts and look at the photos.

EXTRA Use your text to make an audio guide for British visitors.

➡ **Workbook** *Wordbank 1–3, 7*

Unit 3

How did you do?
Answer these questions about your text.

How can you do better?
If your answer is "no", follow the tips below.

Content	**Tips**
Have you given enough information about the person behind your street name?	• Check your mindmap or table: Highlight information that is not in your text. • Decide what information to add to your text.
Structure	
Have you used paragraphs to organize your information?	• Read the text again and look for places where you could start a new paragraph.
Does your first paragraph say what you are going to write about?	• Read your paragraphs again and make notes about their content. • Use your notes to revise your introduction.
Does your conclusion go well with the rest of the text?	In this text, you are writing about two things: • a building or a street • a person Your conclusion should bring these ideas together. For example, you could say how you think the person would feel, if he or she knew that a place was named after them. ➡ p. 51, Structuring a text
Language	
Could you find the right words to describe your person and what he or she did?	• Look at the table in exercise 2 a) on page 48. Decide what kind of words you need: adjectives, nouns or verbs. If you can't find the words you need in the table look them up in a dictionary.

Did you use the passive to talk about the history of places? For example: *The school was named after Max Planck in 1947.*	• Go back and check where you can use a passive sentence to improve your text. ➡ p. 55 ex.3

4 Unit

Leistungsmessung Unit 4

My trip to Ireland

Lernfeld S. 64–65: Die S können Hörtexten **Informationen über Irland und Nordirland** entnehmen und sich zu den darin beschriebenen Angeboten/Sehenswürdigkeiten äußern.

Text file: zu Unit 4 passen **Text 6** und **7**.

Lewis

1 Impressions of Ireland

Look at the photos for two minutes. Then close your books and say what you remember.

A: There's a picture of huge cliffs by the sea. Two people are lying at the edge of the cliff. Scary!
B: OK. My turn. I remember some signs …

➡ pp. 26–27 Look at Ireland on the map. Say what you notice about the island.

2) Lewis's trip starts in Edinburgh. From there he travels to Belfast across the North Channel. From there he goes north, then south to Ireland. He goes to Dublin, the capital of Ireland, and then to the west coast.

2 Lewis's trip

Lewis McCray from Edinburgh is visiting his Aunt Mary and Uncle Frank in Belfast. They're taking him on a tour of Ireland.

➡ pp. 26–27 Find Lewis's route around Ireland.

1, 2 • FöFo 4.1

Unit **4**

3 Attractions 2 ▶ 20–22

a) You will hear about three attractions.
→ pp. 26–27 Listen and find where they are on the map.
Say what you can do at each one.

b) Choose one of the attractions.
Explain why you would like to go there.

Your task

Your task for this unit: In a team, make a **brochure** with **practical** tips for Irish students who want to visit Germany.

→ Workbook 1 (p. 46)

National Leprechaun Museum in Dublin: a museum about Irish folk tales, fairy tales and magical stories, especially about people who are very small. They are called leprechauns. You can travel through a tunnel to the otherworld, walk through magical forests and even become one of the small people!

Titanic Belfast Experience: brings the Titanic, the most famous ship in the world, which hit an iceberg in 1912, back to life. You can see how the ship was built, have a look inside and listen to people who were on the Titanic when it sank. You can even travel below the sea and look at its resting place.

The Burren on Ireland's west coast: you can go riding on horses and ponies through the countryside and on sandy beaches with a view of cliffs and islands.

4 Part A

Lernfeld S. 66: Die S können einem Lesetext **Charaktereigenschaften einer Person** entnehmen und diese mit Textstellen belegen.

1 👆 Belfast and the **northern** coast
+western, southern, eastern

2▶23	Uncle F.:	Can you pass the **coffee**?
	Lewis:	May I have some too, please?
	Aunt M.:	Of course not! You mustn't drink coffee at your age! Is that what you do at home?
5	Lewis:	Er … sometimes.
	Aunt M.:	Well, it's not good for you. But what you can do, is help me to clear the table.
	Lewis:	Where are we going today?
	Uncle F.	To the **Giant's**°**Causeway**, about an hour
10		in the car from Belfast. But it might as well be the other side of the moon.

Box "möglich – wahrscheinlich – sicherlich", Voc, S. 188

	Lewis:	I don't understand.
	Uncle F.	You will … Now go and help your aunt!

❖

2▶24	Uncle F.	Don't drive so fast, Mary. I want to read
15		this to Lewis. "The cliffs are made of tall stone **columns**. In some places, the columns rise up nearly 30 metres from the water, while in others, they are like steps that form a wide stone path down
20		to the sea."
	Lewis:	What's so special about cliffs?
	Uncle F.:	You'll see!

❖

2▶25	Lewis:	Wow! This *is* like being on the moon! Who built this place?
25	Aunt M.:	There's a legend that it's the work of an Irish giant called Finn McCool.
	Lewis:	McCool? Sounds like the name of a DJ.
	Aunt M.:	°Does it now? But no, he was a giant, and a proud one too, who couldn't say no to
30		a challenge.
	Lewis:	That sounds more like me.
	Aunt M.:	Well, to go on with my story: One day a Scottish giant challenged Finn McCool to a fight. Finn of course agreed. But
35		because he couldn't swim, he built a stone path all the way to the Scottish coast. The giants met in the middle, fought°fiercely, and Finn won. After the fight, the Scottish giant was so scared
40		that Finn would follow him to Scotland, he pulled up the stones as he ran back home. What you see is all that is left.
	Uncle F.:	Where did you hear *that* story? I know a different legend. Shall I tell you?
45	Lewis:	Later. Right now I'd like to explore.
	Aunt M.	Careful or you'll fall and break your neck!

❖

	Uncle F.:	What about some music?
	Aunt M.:	It's only adverts.
	Uncle F.:	That advert is about the Titanic museum.
50		It's where we're going tomorrow.
	Lewis:	Really? Fantastic.

2▶2

2 Sounds like me

Say which adjectives best describe Lewis.
Find lines in the text which show this.

> careful · **curious** · excited · **impolite** · nervous · **polite** · proud · shocked · shy

Early finisher Describe the character of Aunt Mary or Uncle Frank.

3 Legends

Did someone really build the Giant's Causeway?
Say why you think legends say so.

> *I think people tell legends because …*

> *If you want to explain something …*

🌐 Find out how the Giant's Causeway was really formed. **Follow the link:** die S recherchieren online weiter.

➡ **Text Files 6** and **7** (pp. 106–111) ➡ **Workbook** 2 (p. 46)

Text File 6: Finn McCool (the legend behind the Giant's Causeway)
Text File 7: The Titanic

Moments in Irish history

Read about some key moments in Irish history.

1801

The Act of Union made Ireland part of the United Kingdom, with one parliament for all its countries. 121 years later, in 1922, southern Ireland left the UK. It became a **republic** in 1949. Northern Ireland chose to stay in the UK.

Irish flag before 1801   GB flag before 1801   UK flag from 1801

👉 **Find out** more about the long history of Ireland's relationship with Britain.
Why did southern Ireland leave the UK?
Why did the North keep its link with Britain?

1909 to 1911

The Titanic, the world's largest **passenger** ship at that time, was built in Belfast.
In April 1912, it **sailed** for the first and last time.

Building the Titanic in Belfast

👉 **Find out** about the Belfast shipyards and what happened to the Titanic. ➡ Text File 7

1998

The Belfast Agreement ended a 30-year **conflict** between **supporters** and **opponents** of Northern Ireland's **union** with Britain. Northern Ireland will now stay in the UK, but it will also have **closer** links with the Republic. During the conflict, over 3,000 people were killed.

Wall painting, Belfast

👉 **Find out** about four people who won the Nobel Peace Prize for their work on bringing peace to Northern Ireland.

1845 to 1849

The Great Famine started when a potato **disease** hit the country. Potatoes were then the main food for **half** the **population**, so millions of people **went hungry**. About a million died, and over a million left Ireland for ever.

Deserted village from the time of the Great Famine

👉 **Find out** why so many people died. Learn more about emigration from Ireland.

1973

The EEC (now the **EU**) **welcomed** the UK and Ireland as new members. **Membership** has been good for both parts of Ireland, but **especially** the Republic, which is now much richer than it was in the 1970s.

EEC members 1973

👉 **Find out** how the republic of Ireland has become a richer country.

2003

Google opened its European **headquarters** in Dublin. This continued the 1990s **boom** that made Ireland a big world centre for **high-tech companies**.

Dublin **Docklands**, where many big **IT** companies have their offices.

Follow the link: die S recherchieren auf dieser Seite zu verschiedenen Themen online weiter.

➡ Workbook 3 (p. 47)

4 Part A Practice

   3 · FöFo 4.2

1 WORDS Countries

Lernfeld: Die S können Wörter des **Wortfeldes** *countries* nach verschiedenen Strukturen ordnen.

You choose Choose one way to order these words: a, b or c. Then choose 25 words and try it out.

Neigungsdifferenzierung: Die S wählen die Methode, die am besten zu ihnen passt.

Box "Pounds and euros", Voc, S. 189

battle · beautiful · ⁺border · ⁺change money · coast · county · crown · culture · ⁺currency · defend · demonstration · enemy · ⁺EU · ⁺euro · Europe · flag · ⁺ID card · invade · island · king · land · language · mayor · ⁺nation · navy · parliament · ⁺passport · ⁺peace · peaceful · police officer · ⁺police station · ⁺population · pound · ⁺president · queen · ⁺republic · royal · ⁺state · traditional · travel · UK · village · ⁺visa · visit

a) Copy the table and add the nouns from the box. Then add the verbs or adjectives that go with the nouns. Think of more words for each noun, e.g. *passport + show*.

noun	verb	adjective
battle		
border		

c) Draw a picture with the words and label them.

b) Write the words in a mind map.

➡ Workbook 4 *(p. 48)*

2 REVISION Travelling to other countries *(Modal verbs)*

Lernfeld: Die S wiederholen **Modalverben**.

YT

a) Choose a country and write six rules for travelling there. Use *can, can't, must, mustn't* or *needn't*.

carry a knife in your bag · change money · get a visa · pay in euros · see a doctor · show your ID card · show your passport · take your pet/laptop/… · visit a police station

1 If you travel to the UK or Ireland, you must show your ID card or passport.
2 If you travel to Spain, you needn't …

More help ➡ p. 122

More help: Die S ergänzen Modalverben in den Sätzen.

b) Give advice to someone who is going to another country. You can use ideas from the table.

If you lose your passport/ID card	you could	buy some in a shop
If you don't have the right currency	you should	ask if they speak English
If you don't speak the language	you must	go to a police station
If you don't have the right clothes		go to a bank
If your money is stolen		have a problem at the airport
…		…

Early finisher ➡ *p. 129* ➡ GF 6.1: Modal verbs *(p. 165)* ➡ Workbook 5 *(p. 48)*

Early finisher: *matching exercise* oder *Quiz*.

68

KV 17 • FöFo 4.2

Part A Practice 4

Lernfeld S. 69: Die S arbeiten mit anderen in einem Team, in dem sie gemeinsam ein Projekt planen, Aufgaben verteilen, einen Zeitplan erstellen, das Projekt durchführen und über die Durchführung reflektieren.

3 Study skills: Teamwork

This page will show you how to work in a team.

a) When you work in a team, everyone has a special job. Match these four jobs to the speech bubbles.

1 coordinator
2 writer
3 picture and layout editor
4 language watchdog

1D · 2A · 3B · 4C

A I do *research*. When I find the information we need, I write the texts.

B I look for pictures, or I draw them. Then I put the pictures and the texts together so that our *results* look good.

C I check all the texts and make sure there are no mistakes. I also *suggest* how we can improve our text.

D I plan our *discussions* and take notes on our *decisions*. I also check that everyone does their job at the right time.

b) Work in teams of four. Choose one of these topics and make a brochure on it.

1 The Titanic
2 Irish writers
3 Horse riding in Ireland
4 Dublin for kids

KV 17: Project sheet hilft bei der Projektplanung.

Decide who will do what job and make a timetable for all the work. Then make your brochure.
www Find more information. You can also get information about the Titanic in the *Text File*.

Text File 7 (pp. 110–111)

c) Swap brochures with another team. In your team, say what you think about the other brochure.

d) **Think**: Think of at least two reasons why teamwork helped you, and write them down.
Pair: Compare your reasons. Number them 1 *(most important)*, 2, 3, etc.
Share: Join two other pairs and agree on the four most important reasons.

e) In your team, talk about your teamwork. Did each member of the team have the right job? Did the team do the task successfully?

Study skills

Teamwork
Wenn wir im Team arbeiten, kann ich folgende Aufgaben übernehmen: …
Ein Team kann …

➡ *SF 19: Teamwork (p. 151)*

➡ *Workbook 6–7 (p. 49)*

4 Part B

Lernfeld S. 70–71: Die S können kurzen Texten (hier: *posts*) **Informationen zu Sehenswürdigkeiten** entnehmen und diese in einer Tabelle anordnen. Sie können auf die *posts* anderer mit eigenen Kommentaren reagieren.

1 Lewis's travel posts

30 minutes ago

 Lewis McCray I've just heard angels singing!

 Chloe Carr Where? Are you in heaven?

 Lewis McCray Not yet! ;)))) I was in St Patrick's Cathedral. Uncle Frank and Aunt Mary took me there to hear the boys' choir. We weren't allowed to take photos inside, but I found this on the Internet. And I talked to one of the boys after the service. He told me the 21 choir boys go to the cathedral school. They're allowed to miss lessons because they have to sing at two services every day! It's a real job and they get paid!

 Chloe Carr I'd love to have a job like that! Could I join the choir?

Yesterday

 Lewis McCray Check this video out! I've been to lots of these places!

Länge: 7:21

… and here's Dublin at night. This area is called Temple Bar.

Music and dancing is EVERYWHERE!

 Chloe Carr I wish I could see you doing an Irish dance, Lewis!

 Lewis McCray Irish dance? No way! I wanted to go into a nightclub! There are hundreds of them. But Uncle Frank was like: "Stop. You aren't allowed in there!" I'll have to wait till I'm 18 … Unfair! : (((

 Jack Boyd Who wants to go to nightclubs? There are better things to look forward to. Like when I'm 18, I'll be allowed to ride my brother's motorbike!

4 • FöFo 4.3   Part B   4

Yesterday

 Chloe Carr I'm listening to U2 songs and thinking about you. ♥
Have you seen any °leprechauns yet?

 Lewis McCray Yes! Here's one of the little people!

 Luke Reid I thought leprechauns wore green <u>suits</u> and hats, funny shoes and <u>smoked</u> a <u>pipe</u>! That one looks like a little girl!

 Chloe Carr Looks <u>like</u> <u>she wasn't able to climb</u> onto the chair!   +as if

 Lewis McCray I <u>had to help</u> her. And she thanked me with a pot of gold!
PS This photo is REAL! (2 hours ago – National Leprechaun Museum)

Two days ago

 Lewis McCray Today we crossed the border into southern Ireland. We stopped at a shop, but I <u>wasn't able to pay</u> for this chocolate. Welcome to the eurozone!

 Luke Reid Hey, Lewis. We learned all about Ireland in geography last year! Maybe you were ill that day? ;))))

 Jack Boyd So you <u>won't be able to buy</u> any cool souvenirs!

2a) <u>St. Patrick's Cathedral:</u> what he did: heard boys' choir, talked to one of the boys after the service • what he didn't do: take photos, join the choir
<u>Temple Bar:</u> what he did: enjoyed Dublin at night with music everywhere • what he didn't do: do an Irish dance, go into a nightclub
<u>Leprechaun Museum:</u> what he did: helped the girl to climb onto the chair
<u>Southern Ireland:</u> crossed the border, stopped at a shop • what he didn't do: buy chocolate, pay for chocolate

2 In Dublin

a) Copy and complete the table.

place	what Lewis did	what he didn't do
St Patrick's Cathedral	heard choir ...	take photos
Temple Bar	...	

b) Add a comment to each one of Lewis's posts. Read one of your comments to the class.

c) Watch the video Lewis posted for his friends.

3 Have a go

Lernfeld: Die S verwenden **vorbewusst** das *modal substitute* „be allowed to".

👥 Talk about what you will be allowed to do after your eighteenth birthday.

When I'm 18, I'll be allowed to ride a motorbike.

I wouldn't want to ride a motorbike. But when I'm 18, I'll also be allowed to …

71

4 Part B Practice

5 • Folie 14 • FöFo 4.3 • LAS 4.1

Lernfeld S. 72: Die S verwenden die *modal substitutes be allowed to, have to, must, be able to*.

YT Looking at language

a) In the present tense, you can use have to or must.
   We **have to** be at the station at 7:45. / We **must** be at the station at 7:45.

In the past and future, you can only use a form of have to.
Complete these sentences from 1 on pages 70–71:
   Simple past: I ... help her onto the chair.   Future: I' ... wait till I'm 18.   had to • I'll have to

b) In the past and future, be able to or be allowed to are used instead of can.
   Complete these sentences from 1 on pages 70–71:
   Simple past: We ... to take photos.   Future: When I'm 18, ... to ride my brother's motorbike!
                I ... to pay for this chocolate.   So you ... to buy any cool souvenirs.
   Choose the right answer: weren't allowed • wasn't able
      For German *können*, we use (be able to) / be allowed to.   I'll be allowed • won't be able
      For German *dürfen*, we use be able to / (be allowed to).

➡ GF 6.2: Modal substitutes (pp. 166–167)

1 Hostel from hell (have to, be allowed to: Simple past)

On holiday, you stayed at an awful hostel.
Read the hostel rules and write sentences.
We had to be in bed by 8 pm.
We were only allowed to sleep till …

Early finisher Think of more awful rules and write similar sentences.
We had to clean our rooms with a toothbrush.

1. You must be in bed by 8 pm.
2. You can only sleep here till 5.30 am.
3. You must have a cold shower every morning.
4. You must clean your room before breakfast.
5. You can only have one piece of bread for breakfast.
6. You must leave the building to use your mobile.
7. You can only play games between 6:30 pm and 6:40 pm.
8. You must use earphones when you listen to music.

2 … till 5.30 am. • 3 We had to have a cold ➡ **Workbook** 8 (p. 50) shower every morning. • 4 We had to clean our rooms before breakfast. • 5 We were only allowed to have one piece of bread for breakfast. • 6 We had to leave the building to use our mobile phones. • 7 We were only allowed to play games between 6.30 pm and 6.40 pm. • 8 We had to use earphones when we were listening to music.

2 You'll have to revise …
(have to, be able to, be allowed to: Future)

A new classmate has some questions about next week's English test. Write answers.

1. Will I have to revise for the test?
   Yes, you'll have to revise the last unit.
2. What about dictionaries?
   You will/won't be allowed to use …
3. And electronic dictionaries, mobile phones?
   No, you won't … / Yes, you will …
4. Will I have to arrive early?
5. Will we be able to work together?
6. Will I be allowed to sit where I want?
7. Will I have to bring my own paper for the test?
8. Will I be able to leave when I'm finished?

2 You won't be allowed to use dictionaries. • 3 No, you won't be allowed to use things like that. • 4 Yes, you'll have to be there just before the test.

More help ➡ p. 122 ➡ **Workbook** 9–10 (pp. 50–51)

More help: Die S ergänzen nur *will/won't* und ordnen dann die Sätze den Fragen zu.

5 No, you'll have to work on your own. • 6 No, you'll have to sit where the teacher says. • 7 No, you'll be able to get it from the teacher. • 8 No, you'll have to stay until everybody is finished.

3 I won't be able to go swimming

a) Choose one of these places to visit.
   Make notes on advantages and disadvantages.

   Ireland • a small island in the Atlantic •
   Greenland • the moon • …

   the moon: + good view of the earth, a …
             − no swimming, …

More help: Liste von Vor- und Nachteilen zur Auswahl.

More help ➡ p. 122

b) 👥 Say which place you've chosen.
   Talk about the advantages and disadvantages.

   I've chosen the moon. I'll be able to get a great view of the Earth.   *But I won't be able to go swimming.*   *And I'll have to …*

Early finisher ➡ p. 130

Early finisher: Sprachaufgabe mit Rätsel.

▶ The world behind the picture   4

Lernfeld S. 73: Die S können **interkulturelle Missverständnisse** in einem Film beobachten, beschreiben und analysieren. Sie analysieren wie **Gefühle in einem Film** umgesetzt werden (Musik, Farbe, Gesichtsausdruck, Körpersprache, Umgang mit anderen Menschen).

1 Yu Ming is ainm dom

Länge: 13:28

a) Look at the stills from the film.
   Say what you think it might be about.

b) Watch the film and say where the action is:
   1 at the **beginning**   in China, in a grocery store and a library
   2 after the plane lands   Dublin Airport · streets of Dublin
   3 at the end of the film   in Connemara

c) There are a lot of misunderstandings in the film. Explain what these people think at first.
   1 Yu Ming: when he learns Irish at the beginning.   that Irish is spoken in Ireland
   2 The blond man: in the hostel.   that Yu Ming speaks Chinese
   3 Yu Ming: when nobody understands him.
   4 The barman: when Paddy talks to Yu Ming.

3 that he doesn't speak Irish well enough · 4 that Paddy speaks Chinese

d) Say which three languages you hear in the film. Explain what you find out about Irish (Gaelic) in Ireland.   English, Irish, Chinese · Irish is an official language of Ireland but is only spoken by a small minority

e) It's not always easy to understand each other across cultures. Explain:
   1 how people react when they cannot understand Yu Ming.
   2 why the man at the hostel asks another Asian **guest** for help with Yu Ming.

f) **EXTRA** What's your favourite scene in the film? Explain why.

e) 1 they speak more slowly or loudly or clearly because they think that might help · they use their hands, feet and faces (barman) ·
2 he thinks Yu Ming speaks Chinese and wants the other Asian man to translate, but the man speaks Mongolian, not Chinese

2 Making the film: Feelings

a) Say how you think Yu Ming feels …
   1 in his job at the beginning of the film.
   2 when he is learning Irish (**Gaelic**).
   3 when he arrives at the airport.
   4 when he is walking around Dublin.
   5 when people don't understand him.
   6 at the end of the film.

b) 👥 Work in groups of five.
   Here are five ways that film-makers can show their characters' feelings:
   1 music
   2 colour
   3 **facial expressions**
   4 body language
   5 **interaction** with other people.

   Each student chooses one of these five ways.

   Look carefully at the parts 1–6 from 2a).
   Watch the film again.
   Say where you saw the way of showing feelings which you chose.

 Access to cultures

Irish is spoken as an everyday language in some parts of the west coast.
Name countries where different languages are spoken in different regions, e.g. Canada.
Are there regions with different languages in your country?

2a) mögliche Antworten: 1 bored, sad, unhappy, disillusioned, horrible · 2 confident, determined, serious · 3 excited, confident, curious ·
4 shy, insecure, cautious, lonely · 5 incompetent, disillusioned, foolish, stupid, horrible, lonely · 6 happy, confident, competent

4 Part C
FöFo 4.6

Lernfeld S. 74: Die S können einem Text Informationen zu Personen entnehmen und eine Situation in Form eines Dialogs weiterentwickeln.

1 Arrival in the Burren

2 ▶ 31 | 5 minutes ago

Lewis McCray We're at the horse-riding centre on the west coast. Aunt Mary fell asleep in the car just outside Dublin and only woke up when we arrived! The owner's **weird** daughter showed us our cottage. She looks just like a °**VAMPIRE**. Black hair, black clothes and a very white face! She's taking us on the horse **ride** tomorrow. SCARY!
We have to be up EARLY (6 am!!!) for the ride. Help! I've never been on a horse.

Chloe Carr Be careful. If you're in °**Countess** Dracula's castle, I hope you'll still **be alive** for the ride tomorrow!! ☺

2 ▶ 32

TUESDAY 15 APRIL   127 days since Dad died

Mum says that I have to go on the horse ride with her tomorrow because it's a big group and she can't do it on her own. I <u>had planned</u> to ride Raven down to the beach, so we had a big **argument**. That never happened when Dad was alive. I **miss** him so much!

The worst thing is that I have to be friendly to the guests too. "They're here to have a good time, Ashling," Mum always says. Yeah, Mum, right. But what about me? I'm not having a good time! I can't even listen to my music. "It's too loud. Think of our guests, please!" Guests, guests, It's all about the guests here. I can't do anything I want to at home – and the people who live **round here stare** at me as if I'm mad. If we lived in the city, people wouldn't **care** what I looked like. But I'd miss the horses …

Box "(to) care", Voc, S. 191

When the last guests arrived, Mum <u>had already gone</u> to bed. So I showed them their cottage and their sandwiches and drinks. They <u>were starving</u> because they <u>hadn't had</u> anything to eat since lunch. They <u>had travelled</u> all the way from Dublin. They sound funny, but not like Dubliners. I think they're from Northern Ireland. The boy wanted to talk about the ride tomorrow – but I just said goodnight and left them to **unpack**.   +pack

When I got back to my room, I saw a blue light in the cottage. I think it was that boy on his computer. Was he writing, like me? No, I'm sure he talks more than he writes. He was probably chatting or playing a game … The lights are out now, so he must be asleep. I hope he doesn't talk too much tomorrow. Oh, **God** – I hope they know how to ride! The worst thing is guests who don't know how to ride …

Ashling

2 Lewis and Ashling

👥 Make groups of four.
Each students does one of the following:

a) Explain why Lewis calls Ashling a vampire.
b) Say what you have learned about Ashling and her family from her diary.
c) List what Ashling likes and **dislikes** about her life in the Burren.
d) Say what Ashling thinks of the new guests.

3 On the horse ride

Imagine Lewis and Ashling talk during the horse ride. What might they say?
Write a dialogue.

Early finisher   Find another early finisher.
Act out each other's dialogues.

2a) her black hair, black clothes and very white face remind him of pictures of vampires he has seen in films and books • b) Ashling has to help her mother with the guests • has arguments with her mother which never happened when her dad was still alive • c) likes: riding Raven, listening to music, writing in her diary, … • dislikes: going on horse rides with the guests, not being able to do anything she wants, that the people in the Burren stare at her, … • d) sound funny • that the boy talks more than he writes • she hopes that he won't talk too much the next day on the ride

6 • FöFo 4.4

Part C Practice 4

1 Pronunciation (Consonants) 🎧

33 a) Look at the word pairs below. Then listen. For each pair, write down the word you hear.
👥 Compare your answers.

1 white – [wide]   4 [side] – sight   7 [cheap] – jeep   10 [nod] – not
2 feed – [feet]   5 bang – [bank]   8 pick – [pig]   11 [choose] – juice
3 God – [got]   6 [docks] – dogs   9 card – [cart]   12 thing – [think]

34 b) Listen and write down the missing word.

        1 card · 2 cart · 3 wide · 4 white ·
        5 sights · 6 sides · 7 back ·
        8 bag · 9 feet · 10 feed ·
        11 bang · 12 bank

1 the red ...   7 put it in the ... of the car
2 with a red ...   8 put your ... in the car
3 a lovely ... beach   9 on your own two ...
4 lots of lovely ... beaches   10 time to ... her
5 all the different ... in Dublin   11 and then it went ...
6 on different ... in the match   12 we went to the ...

More help ➔ p. 123
More help: Die wählen aus je zwei Wörtern das richtige aus.

➔ **Workbook** 11 (p. 51)

Lernfeld: Die S können Gesprächen zwischen deutsch- und englischsprachigen Muttersprachlern verfolgen und angeben, welche **Kommunikationsprobleme** sie haben.

2 At the hotel   2 🔊 35–38

YT

👥 At a hotel, you hear some conversations between a tour guide and some tourists.

Listen to the four conversations.
Take turns to explain in German why there are misunderstandings.

➔ **Workbook** 12 (p. 52)

TIP
Don't translate every detail. Think about what is important and interesting: in these conversations what the people understand and don't understand.

1 *white* statt *wide* · *choose* statt *juice* · 2 *back* statt *bag* · *sheep* statt *ship* · 3 *cart* statt *card* · 4 *not* statt *nod*

Lernfeld: Die S können in Hörtexten mit mehreren Sprechern hören, dass die Sprecher aus unterschiedlichen Regionen kommen, und bestimmen, welcher Sprecher Standard-Englisch spricht.

3 Regional accents 🎧   2 🔊 39–45

a) Listen to seven tour guides.
Say where they are giving their tours.
Which one speaks standard English?

b) Listen to how the standard English speaker says these words:

> everyone · guide · here · name · tour · thirty

Then listen to the first guide again, and try to say the words like he does.

c) Listen again to the other tour guides and to how they say the same six words.
Say which accent you find easiest to understand. Which one is the most difficult?

➔ **Workbook** 13–14 (p. 52)

🌐 Access to cultures

In the UK and Ireland, people often speak with **regional accents**, so a Londoner can sound very different from someone from Liverpool. And in Scotland, Wales and Ireland, they also have their own English accents.

A regional accent isn't always easy to understand, but everyone in the UK and Ireland understands standard English. You often hear **standard** English on the BBC, and you also learn it in this book.

Say if the situation in your country is the same.
Say which accents you find harder to understand.
Is there a standard accent?

a) 1 Northern Ireland/Belfast · 2 Ireland (Best-of-Ireland tour) · 3 Liverpool · 4 Glasgow ·
5 Cambridge (Standard English accent) · 6 London's East End · 7 Cardiff

75

4 Part C Practice

Lernfeld S. 76: Die S sprechen über Dinge, die vor etwas anderem in der Vergangenheit geschehen sind *(past perfect)*.

7 • Folie 15, 16 • FöFo 4.6 • LAS 4.2

4 REVISION I had a weird dream (Simple past)

Complete Chloe's message. Use the simple past of the verbs in the box.

Chloe Carr Last night I ¹... this weird dream. You and I ²... on our way up a rocky hill with other kids from our class. Our German teacher Miss Kunzel ³... already at the top. She ⁴... angry and ⁵... at us to hurry. I ⁶... to get into trouble, so I ⁷... up the hill like mad. When I ⁸... the top, I ⁹... around but you ¹⁰... there. Then I ¹¹... you at the bottom of the hill. You had fallen all the way down. I ¹²... you, but you ¹³...You ¹⁴... hurt, and I was sure you had broken your leg. Lewis, tell me you're OK.

(not) answer ·
be (3 x) · (not) be ·
call · have ·
look (2 x) · reach ·
run · see · shout ·
(not) want

More help: Verben sind den Lücken schon zugeordnet.

More help ➔ p. 123

➔ Workbook 15 (p. 53)

1 had · 2 were · 3 was · 4 looked · 5 shouted · 6 didn't want · 7 ran · 8 reached · 9 looked · 10 weren't · 11 saw · 12 called · 13 didn't answer · 14 we

Language help

We use the **simple past** to say what happened in the past.
To say what happened before this time, we use the **past perfect**.
I *saw* you at the bottom of the hill. You *had fallen* all the way down.
You *were* hurt. I was sure you *had broken* your leg.

We form the **past perfect** with had + past participle.

➔ GF 1.5: Past perfect (p. 158)

When Morph arrived at the station, the train had already left.

5 After the class trip (Past perfect)

Say how the students felt after their class trip.
Use the past perfect for the earlier action.

1 Susan ... (be) happy to be back because she ... (miss) her parents.
   Susan was happy to be back because she had missed her parents.
2 Dan ... (be) unhappy because he ... (lose) his mobile.
3 Sam ... (feel) tired because he ... (not sleep) very well.
4 Peter ... (feel) sick because he ... (eat) too many biscuits.
5 Jill ... (look) worried because her **boyfriend** ... (not phone) her.
6 Tom ... (be) all red because he ... (stay) in the sun too long.
7 Ben ... (look) excited because he ... (meet) a nice girl at the hostel.

+girlfriend

2 was · had lost · 3 felt · hadn't slept · 4 felt · had eaten 5 looked · hadn't phoned · 6 was · had stayed · 7 looked had met

➔ Workbook 16 (p. 53)

6 At the farm in the Burren (Past perfect)

Link the two sentences with the word in the brackets. Use the past perfect for the earlier action.

1 Aunt Mary fell asleep.
  The car arrived at the farm. (when)
  Aunt Mary had fallen asleep when the car ...
2 Ashling's mum went to bed.
  Ashling **welcomed** the guests. (so)
3 The guests were hungry.
  They didn't eat on the journey. (because)
4 Ashling tried to be friendly to the guests.
  Her mum told her to. (because)
5 Lewis couldn't find Ashling.
  She went to her room. (because)
6 Lewis's room was dark.
  He turned off the lights. (because)

1 Aunt Mary had fallen asleep when the car arrived at the farm. • 2 Ashling's mum had gone to bed, so Ashling welcomed the guests. • 3 The guests were hungry because they hadn't eaten on the journey. • 4 Ashling tried to be friendly to the guests because her mum had told her to. • 5 Lewis couldn't find Ashling because she had gone to her room. • 6 Lewis's room was dark because he had turned off the lights.

Early finisher ➔ p. 130   ➔ Workbook 17 (p. 54)

Early finisher: Lückentext zu *prepositions*.

4 · Using time markers in a story — Writing course

8 · Folie 16 · KV 18 A/B · FöFo 4.5

Lernfeld S. 77: Die S können einen Text mit gelungenen Sätzen schreiben, indem sie *time markers* und *linking words* verwenden.

1 Learn how

KV 18 bietet eine Kopie des Textes.

a) Make a table like this. On a copy of the story, underline all the time markers. Then put them in the correct column of your table. s.u.

when sth. happened	what happened first, second, etc.	how much time passed
the Easter holidays	First	for about five minutes
...	...	...

TIP
1. Use time markers to help your reader to see
   – when something happened
   – what happened first, second etc.,
   – how much time passed
2. Use time markers to link sentences.

b) Add these time phrases to your table too. s.u.

> after that · next · last Monday · for two weeks · in the beginning · a few hours ago · for a while · two weeks later · later

c) Now look at these two sentences:
The guests went horse riding.
Ashling's mother prepared their lunch.

Link the sentences in as many ways as you can with phrases from the box.

> before · after · as soon as · while · shortly after that · earlier · First ... then

- <u>While</u> the guests went horse riding, Ashling's mother prepared their lunch.
- The guests went horse riding after ...
- ...

The view from my window

It was <u>the Easter</u> holidays and I had nothing to do because all of my friends were away. <u>Early one morning</u>, I was watching TV, but the show was silly and I <u>soon</u> got bored. So I sat by the window to watch the people go by.

Our flat is on the fifth floor of a corner building at a busy junction, so there are always lots of cars and pedestrians.

<u>First</u> I watched a woman who was walking three little dogs. They had very short legs which moved <u>very quickly</u> and it looked like they were taking her for a walk instead.

<u>Then</u> I watched a little boy and his father. The boy didn't want to walk any more and sat down on the pavement. <u>At first</u> his father waited, but <u>then</u> he became angry and started shouting. This continued <u>for about five minutes</u>. <u>Finally</u> the father picked up the boy and carried him like a baby. The boy kicked and screamed.

<u>Suddenly</u> a white sports car raced down the street. It was going really fast! The traffic light turned red as the car reached the junction and BAM! It drove into a green van. The white car spun around, while the green van hit a parked car. Glass flew everywhere. [+traffic]

<u>Seconds later</u>, I saw a man in a black hat jump out of the white car and run away. I called the police <u>immediately</u>. <u>Five minutes later</u> I heard the siren and ran down to the street. But it was <u>too late</u> – the man in the black hat was gone. I had to wait <u>for an hour</u> while they cleared the road. <u>Finally</u> I had the chance to tell a policeman what I had seen.

2 Now write ...

Write a short story. Use time markers to show the order of events. Remember to start a new paragraph for every new idea.

→ SF 12: Paragraphs and topic sentences (p. 145)
→ Workbook Wordbank 7

3 ... and revise

KV 6: Giving feedback on texts hilft beim Erstellen der Rückmeldung.

a) Give feedback. Read your partner's text and make notes where it is clear/unclear to you when things happened.
Take turns to make comments and corrections.

b) Think about your partner's feedback and what you've learned on this page. Decide what to change and write a final draft.

→ SF 13: Time markers (p. 146); SF 14: Feedback – writing (p. 146)
→ Workbook 18 (p. 54)

(a +b) **when:** early one morning · seconds later · 5 minutes later · last Monday · a few hours ago · two weeks later
what happened first etc.: finally · after that · next · in the beginning · later
how much time passed: soon · very quickly · suddenly · seconds later · immediately · 5 minutes later · too late · for an hour · for two weeks · for a while

4 Text

Lernfeld S. 78–79: Die S können einem Text Informationen zu Lehrwerksfiguren entnehmen und deren Gedanken entwickeln und aufschreiben.

🔊 The horse ride

Ashling · Lewis

Part 1

2 ▶ 46   It was just as Ashling had expected. Nine guests and **none** of them could ride very well. At least the four old **couples** had ridden before, but the boy
5 had never sat on a horse – ever.
"Still," she thought, "he's not so bad for a city boy from Edinburgh."
They were on a four-hour ride into the Burren. It was starting to rain a little and the old couples
10 were so slow. The ride would take five hours like this. Or even longer! Why did these city **folk** come here? They were like fish out of water °**on horseback** in the country.
At least she hadn't had to talk very much yet. She
15 was at the front of the group while her mother moved from person to person along the **line** and chatted happily with them all. She showed them the views and told them why the area was so rocky. But now, as they were passing some old stone
20 walls, her mother said, "We'll come to a very interesting area later. Ashling will tell you all about it. She knows more about the history of the Burren than I do."
"Thanks, Mum," Ashling thought.

❖

25 The rain was getting heavier when Ashling's mother called out to her, "Wait, please, Ashling." Ashling stopped and turned her horse. "**What's up?**"
"Well," her mother started, "it's like this …"
30 One of the old men went on. "Some of us old folk are feeling a bit cold in this rain, dear, so …"

"So we're going to take the short **trail** back," her mother finished.
"Oh, OK," Ashling said and began to walk her
35 horse back towards the others.
"No, Ashling, wait. I'll take most of us back on the short trail but Lewis would like to go the long way round. So he'll go with you."
The boy from Edinburgh smiled up at Ashling. She
40 **sighed**, turned her horse round again and with a "Come on, then," started back up the long trail.

Part 2

"We can go a bit faster if you like," Lewis said.   2 ▶ 47
"**Now that** we haven't got the old folk with us."
45 Ashling stopped her horse and turned round to look at Lewis. Her black hair and clothes, her black horse and the dark clouds behind her made her face seem whiter than ever. Lewis suddenly felt cold.
50 "So you want to go faster, do you?" Ashling asked. "Well, these rocky trails get very **slippery** in the rain. Have you seen all the green **ditches** next to the trail? Some of them have holes in them, big holes. If you're not careful you'll fall off the rocks
55 into a ditch and disappear down a big hole, horse and all. No one will ever find you again."
For a moment Lewis didn't know what to say. Was that a smile on Ashling's lips?
"She's just trying to scare me," he thought. He
60 smiled back at her and said, "Nice story! You should be on the stage. Anyway, that's good. If we go slower, we'll have more time to talk."

As they went up the hill, Lewis talked and talked. Ashling thought he would never stop. He told her
65 about his visits to Belfast and Dublin. She had only been to Dublin twice, when she was much younger and her dad was still alive. She had never been to Belfast.
Lewis was full of questions too. "Who built all
70 these stone walls?"
"Farmers," Ashling answered. "A long time ago. A lot more people lived in the Burren in the old days. Some of these walls are 4,000 years old."
"So where did all the people go?"
75 "Er … well, that's a long story, but I'll show you something on the other side of the hill."
At the top of the hill, Ashling stopped her horse and pointed. Looking down, Lewis could see the ruins of an old church with some gravestones.
80 "That's where they buried lots of people who died in the Great Famine," Ashling told him.
"The Great Famine?"
"Yes, you know, in the 19th century, when the potatoes had a disease and didn't grow. A million
85 people died and another million emigrated. Because potatoes were all that poor people in Ireland had to eat."
"Was there no other food in Ireland?" Lewis asked.
"There was enough food. But the farmers sold it.
90 Lots of it was sold in Britain. And the British government did nothing to stop the exports."
For the second time that day, Lewis didn't know what to say.

Part 3

95 On the way down the hill, Ashling suddenly stopped and got off her horse.
"Can you just wait here for a minute?" she said and started walking off the trail towards a stream.
"I'll come with you," said Lewis.
100 "No, no," Ashling turned round and held her hand up. "There's something I have to do – alone."
Lewis watched as Ashling walked over the rocks to the stream. She knelt down and scooped up some water in her hands then let it fall slowly back into
105 the stream. She stayed there a few minutes, turned round and came back to the horses.
As they went on down the hill towards the end of the trail, Lewis asked, "What was that all about? Back at the stream?"
110 For a while it seemed as if Ashling didn't want to answer. Then she suddenly looked at Lewis and said: "It was about my dad. He loved that stream, so we threw his ashes into it after he died. I like to talk to him there. I really miss him."
115 It was the third time that Lewis didn't know what to say – and now, for the first time, Ashling asked him a question: "So, what's Edinburgh like?"
"Edinburgh?" Lewis said in surprise. He had a lot to say on that topic and was glad to forget about
120 death and dying in the Burren for a while.
"It's a great city," he began, "especially in the summer when the Edinburgh Festival is on. One thing I like to do at the festival is …" and he talked all the way to where Ashling's mother and the
125 others were waiting. This time, Ashling was surprised that she didn't mind listening.

1 The ride across the Burren

Say who the riders are in each part of the story and what they talk about.

More help → p. 123
More help: Es sind *key words* vorgegeben.

2 Ashling and Lewis

Work in groups of four. Each student reads *one* of these parts of the story again:
ll. 50–62 · ll. 71–93 · ll. 95–114 · ll. 115–126
Then explain to the others what you find out about Ashling and/or Lewis in your part.

3 Silent thoughts

You choose Choose a, b or c. Write a few sentences about

Neigungsdifferenzierung: Die S wählen aus unterschiedlichen Situationen/Perspektiven.

a) what Ashling thinks about Lewis before and after the ride.
b) what Lewis might think when he hears about the Famine.
c) what Lewis might think when Ashing tells him about her father.

→ Workbook 19 (p. 55)

1) Part 1: Ashling, nine guests (four couples + Lewis), Ashling's mum · The Burren: the views, why the area is rocky / the cold, splitting up the group · Part 2: Lewis + Ashling · slippery trails, ditches, holes you can fall into / Belfast and Dublin / the Great Famine / the potato disease and emigration, the role of the British government · Part 3: L. and A. · Ashling's dad / Edinburgh Festival

Unit 4

Your task

Die komplette Lernaufgabe wird in **Teamwork** bearbeitet.

A brochure for students from Ireland

Students at your partner school in Ireland want to visit your area.
👥 Work in a team with four students. Make a brochure with tips for the visit.

STEP 1
👥 Make a checklist with the main points. Think of what you could say about each point, for example:

• tips on travel	• suggestions about where to stay
If you fly from Belfast you'll have to change in London. But if you travel from Dublin …	There's a very good hostel in …
If you live in the Republic, you won't have to …	The *Pension* in the old town is cheap and …

• attractions and activities in your area	• what your guests will be able to do, see, …
The countryside around … is very beautiful.	Why not pack some strong boots?
Our local chocolate museum is a big attraction.	Then you'll be able to …

STEP 2
👥 Choose your team roles: writer, picture and layout editor, language watchdog or coordinator.
Then the coordinator asks each member to do one of these jobs and suggests the best order for them.
• get information and write the texts
• check the language
• find good pictures that go with the brochures
The coordinator says when each job must be done before the next meeting.

➡ *SF 19: Teamwork (p. 151)*

STEP 3
Before the meeting, each team member checks his/her own work so far.

How am I doing?
Answer the questions about your role.

How can I do better?
Follow these tips if you need to.

Writer
- Have I found all the information we need?
- Have I organized the information clearly in my texts?

- Read through the checklist from Step 1 and make sure you have all your main points.
- Check that you have enough information for each point. Add more information, if necessary.
- Check the tips on writing paragraphs.

Picture and layout editor
- Have I found good pictures for the brochure?

- Use the checklist from Step 1 to make sure that you have pictures for the main points.
- Ask the writer to show you his/her text and check that your pictures go with it. ➡ *p. 38*

Language watchdog
- Have I checked everything I need to?

- Make sure that the writer has used the right travel vocabulary. ➡ *p. 68, ex. 2*
- Check if the writer has used phrases like *you'll be able to, you'll have to, you won't have to*, etc. If not, make suggestions about where to use them.
- Look out for spelling and grammar mistakes.

Coordinator
- Have I prepared everything for the meeting?

Remember, <u>before</u> the meeting you should
- check that the writer has given his/her texts to the language watchdog
- check that the picture editor has a copy of the pictures for everyone to see.
- make a list of discussion points, e.g. headings for the texts, order of the texts in the brochure, position of the pictures, etc.
- have a plan for the next steps, e.g. printing or writing the final version

STEP 4
At the team meeting, the coordinator leads the discussion.
The team agrees on the final steps, who does what, and when the brochure must be ready.
When your brochure is finished, swap with another group and read theirs.

EXTRA Give feedback to the other group about their brochure.

➡ *Inside back cover: Giving feedback*
➡ **Workbook** *Wordbank 4–5, 7*

Unit 5 — Leistungsmessung Unit 5

Text File: zu Unit 5 passt Text 8.

Extraordinary Scotland

1 Skye Hunter is performing in the Edinburgh **Fringe** Festival. I met Skye on the Royal Mile, where she was **promoting** her new show with the rest of the cast. — Lewis

2 Listen to my interview with Angus MacLeod [məˈklaʊ] from Glasgow and find out how **bagpipes** work!

3 **LOOK OUT**!!! The Fringe Festival is coming!

2c) <u>Skye:</u> Do you have a play in this years' Fringe Festival? (The Road to Red Cow Valley, she wrote it herself) • What do you like about the Fringe? (seeing theatre groups from all over the world) • When did you start acting? (at the age of 7, her school's Christmas play) • Is it true that you are in a theatre company in Edinburgh? (yes, Little Red Riding Hood theatre group) • What's the best part of being in a play? (being on stage) • What's the worst part? (being nervous before going on stage) • How many plays will you do this year? (six

2c) Angus: Why did you want to learn the bagpipes? (family tradition) • Does your dad play? (yes, also grandfather, great-grandfather did it) • When did you first make that strange sound? (at the age of 6) • Can you explain how the bagpipes work? (there are 5 pipes; with the blowpipe, the bag is filled with air; the bag is pressed with your arm; when the air goes out, three pipes make a tone, the melody is played on fourth pipe)

Unit 5

1 • KV 19 • FöFo 5.1

Lernfeld S. 82–83: Die S können sich dazu äußern, was in sozialen Netzwerken gepostet wird und sich ein Bild über andere Personen machen und die begründen. Sie sprechen darüber, wie sie selbst soziale Netzwerke nutzen.

4 A girl and her dog: Lauren Reid and her dog Shadow compete in sheepdog trials in the Scottish Highlands.

5 On board the yacht Wee Lass Katie MacNeil, Iain Ferguson and the rest of their class from the Isle of Barra learn how to identify dolphins.

1 Social media and you

Talk about the kind of information, photos and videos you post or watch on the internet. Then report to the class.

2 Lewis's social media page

a) Describe the photo you like most. Say why you like it and what you'd like to find out about the people or situation.

b) → pp. 26–27
Find Edinburgh and the other places Lewis writes about in his captions.
Say what part of Scotland they're in.

c) Listen to Lewis and write down his questions to Angus, Skye, Lauren and Katie.   3 ▸ 01–04

Listen again and take notes on the answer to the questions. Use your notes to describe their hobbies.

What else would you like to know? Write down other questions you'd like to ask.

3 The Fringe ▶ Länge: 3:03

Watch the film about the Edinburgh Fringe. Take notes about the kind of performers you see.
Say which performers or show you found the most interesting. Give reasons.

→ Workbook 1 (p. 60)

Your task

Interview someone who plays an instrument or has an unusual hobby. [+usual]
Make a poster about the interview and present it to the class.

c) **Lauren:** Can you tell us a bit about yourself? (Lauren Reid, 15, lives on sheep farm) • What's your special hobby? (sheepdog trials) • What does a sheepdog do? (works with you in the fields, moves sheep) • What do you do at a sheepdog trial? (same things, but you must be quicker and better than the others) • Who takes part in the trials? (no kids, mostly men) • Why do some men not like it that you take part? (they don't want to lose to a girl) • Does this make it harder for you? (no, her dog Shadow and her mum and dad help)

2c) **Katie:** Do you spend a lot of your free time out at sea? (yes, at weekends, when the weather is fine) • What got you interested in dolphins? (a workshop with our class) • Why do you collect information about dolphins? (dolphins are in danger) • What enemies do dolphins have? (people)

Part A

1 Extraordinary west coast

Dolphin watching near Barra

A team of students from Castlebay Community School is helping the Western Isles Dolphin Trust's (WIDT) research on Barra's dolphins

5 When the WIDT was looking for volunteers to make dolphin sightings near the Isle of Barra in the Western Isles, students from the island's community school put their hands up.

Classroom at sea

10 On the Trust's yacht, the Wee Lass, Castlebay students learned how to watch, photograph and identify dolphins.

"Scientists don't know much about the dolphins on Scotland's west coast," said Katie MacNeil, 14, "so 15 sightings are important for research."

Katie explained: "Pollution is a huge problem for dolphins. And fishing – they get caught in the nets of big fishing boats. So if we know where they spend their time and what they do there, we can protect them better. They can't protect themselves from us." 20

"I've seen dolphins around Barra before," said Katie's classmate Iain Ferguson, 15, "but I couldn't identify them. You can't teach yourself to do that. Someone has to show you. You identify each dolphin by its dorsal fin, so you need photos. Taking good 25 photos of fins is one thing I've learned to do."

Teamwork

Other students learned how to record the exact locations of the sightings. "So we can monitor a dolphin's movements over time and see where it 30 goes," said Katie. "It's all about teamwork. When we help each other we can make exact sightings."

New skills and hard work

With their new skills, the students continue their work on their island home. "When the sea is rough, I 35 look for dolphins from land," Iain explained. "And when I make a sighting, I can identify the dolphin and record its exact location, all on my own."

In calm weather, the students go out together in small sailing boats or kayaks to look for dolphins. 40

"We phone each other first before we go out in boats," Katie said. "You shouldn't do that alone. You have to look after yourself at sea. We don't often see dolphins. It's hard work and I get seasick sometimes. But I tell myself it's worth it to protect these beautiful 45 animals."

2 Understanding the article

a) Make notes on what you learned about:

1 the west coast of Scotland
2 the WIDT
3 dolphins
4 the students of Castlebay Community School.

b) Use your notes to compare your ideas. Take turns.

3 EXTRA Our English lesson

Your parents ask you and your friend what you did in English today.
Tell your parents about the article on dolphins. Use your notes from 2 to explain the main points in German.

Part A Practice 5

2 • Folie 17 • LAS 5.1

1 Looking for dolphins 🎧

Lernfeld: Die S können Vermutungen darüber anstellen, was in einem bestimmten Kontext zu hören sein wird und dies dann anhand des Hörens überprüfen.

3 ▶ 06–08

a) Think of all the sounds you might hear if you were on the *Wee Lass*. Write them down. Then listen and check if you hear them.

b) Listen again. Say which of these things happened on the boat. Say what you can remember about them.
The Castlebay students …

- listened to music
- listened to dolphins
- saw dolphins
- swam with dolphins
- got seasick
- fell off the boat
- took photos of each other
- took photos of dolphins
- got wet
- arrived back later than planned

the skipper listened to dolphins, the kids saw dolphins, some kids got seasick, the kids took photos of dolphins, they got wet in a storm

c) Would you like to go on a trip on the *Wee Lass*? Give reasons.

2 After the boat trip (Reflexive pronouns)

a) Finish the sentences with the right pronoun.

> myself · yourself · himself · herself ·
> ourselves · yourselves · themselves

1 When Iain got home, he made **himself** a cup of tea.
2 "I'm hungry," said Iain's dad. "Let's cook … something for dinner." **ourselves**
3 "Be careful with that knife, Dad," said Iain, "or you'll cut …" **yourself**
4 "Too late," said his dad, "but I haven't hurt … badly." **myself**
5 When the food was ready, Iain and his dad got … something to drink. **themselves**
6 "Shall we **keep** some food for Mum?", asked Iain. "Or will she look after …?" **herself**

b) In English, not as many verbs need a reflexive pronoun as in German.
👥 Read the dialogue.
Decide where you need pronouns.

Mrs M: Sit ¹… down, Katie. You must be tired.
Katie: Don't worry ²…, Mum. I feel ³… fine.
Mrs M: You just **relax** ⁴… Katie. Here's some soup. It's hot, so don't burn ⁵…. **yourself**
Katie: Mmm, thanks. Delicious!
Mrs M: So you heard dolphins today. I can't imagine ⁶… what they sound like.
Katie: Mum, they're amazing! And we really have to help them, because they can't help ⁷… **themselves**

➡ GF 7.1: Reflexive pronouns (pp. 167–168)
➡ Workbook 3–4 (p. 61)

3 Katie and Iain help each other (each other)

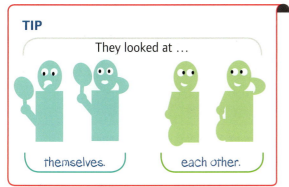

TIP
They looked at …
themselves. each other.

Make sentences with **each other** which show that Katie and Iain are good friends.

help	give	send	phone	parties	presents
invite	buy	miss		texts	homework
argue with		look after			

1 Katie and Iain help each other with their homework.
2 They usually phone each other at weekends.
3 They never …

➡ GF 7.2: themselves or each other (p. 168)

More help ➡ p. 124   **Early finisher** ➡ p. 131

More help: Es sind Lückensätze vorgegeben.   **Early finisher:** Zwei Rätsel zur Auswahl.

3 They never argue with each other. • 4 They always invite each other to parties. • 5 They buy each other presents. • 6 They help each other. • 7 They look after each other. • 8 They send each other texts every day …

➡ Workbook 5 (p. 61)

85

5 Background file

Lernfeld S. 86: Die S können einen Text mit **Informationen zu Schottland** lesen und Schottland mit ihrer Heimatregion vergleichen.

This is Scotland

The Highlands
Scotland has some of the world's most beautiful countryside. Maybe the best place to enjoy it is in the Highlands with their °snowy mountains, green °glens, °wonderful °lochs (one even with a monster!), and lots of wild animals.

● Urquhart Castle, Loch Ness [ˈɜːkət]

°Rival cities
Scotland's two main cities, only 60 km away from each other, have long been rivals.
Edinburgh, the °capital, with its °stunning °historical centre, is a UNESCO °World Heritage Site and home to the world's biggest arts festival.
Glasgow, the largest city and Edinburgh's "°ugly sister", was once a centre of °shipbuilding and other °industries. These have °declined, but the city now offers great museums and exciting nightlife.

● National Gallery, Edinburgh, with the UK and Scottish flags
● Cycle °Arc Bridge, Glasgow

°Traditions
°**Kilts** are traditional °clothing for men. They're worn at °weddings and °céilidhs or on fun nights out.
A °**tartan** is the °pattern on kilts and other clothes. It shows the family or °clan of the man who is wearing it.
Bagpipes are played every day in towns and cities all over Scotland – by street musicians, at weddings, at Highland dancing and at many other events.

● Shop window, Edinburgh
● Street °piper, Edinburgh

Find out more about Scottish traditions.

Scotland and England
In 1314, the Scots °defeated the English at Bannockburn. The battle is still celebrated in Scotland today.
In those days, the two countries were often at °war. But in 1603, Scotland's King James also became king of England. A century later, the two countries formed the kingdom of Great Britain.
But the Scots have always seen themselves as a different nation. From the late 20th century, many Scots wanted to be °independent again. However, in a 2014 °referendum, 55.3 °% of the population decided that it was better to stay in the UK.

● Bannockburn celebration, 2014 [ˈbænəkbɜːn]

Compare Scotland with your region.
Think about the countryside and cities, traditions and important historical events.

➔ Workbook 6 (p. 62)

5 ▶ The world behind the picture

Lernfeld: Die S können **Bildunterschriften** zu *film stills* verfassen und nach Anschauen des Films in die richtige Reihenfolge bringen. Sie können ein *voice-over* zu einer Filmsequenz verfassen und mit dem Original vergleichen.

1 Escape to ... Scotland (+escape (v.))

a) 👥 Look at the film stills. Describe each one. Take turns. Agree on captions for each still and write them down. *an afternoon in town · traditional music · Scottish animals · Scotland is beautiful in summer and winter*

b) 👥 Watch the film and put your captions in the right order. ⟨Länge: 2:59⟩

c) The film will be shown in four parts.
Your teacher will say which part each pair should watch.
👥 Take notes while you watch your part.

d) 👥 Use your notes to write a short voice-over for your part of the film. You should:
– describe what the film shows, e.g.
Here an old train is crossing a bridge.
– make a comment, e.g.
I'd love to travel through Scotland by train.
Make sure your voice-over is not too long.

e) Join pairs who watched the other parts of the film.
Your teacher will play the whole film again.
👥 Each pair reads the voice-over for their part.

f) 👥 Now watch a version of the film with a voice-over.
Compare your voice-over to the film's.
What else did you learn?

2 Making the film: Split screen and music

Lernfeld: Die S können die Wirkung von Filmtechniken wie *split screen* und *music changes* analysieren.

👥 Partner B: Go to page 132.

Partner A:
a) Watch the film again (first version, without voice-over).
Take notes about where the film
• has a split screen
• shows one picture on top of another.
Think of why the film-maker does this. Make notes about your ideas.

Partner A: Split screens: 6 times (summer/winter, train ride, tartan patterns, lakes, wild flowers, making whisky). They show contrasts, two things at the same time, make it more exciting. · Pictures on top of each other: 4 times (making bagpipes, on the battlefield, a cross, various historical sites). They show that past/present, tradition/modern life belong together.

b) Talk to your partner. Use your notes to say what you noticed about the split screen.
Then listen to what your partner tells you about music changes in the film.

Partner B: Music changes: Part 2 – from bagpipes and drums (traditional Scotland) to faster music (modern city life) · Part 3 – to slower melody (nature/wildlife) · Part 4 – to fast melody from before (back to the city)

5 Part B

FöFo 5.4

Lernfeld S. 88: Die S können einer Bildgeschichte folgen und ihr entnehmen, wie sich die Protagonisten fühlen. Sie können auch über den Inhalt eines Theaterstückes spekulieren.

1 🔊 Star performers 3 ▶ 09

2 At the rehearsal

a) Say who these people are and how they feel:
Lewis • Sandra • Skye

Lewis is the boy we met ...   *I think ...*

b) Look at the first picture again. What do you think the play is about? What will happen next?

Write the next few lines of dialogue and stage directions.

2a) Lewis is the boy we first met in Northern Ireland, where he was visiting his aunt and uncle. I think he is very nice/friendly when he talks to Skye. • Sandra seems to be the director of the play. She's nervous and also a little angry when Skye misses her cue. She also seems to be worried that the play won't be a success at the Fringe. • Skye has one of the lead roles in the play. She is sad when Sandra picks on her, and she feels angry and hurt and wants to quit.

Part B 5

Lernfeld S. 89: Die S können einem Chat entnehmen, wie die Figuren zueinander stehen und dies begründen.

3 Time for a chat

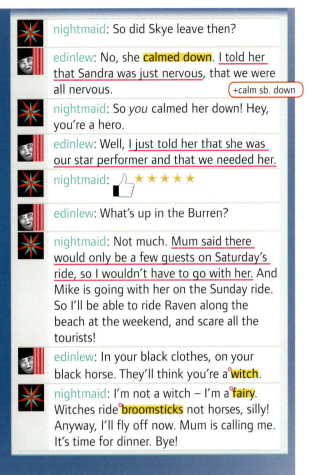

4 Good friends?

a) What are the real names of *edinlew* and *nightmaid*? Explain how you know. Say what you know about them.

b) Say which of these sentences you think best describes the relationship between *edinlew* and *nightmaid*. Give reasons for your opinion.
   1 They really like each other now.
   2 They know a lot more about each other now.
   3 Edinlew still talks, nightmaid listens.

More help ➔ p. 124 ➔ **Text File 8** (pp. 112–115)

More help: bietet Ideen für mögliche Begründungen. | **Text File 8:** The Off-side Trap

5 Have a go

Lernfeld: Die S verwenden vorbewusst indirekte Rede.

Report what *nightmaid* said to *edinlew*.

Nightmaid told *Edinlew* that
1 she was free.
2 her Mum wasn't …
3 he …
4 she …
5 it …

2 … home yet. • 3 … was a hero. • 4 … was not a witch. • 5 … was time for dinner

4a) edinlew = Lewis (edin = Edinburgh, lew= Lewis): visited Uncle Frank/ Aunt Mary in Belfast • went on trips to Giant's Causeway, Dublin, the Burren • met Ashling in the Burren • went out for a ride with her • has a website: "Extraordinary Scotland" • will perform at the Fringe
nightmaid = Ashling (night = Lewis thought she was dark, vampire, creature of the night) • lives with her mum in the Burren • lost her dad • met Lewis on a horse ride • loves riding • often wears black clothes

5 Part B Practice

4 • LAS 5.2

Lernfeld S. 90–91: Die S können wiedergeben, was andere gesagt haben. Dabei verwenden sie *indirect speech*.

YT Looking at language

Look at sentence 1 to see how the verb changes when you report what somebody said. Then read the other speech bubbles and write the sentences in indirect speech. Say how the verb changes. You can check on p. 89.

➡ GF 8: Indirect speech (pp. 168–169)

YT 1 Skye said she was nervous (Indirect speech)

Imagine you're Lewis. Report to Ashling what these people said on the first night of the play.

Skye said she was so nervous. She said so …

Sandra said we … She said she …

Dad said …

More help ➡ p. 125 ➡ Workbook 7 (p. 62)

More help: Die S ergänzen Lückensätze.

Skye said so many people would be there. • … she had a funny feeling in her stomach. • Sandra said we looked great in our costumes. • … she was really proud of us all. • … she couldn't understand why everyone was so nervous. • … we would have a party on the last night. • Dad said he couldn't wait to see me on stage. • … it was a great play. • … he would have to see it again.

YT 2 Jana said she could speak Chinese (Indirect speech)

Work in groups of three.
Take turns to play A, B and C.

A: I can speak Chinese.
B: What did Jana say?
C: She said she could speak Chinese.

Use the sentences on the right.

I'm a Hertha fan. | I can speak Chinese.
I can't do my homework today. | There's a snake near the board.
I live in a palace. | Hamburgers cost 50 cents in the school shop.
Beyoncé is my friend on Facebook. | I'll be 18 on my next birthday.
It will be quite warm tomorrow. | Partner B can't hear very well.
These exercises are easy. | I like Scottish music.
Our teacher won't give us homework today. | The window is broken.

She said she was a Hertha fan. • … she could speak Chinese. • … she couldn't do her homework today. • … there was a snake near the board. • … she lived in a palace. • … hamburgers cost 50 cents in the school shop. • … Beyoncé was her friend on Facebook. • … she would be 18 on her next birthday. • … it would be quite warm the next day. • … Partner B couldn't hear very well. • … these exercises were easy. • … she liked Scottish music. • … our teacher wouldn't give us homework today. • … the window was broken.

➡ Workbook 8 (p. 63)

5, 6 • Folie 18 • FöFo 5.4

Part B Practice 5

3 An interview about the internet and social media

a) Ask your partner these questions and write down his/her answers.

1. Can you use the internet at home? Are you allowed to use it **whenever** you want?
2. Do you use social media
   - on your home computer?
   - on your phone?
   - at school?

   Box "whenever, wherever, whatever, whoever", Voc, S. 195

3. What is your favourite social media site?
4. Do you have a blog?
   What kind of posts do you write?
5. Do you chat online with your friends? When?
6. How often do you watch online videos?
7. Do you listen to music online? On what sites?
8. Which is your favourite online activity?
   - writing posts on a social media **platform**
   - watching videos
   - listening to music

b) Work with students from other pairs. Say what you learned about your partner in a).

Jana told me that she had a music blog. She said that she wrote …

Zoe said that she listened to music online.

Peter said he didn't often listen to music online.

Early finisher → p. 131

→ Workbook 9–10 (pp. 63–64)

Early finisher: Abgewandeltes Stadt–Land–Fluss-Spiel.

4 WORDS Music and entertainment

a) Start a table. Add words from the box under the right heading. Be careful! Some words don't go under any of the headings.

verbs	instruments	events	people
…	…	…	

b) Add other words you know to the lists.
   Compare your list with a partner's.
   More help → p. 125 **More help:** In einer Box sind bekannte Wörter vorgegeben.

band · bus · choir · chorus · ⁺**comedian** ·
comedy · concert · drums · ⁺**entertainment** ·
festival · flag · guitar · musical · musician ·
pedestrian · perform · piano ·
play an instrument · poster · rhythm · shop ·
show · sing (along) · singer · song · telephone

c) Write five sentences about a musical event you have seen or would like to see.
   The 5 Ws (When? Where? What? Who? Why?) can help you to find ideas.

2a) verbs: perform · play an instrument · shop · sing (along) ·
instruments: drums · guitar · piano · events: comedy · concert ·
festival · musical · show · people: band · choir · comedian · musician · pedestrian · singer · words that don't fit: bus, chorus, entertainment, flag, poster, rhythm, song, telephone

→ Workbook 11 (p. 64)

5 An arts festival in Dresden

11 You are visiting Dresden with a British friend.
You hear a report on the *Elbhangfest*. Listen, then tell your friend what you could do there.

TIP
Concentrate on things that **interest** you and your friend and give information about them.

Lernfeld: Die S können einem Hörtext wichtige Informationen zu einer Veranstaltung entnehmen und diese auf Englisch weitergeben.

The Elbhangfest is a big festival in Dresden. There are lots of events happening along the Elbe River, for example concerts, plays, readings, sports events and art exhibitions. If you like music, you can go to classical or rock concerts, or you can listen to choir or folk or brass music. You can also bring your own instrument and play in the streets. You can attend the big parade and watch people dressed up in historical costumes. Some people also open up their private houses for visitors to check out. All in all, there are more than 200 events along the Elbe River.

→ Workbook 12 (p. 65)

5 Part B Practice

Lernfeld S. 92: Die S können eine gute **Präsentation** halten, indem sie in der Vorbereitung einzelne, wichtige Schritte berücksichtigen.

 7 • KV 21 • FöFo 5.5

6 Study skills: A good presentation

The Western Isles Dolphin Trust works to protect dolphins. This page will help you to prepare and give a good presentation about a place, animal, river, … that needs protection in your area.

Preparing and giving your presentation

1 Do your research.
   - Find out more about your place/animal/…
   - Make notes on the points you want to talk about.

2 Look up words you need in a *German-English dictionary*.
   - Explain the meaning of important words in your presentation on a **handout** – or write them on a **transparency** or the board.
   - Don't just use the first translation you find.
   - Make sure you find the right translation for your context.
   For example, what English word do you need for *Beute* in this sentence:

   Das Reh ist die bevorzugte **Beute** des Luchses.

➡ SF 6: German-English dictionaries (p. 142)

Beute
1. *(Diebesgut)* loot; haul; *(im Krieg)* booty; spoils *(of war) (pl)*; **reiche** o. **fette Beute machen** make a big haul; **eine Beute von mehreren Millionen Euro** a multi-million-euro haul
2. *(von Tieren; auch übertragen: Opfer)* prey; **leichte Beute sein (für)** be (an) easy prey (to/for)

KEY VOCABULARY
lynx – Luchs
habitat – Lebensraum
coat – Fell
predator – Raubtier

The Eurasian lynx *(Lynx lynx)*

3 Write down your presentation and make notes on cards with numbers.

4 Practise your presentation in front of a mirror, your family, a friend, …

5 Give your presentation.
   - before you begin, make sure you have everything ready (cards, handout, …)
   - wait till your classmates are quiet then tell them what your presentation is about
   - use your cards, but look at your classmates when you speak, not at your notes
   - speak slowly, loudly and clearly
   - finish your talk and ask for questions

➡ SF 23: Presentations (p. 153)
➡ Workbook 13 (p. 65)

Mithilfe von **KV 21: Giving feedback on a presentation** können die S Rückmeldungen zu den Präsentationen geben.

Speech bubbles:
- My presentation today is about …
- First I'm going to talk about …
- After that, I'll tell you …
- It … because … so … but …
- The picture on the handout is …
- "Territory": that's where the lynx lives. In German it's …
- This photo shows …
- That's the end of my presentation.
- Are there any questions?
- Thank you for listening.

Study skills

A good presentation
Für eine gute Präsentation muss ich Folgendes beachten:
– …
– …

➡ SF 23: Presentations (p. 153)

5 Writing course — The elements of writing

FöFo 5.6

Lernfeld S. 93: Die S können verschiedene Strategien zum Schreiben nutzen, um einen guten Text zu verfassen.

1 Learn how

You've learned different writing skills in this school year. Here you will learn how to choose which skills you need and how to combine them when you write a longer text.

2 Now write …

a) Decide what you're going to write about: you can write about a film, a game or a book. Or you can write a story.

b) Read the tips and choose the ones that might help you. Make notes on these tips. Then write a first draft of your text.

→ **Workbook** Wordbank 7

3 … and revise

a) Read your text again carefully. Look at the tips you wrote down. Can you use them to improve your text more? Correct any grammar or spelling mistakes.

b) 👥 Give feedback. Read your partner's text and make notes. Take turns to make comments and corrections. **KV 6: Giving feedback on texts** hilft beim Erstellen der Rückmledung.

c) Think about your partner's feedback and what you've learned on this page. Decide what to change and write a second draft.

EXTRA Put together a class magazine with all the reviews for each member of your class.

→ SF 10: Good sentences (p. 144); SF 11: Structuring texts (p. 145); SF 12: Paragraphs (p. 145); SF 15: Revising texts (p. 147)

→ **Workbook** 14 (p. 66)

TIPS – UNIT 2
1. Before you start writing, make a °mind map or table to collect and organize your memories and ideas.
2. The 5 **Ws** (When? Where? What? Who? Why?) can help you to find ideas.
3. Start a new paragraph for every new idea.
4. Use a topic sentence in each paragraph. In the other sentences add details or examples.

TIPS – UNIT 3
1. Organize your ideas and plan your paragraphs.
2. Write your text. Remember to
   - say what the text is about (first paragraph)
   - use topic sentences in the body of the text
   - find a good way to end your text.
3. Read your text. Check your topic sentence and decide if the paragraphs are in a good order.
4. Change the order of the paragraphs if necessary.

TIPS – UNIT 1
1. Use different adjectives (*bright, fantastic, dark,* …) to describe people, things and places – not just *good, bad* and *nice.* Use adverbs (*quietly, slowly,* …) for actions. Use *really, very, a bit,* etc. (*really slowly, very quietly, a bit dark*) to be more exact.
2. Use time phrases (*last week, tomorrow,* …) to tell your reader when things happened.
3. Use linking words (*and, but, because,* …) and relative clauses to link short sentences.

TIPS – UNIT 4
1. Use time markers to help your reader to see
   - when something happened
   - what happened first, second, etc.
   - how much time passed.
2. Use time markers to link sentences.

5 Text

Lernfeld S. 94–96: Die S können einen Lesetext verstehen und zeigen dies, indem sie einzelnen Textteilen Überschriften geben, Fragen zum Text entwickeln und ein Ereignis innerhalb der Geschichte weiterschreiben.

Missing

Look at the pictures and say what the characters are thinking or feeling. Discuss what the pictures tell you about the story.

1

Lauren looked across the green field where the sheepdog trials were taking place. On the right, a mountain of brown **heather** and grey rock rose up. On the left, the field ended at the edge of a high cliff. Far **below**, she could see the dark waters of Loch Ness with the ruins of Urquhart Castle next to it. She wondered why there was no fence or wall at the edge of the field. That cliff was dangerous … When it was Lauren's turn, one black sheep moved away from the group of four and stood next to some rocks at the edge of the cliff.

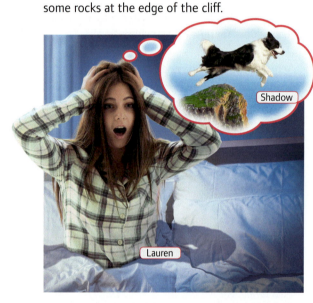

"I'll lose some points for that," Lauren thought. She could feel the **tension** in her arms and throat. She wanted to win this trial. She took a deep breath and gave a short **whistle**. Her black and white sheepdog, Shadow, raced off towards the black sheep. But Lauren could see that he was getting too near to the nervous animal. The sheep turned, panicked, and ran over the edge of the cliff. She imagined its body falling, falling, falling … then, while she watched **in horror**, Shadow followed it. He jumped over the rocks into the air. Lauren screamed "Shadow!!!"

In the bed next to her, Beth heard her sister make a strange **noise**: "Aaaahooww!" She **reached over**, touched Lauren's face softly with her fingers and whispered, "Wake up! You're having a bad dream." Lauren opened her eyes and looked at Beth. Then she sat up in bed and looked out of the window at the barn where the dogs slept. Shadow was in there, warm and **dry**. "But," she thought, "a dream like that could be a bad sign …"

2

Lauren got off the bus outside her school in Inverness. Two boys, Callum Macdonald and Ross Fraser, followed her. All three lived on farms in the same valley.

"Do you think your dad will **beat** Lauren at the trials on Saturday?" Callum asked Ross.

"**Aye**, of course he will," Ross answered with a smile. "Believe me, I know."

"How do you know?"

"**Och**, I just know."

"I think her dog Shadow can **read her mind**," Callum continued. "That's why they're such a good team."

"My dad has been a **shepherd** for 25 years. Lauren's just a wee girl."

"But she beat a lot of older shepherds last time," Callum said. "I think you're just **jealous** because you weren't good enough to get into the main trials."

"Don't be stupid. I'm not really interested in sheepdog trials any more. And anyway," Ross went on, "why do you care? I didn't know you liked Lauren. What's that all about, eh? I think …"

Callum pushed Ross away and walked quickly in through the school gates.

3

When Lauren got on the school bus the next morning, the seat next to Callum was empty, so she sat down next to him.

"Where's Ross?" she asked.

"He's not coming to school. His mother said he wasn't well," Callum told her.

"I feel ill too. I **hate** Thursdays."

"Aye, I'm sure you'd just love to stay at home with Shadow, right? And practise for Saturday's trials?"

"Aye," Lauren nodded, "but Mum and Dad wouldn't let me."

4

15 That afternoon, the school bus stopped at the farm gate and Lauren got off. Where was Shadow? She didn't understand. He was always there when she came home from school – he heard the bus and ran to the gate. She called his name but there was still no sign of him, so she started to walk slowly from the road to the farmhouse.

75 "He must be in the fields with Dad," she thought, but when she reached the house, she found her dad in the kitchen with her mum and sister. No one knew where Shadow was.

5

16 When the sun went down at twenty past ten that
80 evening, Lauren was still outside. She had walked around the whole farm and looked everywhere for Shadow. She was still walking and calling his name when her mum and dad came to pick her up.
"The poor girl's so worried," Lauren's mum said.
85 "I know, but it'll be dark soon," said her dad. He opened the car window and called to his daughter: "Come on, Lauren. We'll have to go home now. We can look again in the morning." Lauren looked at her dad, then down at the ground
90 and burst into tears.

6

17 As they arrived at their farm gate, another car stopped – a police car. A policeman and a policewoman got out.
95 "It's not about our dog, is it?" Lauren's dad asked. "Your dog?" the policewoman shook her head. "No, it's about Ross Fraser. Have you seen him? Has he been at your house today?"
"Ross? No. Why, what's happened?"
100 "He's missing."
Lauren opened the door and got out of the car. "Ross wasn't at school today," she told the police officers. "His mum said he was ill."
"Aye," the policeman said. "He was at home in bed
105 this morning but then he just, well, disappeared. No one has seen him since then."
Lauren's mouth fell open as she stared at the police officers. "My dog Shadow has disappeared too!"
"Is that right?" the policewoman asked. "OK, now tell us all about it."

7

110 From her window Lauren watched the lights on the mountain above the farm. About forty police officers and volunteers were looking for Ross in the dark night. She wanted to go too – maybe she would find Shadow up there – but no children
115 were allowed. She watched until her eyes got heavy and the lights started to dance.
Then she was running through the heather. She saw something in front of her. It was running fast. It was Shadow, she was sure, but she couldn't
120 reach him. She called him and suddenly, there he was, just a few metres away. He turned and barked, but the bark sounded wrong: bang, bang, bang.
Her mother shook her gently awake. Lauren
125 opened her eyes.
"I knocked but you were asleep," her mother said. "They've found Ross. He's hurt his foot, but he's all right. And guess what … Shadow was with him!"

8

130 On Friday evening, Callum sat next to Ross's bed in the Ross Memorial Hospital.
"I see they named this place after you," he said. Ross smiled but didn't say anything.
"So what happened?" Callum asked. "I thought
135 you were ill in bed."
"Well, I wasn't really ill, you see … it was like this." And he told Callum his story.

Lauren

9

3 ▶20 "And in second place, with 137 points, from down the road in Beauly, Lauren Reid, just 15 years old,
140 with Shadow."

The crowd cheered, and Lauren and Shadow went to get their prize. Next came the winner, Mr Fraser, Ross's dad. He held up the trophy and then he spoke to the crowd.

Lauren
Shadow

145 "I know you've all heard that we had a bit of an adventure this week down in Beauly. My son Ross was missing – and Lauren's dog Shadow too. Well, Ross fell and hurt his foot out on the mountain and Shadow stayed with him till he was found in the
150 middle of the night. Shadow and Lauren, thank you for that. And this morning, Ross told me a story. I'm not going to repeat that here, but what it means is that, actually, Lauren and Shadow are the real winners of the trial today. So this trophy here,
155 Lauren ... this trophy is yours."

 Access to cultures

Sheepdogs are trained to help people with their work. Sheepdog trials test how well the people and the dogs work together. They take place all over the British Isles.
Talk about ways that animals help people with their work in your country.
Are there competitions like sheepdog trials?

---

1 Understanding together

a) Compare the ideas you had before you read the story with what really happens.
b) Give each part of the story a title, e.g.
   1 A bad dream.
   Then think of two questions about each part and write them down.
c) Compare your titles with another pair. Then answer the other pair's questions. Make sure that you all understand the story.

2 Ross's story – Part 1

Write the story Ross tells Callum at the hospital. You could write about:

1 why Ross was out on the mountain
2 why Shadow was with him
3 how he hurt his foot
4 how he was found.

More help ➔ *p. 125*

More help: bietet einige Ideen.

3 Ross's story – Part 2   3 ▶21

a) Listen and take notes on what Ross tells Callum. Use points 1–4 from the last task. Compare your notes and agree on what happened.

b) Compare the story you have just heard with the story you wrote in 2.
Explain which you like better and why.

4 What would they say?

You choose Do a), b) or c).

Neigungsdifferenzierung: Die wählen aus verschiedenen Szen

What would these people say? Write one or two sentences. Find a partner who has chosen the same task and read out your sentences.

a) Lauren when she meets Ross at school.
b) Mr Fraser when he takes Ross home.
c) Ross when he next sees Shadow.

➔ Workbook *15–16 (pp. 66–67)*

Unit **5**

Your task

> Diese Lernaufgabe kann im normalen Unterricht oder als Projekt durchgeführt werden, in Einzel-, Partner- oder Kleingruppenarbeit.

A UK music channel is preparing a programme about the hobbies of young people.
They have asked viewers from around the world to send in their stories or film clips.
Interview someone who plays an instrument, sings in a choir, band, etc. <u>or</u> who has an unusual hobby.

You choose a) or b)

a) Make a **poster** about your interview and present it.
b) Make a **film** presentation about your interview.

> **Neigungsdifferenzierung:** Die S wählen zwischen Video oder Poster.

Step 1
👥 Brainstorm ideas about people you could interview. Discuss what questions you could ask.

My cousin plays in an orchestra. I could interview him.

You could ask him how long he has to practise every day.

…

Step 2
Write down your questions. Remember you will do the interview in the language of your interview partner.

2 Warum wolltest du Flöte spielen?
3 …

3 Wann hast du mit deinem Hobby angefangen?
4 …

Step 3
Do your interview. Take notes on the answers to your questions or record them.

Step 4
Take photos of the person and things they use, e.g an instrument, equipment for a hobby, etc.   **or** Film the person and show them while they are playing an instrument, doing their hobby, etc.

Step 5
Prepare texts for your poster <u>or</u> a script for your film presentation.
Use your German notes to write your texts in English. ➡ *SF 16: Mediation, (p. 148)*
Use a dictionary to look up key words you don't know. ➡ *p. 92, 6 Study skills, 2*

Step 6
Put your poster together. Use text and photos. **or** Make a film presentation about your interview. Use some of the scenes you filmed.

Step 7
Give a presentation of your poster in class. **or** Show your film clip to the class.
➡ *p. 92, 6 Study skills*

Step 8
Use the checklist on the inside back cover to give feedback on one of the presentations or film clips.

1 Text File

 Underground etiquette

KNOW THE CODE

TIP № 1

There's lots of time,
No need to worry,
You're not the one who's in a hurry.
Yet people who are running late
Most certainly won't want to wait
Till you have travelled up or down.
Stand on the right, don't make them frown.

KNOW THE CODE

TIP № 4

If you are young and fit and strong,
Then, even if your journey's long,
Remember there are people who
Are not as young and fit as you.
So why not offer them your seat
And stand instead upon your feet?

a) Look at the illustrations in each tip.
Describe the situation in each one.
Then listen to the rhymes.
For each rhyme, sum up the tip in one short sentence.

b) Choose your favourite rhyme.
Say why you like it.
Learn it by heart and say it to the class, or read it aloud.

---

yet [jet] aber   **certainly** ['sɜːtnlɪ] sicherlich

c) Tips No. 2 and No. 5 are missing.
Say what you think they could be.
Think of as many tips as you can about how to behave on trains or buses.

d) Is it a good idea to use rhyme to give people tips about how to behave?
Give reasons for your opinion.
Write a rhyme for another tip.

---

destination [ˌdestɪˈneɪʃn] Ziel **plain** [pleɪn] deutlich, offensichtlich **delay** [dɪˈleɪ] Verspätung **rather** [ˈrɑːðə] ziemlich
please sb. [pliːz] jm. eine Freude machen

1 Text File

Text 2 — London shapes

a) Listen to the poems. Then read them aloud.

b) Think of London shapes you could write a poem about.

— Tower Bridge!   — A policeman's helmet.   — …

c) Choose one shape. Then write a shape poem.

---

whispering gallery ein Ort, an dem sich Personen über eine große Entfernung in normaler Lautstärke unterhalten können
spy [spaɪ] erspähen   **gherkin** [ˈgɜːkɪn] Gewürzgurke   **steeple** [ˈstiːpl] Kirchturm   **wind its way** [waɪnd] sich schlängeln
sweeping [ˈswiːpɪŋ] weit ausholend

Text File 2

Text 3
Jerry
by Laurence Harger and Cecile Rossant

Chapter 5 The magic hit

Paige walked along to the big COMPANY shop and set up her table in front of the shop window with all its adverts. ONE PHONE FOR THE WHOLE WORLD. NO MORE LONELY DAYS OR NIGHTS – WITH PERFECT PAL, YOU'LL ALWAYS HAVE COMPANY.

She put her sign on the table: Matches' Magic Show. Then she placed her hat for money in front of it and got everything else that she needed out of her bag: the cards, the coins, the small cups and larger boxes.

When she started on her magic routine, a few people stopped to watch: an old man with a walking stick, a young boy with his mother.

"Look, Mummy. She's doing magic like on TV!" Soon five or six people, a small crowd, stood in front of her table. At the end of every trick the little boy clapped, the old man smiled kindly and a teenage boy in a bright blue jacket, with a COMPANY phone in his hand, shook his head and rolled his eyes.

"OK," Paige thought and gave him a hard look. "I know I'm not very good yet, you tosser[1], so why don't you just …"

Suddenly Paige felt that someone was standing behind her. She turned round quickly to see Knuckles. He was dressed as usual in an army pullover and trousers. He moved his face towards her and gave her a horrible smile. She saw the big gap in his front teeth and felt his hot breath on her face.

Knuckles pulled a five-pound note out of his trouser pocket and held it up.

"See this?" he said.

"Yes," Paige nodded at him. "It's a five-pound note."

"Right," Knuckles agreed. "I bet you a fiver[2] I can work out how you do your next trick. If I'm right, I win a fiver from you. If you win, you get this." He waved the money around for everyone to see.

Paige looked at the coins in her hat and said, "All right."

She took a pack of cards and spread them across her table so that everyone could see they were normal playing cards. She picked them up and began to shuffle[3] them. Then she held them out to Knuckles. "Pick a card," she said to him, "any card."

Knuckles picked a card from the pack.

"Now, don't let me see the card, but show it to everyone else, so they can see what it is."

As Paige went on with her trick she thought, "This is the easiest trick in the world, but I don't think Knuckles will get it …"

At the end of the trick, Paige placed one card after another on the table. "Not that one," she said. "Not that one. Not that one …"

Finally she looked up at Knuckles as she placed the Queen of Spades[4] on the table for everyone to see.

"Was that your card?" she asked. "The Queen of Spades?"

Everyone in the crowd began to clap and Paige smiled at the big boy in his army clothes. Knuckles didn't smile back.

---

[1] **tosser** ['tɒsə] *(infml)* Vollidiot/in   [2] **I bet you a fiver.** [bet], ['faɪvə] Ich wette mit dir um 5 Pfund.   [3] **shuffle** ['ʃʌfl] *(Kartenspiel)* mischen   [4] **Spades** [speɪdz] *(Kartenspiel)* Pik

2 Text File

"No," he said. "That wasn't my card."
The crowd booed him. "Don't be a cheat¹," the old man said. "Give the young lady her fiver."
"Don't you call me a cheat," Knuckles threatened². "She's the only cheat here."
"Cheat, cheat, cheat," the crowd began to chant and Knuckles went wild. He put his hands under Paige's table and threw it into the air. Her cards, her hat, coins and boxes flew everywhere. Suddenly everyone was shouting. The noise was so loud that all the customers³, the shop assistants and a security guard⁴ came out of the COMPANY shop to find out what was happening.
"Oi!" the guard shouted at Knuckles as he stood over Paige, who was picking her things up off the ground. "Get lost, will you! You're scaring our customers away."
"You get lost!" Knuckles shouted. He walked over, grabbed the guard's hat and ran off along the street. The security guard started to run after him but soon stopped. He turned back to Paige.
"Hurry up," he told her. "Pack up and get out of here. And don't let me catch you here again, or I'll call the police."
Then he spoke to the big crowd of customers outside the shop.
"Sorry about that, ladies and gents, but the show's over now, so if you'd like to go back inside …"
Slowly, the crowd of COMPANY customers started to move into the shop again. The security guard followed them, and as he entered the shop his hand flew up to his mouth.
"What the …? Who did that?"
Paige had all her things together again now and went to look in the shop too. Across the walls, and the counters, she could see slogans in big, bright red letters: "EVERY TEXT YOU SEND, EVERY CALL YOU MAKE, WE'LL BE WATCHING YOU! THE COMPANY" the slogans said. "YOUR PERFECT PAL IS THE COMPANY'S PERFECT SPY⁵!" And "DUMP⁶ YOUR COMPANY PHONE! DO IT TODAY! THE GROUP"
A big smile spread across Paige's face. "Yes!" she said under her breath, clenched her fist⁷ and started to walk away. She stopped when the teenager in the bright blue jacket stood in her way. He held out a five-pound note to her. She took it automatically.
"Here," the boy said, "you won this. That kid had no idea how you did that trick."
Then he turned round and walked quickly away before Paige could say a word. She just stood there and watched him with her mouth open. When he disappeared round a corner she looked down at the note in her hands. Next to the picture of the Queen was a telephone number and a smiley face.

a) Say …
   – how Knuckles behaves towards Paige
   – what Paige thinks when she sees the slogans on the walls of COMPANY

b) You've read one chapter of *Jerry*.
   Say what you think the book is about.

---

¹ **cheat** [tʃiːt] Mogler/in   ² **threaten sb.** [ˈθretn] jm. drohen   ³ **customer** [ˈkʌstəmə] Kunde/Kundin   ⁴ **security guard** [sɪˈkjʊərəti ˌgɑːd] Wachmann   ⁵ **spy** [spaɪ] Spion/in   ⁶ **dump sth.** [dʌmp] etwas wegwerfen   ⁷ **clench your fist** [klentʃ] die Faust ballen

Text File 3

Text 4 — A Liverpool street [3] [28]

PENNY LANE *(John Lennon and Paul McCartney)*

In Penny Lane there is a barber showing photographs
Of every head he's had the pleasure to know
And all the people that come and go
Stop and say hello

5 On the corner is a banker with a motorcar
The little children laugh at him behind his back
And the banker never wears a mac in the pouring rain
Very strange

10 Penny Lane is in my ears and in my eyes
There beneath the blue suburban skies
I sit and meanwhile back in

Penny Lane there is a fireman with an hourglass
And in his pocket is a portrait of the Queen
15 He likes to keep his fire engine clean
It's a clean machine

Penny Lane is in my ears and in my eyes
A four of fish and finger pies
In summer meanwhile back

20 Behind the shelter in the middle of a roundabout
A pretty nurse is selling poppies from a tray
And though she feels as if she's in a play
She is anyway

Penny Lane, the barber shaves another customer
25 We see the banker sitting waiting for a trim
Then the fireman rushes in from the pouring rain
Very strange

Penny Lane is in my ears and in my eyes
There beneath the blue suburban skies
30 I sit and meanwhile back

Penny Lane is in my ears and in my eyes
There beneath the blue suburban skies
Penny Lane

Penny Lane is the name of a Liverpool street near where two of the Beatles, John Lennon and Paul McCartney, grew up. In the song *Penny Lane*, the two young musicians describe the kind of people that they saw while they were waiting for a bus to take them into the city centre.

a) Read or listen to the song and make a list of the people, what they're doing and what else you learn about them.
barber
…
Say what other people you think might live in this part of town.

b) Think of a street you know where you can see lots of different people. What kind of people are they and why do they come to this street?

c) Tell your partner about the street you chose and the people you can see there.

---

barber ['bɑːbə] (Herren-)Friseur   **pleasure** ['pleʒə] Vergnügen   **mac** [mæk] Regenmantel   **pouring** ['pɔːrɪŋ] strömend   **beneath** [bɪ'niːθ] unter   **suburban** [sə'bɜːbən] vorstädtisch   **meanwhile** ['miːnwaɪl] unterdessen   **hourglass** ['aʊəglɑːs] Sanduhr   **fire engine** ['faɪər ˌendʒɪn] Feuerwehrauto   **pie** [paɪ] Pastete   **shelter** ['ʃeltə] Wartehäuschen   **roundabout** ['raʊndəbaʊt] Kreisverkehr   **nurse** [nɜːs] Krankenschwester   **poppy** ['pɒpɪ] Mohn(blume)   **tray** [treɪ] Tablett   **(to) shave** [ʃeɪv] rasieren   **customer** ['kʌstəmə] Kunde, Kundin   **trim** [trɪm] Schnitt   **(to) rush in** [rʌʃ_'ɪn] hineinstürzen

3 Text File

Juggling with Gerbils

a) Listen to the poems. Then read them to yourself.

When you are called names, remember

If bullies mock and reject you
Repeat after the poet, please:
A cat's a wonderful creature
That does not converse with its fleas

Mr Ifonly

Mr Ifonly sat down and he sighed,
I could have done more if only I had tried
If only I had followed my true intent
If only I had done the things that I meant
If only I had done the things that I could
And not simply done the things that I should
If only a day had lasted a year
And I had not lived in constant fear
Mr Ifonly sat down and he cried:
I could really have lived if only I had tried!
Now life has passed me by and it's such a crime,
Said Mr Ifonly who had run out of time

The Panther's Heart

Although he still pads about behind
The bars of his solitary cage,
Although he still looks up nightly
At the moonstruck mountains
And the falling snow,
The panther's heart
Stopped long ago.

---

call sb. names jn. beschimpfen **mock** verspotten **reject** [rɪˈdʒekt] zurückweisen **flea** [fliː] Floh **mean** beabsichtigen
fear [fɪə] Angst **run out of time** keine Zeit mehr haben **although** [ɔːlˈðəʊ] obwohl **pad about** herumtappen

Text File 3

My Neighbours' Rabbit

On the wall between my neighbours' garden and mine
a rabbit is sitting, shivering with cold.
They've been away some days now.
They've left out water and dry food
(though the rain's put paid to that).
What they haven't left behind is love.
They've asked no one to call in,
to stroke it, to make sure it's OK.
Having made it dependent upon them
they've abandoned it.
I take it from the wall,
feed it some apple, feel
how warm it grows, a furry volcano,
as warm as my absent neighbours are cold.
I marvel at how many sizes
the human heart comes in.
Some hearts have room inside them for a hutchful of rabbits,
some are so small
not even one rabbit would fit inside.
Perhaps my neighbours possess such hearts –
hearts that keep on shrinking,
that grow smaller and smaller until finally
nothing will fit inside, not even
the breath of a solitary rabbit.

---

b) Say which poems are about
  – how cruel people can be
  – unhappy people
  Which poems give the reader advice?
  Give reasons for your answers.

c) Say which poem you like most and why.

The poet and writer **Brian Patten** was born in Liverpool in 1946. He left school at 15 and worked for a local newspaper, where he wrote articles on pop music.
In the 1960s he was one of the group of three "Liverpool Poets" (the others were Adrian Henri and Roger McGough). The "Liverpool Poets" wanted to make poetry more popular in everyday life. In 1967 they published a book of poems called *The Mersey Sound*, which became a bestseller.
Brian writes for adults and children. He often reads his poems on stage. The poems above are from *Juggling with Gerbils*, a book of poetry for children which came out in 2000.

---

put paid to sth. etwas zunichtemachen **stroke** [strəʊk] streicheln **dependent upon sb./sth.** [dɪˈpendənt] von jm./etwas abhängig **abandon** [əˈbændən] im Stich lassen **furry** [ˈfɜːri] kuschelig **marvel at sth.** [ˈmɑːvəl] staunen über etwas **hutchful of** [ˈhʌtʃfʊl] Käfig voller

4 Text File

Text 6 — Finn McCool

The legend of Finn McCool, an Irish giant, tells how Finn builds a bridge or causeway between Ireland and Scotland so that he can fight a Scottish giant. There are two versions of this legend. In the one you read about on page 67, the two giants fight in the middle of the causeway. Finn is the winner, and the Scottish giant runs home as fast as he can. On his way he pulls up all the stones and destroys the bridge. He is so afraid of Finn that he never wants to fight him again.
The second version of the legend tells a different story. You can read it below.

33 Long ago, there was a giant called Finn McCool. He lived on the northern coast of Ireland with Oonagh [ˈuːnə], his wife. At 54 foot[1], he was half as tall as the tallest oak tree. He was, people said, the tallest
5 giant in the British Isles.
Finn was strong too. He could lift rocks the size of elephants and throw them for 50 miles and more. People said he was the strongest giant in the whole of the British Isles.
10 And Finn was handsome[2]. He had thick yellow hair that shone like gold in the morning sunshine. His nose was as noble as the nose of a king, and his eyes bluer than the blue, blue sea between Scotland and Ireland. Nowhere in the British Isles
15 was there a giant more handsome than Finn, people said.

❖

34 One morning, as Oonagh was preparing breakfast, Finn called to her and spoke:
"I forgot to tell you, but I'll be away for a few
20 days."
"And where are you going?" Oonagh asked.
"To Carlingford. The giant Ruscaire [ˈrʌskərə] has challenged me to a fight."
Oonagh frowned. "You could say no."
25 "Are you mad?" said Finn. "If I didn't accept a challenge, people would think I was afraid. They might even think Ruscaire is stronger than me."
"Would that matter[3]?" Oonagh asked.

"Would that *matter*? Of course it would matter.
30 Anyway, I'll only be gone for a few days."
"Exactly," said Oonagh. "A few days this week, a few days next week. Week in, week out, you walk from one end of Ireland to the other. And why? To fight with other giants! Well, I'm tired of it, Finn
35 McCool. You're like a little boy. It's time you stopped fighting and grew up."
"Oonagh," said Finn. "People say I'm the strongest giant in the British Isles. I have a reputation[4], and I mean to defend it."
40 "There are other ways to defend a reputation, Finn McCool," Oonagh replied.
"You can keep them to yourself," said Finn. "*I* don't want to know." And he picked up his sword and his club[5] and walked out of the house.

❖

45 When Finn arrived in Carlingford, Ruscaire was waiting for him. They fought for three days. On the first day, they fought with clubs. On the second day, they fought with swords. And on the third day, they fought with their bare hands.
50 "All right, Finn, you win," said Ruscaire, as he lay face down on the ground with Finn's knee pressing against his back. "But there'll be another day."
"There will!" said Finn. "Another day, another fight, another victory[6]."
55 With that, he left Ruscaire and made his way home.

❖

---

[1] **54 foot** [fʊt] 54 Fuß groß *(ca. 16,5 m)*   [2] **handsome** [ˈhænsəm] gut aussehend   [3] **Would that matter?** Wäre das schlimm?
[4] **reputation** [ˌrepjʊˈteɪʃn] Ruf   [5] **club** Knüppel   [6] **victory** [ˈvɪktəri] Sieg

Text File 4

When Finn got back to the northern coast, it was already dark. Oonagh was fast asleep. Finn climbed into bed and, soon, he was dreaming of the battles he had fought and the victories he had won. Then suddenly, in the early hours, he was torn from his sleep by a terrible roar:
"Finnnnn … Finn McCool," cried a voice like an erupting volcano. "Finnnnn …"
Oonagh woke up too.

"Is that thunder?" she asked.
"No", said Finn. "It's somebody calling me."
"Finnnnn …" roared the voice.
A moment later, there was a loud bang outside. Finn ran to the door. In front of the house he saw a huge rock with a message carved[1] into it. He read it out loud:

[ˌbenənˈdɒnə]

"Benandonner – the Scottish giant!" said Finn. "He *can't* be stronger than me."
"Well," said Oonagh. "With a voice like thunder that carries across the sea, he must be quite big. And if he's big, he's probably quite strong. And who knows? He might be a handsome fellow, too."
"I must challenge him to a fight," said Finn.
"Must you really?"
"Of course I must," growled[2] Finn. "But first I'm going to finish my sleep."
And with that, he went back to bed.

The next day, Finn carved a message into a rock:

Then he hurled[3] the rock over the sea to Scotland. Before long, a rock with Benandonner's answer came flying through the air. Finn caught it in one hand and read out loud:

"Well," said Oonagh. "That solves that problem."
"It solves nothing," shouted Finn. "Do you really believe that he cannot swim? In truth, he is afraid. He wants to call himself the strongest giant, but without a fight."
"Let him," said Oonagh. "It does no harm[4]."
"He's bluffing, said Finn, "but I will call his bluff[5]. Of that you can be sure."
"I'm sure you know best what to do, Finn McCool," Oonagh sighed. "And now, if you'll excuse me, I'll have to go. King Cormac has invited me to lunch."

When Oonagh returned from lunch with the king, she could hardly believe her eyes. In front of her house was a pile[6] of rocks 40 foot high, and at least a mile long.
"Finn!" she called angrily. "What in heaven's name have you been doing?"
"Collecting rocks," Finn replied.
"I can see that," said Oonagh "but I don't want to have a huge wall of rocks in front of my house."
Finn smiled. "They'll be gone soon. Don't worry."
For the next six days, Finn walked all over Ireland, collecting the biggest rocks he could find. With each day, the pile became longer and higher.
"Finn," cried Oonagh. "I thought you said the rocks wouldn't be here for long."
"They won't be," Finn answered.
"What are you going to do with them?"

---

[1] **carved** [kɑːvd] gehauen [2] **growl** [graʊl] knurren, brummen [3] **hurl** [hɜːl] schleudern [4] **It does no harm.** [hɑːm] Es schadet nichts. [5] **call sb's bluff** [blʌf] jn. auf die Probe stellen [6] **pile** [paɪl] Stapel, Haufen

"I'm going to build a causeway, Oonagh," Finn explained. "Between Ireland and Scotland, so that Benandonner can come over here and accept my challenge."

Once Finn had collected enough rocks, he began to build the bridge to Scotland. One after the other, he hurled the rocks into the sea and day by day the bridge grew until finally it was complete.

"So," said Finn to Oonagh, "you'll be pleased to see that the pile of rocks in front of the house has disappeared. It now forms a causeway across the sea to Scotland."

"Aye," said Oonagh with a smile. "The Giant's Causeway."

"And now," said Finn, "I'll tell Benandonner that he can cross the water." He picked up a rock and carved a message into it. Then he threw the rock across the sea to Scotland.

❖

It was a fine day. Finn stood on the Irish side of the causeway, waiting for Benandonner to arrive. In the distance[1] he could hear footsteps, each as loud as a clap of thunder. Then suddenly, the Scottish giant came into view. Finn shuddered[2]. "He must be 75 foot!" he thought.

Quickly, he picked up his sword and his club and hurried back to his house.

Oonagh was surprised to see him.

"Have you beaten Benandonner already?"

"There's no time for joking, Oonagh. "I wouldn't have a chance against Benandonner. He's huge. And he'll be here any minute. What can I do?"

"You aren't afraid of a Scottish giant, Finn McCool?" Oonagh asked.

"Of course not," Finn replied. "It's just … er …"

"Never mind[3]," said Oonagh. "Take this."

"A bonnet[4]?" said Finn in surprise.

"Yes, a bonnet. Now put it on your head and lie down on that bed over there."

Finn did as Oonagh said. Oonagh then fetched some blankets and covered Finn with them. Then she went to a cupboard and took out a rattle[5].

"Hold this in your hand," she said.

Finn did as he was told. Moments later there was a loud knock on the door.

❖

Oonagh opened the door and looked up. Benandonner was indeed much taller than Finn, and probably much stronger. But there was nothing handsome about him at all. His red stringy hair fell over a face which was covered in pimples the size of apples. His eyes were greener than poison[6] and his huge nose was like a parrot's beak. Through his open mouth Oonagh could see a long row of sharp, crooked, yellow teeth.

"Good morning, sir," said Oonagh. "And what can I do for you?"

"My name is Benandonner," said the giant. "I'm looking for Finn McCool."

"Benandonner!" said Oonagh. "Finn is expecting you. He's out now, but he'll be back soon. Won't you come in and sit down while you're waiting?"

Benandonner came in and took a seat.

"I hope you don't mind if I work at the stove[7]," said Oonagh. "I'm making the baby's breakfast," she added, pointing to Finn in the bed in the corner.

"That's a fine big baby," said Benandonner.

"He is indeed." Oonagh replied. "And just like his father. Finn is very proud of him, of course."

"He must be," said Benandonner.

---

[1] **distance** ['dɪstəns] Ferne [2] **shudder** ['ʃʌdə] erschaudern [3] **Never mind.** [maɪnd] Mach dir nichts draus. [4] **bonnet** ['bɒnɪt] Haube [5] **rattle** ['rætl] Rassel [6] **poison** ['pɔɪzn] Gift [7] **stove** [stəʊv] Herd

Text File 4

"Anyway," said Oonagh. "I'm making steak and
185　pancakes. Would you like some yourself?"
"Yes, please," said Benandonner.
At the stove, Oonagh made two huge pancakes.
Into the second one she threw a handful of stones.
When it was cooked, she put it on a plate and gave
190　it to Benandonner. Then she took the other
pancake and began to feed it to Finn."
"Ouch!" cried Benandonner.

"What's the matter?" Oonagh asked.
"I've just broken a tooth," said the giant.
195　"On a pancake so soft?" cried Oonagh. "Oh, dear!
I *am* sorry. But don't worry, I'm sure you'll enjoy
your steak."
Oonagh went back to the stove. With a sharp knife
she cut a pocket into one of the steaks and pushed
200　a plank[1] of oak into it. Then she put it on a plate
and gave it to Benandonner.
"Thank you," said the giant. "It smells delicious."
Benandonner closed his mouth on the steak and
his sharp teeth sank into the plank of oak."
205　"Mmmmmmmmmmmm," he whined[2].
"I'm glad you're enjoying it," Oonagh smiled.
Benandonner shook his head wildly and pointed at
the steak between his teeth. It was clear that he
couldn't open his mouth.
210　"Good heavens," said Oonagh. "Your teeth are
stuck – in such a tender piece of steak! Sure it was
no problem at all for Baby Finn."
Benandonner pulled and grunted[3] until finally he
managed to free his teeth. Then he put the steak
215　back onto his plate. "I'm sorry," he said, "but I
can't eat this."
"No need to worry," said Oonagh. "I can give it to
Baby Finn for his lunch."

"What a strong little baby he is," said
220　Benandonner.
"Yes," said Oonagh. "He's going to be just as
strong as his father when he grows up."
Benandonner stood up.
"Well," he said. "It doesn't look as if Finn will be
225　back very soon."
"You don't want to go, surely?" cried Oonagh.
"Finn will be here very soon, and he'll be
disappointed[4] if he doesn't see you."
"To be honest[5]," said Benandonner, "I have some
230　important business back in Scotland. I really must
be on my way."
With that, he ran out of the house as fast as his
feet could take him.

❖

"Well," said Finn, "You saved me."
235　Oonagh smiled. "Why don't we go out for a walk?
You can show me the causeway you built. I've not
seen it yet, you know."
They walked down to the sea.
"So where is it?" Oonagh asked.
240　"I don't believe it," said Finn. "Look, there's the
beginning of the causeway," he said, and pointed
to the Giant's Causeway as we know it today. "But
the rest has disappeared. Benandonner must have
destroyed it on his way back to Scotland."
245　"He must be scared of you, Finn," said Oonagh.
"Very scared."

a) Work in threes. Each partner takes one
character – Finn, Oonagh or Benandonner.
Choose three adjectives to describe your
character. Explain your choice.

b) Explain why Benandonner destroyed the
Giant's Causeway.

c) `You choose` Do i) or ii).
　i) Draw a picture of a scene from the story.
　ii) The legend explains the origins of the
　　 Giant's Causeway, but it also has a moral.
　　 Explain what you think the moral is.

---

[1] **plank** [plæŋk] Brett　　[2] **whine** [waɪn] heulen, jammern　　[3] **grunt** [ɡrʌnt] grunzen　　[4] **disappointed** [ˌdɪsəˈpɔɪntɪd] enttäuscht　　[5] **honest** [ˈɒnɪst] ehrlich

4 Text File

Text 7 The Titanic

Crossing the Atlantic

When people travel to New York from Frankfurt or London today, they usually go by plane. The flight takes between six and nine hours. But in the early 1900s, there were no planes. Back then, millions of people left Europe and crossed the Atlantic Ocean to go to America. They all crossed the Atlantic by ship. It took about a week.

In 1911, a new steamer[1] was built in Belfast for a Liverpool company, White Star Line. It was bigger and more comfortable than any other ship in the world. That ship was the Titanic, and in April 1912 it was ready for its first transatlantic journey.

early 20th century
➤ about 7 days

early 21st century
➤ 6 to 9 hours

1 How has travelling across the Atlantic changed since the early 20th century? Use phrases from the box.

> today / these days / in the early 1900s / back then / …
> It takes/took … hours/days/weeks … to go by plane/ship …
> The journey by plane/ship takes/took …

A big ship

The White Star Line wanted people to believe that their ship was not only the biggest, but also the strongest and safest[2] ship in the world. They named it Titanic. Newspapers called the ship "unsinkable". The Titanic was like a big hotel on water with restaurants, a swimming pool and comfortable rooms for first and second-class passengers[3]. It also had space for hundreds of third-class passengers who couldn't pay much for a ticket. This was a time when large numbers of emigrants were leaving Great Britain and Ireland and other parts of Europe for political and economic[4] reasons. They were hoping for a better life in America.

The Titanic's dimensions

Car | Bus | Airbus A380

The Titanic in numbers

Length	269 m
Width	28 m
Height	53 m
Passengers	about 2,200

2 Look at the text, diagram and table above.
Talk to a partner about the Titanic's dimensions. The phrases in the box can help you.

> This diagram shows … / gives information about …
> From the diagram you can see that …
> The Titanic was (about) as big as three …
> It was … metres long/wide/high.
> It could carry … passengers.

---

[1] **steamer** ['stiːmə] Dampfschiff [2] **safe** [seɪf] sicher [3] **passenger** ['pæsɪndʒə] Reisende(r) [4] **economic** [iːkə'nɒmɪk] wirtschaftlich

Text File 4

3 Read *The Titanic's first and last journey* and sum up the events in 5–6 sentences.
👥 Compare with a partner.

The Titanic's first and last journey

On 10 April 1912, the Titanic left Southampton for New York with about 2,200 people on board. On the journey, there were warnings from other ships about icebergs, but the captain didn't take them seriously[1]. On the night of 14 April, people suddenly saw an iceberg in front of the ship, but it was already too late. The ship hit the iceberg. The collision left six small holes in the ship's hull[2]. Water began to fill the bow[3] of the ship. At first the people were calm because they didn't believe that the Titanic could sink. But soon everyone knew that the ship was in trouble.

The Titanic only had enough lifeboats for about half of the people on board. The captain said that women and children must go first. Many lifeboats left the ship only half full because no one knew how many people they could take.

Two and a half hours later, the Titanic broke into two parts, filled with water and sank. There were still over 1,000 people on board. In the end, about 1,500 people drowned or froze to death in the ice-cold water.

Illustration of the sinking Titanic

The ship's captain, Edward Smith

Diagram: Position of the Titanic and the iceberg

Passengers

Most of the passengers on the Titanic were travelling third-class. They were not allowed to visit the parts of the ship that were for first-class and second-class passengers only.

- 38% / 325 – first class
- 59% / 285 – second class
- 75% / 710 – third class
- died

- first class
- second class
- third class
- lifeboats

Diagram of the classes and the lifeboats of the Titanic

4 Look at the diagrams. Say why you think so many third-class passengers died. The language box can help you.

> The green/blue/red part is …
> …-class passengers were near / far from the lifeboats.
> … passengers were in the first/… class.
> … per cent of the first-class/… passengers died/survived.

---

[1] **take sth. seriously** ['sɪərɪəsli] etwas ernst nehmen [2] **hull** [hʌl] Rumpf [3] **bow** [baʊ] Bug [4] **stern** [stɜːn] Heck

5 Text File

Text 8: *The Off-side Trap*[1] by Mary Colson

a) Describe the pictures on pp. 112–115. Say why you think the characters look different in grey than in colour.

b) Read the play. Choose three examples of where the characters say something different from what they think.
   Compare your examples.

EXTRA Act out the play.

Setting
Football club disco.

Maxine really fancies Paul and he quite likes her. They're thirteen years old. He's hugely into football – she knows nothing about it but has to pretend she does in order to make conversation. While their thoughts are being spoken, Maxine and Paul are experiencing awkward silences, looking ill at ease and searching for something to say. There is a prevailing embarrassed awkwardness throughout their dialogue. → Text in English and German (p. 197)

List of characters
Maxine, Maxine 1 *(her thoughts)*
Paul, Paul 1 *(his thoughts)*
Dave *(Paul's friend)*
Shelly *(Maxine's friend)*

Maxine	Hi, Paul.
Maxine 1	OK, done it. Made contact.
Paul	All right, Maxine.
Maxine 1	He doesn't sound very pleased to see me.
5 Paul	What you up to?
Paul 1	Tell me I didn't say that – talk about stating the blinking obvious![2]
Maxine	Oh, you know, nothing much.
10 Paul	Right.
Pause.	
Maxine 1	Come on, come on. Say something.
Paul 1	What do I say now?
Pause.	
15 Paul	So … um …
Maxine	*(at the same time)* What did you … Oh, sorry.
Maxine 1	Oh no – how clumsy[3] was that?
Paul	No, you first.
20 Paul 1	Come on, man, be cool.
Maxine	I was just going to ask what you did today. Did you play?
Maxine 1	That's better. More confident. Dead cas[4].
25 Paul	Yeah. Well, I was sub[5].
Paul 1	I sound like a half–wit! I haven't said a normal sentence yet. What's she going to think?
Maxine	I see. Whereabouts did you play, then? On the wing?

---

[1] **off-side trap** [ˈɒfsaɪd træp] Abseitsfalle   [2] **Talk about stating the blinking obvious!** [ˈblɪŋkɪŋ] *(infml)*, [ˈɒbviəs] Musste ich etwas so Offensichtliches sagen?!   [3] **clumsy** [ˈklʌmzi] ungeschickt   [4] **dead cas** [ded ˈkæʒ] *(infml)* (= **casual**, [ˈkæʒjʊl]) total locker
[5] **sub** [sʌb] *(infml)* (= **substitute**, [ˈsʌbstɪtjuːt]) Ersatzspieler/in

112

Text File 5

	Maxine 1	Did that sound technical enough? Do you even have wings in footie? I wish I'd listened to our Stuart when he used to go on.	Maxine	What sort of music do you like?
35	Paul	No, I went on for[1] Dave in midfield.	Maxine 1	He must like some music – even if it's heavy metal.
	Paul 1	A sentence! At last!	70 Paul	I like rap, you know, Eminem and such.
	Maxine	Good match, was it?	Paul 1	That sounds pretty cool.
	Maxine 1	Smooth[2].	Maxine	Isn't he the one who's been done for[7] attacking somebody?
	Paul	Not really, we lost 3–1.	Maxine 1	Oh, I can't stand[8] rap! Even heavy metal would've been better than rap.
		❖	75 Paul	Yeah, but that's just the way it is in America – you just have to accept it.
40	Maxine	Oh, sorry.	Paul 1	She must think I'm pretty cool now.
	Maxine 1	Why'd I have to put my foot in it[3]?	Maxine	What? You have to accept people killing each other?
	Paul 1	Oh God! What now?	80 Maxine 1	I can't believe he's saying this.
	Maxine	So do you play in a league or something?	Paul 1	Oh here we go – what is it with girls and violence[9]? It's not as if it's really happening, is it?
45	Maxine 1	This is awful.	85 Paul	It's just the way it is in the States, Maxine, it's the law[10] of the gun[11].
	Paul	Yeah, but it's nothing great or anything. It's just a local Saturday league.	Paul 1	She'll soon see I'm right.
	Paul 1	Is she as bored as I am?	Maxine	I'm sorry, Paul, but I don't think it's fun to point guns at people or beat them up. It's barbaric.
50	Maxine 1	This has to be the most boring conversation I've ever had.	90	
	Maxine	So do you want to dance? I like this one.	Maxine 1	How naïve can he be?
	Maxine 1	Anything to avoid[4] talking!		
55	Paul	I'm not much good at dancing, actually.		
	Paul 1	I can't dance at all – nightmare[5]. I'm not having Gav and that lot laughing at me – no way.		
60	Maxine	Neither am I[6] really – Shelly always says I've got one dance that I do whatever the song is. I don't think that's true but she says it is.		
	Maxine 1	I really like this one – I might just go and join Shell and Rach anyway if he won't dance with me.		
65		❖		

---

[1] **go on for sb.** für jn. eingewechselt werden [2] **smooth** [smuːð] cool [3] **put my foot in it** ins Fettnäpfchen treten
[4] **avoid** [əˈvɔɪd] vermeiden [5] **nightmare** [ˈnaɪtmɛə] Albtraum [6] **Neither am I.** Ich auch nicht. [7] **be done for doing sth.** wegen etwas bestraft werden [8] **stand sth.** etwas ertragen, etwas aushalten [9] **violence** [ˈvaɪələns] Gewalt [10] **law** [lɔː] Gesetz
[11] **gun** [ɡʌn] Schusswaffe

5 Text File

Paul 1	Oh God.	
Paul	So you don't ever watch anything violent at all?	
95 Maxine	No, I don't.	
Paul	I expect you watch *EastEnders* and *Neighbours*[1] and stuff though, don't you?	
Maxine	Yeah, who doesn't?	
100 Paul	What about the explosions they had at the car yard[2] and all the slagging off[3] they do?	
Maxine 1	What's he getting at? What's he saying?	
105 Maxine	Well, yeah, but it's only a story, isn't it? It's not real.	
Paul 1	Is she thick[4] or what?	
Paul	But it's supposed to[5] reflect society[6] so it seems like it's real.	
110 Maxine	I suppose so[7].	
Paul 1	At last! She's starting to get the picture. Cor, took her a while.	
Maxine 1	I don't get this. Does he think it's real people? And when you think about it, they've had murders[8], crimes[9], assaults[10], drugs – all the things that happen in real life.	
Maxine	Yeah, so?	
Paul	So it's not just in America that it's violent – it's here too, it's just we don't have as many guns.	
Paul 1	Made it!	
Maxine 1	Wow, that's a really thoughtful thing to say.	
125 Maxine	You've got a really mature[11] attitude[12] towards things, Paul.	
Paul 1	I'm in here.	
Maxine 1	He's so nice and mature – not like those silly boys who talk about gangs and guns all the time.	
Paul	Yeah, well, you've got to, haven't you?	
Paul 1	Go on, my son!	
Maxine	Yeah.	
Maxine 1	He's gorgeous[13].	
135 Paul 1	She's all right is Maxine. Dave'll be dead jealous[14].	
Maxine 1	I've got to tell Shell, she'll be so envious[15]!	
Maxine 140 and Paul	I've just got to . . .	
Paul	Oh, sorry. After you.	
Maxine 1	He's such a gentleman!	
Maxine	I was just going to ask you if you could hold my coke whilst I go to the loo.	
145 Maxine 1	How embarrassing[16]! I hate my bladder[17].	
Paul	Oh yeah, sure.	
Maxine	I'll be back in a sec.	
Paul	Right.	

Maxine leaves Paul and walks over to Shelly who's standing near the girls' toilets. Paul remains where he is and his friend Dave comes over.

Maxine	Oh, Shell, I spoke to him! He's absolutely gorgeous!
Shelly	What'd he say? It looked like you were getting on[18] really well.

---

[1] **EastEnders, Neighbours** beliebte britische TV-Serien [2] **yard** [jɑːd] Hof [3] **slag sb. off** [slæg] *(infml)* jn. runtermachen [4] **thick** [θɪk] dumm [5] **be supposed to do sth.** [səˈpəʊzd] etwas tun sollen [6] **society** [səˈsaɪəti] die Gesellschaft [7] **I suppose so.** [səˈpəʊz] Das nehme ich an. [8] **murder** [ˈmɜːdə] Mord [9] **crime** [kraɪm] Straftat, Verbrechen [10] **assault** [əˈsɔːlt] Körperverletzung [11] **mature** [məˈtjʊə] reif [12] **attitude** [ˈætɪtjuːd] Einstellung, Haltung [13] **gorgeous** [ˈgɔːdʒəs] fantastisch, traumhaft [14] **dead jealous** [ˈdʒeləs] *(infml)* total neidisch [15] **envious** [ˈenvɪəs] neidisch [16] **embarrassing** [ɪmˈbærəsɪŋ] peinlich [17] **bladder** [ˈblædə] Blase [18] **get on** sich verstehen

	Maxine	Oh, you know, we just talked about telly and stuff.	
155	Shelly	Well? Are you going out with him or what?	
	Maxine	Well he hasn't asked me yet but …	
	Dave	How's it going with the lovely Maxine, then?	
160	Paul	All right, actually. She is pretty stunning[1], isn't she?	
	Dave	I'll say, she's a babe. What were you talking about? You've been chatting for ages.	
165	Paul	Oh, you know, footie, telly – the usual sort of stuff.	
	Dave	Get in[2] there, my man!	
	Paul	Shut up[3], Dave, she's coming back.	
170	Dave	See you later, Romeo.	
	Maxine	Hiya.	
	Maxine 1	He looks different somehow.	
	Paul	Hi.	
	Paul 1	Dave's right; she *is* a babe.	
175	Maxine	Thanks for holding my drink.	
	Paul	No worries.	
	A beat[4].		
	Paul	So … uh … Do you want to dance? I'm not very good, like I said, but if you want to …	
180			
	Paul 1	Oh God, please say no!	

	Maxine	No, that's OK. I'm happy just talking.
	Paul	Well, if that's what you want, that's fine with me.
	They smile happily at each other.	
185	Maxine	I think we're really similar, don't you?
	Paul	Yeah, I suppose we are.
	Maxine	I mean, we've got similar friends, like the same sorts of things, music and stuff. We even hang around the same places.
190		
	Paul	Yeah.
	A beat.	
		Um … Maybe we could um … go out some time – to the cinema – um … There's a really good new film out – the one with Leonardo DiCaprio and um … Jennifer Aniston, I think.
195		
	Maxine	I'd love to go.
	Maxine 1	Leo's so sweet!
200	Paul	Great.
	Paul 1	Jennifer Aniston's such a stunner[5].
	Maxine	I've wanted to see it for ages.
	Paul	But it's only been out about a week.
	Maxine	Oh, well, I've read loads about it – it sounds really good.
205		
	Maxine 1	I can't believe he wants to see this film. Most lads hate Leo.
	Paul	Yeah, I think it's good to see all sorts of different films.
210	Maxine	Mm. When do you want to go?
	Paul	How about tomorrow night?
	Maxine	Great.
	Maxine 1	Fantastic – a night with Paul and Leo!
	Paul 1	I can't believe it – I get to see Jennifer Aniston and Maxine at the same time! And I get to see Leonardo DiCaprio looking a right idiot pretending to be an ugly midfielder – I bet he can't even kick the ball straight. I'm a genius[6]!
215		
220		
	Maxine 1 and Paul 1	Cool.

---

[1] **stunning** ['stʌnɪŋ] atemberaubend   [2] **Get in!** *(infml)* Mach doch!   [3] **Shut up!** [ʃʌt‿'ʌp] Halt die Klappe!
[4] **beat** [biːt] Pause   [5] **stunner** ['stʌnə] *(infml)* Wucht   [6] **genius** ['dʒiːnɪəs] Genie

1 More help

Part A Practice

1 WORDS City holidays ← *p. 12*

Can you find the verb-noun combinations in the snakes?

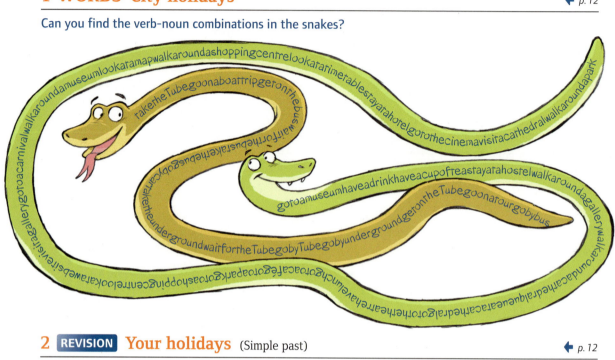

2 REVISION Your holidays (Simple past) ← *p. 12*

Make questions for a partner.

Did you	stay at home / go away? make new friends? do any sports? visit friends/family?

What did you Where did you How did you	do/see/play there? go/stay? travel/get there?

Go back to c) on p. 12.

4 REVISION A message from London (Simple past or present perfect?) ← *p. 13*

Complete Emily's message with the correct tenses. Look closely at the signal words for the simple past or the present perfect. They can help you to choose the right tense.

Hey Amelia,
Hi from London. I ¹… (arrive) on Friday evening (with Mum and Dad), so we ²… (already do) a few things. Yesterday morning we ³… (go) up to the roof of a building where we ⁴… (have) a great view. On the roof we ⁵… (meet) two boys – Luke and Mo. They ⁶… (give) us some tips. Luke ⁷… (tell) us about a carnival at a place called Notting Hill.
After lunch we ⁸… (visit) St Paul's Cathedral and then we ⁹… (take) a red London bus to Hyde Park. It ¹⁰… (be) beautiful there, and it's really huge. ¹¹… you ¹²… (ever be) there?
There are lots of places that we ¹³… (not be) to – like Buckingham Palace, so I ¹⁴… (not have) tea with the Queen yet! (LoL) And we ¹⁵… (not visit) any museums yet, but Mum has plans!
¹⁶… you ¹⁷… (enjoy) your trip to France last week? What ¹⁸… (be) the weather like there? In London it ¹⁹… (not rain) yet! Hugs, Emily xxx

More help 1

Part B Practice

1 REVISION How can I get there? 💬
← p. 18

b) 👥 You're at Leicester Square tube station.
Ask the way to other places on the map.
You can use these phrases to answer your partner's questions.

> Go along … Street. ·
> Cross … Road near the … ·
> Turn left between the … and the … ·
> Turn right behind the church/… ·
> Go past the hotel/… ·
> Go straight on until you get to …

How can I get to Covent Garden Market, please?

Walk along Cranbourn Street. Then turn right into …

Part C Practice

2 I've been living here … (Present perfect progressive)
← p. 21

Complete Mo's sentences with *for* or *since*.

I'm a Londoner. I've been living here …

1 I'm a Londoner. I've been living here … I was three.
2 I like languages. I've been learning German at school … three years.
3 My sister Mishal loves music. She's been singing in a band … over a year.
4 I have a blog. I've been writing posts … last March.
5 My friend Luke and I love cricket. We've been playing in the same team … a long time.
6 Luke is a big fan of Notting Hill Carnival. He's been going there … he was twelve.

3 How long … ? 💬
← p. 21

b) 👥 Swap profiles.
Ask and answer like this:

How long have you been living in Berlin?

I've been living in Berlin for thirteen years.

How long have you been going to … Gymnasium?

Here are some example answers to questions about hobbies and sport.

I've been

learning the piano
playing the drums
playing computer games
playing football
going swimming
doing judo
collecting comics
taking photos

for
ten months.
a long time.
three years.
my whole life.

since
April.
Year 5.
last summer.
I was little.

117

2 More help

Lead-in

2 A long journey
← p. 28

c) Listen again. Say how the girl feels and how she shows her feelings when:

- her parents speak about her when they think she's asleep.
- her mother asks her if she wants to stop for lunch.
- her mother wants to listen to the weather report.
- her father asks her to explain some Welsh words.
- her father asks if she'd like to go on a train.
- her mother asks her the name of a lake.

You can find ideas in the box.

- She feels angry/bored/sad/unhappy.
- She speaks loudly / in an angry voice.
- She shouts.
- She makes a funny sound.
- She says she doesn't want to …
- She says her mother/father can/can't/should …

Part A Practice

1 WORDS Jobs
← p. 31

b) Write sentences for the other jobs in the box.
1 … in films or plays or TV shows.
2 … draw or paint pictures.
3 … work on a farm.
4 … are doctors for people's teeth.
5 … make furniture.

actor · ⁺architect · artist · ⁺astronaut · carpenter · dentist · farmer · ⁺hairdresser · ⁺musician · ⁺painter · scientist

2 REVISION Tom thinks he'll be an astronaut (will-future)
← p. 31

a) What do you think you'll be or do in the future? Copy the chart and add ideas.
Then make appointments with three classmates and interview them.

You can use these ideas about your future.

live in another town/country   be a star
have a family   become a farmer/teacher/…
go on a bike tour across the Sahara   travel to Mars …   be rich and famous

What we will be/do	Me	Partner A	Partner B	Partner C
in 5 years				
in 10 years				
in 20 years				

More help 2

Part C Practice

2 If I were a police officer ... (Conditional 2)   ← p. 36

Think of six jobs. Write a sentence about what you could or would do in each job.
If I were a police officer, I'd catch lots of thieves.
If I became a cameraman, I could film action movies.

Match the ideas in the boxes to make more sentences.

If ...	I would / I could ...
architect	be nice to my students.
artist	grow vegetables in my fields.
carpenter	paint pictures of famous people.
designer	build the highest building in the world.
hairdresser	play songs in the pedestrian zone.
farmer	make a desk for my room.
musician	make beautiful clothes.
teacher	cut my friends' hair for free.

➡ Workbook 1–2 (p. xxx)

3 What would happen if ...? (Conditional 2)   ← p. 37

a) Make notes like this. You can use the ideas from the list.

Idea	+	–
run away to London	see Mo and Luke	no place to live
shout at Dylan		
walk alone in the hills		
invite classmates home		
stop speaking Welsh		
ask a teacher for help		

- laugh at her
- shout back
- feel sad
- lose her way
- be more friendly
- become her friends
- give her some good tips
- have time to think
- not learn the language
- not feel at home in North Wales

Text

2 A fair punishment   ← p. 42

a) What do you think about Dylan and Emily's punishment?
   Read the statements below. Choose the five that you agree with most and write them down.

FAIR BECAUSE ...
- It's very dangerous on the roof.
- They knew that they weren't allowed to go up.
- They're lucky that they didn't fall.
- Mrs Grant was right to be angry. She's responsible for a lot of students.
- Mrs Grant didn't send Dylan and Emily home. They only had to wash the floors.

NOT FAIR BECAUSE ...
- The kids only looked at the stars and sang. They didn't do anything dangerous.
- The door to the roof was open.
- Mrs Grant didn't listen when Dylan tried to explain why they were on the roof.
- It isn't right to tell children to clean toilets.
- It would be enough to wash the corridor floors.

3 More help

Part A Practice

2 WORDS John Lennon was a famous musician p. 48

a) Match six of the people from the column on the left with things that they did on the right to make six sentences like this: *John Lennon was a famous musician who wrote Imagine and other songs.*

John Lennon was a famous musician		wrote *Imagine*.
Cate Blanchett is an Australian actor		**built** the Eiffel Tower.
Galileo Galilei was an Italian scientist		**designed** the *Reichstag* building.
Gustave Eiffel was a French engineer	… who …	**founded** the Boy Scouts.
Norman Foster is a British architect		**invented** the thermometer.
Robert Baden-Powell was a British soldier		**played** in *The Hobbit*.
Steffi Graf is a German sportsperson		**won** the Wimbledon Singles.

3 REVISION Crossword clues (Relative pronouns) ← p. 48

Use these ideas and relative pronouns to write clues for the crossword.

1 thing · you see · sky at night
 – *A thing which you can see in the sky at night.*
2 person · works · with you · class
 – *A person who works with you in class.*
3 black thing · people use · make fire
4 person · sings
5 things · people wear · nose · see
6 thing · you use · clean the floor
7 Welsh boy · likes · Beatles
8 something · at the end · arm
9 thing · takes people · upstairs
10 animal · swims · river or sea
11 white animal · you see · countryside

5 Gwen's photos (Contact clauses) p. 49

Decide if you can make sentences **without** a relative pronoun or if you have to use **which** or **who**.
TIP: Never leave out *who* or *which* if they come directly before the verb.

1 These are the shops ~~which~~ Gareth *wanted* to see.
2 This is the shop **which sells** John Lennon sunglasses.
3 These are the sunglasses … Gareth bought there.
4 This is one of the ferries … crosses the Mersey.
5 This is the Chinese gate … we saw on our walk.
6 These are the kids … gave us tickets for the match.
7 This is the shop … they work in.
8 This is the fruit … looks like green bananas.

120

More help 3

Part B Practice

2 They aren't worn at Igbo festivals (Passive: simple present) ← p. 54

Correct the wrong information in each sentence and complete the sentences.

1 Goat face masks are worn at Igbo festivals.
   – No, they aren't worn at Igbo festivals.
   They're worn at Ogoni festivals.
2 Goat face masks are worn by young women and girls.
   – No, they ... by young women and girls.
   They ... by boys and young men.
3 An Udu is made of wood.
   – No, it ... of wood. It ... of clay.
4 Udus are played by men and older boys.
   – No, they ... by men and older boys.
   They ... by women.
5 Djembe drums are also called water pot drums.
   – No, they ... water pot drums.
   Udus ... water pot drums.
6 The djembe is used every day.
   – No, it ... every day. It ... at special events.
7 The djembe is played with sticks.
   – No, it ... with sticks. It ... with bare hands.

4 Oliver Twist was written by ... (Passive with *by*) ← p. 55

a) Make sentences like the ones in the examples.
   Use the verb in the correct form and choose the correct name on the right.
   Oliver Twist • write • Charles Dickens
   The 2014 World Cup • win • Germany

   Oliver Twist was **written** by Charles Dickens.
   The 2014 World Cup was **won** by Germany.

Romeo and Juliet	write
Treasure Island	
The 1966 World Cup	win
The 2010 Eurovision Song Contest	
Imagine	sing
We Are The Champions	
Hadrian's Wall	build
The Eiffel Tower	
The Mona Lisa	paint

Lena (Germany)   Emperor Hadrian
England   Gustave Eiffel
Queen   John Lennon
Robert Louis Stevenson
                        Leonardo da Vinci
William Shakespeare

Part C Practice

2 Study skills: Ordering and structuring topic vocabulary ← p. 58

c) Add these words to a copy of the diagram in b).
   They can go under these headings, but you decide where to put them exactly.

STADIUM	PEOPLE				COMPETITIONS
goal	cards	midfielder	socks		FA Cup
penalty area	defender	penalty	song		FIFA World Cup
refreshment stalls	flag	shin guards	striker		
terrace	foul	shirt	substitute		
ticket office	gloves	shorts	watch		

4 More help

Part A Practice

2 REVISION Travelling to other countries (Modal verbs) ← p. 68

a) Complete these rules for travelling. Use can, can't, must, mustn't or needn't.

If you travel	to the UK or Ireland, to Spain, by plane, to the USA, to Austria, to India,	you	must	show your ID card or passport. change money. carry a knife in your bag. pay in euros. take your pet. get a visa.

Part B Practice

2 You'll have to revise ... (have to, be able to, be allowed to: Future) ← p. 72

On the left are some questions from a new classmate about next week's English test.
Match the answers (a–h) to the questions and complete them with will or won't.

1 Will I have to revise for the test?
2 What about dictionaries?
3 And electronic dictionaries, mobile phones?
4 Will I have to arrive early?
5 Will we be able to work together?
6 Will I be allowed to sit where I want.
7 Will I have to bring my own paper for the test?
8 Will I be able to leave when I'm finished?

a) No, you ... be able to get it from the teacher.
b) No, you ... be allowed to use dictionaries.
c) No, you ... be allowed to use things like that.
d) No, you ... have to sit where the teacher says.
e) No, you ... have to work on your own.
f) Yes, you ... have to revise the last unit.
g) You ... have to be there just before the test.
h) You ... have to stay until everybody is finished.

3 I won't be able to go swimming ← p. 72

a) Choose one of these places to visit.

> Ireland · a small island in the Atlantic ·
> Greenland · the moon · Mallorca ·
> Berlin · Africa

Choose advantages and disadvantages from
the lists on the right or use your own ideas.
the moon:
+ good view of the earth:
   I'll be able to have a good view of the earth
− no swimming: I won't be able to ...

Advantages	Disadvantages
see wild animals	too cold to have fun
beautiful countryside	dangerous alone
cheap	dirty
friendly local people	expensive
good for swimming	full of tourists
good for walks	too hot to have fun
good music	lonely
good view of the earth	far from home
museums	no swimming
practise my English	rainy
tasty food	mobile phone problems

More help 4

Part C Practice

1 Pronunciation (Consonants)
→ p. 75

b) Listen. Which of the words in brackets do you hear? Write it down.

1 the red ... (card/cart)
2 with a red ... (card/cart)
3 a lovely ... beach (white/wide)
4 lovely ... beaches (white/wide)
5 all the different ... in Dublin (sides/sights)
6 on different ... in the match (sides/sights)
7 put it in the ... of the car (back/bag)
8 put your ... in the car (back/bag)
9 on your own two ... (feed/feet)
10 time to ... her (feed/feet)
11 then it went ... (bang/bank)
12 we went to the ... (bang/bank)

1 card
2 cart
3 ...

4 REVISION I had a weird dream (Simple past)
→ p. 76

Complete Chloe's message. Use the simple past of the verbs in brackets.

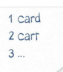 **Chloe Carr** Last night I ¹... (have) this weird dream. You and I ²... (be) on our way up a rocky hill with other kids from our class. Our German teacher Miss Kunzel ³... (be) already at the top. She ⁴... (look) angry and ⁵... (shout) at us to hurry. I ⁶... (not want) to get into trouble, so I ⁷... (run) up the hill like mad. When I ⁸... (reach) the top, I ⁹... (look) around but you ¹⁰... (not be) there. Then I ¹¹... (see) you at the bottom of the hill. You had fallen all the way down. I ¹²... (call) you, but you ¹³... (not answer). You ¹⁴... (be) hurt, and I was sure you had broken your leg. Lewis, tell me you're OK.

1 had
2 were
3 ...

Text

1 The ride across the Burren
→ p. 79

Say who the riders are in each part of the story and what they talk about.
Find these key words in the story:

PEOPLE		TOPICS	
Ashling	old people	Burren	cold
Lewis	Ashling's mother	Great Famine	big holes
		rain	Dad's ashes

Use the words in sentences when you talk to your partner.

123

5 More help

Part A Practice

3 Katie and Iain help each other *(each other)* p. 85

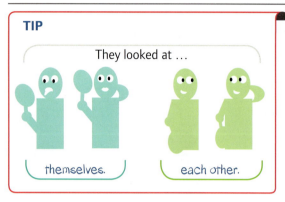

The sentences below show that Katie and Iain are good friends. Complete the sentences with verbs from the box and *each other*.

> give   help   send
> miss   phone   argue   invite

1 Katie and Iain *help each other* with their homework.
2 They usually … at weekends.
3 They never … with …
4 They always … to their parties.
5 They … texts every day.
6 They … presents on their birthdays.
7 They … when they're on holiday with their families.

Part B

4 Good friends? 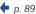 p. 89

b) Say which of these sentences you think best describes the relationship between *edinlew* and *nightmaid*.
  1 They really like each other now.
  2 They know a lot more about each other now.
  3 Edinlew still talks, nightmaid listens.

Give reasons for your opinion.
Look at the information in the boxes below.

> Sorry, but I don't agree. In my opinion …

> I think sentence number … is the best description because …

What Lewis thought about Ashling:

> The owner's weird daughter looks just like a VAMPIRE. Black hair, black clothes and a very white face! SCARY! (p. 74)

> Her black hair and clothes, her black horse and the dark clouds behind her made her face seem whiter than ever. Lewis suddenly felt cold. (p. 78)

> Ashling asked him a question: "So, what's Edinburgh like?" "Edinburgh?" Lewis said in surprise. (p. 79)

> "She's just trying to scare me," (p. 78)

What Ashling thought about Lewis:

> He was probably chatting or playing a game … I hope he doesn't talk too much tomorrow. (p. 74)

> As they went up the hill, Lewis talked and talked. Ashling thought he would never stop. (p. 78)

> He talked all the way to where Ashling's mother and the others were waiting. This time, Ashling was surprised that she didn't mind listening. (p. 79)

5 More help

Part B Practice

1 Skye said she was nervous (Indirect speech) ← p. 90

Imagine you're Lewis. Report to Ashling what these people said on the first night of the play.
You always need to change the verb. Often you need to change the pronoun too, e.g. I → she.

Skye
- I'm so nervous.
- So many people will be there.
- I have a funny feeling in my stomach.

Sandra
- You look great in your costumes.
- I can't understand why everyone is so nervous.
- I'm really proud of you all.
- We'll have a party on the last night.

Mr McCray
- It's a great play.
- I'll have to see it again.
- I can't wait to see you on stage.

Skye said she was so nervous. She said so many people ... be there. She said ... ... a funny feeling in ... stomach.

Sandra said ... ... great in ... costumes. She said ... ... really proud of ... all. She said ... ... understand why everyone ... so nervous. She said we ... have a party on the last night.

Dad said ... ... wait to see ... on stage.
He said it ... a great play.
He said ... ... have to see it again.

4 WORDS Music and entertainment ← p. 91

b) Add more words from this box to the lists you started in a). Add any more that you know.
 Compare your lists.

verbs	instruments	events	people
...	...	...	

act · actor · artist · audition · author · cameraman · carnival · cheer · dance · dancer · director · disco · drum · drummer · drums · edit · film · fun park · guitar · juggle · juggler · model · New Year's Eve · parade · piano · play · reader · recorder · sleepover · star · street artist · theatre · winner · writer

Text

2 Ross's story – Part 1 ← p. 96

Write the story Ross tells Callum at the hospital. Here are some ideas, but you can use your own too.

1 I was out on the mountainside because I wanted to
   - kill/sell/hurt/... Shadow.
   - find a doctor because I felt so ill.
   - write Lauren a love-letter because I'm jealous of Callum and I want Lauren for myself.

2 Shadow was with me because
   - I stole him from the farm.
   - he likes me and enjoys long walks in the countryside.
   - he wanted to leave the farm and live somewhere else.

3 I hurt my foot
   - because it was dark.
   - because Shadow bit me.
   - because the Loch Ness monster bit me.

4 They found me when
   - Shadow barked and told the volunteers where we were.
   - I phoned the police on my mobile.
   - I was taking the Loch Ness monster to the police station.

125

Early finisher

Die S können ihre Antworten selbstständig mit den Lösungen auf S. 250–251 abgleichen.

Hidden words
← p. 12, 3 **REVISION** Have you ever …?

a) Copy the grid.

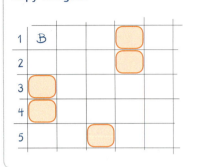

Write in the simple past of these verbs.

1 BEGIN
2 CHOOSE
3 DRIVE
4 HEAR
5 THROW

Use the letters in the orange boxes to make the name of a famous London building.

b) Copy the grid.

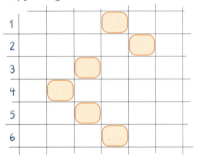

Write in the past participle of these verbs.

1 AGREE
2 BECOME
3 CHOOSE
4 DRIVE
5 JUMP
6 PLAY

Use the letters in the orange boxes to make the name of a game.

True or false?
← p. 21, 3 How long …?

Read the **black** sentences. Then decide if the green sentences are true or false. Correct the false sentences.

1 We moved here in 2010. Our neighbours moved here one year after us.
   a) Our neighbours have been living here since 2009.
   b) We have been living here longer than our neighbours.
   c) Our neighbours have been living here for two years.

2 I got up at 7 o'clock and had breakfast at 8. It started raining during breakfast. It's 3 o'clock in the afternoon now and it is still raining.
   a) It has been raining for 8 hours.
   b) It has been raining since 7 o'clock.
   c) It has been raining since breakfast.

3 Mrs Adams got to the bus stop at 10:10. Mrs Bell got there 5 minutes before Mrs Adams. When Mrs Crown got to the bus stop, nobody was waiting there. After 10 minutes Mrs Bell came. It is now 10:15.
   a) Mrs Crown has been waiting the longest.
   b) Mrs Bell has been waiting for the bus since 10 o'clock.
   c) Mrs Crown has been waiting for 15 minutes.

Early finisher

Word games
← p. 31, 3 **REVISION** If I don't go to bed …

Do a) or b).

a) Find the fourth word

1	music	musician
	science	???

2	guitar	instrument
	table	???

3	cloud	cloudy
	???	rocky

4	farmer	farm
	teacher	???

5	drive	car
	???	plane

6	carpenter	furniture
	???	pictures

7	hairdresser	hair
	???	teeth

8	April	spring
	October	???

9	shoe	foot
	???	hand

b) Words from a Welsh village

A village in Wales has the longest place name in Europe:
Llanfairpwllgwyngyllgogerychwyrndrobwllllantysiliogogogoch.
It also has a shorter name: *Llanfairpwll*. Make as many words as you can from the shorter name.

Number memory game
← p. 39, 3 Making a video

These numbers are all in Philip's report on page 38.
Can you remember what they are?
Match them to the phrases on the right.

13   2   1,085

10   2   59

24   6

- the number of students in the class
- the time they started the walk
- the walk through the forest in hours
- the walk in kilometres
- the climb to the summit in metres
- the time the students reached the summit
- the time they arrived at the hostel
- the number of chocolate bars they ate

3 Early finisher

Strange answers

← *p. 48,* 2 WORDS John Lennon …

Gareth, Gwen and Morgan are walking through Liverpool. Gareth is listening to music.
So he can't hear the others very well and gives some strange answers.

Gareth thinks Gwen said: "What are you listening to?"

Read these dialogues. Say what Gareth thinks Gwen and Morgan said.

1 Morgan: Who's your favourite Beatle?
   Gareth: I don't really like any of our teachers.

Gareth thinks Morgan said: "…"

2 Gwen: When are we meeting the others?
   Gareth: Back at the hostel.

3 Gwen: Do you like it here?
   Gareth: What a silly question. You know I live in Bangor.

4 Morgan: I'm thirsty.
   Gareth: Don't be silly. You're only sixteen.

5 Gwen: Take your earphones out!
   Gareth: I'm not shouting – you are.

What am I?

← *p. 49,* 5 Gwen's photos

Try and answer these puzzles. If you need help, match them to the answers below.

1 I'm a place that begins with P and ends with E and has thousands of letters.
2 I'm a five-letter word which becomes shorter if you add two letters.
3 I am something people answer, but I never ask them questions.
4 I am something everyone has. I go up but I never go down.
5 I am something you can't use until somebody breaks me.
6 I am something that has a neck but no head.

A egg   B phone   C bottle   D short   E post office   F age

Early finisher 4

The right words
← p. 68, 2 Travelling to other countries

Do a) or b).

a) Country words

Match a word in a yellow box to a word in a green box.

b) In English-speaking countries

Choose the best word to finish the sentence below.

When you visit English-speaking countries, it's important to be ... and friendly.

Now do this quiz to find out what kind of person you are.
How would you answer in these situations? Choose a), b) or c).
Then work out your result on page 251.

1. A: Thank you for your help.
   You: a) OK.
   b) That's OK.
   c) You're welcome.

2. B: Have a good weekend.
   You: a) Thank you. You too.
   b) I will.
   c) Thanks.

3. C: What would you like to drink?
   You: a) I want a glass of water.
   b) Can I have glass of water?
   c) I'd like a glass of water, please.

   C: Here you are.
   You: a) That's a very small glass.
   b) Thanks.
   c) OK.

4. D: Hello, can I help you?
   You: a) Yes. Where is the post office?
   b) Yes, please. Can you tell me where the post office is?
   c) I want to find the post office.

   D: Go along this road and it's on the left.
   You: a) Thank you very much.
   b) Is it?
   c) OK.

5. E: Are you feeling tired?
   You: a) What do you think?
   b) Yes, I am a little tired actually.
   c) Of course I am. I've been walking for hours.

6. F: Sorry I'm late.
   You: a) I've been waiting for 20 minutes.
   b) That's OK.
   c) Don't worry – I've only just arrived.

4 Early finisher

The right verbs
← p. 72, 3 I won't be able to go swimming

a) First choose the correct verb for phrases 1–8.

1 *hear / listen* to the radio	1 listen
2 *put / take* off your coat	2 ...
3 *do / make* your homework	
4 *carry / wear* a bag	
5 *drive / ride* a motorbike	
6 *make / take* photos	
7 *say / tell* your friends	
8 *clean / wash* your hair	

b) Use letters from the correct verbs to make the name of a country.

1 last letter	liste(n) N
2 first letter	...
3 second letter	
4 first letter	
5 third letter	
6 second letter	
7 third letter	
8 third letter	

When is Tina's birthday?
← p. 76, 6 At the farm in the Burren

Complete this text with the correct prepositions and you will find out when Tina's birthday is.
Use *at*, *in* or *on*.

Tina's birthday isn't in the shortest month of the year. It isn't in one of the longest either. That means it must be ¹... April, June, September or November. But when is it? Her birthday isn't ²... the autumn, so it must be ³... the spring or the summer. When Tina was 'sweet sixteen' she had a big party. She didn't have one the year before because her 15th birthday was ⁴... a Thursday, and ⁵... Friday morning she had a test at school. She couldn't have a party ⁶... the weekend because her father had planned dinner in a restaurant ⁷... Friday evening to celebrate her mother's 40th birthday. And her mother had already organized a big party for her friends ⁸... Saturday. But this year Tina started planning very early. She decided to have a garden party because the weather is usually good ⁹... her birthday. And it doesn't get dark very early. The party started ¹⁰... 5 o'clock ¹¹... the afternoon and finished late ¹²... night. The last friends left ¹³... 4 o'clock ¹⁴... the morning!

Now you should know the month, but what date is Tina's birthday? Is it ¹⁵... the 5th, 6th, 7th or 8th? Count how many times you used the preposition **on** and you will know! And if you need a bit more help, the month and the date are the same!

Early finisher 5

Work it out
← p. 85, 3 Katie and Iain help each other

Do a) or b).

a) Are you good friends?

Complete these questions. The scrambled letters will help you to find the missing verbs.

Do you and your best friend
1 … each other every weekend?
2 … each other's birthdays?
3 … to each other about problems at home?
4 … or … each other every day?
5 … each other … at Christmas?

Mere berm   ESE
   K E A S P
pen the tox
   spy beer Nuts

b) Where do they live?

Copy the map of the street.

Then read the text and work out where A, B, C, D, E and F live.
Write the letters on your drawing of the map.

When **A** comes out of his house in the morning, **D** comes out of her house opposite and they say hello to each other. **A** turns right and goes past **C**'s house on the way to the station, but they never see each other because **C** works at night. **C** and **E** met each other when they were students and lived together for five years. But they argued with each other so much that **E** moved to the other end of the street. **E** and **D** became friends and they often talk to each other over the garden fence. **D** and **B** have lived next to each other for ten years but they have never spoken to each other. Nobody knows why. **F** and **A** both have cats so they look after each other's cats when one of them is on holiday.

A game without a name
← p. 91, 3 An interview about the internet …

This game is like the German game *Stadt, Land, Fluss*.
You can play it alone or with another Early Finisher.

1 Make a table like this: ⟶

CITY or COUNTRY	HOBBY	SINGER or GROUP	ACTOR	FOOD or DRINK
…	…	…	…	…

2 Take the first letter of your name or the name of somebody in your family.

3 Give yourself three minutes and see if you can complete the table.

If you play with another person,
• take turns to choose a letter
• see who can complete the table first.

There is no name for this game in English. Try to think of a good name.

Partner pages

6 Everyday English Small talk   ← p. 13

c) Partner A:
You're at a tourist sight in London (choose your sight).
You want a photo of yourself at the sight and ask a person who is standing there. He/she takes the photo and starts to talk to you.
Have a nice conversation with him/her.

3 Which is oldest? (Passive: simple past)   ← p. 55

b) Partner A: Ask the questions about 1, 3 and 5.

When was Liverpool Cathedral started?

Liverpool Cathedral
start
finish

Mona Lisa
paint
1503–1507

Berlin Underground
open

Treasure Island
write
1881–1883

Lift
invent

1

Cologne Cathedral
start
finish

2

Portrait of Ludwig van Beethoven
paint
1820

3

London Underground
open

4

Oliver Twist
write
1837–1839

5

°Escalator
invent

2 Making the film: Split screen and music   ← p. 87

Partner B:
a) Watch the film again (first version, without voice-over).

   Take notes on the places where the music changes.
   Think about the effect these changes have on the film.
   Make notes about your ideas.

b) Listen to your partner. He or she will tell you about how the film uses a split screen.
   Then tell your partner your ideas about the music changes in the film.

Partner pages

5 The slave trade
← p. 53

Each partner chooses one of the texts on this page or page 134.

1 The trade triangle:
Selling people to get rich

In the 17th and 18th centuries, millions of Africans were taken from their homes and sold into slavery. This is how the triangle worked:
1. British °traders °exported goods to West Africa.
2. In West Africa, many of these traders took African people as captives, sometimes with the help of other Africans. Why? Because they wanted to take them across the ocean and sell them as slaves.
3. When they sold their captives in America, the traders often got °products like °sugar or °coffee instead of money. Back in Europe, they could sell these products and, in this way, they became very rich.

The captive Africans lived the rest of their lives far from their homes. They had to work very hard, but they earned nothing. The slave trade was one reason why Britain became such a rich and strong country.

→ Raw materials (sugar, coffee, tobacco)
→ Manufactured goods (clothes, pots, cheap jewels)
→ Enslaved Africans

2 From West Africa to America:
The captives' journey

The journey from Africa to America took about eight weeks. During that time the captives lived in terrible conditions. Hundreds of men, women and children had to stay in a °tiny area below deck. They travelled like goods, not like people. It was hard to sit and impossible to stand. Many died during the journey, and the sea was their grave. Those who arrived had to work as slaves on big plantations for the rest of their lives.

133

Partner pages

5 The slave trade ← p. 53

Each partner chooses one of the texts on this page or page 133.

3 Life on the plantations

Plantations were big farms. The farmers were white Europeans who used slaves because they didn't want to pay people to work.

Life for slaves was hard and cruel:
- They had long working days.
- Usually, they didn't get enough food.
- Living conditions were awful.
- There were often °brutal punishments.
- All of this meant that they often became ill.

All slaves had to work – children, men and women. Many of them died young because of this terrible life.

4 The battle against slavery

Protest on the plantations
Captive Africans protested against slavery in many ways. Some worked slowly or pretended to be sick. Some °rebelled against their European masters. Many tried to hold onto their culture and sang traditional songs or told old African stories.

Protest in Britain
In 18th century Britain, people began to change their ideas about slavery. One key figure in this change was Olaudah Equiano (c. 1745–1797).
Equiano's master sent him to Britain while he was still a slave. There he learned to read and write and, later, bought his °freedom. He wrote a book about the cruel life of slaves and gave talks on the topic all around Great Britain and Ireland. His book became a bestseller.

First steps to freedom
In 1807, the UK parliament °prohibited the slave trade, and the British navy tried to stop ships which carried slaves. In 1833, parliament prohibited slavery °completely. These were important steps, but the fight was not over. In many other countries, slavery was still allowed.

Partner pages

6 Everyday English Small talk ← p. 13

c) Partner B:
You're from Britain. At a tourist sight in London (your partner will tell you which sight) you meet a visitor from Germany.
You start talking to him/her and have a nice conversation.

3 Which is oldest? (Passive: simple past) ← p. 55

b) Partner B: Ask the questions about 2 and 4.

Liverpool Cathedral was started …

Liverpool Cathedral
start 1907
finish 1978

Mona Lisa
paint

Berlin Underground
open 1902

Treasure Island
write

Lift
invent 1852

1 Cologne Cathedral
start 1248
finish 1880

2 Portrait of Ludwig van Beethoven
paint

3 London Underground
open 1863

4 Oliver Twist
write

5 °Escalator
invent 1895

135

Sports words

Basketball

- scoreboard [ˈskɔːbɔːd] Anzeigetafel
- lines (pl) Linien
- seats

court [kɔːt] Spielfeld • **referee** [ˌrefəˈriː] Schiedsrichter/in

- guard [gɑːd] Deckung
- forward [ˈfɔːwəd] Angriffsspieler/in
- shirt
- shorts
- boot
- hoop [huːp] Korbring
- backboard [ˈbækbɔːd] Korbbrett
- net [net] Netz
- basketball

Tennis

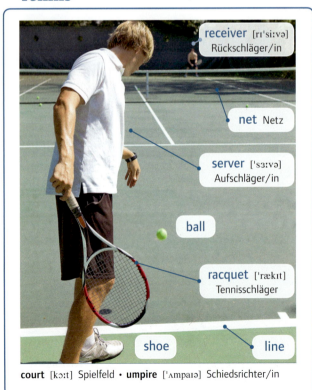

- receiver [rɪˈsiːvə] Rückschläger/in
- net Netz
- server [ˈsɜːvə] Aufschläger/in
- ball
- racquet [ˈrækɪt] Tennisschläger
- shoe
- line

court [kɔːt] Spielfeld • **umpire** [ˈʌmpaɪə] Schiedsrichter/in

136

Sports words

Volleyball

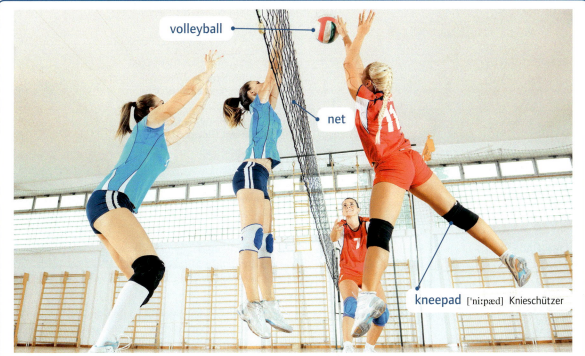

court [kɔːt] Spielfeld • **referee** erste(r) Schiedsrichter/in • **left/centre/right forward** linke(r)/mittlere(r)/rechte(r) Netzspieler/in • **left/centre/right back** linke(r)/mittlere(r)/rechte(r) Abwehrspieler/in • **server** Aufgeber/in

Hockey

pitch [pɪtʃ] Spielfeld • **referee** Schiedsrichter/in • **centre forward** [ˌsentə ˈfɔːwəd] Mittelstürmer/in • **left/right wing** linke(r)/rechte(r) Flügelspieler/in • **left/right inner** linke(r)/rechte(r) Innenfeldspieler/in • **left/right half** linke(r)/rechte(r) Mittelfeldspieler/in • **centre half** Mittelfeldspieler/in • **left/right back** linke(r)/rechte(r) Verteidiger/in

137

Skills File

Skills File – Inhalt   Seite

STUDY SKILLS
- SF 1 Ordering and structuring topic vocabulary 139
- SF 2 Study posters (Revision) 140
- SF 3 Making notes with a crib sheet (Revision) 140

READING SKILLS
- SF 4 Understanding new words (Revision) 141
- SF 5 Working with an English–German dictionary 141
- SF 6 Using a German–English dictionary 142
- SF 7 Scanning (Revision) 142
- SF 8 Taking notes (Revision) 143
- SF 9 Marking up a text (Revision) 143

WRITING SKILLS
- SF 10 Good sentences 144
- SF 11 Structuring a text 145
- SF 12 Paragraphs and topic sentences 145
- SF 13 Using time markers in a story 146
- SF 14 Giving feedback – writing 146
- SF 15 Revising your text 147

LANGUAGE SKILLS
- SF 16 Mediation (Revision) 148
- SF 17 Listening (Revision) 149
- SF 18 Speaking (Revision) 150

PROJECT AND PRESENTATION SKILLS
- SF 19 Teamwork 151
- SF 20 Internet research (Finding information for a project) 151
- SF 21 Describing and presenting pictures (Revision) 152
- SF 22 Putting a page together (Revision) 152
- SF 23 Giving a presentation (Revision) 153
- SF 24 Peer feedback (Revision) 153

In diesem **Skills File** findest du **Lernhilfen und Methoden,** die dir z.B. den Umgang mit Texten erleichtern, beim Schreiben von eigenen Texten und bei der Sprachmittlung helfen oder Tipps zum Vorbereiten von Präsentationen geben.

Alles, was du auf den *Study skills-* und *Writing course*-Seiten in den Units gelernt hast, wird hier nochmal aufgenommen und erläutert.

Einige der Einträge wie z.B. **Study posters** kennst du schon aus Band 1 oder 2. Sie sollen dich an das schon Gelernte erinnern. Du erkennst sie am Zusatz **(Revision)**.

Skills File

STUDY SKILLS

SF 1 Ordering and structuring topic vocabulary
➜ p. 58

Warum soll ich Wortschatz sammeln und strukturieren?

Wenn du einen Text zu einem bestimmten Thema schreiben sollst, kann es dir helfen, vorab Vokabeln dazu zu sammeln und zu ordnen, damit dein Text einen abwechslungsreichen Wortschatz hat und sich gut liest. Oft wird auch schon beim Sammeln eine Gliederung des Themas erkennbar. Dadurch merkst du auch schnell, welche Wörter du ggf. noch in einem Wörterbuch nachschlagen musst.

Diese Art, Wortschatz zu sammeln und zu ordnen, hilft dir auch Vokabeln zu lernen oder zu wiederholen und sie zu vernetzen, so dass sie besser in deinem Gedächtnis bleiben.

Wie strukturiere ich den Wortschatz?

Für das Ordnen der Wörter gibt es verschiedene Möglichkeiten. Du solltest unterschiedliche Formen ausprobieren und dann diejenige verwenden, die am besten zu dir oder der Aufgabe passt.

Einige der Formen, die du nutzen kannst, sind:

- Tabellen (**tables**)
- Diagramme (z.B. **tree diagrams**)
- Mindmaps

Wenn du Wortschatz zusammenstellst, um damit einen Text zu einem bestimmten Thema zu schreiben, solltest du unbedingt daran denken, dass du für einen guten Text nicht nur Nomen, sondern auch Verben, Adverbien, Adjektive etc. brauchst, sowie Varianten für Ausdrücke, die häufig vorkommen.

SF 2 REVISION Study posters

Lernplakate sind ein gutes Hilfsmittel, um Informationen darzustellen, die du dir merken möchtest wie z.B. Grammatikregeln.

Was muss ich beachten, wenn ich ein Lernposter erstelle?

- Sammle und notiere alle Informationen zum Thema, die du auf dem Poster darstellen willst.
- Überlege, wie du das, was du dir merken willst, am besten darstellen kannst. Du kannst z.B. Kästen oder Tabellen verwenden, aber auch kleine Zeichnungen.

Skills File

- Finde einen guten Titel für dein Plakat.
- Gestalte dein Plakat. Schreibe groß und gut leserlich.
- Hebe wichtige Punkte hervor, z.B. durch Unterstreichen oder durch unterschiedliche Farben. Verwende aber nicht zu viele verschiedene Farben, denn sonst wird dein Lernposter unübersichtlich.
- Wenn du ein Lernposter zu einer Grammatikregel machst, kannst du auch ein paar Beispielsätze aufschreiben. Am Besten kannst du dir die Regel merken, wenn du dir zwei oder drei eigene Beispielsätze ausdenkst.
- Häng dein Poster zu Hause oder in der Schule an einer Stelle auf, an der du es häufig siehst, so dass sich dir der Inhalt ganz automatisch einprägen kann.

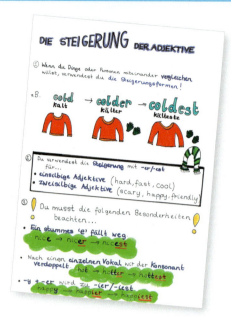

SF 3 REVISION Making notes with a crib sheet

Wozu sind Spickzettel gut?

Ein Spickzettel ermöglicht es auf sehr individuelle Weise

- den Inhalt eines Textes so zusammenzufassen, dass du ihn dir gut merken kannst
- jemandem von einem Erlebnis oder über ein Thema zu berichten
- einen kleinen Vortrag zu halten und möglichst frei vor Zuhörern zu sprechen.

Was muss ich beachten, wenn ich einen Spickzettel erstelle?

Sei kreativ! Dein Spickzettel ist eine Merkhilfe nur für dich – wichtig ist, dass **du** verstehst, was du notiert oder dargestellt hast. Diese Tipps können dir dabei helfen:

- Verwende ein möglichst kleines Blatt Papier.
- Schreibe keine ganzen Sätze, sondern nur Stichwörter oder Teilsätze.
- Verwende Symbole und kleine Zeichnungen, um Inhalte darzustellen, z.B.:
  - "+" für "and"
  - Smileys für Gefühle, Flaggen für Länder, Strichzeichnungen für Dinge und Personen, über die du schreiben oder sprechen möchtest,
  - Pfeile für Richtungen oder Ortsangaben, eine Sonne für Tag/gutes Wetter usw.
- Arrangiere alles so auf deinem Spickzettel, dass die Reihenfolge der Ereignisse oder Inhalte, die du darstellst und wiedergeben willst für dich deutlich erkennbar ist.

Skills File

READING SKILLS

SF 4 REVISION Understanding new words

Das Nachschlagen unbekannter Wörter kostet Zeit und ist auch nicht immer nötig. Oft geht es auch ohne den Einsatz eines Wörterbuches.

Wie erschließe ich unbekannte Wörter?

- Viele englische Wörter werden ähnlich wie im Deutschen geschrieben oder klingen ähnlich (z.B. *brochure, statue, insect*). Manche sehen auch einem Wort aus anderen Sprachen ähnlich, z.B. *voice (French: voix; Latin: vox)*.
- In manchen Wörtern stecken bekannte Teile, z.B. *bottle opener, snowshoe*.
- Bilder zum Text zeigen oft Dinge, die du im Text vielleicht nicht verstehst.
- Der Kontext, also die Wörter und Sätze um das Wort herum, kann beim Verstehen helfen, z.B. *Let's hurry. The train **departs** in ten minutes.*

Hmm, „brochure" heißt dann vielleicht „Broschüre", oder?

SF 5 Working with an English–German dictionary ➡ p. 32

Wenn du unbekannte Wörter nicht selbst erschließen kannst, nutze ein englisch-deutsches Wörterbuch, entweder in Buchform oder im Internet.

Wie benutze ich ein englisch-deutsches Wörterbuch?

Die **Leitwörter** *(running heads)* oben auf der Seite helfen dir, schnell zu finden, was du suchst. Auf der linken Seite steht das erste Stichwort, auf der rechten Seite das letzte Stichwort der Doppelseite.

- *resign* ist das **Stichwort** *(headword)*. Stichwörter sind alphabetisch geordnet: *r* vor *s*, *ra* vor *re*, *rhe* vor *rhi* usw.
- Die *kursiv* **gedruckten** Hinweise helfen dir, die für deinen Text passende Bedeutung zu finden.
- Die **Ziffern 1, 2** usw. zeigen, dass ein Stichwort unterschiedliche Bedeutungen haben oder unterschiedlichen Wortarten angehören kann (z.B. Adjektiv, Nomen, Verb).
- **Beispielsätze und Redewendungen** sind dem Stichwort zugeordnet.
- **Unregelmäßige Verbformen**, **besondere Pluralformen**, die **Steigerungsformen der Adjektive** und ähnliche Hinweise stehen oft in Klammern oder sind kursiv gedruckt.
- Die **Lautschrift** gibt Auskunft darüber, wie das Wort ausgesprochen und betont wird.

> ► resort
>
> ► **resign** /rɪˈzaɪn/
> **1** Beruf • *als Vorsitzender usw* zurücktreten: *He resigned from the company.* Er verließ das Unternehmen.
> **2** *(job, post)* aufgeben *(Stelle, Posten)*
> **3** **resign oneself to something** sich mit etwas abfinden
> **resignation** /ˌrezɪgˈneɪʃn/
> **1** Beruf • *bei Unternehmen* Kündigung; *von Minister usw* Rücktritt
> **2** **hand in one's resignation** *von Angestelltem* kündigen; *von Minister usw* sein Amt niederlegen
> **3** *Gemütszustand* Resignation
> **resigned** /rɪˈzaɪnd/ *(look, sigh)* resigniert
> **resit¹** /ˌriːˈsɪt/ *Verb* (→ *sit*) BE *(exam)* wiederholen *(Prüfung)*
> **resit²** /ˈriːsɪt/ *Substantiv* • BE Wiederholungsprüfung
> **resolution** /ˌrezəˈluːʃn/
> **1** Politik Beschluss, Resolution
> **2** *bei Problem, Streit* Lösung
> **3** ≈ *Entschiedenheit* Entschlossenheit

> **TIPP**
> Wenn du ein Online-Wörterbuch verwenden möchtest, erkundige dich vorher bei deinem Lehrer/deiner Lehrerin, welche zu empfehlen sind, denn nicht alle sind gleich gut. Fast alle funktionieren aber nach den gleichen Prinzipien wie gedruckte Wörterbücher, sodass du sie problemlos ebenso verwenden kannst.

Skills File

SF 6 Using a German–English dictionary ➜ p. 92

Wann brauche ich ein deutsch-englisches Wörterbuch?

Stell dir vor, du sollst einen Text über deine Lieblingsband/deinen Lieblingsverein schreiben und du möchtest sagen, wie schwer die Band/der Verein kämpfen musste, um Erfolg zu haben. Aber was heißt in diesem Fall „schwer"? In diesem Fall hilft dir ein deutsch-englisches Wörterbuch.

Wie benutze ich ein deutsch-englisches Wörterbuch?

Vieles kennst du von der Arbeit mit einem englisch-deutschen Wörterbuch:

- **Leitwörter** *(running heads)* oben auf den Seiten helfen dir, das gesuchte Wort zu finden.
- Die **Stichwörter** *(headwords)* sind alphabetisch geordnet. Beispielsätze und Redewendungen sind den Stichwörtern zugeordnet.
- Die *kursiv* gedruckten Hinweise helfen dir, die für deinen Text passende Bedeutung zu finden.
- Die **Ziffern 1, 2** usw. zeigen, dass ein Stichwort unterschiedlichen Wortarten angehören kann (z.B. Adjektiv, Nomen, Verb).
- Bei **schwierig auszusprechenden Wörtern** stehen auch Hinweise zu Aussprache und Betonung.
- Bei Wörtern mit vielen Bedeutungen gibt es oft weitere Hilfen und Hinweise.

> **Schwede**
>
> **schwer**
> **1** ↔ *leicht* • *im Gewicht* heavy /ˈhevi/
> **2** *(Essen, Parfüm etc)* heavy /ˈhevi/ *(meal, scent etc)*
> **3** ≈ *mühevoll* hard /hɑːd/: *Sie muss schwer arbeiten.* She has to work hard.
> **4** ≈ *schwierig* difficult /ˈdɪfɪkəlt/, hard /hɑːd/
> **5** *es jemandem schwer machen* make* it difficult for someone
> **6** *sich mit etwas schwer tun* find* something difficult, have* difficulty with something
> **7** ≈ *hart* difficult /ˈdɪfɪkəlt/: *Sie hatte eine schwere Kindheit.* She had a difficult childhood.
> **8** ≈ *schlimm, heftig* serious /ˈsɪəriəs/: *ein schwer kranker Patient* a seriously ill patient
> **9** *schwer verletzt sein* be* seriously injured
>
> **schwer**
> Das deutsche *schwer* hat zwei Hauptbedeutungen:
> – *schwer* in Bezug auf das Gewicht: *heavy*, im übertragenen Sinn auch *serious*, *bad*:
> *ein schwerer Koffer*   *a heavy suitcase*

> **TIPP**
> Nimm nicht einfach die erste Übersetzung, die dir angeboten wird! Lies immer erst den gesamten Wörterbucheintrag, bevor du dich für eine bestimmte Übersetzung entscheidest.

SF 7 **REVISION** Scanning

Wozu ist Scanning gut?

Wenn du in einem Text nach Informationen oder Antworten auf eine Frage suchen sollst, reicht es oft, wenn du den Text nach Schlüsselwörtern *(keywords)* absuchst und nur dort genauer liest, wo du sie findest.

Wie scanne ich einen Text?

- Bevor du auf den Text schaust, überlege dir mögliche *keywords*, nach denen du suchen könntest. Es kann helfen, wenn du sie aufschreibst.
- Stell dir dann die *keywords* gut vor und geh mit deinen Augen sehr schnell durch den Text. Die gesuchten Wörter werden dir sofort „ins Auge springen".
- Du kannst auch mit dem Finger in breiten Bewegungen wie bei einem „S" von oben bis unten durch den Text gehen. Wenn du deine *keywords* gefunden hast, lies dort weiter, um Näheres zu erfahren.

Skills File

SF 8 REVISION Taking notes

Worum geht es beim Notizen machen?

Wenn du beim Lesen oder Zuhören Notizen machst, kannst du dich später besser daran erinnern, wenn du etwas vortragen, nacherzählen oder einen Bericht schreiben sollst.

Wie mache ich Notizen?

In Texten oder Gesprächen gibt es immer wichtige und weniger wichtige Wörter. Die wichtigen Wörter sind sogenannte Schlüsselwörter *(keywords)*, und nur die solltest du notieren. Meist sind das Substantive und Verben, manchmal auch Adjektive oder Zahlen.

Folgende Punkte können dir auch helfen:

- Verwende Ziffern (z.B. „7" statt „seven").
- Verwende Symbole und Abkürzungen, z.B. ✓ („yes") und + („and"). Am besten erfindest du eigene Symbole.
- Bei Verneinungen verwende „not" oder streiche Wörter durch.

Da hab ich wohl ein paar Symbole zu viel benutzt …

SF 9 REVISION Marking up a text

Wann sollte ich einen Text markieren?

Manchmal sollst du einen Sachtext lesen und Wichtiges zusammenfassen oder Fragen dazu beantworten. Dann kann es dir helfen, wichtige Informationen für deine Aufgabenstellung im Text zu markieren.

Wie gehe ich am besten vor?

- Lies dir die Aufgabe genau durch.
- Lies den Text und markiere nur Informationen, die für deine Aufgabe wichtig sind. Nicht jeder Satz enthält Wichtiges, und oft reicht es aus, nur ein oder zwei Wörter in einem Satz zu markieren.
- Hebe wichtige Informationen hervor, z.B. durch
  - Unterstreichen
  - Einkreisen
  - oder Markieren mit einem Textmarker.

Wichtig: Markiere nur auf Fotokopien von Texten oder in deinen eigenen Büchern.

> The Beatles' success story started in 1960, when the young musicians played in clubs in Liverpool and Hamburg. They made their first record, *Love Me Do*, in London in 1962.

> The Beatles' success story started in 1960, when the young musicians played in clubs in Liverpool and Hamburg. They made their first record, *Love Me Do*, in London in 1962.

> The Beatles' success story started in 1960, when the young musicians played in clubs in Liverpool and Hamburg. They made their first record, *Love Me Do*, in London in 1962.

Skills File

WRITING SKILLS

SF 10 Good sentences   ➜ p. 16

Gute Texte bestehen aus guten Sätzen. Gute Sätze machen deinen Text interessanter und anschaulicher. Um gute Sätze zu schreiben, solltest du folgenden Dinge beachten.

Wie kann ich meine Texte lebendiger und besser gestalten?

Die folgenden Techniken helfen dir, dich gut auszudrücken und damit den Stil deiner Texte zu verbessern.

Verwende …

- **Adjektive**, wenn du Dinge, Orte und Menschen näher beschreiben möchtest:
  - a bright face
  - a fantastic trip

- aber die Adjektive good, bad and nice nicht zu häufig in deinem Text. Ersetze sie durch andere Adjektive mit einer ähnlichen bzw. genaueren Bedeutung:
  - a nice teacher: a friendly teacher, a helpful teacher, …
  - a good book: an interesting book, a funny book, …

- **Adverbien**, um Handlungen näher zu beschreiben:
  - They walked home slowly.
  - She talked quietly.

- Ausdrücke wie really, very, a bit etc., um Aussagen zu verdeutlichen oder zu verstärken:
  - It was a really sad story.
  - The houses are very high.

- adverbiale Bestimmungen der Zeit **(time markers)**, um zeitliche Abfolgen oder Zeitpunkte zu verdeutlichen:
  - I am going to London next month.
  - He came home yesterday at 5 o'clock.
  - (➜ SF 13: Using time markers in a story, S. 146)

- **Konjunktionen** wie and, but oder because, um deine Sätze zu verbinden und ihnen eine klare, gut nachvollziehbare Struktur zu geben:
  - We went to the London Eye, but it was very expensive.

- **Relativsätze**, um Sätze zu verbinden oder eine Sache oder eine Person näher zu erklären:
  - This is the shop which sells the best ice cream in Berlin.

Skills File

SF 11 Structuring a text
→ p. 51

Welche Struktur braucht mein Text?

Ein guter Text besteht in der Regel aus den folgenden drei Teilen:

- eine **Einleitung** (introduction):
  hier sagst du, worum es in dem gesamten Text geht. Manchmal formulierst du hier auch ein Problem, das in dem Text erörtert werden soll.

- einen **Haupt- oder Mittelteil** (body):
  dieser Teil ist in mehrere Absätze gegliedert und präsentiert die Details zu deinem Thema.

- einen **Schluss** (conclusion):
  hier gibst du deinem Text ein passendes, interessantes Ende.

SF 12 Paragraphs and topic sentences
→ p. 38

Wozu brauche ich Absätze?

Ein Leser kann einen längeren Text einfacher lesen und schneller verstehen, wenn dieser in Absätze eingeteilt ist.

Was sollte ich bei Absätzen beachten?

- Beginne mit einem interessanten *topic sentence*.
- Fang für jeden neuen Aspekt einen neuen Absatz an.
- Beende deinen Text im letzten Absatz/in den letzten Absätzen mit einer Zusammenfassung oder etwas Persönlichem.

Was sind topic sentences?

Jeder Absatz sollte mit einem Einleitungssatz beginnen. Dieser *topic sentence* beschreibt, worum es in dem Absatz geht.

Wichtige Dinge, die du in einem *topic sentence* ansprechen kannst, sind z.B.

- **Orte:** My trip to <u>Berlin</u> was exciting.
- **Personen:** <u>The Beatles</u> are one of the most famous bands in the world.
- **Aktivitäten:** Lots of people <u>ride their bike</u> every day.

My Trip to Wales

Last summer I wanted to go to Wales because I like the mountains.

First I had to find some information on Wales. So I went to the library and looked for books about Wales. I found a book with some interesting information on hiking tours and I also found a camping guide for Wales. I went home with three books under my arm.

At home I started to plan for my trip. I read all the books and took notes on hiking trails, the weather and the equipment I would need for camping and hiking. After a few days I knew where I wanted to go and what I wanted to do there.

I did not want to go to Wales alone, so I had to find someone to go with me. I called most of my friends and told them about my plan. Some of them did not want to go hiking and others had no money for the trip. But my friend Judith agreed to go with me. We decided to go in late August.

Judith and I spent two lovely weeks in Wales. We went to Snowdonia and enjoyed the fantastic mountains. We stayed in a lovely bed and breakfast and met lots of really nice people. Before we went home we spent two very interesting days in Cardiff.

This was one of the best summer holidays I ever had. Go to Wales – it's fantastic!

Skills File

SF 13 Using time markers in a story
→ p. 77

Zeitangaben *(time marker)* helfen dem Leser, sich in einem Text oder einer Geschichte zeitlich zurechtzufinden. Dazu machen sie einen Text anschaulicher.

Welche Zeitangaben sollte ich machen?

Verwende **time markers**, um …

- die **Reihenfolge von Ereignissen** zu verdeutlichen:

    at first, next, finally, …

- zu zeigen, **wie viel Zeit** zwischen einzelnen Ereignissen **vergeht**:

    for half an hour, just three minutes later, I counted thirty seconds, …

- zu verdeutlichen, **wie langsam oder schnell** etwas passiert:

    immediately, it took hours, faster than I could look, …

- zu sagen, wenn etwas **zeitgleich** passiert:

    while I was waiting, during the lesson, as we came round the corner, …

- die **Ereignisse eines Textes/einer Geschichte** zeitlich einzuordnen:

    two summers ago, last Halloween, on my way home from school yesterday, …

SF 14 Giving feedback – writing
→ p. 17

Warum ist Feedback zu Texten wichtig?

Wenn du einen Text geschrieben hast, ist es oft schwierig, deine Fehler und Schwächen des Textes zu entdecken. Deshalb kann es sehr hilfreich sein, eine Rückmeldung von einem Mitschüler zu bekommen.

Was muss ich bei Feedback zu Texten beachten?

Wenn du jemandem eine Rückmeldung zu einem Text geben sollst, gelten dafür grundsätzlich die gleichen Regeln wie bei jeder anderen Art von Feedback auch. (→ *SF 24: Peer feedback (Revision), S. 153*)

Folgende Schritte helfen, wenn du eine Rückmeldung geben sollst:

1. Lies den Text sorgfältig durch, um dir einen ersten, allgemeinen Eindruck zu verschaffen.

2. Beim zweiten Lesen achte besonders auf die Punkte, zu denen du eine Rückmeldung geben sollst. Bei geschriebenen Texten gehören dazu in der Regel
    - Inhalt,
    - Struktur,
    - Wortwahl und abwechslungsreiche Sätze,
    - Grammatik und Rechtschreibung.

3. Streiche Fehler oder weniger gelungene Teile im Text an und mache dir Notizen zu wichtigen Punkten. Wenn du einen Feedbackbogen hast, benutze ihn und trage dort dein Feedback ein.

PEER FEEDBACK CHECKLIST	☺☺	☺	☺	☹
Content				
Lena's text is:				
· interesting			✓	
· exciting				✓
· funny				✓
· _____				
· easy to understand.		✓		
Language				
You connected short sentences with linking words.		✓		
You connected short sentences with relative clauses.		✓		
You used different adjectives in your description of places, people and things.			✓	
You used time phrases to show the order of events.		✓		
You chose interesting words.				✓
You used adverbs.			✓	

Skills File

4. Beginne deine Rückmeldung mit einer Aufzählung der gelungenen Teile/Aspekte des Textes. Es ist immer gut, positiv anzufangen.

5. Erläutere deine kritischen Anmerkungen und mache Verbesserungsvorschläge. Gib Hinweise, wie dein Partner/deine Partnerin bei der Überarbeitung des Textes vorgehen könnte.

SF 15 Revising your text → *p. 38*

Egal, ob du eine Rückmeldung von einem Partner/einer Partnerin bekommen hast oder nicht – einen Text solltest du auf jeden Fall noch einmal gut prüfen, bevor du ihn z.B. abgibst.

Worauf muss ich achten?

1. **Stimmt die *Gliederung*?**
   Jeder Text braucht
   - eine Einleitung, die in das Thema einführt,
   - einen Hauptteil, der das Thema ausführt,
   - einen Schluss, der alles auf den Punkt bringt.
   (→ *SF 11: Structuring a text, S. 145*)

2. **Stimmt der *Aufbau* der *Absätze*?**
   Jeder Absatz
   - befasst sich mit einem zusammenhängenden Gedanken,
   - beginnt mit einem **topic sentence**, der diesen Gedanken einführt.
   (→ *SF 12: Paragraphs and topic sentences, S. 145*)

3. **Stimmen die *Verknüpfungen*?**
   Gute *linking words*
   - schaffen Verbindungen zwischen Sätzen oder Satzteilen,
   - helfen, Zusammenhänge besser darzustellen und verständlich zu machen.
   (→ *SF 10: Good sentences, S. 144*)

4. **Sind die *Zeitangaben* richtig gesetzt?**
   Time markers
   - helfen, sich z.B. in einer Geschichte zurechtzufinden,
   - machen das Geschehen anschaulicher.
   (→ *SF 13: Using time markers in a story, S. 146*)

5. **Enthält der Text *Adjektive* und *Adverbien*?**
   Adjektive und Adverbien
   - erlauben nähere Beschreibungen von Personen und Dingen
   - machen Texte anschaulicher.

6. **Hat der Text sprachliche/grammatikalische *Fehler*?**
   Überprüfe deinen Text
   - auf Rechtschreibung,
   - grammatischen Formen, z.B. die Verbformen,
   - Satzbau *(word order)* usw.

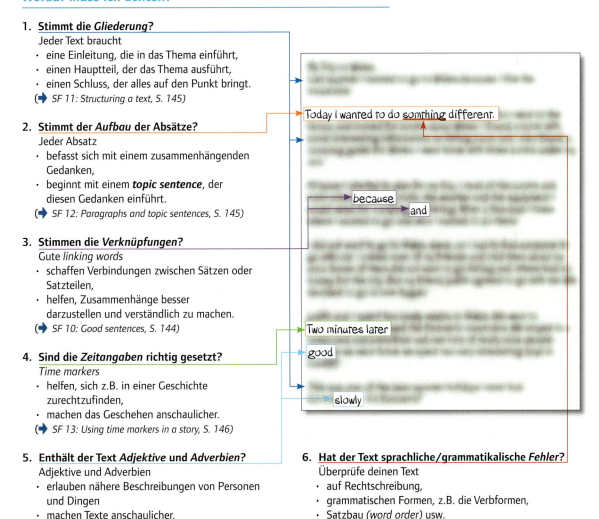

Skills File

LANGUAGE SKILLS

SF 16 REVISION Mediation

Manchmal musst du zwischen zwei Sprachen vermitteln. Das nennt man **mediation**.

Wann brauche ich Mediation?

Hier sind einige Situationen, in denen es sein kann, dass du zwischen Deutsch und Englisch vermitteln musst:

- Du gibst englische Informationen auf deutsch wieder:
  Du fährst z.B. mit deiner Familie nach Großbritannien und deine Großeltern, Eltern oder Geschwister wollen wissen, was jemand gesagt hat oder was auf einer Informationstafel steht.

- Du gibst deutsche Informationen auf englisch wieder:
  Wenn du eine/n Austauschschüler/in aus England (oder einem anderen Land) bei dir zu Hause zu Gast hast, kann es sein, dass er/sie wenig Deutsch spricht und deine Hilfe braucht.

- In schriftlichen Prüfungen musst du manchmal in einem englischen Text gezielt nach Informationen suchen und diese auf Deutsch wiedergeben. Oder du sollst Informationen aus einem deutschen Text auf Englisch wiedergeben.

Worauf muss ich bei Mediation achten?

Übersetze nicht alles wörtlich, sondern gib nur das für die gegebene Situation Wesentliche wieder. Du kannst Unwichtiges weglassen und Sätze umformulieren.

Was kann ich tun, wenn ich ein bestimmtes Wort nicht kenne?

Vielleicht findest du es manchmal schwer, mündliche Aussagen oder schriftliche Textvorlagen in die andere Sprache zu übertragen, z. B. weil

- dein Wortschatz nicht ausreicht
- dir bekannte Wörter „im Stress" nicht einfallen
- spezielle Fachbegriffe auftauchen.

Viele Wörter kannst du umschreiben, z. B. mithilfe von Relativsätzen wie:

It's somebody/a person who …
It's something that you use to …
It's an animal that …
It's a place that/where …

Skills File

SF 17 REVISION Listening

Manchmal kann es schwer sein, einem Hörtext zu folgen, weil du die Sprecher nicht sehen kannst und du dich auch noch auf die Aufgaben zum Hörtext konzentrieren musst. Die folgenden Tipps können dir beim Hörverstehen helfen.

Was kann ich vor dem Hören tun?

- Sieh dir die Aufgabenstellung genau an. Was sollst du heraushören?
- Schau nach Überschriften und Bildern zum Text. Sie können oft schon einige Fragen beantworten helfen: Wer spricht mit wem, wo sind sie, worüber reden sie?
- Überlege, was du selbst zum Thema schon weißt und welche englischen Begriffe daher im Gespräch fallen könnten.

Worauf kann ich während des Hörens achten?

- Lass dich nicht verwirren, wenn es mehrere Sprecher gibt. Versuche, die unterschiedlichen Stimmen Personen zuzuordnen. Das macht es einfacher, dem Gespräch zu folgen.
- Wenn es um generelles Hörverstehen geht, höre gezielt auf die Hintergrundgeräusche. So kannst du herausfinden, ob das Gespräch z.B. am Strand, auf der Straße oder in der Schule stattfindet.
- Sicher wirst du einiges nicht verstehen. Das ist nicht schlimm – versuche aus dem was du alles verstanden hast das Fehlende zu erschließen.

Worauf kann ich beim Hören achten, wenn es um Details geht?

- Gerate nicht in Panik, wenn du denkst, du hättest etwas Wichtiges verpasst. Konzentriere dich auf die nächste wichtige Information.
- Ignoriere Hintergrundgeräusche. Wenn du bestimmte Details heraushören sollst, sind sie unwichtig und lenken nur ab.
- Mach nur kurze Notizen, z.B. Anfangsbuchstaben, Symbole und Stichworte
  (➜ SF 8: Taking notes (Revision), S. 143)
- Je nachdem, welche Details du heraushören sollst, können Signalwörter helfen, dem Hörtext zu folgen und dich auf die Details zu konzentrieren:
  - Aufzählungen: *and, another, too, …*
  - Gegensätze: *although, but, …*
  - Gründe, Folgen: *because, so, so that, …*
  - Vergleiche: *larger/older/… than, as … as, more, most, …*
  - Reihenfolge: *before, after, then, next, later, …*

Was kann ich nach dem Hören tun?

- Vervollständige deine Notizen sofort.
- Wenn möglich, vergleiche mit einem Partner/einer Partnerin, was ihr verstanden habt.
- Wenn dir die Beantwortung einer Frage noch Schwierigkeiten macht, versuche schlau zu kombinieren.

Skills File

SF 18 REVISION Speaking

Lies die beiden Dialoge. Welche Unterschiede erkennst du? Wodurch entstehen sie?

Jen: Hi.
Ben: Hi.
Jen: It's a great parade.
Ben: Yeah.
Jen: Do you like the bands?
Ben: No.
Jen: The food smells good.
Ben: Yeah.
Jen: Do you want some too?
Ben: All right.
Jen: Do you live in Plymouth?
Ben: No.
Jen: …

Ed: Hi there, great parade, isn't it?
Jo: Yeah, I didn't know it was this big.
Ed: Is it your first time here, then?
Jo: That's right, I'm new in Plymouth.
Ed: Okay, so did you come here for the day?
Jo: Yeah, we arrived early this morning … Wow, that food smells good.
Ed: Are you hungry? Look, my friends have this pasties stall over there. Do you want to try one?
Jo: Okay, yes please.
Ed: My name's Ed, by the way.
Jo: Hello Ed, I'm Jo.

Wie kann ich freundlich ein Gespräch führen?

Wenn du dich mit jemandem auf Englisch unterhalten willst, können dir diese Hinweise helfen:

1. Eröffne das Gespräch mit einer freundlichen Anrede oder Frage.
2. Antworte nicht nur mit einem Wort, wenn dich dein Gesprächspartner/deine Gesprächspartnerin etwas fragt.
3. Zeige Interesse an deinem Gesprächspartner/deiner Gesprächspartnerin, indem du auch ein paar Fragen stellst.
4. Erzähle auch etwas von dir, um das Gespräch am Laufen zu halten.
5. Verabschiede dich am Ende freundlich.

1 Hi, can I sit here?
Hello, how are you?
Hi there, are you from Plymouth?

2 Fine, thanks. / Yeah, sure.
Yes, I am. / No, not really.

3 What about you?
I'm Nick and you are …?
Do you like …?
So what do you think …?

4 I'm new here in …
I'm with my friends over there.
I love these …
And I really like …

5 Bye then.
See you.
Have a good time!

Skills File

PROJECT AND PRESENTATION SKILLS

SF 19 Teamwork ➔ p. 69

Bei Projekten arbeitet ihr oft im Team. Dabei solltet ihr eure unterschiedlichen Fähigkeiten und Talente einbringen und bestimmte Regeln beachten.

Was ist wichtig für gutes Teamwork?

Folgende Schritte können helfen, die Arbeit zu organisieren:

1. Legt **Regeln** für die Arbeit in der Gruppe fest, z.B. gegenseitige Unterstützung, pünktliches und zügiges Arbeiten, einander zuhören oder verschiedene Lösungen diskutieren usw.
2. Sammelt Ideen für die Bearbeitung eures Themas (z.B. in einer Mindmap). Wählt gemeinsam Unterthemen aus und legt die **Arbeitsschritte** fest, die für die Bearbeitung nötig sind.
3. **Verteilt Rollen** und Aufgaben nach euren Interessen und Fähigkeiten. Wenn ihr euch nicht einigen könnt, hilft Auslosen oder Würfeln.
   Folgende Rollen solltet ihr auf jeden Fall verteilen:
   – coordinator
   – writer/researcher
   – picture and layout editor
   – language watchdog
4. Macht einen **Zeitplan** für eure Arbeiten, an den sich alle halten sollten.
5. Am Ende der Arbeit sollte ein **Rückblick** stehen: Besprecht, was gelungen war und wo ihr Verbesserungsmöglichkeiten seht.

SF 20 Internet research (Finding information for a presentation) ➔ p. 69

Das Internet ist voller Informationen und es ist nicht einfach, genau die Informationen zu finden, die du benötigst

Wie finde ich die Informationen, die ich brauche?

- Überlege, was die wichtigsten **Stichwörter** für dein Thema sind. Für das Thema "The Beatles in Hamburg" wären *Beatles* und *Hamburg* ein guter Start.
- Gib deine Stichwörter in eine **Suchmaschine** ein. Je mehr gute Stichwörter du eingibst, desto genauer sind die Ergebnisse. In der Infografik rechts kannst du sehen, wie du an ganz spezielle Informationen kommen kannst.
- Sieh dir mehrere **Suchergebnisse** an, um zu sehen, ob sie passen. Wenn du schnell ein bestimmtes Wort wie z.B. *Hamburg* finden willst, dann kannst du mit der Tastenkombination **Strg + F** danach suchen. Das Wort wird dann auf der Seite markiert und du kannst schnell sehen, ob die Information relevant ist.
- Achte darauf, wer die Webseite erstellt hat, um die **Qualität** der Suchergebnisse einzuschätzen. Sind sie eher zuverlässig (Online-Lexikon, bekannte Medien, …) oder eher persönliche Meinungen (Forum, Fan-Seite, …)?

Skills File

- Kopiere nicht einfach ganze Artikel aus dem Internet. Mach dir Notizen und verwende deine eigenen Worte, um die Inhalte wiederzugeben.
- Setz dir ein Zeitlimit für deine Recherche und ordne dann dein Material. Prüfe, ob dir etwas fehlt und suche ggf. gezielt nach nur noch diesen Informationen.
- Leg alle interessanten Materialien zu deinem Thema in einem eigenen Ordner ab. Dann kannst du sie dir später genauer ansehen und auswählen, was du nutzen möchtest.

Was die Suchmaschine auch noch kann:
Definitionen: Wenn du schnell eine Definition für ein Wort suchst, kannst du das mit **define:** tun.
define:prejudice
Konvertieren: Tippe einfach die Einheit, die du schon hast und die, die du wissen möchtest.
50 kilograms in pounds

SF 21 REVISION Describing and presenting pictures

Manchmal sollst du ein Foto vor der Klasse vorstellen. Hier sind ein paar Hilfen.

Wie stelle ich ein Foto vor?

1 Stelle das Foto vor und sage, woher es kommt.

2 Beschreibe das Foto:
   - Sage, was wo zu sehen ist: *at the top/bottom · in the foreground/background · in the middle · on the left/right*
   - Diese Präpositionen sind auch hilfreich: *behind · between · in front of · next to · under · over*
   - Geh bei der Beschreibung in einer bestimmten Reihenfolge vor, z.B. von links nach rechts oder von oben nach unten.

3 Sage, was dir an dem Foto gefällt oder nicht.

4 Wenn du mit der Vorstellung des Fotos fertig bist, bedanke dich fürs Zuhören und frage, ob noch jemand Fragen hat.

1 *I'd like to talk about this photo of … I found it on the internet/in a magazine/…*

2 *In the foreground you can see … I think the people in the photo are talking about …/having fun/ celebrating/…*

3 *I really like/don't like the photo because … It's interesting/boring/exciting/ … because …*

4 *Thank you for listening. Do you have any questions?*

SF 22 REVISION Putting a page together

Wenn du eine Bildseite gestalten sollst, z.B. einen Artikel für eine Schülerzeitung, helfen dir die folgenden Hinweise.

Wie gehe ich am besten vor?

- Sammle und sortiere die Informationen, die auf der Seite stehen sollen.

- Schreibe deinen Text und gib ihm eine klare Struktur.
  (➡ *SF 11: Structuring your text, S. 145*)

- Beginne einen neuen Absatz für jeden neuen Gedanken.
  (➡ *SF 12: Paragraphs and topic sentences, S. 145*)

- Wähle eine passende Überschrift: sie verdeutlicht, worum es in deinem Text geht und macht den Leser neugierig auf deinen Text.

- Wenn es in deinem Text um mehrere Themen geht, dann kannst Du für einzelne Abschnitte auch Zwischenüberschriften verwenden. Das gibt deinem Text eine klare Struktur und hilft dem Leser, sich schnell zu orientieren.

Skills File

SF 23 REVISION Giving a presentation
→ p. 92

Wie bereite ich eine Präsentation vor?

- Trage Informationen zu deinem Thema zusammen.
  (→ SF 20: Internet research (Finding information for your project), S. 151)
- Wähle eine Form der Präsentation aus, die das Thema gut veranschaulicht (Poster, Folie, Tafel, …).
- Schlage Wortschatz nach, den du brauchst.
  (→ SF 6: Using a German-English dictionary, S. 142)
- Mach dir Notizen für deinen Vortrag, z.B. auf nummerierten Karteikarten.
- Bereite deine Medien vor (Poster, Folie, Tafelanschrieb, …). Schreibe groß und für alle gut lesbar.
- Übe deine Präsentation zu Hause vor einem Spiegel oder vor einem kleinen Publikum (Eltern, Großeltern, Freunde). Sprich laut, deutlich und langsam.

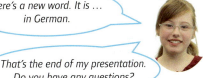

My presentation is about … First I'd like to talk about …

Here's a new word. It is … in German.

That's the end of my presentation. Do you have any questions?

On my poster you can see a photo of … The mind map shows …

Wie halte ich eine gute Präsentation?

- Warte, bis es ruhig ist. Schau die Zuhörer/innen an.
- Erkläre, worüber du sprechen wirst und wie deine Präsentation aufgebaut ist.
- Lies nicht von deinen Karten ab, sondern sprich möglichst frei.
- Bedanke dich fürs Zuhören und frag, ob jemand Fragen hat.

SF 24 REVISION Peer feedback

Gegenseitige Rückmeldungen sind für dich und deine Partner wichtig. Du kannst darin jemanden loben für etwas, das er/sie gut gemacht hat, Hinweise geben, wo deine Partner noch Probleme haben. Du selbst erfährst, was du schon gut kannst und was du anders machen könntest.

Was muss ich beachten?

Bei deiner Rückmeldung solltest du drei Dinge beachten:

- Halte dich an die Punkte, zu denen du Rückmeldung geben sollst, z.B. die Aussprache, Betonung und Verständlichkeit bei einem Dialog, die Rechtschreibfehler in einem Text, das Einhalten eines roten Fadens in einer Geschichte usw. Begründe deine Einschätzungen.
- Gib deine Rückmeldung mit Respekt – niemand soll sich angegriffen fühlen. Nenne zuerst Gelungenes und mache dann Verbesserungsvorschläge zu Punkten, die aus deiner Sicht noch nicht so gelungen sind.
- Wenn du eine Rückmeldung bekommst, überdenke die Vorschläge gut. Korrigiere die Fehler, die andere gefunden haben, und arbeite an den Stellen nach, wo du eventuell Probleme hattest.

What I liked	What you could do better
You chose a great photo. ☺ You spoke clearly and looked at us. …	Next time, say what is happening in the photo. Sometimes you stood in front of the photo. …

Grammar File

Grammar File – Inhalt
Seite

GF 1 **The past** Die Vergangenheit 155
    1.1 REVISION **The simple past** Die einfache Form der Vergangenheit 155
    1.2 REVISION **The present perfect** Das *present perfect* 156
    1.3 REVISION **Present perfect or simple past?** *Present perfect* oder *simple past*? 156
    1.4 **The present perfect progressive** Die Verlaufsform des *present perfect* 157
    1.5 **The past perfect** Das *past perfect* 158

GF 2 **The future** Das Futur 159
    2.1 REVISION **The *will*-future** Das Futur mit *will* 159
    2.2 REVISION **The *going to*-future** Das Futur mit *going to* 160
    2.3 REVISION **The present progressive: future meaning**
               Das *present progressive*: futurische Bedeutung 160
    2.4 **The simple present: future meaning** Das *simple present*: futurische Bedeutung 160

GF 3 **Conditional sentences** Bedingungssätze 161
    3.1 REVISION **Conditional sentences, type 1** Bedingungssätze, Typ 1 161
    3.2 **Conditional sentences, type 2** Bedingungssätze, Typ 2 161

GF 4 **Relative clauses** Relativsätze 162
    4.1 REVISION **Relative pronouns** Relativpronomen 162
    4.2 **Contact clauses** Relativsätze ohne Relativpronomen 163

GF 5 **The passive** Das Passiv 164
    5.1 **Active and passive** Aktiv und Passiv 164
    5.2 **The passive: form** Das Passiv: Form 164
    5.3 **Passive sentences with *by*** Passivsätze mit *by* 164

GF 6 **Modals and their substitutes** Modale Hilfsverben und ihre Ersatzverben 165
    6.1 REVISION **Modal auxiliaries** Modale Hilfsverben 165
    6.2 **(to) be able to – (to) be allowed to – (to) have to** 166

GF 7 **Reflexive pronouns** Reflexivpronomen 167
    7.1 *myself, yourself, himself, herself, itself, ourselves, yourselves, themselves* 167
    7.2 *themselves* or *each other*? 168

GF 8 **Indirect speech** Die indirekte Rede 168
    8.1 **Direct and indirect speech** Direkte und indirekte Rede 168
    8.2 **Indirect speech: tense changes** Indirekte Rede: Veränderungen der Zeitform 169

Grammatical terms (Grammatische Fachbegriffe) 170

Lösungen der Grammar-File-Aufgaben 171

Das **Grammar File** (S. 154–171) fasst die in diesem Englischbuch behandelten grammatischen Themen zusammen. Hier kannst du nachsehen,
– wenn du selbstständig etwas lernen oder etwas wiederholen möchtest,
– wenn du Übungen aus dem *Practice*-Teil deines Englischbuches oder aus dem *Workbook* bearbeitest,
– wenn du dich auf einen Test vorbereiten willst.

Besonders wichtig sind die Stellen mit den **roten Ausrufezeichen** (❗). Sie zeigen, was im Deutschen anders ist, und machen dich auf besondere Fehlerquellen aufmerksam.

Verweise wie ➡ *Unit 1: p. 21, exercises 1–3* zeigen dir, welche **Übungen** zum gerade behandelten grammatischen Thema gehören.

In English: The simple past

In English-Abschnitte enthalten kurze Zusammenfassungen der wichtigsten grammatischen Regeln auf Englisch.

Additional information

Mit **Additional information** sind zusätzliche Informationen gekennzeichnet, die du dir auch gut anschauen solltest.

Die **grammatischen Fachbegriffe** (*grammatical terms*) kannst du auf den Seiten 170–171 nachschlagen.

Am Ende der Abschnitte stehen kleine **Aufgaben** zur **Selbstkontrolle**. Hier kannst du überprüfen, ob du das gerade behandelte Thema verstanden hast. Auf S. 171 kannst du nachsehen, ob deine Lösungen richtig sind.

Grammar File

GF 1 The past — Die Vergangenheit

1.1 REVISION — The simple past — Die einfache Form der Vergangenheit

Last Saturday, Mo and Luke **went** to One New Change. They **didn't want** to go shopping there, they **wanted** to go up on the roof.

On the roof, they **saw** lots of tourists and **heard** lots of different languages. Later, they **talked** to a girl called Emily and her parents. Mo **told** them about the Shard … and about his blog.

| want → want**ed** | arrive → arriv**ed** |
| stop → stopp**ed** | try → tri**ed** |

| go → went | meet → met |
| hear → heard | tell → told |

Mo and Luke **didn't** meet their friends at the shopping centre.
– Who **did** they **meet**? **Did** they **meet** their parents? No, they **didn't**. They met Emily.

➡ Unit 1: p. 12, exercise 2

Wenn du über **Vergangenes** berichtest – z.B., wenn du eine Geschichte erzählst –, benutzt du überwiegend das *simple past*.
Das *simple past* drückt aus, dass etwas **zu einem bestimmten Zeitpunkt** oder **in einem bestimmten Zeitraum** in der Vergangenheit stattfand.

Das *simple past* steht häufig mit Zeitangaben wie **last Saturday, yesterday, two years ago, in 2010**.

◀ Bei **regelmäßigen** Verben hängst du **-ed** an den Infinitiv, um das *simple past* zu bilden.

◀ **Unregelmäßige** Verben haben eine eigene Form für das *simple past*, die du einzeln lernen musst.

➡ Liste der unregelmäßigen Verben, S. 246–247

◀ **Verneinte Aussagesätze** im *simple past* werden mit **didn't** gebildet, **Fragen** mit **did**.

(**Ausnahme**: Verneinungen und Fragen mit dem Verb **be** werden nicht mit **did** gebildet:
Was it expensive? – No, it wasn't.)

Die einfache Form der Vergangenheit

Bejahte Aussagen	Verneinte Aussagen	Fragen
I/You/He/She/It talk**ed** …	I/You/He/She/It **didn't** talk …	**Did** I/you/he/she/it talk …?
We/They talk**ed** …	We/They **didn't** talk …	**Did** we/they talk …?

 In English: The simple past
You use the **simple past**
- when you want to say or ask <u>when</u> something happened
- when you talk about things in the past (e.g. when you tell a story).

I wanted to clean the shelves in the library, but I fell off.

Grammar File

1.2 REVISION The present perfect — Das *present perfect*

Luke **has been** at the shopping centre before.
But he**'s** never **been** up on the roof.
Luke ist schon einmal im Einkaufszentrum gewesen.
Aber er war noch nie auf dem Dach.

Mo **hasn't been** up the Shard yet. It's too expensive.
Have you ever **visited** the Shard?

Emily **has given** Mo her number. Now he can text her.

Auch das **present perfect** wird verwendet, um über etwas zu sprechen, das in der Vergangenheit geschehen ist. Aber es ist nicht wichtig oder gar nicht bekannt, wann das war – ein genauer Zeitpunkt wird nicht genannt.

Das *present perfect* steht oft mit Adverbien der unbestimmten Zeit wie *just, already, often, never, not … yet, before*.

◀ Das *present perfect* wird oft verwendet, wenn man betonen will, dass ein vergangenes Geschehen wichtig für die Gegenwart oder die Zukunft ist: Emily hat Mo ihre Nummer gegeben; jetzt kann Mo ihr Mails schicken.

Das *present perfect* wird mit **have/has + 3. Form des Verbs** (Partizip Perfekt; englisch: *past participle*) gebildet.

visit → visit**ed**	phone → phon**ed**
plan → plann**ed**	copy → copi**ed**
be → **been**	take → **taken**
give → **given**	see → **seen**

◀ Bei **regelmäßigen** Verben hängst du **-ed** an den Infinitiv, um das *past participle* zu bilden (wie bei der Bildung der *simple past*-Form).

◀ **Unregelmäßige** Verben haben eigene *past participle*-Formen, die du einzeln lernen musst.

➡ *Liste der unregelmäßigen Verben, S. 246–247*

➡ Unit 1: p. 12, exercise 3

Das *present perfect*

Bejahte Aussagen	Verneinte Aussagen	Fragen
I've visited …	I haven't visited …	Have I/you/we/they visited …?
You've visited …	You haven't visited …	
He**'s**/She**'s**/It**'s** visited …	He/She/It hasn't visited …	Has he/she/it visited …
(= He/She/It **has** visited …)		
We've/They've visited …	We/They haven't visited …	

🇬🇧 **In English: The present perfect**
You use the **present perfect**
- to say <u>that</u> something has happened (not when it happened).

1.3 REVISION Present perfect or simple past? — *Present perfect* oder *simple past*?

Mo: **Have** you **been** here before?

Luke: Yeah, I **came** with Dad **a few months ago**.
We **bought** mum's birthday present here.

Mo: So, **have** you **been** up on the roof too?

"We only **arrived** *yesterday evening*, so we **haven't seen** much yet."

- *Present perfect:*
  – wenn du sagen willst, **dass** etwas (irgendwann) geschehen ist
  – wenn du fragen willst, **ob** etwas geschehen ist
  Ein Zeitpunkt wird nicht genannt (er ist nicht wichtig oder nicht bekannt).

- *Simple past:*
  – wenn du sagen oder fragen willst, **wann** etwas geschehen ist
  In *simple past*-Sätzen stehen oft genaue Zeitangaben wie *yesterday, last year, an hour ago, in 2012*.

➡ Unit 1: p. 13, exercise 4

Grammar File

Alles verstanden? Dann vervollständige jetzt diese beiden kurzen Dialoge. Wo muss es *simple past* sein, wo *present perfect*? (Auf S. 171 kannst du nachschauen, ob deine Lösungen richtig sind.)

1 Katie: Hannah and I … (decide) to go to that rock concert in Bath. Do you want to come with us?
 Daniel: No, thanks. I … (see) both bands on TV last month, and I … (not like) them.

2 Thomas: Hi Jessica. … (you/just arrive)?
 Jessica: Yes, I'm a bit late. … (the meeting/start yet)?
 Thomas: I think so. Mr Carter … (go in) a few minutes ago.

1.4 The present perfect progressive — Die Verlaufsform des *present perfect*

You've been watching TV for hours.
Du siehst (schon) seit Stunden fern.

Have you been waiting long?
Wartest du schon lange?

How long has she been going to this school?
Wie lange/Seit wann geht sie (schon) auf diese Schule?

Mit dem **present perfect progressive** kannst du ausdrücken, dass etwas in der Vergangenheit begonnen hat und bis jetzt andauert.

❗ Im **Deutschen** benutzen wir meist das Präsens:
 Ich warte hier seit fünf Minuten.
Im **Englischen** steht das *present perfect progressive*:
 I've been waiting here for five minutes.

Das *present perfect progressive*

I've been waiting …
You've been waiting …
He's/She's/It's been waiting …
(= He/She/It **has** been waiting …)
We've/They've been waiting …

Have you been waiting long?
Has he/she/it been waiting long?
How long have they been waiting?
How long has he/she/it been waiting?

Das **present perfect progressive** wird mit **have/has been + ing-Form** gebildet.

❗ Im **Deutschen** verwenden wir „seit", um zu sagen, seit wann oder wie lange etwas schon andauert. Im **Englischen** wird zwischen *since* und *for* unterschieden:

◀ 1 Mit *since* gibt man einen **Zeitpunkt** an:
 since 10 o'clock; since 2012; since Monday morning; since I was born.
 since + Zeitpunkt drückt aus, **seit wann** etwas bereits andauert.

1 *I've been watching* TV *since* 10 o'clock.
Ich sehe seit 10 Uhr fern.

England has been playing better *since* the break.
England spielt besser seit der Halbzeitpause.

◀ 2 Mit *for* gibt man einen **Zeitraum** an:
 for hours; for 14 years; for five minutes; for a long time.
 for + Zeitraum drückt aus, **wie lange** etwas bereits andauert.

2 *I've been waiting* here *for* five minutes, boys.
Ich warte hier (schon) seit fünf Minuten, Jungs.

We've been living here *for* 14 years now.
Wir wohnen jetzt (schon) seit 14 Jahren hier.

since + Zeitpunkt – *for* + Zeitraum

It's **4 o'clock**. Hannah and Declan are in the kitchen.

They've been working in the kitchen …
… **since 3:30**. seit 15 Uhr 30
… **for half an hour**. seit einer halben Stunde

➡ Unit 1: p. 21, exercises 1–3

I've been reading for three hours.

Grammar File

🇬🇧 **In English: The present perfect progressive**
You use the **present perfect progressive**
- to say that something began in the past and is still going on now.

Sieh dir die Bilder an und schreib die dazu passenden Sätze in dein Heft.

1
They – wait – a long time

2
She – read – lunchtime

3
He – play – an hour

Additional information

They**'ve been** in London since last month.
Sie sind seit letztem Monat in London.

We**'ve had** our dog for more than three years now.
Wir haben unseren Hund jetzt seit mehr als drei Jahren.

How long **have** you **known** your boyfriend?
Wie lange kennst du deinen Freund (schon)?

Would you like to visit me in Sydney?
– I'd love to. I**'ve** always **wanted** to go to Australia.
… Ich wollte schon immer nach Australien reisen

❗ Verben, die nicht Tätigkeiten, sondern **Zustände** beschreiben, werden in der Regel **nicht in der Verlaufsform** verwendet (siehe die Beispiele links).

Wichtige Zustandsverben sind

– **be** („sein"), **have** („haben, besitzen"), **own** („besitzen")

– **believe** („glauben"), **know** („wissen, kennen"), **think** („meinen, glauben")

– **like** („mögen"), **love** („lieben"), **want** („wollen, haben wollen")

1.5 The past perfect

Das *past perfect*

Aunt Mary **woke up** when we **arrived**. The owner's daughter **showed** us our cottage.
Tante Mary wachte auf, als wir ankamen. Die Tochter der Besitzerin zeigte uns unser Cottage.

◂ Wie du weißt, gebraucht man überwiegend das *simple past*, wenn man über Vergangenes redet.

When the guests arrived, Mum **had** already **gone** to bed.
Als die Gäste ankamen, war Mutter schon ins Bett gegangen.

I **had planned** to ride down to the beach, so we had a big argument.
Ich hatte geplant, hinunter zum Strand zu reiten, …

◂ Wenn du sagen willst, dass etwas **noch vor etwas anderem in der Vergangenheit** stattgefunden hatte, verwendest du das *past perfect* (deutsch: Vorvergangenheit, Plusquamperfekt).

Handlung 1 *(past perfect)* geschah vor **Handlung 2**:

    1   2
When I **had shown** them their cottage, I **said** good night.

My mother **went** to bed when the guests arrived.
Meine Mutter ging ins Bett, als die Gäste ankamen.
(die Gäste kamen, und sie ging ins Bett)

My mother **had gone** to bed when the guests arrived.
Meine Mutter war ins Bett gegangen, als die Gäste ankamen.
(sie war schon im Bett, als die Gäste ankamen)

❗ Beachte die Bedeutungsunterschiede, je nachdem, ob du das *simple past* oder das *past perfect* verwendest.

Grammar File

Das *past perfect*

Bejahte Aussagen	Verneinte Aussagen	Fragen
I had visited …	I hadn't seen …	Had I closed …?
You had visited …	You hadn't seen …	Had you closed …?
He/She/It had visited …	He/She/It hadn't seen …	Had he/she/it closed …?
We/They had visited …	We/They hadn't seen …	Had we/they closed …?

Das *past perfect* wird mit **had** (Kurzform: **'d**) und der **3. Form des Verbs** (Partizip Perfekt; englisch: *past participle*) gebildet.

*I was sure I **had seen** this before.*
Ich war sicher, dass ich dies schon einmal **gesehen hatte**.

*I was sure I **had been** here before.*
Ich war sicher, dass ich schon einmal hier **gewesen war**.

❗ Das *past perfect* wird immer mit **had** gebildet, egal ob im Deutschen „hatte" oder „war" steht.

➡ Unit 4: p. 76, exercises 5–6

In English: The past perfect
You use the **past perfect**
- for actions that finished before a time in the past.

Sieh dir die Bilder genau an und vervollständige die Sätze.
Wo muss es *simple past* sein, wo *past perfect*?

Holly didn't go to the cinema because …

1. she … (leave) her money at home.
2. the queue … (be) too long.

Matthew bought lots of apples because …

3. they … (be) very cheap.
4. his mother … (ask) him to get some fruit.

GF 2 The future Die Zukunft

2.1 REVISION The *will*-future

Das Futur mit *will*

*When **will** Mum **be** back? – She **won't be** back till tomorrow.*

Mit **will/won't + Infinitiv** sagst du, was in der Zukunft geschehen wird.

*I'm sure you**'ll** soon **speak** Welsh as well as the others.*

◀ Wenn **Vermutungen** geäußert werden, steht häufig *I (don't) think*, *I'm (not) sure*, *maybe* oder *probably*.

*Wales **will get** a lot of rain tomorrow, and it **will be** very windy in Scotland.*

◀ Oft geht es um Dinge, die man nicht beeinflussen kann, z.B. **Vorhersagen** über das Wetter.

*Laugh with the others, then you**'ll feel** better.*
Lach mit den anderen, dann **fühlst** du dich besser.

❗ Im Deutschen benutzen wir oft das Präsens, wenn wir Vermutungen äußern oder Vorhersagen machen. Im Englischen steht das *will-future*.

➡ Unit 2: p. 31, exercise 2

Grammar File

2.2 REVISION The *going to*-future — Das Futur mit *going to*

The Evans family **is going to move** to Wales.
Mrs Evans is happy that they **are going to live** in the country.

Wenn es um **Vorhaben**, **Pläne**, **Absichten** für die Zukunft geht, verwendet man **am/are/is going to** + Infinitiv.

! *going to* hat hier nichts mit „gehen" zu tun. *I'm going to …* bedeutet so viel wie „Ich werde …", „Ich habe vor …".

2.3 REVISION The present progressive: future meaning — Das *present progressive*: futurische Bedeutung

Emily and her new class **are climbing** Mt Snowdon next weekend.

What **are** you **doing** on Sunday? **Are** you **going** skiing again?

Wenn etwas für die Zukunft **fest verabredet** ist, kannst du auch das **present progressive** benutzen. Es muss aber deutlich sein, dass es sich um etwas Zukünftiges handelt, z.B. durch eine Zeitangabe (*next weekend, tomorrow, on Sunday*) oder aus dem Zusammenhang.

(Man nennt diese Verwendung des *present progressive* manchmal *diary future*, weil es dabei oft um Verabredungen geht, die schon im Terminkalender eingetragen sind.)

2.4 The simple present: future meaning — Das *simple present*: futurische Bedeutung

The next train to Cardiff **leaves** at 8:25.
Our French classes **start** on Monday.

Auch das **simple present** kann futurische Bedeutung haben. Es wird verwendet, wenn ein zukünftiges Geschehen durch einen **Fahrplan**, ein **Programm** oder Ähnliches genau festgelegt ist. Verben wie **arrive, leave, go, open, close, start, stop** werden häufig so verwendet.

(Diese Verwendung des *simple present* wird als *timetable future* bezeichnet.)

🇬🇧 **In English: Talking about the future**

You often use the **will-future** to talk about the future.
But …
- you use the **going to-future** for intentions and plans for the future
- you can use the **present progressive** to talk about what you have arranged to do in the future
- you can use the **simple present** for future events that are listed in a timetable or programme.

Schreibe die Sätze mit der passenden Futurform in dein Heft.

1. Do you think it … tomorrow? (will rain / is raining)
2. Have you got any plans for this summer? – Yes, we … to Spain. ('ll fly / 're going to fly)
3. Do you like your new flat? – Well, it's too small, really. We … out again. We've already started looking. ('ll move / 're going to move)
4. Are you free next Friday? – No, I … Julian. ('ll meet / 'm meeting)

I hope it will be warmer tomorrow.

Grammar File

GF 3 Conditional sentences Bedingungssätze

3.1 REVISION Conditional sentences, type 1 — Bedingungssätze, Typ 1

Emily: **If** I **hear** one more word of Welsh, I**'ll scream**!
Wenn ich noch ein walisisches Wort höre, dann schreie ich!

Dad: You**'ll** soon **speak** Welsh as well as the others **if** you **don't give up**.
Du wirst bald genauso gut Walisisch sprechen wie die anderen, wenn du nicht aufgibst.

Dad: **If** you **laugh** with the others, you **won't feel** so bad.
Wenn du mit den anderen lachst, fühlst du dich nicht so schlecht.

Emily: I **can't laugh** at their jokes if I don't understand them, Dad.

Dad: If they speak too fast, **ask** them to slow down.

➡ Unit 2: p. 31, exercise 3

Bedingungssätze vom Typ 1 sind „**Was ist, wenn …**"-Sätze: Sie beschreiben, was unter bestimmten Bedingungen geschieht oder nicht geschieht.

Die Bedingung steht im *if*-Satz. Der Hauptsatz sagt aus, was passiert, wenn die Bedingung erfüllt wird:

Bedingung	Folge für die Zukunft
If it **rains**,	we**'ll stay** at home.
simple present	*will-future*

Im *if*-Satz steht das *simple present*. Im Hauptsatz steht meist das *will-future*.

◀ Im Hauptsatz können auch *can, must, could, should* + Infinitiv oder ein Imperativ stehen.

3.2 Conditional sentences, type 2 — Bedingungssätze, Typ 2

Dylan: **If** you **gave** me a pound for every trip, I **would be** rich.
Wenn du mir für jeden Ausflug ein Pfund geben würdest, dann wäre ich reich.

❗ Kein *would* im *if*-Satz! Nicht: *If you ~~would give~~ me …*

Dylan: **If** I **had** a kayak, I**'d paddle** right down from the top to this pool.
Wenn ich ein Kajak hätte, würde ich geradewegs … hinunterpaddeln.

Emily **wouldn't feel** so bad **if** her Welsh **was** better.
Emily würde sich nicht so schlecht fühlen, wenn ihr Walisisch besser wäre.

If Philip read the message, he **could get** the wrong idea.
… könnte er das missverstehen.

If I were a cat, I'd be nice to Morphs.

➡ Unit 2: pp. 36–37, exercises 1–4

Bedingungssätze vom Typ 2 sind „**Was wäre, wenn …**"-Sätze: Sie drücken aus, dass etwas nicht sehr wahrscheinlich oder sogar unmöglich ist:

1 **If** we **met** Emily in Wales, we **would go** climbing together.

2 "**If** I **were** you, I**'d go** down the waterfall inside a beach ball", said Philip.

Es ist unwahrscheinlich, dass wir Emily in Wales treffen (Satz 1), und Philip ist nun einmal nicht Dylan (Satz 2). Die Sprecher/innen drücken nur aus, was geschehen würde oder der Fall wäre, wenn …

Bedingung	Folge für die Zukunft
If you **did** that,	you **would die**.
simple past	*would + infinitive*

Im *if*-Satz steht das *simple past*. Im Hauptsatz steht meist *would* + Infinitiv (Kurzform: *'d*).

◀ Im Hauptsatz kann auch *could* („könnte") + Infinitiv stehen.

❗ Beachte, dass nach *I* im *if*-Satz oft **were** statt **was** steht:
If I were a cat …
(*If I was* … ist aber ebenfalls möglich.)

Grammar File

🇬🇧 **In English: Conditional sentences**
- **Type 1:**

simple present	will-future or can/must/should + infinitive
If she **wins** the competition,	she **will be** the star of the whole school.

  The speaker thinks there is a good chance that she will win the competition.

- **Type 2:**

simple past	would + infinitive or could + infinitive
If she **won** the competition,	she **would be** the star of the whole school.

  The speaker thinks it is less probable that she will win the competition.

Vervollständige die Sätze in deinem Heft. Achte auf die richtige Form der Verben.
1. *If the weather **is** nice, we … (have) a picnic in the park.*
2. ***Would** you **change** anything if you … (be) the head teacher at your school?*
3. *What **would** you **do** if your classmates … (make) fun of you?*
4. *If we really **go** to Wales this summer, I … (try) to climb Mount Snowdon.*
5. *If I **had** more money, I … (travel) all over Europe in the summer.*
6. *If you … (not hurry up) now, you**'ll be** late for school.*

GF 4 Relative clauses Relativsätze

4.1 REVISION Relative pronouns — Relativpronomen

Mit **Relativsätzen** beschreibt man genauer, über wen oder was man spricht.

*These shops are for **tourists who like the Beatles**.*
Diese Läden sind für Touristen, die die Beatles mögen.

◀ Das Relativpronomen **who** steht in Relativsätzen, die **Personen** beschreiben:
The **girl/boy/student/tourists who** …

*It's a **market which sells food and clothes**.*

◀ Das Relativpronomen **which** steht in Relativsätzen, die **Dinge** (und Tiere) beschreiben:
The **market/bag/dogs/places which** …

*John Lennon is **the Beatle that Gareth likes best**.*
*Mathew Street is the **street that's full of tourist shops**.*

◀ Das Relativpronomen **that** wird für Personen und Dinge verwendet.

❗ **Beachte**

*… for tourists **who like** the Beatles.*
*… für Touristen, **die** die Beatles **mögen**.*

– die unterschiedliche **Wortstellung** in englischen und deutschen Relativsätzen

*What was the name of the market **that we went to**?*
*Wie hieß der Markt, **zu** dem wir gegangen sind?*

– die **Stellung der Präposition** in englischen Relativsätzen.

➡ Unit 3: p. 48, exercises 2–3

🇬🇧 **In English: Relative Pronouns**
You use
- **who** for people
- **which** for things
- **that** for people and things.

Grammar File

4.2 Contact clauses

Relativsätze ohne Relativpronomen

Das Relativpronomen kann **Subjekt** oder **Objekt** sein.

	subject	
Gareth is the boy	who	**likes** the Beatles.
… der Junge,	der	die Beatles mag.
Where are the shops	which	**sell** Beatles souvenirs?
… die Läden,	die	Beatles-Souvenirs verkaufen?

◀ Hier sind die Relativpronomen **Subjekt** des **Relativsatzes**. Sie stehen **direkt vor dem Verb**.

	object	subject	
John is the Beatle	who	Gareth	**likes** best.
… der Beatle,	den	Gareth	am liebsten mag.
Remember the plan	that	we	**made**, Gareth?
… an den Plan,	den	wir	gemacht haben, …?

◀ Hier sind die Relativpronomen **Objekt** des Relativsatzes. Auf das Relativpronomen folgt das Subjekt des Relativsatzes, und dann das Verb.

John is the Beatle		Gareth	**likes** best.
Remember the plan		we	**made**, Gareth?

Wenn das Relativpronomen **Objekt** ist, wird es oft **weggelassen**. (Das ist im Deutschen nicht möglich.) Relativsätze ohne Relativpronomen werden **contact clauses** genannt.

❗ **Vorsicht:**
Wenn das **Relativpronomen direkt vor dem Verb** steht, dann ist es **Subjekt** und **darf nicht weggelassen werden**.

Where's the shop (that **sells**) plantains?

➡ Unit 3: p. 49, exercises 4–5

🇬🇧 **In English: Contact clauses**
- The relative pronoun can be the subject or the object of the relative clause.
- When the relative pronoun is the object of the relative clause, you can leave it out.
- A relative clause without a relative pronoun is called a **contact clause**.

In welchen Sätzen kannst du das **Relativpronomen** weglassen? Schreibe die Sätze als **contact clauses** in dein Heft.

1 It is Gareth **who** thinks that plantains are green bananas.
2 Look, that's the cathedral **that** the choir went to for the concert.
3 Chinatown Arch is the gate **that** Gwen saw in the guidebook.
4 Gwen is the girl **who** wanted to go to Greaty.
5 It was Morgan's plan **that** made everybody happy.
6 Birkenhead is the town **which** you can see across the Mersey.

These are the books I like best.

Grammar File

GF 5 The passive Das Passiv

5.1 Active and passive — Aktiv und Passiv

subject	verb (active)	
Young men	**wear**	masks with animal faces.

Junge Männer tragen Masken mit Tiergesichtern.

subject	verb (passive)	
Animal masks	**are worn**	in Nigeria today.

Tiermasken werden heute in Nigeria getragen.

◀ Mit einem **Aktivsatz** drückst du aus, **wer oder was etwas tut**. Das Subjekt des Aktivsatzes führt die Handlung aus. Der Beispielsatz sagt etwas über junge Männer aus – nämlich, dass sie Masken tragen.

◀ **Passivsätze** drücken aus, **mit wem oder was etwas geschieht**. Der Beispielsatz sagt etwas über Tiermasken aus – nämlich, dass sie in Nigeria getragen werden.

The slavery museum **was founded** to tell the story of slavery.
Das Sklaverei-Museum wurde gegründet, um die Geschichte der Sklaverei zu erzählen.

Two computers **were stolen** from the museum's office last night.

The car crashed into a wall, but the driver **wasn't hurt**.

Were many people **killed** in the plane crash?

Mit einem **Passivsatz** kannst du Handlungen beschreiben, ohne zu sagen, wer die Handlung ausführt. Oft ist gar nicht bekannt oder nicht wichtig, wer die Handlung ausführt.

Daher wird das Passiv oft in Nachrichten und Zeitungsberichten (z.B. über Unfälle oder Verbrechen), in technischen Beschreibungen und auf Schildern verwendet, wenn man den „Täter" oder „Verursacher" nicht nennen kann oder nicht nennen will.

> English is spoken here.
> Hier spricht man Deutsch.
> On parle français.

◀ Im Deutschen verwenden wir oft einen Aktivsatz mit „man" in Situationen, in denen im Englischen ein Passivsatz steht.

5.2 The passive: form — Das Passiv: Form

First, the mud for the houses **is made**.
Then the floors and walls **are built** with the mud.

The goat face mask **was made** in West Africa.
Udus **were used** to carry water.

Das **Passiv** bildest du mit einer **Form von be** und der **3. Form des Verbs** (Partizip Perfekt; past participle).

Simple present: *am/are/is* + **past participle**
The mud **is** made …
The walls **are** built …

Simple past: *was/were* + **past participle**
The mask **was** made …
Udus **were** used …

➡ Unit 3: pp. 54–55, exercises 1–3, 5

➡ Liste der unregelmäßigen Verben, S. 246–247

5.3 Passive sentences with *by* — Passivsätze mit *by*

Udus **are played by** women.
Udus werden von Frauen gespielt.

Over 30 houses **were destroyed by** a storm.
Über 30 Häuser wurden durch ein Unwetter zerstört.

➡ Unit 3: p. 55, exercise 4

Wenn man in einem Passivsatz den „Täter" oder „Verursacher" nennen will, verwendet man die Präposition **by** („von", „durch").

The prize for the best costume was won by …

Grammar File

🇬🇧 In English: The passive

- An **active** sentence describes what somebody (or something) does:
  *The **Hills sell** fruit and vegetables.*
  (You are talking about what the Hills do.)

- A **passive** sentence describes what is done or what happens to people or things; often we do not say who does the action:
  ***Fruit and vegetables are sold** at lots of markets.*
  (You are talking about where people can buy fruit and vegetables.)

- **Passive** sentences are made with a form of **be** + **past participle**.

- You can use **by** in a passive sentence if you want to say who does the action:
  *The song 'Imagine' is sung **by John Lennon**.*

Vervollständige die Passivsätze in deinem Heft mit den Verben aus den Kästchen. Achte auf die richtige Zeitform (*simple present* oder *simple past*).

1 The djembe **is** … with bare hands, not with sticks.
2 The street market in Great Homer Street … 'Greaty'.
3 The new Beatles museum … by the mayor last Saturday.
4 The Beatles Platz in Hamburg … as a monument to the famous band's time in Germany.
5 German … in Germany, Switzerland and Austria.
6 The song 'We will rock you' … by Queen.

build · call · open · play · speak · write

GF 6 Modals and their substitutes — Modale Hilfsverben und ihre Ersatzverben

6.1 REVISION Modal auxiliaries — Modale Hilfsverben

Can, may, must, should usw. sind **modale Hilfsverben** (*modal auxiliaries* oder kurz: *modals*). Sie drücken aus, was jemand tun **kann, darf, muss, soll** usw.

1 *I **can clear** the table.*
  ***Can** you **wash** the dishes?*

1 Modale Hilfsverben werden zusammen mit dem Infinitiv eines Vollverbs verwendet. Frage und Verneinung werden ohne *do/does/did* gebildet.

2 *Yes, I **can**. / No, I **can't**.*

2 Nur in Kurzantworten können modale Hilfsverben allein stehen.

3 *I **must help** Dad in the garden now.*
  *We **should visit** Grandma tomorrow.*

3 Modale Hilfsverben beziehen sich in der Regel auf die Gegenwart oder die Zukunft.

❗ Vorsicht bei **must**, **mustn't** und **needn't**:

*You **must feed** the cats. They're hungry.*

- Mit **must** drückt man aus, dass jemand etwas **tun muss**.

*You **needn't feed** the dogs. Mum has fed them already.*

- Mit **needn't** drückt man aus, dass jemand etwas **nicht tun muss**.

*You **mustn't feed** the birds. Bread is bad for them.*

- Mit **mustn't** drückt man aus, dass jemand etwas **nicht tun darf**.

➡ Unit 4: p. 68, exercise 2

I mustn't make him angry.

165 one hundred and sixty-five

Grammar File

6.2 (to) be able to – (to) be allowed to – (to) have to

I forgot my key, but I **was able to get** in through the window.
Tomorrow is Saturday, so we**'ll be able to sleep** a bit longer.

Were you **allowed to take** photos at the concert?
– Yes, we were.
You**'ll be allowed to go** to discos when you're a bit older.

I felt so ill that I **had to stay** in bed.

If it doesn't work the first time, you**'ll have to try** again.

1 I**'m not allowed to go** to parties.
 Have you got a minute? I **have to talk** to you.

2 I looked everywhere, but I **couldn't find** my key.
 I **could hear** music, but I **couldn't see** anybody.

3 **Did** you **have to wait** long?
 You **don't have to show** your passport when you cross the border.

➡ Unit 4: p. 72, exercises 1–3

(to) be able to – (to) be allowed to – (to) have to

Wenn es um „können", „dürfen", „müssen" in der **Vergangenheit** oder der **Zukunft** geht, werden meist **Ersatzverben** verwendet:

◄ „können": (to) **be able to**
 – jemand konnte etwas tun (Vergangenheit):
  was/were able to …
 – jemand wird etwas tun können (Zukunft):
  will be able to …

◄ „dürfen": (to) **be allowed to**
 – jemand durfte etwas tun (Vergangenheit):
  was/were allowed to …
 – jemand wird etwas tun dürfen (Zukunft):
  will be allowed to …

◄ „müssen": (to) **have to**
 – jemand musste etwas tun (Vergangenheit):
  had to …
 – jemand wird etwas tun müssen (Zukunft):
  will have to …

❗ Beachte die folgenden Hinweise:

1 Alle Ersatzverben können auch im *simple present* verwendet werden.

2 Zu *can* gibt es auch die Vergangenheitsform *could*, die überwiegend in verneinten Sätzen vorkommt. Die bejahte Form *could* wird häufig mit Verben der Wahrnehmung (*see, hear, …*) verwendet.

3 Das Ersatzverb *(to) have to* bildet Fragen und Verneinungen im *simple present* und *simple past* mit *do/does/did*.

🇬🇧 **In English: Modals and their substitutes**

- **Modal auxiliaries** like *can, may, must, should,* etc.
  - are followed by an infinitive (without *to*): You should feed the cats now.
  - never have *do/does/did* in questions and negatives: Sorry, I can't help you.
  - are usually used to talk about the present or the future: Could I have a glass of water, please? (present)
   Can we go to the zoo tomorrow? (future)

- **Substitutes** are used to form other tenses:
  can („können") – (to) be able to: The driver was able to stop the car.
   I'll be able to buy a new car with this money.

  can, may („dürfen") – (to) be allowed to: We weren't allowed to use a dictionary.
   I'll be allowed to drive next year.

  must („müssen") – (to) have to: We didn't have to wait long.
   We'll have to work very hard next month.

Grammar File

Vervollständige das Gespräch mit Formen von *have to* (2x), *be able to, be allowed to* und *not be allowed to*:

1 Katie: *My mother is so strict. Yesterday I wanted to go out, but I … stay in and tidy my room.*
2 Hannah: *My parents are strict too. I'm sure I … go to Jessica's party on Friday.*
3 Daniel: *Well, I think I … go, but I … be home by ten again, as usual.*
4 Holly: *I'm going to a music festival on Friday, so I … go to the party.*

GF 7 Reflexive pronouns Reflexivpronomen

7.1 myself, yourself, himself, herself, itself, ourselves, yourselves, themselves

*You have to **look after yourself** at sea.*
Auf dem Meer muss man auf **sich aufpassen**.

*Dolphins can't **protect themselves** from fishing boats.*
Delfine können **sich** nicht vor Fischerbooten **schützen**.

Reflexive pronouns

Singular		Plural	
myself	(ich) mir/mich	ourselves	(wir) uns
yourself	(du) dir/dich	yourselves	(ihr) euch
himself	(er) sich	themselves	(sie) sich
herself	(sie) sich		
itself	(er/sie/es) sich		

*When I was little, I always **felt** scared in the dark. When my parents were out, I often tried to **hide** in a cupboard. But that all **changed** when I got older, and now I don't **worry** any more.*

➡ Unit 5: p. 85, exercise 2

myself, yourself, himself, herself, itself, ourselves, yourselves, themselves

Reflexivpronomen bezeichnen dieselbe Person oder Sache wie das Subjekt des Satzes:

***John** went home and made **himself** a cup of tea.*
***John** ging heim und machte **sich** eine Tasse Tee.*

Das Reflexivpronomen **himself** bezieht sich zurück auf das Subjekt **John**.

Die Betonung liegt auf der zweiten Silbe:
myself [maɪˈself] usw.
ourselves [aʊəˈselvz] usw.

❗ Es gibt eine Reihe von Verben, die im Deutschen mit „sich" gebraucht werden, im Englischen aber **ohne Reflexivpronomen**. Beispiele:

(to) change	sich ändern
(to) feel	sich fühlen
(to) hide	sich verstecken
(to) imagine	sich (etwas) vorstellen
(to) meet	sich treffen
(to) move	sich bewegen
(to) relax	sich entspannen
(to) remember	sich erinnern
(to) sit down	sich hinsetzen
(to) wonder	sich fragen
(to) worry	sich Sorgen machen

Merke dir auch diese Wendungen:

*Enjoy **yourself**.* Viel Spaß! / Amüsier dich gut!
*Help **yourself**.* Greif zu! / Bedien dich!

Morph is enjoying himself by the sea.

Grammar File

 In English: Reflexive pronouns
A **reflexive pronoun** (e.g. *myself, themselves*) refers back to the subject of the sentence (e.g. *I, my sisters*).
I cut **myself** *with a breadknife.*   *My sisters* *can look after* **themselves**.

7.2 **themselves** or **each other**?   *themselves* oder *each other*?

Das Reflexivpronomen **themselves** steht für „**sich**" im Sinne von „**sich selbst**".

Finn and Asif are taking photos of **themselves**.
Finn und Asif machen Fotos von **sich (selbst)**.

Wenn „**sich gegenseitig**", „**einander**" gemeint ist, verwendest du **each other**.

Now they are taking photos of **each other**.
Jetzt fotografieren sie **sich gegenseitig**.

➡ Unit 5: p.85, exercise 3

Sieh dir die Bilder an und vervollständige die Sätze. Brauchst du *themselves* oder *each other*?

1 They're laughing at …

2 They might hurt …

3 They're teaching … German.

4 They're talking to … on the phone.

GF 8 Indirect speech   Die indirekte Rede

8.1 Direct and indirect speech   Direkte und indirekte Rede

Direct speech	*Skye says, "It's too noisy."* Skye sagt: „**Es ist zu laut**."	◀ In der **direkten Rede** *(direct speech)* gibt man **wörtlich** wieder, was jemand sagt oder schreibt (oder gesagt oder geschrieben hat). Direkte Rede steht gewöhnlich in Anführungszeichen.
Indirect speech	*Skye* **says (that)** *it's too noisy.* Skye **sagt, dass** es zu laut ist.	◀ In der **indirekten Rede** *(indirect speech* oder *reported speech)* **berichtet** man, was jemand sagt oder schreibt (oder gesagt oder geschrieben hat). Die indirekte Rede wird mit Verben wie *say, tell sb., add, answer, explain, write* eingeleitet. ❗ Im Englischen steht vor der indirekten Rede **kein Komma**, und das Wort *that* („dass") wird oft weggelassen.

Grammar File

8.2 Indirect speech: tense changes
Indirekte Rede: Veränderungen der Zeitform

I'm tired of it. I don't want to be in this play any more!

Skye **told** Lewis that she **was** tired of it.
She **said** she **didn't want** to be in the play any more.
Skye erzählte Lewis, dass sie es satt habe.
Sie sagte, dass sie bei dem Stück nicht mehr mitmachen wollte.

Wenn das einleitende Verb im **simple past** steht (*she said, she told me* usw.), werden in der indirekten Rede meist andere Zeitformen verwendet als in der direkten Rede: Die Zeitformen der direkten Rede werden um eine Zeitstufe in die Vergangenheit „zurückverschoben" (auf Englisch nennt man das *backshift of tenses*).

◀ So wird z.B. das *simple present* der direkten Rede in der indirekten Rede „zurückverschoben" zum *simple past*:
"I'm ..." → she **was** ...
"I **don't want** ..." → she **didn't want** ...

Tense changes

	Direct speech	Indirect speech
present → **past**	"We **need** you."	Lewis **told** Skye that they **needed** her.
	"No one **is missing** their cues."	Sandra **said** no one **was missing** their cues.
***will*-future** → **would + infinitive**	"We**'ll** never **get** it right."	Sandra **said** they **would** never **get** it right.
can → **could**	"I **can't** **hear** the cue."	Skye **said** she **couldn't** **hear** the cue.
past → **past perfect** [1]	"Skye **started** to cry."	Lewis **said** that Skye **had started** to cry.

[1] *Past tense*-Formen der direkten Rede werden in der indirekten Rede oft beibehalten, also nicht ins *past perfect* verändert: Lewis **said** that Skye **started** to cry.

Ella (zu Lucy): *"I'll call you when we're back."*

(Lucy berichtet ihrer Schwester:)
Ella told me that **she** would call **me** when **they** were back.

(Ella berichtet ihrem Vater:)
I told Lucy that **I** would call **her** when **we** were back.

◀ Wie im Deutschen werden in der indirekten Rede die Pronomen verändert, je nachdem, wer wem berichtet.

➡ Unit 5: pp. 90–91, exercises 1–3

🇬🇧 In English: Indirect speech
- In **direct speech**, we repeat word for word what someone has said or written.
  We usually use quotation marks: *"I'm tired," she said.*
  In **indirect speech**, we report what someone has said or written: *She said/told me that she was tired.*
- If the **reporting verb** is in the **past** (*said, told*, etc.), there is usually a change of tenses – the verb forms move back a step into the past ("backshift of tenses"):
  present → **past**, *will* → **would**, *can* → **could**.

Berichte, was Iain gesagt hat. Schreib die Sätze in der indirekten Rede in dein Heft. Achte darauf, die richtigen Pronomen zu verwenden.

1 *"I love helping to make dolphin sightings."* — Iain said he …
2 *"Identifying dolphins isn't easy."* — He explained that identifying dolphins …
3 *"We're all looking forward to our next trip."* — He told me they …
4 *"We'll go out in our kayaks tomorrow."* — He said that …
5 *"You have to look after yourself at sea."* — He also said you …
6 *"You can't go out alone."* — He added that …

Grammar File

Grammatical terms (Grammatische Fachbegriffe)

Term	German	Example
active ['æktɪv]	Aktiv	A heavy storm **destroyed** twelve houses.
adjective ['ædʒɪktɪv]	Adjektiv (Eigenschaftswort)	good, new, green, interesting, …
adverb ['ædvɜːb]	Adverb	today, there, outside, very, …
adverb of frequency ['friːkwənsi]	Häufigkeitsadverb	always, usually, often, sometimes, never
adverb of indefinite time [ɪn'defɪnət]	Adverb der unbestimmten Zeit	already, ever, just, never, before, yet, …
adverb of manner ['mænə]	Adverb der Art und Weise	nicely, happily, quietly, slowly, well, fast, …
article ['ɑːtɪkl]	Artikel	the, a, an
backshift of tenses ['bækʃɪft]	Rückverschiebung der Zeitformen	"I'm tired." → She said (that) she **was** tired.
comparative [kəm'pærətɪv]	Komparativ (1. Steigerungsform)	older; more expensive
comparison [kəm'pærɪsn]	Steigerung	old – older – oldest; expensive – more expensive – most expensive
compound ['kɒmpaʊnd]	Zusammensetzung	somebody, anyone, something, …
conditional sentence [kən'dɪʃənl]	Bedingungssatz	If I see Sam, I'll tell him.
conjunction [kən'dʒʌŋkʃn]	Konjunktion	and, but, …; because, when, …
direct speech [ˌdaɪrekt 'spiːtʃ]	direkte Rede	"I'm tired."
contact clause ['kɒntækt klɔːz]	Relativsatz ohne Relativpronomen	Here's the report **I've written**.
going to-future ['fjuːtʃə]	Futur mit *going to*	I**'m going to watch** TV tonight.
imperative [ɪm'perətɪv]	Imperativ (Befehlsform)	Open your books. Don't talk.
indirect speech [ˌɪndərekt 'spiːtʃ]	indirekte Rede	She said (that) **she was tired**.
infinitive [ɪn'fɪnətɪv]	Infinitiv (Grundform des Verbs)	(to) open, (to) go, …
irregular verb [ɪ'regjələ]	unregelmäßiges Verb	(to) go – went – gone, (to) see – saw – seen, …
modal auxiliaries [ˌməʊdl ɔːg'zɪliəri]	modales Hilfsverb, Modalverb	can, may, might, needn't, should, must, …
negative statement ['negətɪv]	verneinter Aussagesatz	I don't like oranges.
noun [naʊn]	Nomen, Substantiv	Justin, girl, man, time, name, …
object ['ɒbdʒɪkt]	Objekt	Justin has **a new camera**.
object question	Objektfrage, Frage nach dem Objekt	**Who did** Mrs Pascoe **invite** to tea?
passive ['pæsɪv]	Passiv	Twelve houses **were destroyed** by a storm.
past participle [ˌpɑːst 'pɑːtɪsɪpl]	Partizip Perfekt	checked, phoned, tried, gone, eaten, …
past perfect [ˌpɑːst 'pɜːfɪkt]	*past perfect* (Vorvergangenheit, Plusquamperfekt)	I **had** already **gone** to bed when they arrived.
past progressive [ˌpɑːst prə'gresɪv]	Verlaufsform der Vergangenheit	Olivia **was playing** cards.
personal pronoun [ˌpɜːsənl 'prəʊnaʊn]	Personalpronomen (persönliches Fürwort)	I, you, he, she, it, we, they; me, you, him, her, it, us, them
plural ['plʊərəl]	Plural, Mehrzahl	
positive statement ['pɒzətɪv]	bejahter Aussagesatz	I like oranges.
possessive determiner [pə'zesɪv dɪ'tɜːmɪnə]	Possessivbegleiter (besitzanzeigender Begleiter)	my, your, his, her, its, our, their
possessive form [pə'zesɪv 'fɔːm]	s-Genitiv	Sam's sister, the Blackwells' house, …
preposition [ˌprepə'zɪʃn]	Präposition	after, at, in, into, near, next to, …
present perfect [ˌpreznt 'pɜːfɪkt]	*present perfect*	We**'ve made** some scones for you.
present perfect progressive [ˌpreznt ˌpɜːfɪkt prə'gresɪv]	Verlaufsform des *present perfect*	He**'s been watching** TV for hours.
present progressive [ˌpreznt prə'gresɪv]	Verlaufsform der Gegenwart	Olivia **is playing** cards.
pronoun ['prəʊnaʊn]	Pronomen (Fürwort)	
question tag ['kwestʃn tæg]	Frageanhängsel	isn't he?, are you?, can't we?, …
question word ['kwestʃn wɜːd]	Fragewort	who?, what?, when?, where?, how?, …
reflexive pronoun [rɪˌfleksɪv 'prəʊnaʊn]	Reflexivpronomen	myself, yourself, themselves, …
regular verb ['regjələ]	regelmäßiges Verb	(to) help – helped, (to) look – looked, …
relative clause [ˌrelətɪv 'klɔːz]	Relativsatz	I like teachers **who laugh a lot**.
relative pronoun [ˌrelətɪv 'prəʊnaʊn]	Relativpronomen	who – which – that
short answer [ˌʃɔːt 'ɑːnsə]	Kurzantwort	Yes, I am. / No, we don't. / …
simple past [ˌsɪmpl 'pɑːst]	einfache Form der Vergangenheit	Olivia **played** cards last Friday.
simple present [ˌsɪmpl 'preznt]	einfache Form der Gegenwart	Olivia **plays** cards every Friday evening.

Grammar File

singular [ˈsɪŋgjələ]	Singular, Einzahl	
statement [ˈsteɪtmənt]	Aussage(satz)	
sub-clause [ˈsʌbklɔːz]	Nebensatz	I like Plymouth **because I like** the sea.
subject [ˈsʌbdʒɪkt]	Subjekt	**Justin/He** has a new camera.
subject question	Subjektfrage, Frage nach dem Subjekt	**Who invited** the Coopers to tea?
substitute [ˈsʌbstɪtjuːt]	Ersatzverb (eines Modalverbs)	be able to, be allowed to, have to
superlative [suˈpɜːlətɪv]	Superlativ (2. Steigerungsform)	(the) oldest; (the) most expensive
verb [vɜːb]	1. Verb; 2. Prädikat	go, help, look, see, … Reading **can be** fun.
will-future [ˈfjuːtʃə]	Futur mit *will*	I'm sure you**'ll like** the new maths teacher.
yes/no question	Entscheidungsfrage	Are you 14? Do you like oranges?

Lösungen der Grammar-File-Aufgaben

p. 157
1 Katie: *Hannah and I* **have decided** *to go to that rock concert in Bath. Do you want to come with us?*
Daniel: *No, thanks. I* **saw** *both bands on TV last month, and I* **didn't like** *them.*
2 Thomas: *Hi Jessica.* **Have** *you* **just arrived**?
Jessica: *Yes, I'm a bit late.* **Has** *the meeting* **started yet**?
Thomas: *I think so. Mr Carter* **went in** *a few minutes ago.*

p. 158
1 *They***'ve been waiting for** *a long time.*
2 *She***'s been reading since** *lunchtime.*
3 *He***'s been playing for** *an hour.*

p. 159
1 *Holly didn't go to the cinema because she* **had left** *her money at home.*
2 *Holly didn't go to the cinema because the queue* **was** *too long.*
3 *Matthew bought lots of apples because they* **were** *very cheap.*
4 *Matthew bought lots of apples because his mother* **had asked** *him to get some fruit.*

p. 160
1 *Do you think it* **will rain** *tomorrow?*
2 *Have you got any plans for this summer? – Yes, we***'re going to fly** *to Spain.*
3 *Do you like your new flat? – Well, it's too small really. We***'re going to move** *out again. We've already started looking.*
4 *Are you free next Friday? – No, I***'m meeting** *Julian.*

p. 162
1 *If the weather* **is** *nice, we***'ll have** *a picnic in the park.*
2 **Would** *you* **change** *anything if you* **were** *the headteacher at your school?*
3 *What* **would** *you* **do** *if your classmates* **made** *fun of you?*
4 *If we really* **go** *to Wales this summer, I***'ll try** *to climb Mount Snowdon.*
5 *If I* **had** *more money, I* **would travel** *(I***'d travel***) all over Europe in the summer.*
6 *If you* **don't hurry** *up now, you***'ll be** *late for school.*

p. 163 **Sätze 2, 3, 6:**
2 *Look, that's the cathedral the choir went to for the concert.*
3 *Chinatown Arch is the gate Gwen saw in the guidebook.*
6 *Birkenhead is the town you can see across the Mersey.*

p. 165
1 *The djembe* **is played** *with bare hands, not with sticks.*
2 *The street market in Great Homer Street* **is called** *'Greaty'.*
3 *The new Beatles museum* **was opened** *by the mayor last Saturday.*
4 *The Beatles Platz in Hamburg* **was built** *as a monument to the famous band's time in Germany.*
5 *German* **is spoken** *in Germany, Switzerland and Austria.*
6 *The song 'We will rock you'* **was written** *by Queen.*

p. 167
1 Katie: *My mother is so strict. Yesterday I wanted to go out, but I* **had to** *stay in and tidy my room.*
2 Hannah: *My parents are strict too. I'm sure I* **won't be allowed to** *go to Jessica's party on Friday.*
3 Daniel: *Well, I think I***'ll be allowed to** *go, but I***'ll have to** *be home by ten again, as usual.*
4 Holly: *I'm going to a music festival on Friday, so I* **won't be able to** *go to the party.*

p. 168
1 *They're laughing at each other.*
2 *They might hurt themselves.*
3 *They're teaching themselves German.*
4 *They're talking to each other on the phone.*

p. 169
1 *Iain said he loved helping to make dolphin sightings.*
2 *He explained that identifying dolphins wasn't easy.*
3 *He told me they were all looking forward to their next trip.*
4 *He said that they would go out in their kayaks tomorrow.*
5 *He said you had to look after yourself at sea.*
6 *He added that you couldn't go out alone.*

Vocabulary

Das **Vocabulary** (S. 172 – 197) enthält alle Wörter und Wendungen deines Englischbuches, die du lernen musst. Sie stehen in der Reihenfolge, in der sie im Buch zum ersten Mal vorkommen.

Hier siehst du, wie das **Vocabulary** aufgebaut ist:

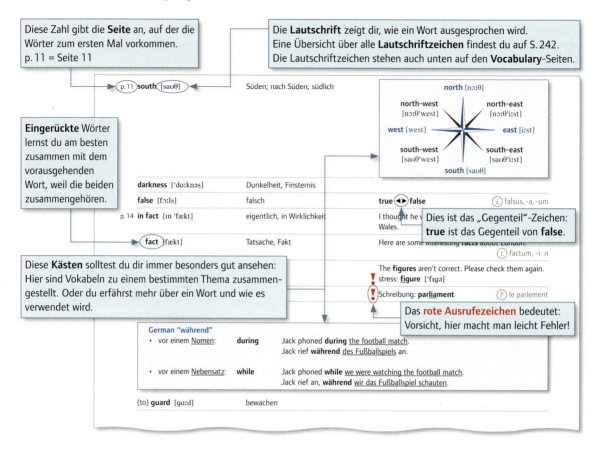

Im **Vocabulary** werden folgende **Abkürzungen** verwendet:

p. = page (Seite)   pp. = pages (Seiten)

sth. = something (etwas)   sb. = somebody (jemand)

jn. = jemanden   jm. = jemandem

pl = plural (Mehrzahl)

infml = informal (umgangssprachlich)

(F) = verwandtes Wort im Französischen

(L) = verwandtes Wort im Lateinischen

Wenn du **nachschlagen** möchtest, was ein englisches Wort bedeutet oder wie man es ausspricht, dann verwende das **English – German Dictionary** auf den Seiten 198 – 220. Und wenn du vergessen hast, wie etwas auf Englisch heißt, dann kann dir das **German – English Dictionary** auf den Seiten 221 – 242 eine erste Hilfe sein.

[iː] green · [i] happy · [ɪ] big · [e] red · [æ] cat · [ɑː] class · [ɒ] song · [ɔː] door · [uː] blue · [ʊ] book · [ʌ] mum · [ɜː] girl · [ə] a partner

Unit 1 Vocabulary

Unit 1 This is London

pp. 8/9 | **the best thing about …** | das Beste an … | **The best thing about** the film was the music.

Part A

p. 10	**huge** [hjuːdʒ]	riesig, sehr groß	Little Andrew got a **huge** teddy bear for his birthday.
	as soon as [əz ˈsuːn‿əz]	sobald, sowie	I'll call you **as soon as** I'm home.
	cathedral [kəˈθiːdrəl]	Kathedrale, Dom	❗ Betonung: ca**th**edral [kəˈθiːdrəl] (F) la cathédrale
	palace [ˈpæləs]	Palast, Schloss	❗ Betonung: **pa**lace [ˈpæləs] (F) le palais
	Welsh [welʃ]	Walisisch; walisisch	Some people in Wales speak English and **Welsh**.
	(to) reply (to) [rɪˈplaɪ]	antworten (auf); erwidern, entgegnen	Why didn't you **reply to** my email? "That isn't London Bridge," he **replied**. "It's Tower Bridge."
	Europe [ˈjʊərəp]	Europa	
	western [ˈwestən]	westlich, West-	Spain is one of the biggest countries in **western** Europe.
	I see.	Aha! / Verstehe.	
	lift [lɪft]	Fahrstuhl, Aufzug	
	amazing [əˈmeɪzɪŋ]	erstaunlich, unglaublich	
	How do you know …?	Woher weißt/kennst du …?	**How do you know** so much about cows? – My grandparents have a farm.
	post [pəʊst]	Posting *(auf Blog)*, Blog-Eintrag	
	carnival [ˈkɑːnɪvl]	Karneval, Fasching	**Carnival** is a big event in German cities like Cologne and Mainz, but people in Britain don't celebrate it. ❗ In Großbritannien wird mit **carnival** jegliche Art von Straßenumzügen mit Musik- und Tanzgruppen, Festwagen u.Ä. bezeichnet.
	test [test]	Test	
	(to) be into sth. *(infml)*	etwas mögen, auf etwas stehen	My sister **is into** reggae at the moment.
	(to) enjoy [ɪnˈdʒɔɪ]	genießen	The film was fantastic. I really **enjoyed** it.
	by the way [ˌbaɪ ðə ˈweɪ]	übrigens	Oh, **by the way,** Grandma called this morning.
p. 11	**south** [saʊθ]	Süden; nach Süden; südlich	**north** [nɔːθ] **north-west** [ˌnɔːθˈwest] **north-east** [ˌnɔːθˈiːst] **west** [west] **east** [iːst] **south-west** [ˌsaʊθˈwest] **south-east** [ˌsaʊθˈiːst] **south** [saʊθ]
	darkness [ˈdɑːknəs]	Dunkelheit, Finsternis	
	clue [kluː]	(Lösungs-)Hinweis; Anhaltspunkt	Nobody knows who killed the man. The police are still looking for **clues** in his house.
	skyline [ˈskaɪlaɪn]	Skyline; Horizont	
	false [fɔːls]	falsch	true ◄► false (L) falsus, -a, -um

[eɪ] n**a**me · [aɪ] t**i**me · [ɔɪ] b**oy** · [əʊ] **o**ld ·
[aʊ] t**ow**n · [ɪə] h**ere** · [eə] wh**ere** · [ʊə] t**our**

Vocabulary Unit 1

p. 12	(to) **go together**	zusammenpassen, zueinander passen	I don't think pink and orange **go together**.
	the Tube [tjuːb] *(no pl)*	die U-Bahn *(in London)*	English: **on** the Tube German: **in** der U-Bahn
	the underground [ˈʌndəgraʊnd] *(no pl)*	die U-Bahn	In London, **the underground** is called "the Tube".
	(to) **stay (at/with)** [steɪ]	(vorübergehend) wohnen, übernachten (in/bei)	Did you **stay at** a hotel? – No, we didn't. We **stayed with** my grandma.
	timetable [ˈtaɪmteɪbl]	Fahrplan	❗ **timetable** = 1. Stundenplan; 2. Fahrplan
	gallery [ˈgæləri]	Galerie	❗ Betonung: **gallery** [ˈgæləri] (F) la galerie
	restaurant [ˈrestrɒnt]	Restaurant	(F) le restaurant
p. 13	**stress** [stres]	Betonung	Where's the **stress** in "gallery"? – On the first syllable.
	stress mark [ˈstres mɑːk]	Betonungszeichen	
	small talk	Smalltalk *(spontan geführtes Gespräch in umgangssprachlichem Ton)*	
	culture [ˈkʌltʃə]	Kultur	❗ stress: **culture** [ˈkʌltʃə] (F) la culture (L) cultura, -ae f
	(to) **expect** sth. [ɪkˈspekt]	etwas erwarten	(L) exspectare

Part B

p. 14	**attraction** [əˈtrækʃn]	Attraktion; Anziehungspunkt	The British Museum is one of London's biggest tourist **attractions**. (F) l'attraction (f) (L) trahere *(ziehen)*
	natural history [ˌnætʃrəl ˈhɪstri]	Naturkunde	
	entry [ˈentri]	Eintritt, Zutritt	**Entry** into museums is usually free in Britain. (F) l'entrée (f)
	in fact [ɪn ˈfækt]	eigentlich, in Wirklichkeit	I thought he was English, but **in fact** he was from Wales.
	fact [fækt]	Tatsache, Fakt	Here are some interesting **facts** about London. (L) factum, -i n
	the UK (the United Kingdom) [ˌjuː ˈkeɪ], [juːˌnaɪtɪd ˈkɪŋdəm]	das Vereinigte Königreich	**the UK** = Great Britain (England, Scotland, Wales) and Northern Ireland
	(to) **reserve** [rɪˈzɜːv]	reservieren, buchen	We'll have to **reserve** a table if we want to eat there. (F) réserver
	step [step]	Stufe	❗ **step** = 1. Stufe; 2. Schritt **steps**
	chance [tʃɑːns]	Gelegenheit, Möglichkeit, Chance	If you have the **chance**, you should go to the British Museum. (F) la chance
p. 15	**figure** [ˈfɪgə]	Zahl, Ziffer	The **figures** aren't correct. Please check them again. ❗ stress: **figure** [ˈfɪgə]
	less (than) [les]	weniger (als)	I have **less** money than you. = You have more money than me.
	tortoise [ˈtɔːtəs]	(Land-)Schildkröte	a **tortoise**

[b] **b**oat · [p] **p**ool · [d] **d**ad · [t] **t**en · [g] **g**ood · [k] **c**at
[m] **m**um · [n] **n**o · [ŋ] so**ng** · [l] **h**ello · [r] **r**ed · [w] **w**e · [j] **y**ou

Unit 1 Vocabulary

on top of each other	übereinander, aufeinander	Can you put all those plates **on top of each other**, please?
parliament ['pɑːləmənt]	Parlament	❗ Schreibung: **parli̲ament** (F) le parlement
at one time	zur selben Zeit, gleichzeitig	It's hard to understand if everyone talks **at one time**.
Christmas ['krɪsməs]	Weihnachten	❗ Der 1. Weihnachtsfeiertag heißt **Christmas Day**.
ticket office ['tɪkɪt ˌɒfɪs]	Fahrkartenschalter; Kasse *(für den Verkauf von Eintrittskarten)*	
detail ['diːteɪl]	Detail, Einzelheit	❗ stress: **de̲tail** ['diːteɪl] (F) le détail
adult ['ædʌlt]	Erwachsene(r)	Free entry for children. **Adults** pay £ 1.50. (F) l'adulte *(m/f)*
a family of four	eine vierköpfige Familie	
during ['djʊərɪŋ]	während	

> **German "während"**
> - vor einem <u>Nomen</u>:   **during**   Jack phoned **during** <u>the football match</u>.
>   Jack rief **während** <u>des Fußballspiels</u> an.
>
> - vor einem <u>Nebensatz</u>:   **while**   Jack phoned **while** <u>we were watching the football match</u>.
>   Jack rief an, **während** <u>wir das Fußballspiel schauten</u>.

(to) guard [gɑːd]	bewachen	
raven ['reɪvn]	Rabe	a **raven**
blood [blʌd]	Blut	
(to) be home to sth.	Heimat sein für etwas; etwas beheimaten	The Amazon area **is home to** the world's largest rainforest.
jewels *(pl)* ['dʒuːəlz]	Juwelen	❗ stress: **je̲wels** ['dʒuːəlz]
education [ˌedʒuˈkeɪʃn]	(Schul-, Aus-)Bildung; Erziehung	You need a good **education** if you want to get a good job. (F) l'éducation *(f)* (L) educere *(großziehen)*
p. 16 **instead of** [ɪnˈsted əv]	anstelle von, statt	❗ • **instead of** = <u>anstelle von</u> – I'd like chips **instead of** rice, please. • **instead** = <u>stattdessen</u> – I don't like rice. Can I have chips **instead**?
exact [ɪgˈzækt]	genau	What's the **exact** size of London? Do you know?
linking word [ˈlɪŋkɪŋ wɜːd]	Bindewort	
(to) link [lɪŋk]	verbinden, verknüpfen	You can **link** two sentences with "and", for example.
queue [kjuː]	Schlange, Reihe *(wartender Menschen)*	a **queue** They're queuing in front of the cinema.
worth [wɜːθ]	wert	The correct answer is **worth** five points.
(to) roar [rɔː]	brüllen	
crowded ['kraʊdɪd]	voller Menschen; überfüllt	The old city centre is often **crowded** with tourists.

[f] **f**ather · [v] ri**v**er · [s] **s**ister · [z] plea**s**e · [ʃ] **sh**op · [ʒ] televi**s**ion ·
[tʃ] **t**eacher · [dʒ] **G**ermany · [θ] **th**anks · [ð] **th**is · [h] **h**ere

Vocabulary   Unit 1

p. 17	**feedback** [ˈfiːdbæk]	Rückmeldung, Feedback	The hotel wants to get some **feedback** from the people who have stayed there.
	(to) improve [ɪmˈpruːv]	verbessern; sich verbessern	This book helps you to **improve** your English. Your English will **improve** if you watch English films.
	(to) react (to) [riˈækt]	reagieren (auf)	I called him but he didn't **react**. (F) réagir
	content [ˈkɒntent]	Inhalt	(F) le contenu
	(to) connect [kəˈnekt]	verbinden, verknüpfen	= (to) link
	(to) point sth. **out (to** sb.**)** [ˌpɔɪnt ˈaʊt]	(jn.) auf etwas hinweisen	"Be careful!" he said, and **pointed out** a snake in the grass.
	spelling [ˈspelɪŋ]	Rechtschreibung; Schreibweise	
p. 18	**line** [laɪn]	(U-Bahn-)Linie	(F) la ligne (L) linea, -ae f
	northbound [ˈnɔːθbaʊnd]	Richtung Norden	northbound ↑ westbound ←→ eastbound ↓ southbound
	(to) change [tʃeɪndʒ]	umsteigen	Take the Bakerloo Line southbound and **change** to the Central Line westbound at Oxford Circus. (F) changer
p. 19	**(to) be slow**	nachgehen *(Uhr)*	It's twenty past eight. – No, it isn't. It's half past eight. Your watch **is slow**. (to) **be slow** ◄► (to) **be fast**
	(to) work	funktionieren	I need your help. My computer doesn't **work**.
	(to) head for sth. [hed]	auf etwas zusteuern/zugehen/zufahren	As soon as we arrived at the coast, we **headed for** the beach.
	announcement [əˈnaʊnsmənt]	Durchsage, Ansage	We'll have to wait for the **announcement** to find out where our train leaves. (F) l'annonce (f)
	message [ˈmesɪdʒ]	Botschaft, Aussage	❗ **message** = (F) le message 1. Nachricht – John left a **message** for you. 2. Botschaft – I think the poem has an interesting **message**.
	platform [ˈplætfɔːm]	Bahnsteig, Gleis	

Part C

p. 20	**(to) be on**	eingeschaltet sein, an sein *(Radio, Licht usw.)*; laufen, übertragen werden *(Programm, Sendung)*	The lights **are on**, so they must be at home. (to) **be on** ◄► (to) **be off** Can we watch TV, Mum? The football **is on**.
	No way! [ˌnəʊ ˈweɪ]	Auf keinen Fall! / Kommt nicht in Frage!	Dad, can you give me £120 for a new pair of jeans? – £120? **No way!** You can have £70.
	for hours/weeks/…	seit Stunden/Wochen/…	"You've been watching TV **for hours**." –
	since 10 o'clock/last week/… [sɪns]	seit 10 Uhr/letzter Woche/…	"No, I haven't. I've been watching TV **since 10**."
	And anyway, … [ˈeniweɪ]	Und überhaupt, …	I don't have time to go. **And anyway**, it's too expensive.
	try [traɪ]	Versuch	verb: (to) **try** – noun: **try**

[iː] green · [i] happy · [ɪ] big · [e] red · [æ] cat · [ɑː] class · [ɒ] song
[ɔː] door · [uː] blue · [ʊ] book · [ʌ] mum · [ɜː] girl · [ə] a partner

Unit 1 Vocabulary

remote control [rɪˌməʊt kənˈtrəʊl] (*kurz auch:* **remote**)	Fernbedienung		**remote controls**
(to) **turn** sth. **up/down** [tɜːn]	etwas lauter/leiser stellen		Can you **turn up** the radio? I want to hear the news.

> **(to) turn**
> 1. The London Eye **turns** very slowly. — sich drehen
> 2. The woman **turned** (*auch:* **turned round / turned around**) and looked at me. — sich umdrehen
> 3. The boy **turned to** his father and smiled. — sich jm. zuwenden
> 4. Please **turn on** the TV. And **turn up** the sound. — einschalten ... lauter stellen
> 5. First you **turn left**. Then you **turn right**. — (nach) links/rechts abbiegen

each other [iːtʃ_ˈʌðə]	sich (gegenseitig), einander	Luke looked at Mo and Mo looked at Luke. = Luke and Mo looked at **each other**.
pub [pʌb]	Kneipe, Lokal	
a while [waɪl]	eine Weile, einige Zeit	First we watched the monkeys **for a while**. (… eine Weile, eine Zeit lang)
tap [tæp]	(*leichtes*) Klopfen	In the middle of night, we heard a **tap** on the door.
Off you go now. [ɒf]	Ab mit euch jetzt! / Los mit euch jetzt!	

> **off**
> 1. **weg, los** — The thieves took our bag and ran **off**. She turned around and walked **off**.
> 2. **von … herunter** — He fell **off** his bike and broke his leg. She jumped **off** the wall and ran away.
>
> • (to) **get off** the bus/boat/plane — aus dem Bus/Boot/Flugzeug aussteigen
> • (to) **take** sth. **off** — etwas ausziehen (*Kleidung*); etwas absetzen (*Hut, Helm*)
> • (to) **turn** sth. **off** — etwas ausschalten (*Radio, Fernsehen, Licht*)

	towards the station/Mr Bell [təˈwɔːdz]	auf den Bahnhof/Mr Bell zu, in Richtung Bahnhof/Mr Bell	When the fire started, everyone ran **towards** the door.
p. 21	**tense** [tens]	(grammatische) Zeit, Tempus	the **past tense**, the **present tense**, the **future tense** ⓛ tempus, -oris *n*
	(to) **go on**	im Gang sein; andauern	The film was so boring, and it **went on** for hours.
	situation [ˌsɪtʃuˈeɪʃn]	Situation	❗ stress: **situ**a**tion** [ˌsɪtʃuˈeɪʃn] Ⓕ la situation
p. 22	**route** [ruːt]	Strecke, Route	Ⓕ la route
	speed [spiːd]	Geschwindigkeit	
	It was a pity that … [ˈpɪti]	Es war schade, dass …	**It's a pity that** Jake can't come to our party.

The Notting Hill Carnival Parade

p. 24	(to) **hold onto** sth. [həʊld], **held, held** [held]	sich an etwas festhalten	She **held onto** the table and tried to stand up.
	(to) **scan** sth. **(for** sth.**)** [skæn]	etwas (nach etwas) absuchen	I **scanned** the crowd/the garden for my sister but couldn't see her.
	(to) **fill** [fɪl]	füllen	
	pavement [ˈpeɪvmənt]	Gehweg, Bürgersteig	

Vocabulary Unit 2

available [əˈveɪləbl]	erhältlich, verfügbar; erreichbar *(am Telefon)*	Tickets for the concert will be **available** soon.
all around her	überall um sie herum	Suddenly there was darkness **all around** her.
whistle [ˈwɪsl]	(Triller-)Pfeife	a **whistle**
(to) **blow the whistle** [bləʊ], **blew** [bluː], **blown** [bləʊn]	pfeifen *(auf der Trillerpfeife)*	
(to) **panic** [ˈpænɪk]	in Panik geraten	❗ spelling: -ing form: **panicking**; simple past: **panicked** (F) paniquer
exactly [ɪgˈzæktli]	genau	❗ • adjective: **exact** – What's the **exact** size of Spain? • adverb: **exactly** – Sue and Jack are **exactly** the same size. (F) exactement
(to) **bend down** [bend], **bent**, **bent** [bent]	sich hinunterbeugen, sich bücken	She saw a coin on the ground and **bent down** to pick it up.
rope [rəʊp]	Seil	
wing [wɪŋ]	Flügel	**wing**
rainbow [ˈreɪnbəʊ]	Regenbogen	
dizzy [ˈdɪzi]	schwindlig	All the noise and the lights made her feel **dizzy**.
hip [hɪp]	Hüfte	
you	man	How do **you** say that in English? (Wie sagt man …?) That's not how **you** do it! (So macht man das nicht!)
rhythm [ˈrɪðəm]	Rhythmus	(F) le rythme
p.25 (to) **scare** sb. [skeə]	jn. erschrecken; jm. Angst machen	verb: (to) **scare** – adjectives: **scared** (verängstigt) **scary** (unheimlich)
loudspeaker [ˌlaʊdˈspiːkə]	Lautsprecher; Megaphon	
(to) **mind** [maɪnd]	etwas dagegen haben	

(to) **mind**	
He **won't mind** if we sit down here for a while. I'd like to ask you a question, **if you don't mind**. **Do you mind** if I open the window?	Es wird ihm nichts ausmachen. … / Er wird nichts dagegen haben, … …, wenn Sie nichts dagegen haben. Stört es Sie, …? / Haben Sie etwas dagegen, …?

(to) **rest** [rest]	ruhen, sich ausruhen	They sat down in the park to **rest** for a moment.
no sign of … [saɪn]	keine Spur von …	We scanned the crowd, but there was **no sign of** my sister.
…, he said **under his breath**. [breθ]	…, sagte er flüsternd / murmelte er.	

Unit 2 Welcome to Snowdonia
Part A

p.30 **empty** [ˈempti]	leer	**full** ◄► **empty**
scientist [ˈsaɪəntɪst]	Naturwissenschaftler/in	someone who has studied science (L) scientia, -ae f *(Wissen)*
(to) **study** [ˈstʌdi]	studieren; untersuchen, beobachten; lernen	She **studied** English in Dublin in the 1980s. His dream was to **study** seals on the Welsh coast. There's a test on Monday so I have to **study** at the weekend. (L) studere

Unit 2 Vocabulary

workshop [ˈwɜːkʃɒp]	Werkstatt	❗ **workshop** = 1. Werkstatt; 2. Lehrgang, Workshop	
carpenter [ˈkɑːpəntə]	Tischler/in, Zimmerer/Zimmerin	someone who works with wood to make things like tables, chairs, etc.	
furniture [ˈfɜːnɪtʃə] *(no pl)*	Möbel	❗ **furniture** hat keinen Plural: The **furniture is** new. Die **Möbel sind** neu. **ein** Möbel(stück) = **a piece of** furniture	
oil [ɔɪl]	Öl		
a piece of … [piːs]	ein Stück …	a piece of wood a piece of paper	
hammer [ˈhæmə]	Hammer		
(to) come over (to)	herüberkommen (zu/nach), vorbeikommen (bei)	Why don't you **come over to** our place on Friday evening?	
probably [ˈprɒbəbli]	wahrscheinlich	❗ • adverb: **probably** („wahrscheinlich") – Jake is late. He's **probably** missed the bus again. • adjective: **probable** („wahrscheinlich") – How **probable** is a white Christmas this year?	
(to) make fun of sb./sth.	sich über jn./etwas lustig machen	Don't **make fun of** me or I'll tell Mum!	
(to) give up	aufgeben		
tonight [təˈnaɪt]	heute Nacht, heute Abend		
p. 31 architect [ˈɑːkɪtekt]	Architekt/in	❗ stress: **ar**chitect [ˈɑːkɪtekt] *(F)* l'architecte *(m/f)* *(L)* architectus, -i m	
astronaut [ˈæstrənɔːt]	Astronaut/in	❗ stress: **as**tronaut [ˈæstrənɔːt] *(F)* l'astronaute *(m/f)* *(L)* nauta, -ae m *(Seemann)*	
hairdresser [ˈheədresə]	Friseur/in		
musician [mjuˈzɪʃn]	Musiker/in	someone who plays an instrument *(F)* le musicien, la musicienne	
painter [ˈpeɪntə]	Maler/in	*(F)* le/la peintre	
natural [ˈnætʃrəl]	natürlich	the **natural** world = die Welt der Natur, die Natur *(L)* natura, ae f *(Geburt; Wesen)*	
p. 32 headword [ˈhedwɜːd]	Stichwort *(im Wörterbuch)*		
part of speech [ˌpɑːt əv ˈspiːtʃ]	Wortart	Nouns, verbs, adjectives, etc. are all **parts of speech**.	
translation [trænsˈleɪʃn]	Übersetzung	verb: (to) **translate** – noun: **translation** *(L)* transferre *(hinübertragen)*	
coal [kəʊl]	Kohle		
underground [ˌʌndəˈɡraʊnd]	unterirdisch, unter der Erde	Some animals – like rabbits – live **underground**.	
(to) ground sb. [ɡraʊnd]	jm. Hausarrest/Ausgehverbot erteilen	If you come home so late again, I'll **ground** you for two weeks.	
official [əˈfɪʃl] *(adj)*	amtlich, Amts-	❗ stress: of**fic**ial [əˈfɪʃl] *(F)* officiel, le	
official [əˈfɪʃl] *(n)*	Beamte(r), Beamtin	*(L)* officium, -i n *(Dienst)*	
police *(pl)* [pəˈliːs]	Polizei	❗ **police** ist ein Pluralwort! *English:* The **police are** on **their** way. *German:* Die **Polizei ist** auf dem Weg.	

[f] father • [v] river • [s] sister • [z] please • [ʃ] shop • [ʒ] television •
[tʃ] teacher • [dʒ] Germany • [θ] thanks • [ð] this • [h] here

Vocabulary   Unit 2

(to) look after/around/for/…

• (to) **look after** sb.	I often have to **look after** my little brother.	aufpassen auf; sich kümmern um
• (to) **look around**	I like your new flat. Can I **look around**?	sich umsehen
• (to) **look for** sb./sth.	I'm **looking for** my keys. Have you seen them?	suchen
• (to) **look forward to** sth.	We're all **looking forward to** the summer holidays.	sich freuen auf
• (to) **look into** sth.	The officials are going to **look into** the problem.	untersuchen, prüfen
• (to) **look up**	She heard a noise and **looked up** from her book.	hochsehen, aufschauen
• (to) **look** sth. **up**	I don't understand this word. I'll have to **look** it **up**.	nachschlagen (Wörter, Informationen)

(to) come across/down/over/…

• (to) **come across** sb./sth.	Later we **came across** a beautiful village.	stoßen auf, (zufällig) treffen
• (to) **come down with** sth.	Jack can't take part. He's **come down with** a cold.	bekommen (Krankheit), erkranken an
• (to) **come over**	John **came over** to watch the football with us.	herüberkommen, vorbeikommen
• (to) **come up with** sth.	Then my sister **came up with** a brilliant idea.	haben, kommen auf (Idee, Vorschlag)

Part B

p. 34	**national** [ˈnæʃnəl]	national, National-	❗ stress: **national** [ˈnæʃnəl] (F) national, e (L) natio, -onis f
	altogether [ˌɔːltəˈgeðə]	insgesamt, alles in allem	We've raised a lot of money for charity – £ 400 **altogether**.
	hostel [ˈhɒstl]	Herberge, Wohnheim	
	(to) **wonder** [ˈwʌndə]	sich fragen, gern wissen wollen	Have you ever **wondered** why we have Christmas trees?
	(to) **pretend** [prɪˈtend]	so tun, als ob	He **pretended** to be ill so that he could miss school. The boys shouted after her, but she **pretended** not to hear them.
	Me neither. [ˈnaɪðə], [ˈniːðə]	Ich auch nicht.	"I don't know the answer." – "**Me neither.**" Me too. ◀▶ Me neither.
	(to) **go by**	vergehen, vorübergehen (Zeit)	Time always **goes by** too quickly in the holidays.
	stupid [ˈstjuːpɪd]	dumm, blöd	stupid ◀▶ clever (F) stupide
	downstream [ˌdaʊnˈstriːm]	flussabwärts	
	edge [edʒ]	Rand, Kante	The ball rolled down the hill and dropped off the **edge** of the cliff.
	(to) **reach** [riːtʃ]	erreichen	If we leave now, we'll **reach** Wales before dinner.
	stick [stɪk]	Stock	
	(to) **grab** [græb]	schnappen, packen	I was late, so I **grabbed** my school bag and ran to the bus stop.
p. 35	**steep** [stiːp]	steil	You can't ride your bike up that hill. It's too **steep**.
	(to) **sing along (with** sb.**)**	(mit jm.) mitsingen	
	(to) **join in (**sth.**)**	(bei etwas) mitmachen	

[iː] green • [i] happy • [ɪ] big • [e] red • [æ] cat • [ɑː] class • [ɒ] song
[ɔː] door • [uː] blue • [ʊ] book • [ʌ] mum • [ɜː] girl • [ə] a partner

180   one hundred and eighty

Unit 2 Vocabulary

before long	schon bald	The afternoon passed quickly and **before long** it was time to say goodbye.
(to) **tell** sb. **(not) to do** sth.	jn. auffordern, etwas (nicht) zu tun; jm. sagen, dass er/sie etwas (nicht) tun soll	The teacher **told** the students **to** be quiet. How often do I have to **tell** you **not to** hit your brother?
p. 36 **warning** [ˈwɔːnɪŋ]	Warnung	
movie [ˈmuːvi]	Film	
p. 37 **head teacher** [ˌhed ˈtiːtʃə]	Schulleiter/in	
(to) **allow** [əˈlaʊ]	erlauben, zulassen	❗ • (to) **allow** = <u>erlauben, zulassen</u> – **Does** your school **allow** you to use mobiles? • (to) **be allowed to do** sth. = <u>etwas tun dürfen</u> – **Are** you **allowed to use** mobiles at school?
p. 38 **topic sentence** [ˌtɒpɪk ˈsentəns]	*Satz, der in das Thema eines Absatzes einführt*	
(to) **be connected** [kəˈnektɪd]	verbunden sein	

> **Numbers**
> • *English:* **3.5** = three **point** five
>   *German:* **3,5** = drei **Komma** fünf
>   Im Englischen steht ein **Punkt**, im Deutschen ein **Komma**.
> • *English:* **1,500** = one thousand five hundred
>   *German:* **1.500** = eintausendfünfhundert
>   Im Englischen steht oft ein **Komma** in Zahlen, die größer als 1 000 sind. Im Deutschen steht dort manchmal ein **Punkt**.

climb [klaɪm]	Aufstieg, Anstieg	verb: (to) **climb** – noun: **climb**
summit [ˈsʌmɪt]	Gipfel	summit Ⓕ le sommet Ⓛ summus, -a, -um (höchster)
(to) **manage** sth. [ˈmænɪdʒ]	etwas schaffen; etwas zustande bringen	We wanted to be back home at 6, but we didn't **manage** it. I didn't **manage** to visit the Tower while I was in London.
(to) **continue** sth. [kənˈtɪnjuː]	etwas fortsetzen	We went inside and **continued** our conversation.
downhill [ˌdaʊnˈhɪl]	bergab	**downhill** ◄► **uphill** (bergauf) **downstream** ◄► **upstream** (flussaufwärts)
energy [ˈenədʒi]	Energie, Kraft	❗ stress: **energy** [ˈenədʒi] Ⓕ l'énergie (f)
a total of … [ˈtəʊtl]	eine Gesamtsumme von …; insgesamt	We raised **a total of** £400 for charity.
bar [bɑː]	Riegel *(Schokolade, Müsli)*, Tafel *(Schokolade)*	
hero [ˈhɪərəʊ], *pl* **heroes**	Held/in	Ⓕ le héros, la héroïne
(to) **revise** [rɪˈvaɪz]	überarbeiten; *(Lernstoff)* wiederholen	He had to **revise** his work because there were too many mistakes. I have a test tomorrow, so I must **revise** tonight. Ⓕ réviser
(to) **organize** [ˈɔːɡənaɪz]	organisieren; ordnen	❗ stress: **organize** [ˈɔːɡənaɪz] Ⓕ organiser
(to) **add (to)** [æd]	hinzufügen, addieren (zu)	Ⓛ addere
p. 39 **difficult** [ˈdɪfɪkəlt]	schwierig, schwer	**easy** ◄► **difficult**
carrot [ˈkærət]	Möhre, Karotte	❗ stress: **carrot** [ˈkærət]

[eɪ] name • [aɪ] time • [ɔɪ] boy • [əʊ] old •
[aʊ] town • [ɪə] here • [eə] where • [ʊə] tour

Vocabulary   Unit 2

Snowdonia at night

p. 40	(to) **press** [pres]	drücken	
	finally [ˈfaɪnəli]	endlich, schließlich	He tried again and again to open the door, and **finally** he managed it. (F) finalement (L) finis, -is m (Ende, Ziel)
	(to) **be able to do** sth. [ˈeɪbl]	etwas tun können; fähig sein / in der Lage sein, etwas zu tun	Finally the rain stopped and we **were able to** go home.
	meal [miːl]	Mahlzeit, Essen	Me and my sister always prepare the evening **meal** on Fridays.
	(to) **keep doing** sth. [kiːp], **kept, kept** [kept]	etwas immer wieder / immer weiter tun; etwas ständig tun	I tried to speak, but he **kept interrupting** me. **Keep smiling** – and never give up.
	silently [ˈsaɪləntli]	lautlos; schweigend	adverb: **silently** – adjective: **silent** (still, leise) (L) silentium, -i n (Schweigen)
	corridor [ˈkɒrɪdɔː]	Gang, Korridor	a **corridor**
	star [stɑː]	Stern	
	magical [ˈmædʒɪkl]	zauberhaft, wundervoll; magisch	The first time I was on stage with my band was one of the most **magical** moments in my life.
	(to) **lie down** [ˌlaɪ ˈdaʊn], **lay** [leɪ], **lain** [leɪn]	sich hinlegen	I'm so tired. I think I'll **lie down** for half an hour. (to) **lie down** ◄► (to) **get up**
	busy [ˈbɪzi]	belebt, geschäftig, hektisch	It was too **busy** in the dining room, so we went upstairs. (*etwa*: Im Esszimmer war zu viel los, …) The week before Christmas is a **busy** time for most shops.
	(to) **clear** [klɪə]	räumen; abräumen	(to) **clear** the table / the dishes / your desk / the road
	breeze [briːz]	Brise	
	(to) **have a look (at** sth.**)**	nachschauen; einen Blick auf etwas werfen	What was that noise in the garden? – I don't know. Let's go and **have a look**.
	(to) **sit up**	sich aufsetzen	The sound of a bell woke her. She **sat up** and opened her eyes.
	wooden [ˈwʊdn]	hölzern; Holz-	a **wooden** puppet
	wide [waɪd]	weit; breit	"Open your mouth **wide**, please," said the dentist. I don't think the Elbe is as **wide** as the Mississippi.
	figure [ˈfɪɡə]	Figur, Gestalt	❗ **figure** = 1. Figur, Gestalt; 2. Zahl, Ziffer stress: **figure** [ˈfɪɡə] (L) figura, -ae f
p. 41	**note** [nəʊt]	Note *(Musik)*	❗ **note** = 1. Notiz, Mitteilung; 2. Note
	such a … [sʌtʃ]	so ein/e …; solch ein/e …	**such a** thing/person = a thing/person like that

such a + noun	so + adjective
Olivia is **such a** nice **person**. … so ein netter Mensch It was **such a** good **film** that I watched it twice. … so ein guter Film	Olivia is **so nice**. … so nett The film was **so good** that I watched it twice. … so gut

Unit 3   Vocabulary

(to) **make** sth. **up**	sich etwas ausdenken	Today we had to **make up** a story and tell it to our classmates.
(to) **argue** [ˈɑːgjuː]	streiten; sich streiten	My brother and sister **argue** from morning till night. "But, Mum …," he said. "**Don't argue**," she replied. („Widersprich mir nicht" …)
bite [baɪt]	Biss, Bissen	
director [dəˈrektə]	Leiter/in	⒡ le directeur, la directrice
office [ˈɒfɪs]	Büro	ⓛ officium, -i n (Dienst)
p. 42 **how to do** sth.	wie man etwas macht / machen kann / machen soll	I don't know **how to do** this exercise. Can you help me?

> **Question word + to-infinitive: how to … / what to … / who to … / where to …**
> Can you tell me **how to get** to the station?   Können Sie mir sagen, wie ich zum Bahnhof komme/kommen kann?
> I don't know **what to do**.   Ich weiß nicht, was ich tun soll.
> I need help, but I don't know **who to ask**.   Ich brauche Hilfe, aber ich weiß nicht, wen ich fragen kann/soll.
> We had no idea **where to go**.   Wir hatten keine Ahnung, wohin wir gehen sollten.

(to) **behave** [bɪˈheɪv]	sich verhalten, sich benehmen	If you **behave** like that again, I'll ground you for a month.
mop [mɒp]	Wischmopp	noun: **mop** – verb: (to) **mop** (wischen (Fußboden))

He's **mopping** the floor.

(to) **splash** sb. [splæʃ]	jn. nass spritzen	
punishment [ˈpʌnɪʃmənt]	Bestrafung, Strafe	
point of view [ˌpɔɪnt_əv ˈvjuː]	Standpunkt	*English:* from my **point of view** *German:* von meinem **Standpunkt** aus gesehen; aus meiner **Sicht** ⒡ le point de vue

Unit 3   A weekend in Liverpool

p. 45 (to) **explore** [ɪkˈsplɔː]	erkunden, erforschen	It's exciting to **explore** new places. ⒡ explorer ⓛ explorare
cruise [kruːz]	Kreuzfahrt, Schiffsreise, Bootsfahrt	

They're going on a **cruise**.

international [ˌɪntəˈnæʃnəl]	international	national ◄► **international** ⒡ international, e ⓛ inter nationes (zwischen den Völkern)
slavery [ˈsleɪvəri]	Sklaverei	
slave [sleɪv]	Sklave, Sklavin	⒡ l'esclave (m/f)

[f] **f**ather • [v] ri**v**er • [s] **s**ister • [z] plea**s**e • [ʃ] **sh**op • [ʒ] televi**s**ion •
[tʃ] **t**ea**ch**er • [dʒ] **G**ermany • [θ] **th**anks • [ð] **th**is • [h] **h**ere

Vocabulary Unit 3

Part A

p. 46	**stuff** [stʌf] *(infml)*	Zeug, Kram	What's the red **stuff** on your shirt? Ketchup?
	after that	danach	First I feed my cats. **After that** I have breakfast. **after that** ◀▶ **before that** (davor)
	normal [ˈnɔːməl]	normal	❗ stress: **normal** [ˈnɔːməl] (F) normal, e
	(to) protest [prəˈtest]	protestieren	(F) protester
	protest [ˈprəʊtest]	Protest	❗ verb: (to) **protest** [prəˈtest] – noun: **protest** [ˈprəʊtest]
p. 47	**guidebook** [ˈɡaɪdbʊk]	Reiseführer	
	quite [kwaɪt]	ziemlich; völlig, ganz	It's **quite** cold. You should take a coat. You're **quite** right. It was my mistake.
	banana [bəˈnɑːnə]	Banane	(F) la banane
	actually [ˈæktʃuəli]	eigentlich; übrigens; tatsächlich	

> **actually**
> Das Wort **actually** kann im Deutschen – je nach Situation – mit **eigentlich, übrigens, tatsächlich** wiedergegeben werden. Manchmal hat es auch überhaupt keine Entsprechung.
>
> Man verwendet **actually**,
> - wenn man jemanden höflich darauf hinweisen möchte, dass er/sie etwas Falsches gesagt hat
>
>   I'm not English, **actually**: I'm Welsh.
>   **Actually**, London is bigger than Paris.
>
> - wenn man ausdrücken möchte, dass etwas in Wirklichkeit anders ist oder war, als man erwartet hat
>
>   I didn't think I would enjoy the party, but it was **actually** fun.
>
> - als entschuldigende Einleitung, wenn man etwas Unangenehmes mitzuteilen hat.
>
>   When are you going to give me my MP3 player back?
>   – **Actually**, I can't. I've lost it.

	(to) cook [kʊk]	kochen; zubereiten	
p. 48	**well-known** [ˌwelˈnəʊn], [ˈwelˌnəʊn]	bekannt, wohlbekannt	❗ spelling: Lady Gaga is **well known** all over the world. She's a **well-known** singer.
	engineer [ˌendʒɪˈnɪə]	Ingenieur/in	(F) l'ingénieur (L) ingenium, -i n (Begabung)
	sportsperson [ˈspɔːtspɜːsn]	Sportler/in	
	soldier [ˈsəʊldʒə]	Soldat/in	(F) le soldat, la soldate
	(to) design [dɪˈzaɪn]	entwerfen, konstruieren, entwickeln	What's your uncle's job? – He **designs** cars. (L) signum, -i n (Zeichen, Bild)
	design [dɪˈzaɪn]	Design; Gestaltung; Konstruktion	
	(to) found [faʊnd]	gründen	❗ (to) **found** – **founded** – **founded** (gründen) (to) **find** – **found** – **found** (finden)
	(to) invent [ɪnˈvent]	erfinden	(F) inventer (L) invenire
	crossword [ˈkrɒswɜːd]	Kreuzworträtsel	
p. 49	**member** [ˈmembə]	Mitglied	(F) le membre (L) membrum, -i n
p. 51	**introduction** [ˌɪntrəˈdʌkʃn]	Einleitung, Einführung	(F) l'introduction (f)
	body [ˈbɒdi]	Hauptteil *(eines Textes)*	
	conclusion [kənˈkluːʒn]	Schluss(folgerung)	(F) la conclusion
	several [ˈsevrəl]	mehrere, verschiedene	**Several** shops here sell John Lennon sunglasses.

Unit 3   Vocabulary

opinion [əˈpɪnjən]	Meinung	*English:* **In my opinion** … *German:* **Meiner Meinung nach** … (F) l'opinion (f) (L) opinio, -onis f
(to) end [end]	enden; beenden	(to) start ◄► (to) end
schedule [ˈʃedjuːl]	(Zeit-)Plan, Programm	The starting time could change, so check the **schedule** before you come.
(to) get/have a day off [ɒf]	einen Tag frei bekommen/haben	When Mum and Dad **have a day off**, we often go surfing or sailing.
(to) earn [ɜːn]	verdienen *(Geld)*	
experience [ɪkˈspɪəriəns] *(no pl)*	Erfahrung(en)	We'd love to hear about your **experience** during your trip to Liverpool. (F) l'expérience (f) (L) peritus, -a, -um *(erfahren)*
As John Lennon said …	Wie John Lennon (einmal) sagte …	**As** you know, Liverpool is the home of the Beatles.
(to) be born [bɔːn]	geboren sein/werden	*English:* I **was born** in 1998. (*not:* I am born in …) *German:* Ich **bin** 1998 **geboren**.
(to) grow up [ˌgrəʊˈʌp], **grew up** [ˌgruːˈʌp], **grown up** [ˌgrəʊnˈʌp]	erwachsen werden; aufwachsen	When I **grow up**, I want to be an artist. When my grandparents were **growing up**, there was no internet.
modern [ˈmɒdən]	modern	❗ stress: m**o**dern [ˈmɒdən] (F) moderne
success [səkˈses]	Erfolg	(F) le succès
(to) perform [pəˈfɔːm]	auftreten *(Künstler/in)*	The Beatles first **performed** in the USA in 1964.
popular (with) [ˈpɒpjələ]	populär, beliebt (bei)	*English:* Beatles songs are very **popular with** people who were born in the 1950s and 1960s. *German:* … beliebt **bei** … (F) populaire (L) populus, -i m *(Volk)*
monument (to) [ˈmɒnjumənt]	Denkmal, Monument (für/zum Gedenken an)	(F) le monument (L) monumentum, -i n
a **one-hour** concert	ein einstündiges Konzert	*English:* a **one-hour** concert • a **three-week** holiday • a **30-minute** ride *German:* ein **einstündiges** Konzert • ein **dreiwöchiger** Urlaub • eine **30-minütige** Fahrt
(to) remember sth.	an etwas denken; sich etwas merken	**Remember**: The simple past of *do* is *did*. I can never **remember** your phone number. ❗ (to) **remember** sth. = **1.** sich an etwas erinnern; **2.** an etwas denken *(etwas nicht vergessen)*; **3.** sich etwas merken
if	ob	❗ **if** = **1.** ob – I don't know **if** I can come to your party. **2.** wenn, falls – I'll come to your party **if** I can.
way [weɪ]	Art und Weise	

way ("Art und Weise")	
Try to introduce your topic **in an interesting way**.	auf eine interessante Art und Weise
In this way, you will make sure that everyone enjoys your talk.	auf diese Weise
I like **the way** Oliver ended his talk.	die Art und Weise, wie …
John is like his father **in some/many ways**.	in mancher/vielerlei Hinsicht

Vocabulary   Unit 3

Part B

p.52	(to) **lead** [liːd], **led, led** [led]	führen, leiten	This road **leads** to the next village.
	leader ['liːdə]	Leiter/in	Our Maths teacher is also **leader** of our school choir.
	trade [treɪd]	Handel	the activity of buying and selling
	mask [mɑːsk]	Maske	
	horn [hɔːn]	Horn	
	people ['piːpl]	Volk	(L) populus, -i m
	clay [kleɪ]	Ton, Lehm	
	shape [ʃeɪp]	Form, Gestalt	*English:* Those glasses **are** an interesting **shape**. *German:* Die Brille **hat** eine interessante **Form**.
	pot [pɒt]	Gefäß; Topf	**several pots**
	(to) **carry** ['kæri]	tragen; befördern	❗ He's **carrying** a heavy box. (Er trägt eine schwere Kiste.) He's **wearing** jeans and a red T-shirt. (Er trägt Jeans und ein rotes T-Shirt.) This ferry doesn't **carry** more than two cars.
	bare [beə]	nackt, bloß (*Hände, Arme, Füße*)	
	respect [rɪ'spekt]	Respekt, Achtung	
	ancestor ['ænsestə]	Vorfahr/in	Our **ancestors** lived shorter lives than we do. (F) l'ancêtre (m)
p.53	**captive** ['kæptɪv]	Gefangene(r)	(L) captivus, -i m
	plantation [plɑːn'teɪʃn]	Plantage	
	cruel ['kruːl]	grausam	I don't like zoos. I think it's **cruel** to put animals in cages. (F) cruel, le (L) crudelis, -e
	(to) **survive** [sə'vaɪv]	überleben	(F) survivre (L) vivere (leben)
	conditions (*pl*) [kən'dɪʃnz]	Verhältnisse, Bedingungen	It's too cold and too noisy in this office. I can't work in these **conditions**. (F) les conditions (f) (L) condicio, -onis f
	triangle ['traɪæŋgl]	Dreieck	(F) le triangle
p.54	**room** [ruːm]	Platz	There's not enough **room** for all of us in the car.
	material [mə'tɪəriəl]	Material, Stoff	(F) le matériel
	(to) **cover** ['kʌvə]	bedecken, zudecken	It was cold so she **covered** her baby with her jacket. His desk is always **covered** with books and articles.
p.55	**contest** ['kɒntest]	Wettbewerb	
	goal net ['gəʊl net]	Tornetz	goal net — goal
	airport ['eəpɔːt]	Flughafen	(F) l'aéroport (m) (L) portus, -us m (Hafen)

[b] **b**oat · [p] **p**ool · [d] **d**ad · [t] **t**en · [g] **g**ood · [k] **k**at
[m] **m**um · [n] **n**o · [ŋ] so**ng** · [l] **h**ello · [r] **r**ed · [w] **w**e · [j] **y**ou

Unit 3 Vocabulary

	community [kə'mju:nəti]	Gemeinde; Gemeinschaft	Bayern Munich has a big **community** of fans all over Germany. ⓛ communis, -e *(gemeinsam)*
	mosque [mɒsk]	Moschee	

Part C

p. 56	**score** [skɔ:]	Spielstand; Punktestand	*English:* What's the **score**? *German:* Wie steht es?
	final ['faɪnl]	letzte(r, s), End-	The **final** score was 2 : 0. *(you say: two nil)*
p. 57	**sunshine** ['sʌnʃaɪn]	Sonnenschein	
p. 58	**referee** [ˌrefə'ri:]	Schiedsrichter/in	
	goalkeeper ['gəʊlki:pə]	Torwart, Torfrau	
	(to) **order** ['ɔ:də]	ordnen	❗ (to) **order** = **1.** ordnen; **2.** bestellen the right **order** = die richtige Reihenfolge
	(to) **structure** ['strʌktʃə]	strukturieren, gliedern	Ⓕ structurer
	equipment [ɪ'kwɪpmənt] *(no pl)*	Ausrüstung	Ⓕ l'équipment *(m)*
	stadium ['steɪdiəm]	Stadion	Ⓕ le stade
	pitch [pɪtʃ]	(Sport-)Platz, Spielfeld	
	manager ['mænɪdʒə]	Trainer/in *(von Sportmannschaften)*	
	scarf [skɑ:f], *pl* **scarves** [skɑ:vz]	Schal	
	free kick [ˌfri: 'kɪk]	Freistoß	
p. 59	**bully** ['bʊli]	(Schul-)Tyrann	
	(to) **solve** [sɒlv]	lösen	We had a lot of problems at first, but in the end we **solved** them all. ⓛ solvere
	slow motion [ˌsləʊ 'məʊʃn]	Zeitlupe	

A Liverpool hero

p. 60	it was **no** different	es war nicht anders	The weather in June was **no** better than in May.
	canal [kə'næl]	Kanal	Ⓕ le canal
	(to) **shine** [ʃaɪn], **shone, shone** [ʃɒn]	scheinen *(Sonne)*	
	laughter ['lɑ:ftə]	Gelächter	verb: (to) **laugh** – noun: **laughter**
	surface ['sɜ:fɪs]	Oberfläche	Ⓕ la surface
	(to) **seem (to be/do)** [si:m]	(zu sein/zu tun) scheinen	He **seems (to be)** very sad. What's wrong?
	(to) **burn** [bɜ:n]	brennen; verbrennen	The lights in the flat are **burning**. They must be in. Don't **burn** the magazines. I haven't read them yet.
	(to) **drown** [draʊn]	ertrinken	She jumped into the river to save the boy from **drowning**.

[f] father · [v] river · [s] sister · [z] please · [ʃ] shop · [ʒ] television ·
[tʃ] teacher · [dʒ] Germany · [θ] thanks · [ð] this · [h] here

Vocabulary   Unit 4

	nowhere [ˈnəʊweə]	nirgendwo; nirgendwohin	*English:* **out of nowhere** *German:* (wie) aus dem Nichts
	(to) **dive in** [daɪv ˈɪn]	hineinspringen	
p. 61	(to) **marry** sb. [ˈmæri]	jn. heiraten	verb: (to) **marry** – adjective: **married**
	career [kəˈrɪə]	Karriere	Choosing a **career** as a police officer is one way to help your community. (F) la carrière
	sailor [ˈseɪlə]	Seemann, Matrose, Matrosin	
	body [ˈbɒdi]	Leiche	
	local [ˈləʊkl]	örtlich, Lokal-; am/vom Ort	We like to buy food from **local** farmers. (F) local, e (L) locus, -i m (Ort)
	(to) **spread, spread, spread** [spred]	(sich) ausbreiten, verbreiten	The fire quickly **spread** to other parts of the building.
	funeral [ˈfjuːnərəl]	Trauerfeier	
	(to) **take place** [teɪk ˈpleɪs]	stattfinden	Our next school trip will **take place** in October.
	(to) **name** [neɪm]	(be)nennen	**Name** three pop bands that you like.

Unit 4   My trip to Ireland

p. 64	**impression** [ɪmˈpreʃn]	Eindruck	(F) l'impression (f)
p. 65	**brochure** [ˈbrəʊʃə]	Broschüre, Prospekt	❗ stress: **brochure** [ˈbrəʊʃə] (F) la brochure
	practical [ˈpræktɪkl]	praktisch	Your ideas are good, but can you give me some **practical** help, too? (F) pratique

Part A

p. 66 **northern** [ˈnɔːðən]	nördlich, Nord-	

northern [ˈnɔːðən]
western [ˈwestən]   eastern [ˈiːstən]
southern [ˈsʌðən]

❗ Aussprache: **south** [saʊθ] – **southern** [ˈsʌðən]

coffee [ˈkɒfi]	Kaffee		(F) le café
giant [ˈdʒaɪənt]	Riese		(F) le géant
it **might** be the other side [maɪt]	es könnte die andere Seite sein		You **might** see the Queen if you wait outside Buckingham Palace. (= Maybe you'll see the Queen if you wait …)

möglich – wahrscheinlich – sicherlich

	may			sind jetzt **vielleicht** zu Hause.
	might			**könnten** jetzt (**vielleicht**) zu Hause sein.
My parents	could	be at home now.	Meine Eltern	**könnten** jetzt zu Hause sein.
	should			**sollten/müssten eigentlich** jetzt zu Hause sein.
	must			**müssen** jetzt zu Hause sein.

as well [əz ˈwel]	auch, ebenso	We don't only sell books, we sell magazines **as well**. You might **as well** stay here tonight. (Du könntest heute Nacht ebenso gut hier bleiben.)

Unit 4 Vocabulary

column ['kɒləm]	Säule		(F) la colonne
(to) rise up [ˌraɪz_'ʌp], rose [rəʊz], risen ['rɪzn]	aufragen, emporragen (Berge, Säulen, Türme, …)		
nearly ['nɪəli]	fast, beinahe	= almost	
(to) form [fɔːm]	bilden, formen		(L) forma, -ae f (Form, Gestalt)
proud (of) [praʊd]	stolz (auf)	She's a very good student. We're **proud of** her.	
challenge ['tʃælɪndʒ]	Herausforderung	My first day at *Gymnasium* was a **challenge** for me.	
(to) challenge sb. (to sth.) ['tʃælɪndʒ]	jn. herausfordern (zu etwas)	We **challenged** them **to** a game of basketball. Maths doesn't really **challenge** me at the moment.	
(to) be left [left]	übrig sein	There **aren't** any biscuits **left**. I've eaten them all.	
Shall I …? [ʃæl]	Soll ich …?	It's hot in here. **Shall I** open the window?	
advert ['ædvɜːt]	Werbespot, Werbung; Anzeige, Inserat	We bought our dog after we saw an **advert** in the local paper.	
curious ['kjʊəriəs]	wissbegierig, neugierig	My brother is very **curious** and always wants to learn everything about everything. (F) curieux, se (L) cura, -ae f (Sorge, Neugier)	
polite [pə'laɪt]	höflich		(F) poli, e
impolite [ˌɪmpə'laɪt]	unhöflich	**polite** ◄► **impolite**	(F) impoli, e
p. 68 border ['bɔːdə]	Grenze	Spain only has a **border** with Portugal and France.	
(to) change [tʃeɪndʒ]	wechseln, umtauschen (Geld)	Don't forget to **change** money if you want to travel to Britain.	(F) changer
currency ['kʌrənsi]	Währung	Until 2001, Germany's **currency** was the *Deutsche Mark*.	
the EU [ˌiː 'juː] (the European Union [ˌjʊərəpiːən 'juːniən])	die Europäische Union		
euro (€) ['jʊərəʊ]	Euro		

Pounds and euros

In **Britain**, you pay with **pounds** and **pence**.

You say:	You write:
fifty p [piː] / fifty pence [pens]	50 p
one pound / a pound	£ 1
two pounds fifty	£ 2.50

In **Germany**, you pay with **euros** and **cents**.

You say:	You write:
fifty cents [sents]	€ 0.50
one euro / a euro	€ 1
two euros fifty	€ 2.50

ID card [ˌaɪ 'diː kɑːd]	Personalausweis		
nation ['neɪʃn]	Nation, Volk		(F) la nation (L) natio, -onis f
passport ['pɑːspɔːt]	(Reise-)Pass		(F) le passeport
peace [piːs]	Friede, Frieden	**peace** ◄► **war**	(F) la paix (L) pax, pacis f
police station [pə'liːs steɪʃn]	Polizeiwache, -revier		
population [ˌpɒpjʊ'leɪʃn]	Bevölkerung, Einwohner(zahl)		(F) la population (L) populus, -i m
president ['prezɪdənt]	Präsident/in	❗ stress: **pre**sident ['prezɪdənt]	(F) le président, la présidente
republic [rɪ'pʌblɪk]	Republik	❗ stress: re**pub**lic [rɪ'pʌblɪk]	(L) res publica f
state [steɪt]	Staat	(F) l'état (m)	(L) status, -us m (Zustand)

[eɪ] name · [aɪ] time · [ɔɪ] boy · [əʊ] old ·
[aʊ] town · [ɪə] here · [eə] where · [ʊə] tour

Vocabulary   Unit 4

visa [ˈviːzə]	Visum	Germans need a **visa** if they travel to India.
pet [pet]	Haustier	
(to) **steal** [stiːl], **stole** [stəʊl], **stolen** [ˈstəʊlən]	stehlen	Where is your bike? – Somebody has **stolen** it.
bank [bæŋk]	Bank	(F) la banque
p.69 **coordinator** [kəʊˈɔːdɪneɪtə]	Koordinator/in	
layout [ˈleɪaʊt]	Layout, Gestaltung	
editor [ˈedɪtə]	Redakteur/in; Herausgeber/in	(F) l'éditeur (m), l'éditrice (f) (L) edere (bekanntmachen)
research (no pl) [ˈriːsɜːtʃ]	Recherche, Forschung(en)	I have to do some **research** on Ireland for homework.
result [rɪˈzʌlt]	Ergebnis, Resultat	Have you heard the football **results**? Did we win? (F) le résultat
(to) **suggest** sth. **(to** sb.) [səˈdʒest]	(jm.) etwas vorschlagen	English: Dad **suggested that we go** to the cinema. German: Dad **schlug vor**, ins Kino **zu gehen**. ❗ (not: Dad suggested to go …)
discussion [dɪˈskʌʃn]	Diskussion	(F) la discussion
decision [dɪˈsɪʒn]	Entscheidung	verb: (to) **decide** – noun: **decision** (F) la décision

Part B

p.70 **angel** [ˈeɪndʒl]	Engel	(F) l'ange (m)
heaven [ˈhevn]	Himmel (im religiösen Sinn)	❗ clouds in the **sky** angels in **heaven**
service [ˈsɜːvɪs]	Gottesdienst	(L) servire (dienen)
(to) **check** sth. **out** [ˌtʃək ˈaʊt] (infml)	sich etwas anschauen, anhören; etwas ausprobieren	Our new CD is called "No sky in heaven". **Check it out**!
He was like: "Stop …" (infml)	Und er so: „Stop …"	
motorbike [ˈməʊtəbaɪk]	Motorrad	
p.71 **suit** [suːt]	Anzug	
(to) **smoke** [sməʊk]	rauchen	
pipe [paɪp]	(Tabaks-)Pfeife	

motorbikes   pipe (F) la pipe   suit

He's **smoking** a **pipe**.

like (infml)	als ob	What's he doing? – He looks **like** he's crying. ❗ Diese umgangssprachliche Verwendung von **like** wird von manchen als falsches Englisch empfunden. Besonders im Schriftlichen solltest du **as if** für das deutsche „als ob" benutzen: He looks **as if** he's crying.
p.72 **hell** [hel]	Hölle	**heaven** ◄► **hell**
by 8 pm [baɪ]	bis (spätestens) 20 Uhr	You must be here **by** 8 pm. (= not later than 8 pm)
(to) **have a shower** [ˈʃaʊə]	(sich) duschen	English: First I make tea, then I **have a shower**. German: …, dann dusche ich (mich).
electronic [ɪˌlekˈtrɒnɪk]	elektronisch	(F) électronique

Unit 4 Vocabulary

the Atlantic (Ocean) [ətˈlæntɪk]	der Atlantik, der Atlantische Ozean	
p.73 **beginning** [bɪˈgɪnɪŋ]	Anfang, Beginn	verb: (to) **begin** – noun: **beginning**
guest [gest]	Gast	
facial expression [ˌfeɪʃl_ɪkˈspreʃn]	Gesichtsausdruck, Mimik	
interaction [ˌɪntərˈækʃn]	Interaktion, Umgang	(L) agere (tun, handeln)

Part C

p.74 **arrival** [əˈraɪvl]	Ankunft	verb: (to) **arrive** – noun: **arrival** (F) l'arrivée (f)
weird [wɪəd]	seltsam, komisch	I have a **weird** feeling that something is wrong.
ride [raɪd]	Ritt, Ausritt	
(to) be alive [əˈlaɪv]	leben, am Leben sein	(to) **be alive** ◄► (to) **be dead**
argument [ˈɑːgjumənt]	Streit, Auseinandersetzung	❗ stress: **argument** [ˈɑːgjumənt]
(to) miss [mɪs]	vermissen	I enjoyed my trip to France, but I **missed** my friends. ❗ (to) **miss** = 1. verpassen; 2. vermissen
round here [ˌraʊnd ˈhɪə]	hier in der Gegend	**Round here**, we're all United fans.
(to) stare (at sb./sth.**)** [steə]	(jn./etwas an)starren	You shouldn't **stare at** people. It's impolite.
(to) care about sth. [keə]	etwas wichtig nehmen	(L) curare (sorgen für)

> **(to) care**
> 1. I **don't care** about money.   Geld ist mir egal.
> 2. In the city, people **wouldn't care** what I looked like.   In der Großstadt wäre es den Leuten egal, wie ich aussehe / würde sich niemand darum kümmern, wie ich aussehe.
> 3. I really **care** about animals.   Tiere liegen mir sehr am Herzen. / Tiere sind mir sehr wichtig.
> 4. Her parents are really rich. – Who **cares**?   Ihre Eltern sind richtig reich. – Na und? / Wen interessiert das?

(to) be starving [ˈstɑːvɪŋ]	einen Riesenhunger haben	
(to) unpack [ˌʌnˈpæk]	auspacken	(to) **pack** (packen, einpacken) ◄► (to) **unpack**
God [gɒd]	Gott	
(to) dislike [dɪsˈlaɪk]	nicht mögen, nicht leiden können	(to) **like** ◄► (to) **dislike**
p.75 **bang** [bæŋ]	Knall	
regional [ˈriːdʒənl]	regional	local – **regional** – national – international (F) régional, e
accent [ˈæksənt]	Akzent	❗ stress: **accent** [ˈæksənt] (F) l'accent (m)
standard [ˈstændəd]	Standard; Standard-	(F) le standard
p.76 **boyfriend** [ˈbɔɪfrend]	Freund	
girlfriend [ˈgɜːlfrend]	Freundin	
(to) welcome sb. **(to)** [ˈwelkəm]	jn. begrüßen (in), jn. willkommen heißen (in)	I'll make tea. Can you **welcome** the guests?
p.77 **(to) pass** [pɑːs]	vergehen, vorübergehen (Zeit)	The lesson was so interesting that the time **passed** really quickly. (F) passer
next [nekst]	als Nächstes	That was nice. What are we going to do **next**?
Easter [ˈiːstə]	Ostern	

[f] **f**ather · [v] ri**v**er · [s] **s**i**s**ter · [z] plea**s**e · [ʃ] **sh**op · [ʒ] televi**s**ion ·
[tʃ] **t**ea**ch**er · [dʒ] **G**ermany · [θ] **th**anks · [ð] **th**is · [h] **h**ere

Vocabulary   Unit 4

junction [ˈdʒʌŋkʃn]	(Straßen-)Kreuzung	
pedestrian [pəˈdestriən]	Fußgänger/in	
(to) **walk the dog**	mit dem Hund rausgehen, den Hund ausführen	He's **walking the dog.**
(to) **kick** [kɪk]	treten	
(to) **race** [reɪs]	rasen	A car is **racing** down the street.
traffic light [ˈtræfɪk laɪt] (oft auch: **traffic lights** (pl))	(Verkehrs-)Ampel	
traffic [ˈtræfɪk]	Verkehr	
(to) **turn** red/brown/cold/… [tɜːn]	rot/braun/kalt/… werden	❗ turn = „werden" wird hauptsächlich für Farbveränderungen und Wetterwechsel verwendet.
van [væn]	Transporter, Lieferwagen	
(to) **spin around** [ˌspɪn əˈraʊnd], **spun, spun** [spʌn]	sich (im Kreis) drehen; herumwirbeln	The girl **spun around** until she fell to the ground.
(to) **park** [pɑːk]	parken	
immediately [ɪˈmiːdiətli]	sofort	My dog comes **immediately** when I call her. Ⓕ **immédiatement**
siren [ˈsaɪrən]	Sirene	❗ stress: **siren** [ˈsaɪrən]
(to) **be gone** [gɒn]	weg sein, nicht (mehr) da sein	I don't know where Steve is. He was here two minutes ago and now he**'s gone**.

The horse ride

p. 78 **none (of …)** [nʌn]	keine(r, s) (von …)	He had 11 cousins but **none of** them lived near him.
a couple [ˈkʌpl]	ein Paar; ein paar	**a young couple** **a couple of sandwiches**
folk (pl) [fəʊk] (infml)	Leute	The **folk** round here are very friendly to tourists.
line [laɪn]	Reihe	❗ line = 1. Linie; 2. Zeile; 3. Reihe
What's up?	Was gibt's? / Was ist los?	Can you come and help me? – Why, **what's up?**
trail [treɪl]	Weg, Pfad	There are lots of good riding **trails** in the hills behind our house.
(to) **sigh** [saɪ]	seufzen	
Now that …	Jetzt, wo … / Nun, da …	**Now that** the school year is nearly over, we can make plans for the holidays.
slippery [ˈslɪpəri]	rutschig, glatt	
ditch [dɪtʃ]	Graben	
p. 79 **in the old days**	früher (einmal)	**In the old days**, there were no cars. People walked or rode horses.
gravestone [ˈgreɪvstəʊn]	Grabstein	a **gravestone**
(to) **bury** [ˈberi]	begraben, beerdigen	He died on holiday in Spain and was **buried** there.

[iː] green · [i] happy · [ɪ] big · [e] red · [æ] cat · [ɑː] class · [ɒ] song · [ɔː] door · [uː] blue · [ʊ] book · [ʌ] mum · [ɜː] girl · [ə] a partner

Unit 5 Vocabulary

famine [ˈfæmɪn]	Hungersnot		ⓛ fames, -is f (Hunger)
disease [dɪˈziːz]	*(ansteckende)* Krankheit	❗ • **disease** wird für ansteckende oder sehr ernsthafte Erkrankungen verwendet: She has a blood **disease**. Thousands of trees died from **disease**. • Das allgemeinere Wort für „Krankheit" ist **illness**: After a week of **illness**, she went back to school.	
(to) **emigrate** [ˈemɪɡreɪt]	auswandern, emigrieren		⒡ émigrer
government [ˈɡʌvənmənt]	Regierung		⒡ le gouvernement
export [ˈekspɔːt]	Export, Ausfuhr		⒡ l'export *(m)*
stream [striːm]	Bach	She stopped at the **stream** and drank some water.	
ashes *(pl)* [ˈæʃɪz]	Asche *(sterbliche Überreste)*	❗ • **ash** („Asche") wird verwendet für das, was übrig bleibt, wenn Holz, Papier, Kohle, Tabak verbrennt. • **ashes** *(pl)* („Asche") wird verwendet, – für die sterblichen Überreste nach der Einäscherung eines Verstorbenen; – für die Überreste nach einem Brand (z.B. eines Hauses).	
glad [ɡlæd]	froh, dankbar		
death [deθ]	Tod		
especially [ɪˈspeʃli]	besonders, vor allem	I love chocolate, **especially** chocolate from Belgium.	
thought [θɔːt]	Gedanke	verb: (to) **think, thought, thought** – noun: **thought**	

Unit 5 Extraordinary Scotland

p. 82 **extraordinary** [ɪkˈstrɔːdnri]	außergewöhnlich	⒡ extraordinaire ⓛ extra *(außerhalb von)*; ordo, -inis f *(Reihe)*	
(to) **promote** sth. [prəˈməʊt]	Werbung machen für etwas	Shakira is on tour. She's **promoting** her new album.	
bagpipes *(pl)* [ˈbæɡpaɪps]	Dudelsack		
Look out!	Achtung! / Aufgepasst!	**Look out**, a car's coming!	
p. 83 (to) **compete in** sth. [kəmˈpiːt]	an etwas teilnehmen *(Wettkampf)*		
sheepdog [ˈʃiːpdɒɡ]	Hütehund	❗ Mit **sheepdog** werden in Großbritannien oft Border Collies bezeichnet, da Schäfer meist diese Hunderasse als Hütehund einsetzen.	
trials *(pl)* [ˈtraɪəlz]	Turnier, Wettkampf		
the Highlands *(pl)* [ˈhaɪləndz]	das schottische Hochland		
on board [bɔːd]	an Bord	English: **on board** the ship/ferry German: **an Bord** des Schiffes/der Fähre	
yacht [jɒt]	Jacht	❗ pronunciation: **yacht** [jɒt]	
wee [wiː] *(bes. Scottish English, infml)*	klein	I live in a **wee** house in the Highlands. (= little, small)	
isle [aɪl]	*(kleine)* Insel, Eiland	❗ Das Wort **isle** wird vor allem in dichterischer Sprache und in Eigennamen verwendet. ⒡ l'île (f) ⓛ insula, -ae f	

Vocabulary   Unit 5

(to) **identify** sb./sth. **(by** sth.**)** [aɪˈdentɪfaɪ]	jn./etwas identifizieren (anhand von etwas)	She **identified** the thief **by** his very big nose. (F) **identifier**
dolphin [ˈdɒlfɪn]	Delfin	❗ stress: **dolphin** [ˈdɒlfɪn]
social media *(pl)* [ˌsəʊʃl ˈmiːdɪə]	soziale Medien	
unusual [ʌnˈjuːʒuəl]	ungewöhnlich	Snow is very **unusual** in June.
usual [ˈjuːʒuəl]	gewöhnlich, üblich	adjective: **usual** – Dad came home earlier than **usual**. adverb: **usually** – He **usually** comes home later.

Part A

p. 84	**volunteer** [ˌvɒlənˈtɪə]	Freiwillige(r), Ehrenamtliche(r)	(F) le/la **volontaire**
	sighting [ˈsaɪtɪŋ]	Sichtung	The first **sighting** of the Loch Ness monster was in 1933.
	(to) **put your hand up**	sich melden	**Put your hand up** if you know the answer.
	(to) **photograph** [ˈfəʊtəɡrɑːf]	fotografieren	
	pollution [pəˈluːʃn]	(Umwelt-)Verschmutzung	(F) la **pollution**
	(to) **spend time/money (on)** [spend], **spent, spent** [spent]	Zeit verbringen (mit); Geld ausgeben (für)	Mum says I **spend** too much time in front of my computer. My brother **spends** a lot of money **on** DVDs.
	(to) **protect** sb./sth. **(from** sb./sth.**)** [prəˈtekt]	jn./etwas (be)schützen (vor jm./etwas)	Wear a hat to **protect** your head **from** the sun. Animals might get dangerous if they're trying to **protect** their young. (F) **protéger**
	(to) **teach** [tiːtʃ], **taught, taught** [tɔːt]	unterrichten, lehren	Mr Schwarz is a teacher. He **teaches** English. My sister is **teaching** me to play the guitar. (= … bringt mir das Gitarrespielen bei.)
	dorsal fin [ˌdɔːsl ˈfɪn]	Rückenflosse	
	(to) **record** [rɪˈkɔːd]	aufzeichnen *(Musik, Daten);* dokumentieren *(Daten)*	The Beatles **recorded** their albums in London. I **recorded** every little detail in my little black book.
	location [ləʊˈkeɪʃn]	Position, Standort	(L) **locus**, -i *m (Ort)*
	(to) **monitor** [ˈmɒnɪtə]	nachverfolgen; überwachen	Almost everything we do on the internet can be **monitored** by somebody.
	movement [ˈmuːvmənt]	Bewegung	verb: (to) **move** – noun: **movement** (F) le **mouvement** (L) **movere** *(bewegen)*
	rough [rʌf]	stürmisch, rau *(See)*	The sea was so **rough** that we stayed in the harbour.
	calm [kɑːm]	ruhig	My mum has a very **calm** voice. (F) **calme**
	seasick [ˈsiːsɪk]	seekrank	I always get **seasick** on a boat when the sea is rough.
p. 85	(to) **keep** [kiːp], **kept, kept** [kept]	aufheben, aufsparen; aufbewahren	Don't spend all your money now. **Keep** some for later. You should always **keep** milk in a cool place.
	(to) **relax** [rɪˈlæks]	sich entspannen, sich ausruhen	
p. 87	(to) **escape** [ɪˈskeɪp]	fliehen	His grandfather **escaped** from Germany in 1940.
	escape [ɪˈskeɪp]	Flucht	

Unit 5 Vocabulary

	split screen [splɪt ˈskriːn]	geteilter Bildschirm; Bildschirm(auf)teilung	

Part B

p. 88	**cue** [kjuː]	Stichwort, Signal *(Theater)*	He says "Where is she?" and that's your **cue** to enter.
	fault [fɔːlt]	Schuld, Fehler	Why didn't you wake me up this morning? It's your **fault** that I'll be late for school.
	backstage [ˌbækˈsteɪdʒ]	hinter der Bühne	another word for "behind the stage"
	rehearsal [rɪˈhɜːsl]	Probe *(Theater)*	
	no one else [els]	niemand anders; niemand sonst	**No one else** has to help at home as much as I do.

> **… else**
> Oh Dad, why can't I go to Henry's party? **Everybody else** is allowed to go. alle anderen; sonst jeder
> I'm so tired. **Someone else** will have to wash the dishes. jemand anders
> Do you need **anything else** from the shops? sonst noch etwas
> **What else** can you tell us about Scotland? was (sonst) noch
> **Who else** wants to go to the festival in Edinburgh? wer (sonst) noch

	(to) **concentrate (on** sth.**)** [ˈkɒnsntreɪt]	sich konzentrieren (auf etwas)	Please be quiet. I can't **concentrate** on my work. ❗ stress: **concentrate** [ˈkɒnsntreɪt] (F) se concentrer
	(to) **pick on** sb. [pɪk] *(infml)*	auf jm. herumhacken	It's not nice to **pick on** people if they're fat.
	(to) **be tired of** sth. [ˈtaɪəd]	genug von etwas haben; etwas satt haben	I'm **tired of** this book. It's too long and very boring.
	position [pəˈzɪʃn]	Platz, Position	❗ stress: **position** [pəˈzɪʃn] (F) la position (L) ponere *(stellen)*
p. 89	**tough** [tʌf]	(knall)hart, schwierig	Starting at a new school is a **tough** thing for most students.
	(to) **tread on** sb.'s **toes** [tred], **trod** [trɒd], **trodden** [ˈtrɒdn] *(infml)*	jm. auf die Füße/Zehen treten *(auch im übertragenen Sinne)*	Hey, look out – you just **trod on** my **toes**! Maybe I'm **treading on** some people's **toes** here, but I think I could do the job better than everybody else.
	(to) **give** sb. **a hard time** *(infml)*	jn. fertig machen, jm. einheizen; jm. das Leben schwer machen	
	(to) **calm down** [ˌkɑːm ˈdaʊn]	sich beruhigen	English: (to) **calm down** | (to) **calm** sb. **down** German: **sich** beruhigen | **jn.** beruhigen
	description [dɪˈskrɪpʃn]	Beschreibung	verb: (to) **describe** – noun: **description** (F) la description (L) scribere *(schreiben)*
p. 90	**direct** [dəˈrekt], [daɪˈrekt]	direkt	**direct** ◄► **indirect** [ˌɪndəˈrekt], [ˌɪndaɪˈrekt] (F) direct, e / indirect, e
p. 91	**whenever** [ˌwenˈevə]	wann (auch) immer; egal, wann	

> **whenever, wherever, whatever, whoever**
> At my school, we're allowed to use dictionaries **whenever** we want. … wann immer wir wollen
> I'll find you, **wherever** you are. … wo immer du (auch) bist / egal, wo du bist
> We will help you, **whatever** happens. … was immer auch geschieht / egal, was geschieht
> **Whoever** told you that was wrong. Wer immer dir das auch erzählt hat, …

	platform [ˈplætfɔːm]	Plattform	❗ **platform** = 1. Plattform; 2. Bahnsteig, Gleis
	comedian [kəˈmiːdiən]	Komiker/in, Komödiant/in	(F) le comédien, la comédienne

Vocabulary   Unit 5

entertainment [ˌentəˈteɪnmənt]	Unterhaltung	There's usually lots of **entertainment** on a cruise ship: films, shows, concerts, competitions, etc.
(to) **interest** sb. [ˈɪntrəst]	jn. interessieren	❗ • He's **interested in** films. Er interessiert sich für … • Films **interest** him. Filme interessieren ihn.
p. 92 **handout** [ˈhændaʊt]	Handout, Handzettel	
transparency [trænsˈpærənsi]	Folie	
lynx [lɪŋks], *pl* **lynx** *or* **lynxes**	Luchs	
habitat [ˈhæbɪtæt]	Lebensraum	The natural **habitat** of the panda is China. ⓛ habitare *(wohnen)*
coat [kəʊt]	Fell	
predator [ˈpredətə]	Raubtier	❗ pronunciation: **predator** [ˈpredətə] ⓛ praeda, -ae *f (Beute)*
mammal [ˈmæml]	Säugetier	
territory [ˈterətri]	Revier, Territorium	ⓕ le territoire ⓛ terra, -ae *f (Erde, Land)*
p. 93 **element** [ˈelɪmənt]	Element	
necessary [ˈnesəsəri]	notwendig, nötig	You can phone me on my mobile if **necessary**. ⓕ nécessaire ⓛ necesse est *(es ist notwendig)*

Missing

p. 94 **missing** [ˈmɪsɪŋ]	verschollen, vermisst	
heather [ˈheðə]	Heide(kraut)	
below [bɪˈləʊ]	unten, darunter; unter, unterhalb (von)	From the plane, the buildings **below** were so small. Your mouth is **below** your nose.
above [əˈbʌv]	oben, darüber; über, oberhalb (von)	The buildings looked very small from **above**. Your eyes are **above** your nose.
tension [ˈtenʃn]	Spannung, Anspannung	ⓕ la tension
whistle [ˈwɪsl]	Pfiff	❗ **whistle** = 1. pfeifen; 2. Pfiff; 3. (Triller-)Pfeife
in horror [ˈhɒrə]	entsetzt	We watched **in horror** as Messi scored his fifth goal.
noise [nɔɪz]	Geräusch; Lärm	noun: **noise** – adjective: **noisy**
(to) **reach over** [ˌriːtʃ ˈəʊvə]	die Hand ausstrecken	He **reached over** and quietly stole a biscuit.
dry [draɪ]	trocken	**dry** ◄► **wet**
(to) **beat** [biːt], **beat** [biːt], **beaten** [ˈbiːtn]	schlagen; besiegen	I **beat** my father at tennis last Sunday.
(to) **read** sb.'s **mind** [maɪnd]	jemandes Gedanken lesen	Sometimes I wish I could **read your mind**.
shepherd [ˈʃepəd]	Schäfer/in, Schafhirte/-hirtin	

the sky above — heather — shepherd — sheepdog

[iː] green · [i] happy · [ɪ] big · [e] red · [æ] cat · [ɑː] class · [ɒ] song ·
[ɔː] door · [uː] blue · [ʊ] book · [ʌ] mum · [ɜː] girl · [ə] a partner

Unit 5 Vocabulary

	jealous (of) [ˈdʒeləs]	neidisch (auf); eifersüchtig (auf)	You get so much pocket money! I'm really **jealous**. She was **jealous of** her baby brother. She thought her parents loved him more.
	(to) hate [heɪt]	hassen	(to) love ◄► (to) **hate**
p. 95	**(to) burst into tears, burst, burst** [bɜːst]	in Tränen ausbrechen	When I saw that the dog was dead, I immediately **burst into tears**.
	gently [ˈdʒentli]	behutsam, sanft	
	awake [əˈweɪk]	wach	**awake** ◄► asleep
	(to) knock (on sth.**)** [nɒk]	(an)klopfen (an etwas)	I **knocked** and went in.
	memorial [məˈmɔːriəl]	Denkmal; Gedenk-	There's a war **memorial** by the church in our village. ⓛ memoria, -ae f (Erinnerung)
p. 96	**in second place**	auf dem zweiten Platz; an zweiter Stelle	ⓛ secundus, -a, -um (zweiter)

5 Text File

The Off-side Trap by Mary Colson

Setting	Schauplatz
Football club disco.	Disco im Fußballclub.
Maxine really fancies Paul and he quite likes her. They're thirteen years old. He's hugely into football – she knows nothing about it but has to pretend she does in order to make conversation. While their thoughts are being spoken, Maxine and Paul are experiencing awkward silences, looking ill at ease and searching for something to say. There is a prevailing embarrassed awkwardness throughout their dialogue.	Maxine findet Paul echt toll und er mag sie auch irgendwie. Sie sind 13. Er steht voll auf Fußball – sie hat keine Ahnung davon, muss aber so tun als ob, um sich mit ihm zu unterhalten. Während Maxines und Pauls Gedanken gesprochen werden, ertragen die beiden eine peinliche Stille, in der sie sich nicht wohl fühlen und überlegen, was sie sagen könnten. Das ganze Gespräch hindurch wirken sie verlegen und unbeholfen.

Dictionary

Das **Dictionary** besteht aus **zwei alphabetischen Wörterlisten**:
English – German (S. 198–220)   und   **German – English** (S. 221–242)

Im **English – German Dictionary** kannst du nachschlagen, wenn du wissen möchtest, was ein englisches Wort bedeutet, wie man es ausspricht oder wie es geschrieben wird.

Im **Dictionary** werden folgende **Abkürzungen und Symbole** verwendet:

   sth. = something (etwas)   sb. = somebody (jemand)   jn. = jemanden   jm. = jemandem
   pl = *plural* (Mehrzahl)   *infml* = *informal* (umgangssprachlich)
   ° Mit diesem Kringel sind Wörter markiert, die nicht zum Lernwortschatz gehören.

▶ Der Pfeil weist auf Kästen im **Vocabulary** (S. 172–197) hin, in denen du weitere Informationen zu diesem Wort findest.

Die **Fundstellenangaben** zeigen, wo ein Wort zum ersten Mal vorkommt.
I = Band 1;   II = Band 2;   III 1 (15) = Band 3, Unit 1, Seite 15

Tipps zur Arbeit mit einem Wörterbuch findest du im Skills File auf Seite 141.

A

a [ə]:
  1. ein, eine I
  2. **once a week** einmal pro Woche II
°**abbey** ['æbi] Abtei, Kloster
abbreviation [əˌbriːvi'eɪʃn] Abkürzung II
able ['eɪbl]: **be able to do sth.** etwas tun können; fähig sein / in der Lage sein, etwas zu tun III 2 (40)
about [ə'baʊt]:
  1. **about you/…** über dich/… I **about yourself** über dich selbst I **It's about …** Es geht um … / Es handelt von … **know about sth.** sich mit etwas auskennen; über etwas Bescheid wissen II **the best thing about …** das Beste an … III 1 (8) **What about you?** Und du? / Und was ist mit dir?; Und ihr? / Und was ist mit euch? I **What is the story about?** Wovon handelt die Geschichte? / Worum geht es in der Geschichte? I
  2. **about 300** ungefähr 300 II
above [ə'bʌv] oben, darüber; über, oberhalb (von) III 5 (94)
accent ['æksənt] Akzent III 4 (75)
access ['ækses] Zugang, Zutritt I
°**accompany** [ə'kʌmpəni] begleiten
across [ə'krɒs]: **across the street** (quer) über die Straße II
act [ækt] schauspielern II
°**Act of Union** [ækt] Vereinigungsgesetz
act out [ˌækt_'aʊt] vorspielen I
action ['ækʃn] Action; Handlung, Tat I
°**active** ['æktɪv] aktiv
activity [æk'tɪvəti] Aktivität I **free-time activities** Freizeitaktivitäten I
actor ['æktə] Schauspieler/in I
actually ['æktʃuəli] eigentlich; übrigens; tatsächlich III 3 (47)
  ▶ S. 184 actually

add (to) [æd] hinzufügen, ergänzen, addieren (zu) III 2 (38)
adder ['ædə] Kreuzotter II
address [ə'dres] Adresse, Anschrift I
adjective ['ædʒɪktɪv] Adjektiv II
°**admire** [əd'maɪə] bewundern
adopted [ə'dɒptɪd] adoptiert, Adoptiv- II
adult ['ædʌlt] Erwachsene(r) III 1 (15)
°**advantage** [əd'vɑːntɪdʒ] Vorteil
adventure [əd'ventʃə] Abenteuer II
adverb ['ædvɜːb] Adverb II
advert ['ædvɜːt] Werbespot, Werbung III 4 (66)
°**advice** [əd'vaɪs] Rat(schlag)
°**afraid** [ə'freɪd]: **be afraid** Angst haben
after ['ɑːftə]:
  1. **after breakfast** nach dem Frühstück I **right after you** gleich nach dir II **after that** danach III 3 (46)
  2. **nachdem … just after …** gleich nachdem …; kurz nachdem … II
  3. **run after sb.** hinter jm. herrennen I
afternoon [ˌɑːftə'nuːn] Nachmittag I **in the afternoon** nachmittags, am Nachmittag I **on Saturday afternoon** am Samstagnachmittag I **this afternoon** heute Nachmittag II
again [ə'gen] wieder; noch einmal I **again and again** immer wieder II
against [ə'genst] gegen I
age [eɪdʒ] Alter I **… is your age … ist in deinem Alter; … ist so alt wie du** II
ago [ə'gəʊ]: **two days ago** vor zwei Tagen I
agree [ə'griː]: **agree with sb.** jm. zustimmen I **agree on sth.** sich auf etwas einigen I
°**agreement** [ə'griːmənt] Abkommen
air [eə] Luft II
airport ['eəpɔːt] Flughafen III 3 (55)
°**album** ['ælbəm] Album
alive [ə'laɪv]: **be alive** leben, am Leben sein III 4 (74)

all [ɔːl] alles; alle I **all around her** überall um sie herum III 1 (24) **all of Plymouth** ganz Plymouth, das ganze Plymouth I **all alone** ganz allein II **all day** den ganzen Tag II °**all over this land** im ganzen Land **all the time** die ganze Zeit II **one all** eins zu eins; eins beide III 3 (56)
allow [ə'laʊ] erlauben, zulassen III 2 (37) **be allowed to do sth.** etwas tun dürfen II
all right [ˌɔːl 'raɪt] okay; in Ordnung I
almost ['ɔːlməʊst] fast, beinahe I
alone [ə'ləʊn] allein II **all alone** ganz allein II
along [ə'lɒŋ]: **along the street / …** die Straße / … entlang I **sing along (with sb.)** (mit jm.) mitsingen III 2 (35)
aloud [ə'laʊd]: **read aloud** laut (vor)lesen II
already [ɔːl'redi] schon, bereits II
also ['ɔːlsəʊ] auch I
altogether [ˌɔːltə'geðə] insgesamt, alles in allem III 2 (34)
always ['ɔːlweɪz] immer I
am: 4 am [ˌeɪ_'em] 4 Uhr morgens I
amazing [ə'meɪzɪŋ] erstaunlich, unglaublich III 1 (10)
an [æn], [ən] ein, eine I
ancestor ['ænsestə] Vorfahr/in III 3 (52)
and [ænd], [ənd] und I
angel ['eɪndʒl] Engel III 4 (70)
°**Anglican** ['æŋlɪkən] anglikanisch
angry ['æŋgri] wütend I **angry with sb.** wütend, böse auf jn. II
animal ['ænɪml] Tier I **my favourite animal** mein Lieblingstier I
announcement [ə'naʊnsmənt] Durchsage, Ansage III 1 (19)
another [ə'nʌðə]:
  1. ein(e) andere(r, s) I
  2. noch ein(e) I
answer ['ɑːnsə]:
  1. antworten; beantworten I **answer**

English – German

the phone ans Telefon gehen II
2. Antwort I
ant [ænt] Ameise I
any ['eni]: **Are there any ...?** Gibt es (irgendwelche) ...? I **not ... any more** nicht mehr II **There aren't any ...** Es gibt keine / Es sind keine ... I
anybody ['enibɒdi]: anybody? (irgend)jemand? II **not ... anybody** niemand II
anyone ['eniwʌn]: anyone? (irgend)jemand? II **not ... anyone** niemand II
anything ['eniθɪŋ]: anything? (irgend)etwas? II **not ... anything** nichts II
Anyway, ... ['eniweɪ] Jedenfalls, ... / Aber egal, ... II **And anyway, ...** Und überhaupt, ... III 1 (20)
apartment [ə'pɑːtmənt] Wohnung I
appear [ə'pɪə] erscheinen, auftauchen II
apple ['æpl] Apfel II
appointment [ə'pɔɪntmənt] Verabredung, Termin I
April ['eɪprəl] April I
aquarium [ə'kweəriəm] Aquarium; Aquarienhaus I
°**arc** [ɑːk] Bogen
°**arch** [ɑːtʃ] Bogen
architect ['ɑːkɪtekt] Architekt/in III 2 (31)
°**architecture** ['ɑːkɪtektʃə] Architektur
°**archive** ['ɑːkaɪv] Archiv
are [ɑː] bist; sind; seid I **Are you ...?** Bist du ...? I **The DVDs are ...** Die DVDs kosten ... I
area ['eəriə] Bereich; Gebiet, Gegend I
aren't [ɑːnt]: **you aren't ...** du bist nicht ...; du bist kein/e ...; ihr seid nicht ...; ihr seid kein/e ... I
argue ['ɑːɡjuː] streiten; sich streiten III 2 (41)
argument ['ɑːɡjumənt]:
1. Streit, Auseinandersetzung III 4 (74)
°2. Argument
arm [ɑːm] Arm II **take sb. by the arm** jn. am Arm nehmen II
armchair ['ɑːmtʃeə] Sessel I
around [ə'raʊnd]:
1. **around the library / ...** in der Bücherei / ... umher I **all around her** überall um sie herum III 1 (24) **look around (the farm)** sich (auf der Farm) umsehen II
▶ S. 180 (to) look ...
walk/run/... around herumlaufen, umherspazieren / herumrennen, umherrennen II
2. um ... herum II **around 6 pm** um 18 Uhr herum, gegen 18 Uhr II
arrange [ə'reɪndʒ] anordnen I
arrival [ə'raɪvl] Ankunft III 4 (74)
arrive [ə'raɪv] ankommen, eintreffen I
art [ɑːt] Kunst II
article ['ɑːtɪkl] Artikel II

artist ['ɑːtɪst] Künstler/in II **street artist** Straßenkünstler/in II
as [æz], [əz]:
1. als, während II
2. **(not) as big as** (nicht) so groß wie II
3. **as a child** als Kind II **She works as a teacher.** Sie arbeitet als Lehrerin. II
4. **as he said ...** Wie er (einmal) sagte ... III 3 (51)
5. **as soon as** sobald, sowie III 1 (10)
6. **as if** als ob III 4 (71)
ash [æʃ] Asche III 4 (79) **ashes** (pl) Asche (sterbliche Überreste) III 4 (79)
ask [ɑːsk] fragen II **ask a question** eine Frage stellen I **ask for sth.** um etwas bitten II **ask sb. the way** jn. nach dem Weg fragen II **ask sb. to do sth.** jemanden bitten, etwas zu tun I
asleep [ə'sliːp]: **be asleep** schlafen II
°**assess** [ə'ses] einschätzen
assistant [ə'sɪstənt] (auch **shop assistant**) Verkäufer/in II
astronaut ['æstrənɔːt] Astronaut/in III 2 (31)
as well [əz 'wel] auch, ebenso III 4 (66)
at [æt], [ət] an, bei, in I **at 14 Dean Street** in der Deanstraße 14 I **at first** zuerst, anfangs, am Anfang II **at Grandma's (house/flat)** bei Oma II **at home** daheim, zu Hause I **at last** endlich, schließlich II **at least** zumindest, wenigstens II **at lunchtime** mittags I **at night** nachts, in der Nacht I **at school** in der Schule I **at the moment** gerade, im Moment I **at the top (of)** oben, am oberen Ende, an der Spitze (von) II **at the weekend** am Wochenende I
ate [et], [eɪt] siehe **eat**
Atlantic [ət'læntɪk]: **the Atlantic (Ocean)** der Atlantik, der Atlantische Ozean III 4 (72)
attack [ə'tæk] angreifen II
attic ['ætɪk] Dachboden I **in the attic** auf dem Dachboden I
°**attract** [ə'trækt] anziehen, anlocken
attraction [ə'trækʃn] Attraktion; Anziehungspunkt III 1 (14)
audience ['ɔːdiəns] Publikum, Zuschauer/innen, Zuhörer/innen II
audition [ɔː'dɪʃn] Vorsprechen, Vorsingen, Vorspielen I
August ['ɔːɡəst] August I
aunt [ɑːnt] Tante I
author ['ɔːθə] Autor/in I
autumn ['ɔːtəm] Herbst I
available [ə'veɪləbl] erhältlich, verfügbar; erreichbar (Telefon) III 1 (24)
awake [ə'weɪk] wach III 5 (95)
away [ə'weɪ] weg, fort I
awful ['ɔːfl] schrecklich, fürchterlich II
°**aye** [aɪ] ja (bes. schottisch, nordenglisch)

B

back [bæk]:
1. zurück I
2. Rücken II
3. **from the back of the bus** aus dem hinteren Teil des Busses II
background ['bækɡraʊnd] Hintergrund II **background file** Hintergrundinformation(en) I
backstage [ˌbæk'steɪdʒ] hinter der Bühne III 5 (88)
bacon ['beɪkən] Schinkenspeck II
bad [bæd] schlecht, schlimm I **go bad** (fish, cheese, eggs) schlecht werden II
bag [bæɡ] Tasche, Beutel, Tüte I **school bag** Schultasche I
bagpipes (pl) ['bæɡpaɪps] Dudelsack III 5 (82)
ball [bɔːl] Ball I
banana [bə'nɑːnə] Banane III 3 (47)
band [bænd] Band, (Musik-)Gruppe II
bang [bæŋ] Knall III 4 (75)
bank [bæŋk] Bank III 4 (68)
bar [bɑː] Riegel (Schokolade, Müsli), Tafel (Schokolade) III 2 (38)
bare [beə] nackt, bloß (Hände, Arme, Füße) III 3 (52)
bark [bɑːk]:
1. bellen I
2. Bellen III 5 (95)
barman ['bɑːmən], pl **barmen** ['bɑːmən] Barkeeper III 1 (20)
barn [bɑːn] Scheune II
basket ['bɑːskɪt] Korb I
basketball ['bɑːskɪtbɔːl] Basketball I
°**bass** [beɪs] Bassgitarre
bath [bɑːθ] Bad II
bathroom ['bɑːθruːm] Badezimmer I
battle ['bætl] Schlacht; Kampf II
be [bi], **was/were, been**: sein I
beach [biːtʃ] Strand I
bear [beə] Bär I
beard [bɪəd] Bart II
beautiful ['bjuːtɪfl] schön II
beat [biːt], **beat, beaten** schlagen; besiegen III 5 (94)
beaten ['biːtn] siehe **beat**
became [bɪ'keɪm] siehe **become**
because [bɪ'kɒz] weil I °**because of** wegen
become [bɪ'kʌm], **became, become** werden II
bed [bed] Bett I **bed and breakfast** Frühstückspension; Zimmer mit Frühstück III 1 (12)
bedroom ['bedruːm] Schlafzimmer I
beef [biːf]: **roast beef** Rinderbraten I
°**Beefeater** ['biːfiːtə] Torwächter des Towers von London
been [biːn]:
1. siehe **be**
2. **Have you ever been to ...?** ... Bist du schon in ... gewesen? I

Dictionary

beep [biːp] piepen II
before [bɪˈfɔː]:
1. bevor I
2. vor I **before school/lessons** vor der Schule (vor Schulbeginn) / vorm Unterricht I **before long** schon bald III 2 (35) **before that** davor III 3 (46)
3. (vorher) schon mal II **not/never before** (vorher) noch nie II
began [bɪˈgæn] siehe **begin**
begin [bɪˈgɪn], **began, begun** beginnen, anfangen II
beginning [bɪˈgɪnɪŋ] Anfang, Beginn III 4 (73) **in the beginning** anfangs, zuerst III 4 (73)
begun [bɪˈgʌn] siehe **begun**
behave [bɪˈheɪv] sich verhalten, sich benehmen III 2 (42)
behind [bɪˈhaɪnd] hinter I **from behind** von hinten II **right behind you** direkt hinter dir, genau hinter dir II
believe [bɪˈliːv] glauben I
bell [bel] Klingel, Glocke I
below [bɪˈləʊ] unten, darunter; unter, unterhalb (von) III 5 (94)
bend down [bend], **bent, bent** sich hinunterbeugen, sich bücken III 1 (24)
bent [bent] siehe **bend**
best [best]: **the best** der/die/das beste; die besten; am besten I **the best thing about …** das Beste an … III 1 (8)
better [ˈbetə] besser I **better than ever** besser als je zuvor II
between [bɪˈtwiːn] zwischen I
big [bɪg] groß I **big wheel** Riesenrad I **the biggest** der/die/das größte; am größten I
bike [baɪk] Fahrrad I **ride a bike** Fahrrad fahren I
°**bilingual** [ˌbaɪˈlɪŋgwəl] zweisprachig
bird [bɜːd] Vogel I
birthday [ˈbɜːθdeɪ] Geburtstag I **My birthday is in May.** Ich habe im Mai Geburtstag. I **My birthday is on 5th May.** Ich habe am 5. May Geburtstag. I **When's your birthday?** Wann hast du Geburtstag? I
biscuit [ˈbɪskɪt] Keks, Plätzchen I
bit [bɪt]:
1. siehe **bite**
2. a bit ein bisschen, etwas II
bite [baɪt]:
1. (bit, bitten) beißen I
2. Biss, Bissen III 2 (41)
bitten [ˈbɪtn] siehe **bite**
black [blæk] schwarz I
blew [bluː] siehe **blow**
blog [blɒg] Blog (Weblog, digitales Tagebuch) II
blogger [ˈblɒgə] Blogger/in III 1 (11)
blond (bei Frauen oft: **blonde**) [blɒnd] blond I
blood [blʌd] Blut III 1 (15)
blow [bləʊ], **blew, blown: blow sth. out** etwas auspusten, ausblasen II

blow (a whistle) pfeifen (auf der Trillerpfeife) III 1 (24)
blown [bləʊn] siehe **blow**
blue [bluː] blau I
board [bɔːd]:
1. (Wand-)Tafel I
2. on board an Bord III 5 (83) **on board the ship** an Bord des Schiffes III 5 (83)
boarding school [ˈbɔːdɪŋ skuːl] Internat II
boat [bəʊt] Boot, Schiff I
body [ˈbɒdi]:
1. Körper I **part of the body** Körperteil II
2. Leiche III 3 (61)
3. Hauptteil (eines Textes) III 3 (51)
book [bʊk] Buch I
bookshop [ˈbʊkʃɒp] Buchladen, Buchhandlung I
°**boom** [buːm] Aufschwung
boot [buːt] Stiefel II
border [ˈbɔːdə] Grenze III 4 (68)
bored [bɔːd]: **be/feel bored** gelangweilt sein, sich langweilen II
boring [ˈbɔːrɪŋ] langweilig I
born [bɔːn]: **be born** geboren sein/werden III 3 (51) **I was born in 1998.** Ich bin 1998 geboren. III 3 (51)
both [bəʊθ] beide I
bottle [ˈbɒtl] Flasche I
bottom [ˈbɒtəm]: **at the bottom** unten, am unteren Ende (von) II
bought [bɔːt] siehe **buy**
bow [baʊ] sich verneigen, sich verbeugen II
bowl [bəʊl] Schüssel II
box [bɒks] Kasten, Kiste, Kästchen I **telephone box** Telefonzelle III 1 (15)
boy [bɔɪ] Junge I
boyfriend [ˈbɔɪfrend] Freund III 4 (76)
°**Boy Scouts** [ˌbɔɪ ˈskaʊts] Pfadfinder
°**bracket** [ˈbrækɪt] Klammer (in Texten)
bread [bred] Brot I
break [breɪk]:
1. Pause I
2. (broke, broken) zerbrechen, kaputt machen I; brechen, kaputt gehen I
breakfast [ˈbrekfəst] Frühstück I **have breakfast** frühstücken I **bed and breakfast** Frühstückspension; Zimmer mit Frühstück III 1 (12)
°**breakthrough** [ˈbreɪkθruː] Durchbruch
breath [breθ] Atem, Atemzug II **he said … under his breath** …, sagte er flüsternd / murmelte er. III 1 (25)
breeze [briːz] Brise III 2 (40)
bridge [brɪdʒ] Brücke II
bright [braɪt] strahlend, leuchtend, hell I
brilliant [ˈbrɪliənt] glänzend, großartig, genial II
bring [brɪŋ], **brought, brought** (mit-, her)bringen II **bring in** (hay) einbringen (Heu) II
British [ˈbrɪtɪʃ] britisch I

brochure [ˈbrəʊʃə] Broschüre, Prospekt III 4 (65)
broke [brəʊk] siehe **break**
broken [ˈbrəʊkən]:
1. siehe **break**
2. zerbrochen, kaputt; gebrochen II
°**broomstick** [ˈbruːmstɪk] Besenstiel
brother [ˈbrʌðə] Bruder I
brought [brɔːt] siehe **bring**
brown [braʊn] braun I
°**brutal** [ˈbruːtl] brutal
°**bubble** [ˈbʌbl]: **speech bubble** Sprechblase
bucket [ˈbʌkɪt] Eimer II
build [bɪld], **built, built** bauen II
building [ˈbɪldɪŋ] Gebäude II
built [bɪlt] siehe **build**
bully [ˈbʊli] (Schul-)Tyrann III 3 (59)
burger [ˈbɜːgə] Hamburger II
burn [bɜːn] brennen; verbrennen III 3 (60)
burst [bɜːst], **burst, burst: burst into tears** in Tränen ausbrechen III 5 (95)
bury [ˈberi] begraben, beerdigen III 4 (79)
bus [bʌs] Bus I **go by bus** mit dem Bus fahren I **get on a bus** (in einen Bus) einsteigen II
busy [ˈbɪzi] belebt, geschäftig, hektisch III 2 (40) **be busy** beschäftigt sein; viel zu tun haben I
but [bʌt], [bət] aber I
butterfly [ˈbʌtəflaɪ] Schmetterling I
buy [baɪ], **bought, bought** kaufen I
by [baɪ]:
1. by the sea am Meer I **take sb. by the arm** jn. am Arm nehmen II
2. go by car/bus/… mit dem Auto/Bus/… fahren I
3. by … von … II
4. by 8 pm bis (spätestens) 20 Uhr III 4 (72)
5. by the way [ˌbaɪ ðə ˈweɪ] übrigens III 1 (10)
°**6. by yourself** allein, auf eigene Faust
Bye. [baɪ] Tschüs. I

C

café [ˈkæfeɪ] Café I
cage [keɪdʒ] Käfig I
cake [keɪk] Kuchen I
call [kɔːl]:
1. rufen; anrufen; nennen I **call out the names** die Namen aufrufen II
2. (auch: **phone call**) Anruf, Telefonat II
called [kɔːld]: **be called** heißen, genannt werden I
caller [ˈkɔːlə] Anrufer/in II
calm [kɑːm]:
1. ruhig III 5 (84)
2. calm down sich beruhigen III 5 (89)
calm sb. down jn. beruhigen III 5 (89)
came [keɪm] siehe **come**

English – German

camera [ˈkæmərə] Kamera, Fotoapparat I
cameraman [ˈkæmrəmæn], pl **cameramen** [ˈkæmrəmen] Kameramann I
camping [ˈkæmpɪŋ] Camping, Zelten II   **go camping** zelten gehen II
campsite [ˈkæmpsaɪt] Zeltplatz II
can [kæn], [kən] können I   **we cannot** [ˈkænɒt], **we can't** [kɑːnt] … wir können nicht … I
canal [kəˈnæl] Kanal III 3 (60)
candle [ˈkændl] Kerze II
canteen [kænˈtiːn] Kantine, (Schul-)Mensa I
cap [kæp] Mütze, Kappe II
°**capital** [ˈkæpɪtl] Hauptstadt I
captain [ˈkæptɪn] Kapitän/in I
caption [ˈkæpʃn] Bildunterschrift I
captive [ˈkæptɪv] Gefangene(r) III 3 (53)
car [kɑː] Auto I   **go by car** mit dem Auto fahren I   **get in(to) a car** (in ein Auto) einsteigen I
caravan [ˈkærəvæn] Wohnwagen II
card (to) [kɑːd] Karte (an) I
care [keə]: **care about sth.** etwas wichtig nehmen III 4 (74)   **I don't care about money.** Geld ist mir egal. III 4 (74)   **I really care about animals.** Tiere liegen mir sehr am Herzen. / Tiere sind mir sehr wichtig. III 4 (74)   **Who cares?** Na und? / Wen interessiert das? III 4 (74)
▶ S. 191 (to) care
career [kəˈrɪə] Karriere III 3 (61)
careful [ˈkeəfl] vorsichtig I
°**Caribbean** [ˌkærɪˈbiːən] karibisch
carnival [ˈkɑːnɪvl] Karneval, Fasching III 1 (10)
carpenter [ˈkɑːpəntə] Tischler/in, Zimmerer/Zimmerin III 2 (30)
°**carriage** [ˈkærɪdʒ] Kutsche
carrot [ˈkærət] Möhre, Karotte III 2 (39)
carry [ˈkæri] tragen; befördern III 3 (52)
cart [kɑːt] Karren I
°**cartoon** [kɑːˈtuːn] Cartoon
cash desk [ˈkæʃ desk] Kasse (in Geschäften) II
cast [kɑːst] Besetzung; Mitwirkende (Theaterstück, Film) II
castle [ˈkɑːsl] Burg, Schloss I
cat [kæt] Katze I   **big cat** Großkatze III 5 (92)
catch [kætʃ], **caught, caught** fangen I
cathedral [kəˈθiːdrəl] Kathedrale, Dom III 1 (10)
caught [kɔːt] siehe **catch**
°**causeway** [ˈkɔːzweɪ] Damm
cave [keɪv] Höhle II
°**céilidh** [ˈkeɪli] Tanz- und Musikveranstaltung (bes. in Schottland und Irland)
celebrate [ˈselɪbreɪt] feiern I
celebration [ˌselɪˈbreɪʃn] Feier II
°**Celtic** [ˈseltɪk] keltisch
cent [sent] Cent III 4 (68)
▶ S. 189 Pounds and euros

centre [ˈsentə] Zentrum; Mitte I   **shopping centre** Einkaufszentrum II
century [ˈsentʃəri] Jahrhundert I
chain [tʃeɪn] Kette I
°**chain game** [ˈtʃeɪn geɪm] Kettenspiel
chair [tʃeə] Stuhl I
challenge [ˈtʃælɪndʒ] Herausforderung III 4 (66)
challenge sb. (to sth.) [ˈtʃælɪndʒ] jn. herausfordern (zu etwas) III 4 (66)
champion [ˈtʃæmpiən] Meister/in, Champion I
chance [tʃɑːns] Gelegenheit, Möglichkeit, Chance III 1 (14)
change [tʃeɪndʒ]:
1. (ver)ändern; sich (ver)ändern II
2. wechseln, umtauschen (Geld) III 4 (68)
3. umsteigen III 1 (18)
4. Wechselgeld II
°5. Änderung
chaos [ˈkeɪɒs] Chaos I
character [ˈkærəktə]:
1. Figur, Person (in Roman, Film, Theaterstück) I
°2. Charakter, Wesen
charity [ˈtʃærəti] Wohlfahrtsorganisation; Wohltätigkeit, wohltätige Zwecke II
chat [tʃæt]:
1. chatten III 4 (74); plaudern III 4 (78)
2. Chat III 5 (89)
cheap [tʃiːp] billig, preiswert I
check [tʃek]:
1. Überprüfung, Kontrolle I
2. (über)prüfen, kontrollieren I   **check sth. out** [ˌtʃək_ˈaʊt] (infml) sich etwas anschauen, anhören; etwas ausprobieren III 4 (70)
checklist [ˈtʃeklɪst] Checkliste III 1 (17)
cheer [tʃɪə] jubeln II
cheese [tʃiːz] Käse I
chess [tʃes] Schach I
chest [tʃest] Brust, Brustkorb I
child [tʃaɪld], pl **children** [ˈtʃɪldrən] Kind I
chips (pl) [tʃɪps] Pommes frites II
chocolate [ˈtʃɒklət]:
1. Schokolade I
2. Praline II
choir [ˈkwaɪə] Chor II   °**choir leader** Chorleiter/in
choose [tʃuːz], **chose, chosen** aussuchen, (aus)wählen; sich aussuchen I
chorus [ˈkɔːrəs] Refrain II
chose [tʃəʊz] siehe **choose**
chosen [ˈtʃəʊzn] siehe **choose**
Christmas [ˈkrɪsməs] Weihnachten III 1 (15)   **Christmas Day** 1. Weihnachtstag (25. Dezember) III 1 (15)
church [tʃɜːtʃ] Kirche II
cinema [ˈsɪnəmə] Kino I
circle [ˈsɜːkl] Kreis I
city [ˈsɪti] Stadt, Großstadt I
°**clan** [klæn] Sippe
clap [klæp] (Beifall) klatschen II   **Clap your hands.** Klatscht in die Hände. II

class [klɑːs] (Schul-)Klasse I   °**in class** im Unterricht
classmate [ˈklɑːsmeɪt] Mitschüler/in, Klassenkamerad/in I
classroom [ˈklɑːsruːm] Klassenzimmer I
clause [klɔːz]:   **main clause** Hauptsatz III 2 (36)
clay [kleɪ] Ton, Lehm III 3 (52)
clean [kliːn]:
1. sauber machen, putzen I
2. sauber I
clear [klɪə]:
1. klar, deutlich II
2. räumen; abräumen III 2 (40)
clever [ˈklevə] klug, schlau I
cliff [klɪf] Klippe II
climb [klaɪm]:
1. klettern; hinaufklettern (auf) II
2. Aufstieg, Anstieg III 2 (38)
clock [klɒk] (Wand-, Stand-, Turm-)Uhr I   °**clock face** Zifferblatt   °**clock wheel** Zahnrad (Uhr)
close [kləʊz] schließen II
°**close** [kləʊs] eng
closely [ˈkləʊsli]: **look closely** genau hinschauen II
clothes (pl) [kləʊðz] Kleidung, Kleidungsstücke I
°**clothing** [ˈkləʊðɪŋ] Kleidung
cloud [klaʊd] Wolke II
cloudy [ˈklaʊdi] bewölkt II
clown [klaʊn] Clown II
club [klʌb] Klub I   **join a club** in einen Klub eintreten; sich einem Klub anschließen I
clue [kluː] (Lösungs-)Hinweis; Anhaltspunkt III 1 (11)
coal [kəʊl] Kohle III 2 (32)   **coal mine** Kohlebergwerk III 2 (32)
coast [kəʊst] Küste I
coat [kəʊt]:
1. Mantel II
2. Fell III 5 (92)
cocoa [ˈkəʊkəʊ] Kakao II
coffee [ˈkɒfi] Kaffee III 4 (66)
coin [kɔɪn] Münze I
cola [ˈkəʊlə] Cola I
cold [kəʊld]:
1. kalt I   **be cold** frieren I
2. **have a cold** eine Erkältung haben, erkältet sein II
collect [kəˈlekt] sammeln I
colon [ˈkəʊlən] Doppelpunkt II
colour [ˈkʌlə] Farbe I
column [ˈkɒləm]:
1. Säule III 4 (66)
°2. Spalte
°**combination** [ˌkɒmbɪˈneɪʃn] Verbindung, Kombination
°**combine** [kəmˈbaɪn] kombinieren
come [kʌm], **came, come** kommen I   **come across sth.** stoßen auf etwas, etwas (zufällig) treffen III 2 (32)   **come down with sth.** etwas bekommen (Krankheit), erkranken an etwas III 2 (32)
come in hereinkommen I   **Come on,**

Dictionary

Dad. Na los, Dad! / Komm, Dad! I
come over herüberkommen (zu/nach), vorbeikommen (bei) III 2 (30) **come up with sth.** etwas haben, kommen auf etwas (Idee, Vorschlag) III 2 (32)
▶ S. 180 (to) come …
comedian [kəˈmiːdiən] Komiker/in, Komödiant/in III 5 (91)
comedy [ˈkɒmədi] Comedyshow, Komödie II
comma [ˈkɒmə] Komma II
°**comment** [ˈkɒment] Kommentar
  °**make a comment** einen Kommentar abgeben
°**commentator** [ˈkɒmənteɪtə] (Radio-, Fernseh-)Kommentator/in
community [kəˈmjuːnəti] Gemeinde; Gemeinschaft III 3 (55)
°**company** [ˈkʌmpəni] Firma
compare [kəmˈpeə] vergleichen
compete [kəmˈpiːt]: **compete in sth.** an etwas teilnehmen (Wettkampf) III 5 (83)
competition [ˌkɒmpəˈtɪʃn] Wettbewerb II
°**complete** [kəmˈpliːt] vervollständigen
°**completely** [kəmˈpliːtli] vollständig
computer [kəmˈpjuːtə] Computer I
concentrate [ˈkɒnsntreɪt]: **concentrate (on sth.)** sich konzentrieren (auf etwas) III 5 (88)
concert [ˈkɒnsət] Konzert II **a one-hour concert** ein einstündiges Konzert III 3 (51)
conclusion [kənˈkluːʒn] Schluss(folgerung) III 3 (51)
conditions (pl) [kənˈdɪʃnz] Verhältnisse, Bedingungen III 3 (53)
°**conflict** [ˈkɒnflɪkt] Konflikt
connect [kəˈnekt] verbinden, verknüpfen III 1 (17) **be connected** verbunden sein III 2 (38)
°**conservation** [ˌkɒnsəˈveɪʃn] (Umwelt-)Schutz, Erhaltung
consonant [ˈkɒnsənənt] Konsonant, Mitlaut II
content [ˈkɒntent] Inhalt III 1 (17)
contest [ˈkɒntest] Wettbewerb III 3 (55)
context [ˈkɒntekst] (Satz-, Text-)Zusammenhang, Kontext II
continue [kənˈtɪnjuː]:
1. **continue sth.** etwas fortsetzen III 2 (38)
2. sich fortsetzen, weitergehen III 4 (77)
conversation [ˌkɒnvəˈseɪʃn] Gespräch, Unterhaltung II
cook [kʊk] kochen; zubereiten III 3 (47)
cool [kuːl]:
1. cool I
2. kühl II
3. **cool off** sich abkühlen III 3 (60)
coordinator [kəʊˈɔːdɪneɪtə] Koordinator/in III 4 (69)
copy [ˈkɒpi]:
1. kopieren, abschreiben I
2. Kopie; Exemplar II

corner [ˈkɔːnə] Ecke I **corner shop** Laden an der Ecke; Tante-Emma-Laden I **on the corner of Church Road and London Road** Church Road, Ecke London Road II
cornflakes [ˈkɔːnfleɪks] Cornflakes I
correct [kəˈrekt]:
1. richtig, korrekt II
2. korrigieren, verbessern II
°**correction** [kəˈrekʃn] Korrektur, Berichtigung
corridor [ˈkɒrɪdɔː] Gang, Korridor III 2 (40)
cost [kɒst], **cost, cost** kosten II
costume [ˈkɒstjuːm] Kostüm, Verkleidung II
cottage [ˈkɒtɪdʒ] Häuschen, Cottage II
cough [kɒf]: **have a cough** Husten haben II
could [kʊd], [kəd]:
1. he could … er konnte … I we couldn't … [ˈkʊdnt] wir konnten nicht … I
2. What could be better? Was könnte besser sein? II
▶ S. 188 möglich – wahrscheinlich – sicherlich
count [kaʊnt] zählen I **count to ten** bis zehn zählen
°**countess** [ˈkaʊntəs], [ˈkaʊntes] Gräfin
country [ˈkʌntri] Land (Staat) II
countryside [ˈkʌntrisaɪd] Landschaft, (ländliche) Gegend II
county [ˈkaʊnti] Grafschaft (in Großbritannien) I
couple [ˈkʌpl]: **a couple** ein Paar; ein paar III 4 (78)
course [kɔːs] Kurs, Lehrgang I
courtyard [ˈkɔːtjɑːd] Innenhof II
cousin [ˈkʌzn] Cousin, Cousine I
cover [ˈkʌvə]:
1. bedecken, zudecken III 3 (54)
°2. abdecken
°3. **inside cover** Umschlaginnenseite
cow [kaʊ] Kuh I
crab [kræb] Krebs I
crash [kræʃ] crashen II
cream [kriːm] Sahne I
°**create** [kriˈeɪt] (er)schaffen, hervorbringen
crib sheet [ˈkrɪb ʃiːt] (infml) Spickzettel, Merkzettel I
cricket [ˈkrɪkɪt] Cricket I
°**criterion** [kraɪˈtɪəriən], pl **criteria** Kriterium
cross [krɒs] überqueren; sich kreuzen II
°**cross out** [ˌkrɒs ˈaʊt] durchstreichen
crossword [ˈkrɒswɜːd] Kreuzworträtsel III 3 (48)
crowd [kraʊd] (Menschen-)Menge II
crowded [ˈkraʊdɪd] voller Menschen; überfüllt III 1 (16)
crown [kraʊn] Krone II
cruel [ˈkruːl] grausam III 3 (53)
cruise [kruːz] Kreuzfahrt, Schiffsreise, Bootsfahrt III 3 (45)
cry [kraɪ] schreien; weinen II

cue [kjuː] Stichwort, Signal (Theater) III 5 (88)
culture [ˈkʌltʃə] Kultur III 1 (13)
cup [kʌp]: **a cup of tea** eine Tasse Tee I **World Cup** Weltmeisterschaft III 3 (55)
cupboard [ˈkʌbəd] Schrank I
curious [ˈkjʊəriəs] wissbegierig, neugierig III 4 (66)
currency [ˈkʌrənsi] Währung III 4 (68)
curry [ˈkʌri] Curry(gericht) III 1 (16)
cut [kʌt], **cut, cut** schneiden II **Cut!** Schnitt! (beim Filmen) II

D

dad [dæd] Papa, Vati I
dance [dɑːns]:
1. tanzen I
2. Tanz II
dance floor [ˈdɑːns flɔː] Tanzfläche II
dancer [ˈdɑːnsə] Tänzer/in II
danger [ˈdeɪndʒə] Gefahr II
dangerous [ˈdeɪndʒərəs] gefährlich I
dark [dɑːk]:
1. dunkel I
2. Dunkelheit III 2 (40)
darkness [ˈdɑːknəs] Dunkelheit, Finsternis III 1 (11)
darling [ˈdɑːlɪŋ] Schatz, Liebling III 3 (61)
daughter [ˈdɔːtə] Tochter II
day [deɪ] Tag I **all day** den ganzen Tag II **day of the week** Wochentag I **get/have a day off** einen Tag frei bekommen/haben III 3 (51) **go on day trips** Tagesausflüge machen II
dead [ded] tot I
dear [dɪə]:
1. Oh dear! Oje! II
2. dear liebe(r, s) II
death [deθ] Tod III 4 (79)
December [dɪˈsembə] Dezember I
decide [dɪˈsaɪd] beschließen, sich entscheiden II
decision [dɪˈsɪʒn] Entscheidung III 4 (69)
deck [dek] Deck, Terrasse I
°**decline** [dɪˈklaɪn] zurückgehen
deep [diːp] tief II
deer [dɪə], pl **deer** Reh, Hirsch II
°**defeat** [dɪˈfiːt] besiegen
defend [dɪˈfend]: **defend sb./sth. (against sb./sth.)** jn./etwas verteidigen (gegen jn./etwas) II
°**defender** [dɪˈfendə] Verteidiger/in
delicious [dɪˈlɪʃəs] köstlich, lecker II
demonstration [ˌdemənˈstreɪʃn] Demonstration, Vorführung II
dentist [ˈdentɪst] Zahnarzt/-ärztin II
describe sth. (to sb.) [dɪˈskraɪb] (jm.) etwas beschreiben II
description [dɪˈskrɪpʃn] Beschreibung III 5 (89)
°**deserted** [dɪˈzɜːtɪd] verlassen
design [dɪˈzaɪn]:
1. entwerfen, konstruieren, entwickeln

English – German

III 3 (48)
2. Design; Gestaltung; Konstruktion III 3 (48) **design and technology** Design und Technik I
designer [dɪˈzaɪnə] Designer/in II
desk [desk] Schreibtisch I
dessert [dɪˈzɜːt] Nachtisch, Nachspeise I
destroy [dɪˈstrɔɪ] zerstören II
detail [ˈdiːteɪl] Detail, Einzelheit III 1 (15)
dialogue [ˈdaɪəlɒg] Dialog I
diary [ˈdaɪəri] Tagebuch; Kalender I
dictionary [ˈdɪkʃənri] alphabetisches Wörterverzeichnis, Wörterbuch I
did [dɪd] siehe **do**
die [daɪ] sterben I
different [ˈdɪfrənt] verschieden; anders I **it was no different** es war nicht anders III 3 (60)
difficult [ˈdɪfɪkəlt] schwierig, schwer III 2 (39)
dining room [ˈdaɪnɪŋ ruːm] Esszimmer II
dinner [ˈdɪnə] Abendessen, Abendbrot I **have dinner** zu Abend essen I
°**dinosaur** [ˈdaɪnəsɔː] Dinosaurier I
direct [dəˈrekt], [daɪˈrekt] direkt III 5 (90)
°**directions** (pl) [dəˈrekʃənz]: **stage directions** Regieanweisungen I
director [dəˈrektə]:
1. Leiter/in III 2 (41)
2. Regisseur/in II
dirty [ˈdɜːti] schmutzig II
disappear [ˌdɪsəˈpɪə] verschwinden II
disco [ˈdɪskəʊ] Disko I
°**discuss sth.** [dɪˈskʌs] über etwas diskutieren, etwas besprechen I
discussion [dɪˈskʌʃn] Diskussion III 4 (69)
disease [dɪˈziːz] (ansteckende) Krankheit III 4 (79)
dishes (pl) [ˈdɪʃɪz]: **clear the dishes** das Geschirr abräumen III 2 (40) **wash the dishes** das Geschirr abwaschen, spülen I
dislike [dɪsˈlaɪk] nicht mögen, nicht leiden können III 4 (74)
dislikes [dɪsˈlaɪks]: **likes and dislikes** (pl) Vorlieben und Abneigungen I
°**distance** [ˈdɪstəns] Entfernung I
ditch [dɪtʃ] Graben III 4 (78)
dive in [daɪv ˈɪn] (mit dem Kopf voran) hineinspringen III 3 (60)
divorced [dɪˈvɔːst] geschieden I
dizzy [ˈdɪzi] schwindlig III 2 (24)
do [duː], **did, done** machen, tun I **do sport** Sport treiben I °**Does it now?** Tatsächlich? / Ist das so? I **Don't go.** [dəʊnt] Geh nicht. I **he doesn't have time** er hat keine Zeit I
°**dock** [dɒk] Hafen I
°**dockland(s)** [ˈdɒklænd] Hafenviertel I
doctor [ˈdɒktə] Arzt/Ärztin, Doktor II
dog [dɒg] Hund I **walk the dog** mit dem Hund rausgehen, den Hund ausführen III 4 (77)
dolphin [ˈdɒlfɪn] Delfin III 5 (83)
done [dʌn] siehe **do**
door [dɔː] Tür I

doorbell [ˈdɔːbel] Türklingel II
dorsal fin [ˌdɔːsl ˈfɪn] Rückenflosse III 5 (84)
double [ˈdʌbl] Doppel- I
down [daʊn] hinunter, herunter; nach unten I **down there** dort unten II **up and down** auf und ab; rauf und runter I
downhill [ˌdaʊnˈhɪl] bergab III 2 (38)
downstairs [ˌdaʊnˈsteəz] unten; nach unten (im Haus) I
downstream [ˌdaʊnˈstriːm] flussabwärts III 2 (34)
draft [drɑːft] Entwurf II
drama [ˈdrɑːmə] Schauspiel; darstellende Kunst II
drank [dræŋk] siehe **drink**
draw [drɔː], **drew, drawn** zeichnen I
drawing [ˈdrɔːɪŋ] Zeichnung I
drawn [drɔːn] siehe **draw**
°**dreadlocks** (pl) [ˈdredlɒks] Dreadlocks, Rastalocken I
dream [driːm] Traum I
dress [dres] Kleid I
dress up [ˌdres ˈʌp]:
1. sich verkleiden II
2. sich schick anziehen II
drew [druː] siehe **draw**
drink [drɪŋk]:
1. **(drank, drunk)** trinken I
2. Getränk I
drive [draɪv], **drove, driven** (mit dem Auto) fahren I
driven [ˈdrɪvn] siehe **drive**
drop [drɒp] fallen III 2 (34) **drop sth.** etwas fallen lassen II
drove [drəʊv] siehe **drive**
drown [draʊn] ertrinken III 3 (60)
drum [drʌm] Trommel I **drums** (pl) Schlagzeug I **play the drums** Schlagzeug spielen I
drummer [ˈdrʌmə] Trommler/in; Schlagzeuger/in III 1 (24)
drunk [drʌŋk] siehe **drink**
dry [draɪ] trocken III 5 (94)
during [ˈdjʊərɪŋ] während III 1 (15)
▶ S. 175 German "während"
DVD [ˌdiːviːˈdiː] DVD I

E

each [iːtʃ] jeder, jede, jedes (einzelne) II
each other [iːtʃ ˈʌðə] sich (gegenseitig), einander III 1 (20)
ear [ɪə] Ohr I
early [ˈɜːli] früh I
earn [ɜːn] verdienen (Geld) III 3 (51)
earphones (pl) [ˈɪəfəʊnz] Ohrhörer, Kopfhörer II
earth [ɜːθ] Erde (der Planet) II **on earth** auf der Erde II
east [iːst] Osten; nach Osten; östlich III 1 (11) **eastbound** [ˈiːstbaʊnd] Richtung Osten III 1 (18)
Easter [ˈiːstə] Ostern III 4 (77)

eastern [ˈiːstən] östlich, Ost- III 4 (66)
easy [ˈiːzi] leicht, einfach I
eat [iːt], **ate, eaten** essen I
eaten [ˈiːtn] siehe **eat**
edge [edʒ] Rand, Kante III 2 (34)
edit [ˈedɪt] bearbeiten; schneiden (Film, Video) I
editor [ˈedɪtə] Redakteur/in; Herausgeber/in III 4 (69)
education [ˌedʒuˈkeɪʃn] (Schul-, Aus-) Bildung; Erziehung III 1 (15)
°**EEC** [ˌiː iːˈsiː] EWG (Europäische Wirtschaftsgemeinschaft) I
°**effect** [ɪˈfekt] Wirkung I
e.g. [ˌiː ˈdʒiː] z.B. (zum Beispiel) II
egg [eg] Ei I
°**Egyptian** [iˈdʒɪpʃn] ägyptisch, Ägypter/in I
eight [eɪt] acht I
either [ˈaɪðə], [ˈiːðə]: **not ... either** auch nicht II
electronic [ɪˌlekˈtrɒnɪk] elektronisch III 4 (72)
element [ˈelɪmənt] Element III 5 (93)
elephant [ˈelɪfənt] Elefant I
eleven [ɪˈlevn] elf I
else [els]: **anything else** sonst noch etwas III 5 (88) **everybody else** alle anderen; sonst jeder III 5 (88) **no one else** niemand anders; niemand sonst III 5 (88) **someone else** jemand anders III 5 (88) **what else?** was (sonst) noch? III 5 (88) **who else?** wer (sonst) noch? III 5 (88)
▶ S. 195 else
email [ˈiːmeɪl] E-Mail I
emigrate [ˈemɪgreɪt] auswandern, emigrieren III 4 (79)
empty [ˈempti] leer III 2 (30)
encore [ˈɒŋkɔː] Zugabe II
end [end]:
1. Ende, Schluss I
2. enden; beenden III 3 (51)
ending [ˈendɪŋ] Ende, (Ab-)Schluss II
enemy [ˈenəmi] Feind/in I
energy [ˈenədʒi] Energie, Kraft III 2 (38)
engineer [ˌendʒɪˈnɪə] Ingenieur/in III 3 (48)
English [ˈɪŋglɪʃ] Englisch; englisch I **in English** auf Englisch I
enjoy [ɪnˈdʒɔɪ] genießen III 1 (10) **Enjoy yourself.** Viel Spaß! / Amüsiere dich gut! III 5 (GF/167)
enough [ɪˈnʌf] genug I
enter [ˈentə]:
1. betreten, hineingehen in II
°2. eintragen I
entertainment [ˌentəˈteɪnmənt] Unterhaltung III 5 (91)
entry [ˈentri]:
1. Eintrag, Eintragung (im Tagebuch, Wörterbuch) II
2. Eintritt, Zutritt III 1 (14)
equipment (no pl) [ɪˈkwɪpmənt] Ausrüstung III 3 (58)

Dictionary

escape [ɪˈskeɪp]:
1. fliehen III 5 (87)
2. Flucht III 5 (87)

especially [ɪˈspeʃli] besonders, vor allem III 4 (79)

etc. (et cetera) [etˈsetərə] usw. (und so weiter) II

EU, the [ˌiː ˈjuː] die Europäische Union III 4 (68)

°**Eurasian** [juˈreɪʒn] eurasisch

euro [ˈjʊərəʊ] Euro III 4 (68)
▶ S. 189 Pounds and euros

Europe [ˈjʊərəp] Europa III 1 (10)

European Union, the [ˌjʊərəpiːən ˈjuːniən] die Europäische Union III 4 (68)

eurozone [ˈjʊərəʊzəʊn] Eurozone III 4 (71)

even [ˈiːvn] sogar II **not even** (noch) nicht einmal II

even if [ˈiːvn ˌɪf] selbst wenn II

evening [ˈiːvnɪŋ] Abend I **in the evening** abends, am Abend I **this evening** heute Abend II

event [ɪˈvent] Ereignis II

ever [ˈevə] jemals II **better than ever** besser als je zuvor II **for ever** (für) immer; ewig II

every day/colour/boat [ˈevri] jeder Tag / jede Farbe / jedes Boot I

everybody [ˈevribɒdi] jeder; alle I

everyday [ˈevrideɪ] Alltags- I

everyone [ˈevriwʌn] jeder; alle I

everything [ˈevriθɪŋ] alles II

everywhere [ˈevriweə] überall II

exact [ɪɡˈzækt] genau III 1 (16)

exactly [ɪɡˈzæktli] genau III 1 (24)

example [ɪɡˈzɑːmpl] Beispiel II

except [ɪkˈsept] außer, bis auf II

excited [ɪkˈsaɪtɪd] aufgeregt, gespannt I

exciting [ɪkˈsaɪtɪŋ] aufregend, spannend I

exclamation mark [ˌekskləˈmeɪʃn mɑːk] Ausrufezeichen II

Excuse me, ... [ɪkˈskjuːz miː] Entschuldigung, ... / Entschuldigen Sie, ... II

exercise [ˈeksəsaɪz] Aufgabe, Übung I

exercise book [ˈeksəsaɪz bʊk] Schulheft, Übungsheft I

°**exhibit** [ɪɡˈzɪbɪt] Ausstellungsstück

expect [ɪkˈspekt] erwarten III 1 (13)

°**expenses** (pl) [ɪkˈspensɪz]: **travel expenses** Reisekosten

expensive [ɪkˈspensɪv] teuer I

experience [ɪkˈspɪəriəns]:
1. Erfahrung(en) III 3 (51)
°2. Erlebnis

°**experiment** [ɪkˈsperɪmənt] experimentieren

explain sth. to sb. [ɪkˈspleɪn] jm. etwas erklären, erläutern I

°**explanation** [ˌekspləˈneɪʃn] Erklärung

explore [ɪkˈsplɔː] erkunden, erforschen III 3 (45)

export [ˈekspɔːt] Export, Ausfuhr III 4 (79)

°**export** [ɪkˈspɔːt] ausführen, exportieren

expression [ɪkˈspreʃn] Ausdruck III 4 (73)

extraordinary [ɪkˈstrɔːdnri] außergewöhnlich III 5 (82)

eye [aɪ] Auge I °**in your eyes** aus deiner Sicht; deiner Meinung nach

F

°**fab: the Fab Four** [fæb] die fabelhaften Vier (Bezeichnung für die Beatles)

°**fabulous** [ˈfæbjələs] fabelhaft

face [feɪs] Gesicht I

facial expression [ˌfeɪʃl ɪkˈspreʃn] Gesichtsausdruck, Mimik III 4 (73)

fact [fækt] Tatsache, Fakt III 1 (14) **in fact** eigentlich, in Wirklichkeit III 1 (14)

°**fact sheet** Info-Blatt

fair [feə] fair, gerecht I

°**fairy** [ˈfeəri] Fee

fall [fɔːl], **fell, fallen** fallen, stürzen; hinfallen I **fall asleep** einschlafen I

fallen [ˈfɔːlən] siehe **fall**

false [fɔːls] falsch III 1 (11)

family [ˈfæməli] Familie I **a family of four** eine vierköpfige Familie III 1 (15) **the Bell family** (die) Familie Bell I °**family name** Familienname, Nachname **family tree** (Familien-)Stammbaum I **host family** Gastfamilie I

famine [ˈfæmɪn] Hungersnot III 4 (79)

famous (for) [ˈfeɪməs] berühmt (für, wegen) II

fan [fæn] Fan, Anhänger/in I

fantastic [fænˈtæstɪk] fantastisch I

far [fɑː] weit (entfernt) I **so far** bis jetzt; bis hierher II

farm [fɑːm] Bauernhof, Farm I

farmer [ˈfɑːmə] Bauer/Bäuerin, Landwirt/in I

farmhouse [ˈfɑːmhaʊs] Bauernhaus III 5 (95)

fashion [ˈfæʃn] Mode II

fast [fɑːst] schnell I **be fast** vorgehen (Uhr) III 1 (19)

fat [fæt] dick, fett I

father [ˈfɑːðə] Vater I

fault [fɔːlt] Schuld, Fehler III 5 (88)

favourite [ˈfeɪvərɪt]: **my favourite animal** mein Lieblingstier I

February [ˈfebruəri] Februar I

fed [fed] siehe **feed**

feed [fiːd], **fed, fed** füttern I **feeding time** Fütterungszeit I

feedback (no pl) [ˈfiːdbæk] Rückmeldung, Feedback III 1 (17)

feel [fiːl], **felt, felt** fühlen; sich fühlen I; sich anfühlen III 2 (30) **I feel sick.** Mir ist schlecht. II **I don't feel well** Ich fühle mich nicht gut. / Mir geht's nicht gut. II

feeling [ˈfiːlɪŋ] Gefühl II

feet [fiːt] Plural von **foot** II

fell [fel] siehe **fall**

felt [felt] siehe **feel**

felt pen [felt ˈpen] Filzstift II

fence [fens] Zaun II

ferry [ˈferi] Fähre I

festival [ˈfestɪvl] Fest, Festival II

few [fjuː]: **a few** ein paar, einige II

field [fiːld] Feld, Acker, Weide II

°**fiercely** [ˈfɪəsli]: **fight fiercely** heftig, erbittert kämpfen

fight [faɪt]:
1. (fought, fought) kämpfen I **fight sb.** jn. bekämpfen II
2. Kampf, Schlägerei III 4 (66)

fighter [ˈfaɪtə] Kämpfer/in II

figure [ˈfɪɡə]:
1. Zahl, Ziffer III 1 (15)
2. Figur, Gestalt III 2 (40)

file [faɪl]: **background file** Hintergrundinformation(en) I **grammar file** Zusammenfassung der Grammatik jeder Unit I **skills file** Übersicht über Lern- und Arbeitstechniken I

fill [fɪl] füllen III 1 (24)

film [fɪlm]:
1. filmen I
2. Film I °**film-maker** Filmemacher/in

fin [fɪn] Flosse III 5 (84) **dorsal fin** Rückenflosse III 5 (84)

final [ˈfaɪnl]:
1. Finale, Endspiel I
2. letzte(r, s), End- III 3 (56)

finally [ˈfaɪnəli] endlich, schließlich III 2 (40)

find [faɪnd], **found, found** finden I **Find someone who ...** Finde jemanden, der ... I **find sth. out** etwas herausfinden II °**find out about sth.** sich über etwas informieren

fine [faɪn] fein I **Fine, thanks.** Gut, danke. I

finger [ˈfɪŋɡə] Finger II

finish [ˈfɪnɪʃ]:
1. enden I
2. **finish sth.** etwas beenden; mit etwas fertig werden/sein I
°3. **finish sth.** etwas vervollständigen; etwas abschließen

finished [ˈfɪnɪʃt]: **We're finished.** Wir sind fertig. I

fire [ˈfaɪə] Feuer II

fireplace [ˈfaɪəpleɪs] Kamin II

firework [ˈfaɪəwɜːk] Feuerwerkskörper II

fireworks (pl) [ˈfaɪəwɜːks] Feuerwerk II

first [fɜːst] zuerst, als Erstes I **at first** zuerst, anfangs, am Anfang II **the first day** der erste Tag I

°**first-aid kit** [fɜːst ˈeɪd ˌkɪt] Erste-Hilfe-Kasten

fish [fɪʃ]:
1. pl **fish** Fisch I
2. **fish sth. out** etwas herausfischen III 2 (34)

fishing [ˈfɪʃɪŋ] Fischerei III 5 (84)

five [faɪv] fünf I

flag [flæɡ] Fahne, Flagge II

English – German

flash [flæʃ] Lichtblitz ॥ **a flash of lightning** ein Blitz ॥
flat [flæt] Wohnung ।
flew [fluː] siehe **fly**
floor [flɔː]:
1. Fußboden ।
2. Stock(werk) ॥
flower ['flaʊə] Blume; Blüte ॥
flown [fləʊn] siehe **fly**
fly [flaɪ], **flew, flown** fliegen ॥
folk [fəʊk] (pl, infml) Leute ॥ 4 (78)
follow ['fɒləʊ] folgen ׀ **Follow me.** Folg(t) mir. ׀ °**the following ...** die folgenden ...
food [fuːd] Essen; Lebensmittel; Futter ׀
foot [fʊt], pl **feet** [fiːt] Fuß ॥
football ['fʊtbɔːl] Fußball ॥
°**footpath** ['fʊtpɑːθ] Fußweg, Pfad
footprint ['fʊtprɪnt] Fußabdruck ॥
for [fɔː], [fə] für ׀ **for ever** (für) immer; ewig ॥ **for example** zum Beispiel ׀ **for hours/weeks/...** seit Stunden/Wochen/... ॥ 2 (20) **for miles** meilenweit ॥ **for the first time** zum ersten Mal ॥ 1 (14) **What's for lunch?** Was gibt es zum Mittagessen? ׀ **What's for homework?** Was haben wir als Hausaufgabe auf? ׀
foreground ['fɔːɡraʊnd] Vordergrund ॥
forest ['fɒrɪst] Wald ॥
forget [fə'ɡet], **forgot, forgotten** vergessen ׀
forgot [fə'ɡɒt] siehe **forget**
forgotten [fə'ɡɒtn] siehe **forget**
fork [fɔːk] Gabel ॥
form [fɔːm]:
1. Form ׀
2. bilden, formen ॥ 4 (66)
forward ['fɔːwəd]: **look forward to sth.** sich auf etwas freuen ॥
▶ S. 180 (to) look ...
fought [fɔːt] siehe **fight**
foul [faʊl] Foul ॥ 3 (58)
found [faʊnd]:
1. siehe **find**
2. gründen ॥ 3 (48)
°**fountain** ['faʊntən] Brunnen
four [fɔː] vier ׀ **a family of four** eine vierköpfige Familie ॥ 1 (15)
free [friː]:
1. frei ׀ **free time** Freizeit, freie Zeit ׀ **free-time activities** Freizeitaktivitäten ׀ **free kick** Freistoß ॥ 3 (58)
2. kostenlos ॥ °**for free** umsonst
°**freedom** ['friːdəm] Freiheit ॥
°**freeze frame** ['friːz freɪm] Standbild
French [frentʃ] Französisch ׀
fresh [freʃ] frisch ॥
Friday ['fraɪdeɪ], ['fraɪdi] Freitag ॥
friend [frend] Freund/in ׀
friendly ['frendli] freundlich ׀
fries (pl) [fraɪz] Pommes frites ॥
°**fringe** [frɪndʒ] Rand (das Fringe-Festival findet am Rande des offiziellen Edinburger Festivals statt)
frog [frɒɡ] Frosch ׀

from [frɒm], [frəm] aus, von ׀ **from ... to ...** von ... bis ... ׀
front [frʌnt] Vorderseite ׀ **in front of** vor (räumlich) ׀ **to the front** nach vorne ॥ °**front inside cover** vordere Umschlaginnenseite
frown [fraʊn] die Stirn runzeln ॥
fruit [fruːt] Obst, Früchte; Frucht ׀
fruit salad Obstsalat ׀
full (of) [fʊl] voll ॥ **full sentence** ganzer Satz ॥
full stop [,fʊl 'stɒp] Punkt ॥
fun [fʌn] Spaß ॥ **have fun** Spaß haben, sich amüsieren ׀ **make fun of sb./sth.** sich über jn./etwas lustig machen ॥ 2 (30) **That sounds fun.** Das klingt nach Spaß. ׀ **Was it fun?** Hat es Spaß gemacht? ׀
funeral ['fjuːnərəl] Trauerfeier ॥ 3 (61)
funny ['fʌni] witzig, komisch ׀
fun park ['fʌn pɑːk] Vergnügungspark ॥
furniture (no pl) ['fɜːnɪtʃə] Möbel ॥ 2 (30) **The furniture is new.** Die Möbel sind neu. ॥ 2 (30) **a piece of furniture** ein Möbel(stück) ॥ 2 (30)
further ['fɜːðə] weiter ॥
furthest ['fɜːðɪst] am weitesten ॥
future ['fjuːtʃə]:
1. Zukunft ॥
2. zukünftige(r, s) ॥

G

°**Gaelic** ['ɡeɪlɪk] Gälisch (die irische Sprache)
gallery ['ɡæləri] Galerie ॥ 1 (12)
game [ɡeɪm] Spiel ׀
°**gap** [ɡæp] Lücke **Mind the gap!** etwa: Vorsicht, Lücke!
garage ['ɡærɑːʒ], ['ɡærɪdʒ] Garage ׀
garden ['ɡɑːdn] Garten ׀
gardening ['ɡɑːdnɪŋ] Gärtnern, Gartenarbeit ׀
gate [ɡeɪt] Tor, Pforte, Gatter ॥
gave [ɡeɪv] siehe **give**
gel [dʒel] Gel ॥
°**general** ['dʒenrəl] allgemeine(r, s)
°**generation** [,dʒenə'reɪʃn] Generation ׀
gently ['dʒentli] behutsam, sanft ॥ 5 (95)
geography [dʒi'ɒɡrəfi] Geografie ׀
German ['dʒɜːmən] Deutsch; deutsch ׀ **in German** auf Deutsch ׀
get [ɡet], **got, got**:
1. bekommen ׀ **Did you get it?** (infml) Hast du es mitbekommen/verstanden? ׀ **get paid** Geld bekommen ॥ 4 (70) **get sth.** (sich) etwas besorgen, (sich) etwas holen ॥
2. gelangen, (hin)kommen ׀ **get in touch (with sb.)** (mit jm.) Kontakt aufnehmen; **get** (mit jm.) in Verbindung setzen ׀ **get in(to) a car/taxi** in ein Auto/Taxi einsteigen ॥ **get into**

trouble in Schwierigkeiten geraten, Ärger kriegen ॥ 2 (40) **get on a bus/train/plane** in einen Bus/Zug, in ein Flugzeug einsteigen ॥ **get off a bus/boat** aus einem Bus/Boot aussteigen ׀ **get out of a car** aus einem Auto aussteigen ॥
▶ S. 177 off
3. **get on** vorankommen, zurechtkommen ॥
4. **get up** aufstehen ׀
5. **get angry/cold/...** wütend/kalt/... werden ׀ **get ready (for)** sich fertig machen (für), sich vorbereiten (auf) ॥
ghost [ɡəʊst] Geist, Gespenst ׀
giant ['dʒaɪənt] Riese ॥ 4 (66)
giraffe [dʒə'rɑːf] Giraffe ׀
girl [ɡɜːl] Mädchen ׀
girlfriend ['ɡɜːlfrend] Freundin ॥ 4 (76)
give [ɡɪv], **gave, given**: geben ׀ **give a talk (about)** einen Vortrag / eine Rede halten (über) ॥ **give sb. a lift** jn. mitnehmen ॥ **give sb. a hug** jn. umarmen ॥ **give up** aufgeben ॥ 2 (30)
give sb. a hard time jn. fertig machen, jm. einheizen ॥ 5 (89)
given ['ɡɪvn] siehe **give**
glad [ɡlæd] froh, dankbar ॥ 4 (79)
glass [ɡlɑːs] Glas ॥ **a glass of water** ein Glas Wasser ॥
glasses (pl) ['ɡlɑːsɪz] (eine) Brille ॥
°**glen** [ɡlen] Tal (bes. schottisch)
glove [ɡlʌv] Handschuh ॥
glue [ɡluː] Klebstoff ׀
glue stick ['ɡluː stɪk] Klebestift ׀
go [ɡəʊ], **went, gone**:
1. gehen; fahren ׀ **go by** (time) vergehen, vorübergehen (Zeit) ॥ 2 (34) **go down** untergehen (Sonne) ׀ **go for a walk** spazieren gehen, einen Spaziergang machen ׀ **go green/hard/...** grün/hart/... werden ॥ °**go hungry** hungern **go in** hineingehen ॥ **go on 1.** weiterreden, fortfahren; weitermachen ׀ **2.** im Gang sein; andauern ॥ 1 (21) **go on day trips** Tagesausflüge machen ॥ **go red** rot werden, erröten ॥ **go together** zusammenpassen, zueinander passen ॥ 1 (12) **go with sth.** zu etwas gehören, zu etwas passen ׀ **Here we go.** Los geht's. / Jetzt geht's los. ׀ **I'm going to sing a song.** Ich werde ein Lied singen. / Ich habe vor ein Lied zu singen. ॥
2. **Have a go.** Versuch's mal. ׀
goal [ɡəʊl] Tor (Sport) ॥ 3 (55) **goal net** Tornetz ॥ 3 (55)
goalkeeper ['ɡəʊlkiːpə] Torwart, Torfrau ॥ 3 (58)
goat [ɡəʊt] Ziege ॥
God [ɡɒd] Gott ॥ 4 (74)
go-kart ['ɡəʊ kɑːt] Gokart ॥
gold [ɡəʊld]:
1. Gold ׀
2. golden, Gold- ॥
°**golden** ['ɡəʊldn] golden

Dictionary

gone [gɒn] *siehe* **go be gone** weg sein, nicht (mehr) da sein III 4 (77)
good [gʊd]:
1. gut I **be good at kung fu** gut sein in Kung-Fu; gut Kung-Fu können I **Good luck!** Viel Glück! I **Good morning.** Guten Morgen. I
2. brav II
Goodbye. [ˌgʊdˈbaɪ] Auf Wiedersehen. I
good-looking [ˌgʊdˈlʊkɪŋ] gutaussehend I
goods *(pl)* [gʊdz] Waren, Güter I
got [gɒt]:
1. *siehe* **get**
2. **Have you got …?** Haben Sie …? / Hast du …? / Habt ihr …? II
government [ˈgʌvənmənt] Regierung III 4 (79)
grab [græb] schnappen, packen III 2 (34)
gram (g) [græm] Gramm I
grammar file [ˈgræmə ˌfaɪl] Zusammenfassung der Grammatik I
grandfather [ˈgrænfɑːðə] Großvater I
grandma [ˈgrænmɑː] Oma I **at Grandma's (house/flat)** bei Oma II
grandmother [ˈgrænmʌðə] Großmutter I
grandpa [ˈgrænpɑː] Opa I
grandparents *(pl)* [ˈgrænpeərənts] Großeltern I
grass [grɑːs] Gras; Rasen II
grave [greɪv] Grab II
gravestone [ˈgreɪvstəʊn] Grabstein III 4 (79)
great [greɪt] großartig I
green [griːn] grün I
grew [gruː] *siehe* **grow**
grey [greɪ] grau I
groan [grəʊn]:
1. Stöhnen II
2. stöhnen II
ground [graʊnd]:
1. (Erd-)Boden II °**rugby/football ground** Rugby-/Fußballplatz
2. **ground sb.** jm. Hausarrest/Ausgehverbot erteilen III 2 (32)
group (of) [gruːp] Gruppe I
grow [grəʊ], **grew, grown**:
1. anbauen, anpflanzen I
2. wachsen II
3. **grow up** [ˌgrəʊ ˈʌp] erwachsen werden; aufwachsen III 3 (51)
grown [grəʊn] *siehe* **grow**
guard [gɑːd]:
1. Wachposten, Wache II
2. bewachen III 1 (15)
guess [ges] raten, erraten, schätzen I **Guess what, Dad …** Stell dir vor, Papa … / Weißt du was, Papa … I
guest [gest] Gast III 4 (73)
guide [gaɪd] Fremdenführer/in; Reiseleiter/in II
guidebook [ˈgaɪdbʊk] Reiseführer III 3 (47)
guinea pig [ˈgɪni pɪg] Meerschweinchen I

guitar [gɪˈtɑː] Gitarre I **play the guitar** Gitarre spielen I
gym [dʒɪm] Turnhalle I
gymnastics [dʒɪmˈnæstɪks] Gymnastik, Turnen I

H

habitat [ˈhæbɪtæt] Lebensraum III 5 (92)
had [hæd] *siehe* **have**
hair [heə] Haar, Haare I
hairdresser [ˈheədresə] Friseur/in III 2 (31)
half [hɑːf], *pl* **halves** [hɑːvz] Halbzeit I **half past ten** halb elf (10.30 / 22.30) I **at half-time** zur Halbzeit III 3 (56) °**half the population** die Hälfte der Bevölkerung
hall [hɔːl]: **town hall** Rathaus II
hamburger [ˈhæmbɜːgə] Hamburger II
hammer [ˈhæmə]:
1. Hammer III 2 (30)
2. hämmern III 2 (35)
hamster [ˈhæmstə] Hamster II
hand [hænd]:
1. Hand I **Clap your hands.** Klatscht in die Hände. II **put your hand up** sich melden III 5 (84)
2. **hand sth. in** etwas abgeben; etwas einreichen II
handout [ˈhændaʊt] Handout, Handzettel III 5 (92)
hang [hæŋ], **hung, hung:** hängen II °**hang up** aufhängen
happen (to) [ˈhæpən] geschehen, passieren (mit) II
happy [ˈhæpi] glücklich, froh I
harbour [ˈhɑːbə] Hafen I
hard [hɑːd] schwer, schwierig; hart I **give sb. a hard time** jn. fertig machen, jm. einheizen; III 5 (89) **go hard** *(bread)* hart werden II
°**harmonica** [hɑːˈmɒnɪkə] Mundharmonika
has [hæz]: **he/she has** er/sie hat I
hat [hæt] Hut II
hate [heɪt] hassen III 5 (94)
have [hæv], [həv], **had, had** haben I **Have a go.** Versuch's mal. I **have breakfast** frühstücken I **have lunch/dinner** zu Mittag/Abend essen I **have fun** Spaß haben, sich amüsieren I **have to do** tun müssen I **I'll have a tea/…** Ich nehme einen Tee/… *(beim Essen, im Restaurant)* II **May I have a word with you?** Kann ich Sie kurz sprechen? II
have got [hæv ˈgɒt], [həv ˈgɒt], **had, had** haben II **Have you got …?** Haben Sie …? / Hast du …? / Habt ihr …? I
hay [heɪ] Heu II
he [hiː] er I

head [hed]
1. Kopf I
2. **head for sth.** auf etwas zusteuern/zugehen/zufahren III 1 (19)
headache [ˈhedeɪk]: **have a headache** Kopfschmerzen haben II
°**heading** [ˈhedɪŋ] Überschrift
°**headquarters** [ˌhedˈkwɔːtəz] Zentrale, Hauptsitz
head teacher [ˌhed ˈtiːtʃə] Schulleiter/in III 2 (37)
headword [ˈhedwɜːd] Stichwort *(im Wörterbuch)* III 2 (32)
°**health service** [ˈhelθ ˌsɜːvɪs] Gesundheitswesen
hear [hɪə], **heard, heard** hören I
heard [hɜːd] *siehe* **hear**
heart [hɑːt] Herz I
°**heath** [hiːθ] Heide
heather [ˈheðə] Heide(kraut) III 5 (94)
heaven [ˈhevn] Himmel *(im religiösen Sinn)* III 4 (70)
heavy [ˈhevi] schwer *(von Gewicht)* II **heavy rain** starker Regen, heftiger Regen II
held [held] *siehe* **hold**
hell [hel] Hölle III 4 (72)
Hello. [həˈləʊ] Hallo. / Guten Tag. I
help [help]:
1. Hilfe I
2. helfen I **Help yourself.** Greif zu! / Bedien dich! III 5 (GF/167)
helper [ˈhelpə] Helfer/in I
her [hɜː], [hə]:
1. ihr, ihre I **her best friend** ihr bester Freund / ihre beste Freundin I
2. sie; ihr I
here [hɪə] hier; hierher I **Here we go.** Los geht's. / Jetzt geht's los. I **Here you are.** Bitte sehr. / Hier bitte. II **near here** (hier) in der Nähe I **over here** hier herüber I **up here** hier oben; nach hier oben II
°**heritage** [ˈherɪtɪdʒ]: **World Heritage Site** Welterbestätte
hero [ˈhɪərəʊ], *pl* **heroes** Held/in III 2 (38)
hers [hɜːz] ihrer, ihre, ihrs II
herself [hɜːˈself] sich III 5 (85)
hid [hɪd] *siehe* **hide**
hidden [ˈhɪdn] *siehe* **hide**
hide [haɪd], **hid, hidden** sich verstecken, etwas verstecken I
°**hieroglyphics** *(pl)* [ˌhaɪərəˈglɪfɪks] Hieroglyphen(schrift)
high [haɪ] hoch I
highland [ˈhaɪlənd]: **the Highlands** *(pl)* das schottische Hochland III 5 (83)
highlight [ˈhaɪlaɪt] hervorheben, markieren *(mit Textmarker)* II
°**high-tech company** [ˌhaɪˈtek] High-tech-Firma
hill [hɪl] Hügel I
him [hɪm] ihn; ihm I
himself [hɪmˈself] sich III 5 (85)
hip [hɪp] Hüfte III 1 (24)

English – German

his [hɪz]:
1. **his friend** sein Freund / seine Freundin I
2. seiner, seine, seins II

hiss [hɪs] zischen II

°**historical** [hɪˈstɒrɪkl] historisch

history [ˈhɪstri] Geschichte I **natural history** Naturkunde III 1 (14)

hit [hɪt], **hit, hit**:
1. prallen, stoßen gegen I
2. schlagen II
3. treffen II

hobby [ˈhɒbi] Hobby I

hold [həʊld], **held, held** halten I **Hold on a minute.** Bleib / Bleiben Sie am Apparat. *(am Telefon)* II **hold onto sth.** sich an etwas festhalten III 1 (24) °**hold sth. up** etwas aufhalten, etwas hochhalten

hole [həʊl] Loch II

holiday [ˈhɒlədeɪ] Urlaub II **be on holiday** in Urlaub sein II **go on holiday** in Urlaub fahren II

holidays *(pl)* [ˈhɒlədeɪz] Ferien I

home [həʊm] Heim, Zuhause I **at home** daheim, zu Hause I **be home to ...** Heimat sein für etwas; etwas beheimaten III 1 (15) **come/go home** nach Hause kommen/gehen I

hometown [ˌhəʊmˈtaʊn] Heimatstadt I

homework [ˈhəʊmwɜːk] Hausaufgabe(n) I **Do your homework.** Mach deine Hausaufgaben. I **What's for homework?** Was haben wir als Hausaufgabe auf? I

honour [ˈɒnə] Ehre II

hope [həʊp] hoffen I

horn [hɔːn] Horn III 3 (52)

horror [ˈhɒrə]: **in horror** entsetzt III 5 (94)

horse [hɔːs] Pferd I °**on horseback** [ˈhɔːsbæk] zu Pferd

hospital [ˈhɒspɪtl] Krankenhaus II

host family [ˈhəʊst fæməli] Gastfamilie II

hostel [ˈhɒstl] Herberge, Wohnheim III 2 (34)

hot [hɒt] heiß I

hotel [həʊˈtel] Hotel II

hour [ˈaʊə] Stunde I **an hour** pro Stunde III 1 (15) **a one-hour concert** ein einstündiges Konzert III 3 (51) °**ring out the hour** durch den (Glocken-)Schlag die Uhrzeit bekanntgeben

house [haʊs] Haus I

how [haʊ] wie I **How are you?** Wie geht's? / Wie geht es dir/euch? I **How do you know (about ...)?** Woher weißt/kennst du ...? III 1 (10) **How do you like it?** Wie findest du es (sie/ihn)? / Wie gefällt es (sie/er) dir? I **How many?** Wie viele? I **How much?** Wie viel? I **How much are ...?** Was kosten ...? I **How much is ...?** Was kostet ...? I **How old are you?** Wie alt bist du? I **how to do sth.** wie man etwas macht / machen kann / machen soll III 2 (42)
▶ S. 183 Question words + to-infinitive

°**however** [haʊˈevə] jedoch

hug [hʌg]:
1. jn. umarmen II
2. **give sb. a hug** jn. umarmen II

huge [hjuːdʒ] riesig, sehr groß III 1 (10)

hundred [ˈhʌndrəd]: **a/one hundred** einhundert I

hung [hʌŋ] *siehe* **hang**

hungry [ˈhʌŋgri]: **be hungry** hungrig sein, Hunger haben I °**go hungry** hungern

hurry [ˈhʌri] eilen; sich beeilen II **hurry up** sich beeilen I

hurt [hɜːt], **hurt, hurt**: schmerzen, wehtun; verletzen II

hyphen [ˈhaɪfən] Bindestrich II

I

I [aɪ] ich I **I'm from Plymouth.** Ich bin/komme aus Plymouth. I **I'm two years old.** Ich bin zwei Jahre alt. I

ice [aɪs] Eis II

ice cream [ˌaɪs ˈkriːm] (Speise-)Eis I

iced tea [ˌaɪst ˈtiː] Eistee II

ICT [ˌaɪ siː ˈtiː] Informations- und Kommunikationstechnologie I

ID card [ˌaɪ ˈdiː kɑːd] Personalausweis III 4 (68)

idea [aɪˈdɪə] Idee; Vorstellung I

identify [aɪˈdentɪfaɪ]: **identify sb./sth. (by sth.)** jn./etwas identifizieren (anhand von etwas) III 5 (83)

if [ɪf]:
1. wenn, falls II **even if** selbst wenn II **if-clause** Nebensatz mit *if* III 2 (36)
2. ob III 3 (51)
3. **as if** als ob III 4 (71)

ill [ɪl] krank I

illness [ˈɪlnəs] Krankheit III 4 (79)

imagine sth. [ɪˈmædʒɪn] sich etwas vorstellen I

immediately [ɪˈmiːdiətli] sofort III 4 (77)

impolite [ˌɪmpəˈlaɪt] unhöflich III 4 (66)

important [ɪmˈpɔːtnt] wichtig I

impossible [ɪmˈpɒsəbl] unmöglich II

impression [ɪmˈpreʃn] Eindruck III 4 (64)

improve [ɪmˈpruːv] verbessern; sich verbessern III 1 (17)

in [ɪn] in I **be in** zu Hause sein II **come in** hereinkommen I **in 1580** im Jahr 1580 I **in a loud voice** mit lauter Stimme II °**in class** im Unterricht **in front of** vor *(räumlich)* I **in German** auf Deutsch I **in the afternoon** nachmittags, am Nachmittag I **in the attic** auf dem Dachboden I **in the evening** abends, am Abend I **in the morning** morgens, vormittags, am Morgen/Vormittag I **in the photo** auf dem Foto I **in the world** auf der Welt II

°**independent** [ˌɪndɪˈpendənt] unabhängig

Indian [ˈɪndiən] Inder/in; indisch II

indirect [ˌɪndəˈrekt], [ˌɪndaɪˈrekt] III 5 (90)

°**industry** [ˈɪndəstri] verarbeitende Industrie; Fertigungsindustrie

infinitive [ɪnˈfɪnətɪv] Infinitiv III 2 (36)

°**influence** [ˈɪnfluəns] beeinflussen

information (about/on) *(no pl)* [ˌɪnfəˈmeɪʃn] Information(en) (über) I **Information and Communications Technology** Informations- und Kommunikationstechnologie I

inside [ˌɪnˈsaɪd]:
1. drinnen; nach drinnen I
2. die Innenseite; das Innere III 1 (14)
3. **inside sth.** innerhalb von etwas I
°4. **inside cover** Umschlaginnenseite

instead [ɪnˈsted] stattdessen II **instead of** [ɪnˈsted əv] anstelle von, statt III 1 (16)

instrument [ˈɪnstrəmənt] Instrument I

°**insurance** [ɪnˈʃʊərəns] Versicherung

interaction [ˌɪntərˈækʃn] Interaktion, Umgang III 4 (73)

interest [ˈɪntrəst] interessieren III 5 (91)

interested [ˈɪntrəstɪd]: **be interested (in)** sich interessieren (für), interessiert sein (an) I

interesting [ˈɪntrəstɪŋ] interessant I

international [ˌɪntəˈnæʃnəl] international III 3 (45)

interrupt [ˌɪntəˈrʌpt] unterbrechen II

interview [ˈɪntəvjuː]:
1. Interview II
2. interviewen, befragen I

into [ˈɪntʊ]:
1. **into the kitchen** in die Küche (hinein) I
2. **be into sth.** *(infml)* etwas mögen, auf etwas stehen III 1 (10)

introduce sth./sb. (to sb.) [ˌɪntrəˈdjuːs] etwas/jn. (jm.) vorstellen II

introduction [ˌɪntrəˈdʌkʃn] Einleitung, Einführung III 3 (51)

invade (a country) [ɪnˈveɪd] (in ein Land) einmarschieren I

invent [ɪnˈvent] erfinden III 3 (48)

invitation (to) [ˌɪnvɪˈteɪʃn] Einladung (zu, nach) I

invite sb. (to) [ɪnˈvaɪt] jn. einladen (zu) II

irregular [ɪˈregjələ] unregelmäßig II

is [ɪz]: **Is it Monday?** Ist es Montag? I **Is that you?** Bist du's? / Bist du das? I **The book is ...** Das Buch kostet ... I

island [ˈaɪlənd] Insel I

isle [aɪl] (kleine) Insel, Eiland III 5 (83)

isn't [ˈɪznt]: **he/she/it isn't (= is not)** er/sie/es ist nicht ... I

°**IT** [ˌaɪ ˈtiː] Informationstechnologie

Dictionary

it [ɪt] er, sie, es I
it's ... (= it is) [ɪts] er/sie/es ist ... I
itself [ɪt'self] sich III 5 (85)
its name [ɪts] sein Name / ihr Name I

J

jacket ['dʒækɪt] Jacke II
jam [dʒæm] Marmelade I
January ['dʒænjuəri] Januar I
jealous ['dʒeləs] neidisch (auf); eifersüchtig (auf) III 5 (94)
jeans (pl) [dʒiːnz] Jeans I
jeep [dʒiːp] Jeep III 4 (75)
jewels (pl) ['dʒuːəlz] Juwelen III 1 (15)
jigsaw ['dʒɪgsɔː] Puzzle II
job [dʒɒb]:
1. Job, (Arbeits-)Stelle I
2. Aufgabe II
join [dʒɔɪn]:
1. **join a club** in einen Klub eintreten; sich einem Klub anschließen I
2. **join in (sth.)** (bei etwas) mitmachen III 2 (35)
joke [dʒəʊk] Witz I
journey ['dʒɜːni] Reise, Fahrt II
judo ['dʒuːdəʊ] Judo I
juggle sth. ['dʒʌgl] mit etwas jonglieren II
juggler ['dʒʌglə] Jongleur/in II
juice [dʒuːs] Saft II
July [dʒuˈlaɪ] Juli I
jump [dʒʌmp]:
1. springen I **jump up** aufspringen, hochspringen II
2. Sprung I
junction ['dʒʌŋkʃn] (Straßen-)Kreuzung III 4 (77)
June [dʒuːn] Juni I
just [dʒʌst]:
1. (einfach) nur, bloß I
2. gerade (eben), soeben II **just after ...** gleich nachdem ...; kurz nachdem ... II **just then** genau in dem Moment; gerade dann II
3. **just like** genau wie ... II

K

°**kaleidoscope** [kəˈlaɪdəskəʊp] Kaleidoskop
kayak ['kaɪæk] Kajak III 5 (84)
keep [kiːp], **kept, kept**:
1. aufheben; aufsparen; aufbewahren III 5 (85)
2. **keep doing sth.** etwas immer wieder / immer weiter tun; etwas ständig tun III 2 (40)
°3. **keep fit** gesund/fit bleiben
°4. **keep to a plan** einen Plan einhalten
kept [kept] siehe **keep**

key [kiː]:
1. Schlüssel II
2. Schlüssel- II
keyword ['kiːwɜːd] Schlüsselwort I
kick [kɪk]:
1. treten III 4 (77)
2. **free kick** Freistoß III 3 (58)
kid [kɪd] Kind I
kill [kɪl] töten II
kilogram, kilo (kg) ['kɪləgræm], ['kiːləʊ] Kilogramm, Kilo I
kilometre (km) ['kɪləmiːtə], [kɪ'lɒmɪtə] Kilometer I **square kilometre** Quadratkilometer II
°**kilt** [kɪlt] Schottenrock
kind [kaɪnd]:
1. **a kind of ...** eine Art (von) ... I
2. freundlich, nett II
king [kɪŋ] König I
kingdom ['kɪŋdəm] Königreich III 1 (14)
kiss [kɪs] küssen; sich küssen II
kit [kɪt] Ausrüstung I °**first-aid kit** Erste-Hilfe-Kasten
kitchen ['kɪtʃɪn] Küche I
knee [niː] Knie II
kneel [niːl], **knelt, knelt** knien II
knelt [nelt] siehe **kneel**
knew [njuː] siehe **know**
knife [naɪf], pl **knives** [naɪvz] Messer II
knight [naɪt] Ritter II
knock (on sth.) [nɒk] (an)klopfen (an etwas) III 5 (95)
know [nəʊ], **knew, known** wissen; kennen I **I don't know.** Ich weiß (es) nicht. I **know about sth.** sich mit etwas auskennen; über etwas Bescheid wissen II **..., you know.** ..., weißt du. / ..., wissen Sie. I
known [nəʊn] siehe **know**
kung fu [ˌkʌŋ 'fuː] Kung Fu I

L

label ['leɪbl]:
1. beschriften; etikettieren II
2. Beschriftung; Schild, Etikett II
lain [leɪn] siehe **lie**
lake [leɪk] (Binnen-)See I
lamb [læm] Lamm II
lamp [læmp] Lampe I °**lamp post** Laternenpfahl
land [lænd]:
1. landen, an Land gehen II
2. Land II
language ['læŋgwɪdʒ] Sprache I
laptop ['læptɒp] Laptop III 4 (68)
large [lɑːdʒ] groß II
°**lark** [lɑːk] Lerche
°**lass** [læs] Mädel, Mädchen (bes. schottisch, nordenglisch)
last [lɑːst]:
1. **last Friday** letzten Freitag I **last**

year's ... das ... vom letzten Jahr II
2. **at last** endlich, schließlich I
late [leɪt] spät I **You're late.** Du bist spät dran. / Du bist zu spät. I **stay up late** lang aufbleiben II
later ['leɪtə] später I
°**Latin** ['lætɪn] Latein; lateinisch
laugh [lɑːf] lachen I **laugh at sb./sth.** über jn./etwas lachen; jn. auslachen III 2 (30)
laughter ['lɑːftə] Gelächter III 3 (60)
lay [leɪ] siehe **lie**
layout ['leɪaʊt] Layout, Gestaltung III 4 (69)
lead [liːd], **led, led** führen, leiten III 3 (52)
leader ['liːdə] Leiter/in III 3 (52)
learn [lɜːn] lernen I
least ['liːst]: **at least** zumindest, wenigstens II
leave [liːv], **left, left**:
1. verlassen; zurücklassen I
2. lassen II **leave a message** eine Nachricht hinterlassen II **leave sth.** etwas übrig lassen II °**leave sth. out** etwas auslassen
3. (weg)gehen; abfahren II
led [led] siehe **lead**
left [left]:
1. siehe **leave**
2. linke(r, s); (nach) links II **on the left** links/auf der linken Seite II
3. **be left** übrig sein III 4 (66)
leg [leg] Bein II
legend ['ledʒənd] Legende, Sage II
°**leprechaun** ['leprəkɔːn] Leprechaun, Kobold (Wesen der irischen Mythologie)
less (than) [les] weniger (als) III 1 (15)
lesson ['lesn] (Unterrichts-)Stunde I **before lessons** vorm Unterricht I
let [let], **let, let** lassen I **Let me show you ...** Lass mich dir ... zeigen. I **Let's ...** Lass(t) uns ... I **Let's go to England.** Lass(t) uns nach England gehen/fahren. I
letter ['letə]:
1. Brief I
2. Buchstabe I
library ['laɪbrəri] Bibliothek, Bücherei I
lie [laɪ], **lay, lain** liegen II **lie down** sich hinlegen III 2 (40)
life [laɪf], pl **lives** [laɪvz] Leben I
life jacket ['laɪf dʒækɪt] Schwimmweste I
°**lifetime** ['laɪftaɪm] Leben(szeit)
lift [lɪft]:
1. Mitfahrgelegenheit I **give sb. a lift** jn. mitnehmen II
2. Fahrstuhl, Aufzug III 1 (10)
light [laɪt]:
1. Licht I **traffic light** (Verkehrs-)Ampel (oft auch: **traffic lights** (pl)) III 4 (77)
2. **(lit, lit)** anzünden II **light sth. up** etwas erhellen (aufleuchten lassen) II
lightning (no pl) ['laɪtnɪŋ] Blitz II **a flash of lightning** ein Blitz II

English – German

like [laɪk]:
1. mögen, gernhaben I **I like …** Ich mag … I **I'd like …** Ich hätte gern …/Ich möchte … I **I'd like to go** Ich möchte gehen/Ich würde gern gehen I
2. **like boys** wie Jungen I **just like** genau wie … II **like that** so *(auf diese Weise)* I **like this** so II **What's she like?** Wie ist sie (so)? I **What was it like?** Wie war es? II
3. *(infml)* als ob III 4 (71)
4. **He was like: "Stop!"** *(infml)* Und er so: „Stop!" III 4 (70)
likes and dislikes *(pl)* [ˌlaɪks ən ˈdɪslaɪks] Vorlieben und Abneigungen I
line [laɪn]:
1. Zeile I
2. (U-Bahn-)Linie III 1 (18)
3. Reihe III 4 (78)
°4. **line the streets** die Straßen säumen I
link [lɪŋk]:
1. verbinden, verknüpfen III 1 (16)
linking word Bindewort III 1 (16)
°2. Link, Verknüpfung, Verbindung
lion [ˈlaɪən] Löwe I
lip [lɪp] Lippe II
list [lɪst]:
1. Liste I
2. auflisten III 4 (74)
listen [ˈlɪsn] zuhören, horchen I
listen to sb. jm. zuhören I **listen to sth.** sich etwas anhören I **Listen, Justin.** Hör zu, Justin. I
listener [ˈlɪsənə] Zuhörer/in II
lit [lɪt] *siehe* **light**
litter bin [ˈlɪtə bɪn] Abfalleimer II
little [ˈlɪtl] klein I
live [lɪv] leben; wohnen I
living room [ˈlɪvɪŋ ruːm] Wohnzimmer I
local [ˈləʊkl] örtlich, Lokal-; am/vom Ort; einheimisch III 3 (61)
location [ləʊˈkeɪʃn] Position, Standort III 5 (84)
°**loch** [lɒx], [lɒk] (Binnen-)See in Schottland
lonely [ˈləʊnli] einsam I
long [lɒŋ] lang I **(the) longest …** der/die/das längste …; am längsten II
look [lʊk]:
1. schauen I **Look, …** Sieh mal, …/ Schau mal, … I **look after sb.** auf jn. aufpassen; sich um jn. kümmern I **look at** anschauen, ansehen I **look for sth.** etwas suchen I **look forward to sth.** sich auf etwas freuen II **look happy /…** glücklich /… aussehen I **look into sth.** etwas untersuchen, prüfen III 2 (32) **Look out!** Achtung! Aufgepasst! III 5 (82) **look sth. up** etwas nachschlagen III 2 (32) **look up** hochsehen, aufschauen II
▶ S. 180 (to) look …
2. **have a look** nachschauen I **have a look at sth.** einen Blick auf etwas werfen III 2 (40)

lose [luːz], **lost, lost** verlieren II
lost [lɒst] *siehe* **lose**
lot [lɒt]: **a lot** viel I **That helped us a lot.** Das hat uns sehr geholfen. I **lots of …** viel …, viele … I
loud [laʊd] laut I **in a loud voice** mit lauter Stimme II
loudspeaker [ˌlaʊdˈspiːkə] Lautsprecher; Megaphon III 1 (25)
love [lʌv]:
1. lieben, sehr mögen I **I'd love to …** Ich würde sehr gern … II
2. **Love, …** Alles Liebe, … *(Briefschluss)* II
lovely [ˈlʌvli] schön, hübsch, herrlich, entzückend II
luck [lʌk]: **Good luck!** Viel Glück! I
lucky [ˈlʌki]: **be lucky** Glück haben II **Lucky you.** Du Glückspilz. II
lunch [lʌntʃ] Mittagessen I **have lunch** zu Mittag essen I **What's for lunch?** Was gibt es zum Mittagessen? I
lunchtime [ˈlʌntʃtaɪm] Mittagszeit I **at lunchtime** mittags I
lynx [lɪŋks], *pl* **lynx** or **lynxes** Luchs III 5 (92)

M

°**m** *Abkürzung für* **million** *und* **metre**
mad [mæd] verrückt I **go mad** verrückt werden
made [meɪd]:
1. *siehe* **make**
2. **be made of sth.** aus etwas (gemacht) sein II
magazine [ˌmæɡəˈziːn] Zeitschrift I
magic [ˈmædʒɪk] magisch, Zauber- II
magical [ˈmædʒɪkl] zauberhaft, wundervoll; magisch III 2 (40)
mail [meɪl] E-Mail I
main [meɪn] Haupt- I **main clause** Hauptsatz III 2 (36)
°**majestic** [məˈdʒestɪk] majestätisch
make [meɪk], **made, made:**
1. machen; herstellen I °**make a comment** einen Kommentar abgeben I **make a wish** sich etwas wünschen I **make friends** Freunde finden I **make fun of sb./sth.** sich über jn./etwas lustig machen III 2 (30) **make sb. sth.** jn. zu etwas machen II **make sth. up** sich etwas ausdenken III 2 (41) **make sure that …** sich vergewissern, dass …; darauf achten, dass …; dafür sorgen, dass … II
°2. bilden
make-up [ˈmeɪk ʌp] Make-up II
malaria [məˈleəriə] Malaria III 2 (32)
mall [mɔːl] (großes) Einkaufszentrum I
mammal [ˈmæml] Säugetier III 5 (92)
man [mæn], *pl* **men** [men] Mann I
manage sth. [ˈmænɪdʒ] etwas schaffen; etwas zustande bringen III 2 (38)

manager [ˈmænɪdʒə] Trainer/in *(von Sportmannschaften)* III 3 (58)
°**manufacturing** [ˌmænjuˈfæktʃərɪŋ]: **manufacturing industry** verarbeitende Industrie
many [ˈmeni] viele I **How many?** Wie viele? I
map [mæp] Landkarte; Stadtplan I **on the map** auf der Landkarte; auf dem Stadtplan I
March [mɑːtʃ] März I
mark [mɑːk]:
1. markieren I **mark sth. up** etwas markieren, kennzeichnen II
2. **stress mark** Betonungszeichen III 1 (13)
°**marker** [ˈmɑːkə] Kennzeichnung, Markierung
market [ˈmɑːkɪt] Markt I
married (to) [ˈmærɪd] verheiratet (mit) I
marry sb. [ˈmæri] jn. heiraten III 3 (61)
mask [mɑːsk] Maske III 3 (52)
master [ˈmɑːstə] Meister/in I
match [mætʃ]:
1. Spiel, Wettkampf, Match I
°2. **match sth. (to sth.)** etwas (zu etwas) zuordnen
material [məˈtɪəriəl] Material, Stoff III 3 (54)
maths [mæθs] Mathematik I
matter: What's the matter? [ˈmætə] Was ist denn?/Was ist los? I
°**maximum** [ˈmæksɪməm] Höchstbetrag
May [meɪ] Mai I
may [meɪ] dürfen II **May I have a word with you?** Kann ich Sie kurz sprechen? II **they may be …** sie sind vielleicht … III 4 (66)
▶ S. 188 möglich – wahrscheinlich – sicherlich
maybe [ˈmeɪbi] vielleicht I
mayor [meə] Bürgermeister/in II
me [miː] mich; mir I **Me too.** Ich auch. I
meal [miːl] Mahlzeit, Essen II 2 (40)
mean [miːn], **meant, meant:**
1. bedeuten II
2. meinen II
meaning [ˈmiːnɪŋ] Bedeutung II
meant [ment] *siehe* **mean**
meat [miːt] Fleisch I
°**mediate** [ˈmiːdieɪt] vermitteln *(auch sprachlich)*
media [ˈmiːdiə]: **social media** *(pl)* soziale Medien III 5 (83)
mediation [ˌmiːdiˈeɪʃn] Sprachmittlung, Mediation I
meet [miːt], **met, met:**
1. treffen; kennenlernen I **Nice to meet you.** Freut mich, dich/euch/Sie kennenzulernen. I
2. sich treffen I
°**meeting** [ˈmiːtɪŋ] Begegnung
melt [melt] schmelzen II
member [ˈmembə] Mitglied III 3 (49)
°**membership** [ˈmembəʃɪp] Mitgliedschaft

Dictionary

memorial [məˈmɔːriəl] Denkmal; Gedenk- III 5 (95)
memory [ˈmeməri] Erinnerung II
men [men] *Plural von* **man** I
message [ˈmesɪdʒ]:
1. Nachricht II **text message** SMS II
2. Botschaft, Aussage III 1 (19)

met [met] *siehe* **meet**
metre [ˈmiːtə] Meter I
middle [ˈmɪdl] Mitte I **in the middle** in der Mitte I
°**midfielder** [ˌmɪdˈfiːldə] Mittelfeldspieler/in
midnight [ˈmɪdnaɪt] Mitternacht I
might [maɪt]: **it might be the other side** es könnte die andere Seite sein III 4 (66) °**I might have been born in …** Es mag zwar so sein, dass ich in … geboren bin.
▶ S. 188 möglich – wahrscheinlich – sicherlich
mile [maɪl] Meile *(ca. 1,6 km)* II **for miles** meilenweit II
milk [mɪlk] Milch I
°**Milky Way** [ˌmɪlki ˈweɪ] Milchstraße
million [ˈmɪljən] Million II
mind [maɪnd]:
1. **read sb.'s mind** jemandes Gedanken lesen III 5 (94)
2. etwas dagegen haben III 1 (25)
▶ S. 178 (to) mind
°**3. Mind the gap!** *etwa:* Vorsicht, Lücke!

°**mind map** [ˈmaɪnd mæp] Mindmap
mine [maɪn]:
1. meiner, meine, meins II
2. Bergwerk, Mine III 2 (32) **coal mine** Kohlebergwerk III 2 (32)
3. Mine III 2 (32)
4. abbauen III 2 (32)

minibus [ˈmɪnibʌs] Kleinbus I
minute [ˈmɪnɪt] Minute I **wait a minute** Warte einen Moment. / Moment mal. I **a 30-minute ride** eine 30-minütige Fahrt III 3 (51)
mirror [ˈmɪrə] Spiegel II
miss [mɪs]:
1. verpassen I
2. vermissen III 4 (74)

Miss [mɪs]: **Miss Bell** Frau Bell *(übliche Anrede von Lehrerinnen)* I
missing [ˈmɪsɪŋ] verschollen, vermisst III 5 (94) **the missing words** die fehlenden Wörter I **be missing** fehlen II
mist [mɪst] (leichter) Nebel, Dunst(schleier) II
mistake [mɪˈsteɪk] Fehler II **make a mistake** einen Fehler machen II
°**misunderstanding** [ˌmɪsʌndəˈstændɪŋ] Missverständnis
°**mix** [mɪks]:
1. mischen
2. Mischung

mobile (phone) [ˌməʊbaɪl ˈfəʊn] Mobiltelefon, Handy I

model [ˈmɒdl]:
1. Model II
2. Modell III 1 (16)

modern [ˈmɒdən] modern III 3 (51)
moment [ˈməʊmənt] Moment I **at the moment** gerade, im Moment I
Monday [ˈmʌndeɪ], [ˈmʌndi] Montag I **on Monday** am Montag I
money [ˈmʌni] Geld I
monitor [ˈmɒnɪtə] nachverfolgen; überwachen III 5 (84)
monkey [ˈmʌŋki] Affe I
monster [ˈmɒnstə] Monster I
month [mʌnθ] Monat I
monument (to) [ˈmɒnjumənt] Denkmal, Monument (für / zum Gedenken an) III 3 (51)
moon [muːn] Mond I **at full moon** bei Vollmond I
moonlight [ˈmuːnlaɪt] Mondlicht III 2 (40)
moor [mɔː], [mʊə] Hochmoor II
mop [mɒp]:
1. Wischmopp III 2 (42)
2. wischen *(Fußboden)* III 2 (42)

more [mɔː] mehr I **more beautiful (than)** schöner (als) II **one more photo** noch ein Foto; ein weiteres Foto II
morning [ˈmɔːnɪŋ] Morgen, Vormittag I **Good morning.** Guten Morgen. I **in the morning** morgens, vormittags, am Morgen/Vormittag I **tomorrow morning** morgen früh, morgen Vormittag II
°**moron** [ˈmɔːrɒn] *(infml)* Trottel
mosque [mɒsk] Moschee III 3 (55)
most [məʊst]: **most people** die meisten Menschen II **most of them** die meisten von ihnen II **(the) most beautiful** der/die/das schönste …; am schönsten II
mother [ˈmʌðə] Mutter I
motion [ˈməʊʃn] **slow motion** Zeitlupe III 3 (59)
motorbike [ˈməʊtəbaɪk] Motorrad III 4 (70)
mountain [ˈmaʊntən] Berg II
mouth [maʊθ] Mund; Maul I
move [muːv]:
1. bewegen; sich bewegen I
2. **move (to)** umziehen (nach) II **move in** einziehen II **move into a house** einziehen in ein Haus… II

movement [ˈmuːvmənt] Bewegung III 5 (84)
movie [ˈmuːvi] Film III 2 (36)
MP3 player [ˌem piː ˈθriː ˌpleɪə] MP3-Spieler I
Mr Schwarz [ˈmɪstə] Herr Schwarz I
Mrs Schwarz [ˈmɪsɪz] Frau Schwarz I
much [mʌtʃ] viel I **How much …?** Wie viel …? I **How much are …?** Was kosten …? I **How much is …?** Was kostet …? I
mud [mʌd] Schlamm, Matsch II
mug [mʌg]: **a mug (of)** ein Becher II

mum [mʌm] Mama, Mutti I
°**murder** [ˈmɜːdə] ermorden
museum [mjuˈziːəm] Museum I
music [ˈmjuːzɪk] Musik I
musical [ˈmjuːzɪkl]:
1. Musical II
°2. musikalisch

musician [mjuˈzɪʃn] Musiker/in III 2 (31)
must [mʌst] müssen II **you mustn't do it** [ˈmʌsnt] du darfst es nicht tun II
▶ S. 188 möglich – wahrscheinlich – sicherlich
my [maɪ] mein/e I **My birthday is in May.** Ich habe im Mai Geburtstag. I **My birthday is on 5th August.** Ich habe am 5. August Geburtstag. I **My name is …** Ich heiße … I
myself [maɪˈself] mich, mir III 5 (84)

N

name [neɪm]:
1. Name I **My name is …** Ich heiße … I **What's your name?** Wie heißt du? / Wie heißt ihr? I
2. (be)nennen III 3 (61)

narrow [ˈnærəʊ] schmal, eng II
nation [ˈneɪʃn] Nation, Volk III 4 (68)
national [ˈnæʃnəl] national, National- III 2 (34)
natural [ˈnætʃrəl] natürlich III 2 (31)
natural history Naturkunde III 1 (14)
natural world (Welt der) Natur III 2 (31)
navy [ˈneɪvi] Marine I
near [nɪə] in der Nähe von, nahe (bei) I **near here** (hier) in der Nähe I
nearby [ˈnɪəbaɪ]: **a nearby town** eine nahegelegene Stadt II
nearly [ˈnɪəli] fast, beinahe III 4 (66)
necessary [ˈnesəsəri] notwendig III 5 (93)
neck [nek] Hals II
need [niːd] brauchen, benötigen I **need to do sth.** etwas tun müssen II **you needn't do it** [ˈniːdnt] du musst es nicht tun II
°**negative** [ˈnegətɪv] negativ
neighbour [ˈneɪbə] Nachbar/in II
neither [ˈnaɪðə], [ˈniːðə]: **me neither** Ich auch nicht. III 2 (34)
nervous [ˈnɜːvəs] nervös, aufgeregt II
net [net] Netz III 5 (84) **goal net** Tornetz III 3 (55)
never [ˈnevə] nie, niemals I
new [njuː] neu I
news *(no pl)* [njuːz]:
1. Nachrichten I
2. Neuigkeiten II

New Year's Eve [ˌnjuː jɪəz ˈiːv] Silvester II
next [nekst]:
1. **next year's …** das … vom nächsten Jahr II **the next question** die nächste Frage I
2. als Nächstes III 4 (77)
3. **next to** [ˈnekst tʊ] neben II

English – German

nice [naɪs] nett, schön I **Nice to meet you.** Freut mich, dich/euch/Sie kennenzulernen. I
night [naɪt] Nacht I **at night** nachts, in der Nacht I
nil [nɪl] null, Null III 3 (56)
nine [naɪn] neun I
no [nəʊ]:
1. nein I **No, that's wrong.** Nein, das ist falsch. / Nein, das stimmt nicht. I
2. kein, keine I **it was no different** es war nicht anders III 3 (60) **No way!** Auf keinen Fall! / Kommt nicht in Frage! III 1 (20)
nobody ['nəʊbədi] niemand I
nod [nɒd] nicken II
noise [nɔɪz] Geräusch; Lärm III 5 (94)
noisy ['nɔɪzi] laut, lärmend, voller Lärm II
none (of) [nʌn] keine(r, s) (von …) III 4 (78)
no one ['nəʊ wʌn] niemand I
normal ['nɔːməl] normal III 3 (46)
north [nɔːθ] Norden; nach Norden; nördlich III 1 (11) **northbound** ['nɔːθbaʊnd] Richtung Norden III 1 (18)
north-east [ˌnɔːθ ˈiːst] Nordosten; nach Nordosten; nordöstlich III 1 (11)
northern ['nɔːðən] nördlich, Nord- III 4 (66) **north-west** [ˌnɔːθ'west] Nordwesten; nach Nordwesten; nordwestlich III 1 (11)
nose [nəʊz] Nase I
not [nɒt] nicht I **he/she/it is not** er/sie/es ist nicht … I **not till three** erst um drei, nicht vor drei II **not … yet** noch nicht I
note [nəʊt]:
1. Notiz, Mitteilung I **make notes (on/about sth.)** (sich) Notizen machen (über/zu etwas) (zur Vorbereitung) II **take notes (on/about sth.)** (sich) Notizen machen (über/zu etwas) (beim Lesen oder Zuhören) II
2. Note (Musik) III 2 (41)
nothing ['nʌθɪŋ] (gar) nichts I
noun [naʊn] Nomen, Substantiv III 1 (12)
November [nəʊ'vembə] November I
now [naʊ] nun, jetzt I **°Does it now?** Tatsächlich? / Ist das so? **Now that …** Jetzt, wo … / Nun, da … III 4 (78) **right now** jetzt gerade II
nowhere ['nəʊweə] nirgendwo; nirgendwohin III 3 (60) **out of nowhere** (wie) aus dem Nichts III 3 (60)
number ['nʌmbə] Zahl, Nummer, Ziffer I Anzahl III 2 (39)

O

o [əʊ] Null (in Telefonnummern) I
object ['ɒbdʒɪkt], ['ɒbdʒekt] Objekt II
ocean ['əʊʃn] Ozean I
°Och [ɒx] Ach (bes. schottisch)

o'clock [ə'klɒk]: **at 1 o'clock** um 1 Uhr / um 13 Uhr I
October [ɒk'təʊbə] Oktober I
of [ɒv], [əv] von I
of course [əv 'kɔːs] natürlich, selbstverständlich I
off [ɒf]: **Off you go now.** Ab mit euch jetzt! / Los mit euch jetzt! III 1 (20) **be off** aus(geschaltet) sein (Radio, Licht usw.) III 1 (20) **fall off a bike** vom Fahrrad herunterfallen III 1 (20) **get/have a day off** einen Tag frei bekommen/haben III 3 (51) **run off** wegrennen III 1 (20)
▶ S. 177 off
offer ['ɒfə] anbieten II
office ['ɒfɪs] Büro III 2 (41) **ticket office** Fahrkartenschalter; Kasse (für den Verkauf von Eintrittskarten) III 1 (15)
official [ə'fɪʃl]:
1. amtlich, Amts- III 2 (32)
2. Beamte(r), Beamtin III 2 (32)
often ['ɒfn], ['ɒftən] oft I
oh [əʊ]: **Oh, it's you.** Ach, du bist es. I
oil [ɔɪl] Öl III 2 (30)
old [əʊld] alt I **in the old days** früher (einmal) III 4 (79)
°Olympics, the [ə'lɪmpɪks] Olympiade I
on [ɒn] auf I **be on** eingeschaltet sein, an sein (Radio, Licht usw.); laufen, übertragen werden (Programm, Sendung) III 1 (20) **on earth** auf der Erde III **on Monday** am Montag I **on Monday afternoon** am Montagnachmittag I **on the phone** am Telefon II **on the plane** im Flugzeug II **on the radio** im Radio I **on top of each other** übereinander, aufeinander III 1 (15) **on TV** im Fernsehen III 1 (20) **walk/run/… on** weitergehen/-laufen/… II
once [wʌns]:
1. einmal II **°at once** auf einmal **once a week/year** einmal pro Woche/Jahr I
°**2.** einst
one [wʌn] eins I **a one-hour concert** ein einstündiges Konzert III 3 (51) **one all** eins zu eins; eins beide III 3 (56) **one by one** einzeln; einer nach dem anderen II **one night/day** eines Nachts/Tages II **one-syllable** einsilbige(r, s) II **a white one** ein weißer / eine weiße / ein weißes II **this one** diese(r, s) II **two black ones** zwei schwarze II **Which one?** Welche(r, s)? I
online [ˌɒn'laɪn] online II
only ['əʊnli]:
1. nur, bloß I **the only …** der/die/das einzige …; die einzigen… II
2. erst I
onto ['ɒntʊ] auf (… hinauf) I
open ['əʊpən]:
1. öffnen, aufmachen I; sich öffnen I **opening times** (pl) Öffnungszeiten III 1 (15)
2. geöffnet, offen I

opinion [ə'pɪnjən] Meinung III 3 (51) **in my opinion** meiner Meinung nach III 3 (51)
°**opponent** [ə'pəʊnənt] Gegner/in
opposite ['ɒpəzɪt] gegenüber (von) II
or [ɔː] oder I
orange ['ɒrɪndʒ]:
1. orange I
2. Orange, Apfelsine I
order ['ɔːdə]:
1. Reihenfolge I
2. bestellen II
3. ordnen III 3 (58)
organize ['ɔːɡənaɪz] organisieren; ordnen III 2 (38)
°**original** [ə'rɪdʒənl] original, ursprünglich
other ['ʌðə] andere(r, s) I
otter ['ɒtə] Otter II
our ['aʊə] unser/e I
ours ['aʊəz] unserer, unsere, unseres II
ourselves [ɑː'selvz], [aʊə'selvz] uns III 5 (85)
out ['aʊt]:
1. heraus, hinaus, nach draußen II **out and about** unterwegs II
2. **be out** nicht zu Hause sein, nicht da sein II
3. **out of …** ['aʊt_əv] aus … (heraus/hinaus) I
outdoor ['aʊtdɔː] Außen-, im Freien II
outside [ˌaʊt'saɪd]:
1. draußen; nach draußen II **outside the house** vor dem Haus, außerhalb vom Haus II
2. die Außenseite; das Äußere III 1 (14)
over ['əʊvə]:
1. über I **run over (to)** hinüberrennen (zu/nach) II **over to …** hinüber zu/nach … I **over here** hier herüber II **over there** da drüben, dort drüben II
2. **over 4 years** über 4 Jahre; mehr als 4 Jahre I
3. **be over** vorbei / zu Ende sein I
own [əʊn]:
1. besitzen II
2. **my own room/…** mein eigenes Zimmer/… I
3. **on my/your/their/… own** allein II

P

p [piː] Abkürzung für „pence", „penny" I
pack [pæk] packen III 4 (74)
packet ['pækɪt] Packung, Päckchen II
°**paddle** ['pædl] paddeln
page [peɪdʒ] Seite I **What page are we on?** Auf welcher Seite sind wir? I
paid [peɪd]:
1. siehe **pay**
2. **get paid** Geld bekommen III 4 (70)
paint [peɪnt] (an)streichen; (an)malen I
painted ['peɪntɪd] bemalt, angemalt II
painter ['peɪntə] Maler/in III 2 (31)
pair [peə]: **a pair (of)** ein Paar II

Dictionary

palace ['pæləs] Palast, Schloss III 1 (10)
pancake ['pænkeɪk] Pfannkuchen II
panic ['pænɪk]**, panicked, panicked** in Panik geraten III 1 (24)
paper ['peɪpə]:
1. Zeitung I
2. Papier I

parade [pə'reɪd] Parade, Umzug II
paragraph ['pærəgrɑːf] Absatz *(in einem Text)* I
parents *(pl)* ['peərənts] Eltern I
park [pɑːk]:
1. Park I
2. parken III 4 (77)

parliament ['pɑːləmənt] Parlament III 1 (15)
part [pɑːt] Teil I **part of speech** Wortart III 2 (32) **part of the body** Körperteil II **take part in sth.** an etwas teilnehmen I
partner ['pɑːtnə] Partner/in I
party ['pɑːti] Party I
pass [pɑːs]:
1. vergehen, vorübergehen *(Zeit)* III 4 (77)
2. **pass sth./sb.** an etwas/jm. vorbeigehen/vorbeifahren II
3. **pass sth. around** etwas herumgeben, herumreichen II

°**passenger** ['pæsɪndʒə] Passagier/in
passport ['pɑːspɔːt] (Reise-)Pass III 4 (68)
past [pɑːst]:
1. Vergangenheit I
2. **half past ten** halb elf (10.30 / 22.30) I **quarter past ten** Viertel nach zehn (10.15 / 22.15) I
3. vorbei (an), vorüber (an) II

path [pɑːθ] Pfad, Weg I
°**pattern** ['pætn] Muster
pause [pɔːz] innehalten, pausieren; eine Pause einlegen II
pavement ['peɪvmənt] Gehweg, Bürgersteig III 1 (24)
paw [pɔː] Pfote, Tatze I
pay (for sth.) [peɪ]**, paid, paid** (etwas) bezahlen II **get paid** Geld bekommen III 4 (70)
PE [ˌpiːˈiː] Sportunterricht, Turnen I
peace [piːs] Friede, Frieden III 4 (68)
peaceful ['piːsfl] friedlich; friedfertig II
pedestrian [pə'destriən] Fußgänger/in III 4 (77) **pedestrian zone** Fußgängerzone II
pen [pen] Kugelschreiber, Stift, Füller I
°**penalty** ['penəlti] Elfmeter **penalty area** Strafraum
pence [pens] Pence *(Plural von* **penny***)* I
▶ S. 189 Pounds and euros
pencil ['pensl] Bleistift I
pencil case ['pensl keɪs] Federmäppchen I
people ['piːpl]:
1. *(Singular)* Volk III 3 (52)
2. *(Plural)* Leute, Menschen I

pepper ['pepə] Pfeffer I
°**per cent** [pə 'sent] Prozent

perfect ['pɜːfɪkt] perfekt, ideal I
perform [pə'fɔːm] auftreten *(Künstler/in)* III 3 (51)
performer [pə'fɔːmə] Künstler/in III 5 (88)
person ['pɜːsn] Person I
pet [pet] Haustier III 4 (68)
phone [fəʊn]:
1. Telefon I **answer the phone** ans Telefon gehen II **on the phone** am Telefon II
2. **phone sb.** jn. anrufen II

phone call ['fəʊn kɔːl] *(kurz auch:* **call***)* Anruf; Telefongespräch II
photo ['fəʊtəʊ] Foto I **in the photo** auf dem Foto I **take photos** fotografieren, Fotos machen I
photograph ['fəʊtəgrɑːf] fotografieren III 5 (84)
phrase [freɪz] Ausdruck, (Rede-)Wendung I
Physical Education [ˌfɪzɪkl ˌedʒu'keɪʃn] Sportunterricht, Turnen I
piano [pi'ænəʊ] Klavier, Piano I **play the piano** Klavier spielen I
pick [pɪk]: **pick on sb.** auf jm. herumhacken III 5 (88) **pick sb. up** jn. abholen II **pick sth. up** etwas aufheben *(vom Boden)*, etwas hochheben II
picnic ['pɪknɪk] Picknick I
picture ['pɪktʃə] Bild I **in the picture** auf dem Bild I
piece (of) [piːs] ein Stück ... III 2 (30)
pig [pɪg] Schwein I
pink [pɪŋk] pink, rosa I
pipe [paɪp] Pfeife III 4 (71)
°**piper** ['paɪpə] Dudelsackspieler/in
pitch [pɪtʃ] (Sport-)Platz, Spielfeld III 3 (58)
pity ['pɪti]: **It was a pity that ...** Es war schade, dass ... III 1 (22)
pizza ['piːtsə] Pizza I
place [pleɪs] Ort, Platz, Stelle I **in second place** auf dem zweiten Platz; an zweiter Stelle III 5 (96) **take place** stattfinden III 3 (61)
plan [plæn]:
1. Plan I
2. planen II

plane [pleɪn] Flugzeug II **get on a plane** in ein Flugzeug einsteigen II **on the plane** im Flugzeug II
planet ['plænɪt] Planet I
plant [plɑːnt]:
1. Pflanze II
2. pflanzen II

°**plantain** ['plænteɪn] Kochbanane
plantation [plɑːn'teɪʃn] Plantage III 3 (53)
plaster ['plɑːstə] (Heft-)Pflaster I
plastic ['plæstɪk] Plastik, Kunststoff II
plate [pleɪt] **a plate of ...** ein Teller ... I

platform ['plætfɔːm]:
1. Plattform III 5 (91)
2. Bahnsteig, Gleis III 1 (19)

play [pleɪ]:
1. spielen I **play the drums / the guitar / the piano** Schlagzeug/Gitarre/Klavier spielen I
2. abspielen *(CD, DVD)* I
3. Theaterstück I

player ['pleɪə] Spieler/in I
please [pliːz] bitte I
pm: 4 pm [ˌpiː ˈem] 4 Uhr nachmittags / 16 Uhr I
pocket ['pɒkɪt] Tasche *(Manteltasche, Hosentasche usw.)* II
poem ['pəʊɪm] Gedicht II
point [pɔɪnt]:
1. Punkt I **point: 1.6 (one point six)** 1,6 (eins Komma sechs) III 2 (38) **point of view (on sth.)** Standpunkt (in/über/zu etwas) III 2 (42) **from my point of view** aus meiner Sicht III 2 (42) ▶ S. 181 Numbers
2. **point to sth.** auf etwas zeigen, deuten I
3. **point sth. at sb.** etwas auf jn. richten I
4. **point sth. out (to sb.)** (jn.) auf etwas hinweisen III 1 (17)

police *(pl)* [pə'liːs] Polizei III 2 (32) **police officer** Polizist/in I **police station** Polizeiwache, -revier III 4 (68) **The police are on their way.** Die Polizei ist auf dem Weg. III 2 (32)
policeman [pə'liːsmən] Polizist I
policewoman [pə'liːswʊmən] Polizistin III 5 (95)
polite [pə'laɪt] höflich III 4 (66)
pollution [pə'luːʃn] (Umwelt-)Verschmutzung III 5 (84)
pony ['pəʊni] Pony II
pool [puːl] Schwimmbad, Schwimmbecken I
poor [pɔː], [pʊə] arm I
°**pop (music)** [pɒp] Popmusik
popular (with) ['pɒpjələ] populär, beliebt (bei) III 5 (51)
population [ˌpɒpjuˈleɪʃn] Bevölkerung, Einwohner(zahl) III 4 (68)
position [pə'zɪʃn] Platz, Position III 5 (88)
post [pəʊst]:
1. Posting *(auf Blog)*, Blog-Eintrag III 1 (10)
°2. **lamp post** Laternenpfahl

postcard ['pəʊstkɑːd] Postkarte II
poster ['pəʊstə] Poster I
post office ['pəʊst ˌɒfɪs] Postamt II
pot [pɒt] Gefäß; Topf III 3 (52)
potato [pə'teɪtəʊ]**,** *pl* **potatoes** Kartoffel I
pound [paʊnd] Pfund *(britische Währung)* I
▶ S. 189 Pounds and euros
pour [pɔː] gießen II
practical ['præktɪkl] praktisch III 4 (65)

English – German

practice [ˈpræktɪs] Übung I
practise [ˈpræktɪs] üben, trainieren I
predator [ˈpredətə] Raubtier III 5 (92)
°**Premier League** [ˌpremiə ˈliːg] höchste englische Spielklasse (Fußball)
prepare sth. [prɪˈpeə] etwas vorbereiten I
present [ˈpreznt]:
1. Geschenk I
2. Gegenwart II
°3. vorhanden, anwesend
present sth. (to sb.) [prɪˈzent] (jm.) etwas präsentieren, vorstellen II
presentation [ˌprezn̩ˈteɪʃn] Präsentation, Vorstellung II
president [ˈprezɪdənt] Präsident/in III 4 (68)
press [pres] drücken III 2 (40)
pretend [prɪˈtend] so tun, als ob III 2 (34)
pretty [ˈprɪti] hübsch II
price [praɪs] (Kauf-)Preis I
prince [prɪns] Prinz I
princess [ˌprɪnˈses], [ˈprɪnses] Prinzessin II
prison [ˈprɪzn] Gefängnis I
prize [praɪz] Preis, Gewinn II
probable [ˈprɒbəbl] wahrscheinlich III 2 (30)
probably [ˈprɒbəbli] wahrscheinlich II
problem [ˈprɒbləm] Problem I
°**product** [ˈprɒdʌkt] Produkt, Ware
profile [ˈprəʊfaɪl] Profil; Beschreibung, Porträt I
programme [ˈprəʊɡræm] Programm (auch im Theater usw.); (Radio-, Fernseh-)Sendung I
°**prohibit** [prəˈhɪbɪt] verbieten
project [ˈprɒdʒekt] Projekt II
promise [ˈprɒmɪs] versprechen II
promote sth. [prəˈməʊt]:
1. Werbung machen für etwas III 5 (82)
°2. etwas fördern
pronunciation [prəˌnʌnsiˈeɪʃn] Aussprache I
protect sb./sth. (from sb./sth.) [prəˈtekt] jn./etwas (be)schützen (vor jm./etwas) III 5 (84)
°**protection** [prəˈtekʃn] Schutz
protest [prəˈtest] protestieren III 3 (46)
protest [ˈprəʊtest] Protest III 3 (46)
proud (of) [praʊd] stolz (auf) III 4 (66)
°**provide** [prəˈvaɪd] bereitstellen
pub [pʌb] Kneipe, Lokal III 1 (20)
pull [pʊl] ziehen I **pull sth. out** etwas herausziehen II
pullover [ˈpʊləʊvə] Pullover II
punctuation [ˌpʌŋktʃuˈeɪʃn] Zeichensetzung I
punishment [ˈpʌnɪʃmənt] Bestrafung, Strafe III 2 (42)
puppet [ˈpʌpɪt] Marionette, Handpuppe II
purple [ˈpɜːpl] violett, lila I
push [pʊʃ] drücken, schieben, stoßen I
put [pʊt], **put, put** legen, stellen, (etwas wohin) tun I **put sth. down** etwas hinlegen III 2 (30) **put sth. on** etwas anziehen (Kleidung); etwas aufsetzen (Hut, Helm) II °**put sth. together** etwas zusammenstellen **put your hand up** sich melden III 5 (84)

Q

quarter [ˈkwɔːtə]: **quarter past ten** Viertel nach zehn (10.15 / 22.15) I **quarter to eleven** Viertel vor elf (10.45 / 22.45) I
queen [kwiːn] Königin II
question [ˈkwestʃən] Frage I **question mark** Fragezeichen II
queue [kjuː]:
1. Schlange stehen, sich anstellen II
2. Schlange, Reihe (wartender Menschen) III 1 (16)
quick [kwɪk] schnell II
quiet [ˈkwaɪət] ruhig, still, leise I
quite [kwaɪt] ziemlich; völlig, ganz III 3 (47)
quiz [kwɪz] Quiz, Ratespiel I

R

rabbit [ˈræbɪt] Kaninchen I
race [reɪs]:
1. Rennen, (Wett-)Lauf II
2. rasen III 4 (77)
radio [ˈreɪdiəʊ] Radio I **on the radio** im Radio I
rain [reɪn]:
1. Regen II **heavy rain** starker Regen, heftiger Regen II
2. regnen II
rainbow [ˈreɪnbəʊ] Regenbogen III 1 (24)
raincoat [ˈreɪnkəʊt] Regenmantel II
rainforest [ˈreɪnfɒrɪst] Regenwald II
rainy [ˈreɪni] regnerisch II
raise money (for sth.) [reɪz] Geld sammeln (für etwas) II
rally [ˈræli] Rallye II
ran [ræn] siehe **run**
rang [ræŋ] siehe **ring**
rat [ræt] Ratte I
raven [ˈreɪvn] Rabe III 1 (15)
reach [riːtʃ] erreichen III 2 (34) **reach over** die Hand ausstrecken III 5 (94)
react (to) [riˈækt] reagieren (auf) III 1 (17)
read [riːd], **read** [red], **read** [red] lesen I **read sb.'s mind** jemandes Gedanken lesen III 5 (94)
reader [ˈriːdə] Leser/in II
ready [ˈredi] bereit, fertig I
real [ˈriːəl] echt, wirklich II
really [ˈrɪəli] echt, wirklich I
reason [ˈriːzn] Grund, Begründung II
°**rebel** [ˈrebl] sich auflehnen, rebellieren
recipe [ˈresəpi] (Koch-)Rezept II
°**recognize** [ˈrekəɡnaɪz] erkennen
record [rɪˈkɔːd] aufzeichnen (Musik, Daten); dokumentieren (Daten) III 5 (84)
°**record** [ˈrekɔːd] Schallplatte
recorder [rɪˈkɔːdə] Blockflöte II
red [red] rot I **go red** rot werden, erröten II
referee [ˌrefəˈriː] Schiedsrichter/in III 3 (58)
°**referendum** [ˌrefəˈrendəm] Volksentscheid, Referendum
°**refreshment** [rɪˈfreʃmənt] Imbiss, Erfrischung
°**region** [ˈriːdʒən] Region
regional [ˈriːdʒənl] regional III 4 (75)
regular [ˈreɡjələ] regelmäßig II
rehearsal [rɪˈhɜːsl] Probe (Theater) III 5 (88)
°**rehearse** [rɪˈhɜːs] proben
°**relationship** [rɪˈleɪʃnʃɪp] Verhältnis
relax [rɪˈlæks] sich entspannen, sich ausruhen III 5 (85)
religion [rɪˈlɪdʒən] Religion I
remember sth. [rɪˈmembə]:
1. sich an etwas erinnern I
2. an etwas denken; sich etwas merken III 3 (51)
remote (control) [rɪˌməʊt kənˈtrəʊl] Fernbedienung III 1 (20)
repeat [rɪˈpiːt] wiederholen II
reply (to) [rɪˈplaɪ] antworten (auf); erwidern, entgegnen III 1 (10)
report [rɪˈpɔːt]:
1. Bericht, Reportage II
°2. berichten
°**reporter** [rɪˈpɔːtə] Reporter/in
republic [rɪˈpʌblɪk] Republik III 4 (68)
rescue [ˈreskjuː] retten II
research [ˈriːsɜːtʃ] Recherche, Forschung(en) III 4 (69)
reserve [rɪˈzɜːv] reservieren, buchen III 1 (14)
respect [rɪˈspekt] Respekt, Achtung III 3 (52)
responsible [rɪˈspɒnsəbl] verantwortlich II
rest [rest]:
1. ruhen, sich ausruhen III 1 (25)
2. Rest III 2 (42)
restaurant [ˈrestrɒnt] Restaurant III 1 (12)
result [rɪˈzʌlt] Ergebnis, Resultat III 4 (69)
revise [rɪˈvaɪz] überarbeiten; (Lernstoff) wiederholen III 2 (38)
revision [rɪˈvɪʒn] Wiederholung (des Lernstoffs) II
°**revolution** [ˌrevəˈluːʃn] Revolution
rhyme [raɪm] Reim; Vers I
rhythm [ˈrɪðəm] Rhythmus III 1 (24)
rich [rɪtʃ] reich I
ridden [ˈrɪdn] siehe **ride**
ride [raɪd]:
1. Fahrt I; Ritt, Ausritt III 4 (74)
2. (**rode, ridden**) reiten; (Rad) fahren II **ride a bike** Fahrrad fahren I
riding [ˈraɪdɪŋ] Reiten I

Dictionary

right [raɪt]:
1. richtig ı **sb. is right** jemand hat Recht ı **Yes, that's right.** Ja, das ist richtig. / Ja, das stimmt. ı
2. rechte(r, s); (nach) rechts ıı **on the right** rechts/auf der rechten Seite ıı
3. **right now** jetzt gerade ıı
4. **..., right?** ..., nicht wahr? ıı
5. **right behind you** direkt hinter dir, genau hinter dir ıı **right after you** gleich nach dir ıı

ring [rɪŋ]:
1. **(rang, rung)** klingeln, läuten ıı °**ring out the hour** durch den (Glocken-)Schlag die Uhrzeit bekanntgeben ıı
2. Ring ıı

rise up [ˌraɪz ˈʌp], **rose, risen** aufragen, emporragen *(Berge, Säulen, Türme, …)* ııı 4 (66)

risen [ˈrɪzn] siehe **rise**

°**risk assessment** [ˈrɪsk əˌsesmənt] Risikoeinschätzung

°**rival** [ˈraɪvl] Rivale, Rivalin

river [ˈrɪvə] Fluss ı

road [rəʊd] Straße ı **at 8 Beach Road** in der Beach Road 8 ı **in Beach Road** in der Beach Road ı

roar [rɔː] brüllen ııı 1 (16)

roast beef [ˌrəʊst ˈbiːf] Rinderbraten ı

roast potatoes *(pl)* [ˌrəʊst pəˈteɪtəʊz] im Backofen in Fett gebackene Kartoffeln ı

rock [rɒk]:
1. Fels, Felsen ı
2. **rock (music)** Rockmusik ı

rocky [ˈrɒki] felsig, steinig ıı

rode [rəʊd] siehe **ride**

role [rəʊl] Rolle *(in einem Theaterstück, Film)* ıı

roll [rəʊl] rollen ıı

roof [ruːf] Dach ıı

room [ruːm]:
1. Zimmer, Raum ı
2. Platz ııı 3 (54)

rope [rəʊp] Seil ııı 1 (24)

rose [rəʊz] siehe **rise**

rough [rʌf] stürmisch, rau (See) ııı 5 (84)

round [raʊnd] **round the world** um die Welt ıı **round here** hier in der Gegend ııı 4 (74)

roundabout [ˈraʊndəbaʊt] Kreisverkehr ıı

route [ruːt] Strecke, Route ııı 1 (22)

royal [ˈrɔɪəl] königlich ıı

rubber [ˈrʌbə] Radiergummi ı

rubbish [ˈrʌbɪʃ] Müll, Abfall ı

rucksack [ˈrʌksæk] Rucksack ı

°**rugby** [ˈrʌgbi] Rugby

ruin [ˈruːɪn] Ruine ıı

rule [ruːl] Regel, Vorschrift ı

ruler [ˈruːlə] Lineal ı

run [rʌn], **ran, run** rennen, laufen ı **run after sb.** hinter jm. herrennen ı **run around** herumrennen, umherrennen ıı **run off** wegrennen ııı 1 (20) **run on** weiterlaufen ıı **run over (to)** (zu/nach …) hinüberrennen ıı
▶ S. 177 **off**

rung [rʌŋ] siehe **ring** ıı

runner [ˈrʌnə] Läufer/in ıı

S

sad [sæd] traurig ı

said [sed] siehe **say**

sail [seɪl]:
1. segeln ıı **go sailing** segeln; segeln gehen ı **sailing boat** Segelboot ı
°2. fahren *(Schiff)*, auslaufen, in See stechen

sailor [ˈseɪlə] Seemann, Matrose, Matrosin ııı 3 (61)

salad [ˈsæləd] Salat *(als Gericht oder Beilage)* ı **fruit salad** Obstsalat ı

samba [ˈsæmbə] Samba ı

same [seɪm]: **the same as …** der-/die-/dasselbe wie … ı

sand [sænd] Sand ı

sandwich [ˈsænwɪtʃ], [ˈsænwɪdʒ] Sandwich, (zusammengeklapptes) belegtes Brot ı

sang [sæŋ] siehe **sing**

sat [sæt] siehe **sit**

Saturday [ˈsætədeɪ], [ˈsætədi] Samstag, Sonnabend ı **on Saturday afternoon** am Samstagnachmittag ı

save [seɪv] retten ı

saw [sɔː] siehe **see**

say [seɪ], **said, said** sagen ı **Say hello to … for me.** Grüß … von mir. ıı

scan sth. (for sth.) [skæn] etwas (nach etwas) absuchen ııı 1 (24) **scan a text** einen Text schnell nach bestimmten Wörtern/Informationen absuchen ıı

scare sb. [skeə] jn. erschrecken; jm. Angst machen ııı 1 (25)

scared [skeəd] verängstigt ı

scarf [skɑːf], *pl* **scarves** [skɑːvz] Schal ııı 3 (58)

scary [ˈskeəri] unheimlich, gruselig ı

scene [siːn] Szene ı

schedule [ˈʃedjuːl], [ˈskedjuːl,] (Zeit-)Plan, Programm ııı 3 (51)

school [skuːl] Schule ı **at school** in der Schule ı **before school** vor der Schule *(vor Schulbeginn)* ı **in front of the school** vor der Schule *(vor dem Schulgebäude)* ı **school bag** Schultasche ı

science [ˈsaɪəns] Naturwissenschaft ı

scientist [ˈsaɪəntɪst] Naturwissenschaftler/in ııı 2 (30)

scone [skɒn], [skəʊn] kleines rundes Milchbrötchen, leicht süß ı

°**scoop** [skuːp] schöpfen

score [skɔː]:
1. einen Treffer erzielen, ein Tor schießen ı
2. Spielstand; Punktestand ııı 3 (56)

What's the score? Wie steht es? ııı 3 (56)

scream [skriːm]:
1. schreien ıı
2. Schrei ııı 3 (60)

screen [skriːn] Bildschirm ıı

sea [siː] Meer ı

seagull [ˈsiːgʌl] Möwe ı

seal [siːl] Robbe ı

seasick [ˈsiːsɪk] seekrank ııı 5 (84)

seat [siːt] Sitz, Platz ı

second [ˈsekənd]:
1. zweite(r, s) ı **second biggest** zweitgrößte(r, s) ıı
2. Sekunde ıı

see [siː], **saw, seen** sehen; besuchen ı; *(Arzt)* aufsuchen ıı **I see.** Aha! / Verstehe. ııı 1 (10) **See you.** Bis gleich. / Bis bald. ı **…, you see.** …, weißt du. ıı

seem (to be/do) [siːm] (zu sein/zu tun) scheinen ııı 3 (60)

seen [siːn] siehe **see**

sell [sel], **sold, sold** verkaufen ı

send [send], **sent, sent** schicken, senden ı

sent [sent] siehe **send**

sentence [ˈsentəns] Satz ı **full sentence** ganzer Satz ıı **topic sentence** Satz, der in das Thema eines Absatzes einführt ııı 2 (38)

September [sepˈtembə] September ı

service [ˈsɜːvɪs] Gottesdienst ııı 4 (70)

set [set] Satz, Set ı

seven [ˈsevn] sieben ı

several [ˈsevrəl] mehrere, verschiedene ııı 3 (51)

shadow [ˈʃædəʊ] Schatten ıı

shake [ʃeɪk], **shook, shaken** schütteln ıı

shaken [ʃeɪkn] siehe **shake**

shall [ʃæl]: **Shall I …?** Soll ich …? ııı 4 (66)

shape [ʃeɪp] Form, Gestalt ııı 3 (52) **Those glasses are an interesting shape.** Die Brille hat eine interessante Form. ııı 3 (52)

°**shard** [ʃɑːd] Scherbe

shark [ʃɑːk] Hai ı

sharpener [ˈʃɑːpnə] Anspitzer ı

she [ʃiː] sie ı

sheep [ʃiːp], *pl* **sheep** Schaf ıı

sheepdog [ˈʃiːpdɒg] Hütehund ııı 5 (83)

shelf [ʃelf], *pl* **shelves** [ʃelvz] Regal ı

shepherd [ˈʃepəd] Schäfer/in, Schafhirte/-hirtin ııı 5 (94)

°**shimmer** [ˈʃɪmə] schimmern

°**shin guard** [ˈʃɪn gɑːd] Schienbeinschützer ı

shine [ʃaɪn], **shone, shone** scheinen *(Sonne)* ııı 3 (60)

ship [ʃɪp] Schiff ı

°**shipbuilding** [ˈʃɪpbɪldɪŋ] Schiffbau

°**shipyard** [ˈʃɪpjɑːd] (Schiffs-)Werft

shirt [ʃɜːt] Hemd ıı; Trikot ııı 3 (58)

°**shock** [ʃɒk] schockieren, entsetzen

English – German

shocked [ʃɒkt] schockiert, entsetzt II
shoe [ʃuː] Schuh I
shone [ʃɒn] siehe **shine**
shook [ʃʊk] siehe **shake**
°**shooting star** [ˌʃuːtɪŋ 'stɑː] Sternschnuppe
shop [ʃɒp]:
1. Laden I **corner shop** Laden an der Ecke; Tante-Emma-Laden I **shop assistant** Verkäufer/in II
2. einkaufen II
shopper ['ʃɒpə] (Ein-)Käufer/in II
shopping ['ʃɒpɪŋ]: **do the/some shopping** einkaufen gehen; Einkäufe erledigen II **go shopping** einkaufen gehen I **shopping centre** Einkaufszentrum II **shopping mall** (großes) Einkaufszentrum I
shore [ʃɔː] Ufer, Strand II
short [ʃɔːt] kurz I
shorts (pl) [ʃɔːts] Shorts, kurze Hose I
should [ʃʊd], [ʃəd]: **You should …** Du solltest … / Ihr solltet … / Sie sollten … II
▶ S. 188 möglich – wahrscheinlich – sicherlich
shoulder ['ʃəʊldə] Schulter II
shout [ʃaʊt] schreien, rufen I
show [ʃəʊ]:
1. (showed, shown) zeigen I
2. Show, Vorstellung I
shower ['ʃaʊə] Dusche III 4 (72) **have a shower** (sich) duschen III 4 (72)
shown [ʃəʊn] siehe **show**
shy [ʃaɪ] schüchtern, scheu II
sick [sɪk] krank I **be sick** sich übergeben II **I feel sick.** Mir ist schlecht. I **I'm going to be sick.** Ich muss mich übergeben. II
side [saɪd] Seite I
sigh [saɪ] seufzen III 4 (78)
sights (pl) [saɪts] Sehenswürdigkeiten I
sighting ['saɪtɪŋ] Sichtung III 5 (84)
sign [saɪn] Schild; Zeichen I **no sign of …** keine Spur von … III 1 (25)
silent ['saɪlənt] still, leise III 2 (40)
silently ['saɪləntli] lautlos; schweigend III 2 (40)
silky ['sɪlki] seidig I
silly ['sɪli]:
1. albern; blöd I
2. Dummerchen I
°**silver** ['sɪlvə] silbern
similar (to sth./sb.) ['sɪmələ] (etwas/jm.) ähnlich I
since [sɪns]: **since 10 o'clock / last week** seit 10 Uhr / letzter Woche III 1 (20)
sing [sɪŋ], **sang, sung** singen I **sing along (with sb.)** (mit jm.) mitsingen III 2 (35)
singer ['sɪŋə] Sänger/in I
single ['sɪŋɡl] ledig, alleinstehend I
°**singles** (pl) ['sɪŋɡlz] Einzelturnier
°**sir** [sɜː] Sir (höfliche Anrede, z. B. für Kunden, Vorgesetzte oder Lehrer)
siren ['saɪrən] Sirene III 4 (77)
sister ['sɪstə] Schwester I

sit [sɪt], **sat, sat** sitzen; sich setzen I **sit down** sich hinsetzen I **sit up** sich aufsetzen III 2 (40)
°**site** [saɪt]: **social networking site** eine Website zur Bildung und Unterhaltung sozialer Netzwerke **work site** Arbeitsort **World Heritage Site** Welterbestätte
situation [ˌsɪtʃu'eɪʃn] Situation III 1 (21)
six [sɪks] sechs I
size [saɪz] Größe I **What size tea would you like?** Wie groß soll der/dein Tee sein? II
skates [skeɪts] Inlineskates I
skating ['skeɪtɪŋ] Inlineskaten, Rollschuhlaufen I
skill [skɪl] Fertigkeit II **skills file** Übersicht über Lern- und Arbeitstechniken I **study skills** Lern- und Arbeitstechniken I
skirt [skɜːt] Rock II
sky [skaɪ] Himmel II
skyline ['skaɪlaɪn] Skyline; Horizont III 1 (11)
°**skype** [skaɪp] per Skype telefonieren
slave [sleɪv] Sklave, Sklavin III 3 (45)
slavery ['sleɪvəri] Sklaverei III 3 (45)
sleep [sliːp]:
1. (slept, slept) schlafen I
2. Schlaf III 2 (31)
sleepover ['sliːpəʊvə] Schlafparty I
slept [slept] siehe **sleep**
slippery ['slɪpəri] rutschig, glatt III 4 (78)
slow [sləʊ] langsam I **be slow** nachgehen (Uhr) III 1 (19) **slow motion** Zeitlupe III 3 (59)
small [smɔːl] klein I **small talk** Smalltalk (spontan geführtes Gespräch in umgangssprachlichem Ton) III 1 (13)
smell [smel] riechen I **smell sth.** an etwas riechen I **smell good** gut riechen II
smile [smaɪl]:
1. lächeln I **smile at sb.** jn. anlächeln I
2. Lächeln III 4 (78)
smiley ['smaɪli] Smiley I
smoke [sməʊk] rauchen III 4 (71)
smuggle ['smʌɡl] schmuggeln I
smuggler ['smʌɡlə] Schmuggler/in I
smuggling ['smʌɡlɪŋ] der Schmuggel, das Schmuggeln I
snack [snæk] Snack, Imbiss I
snake [sneɪk] Schlange I
sneeze [sniːz] niesen I
snow [snəʊ] Schnee I
°**snowy** ['snəʊi] verschneit
so [səʊ]:
1. also; deshalb, daher I
2. **so cool/nice** so cool/nett I **so far** bis jetzt; bis hierher II
▶ S. 182 such/so
3. **So?** Und? / Na und? I
4. **so that / so** sodass, damit II

social ['səʊʃl]: **social media** (pl) soziale Medien III 5 (83) °**social services** (pl) Sozialwesen
sock [sɒk] Socke II
sofa ['səʊfə] Sofa I
soft [sɒft] weich I **in a soft voice** sanft II
softly ['sɒftli] sanft III 5 (94) **she sang softly** sie sang leise I
sold [səʊld] siehe **sell**
soldier ['səʊldʒə] Soldat/in III 3 (48)
solo ['səʊləʊ] Solo- II
solve [sɒlv] lösen III 3 (59)
some [sʌm] einige, ein paar; etwas I
somebody ['sʌmbədi] jemand I
someone ['sʌmwʌn] jemand I
something ['sʌmθɪŋ] etwas I
sometimes ['sʌmtaɪmz] manchmal I
son [sʌn] Sohn I
song [sɒŋ] Lied, Song I
soon [suːn] bald I
sore [sɔː] wund II **have a sore throat** Halsschmerzen haben II
sorry ['sɒri]: **(I'm) sorry.** Tut mir leid. / Entschuldigung. I **I'm sorry about …** Es tut mir leid wegen … I
°**soul** [səʊl] Seele
sound [saʊnd]:
1. klingen, sich anhören I
2. Geräusch; Klang I
°3. Ton
soup [suːp] Suppe I
south [saʊθ] Süden; nach Süden; südlich III 1 (11) **southbound** ['saʊθbaʊnd] Richtung Süden III 1 (18)
south-east [ˌsaʊθ'iːst] Südosten; nach Südosten; südöstlich III 1 (11)
southern ['sʌðən] südlich, Süd- III 4 (66)
south-west [ˌsaʊθ'west] Südwesten; nach Südwesten; südwestlich III 1 (11)
souvenir [ˌsuːvə'nɪə] Andenken, Souvenir II
spaghetti [spə'ɡeti] Spagetti I
Spanish ['spænɪʃ] spanisch II
speak [spiːk], **spoke, spoken** sprechen I; reden II **speak to sb.** mit jm. sprechen II
speaker ['spiːkə] Sprecher/in I; Redner/in II
special ['speʃl] besondere(r, s) II
speech [spiːtʃ]:
1. (offizielle) Rede II
2. **part of speech** Wortart III 2 (32)
°**speech bubble** ['spiːtʃ bʌbl] Sprechblase
speed [spiːd] Geschwindigkeit III 1 (22)
°**speed sth. up** [ˌspiːd'ʌp] etwas beschleunigen
spell [spel] buchstabieren I
spelling ['spelɪŋ] Rechtschreibung; Schreibweise III 1 (17)
spend [spend], **spent, spent: spend time (on)** Zeit verbringen (mit) **spend money (on)** Geld ausgeben (für) III 5 (84)

two hundred and fifteen **215**

Dictionary

spent [spent] *siehe* **spend**
spin around [ˌspɪn ə'raʊnd], **spun, spun** sich (im Kreis) drehen; herumwirbeln III 4 (77)
°**spirit** ['spɪrɪt] Geist, Seele
splash sb. [splæʃ] jn. nass spritzen III 3 (42)
split screen [ˌsplɪt 'skriːn] geteilter Bildschirm; Bildschirm(auf)teilung III 5 (87)
spoke [spəʊk] *siehe* **speak**
spoken [spəʊkn] *siehe* **speak**
spoon [spuːn] Löffel ॥ °**a spoonful of sth.** ['spuːnfʊl] ein Esslöffel (voll) etwas
sport [spɔːt] Sport; Sportart I **do sport** Sport treiben I
sportsperson ['spɔːtspɜːsn] Sportler/in III 3 (48)
spot [spɒt] Fleck, Punkt I
spread [spred], **spread, spread** (sich) ausbreiten, verbreiten III 3 (61)
spring [sprɪŋ] Frühling I
spun [spʌn] *siehe* **spin**
square kilometre, sq km [skweə] Quadratkilometer ॥
stadium ['steɪdiəm] Stadion III 3 (58)
stage [steɪdʒ] Bühne ॥ °**stage directions** (pl) Regieanweisungen
stairs (pl) [steəz] Treppe; Treppenstufen ॥
stall [stɔːl] (Markt-)Stand ॥
stamp [stæmp] Stempel ॥
stand [stænd], **stood, stood** stehen; sich (hin)stellen ॥ **stand up** aufstehen III 2 (40)
standard ['stændəd] Standard; Standard- III 4 (75)
star [stɑː]:
1. (Film-, Pop-)Star I
2. Stern III 2 (40) ॥ °**shooting star** Sternschnuppe
stare (at sb./sth.) [steə] (jn./etwas an)starren III 4 (74)
°**starfleet** ['stɑːfliːt] Sternenflotte
start [stɑːt] anfangen, beginnen I
starving ['stɑːvɪŋ]: **be starving** einen Riesenhunger haben III 4 (74)
state [steɪt] Staat III 4 (68)
°**statement** ['steɪtmənt] Aussage
station ['steɪʃn] Bahnhof I
stay [steɪ] bleiben I; *(vorübergehend)* wohnen, übernachten III 1 (12) **stay in touch (with sb.)** (mit jm.) Kontakt halten; (mit jm.) in Verbindung bleiben ॥
stay up late lang aufbleiben ॥
steal [stiːl], **stole, stolen** stehlen III 4 (68)
°**steel** [stiːl] Stahl
steep [stiːp] steil III 2 (35)
steer [stɪə] steuern, lenken I
step [step]:
1. Schritt I
2. Stufe III 1 (14)
stick [stɪk]:
1. Stock III 2 (34)

2. (**stuck, stuck**) **stick sth. into sth.** etwas in etwas stechen, stecken ॥
sticky ['stɪki] klebrig ॥
still [stɪl]:
1. (immer) noch I
2. trotzdem, dennoch ॥
°**3.** Standbild
stole [stəʊl] *siehe* **steal**
stolen [stəʊln] *siehe* **steal**
stomach ['stʌmək] Magen ॥
stone [stəʊn] Stein ॥
stood [stʊd] *siehe* **stand**
stop [stɒp]:
1. anhalten, stoppen I **Stop it!** *(infml)* Hör auf (damit)! / Lass das! ॥
2. Halt; Station, Haltestelle ॥
storm [stɔːm] Sturm, Unwetter, Gewitter ॥ °**take the world by storm** die Welt im Sturm erobern
story ['stɔːri] Geschichte, Erzählung I
°**stowaway** ['stəʊəweɪ] blinde(r) Passagier/in
straight on [streɪt ˈɒn] geradeaus weiter ॥
strange [streɪndʒ] seltsam, komisch I
strawberry ['strɔːbəri] Erdbeere ॥
stream [striːm] Bach III 4 (79)
street [striːt] Straße I **at 14 Dean Street** in der Deanstraße 14 I **in Dean Street** in der Dean Street I **line the streets** die Straßen säumen **street artist** Straßenkünstler/in ॥
stress [stres]:
1. Betonung III 1 (13) **stress mark** Betonungszeichen III 1 (13)
°**2.** betonen
°**striker** ['straɪkə] Angreifer/in, Stürmer/in
strong [strɒŋ] stark, kräftig ॥
structure ['strʌktʃə]:
1. strukturieren, gliedern III 3 (58)
°**2.** Struktur, Gliederung
stuck [stʌk] *siehe* **stick**
student ['stjuːdənt] Schüler/in; Student/in I
studio ['stjuːdiəʊ] Studio I
study ['stʌdi] studieren; untersuchen, beobachten; lernen III 2 (30) **study skills** Lern- und Arbeitstechniken I **study poster** Lernposter ॥
stuff [stʌf] Zeug, Kram III 3 (46)
°**stunning** ['stʌnɪŋ] fantastisch, atemberaubend
stupid ['stjuːpɪd] dumm, blöd III 2 (34)
°**style** [staɪl] Stil
sub-clause ['sʌbklɔːz] Nebensatz I
subject ['sʌbdʒɪkt], ['sʌbdʒekt]:
1. Schulfach I
2. Subjekt ॥
°**substitute** ['sʌbstɪtjuːt] Ersatzspieler/in
subtitle ['sʌbtaɪtl] Untertitel I
success [sək'ses] Erfolg III 3 (51)
°**successful** [sək'sesfl] erfolgreich

such [sʌtʃ]: **such a** so ein/e …; solch ein/e … III 2 (41)
▶ S. 182 such/so
suddenly ['sʌdnli] plötzlich, auf einmal I
°**sugar** ['ʃʊgə] Zucker
suggest sth. (to sb.) [sə'dʒest] (jm.) etwas vorschlagen III 4 (69) **Dad suggested that we go to the cinema.** Papa schlug vor, ins Kino zu gehen.
°**suggestion** [sə'dʒestʃən] Vorschlag
suit [suːt] Anzug III 4 (71)
°**sum sth. up** [ˌsʌm ˈʌp] etwas zusammenfassen
summer ['sʌmə] Sommer I
summit ['sʌmɪt] Gipfel III 2 (38)
sun [sʌn] Sonne I
Sunday ['sʌndeɪ], ['sʌndi] Sonntag I
°**sunflower** ['sʌnflaʊə] Sonnenblume
sung [sʌŋ] *siehe* **sing**
sunglasses (pl) ['sʌnglɑːsɪz] (eine) Sonnenbrille I
sunny ['sʌni] sonnig I
sunshine ['sʌnʃaɪn] Sonnenschein III 3 (57)
°**supporter** [sə'pɔːtə] Befürworter/in
sure [ʃʊə], [ʃɔː] sicher ॥ **make sure that …** sich vergewissern, dass …; darauf achten, dass …; dafür sorgen, dass …I
surface ['sɜːfɪs] Oberfläche III 3 (60)
surprise [sə'praɪz]:
1. Überraschung ॥
°**2.** überraschen
surprised [sə'praɪzd] überrascht I
survive [sə'vaɪv] überleben III 3 (53)
swam [swæm] *siehe* **swim**
°**swap** [swɒp] tauschen
sweet [swiːt] süß ॥
sweets (pl) [swiːts] Süßigkeiten ॥
swim [swɪm], **swam, swum** schwimmen I
swimmer ['swɪmə] Schwimmer/in I
swimming pool ['swɪmɪŋ puːl] Schwimmbad, Schwimmbecken I
sword [sɔːd] Schwert I
swum [swʌm] *siehe* **swim**
syllable ['sɪləbl] Silbe ॥ **one-/two-syllable** ein-/zweisilbig ॥
symbol ['sɪmbl] Symbol ॥

T

table ['teɪbl]:
1. Tisch I **table tennis** Tischtennis ॥
2. Tabelle I
take [teɪk], **took, taken** nehmen, mitnehmen; (weg-, hin)bringen I; *(Zeit)* brauchen; dauern ॥ **take notes (on/about sth.)** (sich) Notizen machen (über/zu etwas) *(beim Lesen oder Zuhören)* I **take part in sth.** an etwas teilnehmen ॥ **take photos** fotografieren, Fotos machen I **take place** stattfinden III 3 (61) ॥ **take sb. by the arm** jn. am

English – German

Arm nehmen ‖ **take sth. off** etwas ausziehen *(Kleidung)*; etwas absetzen *(Hut, Helm)* ‖ **take sth. out** etwas herausnehmen ‖ °**take the world by storm** die Welt im Sturm erobern ‖ °**take turns (to do sth.)** sich abwechseln (etwas zu tun)
▶ S. 177 off
takeaway ['teɪkəweɪ] Restaurant/Imbissgeschäft, das auch Essen zum Mitnehmen verkauft; Essen zum Mitnehmen ‖
taken ['teɪkən] *siehe* **take**
talented ['tæləntɪd] begabt, talentiert ‖
talk [tɔːk]:
1. Vortrag, Referat, Rede ‖ **give a talk (about)** einen Vortrag / eine Rede halten (über) I
2. **talk (to)** reden (mit), sich unterhalten (mit) ‖
tall [tɔːl] groß *(Person)*; hoch *(Gebäude, Baum)* ‖
tap [tæp]:
1. tippen, *(vorsichtig)* klopfen ‖ °**she taps her foot** sie wippt mit dem Fuß
2. *(leichtes)* Klopfen III 1 (20)
°**tartan** ['tɑːtn] Schottenkaro, -stoff
task [tɑːsk] Aufgabe I
taste [teɪst] schmecken I
tasty ['teɪsti] lecker ‖
taught [tɔːt] *siehe* **teach**
taxi ['tæksi] Taxi II
tea [tiː] Tee I; *leichte Nachmittags- oder Abendmahlzeit* ‖
teach [tiːtʃ], **taught, taught** unterrichten, lehren III 5 (84) ‖ **teach sb. to do sth.** jm. etwas beibringen, etwas zu tun III 5 (84)
teacher ['tiːtʃə] Lehrer/in I
team [tiːm] Team, Mannschaft I
tear [tɪə] Träne ‖
teaspoon ['tiːspuːn] Teelöffel ‖
teeth [tiːθ] Plural von **tooth**
telephone ['telɪfəʊn] Telefon ‖ **telephone box** Telefonzelle III 1 (15)
tell [tel], **told, told: tell sb. about sth.** jm. von etwas erzählen; jm. über etwas berichten I ‖ **tell sb. the way (to …)** jm. den Weg (nach …) beschreiben ‖ **tell sb. (not) to do sth.** jn. auffordern, etwas (nicht) zu tun; jm. sagen, dass er/sie etwas (nicht) tun soll III 2 (35)
temperature ['temprətʃə] Temperatur, Fieber ‖ **have a temperature** Fieber haben ‖
ten [ten] zehn I
tennis ['tenɪs] Tennis ‖ **table tennis** Tischtennis ‖
tense [tens] *(grammatische)* Zeit, Tempus III 1 (21)
tension ['tenʃn] Spannung, Anspannung III 5 (94)
tent [tent] Zelt ‖
term [tɜːm] Trimester ‖
°**terrace** ['terəs] Stehtribüne
terrible ['terəbl] schrecklich, furchtbar ‖

territory ['terətri] Revier, Territorium III 5 (92)
test ['test]:
1. Test, (Klassen-)Arbeit III 1 (10) ‖ °**test match** internationales Spiel *(bei Cricket und Rugby)*
2. testen, prüfen III 2 (34)
text [tekst]:
1. Text I
2. *(auch* **text message***)* SMS ‖
3. **text sb.** jm. eine SMS schicken I
than [ðæn], [ðən]: **bigger than** größer als ‖
thank sb. [θæŋk] jm. danken III 4 (71)
thanks ['θæŋks] Danke. I ‖ **thanks to Maya** dank Maya ‖
Thank you. ['θæŋk juː] Danke. I ‖ **Thank you for listening.** Danke, dass ihr zugehört habt. / Danke für eure Aufmerksamkeit. ‖
that [ðæt], [ðət]:
1. **it shows that …** es zeigt, dass … I
2. **that group** die Gruppe (dort), jene Gruppe I
3. **that's** das ist I
4. der/die/das; die *(Relativpronomen)* ‖
5. **that's why** deshalb, darum ‖
the [ðə] der, die, das; die I
theatre ['θɪətə] Theater ‖
their [ðeə] ihr I ‖ **their first day** ihr erster Tag I
theirs [ðeəz] ihrer, ihre, ihrs ‖
them [ðem], [ðəm] sie; ihnen I
theme [θiːm] Thema ‖
themselves [ðəm'selvz] sich III 5 (84)
then [ðen] dann I ‖ **just then** genau in dem Moment; gerade dann ‖
there [ðeə] da, dort; dahin, dorthin I ‖ **down there** dort unten ‖ **over there** da drüben, dort drüben ‖ **There are … ** Es sind/gibt … I ‖ **There's …** Es ist/gibt … I
thermometer [θə'mɒmɪtə] Thermometer ‖
these [ðiːz] diese, die (hier) I
they [ðeɪ] sie *(Plural)* I ‖ **they're (= they are)** sie sind … I
thief [θiːf], *pl* **thieves** [θiːvz] Dieb/in I
thing [θɪŋ] Sache, Ding, Gegenstand I
think [θɪŋk], **thought, thought** denken, glauben I ‖ **think of sth.** sich etwas ausdenken; an etwas denken I
third [θɜːd] dritte(r, s) I ‖ **third biggest** drittgrößte(r, s) ‖
thirsty ['θɜːsti]: **be thirsty** durstig sein, Durst haben I
this [ðɪs]:
1. **This is …** Dies ist … / Das ist … I
2. **this place/break/subject** dieser Ort / diese Pause / dieses Fach I ‖ **this time** dieses Mal ‖ **this afternoon/evening/…** heute Nachmittag/Abend/… ‖ **this year's …** das diesjährige …
those [ðəʊz] die … dort; jene … I
°**though** [ðəʊ] obwohl

thought [θɔːt]:
1. Gedanke III 4 (79)
2. *siehe* **think**
thousand ['θaʊznd] Tausend, tausend III 2 (38)
▶ S. 181 Numbers
three [θriː] drei I
threw [θruː] *siehe* **throw**
throat [θrəʊt] Hals, Kehle ‖ **have a sore throat** Halsschmerzen haben ‖
through [θruː] durch I
throw [θrəʊ], **threw, thrown** werfen I
thrown [θrəʊn] *siehe* **throw**
thunder ['θʌndə] Donner ‖
Thursday ['θɜːzdeɪ], ['θɜːzdi] Donnerstag I
ticket ['tɪkɪt] Eintrittskarte I; Fahrkarte I ‖ **ticket office** Fahrkartenschalter; Kasse *(für den Verkauf von Eintrittskarten)* III 1 (15)
till [tɪl]: **till 1 o'clock** bis 1 Uhr ‖ **not till three** erst um drei, nicht vor drei ‖
time [taɪm]:
1. Zeit; Uhrzeit I ‖ **at one time** zur selben Zeit, gleichzeitig III 1 (15) ‖ **feeding time** Fütterungszeit I ‖ **free time** Freizeit, freie Zeit ‖ **free-time activities** Freizeitaktivitäten I ‖ **What time is it?** Wie spät ist es? I
2. Mal I ‖ **this time** dieses Mal ‖
timetable ['taɪmteɪbl]:
1. Stundenplan I
2. Fahrplan III 1 (12)
tin [tɪn] Dose ‖
°**tiny** ['taɪni] winzig
tip [tɪp] Tipp I
tired ['taɪəd] müde I ‖ **be tired of sth.** genug von etwas haben; etwas satt haben III 5 (88)
title ['taɪtl] Titel, Überschrift I
to [tu], [tə]:
1. zu, nach I ‖ **count to ten** bis zehn zählen ‖ **from … to …** von … bis … I ‖ **to the front** nach vorne ‖
2. **Nice to meet you.** Freut mich, dich/euch/Sie kennenzulernen. I
3. **quarter to eleven** Viertel vor elf (10.45 / 22.45) I
4. um zu ‖
toast [təʊst] Toast(brot) III 2 (41)
°**tobacco** [tə'bækəʊ] Tabak
today [tə'deɪ] heute I
toe [təʊ] Zeh I
together [tə'geðə] zusammen I
toilet ['tɔɪlət] Toilette ‖
told [təʊld] *siehe* **tell**
tomato [tə'mɑːtəʊ] Tomate I
tomorrow [tə'mɒrəʊ] morgen ‖ **tomorrow morning** morgen früh, morgen Vormittag ‖
tongue [tʌŋ] Zunge ‖
tongue-twister ['tʌŋˌtwɪstə] Zungenbrecher I
tonight [tə'naɪt] heute Nacht, heute Abend III 2 (30)

Dictionary

too [tuː]:
1. auch I
2. **too late/cold/big/...** zu spät/kalt/groß/... I

took [tʊk] siehe **take**

°**tool** [tuːl] Werkzeug I

tooth [tuːθ], pl **teeth** [tiːθ] Zahn II

toothache ['tuːθeɪk]: **have a toothache** Zahnschmerzen haben II

top [tɒp]:
1. Spitze II **at the top (of)** oben, am oberen Ende, an der Spitze (von) II **on top of each other** übereinander, aufeinander III 1 (15)
2. Spitzen-, oberste(r, s) I
3. Top, Oberteil I

topic ['tɒpɪk] Thema, Themengebiet II **topic sentence** Satz, der in das Thema eines Absatzes einführt III 2 (38)

torch [tɔːtʃ]:
1. Taschenlampe II
2. Fackel II

tortoise ['tɔːtəs] (Land-)Schildkröte III 1 (15)

°**toss** [tɒs] schleudern I

total ['təʊtl]: **a total of ...** eine Gesamtsumme von ...; insgesamt III 2 (38)

touch [tʌtʃ]:
1. berühren, anfassen I
2. **get in touch (with sb.)** (mit jm.) Kontakt aufnehmen; sich (mit jm.) in Verbindung setzen II **stay in touch (with sb.)** (mit jm.) Kontakt halten; (mit jm.) in Verbindung bleiben II

tough [tʌf] (knall)hart, schwierig III 5 (89)

tour ['tʊər]:
1. **tour (of)** Rundgang, Rundfahrt, Reise (durch) I
°2. auf Tournee gehen; bereisen I

tourist ['tʊərɪst] Tourist/in I

towards [tə'wɔːdz]: **towards the station / John** auf den Bahnhof / John zu, in Richtung Bahnhof / John III 1 (20)

tower ['taʊə] Turm I

town [taʊn] Stadt I **town hall** Rathaus II

toy [tɔɪ] Spielzeug I

tractor ['træktə] Traktor II

trade [treɪd] Handel III 3 (52)

°**trader** ['treɪdə] Kaufmann, Händler I

°**tradition** [trə'dɪʃn] Tradition I

traditional [trə'dɪʃənl] traditionell II

traffic ['træfɪk] Verkehr III 4 (77) **traffic light** (Verkehrs-)Ampel (oft auch: **traffic lights** (pl)) III 4 (77)

trail [treɪl] Weg, Pfad III 4 (78)

train [treɪn]:
1. Zug II **get on a train** in einen Zug einsteigen II
2. trainieren II

trainer ['treɪnə] Turnschuh I

training ['treɪnɪŋ] Training(sstunde) I

translate [træns'leɪt] übersetzen II

translation [træns'leɪʃn] Übersetzung III 2 (32)

transparency [træns'pærənsi] Folie (für Projektor) III 5 (92)

travel ['trævl] reisen I

traveller ['trævələ] Reisende(r) I

tread [tred], **trod, trodden: tread on sb.'s toes** jm. auf die Füße/Zehen treten (auch im übertragenen Sinne) III 5 (89)

°**treasure** ['treʒə] Schatz I

tree [triː] Baum I

trials (pl) ['traɪəlz] Turnier, Wettkampf III 5 (83)

triangle ['traɪæŋgl] Dreieck III 3 (53)

trick [trɪk] Kunststück, Trick II

trip [trɪp] Ausflug; Reise I **go on day trips** Tagesausflüge machen II

trod [trɒd] siehe **tread**

trodden ['trɒdn] siehe **tread**

trophy ['trəʊfi] Pokal; Trophäe I

trouble ['trʌbl]: **be in trouble** in Schwierigkeiten sein; Ärger kriegen I **get into trouble** in Schwierigkeiten geraten, Ärger kriegen III 2 (40)

trousers (pl) ['traʊzəz] Hose II

true [truː] wahr I

°**trust** [trʌst] Stiftung I

truth [truːθ] Wahrheit II

try [traɪ]:
1. (aus)probieren; versuchen I
2. Versuch III 1 (20)

T-shirt ['tiːʃɜːt] T-Shirt I

tube [tjuːb]: **the Tube** die U-Bahn (in London) III 1 (12) **on the Tube** in der U-Bahn III 1 (12)

Tuesday ['tjuːzdeɪ], ['tjuːzdi] Dienstag I **on Tuesday** am Dienstag I

tulip ['tjuːlɪp] Tulpe II

tunnel ['tʌnl] Tunnel II

°**Turkish** ['tɜːkɪʃ] Türkisch; türkisch I

turn [tɜːn]:
1. **(It's) my turn.** Ich bin dran / an der Reihe. I **take turns** sich abwechseln (etwas zu tun) I
2. sich umdrehen III 1 (20) **turn around** sich umdrehen; wenden, umdrehen I **turn round** sich umdrehen III 1 (20) **turn to sb.** sich jm. zuwenden; sich an jn. wenden II
3. **turn sth. down** etwas leiser stellen III 1 (20) **turn sth. off** etwas ausschalten II **turn sth. on** etwas einschalten I **turn sth. up** etwas lauter stellen III 1 (20) ▶ S. 177 off
4. **turn left/right** (nach) links/rechts abbiegen II
5. **turn red/brown/cold** rot/braun/kalt werden III 4 (77)

▶ S. 177 (to) turn

TV [ˌtiː'viː] Fernsehen, Fernsehgerät I **on TV** im Fernsehen III 1 (20)

twelve [twelv] zwölf I

twice [twaɪs] zweimal II

twins (pl) [twɪnz] Zwillinge I

two [tuː] zwei I **two-syllable** zweisilbig II

U

°**ugly** ['ʌgli] hässlich I

UK [ˌjuː 'keɪ]: **the UK** das Vereinigte Königreich III 1 (14)

umbrella [ʌm'brelə] Regenschirm I

uncle ['ʌŋkl] Onkel I

under ['ʌndə] unter I

underground [ˌʌndə'graʊnd] unterirdisch, unter der Erde III 2 (32) **the underground** die U-Bahn III 1 (12)

underline [ˌʌndə'laɪn] unterstreichen II

understand [ˌʌndə'stænd], **understood, understood** verstehen I

understood [ˌʌndə'stʊd] siehe **understand**

unfair [ʌn'feə] unfair, ungerecht III 2 (42)

unhappy [ʌn'hæpi] unglücklich II

uniform ['juːnɪfɔːm] Uniform I

°**union** ['juːniən] Vereinigung, Union I

unit ['juːnɪt] Kapitel, Lektion I

united [juː'naɪtɪd] vereinigt **the United Kingdom** [juːˌnaɪtɪd 'kɪŋdəm] das Vereinigte Königreich III 1 (14)

°**unless ...** [ən'les] es sei denn, ... I

unpack [ˌʌn'pæk] auspacken III 4 (74)

until [ən'tɪl] bis II **not until** erst, nicht vor III 3 (51)

unusual [ʌn'juːʒuəl] ungewöhnlich III 5 (83)

up [ʌp] hinauf, herauf; (nach) oben I **up and down** auf und ab; rauf und runter I **up here** hier oben; nach hier oben II **up to** bis (zu) II **What's up?** Was gibt's? / Was ist los? III 4 (78)

uphill [ˌʌp'hɪl] bergauf III 2 (38)

upstairs [ˌʌp'steəz] oben; nach oben (im Haus) I

upstream [ˌʌp'striːm] flussaufwärts III 2 (38)

us [ʌs], [əs] uns I

use [juːz] benutzen, verwenden I

usual ['juːʒuəl] gewöhnlich, üblich III 5 (83)

usually ['juːʒuəli] meistens, normalerweise, gewöhnlich I

V

valley ['væli] Tal II

°**vampire** ['væmpaɪə] Vampir/in I

van [væn] Transporter, Lieferwagen III 4 (77)

vegetables (pl) ['vedʒtəblz] Gemüse I

vegetarian [ˌvedʒə'teəriən]:
1. Vegetarier/in I
2. vegetarisch II

verb [vɜːb] Verb III 1 (12)

verse [vɜːs] Vers, Strophe II

very ['veri] sehr I

video ['vɪdiəʊ] Video I

video camera ['vɪdiəʊ ˌkæmərə] Videokamera I

English – German

view (of) [vjuː] Aussicht, Blick (auf) II | **point of view (on sth.)** Standpunkt (in/über/zu etwas) III 2 (42)
village [ˈvɪlɪdʒ] Dorf I
visa [ˈviːzə] Visum III 4 (68)
visit [ˈvɪzɪt]:
1. besuchen I
2. Besuch II
visitor [ˈvɪzɪtə] Besucher/in, Gast II
vocabulary [vəˈkæbjələri] Vokabelverzeichnis, Wörterverzeichnis I
voice [vɔɪs] Stimme I | **in a loud voice** mit lauter Stimme II
°**voice-over** Offstimme, Kommentar
volleyball [ˈvɒlibɔːl] Volleyball I
volunteer [ˌvɒlənˈtɪə]:
1. sich freiwillig melden; freiwillig/ehrenamtlich arbeiten (unbezahlt) III 2 (37)
2. Freiwillige(r), Ehrenamtliche(r) III 5 (84)
°**vote** [vəʊt] stimmen; abstimmen
vowel [ˈvaʊəl] Vokal, Selbstlaut II

W

waist [weɪst] Taille II
wait (for) [weɪt] warten (auf) I | **wait a minute** Warte einen Moment. / Moment mal. I | **I can't wait to see …** Ich kann es kaum erwarten, … zu sehen I
wake up [ˌweɪkˈʌp], **woke, woken**:
1. aufwachen I
2. **wake sb. up** jn. (auf)wecken II
walk [wɔːk]:
1. Spaziergang I | **go for a walk** spazieren gehen, einen Spaziergang machen I
2. (zu Fuß) gehen I | **walk around** herumlaufen, umherspazieren I | **walk on** weitergehen I | **walk the dog** mit dem Hund rausgehen, den Hund ausführen III 4 (77)
wall [wɔːl] Mauer; Wand II
wander [ˈwɒndə] herumlaufen; herumirren II
want [wɒnt]: **want sth.** etwas (haben) wollen I | **want to do sth.** etwas tun wollen I
war [wɔː] Krieg III 4 (189) | °**be at war** sich im Krieg befinden; Krieg führen
warm [wɔːm] warm I
warning [ˈwɔːnɪŋ] Warnung III 2 (36)
was [wɒz], [wəz]:
1. siehe **be**
2. **I wish I was there.** Ich wünschte, ich wäre da. II
wash [wɒʃ] waschen, wischen III 2 (42) | **wash the dishes** (pl) das Geschirr abwaschen, spülen II
watch [wɒtʃ]:
1. Armbanduhr I
2. sich etwas anschauen; beobachten I

watch TV fernsehen I | **Watch out!** Pass auf! / Vorsicht! I
°**watchdog** [ˈwɒtʃdɒg] Wächter/in, Aufpasser/in
water [ˈwɔːtə] Wasser I
waterfall [ˈwɔːtəfɔːl] Wasserfall I
°**waterfront** [ˈwɔːtəfrʌnt] Hafenviertel (oft modernisiert und bewohnt)
°**waterproofs** (pl) [ˈwɔːtəpruːfs] wasserdichte Kleidung
wave [weɪv] Welle II
way [weɪ]:
1. Weg I | **ask sb. the way** jn. nach dem Weg fragen II | **No way!** Auf keinen Fall! / Kommt nicht in Frage! III 1 (20) | **on the way to …** auf dem Weg zu/nach … I | **tell sb. the way (to …)** jm. den Weg (nach …) beschreiben II
°**There's no way you'll …** Unmöglich, dass du … I **this/that way** hier entlang/dort entlang; in die Richtung I
2. Art und Weise III 3 (51) | **in an interesting way** auf eine interessante Art und Weise III 3 (51) | **in this way** auf diese Weise III 3 (51) | **the way he …** die Art und Weise, wie er … III 3 (51) | **in some/many ways** in mancher/vielerlei Hinsicht III 3 (51)
▶ S. 185 way
we [wiː] wir I
wear [weə], **wore, worn** tragen (Kleidung) I
weather [ˈweðə] Wetter II
website [ˈwebsaɪt] Website I
°**wedding** [ˈwedɪŋ] Hochzeit
Wednesday [ˈwenzdeɪ], [ˈwenzdi] Mittwoch I
wee [wiː] (Scottish, infml) klein III 5 (83)
week [wiːk] Woche I | **a three-week holiday** ein dreiwöchiger Urlaub III 3 (51)
weekend [ˌwiːkˈend] Wochenende I | **at the weekend** am Wochenende I
weigh [weɪ] wiegen II
weird [wɪəd] seltsam, komisch III 4 (74)
welcome sb. (to) [ˈwelkəm] jn. begrüßen (in), jn. willkommen heißen (in) III 4 (76) | **Welcome to Plymouth.** Willkommen in Plymouth. I
well [wel]:
1. gut II; (gesundheitlich) gut, gesund II | **I don't feel well** Ich fühle mich nicht gut. / Mir geht's nicht gut. I
2. **Well, …** Nun, … / Also, … / Na ja, … I
°**wellies** [ˈweliz] (pl, infml) Gummistiefel
well-known [ˌwelˈnəʊn], [ˈwelˌnəʊn] bekannt, wohlbekannt III 3 (48)
Welsh [welʃ] Walisisch; walisisch III 1 (10)
went [went] siehe **go**
were [wɜː], [wə] siehe **be**
west [west] Westen; nach Westen; westlich III 1 (11) | **westbound** [ˈwestbaʊnd] Richtung Westen III 1 (18) | **western** [ˈwestən] westlich, West- III 1 (10)

western [ˈwestən] westlich, West- III 4 (66)
wet [wet] nass I
whale [weɪl] Wal I
what? [wɒt] was? I | **What about you?** Und du/ihr? / Und was ist mit dir/euch? I | **What about …?** Wie wäre es mit …? I | **What colour …?** Welche Farbe …? I | **What is the story about?** Wovon handelt die Geschichte? Worum geht es in der Geschichte? I | **What programmes …?** Welche Programme …? / Welche Art von Programmen …? I | **What size tea would you like?** Wie groß soll der/dein Tee sein? II | **What time is it?** Wie spät ist es? I | **What would you like to eat?** Was möchtest du essen? I | **What's your name?** Wie heißt du? I | **What's for lunch?** Was gibt es zum Mittagessen? I | **What's for homework?** Was haben wir als Hausaufgabe auf? I | **What's she like?** Wie ist sie? / Wie ist sie so? I | **What's up?** Was gibt's? / Was ist los? III 4 (78) | **I don't know what to do.** Ich weiß nicht, was ich tun soll. III 2 (42)
▶ S. 183 Question words + to-infinitive
whatever [wɒtˈevə] was (auch) immer III 5 (91)
▶ S. 195 whenever etc.
wheel [wiːl]: **big wheel** Riesenrad I
when [wen]:
1. wenn I
2. als I
3. **when?** wann? I
whenever [ˌwenˈevə] wann (auch) immer; egal, wann III 5 (91)
▶ S. 195 whenever etc.
where? [weə] wo? / wohin? / woher? I | **We had no idea where to go.** Wir hatten keine Ahnung, wohin wir gehen sollten. III 2 (42)
▶ S. 183 Question words + to-infinitive
wherever [weərˈevə] wo (auch) immer III 5 (91)
▶ S. 195 whenever etc.
which [wɪtʃ]:
1. **which?** welche(r, s)? I
2. der/die/das; die (Relativpronomen) II
while [waɪl]:
1. während II
2. eine Weile, einige Zeit III 1 (20) | **for a while** eine Weile, eine Zeit lang III 1 (20)
▶ S. 175 German "während"
whisper [ˈwɪspə] flüstern II
whistle [ˈwɪsl]:
1. pfeifen II
2. (Triller-)Pfeife III 1 (24) | **blow a whistle** pfeifen (auf der Trillerpfeife) III 1 (24)
3. Pfiff III 5 (94)
white [waɪt] weiß I

Dictionary

whiteboard [ˈwaɪtbɔːd] Whiteboard, Weißwandtafel III 2 (37)
who [huː]:
1. **Who is there?** Wer ist da? I **Who did you tell?** Wem hast du es erzählt? II **Who does he know?** Wen kennt er? II **I don't know who to ask.** Ich weiß nicht, wen ich fragen kann/soll. III 2 (42)
▶ S. 183 Question words + to-infinitive
2. der/die/das; die (Relativpronomen) II
whoever [huːˈevə] wer (auch) immer III 5 (91)
▶ S. 195 whenever etc.
whole [həʊl] ganze(r, s), gesamte(r, s) II
whose? [huːz] wessen? II
why [waɪ] warum I **that's why** deshalb, darum II
°**wicked** [ˈwɪkɪd] böse, schlecht
wide [waɪd] weit; breit III 2 (40)
wild [waɪld] wild II
°**wildlife** [ˈwaɪldlaɪf] Tier- und Pflanzenwelt
will [wɪl]: **we'll miss the girls (= we will miss the girls)** wir werden die Mädchen verpassen II **I'll have a tea.** Ich nehme einen Tee. (beim Essen, im Restaurant) II
win [wɪn], **won, won** gewinnen I
wind [wɪnd] Wind II
window [ˈwɪndəʊ] Fenster I
windy [ˈwɪndi] windig II
wing [wɪŋ] Flügel III 1 (24)
winner [ˈwɪnə] Gewinner/in, Sieger/in I
winter [ˈwɪntə] Winter I
wise [waɪz] weise II
wish [wɪʃ]:
1. Wunsch I **make a wish** sich etwas wünschen I
2. wünschen II **I wish I was there.** Ich wünschte, ich wäre da. II
°**witch** [wɪtʃ] Hexe
with [wɪð]
1. mit I
2. bei I
without [wɪˈðaʊt] ohne I
woke [wəʊk] siehe **wake**
woken [ˈwəʊkən] siehe **wake**
woman [ˈwʊmən], pl **women** [ˈwɪmɪn] Frau I
won [wʌn] siehe **win**
wonder [ˈwʌndə] sich fragen, gern wissen wollen III 2 (34)
°**wonderful** [ˈwʌndəfl] wunderbar
won't [wəʊnt]: **she won't come (= she will not come)** sie wird nicht kommen II
wood [wʊd] Holz I
wooden [ˈwʊdn] hölzern; Holz- III 2 (40)
word [wɜːd] Wort I **May I have a word with you?** Kann ich Sie kurz sprechen? II **word order** Wortstellung I

wordbank [ˈwɜːdˌbæŋk] „Wortspeicher" I
wore [wɔː] siehe **wear**
work [wɜːk]:
1. arbeiten I °**work sth. out** etwas herausfinden/herausarbeiten
2. Arbeit I
3. funktionieren III 1 (19)
workbook [ˈwɜːkbʊk] Arbeitsheft I
worker [ˈwɜːkə] Arbeiter/in II
worksheet [ˈwɜːkʃiːt] Arbeitsblatt II
workshop [ˈwɜːkʃɒp] Werkstatt III 2 (30); Workshop, Lehrgang II
world [wɜːld] Welt II **in the world** auf der Welt II **natural world** (Welt der) Natur III 2 (31) °**take the world by storm** die Welt im Sturm erobern **World Cup** Weltmeisterschaft III 3 (55) °**World Heritage Site** Welterbestätte
worm [wɜːm] Wurm I
worn [wɔːn] siehe **wear**
worried [ˈwʌrid] besorgt, beunruhigt II
worry (about) [ˈwʌri] sich Sorgen machen (wegen, um) II
worse [wɜːs] schlechter, schlimmer II
worst [wɜːst] der/die/das schlechteste/schlimmste …; am schlechtesten/schlimmsten II
worth [wɜːθ] wert III 1 (16)
would [wʊd]: **I would choose Sam** ich würde Sam wählen II **What would you like to eat?** Was möchtest du essen? I **I'd (= I would) like …** Ich möchte … I
write [raɪt], **wrote, written** schreiben I **write sth. down** etwas aufschreiben II
writer [ˈraɪtə] Schreiber/in III 4 (69); Schriftsteller/in III 4 (69)
written [ˈrɪtn] siehe **write**
wrong [rɒŋ]:
1. falsch, verkehrt I **No, that's wrong.** Nein, das ist falsch. / Nein, das stimmt nicht. I
2. **sb. is wrong** jemand irrt sich; jemand hat Unrecht I
3. **What's wrong with you?** Was fehlt dir?; Was ist los mit dir? II
wrote [rəʊt] siehe **write**

Y

yacht [jɒt] Jacht III 5 (83)
year [jɪə]:
1. Jahr I **last/next year's …** das … vom letzten/nächsten Jahr II **this year's …** das diesjährige … II
2. Jahrgang(sstufe) I
yellow [ˈjeləʊ] gelb I
yes [jes] ja I **Yes, that's right.** Ja, das ist richtig. / Ja, das stimmt. I
yesterday [ˈjestədeɪ], [ˈjestədi] gestern I

yet [jet]: **not … yet** noch nicht I **Have you … yet?** Hast du schon …? II
yoga [ˈjəʊgə] Yoga I
yoghurt [ˈjɒgət] Joghurt I
you [juː]:
1. du; Sie; ihr; dir; dich; euch; Ihnen I
2. man III 1 (24)
young [jʌŋ] jung I
your [jɔː], [jə] dein/e; euer/eure; Ihr/Ihre I
yours [jɔːz] deiner, deine, deins; eurer, eure, eures II
yourself [jɔːˈself] dich, dir; sich (bei „Sie") III 5 (84) **about yourself** über dich selbst I **Enjoy yourself.** Viel Spaß! / Amüsiere dich gut! III 5 (GF/167) **Help yourself.** Greif zu! / Bedien dich! III 5 (GF/167)
yourselves [jɔːˈselvz] euch; sich (bei „Sie") III 5 (85)
yummy [ˈjʌmi] (infml) lecker I

Z

zone [zəʊn]: **pedestrian zone** Fußgängerzone II
zoo [zuː] Zoo I

German – English

Das **German – English Dictionary** enthält den **Lernwortschatz** der Bände 1 bis 3 von *English G Access*. Es kann dir eine erste Hilfe sein, wenn du vergessen hast, wie etwas auf Englisch heißt.

Wenn du wissen möchtest, wo das entsprechende englische Wort zum ersten Mal in *English G Access* vorkommt, dann kannst du im **English – German Dictionary** (S. 198 – 220) nachschlagen.

Im **German – English Dictionary** werden folgende **Abkürzungen** verwendet:

sth. = something (etwas)   sb. = somebody (jemand)   jn. = jemanden   jm. = jemandem
pl = plural (Mehrzahl)   infml = informal (umgangssprachlich)

▶ Der Pfeil weist auf Kästen im **Vocabulary** (S.172 – 197) hin, in denen du weitere Informationen zu diesem Wort findest.

A

ab: auf und ab up and down [ˌʌp_ən ˈdaʊn] **Ab mit euch jetzt!** Off you go now. [ɒf]
abbauen *(Kohle, Erz)* mine [maɪn]
abbiegen: (nach) links/rechts abbiegen turn left/right [tɜːn]
Abend evening [ˈiːvnɪŋ] **am Abend** in the evening **heute Abend** tonight [təˈnaɪt] **zu Abend essen** have dinner [ˈdɪnə]
Abendbrot, Abendessen dinner [ˈdɪnə]
abends in the evening [ˈiːvnɪŋ]
Abenteuer adventure [ədˈventʃə]
aber but [bʌt], [bət] **Aber egal, …** Anyway, … [ˈeniweɪ]
abfahren leave [liːv]
Abfall rubbish [ˈrʌbɪʃ]
Abfalleimer litter bin [ˈlɪtə bɪn]
abgeben: etwas abgeben *(einreichen)* hand sth. in [ˌhænd_ˈɪn]
abholen: jn. abholen pick sb. up [ˌpɪk_ˈʌp]
abkühlen: sich abkühlen cool off
Abkürzung *(Kurzform eines Wortes)* abbreviation [əˌbriːviˈeɪʃn]
Abneigungen: Vorlieben und Abneigungen likes and dislikes *(pl)* [ˌlaɪks_ən ˈdɪslaɪks]
abräumen *(Tisch, Geschirr)* clear [klɪə]
Absatz *(in einem Text)* paragraph [ˈpærəɡrɑːf]
Abschluss ending [ˈendɪŋ]
abschreiben copy [ˈkɒpi]
absetzen: etwas absetzen *(Hut, Helm)* take sth. off [ˌteɪk_ɒf]
▶ S. 177 off
abspielen *(CD usw.)* play [pleɪ]
absuchen: etwas (nach etwas) absuchen scan sth. (for sth.) [skæn]
abwaschen: das Geschirr abwaschen wash the dishes *(pl)* [ˈdɪʃɪz]
acht eight [eɪt]
achten: darauf achten, dass … make sure that …
Achtung *(Respekt)* respect [rɪˈspekt] **Achtung!** *(Aufgepasst!)* Look out!
Acker field [fiːld]
addieren (zu) add (to) [æd]
Adjektiv adjective [ˈædʒɪktɪv]

adoptiert, Adoptiv- adopted [əˈdɒptɪd]
Adresse address [əˈdres]
Adverb adverb [ˈædvɜːb]
Affe monkey [ˈmʌŋki]
ähnlich: etwas/jm. ähnlich similar to sth./sb. [ˈsɪmələ]
Aktivität activity [ækˈtɪvəti]
Akzent accent [ˈæksənt]
albern silly [ˈsɪli]
alle all [ɔːl]; *(jeder)* everyone [ˈevriwʌn], everybody [ˈevribɒdi] **alle anderen** everybody else
▶ S. 195 … else
allein alone [əˈləʊn]; *(ohne Hilfe)* on my/your/their/… own [əʊn]
alleinstehend *(ledig)* single [ˈsɪŋɡl]
alles everything [ˈevriθɪŋ]; all [ɔːl] **alles in allem** *(insgesamt)* altogether [ˌɔːltəˈɡeðə] **vor allem** especially [ɪˈspeʃli]
Alltags- everyday [ˈevrideɪ]
als 1. *(zeitlich)* when [wen]; *(während)* as [æz], [əz] **als Erstes** first [fɜːst] **als Nächstes** next [nekst]
2. **als ob** as if; like *(infml)*
3. **als Kind** as a child
4. **älter als** older than [ðæn], [ðən]
also 1. *(deshalb, daher)* so [səʊ]
2. **Also, …** Well, … [wel]
alt old [əʊld] **Wie alt bist du?** How old are you? **… ist so alt wie du** … is your age [eɪdʒ]
Alter age [eɪdʒ] **… ist in deinem Alter** … is your age [eɪdʒ]
am 1. *(in Ortsangaben)* at [æ], [ət] **am Meer** by the sea [baɪ] **am Telefon** on the phone
2. *(in Zeitangaben)* **am Abend** in the evening **am Montag/Dienstag/…** on Monday/Tuesday/… **am Morgen** in the morning **am Nachmittag** in the afternoon **am Samstagmorgen** on Saturday afternoon **am Wochenende** at the weekend
Ameise ant [ænt]
Ampel traffic light [ˈtræfɪk laɪt] *(oft auch Plural:)* traffic lights
amtlich, Amts- official [əˈfɪʃl]
amüsieren: sich amüsieren have fun [fʌn] **Amüsier dich gut!** Enjoy yourself.

an 1. *(in Ortsangaben)* at [æ], [ət] **an britischen Schulen** at British schools
2. **an sein** *(Radio, Licht usw.)* be on
anbauen *(anpflanzen)* grow [ɡrəʊ]
anbieten offer [ˈɒfə]
andauern *(im Gang sein)* go on
Andenken souvenir [ˌsuːvəˈnɪə]
andere(r, s) other [ˈʌðə] **ein anderer …/eine andere …/ein anderes …** another … [əˈnʌðə] **einer nach dem anderen** one by one **alle anderen** everybody else
▶ S. 195 … else
ändern; sich ändern change [tʃeɪndʒ]
anders *(verschieden)* different [ˈdɪfrənt]
Anfang beginning [bɪˈɡɪnɪŋ]
anfangen start [stɑːt]; begin [bɪˈɡɪn]
anfangs at first [əˈfɜːst]
anfassen touch [tʌtʃ]
anfühlen: sich gut/kalt/… anfühlen feel good/cold/…
angemalt painted [ˈpeɪntɪd]
angreifen attack [əˈtæk]
Angst: jm. Angst machen scare sb. [skeə]
anhalten stop [stɒp]
Anhaltspunkt *(Hinweis)* clue [kluː]
anhören 1. **sich etwas anhören** listen to sth. [ˈlɪsn]; *(probehalber)* check sth. out [ˌtʃek_ˈaʊt] *(infml)*
2. **sich gut anhören** *(gut klingen)* sound good [saʊnd]
anklopfen (an etwas) knock (on sth.) [nɒk]
ankommen arrive [əˈraɪv]
Ankunft arrival [əˈraɪvl]
anlächeln: jn. anlächeln smile at sb. [smaɪl]
anmalen paint [peɪnt]
anordnen *(in eine bestimmte Ordnung bringen)* arrange [əˈreɪndʒ]
anpflanzen grow [ɡrəʊ]
Anruf phone call [ˈfəʊn kɔːl], *(kurz auch:)* call
anrufen call [kɔːl]; phone [fəʊn]
Anrufer/in caller [ˈkɔːlə]
Ansage *(Durchsage)* announcement [əˈnaʊnsmənt]
anschauen: sich etwas anschauen watch sth. [wɒtʃ]; look at sth. [lʊk]; *(probehalber)* check sth. out [ˌtʃek_ˈaʊt] *(infml)*

Dictionary

anschließen: sich einem Klub anschließen join a club [dʒɔɪn]
Anschrift address [əˈdres]
ansehen: sich etwas ansehen watch sth. [wɒtʃ]; look at sth. [lʊk]
Anspannung tension [ˈtenʃn]
Anspitzer sharpener [ˈʃɑːpnə]
anstarren: jn./etwas anstarren stare at sb./sth. [steə]
anstelle von instead of [ɪnˈsted_əv]
anstellen: sich anstellen (Schlange stehen) queue [kjuː]
Anstieg climb [klaɪm]
anstreichen paint [peɪnt]
Antwort answer [ˈɑːnsə]
antworten answer [ˈɑːnsə]; reply [rɪˈplaɪ]
Anzahl number [ˈnʌmbə]
Anzeige (Inserat) advert [ˈædvɜːt]
anziehen: etwas anziehen (Kleidung) put sth. on [ˌpʊt_ˈɒn] **sich schick anziehen** dress up [ˌdres_ˈʌp]
Anzug suit [suːt]
anzünden light [laɪt]
Apfel apple [ˈæpl]
Apfelsine orange [ˈɒrɪndʒ]
Apparat: Bleib/Bleiben Sie am Apparat. Hold on a minute. [ˌhəʊld_ˈɒn], (oft auch kurz:) Hold on.
April April [ˈeɪprəl]
Aquarienhaus aquarium [əˈkweərɪəm]
Aquarium aquarium [əˈkweərɪəm]
Arbeit work [wɜːk]; job [dʒɒb]
arbeiten work [wɜːk]
Arbeiter/in worker [ˈwɜːkə]
Arbeitsblatt worksheet [ˈwɜːkʃiːt]
Arbeitsheft workbook [ˈwɜːkbʊk]
Architekt/in architect [ˈɑːkɪtekt]
Ärger kriegen/haben be in trouble [ˈtrʌbl]; get into trouble
arm poor [pɔː], [pʊə]
Arm arm [ɑːm] **jn. am Arm nehmen** take sb. by the arm
Armbanduhr watch [wɒtʃ]
Art: eine Art (von) … a kind of … [kaɪnd] **Art und Weise** way [weɪ] **auf eine interessante Art und Weise** in an interesting way **die Art und Weise, wie er …** the way he …
▶ S. 185 way ("Art und Weise")
Artikel article [ˈɑːtɪkl]
Arzt/Ärztin doctor [ˈdɒktə]
Asche ash [æʃ]; (sterbliche Überreste) ashes (pl) [ˈæʃɪz]
Astronaut/in astronaut [ˈæstrənɔːt]
Atem, Atemzug breath [breθ]
Atlantik: der Atlantik, der Atlantische Ozean the Atlantic (Ocean) [ətˈlæntɪk]
Attraktion attraction [əˈtrækʃn]
auch too [tuː]; also [ˈɔːlsəʊ]; as well [əz ˈwel] **auch aus Berlin** from Berlin too; also from Berlin **auch nicht** not … either [ˈaɪðə], [ˈiːðə] **Ich auch.** Me too. **Ich auch nicht.** Me neither. [ˈnaɪðə], [ˈniːðə] **wann auch immer** whenever [ˌwenˈevə] **was auch immer** whatever [wɒtˈevə] **wer auch immer** whoever [huːˈevə] **wo auch immer** wherever [weərˈevə]
▶ S. 195 whenever, wherever, whatever, whoever
auf on [ɒn] **auf das Boot (hinauf)** onto the boat [ˈɒntʊ] **auf dem Bild/Foto** in the picture/photo **auf dem Dachboden** in the attic **auf dem Weg zu/nach …** on the way to … **auf den Bahnhof/Mr Bell zu** towards the station/Mr Bell [təˈwɔːdz] **auf der Landkarte/dem Stadtplan** on the map **auf der Welt** in the world **auf Englisch** in English **auf einmal** suddenly [ˈsʌdnli] **auf und ab** up and down **Auf keinen Fall!** No way! [ˌnəʊ ˈweɪ] **Auf welcher Seite sind wir?** What page are we on? **Auf Wiedersehen.** Goodbye.
aufbewahren keep [kiːp]
aufbleiben: lange aufbleiben stay up late
aufeinander (übereinander) on top of each other [iːtʃ_ˈʌðə]
auffordern: jn. auffordern, etwas (nicht) zu tun tell sb. (not) to do sth.
Aufgabe task; exercise [ˈeksəsaɪz]; job
aufgeben give up
Aufgepasst! Look out!
aufgeregt (gespannt) excited [ɪkˈsaɪtɪd]; (nervös) nervous [ˈnɜːvəs]
aufheben 1. (aufsparen) keep [kiːp] 2. **etwas aufheben** (vom Boden) pick sth. up [ˌpɪk_ˈʌp]
aufhören: Hör auf (damit)! Stop it! (infml)
auflisten list [lɪst]
aufmachen open [ˈəʊpən]
aufnehmen: (mit jm.) Kontakt aufnehmen get in touch (with sb.) [tʌtʃ]
aufpassen: auf jn. aufpassen look after sb.
aufragen (Berge, Säulen, Türme, …) rise up [ˌraɪz_ˈʌp]
aufregend (spannend) exciting [ɪkˈsaɪtɪŋ]
aufrufen: die Namen aufrufen call out the names
aufschauen (hochsehen) look up [ˌlʊk_ˈʌp]
aufschreiben: etwas aufschreiben write sth. down [ˌraɪt_ˈdaʊn]
aufsetzen: etwas aufsetzen (Hut, Helm) put sth. on [ˌpʊt_ˈɒn] **sich aufsetzen** sit up
aufsparen (aufheben) keep [kiːp]
aufspringen jump up [ˌdʒʌmp_ˈʌp]
aufstehen get up [ˌget_ˈʌp]; stand up
Aufstieg climb [klaɪm]
aufsuchen (Arzt) see
auftauchen (erscheinen) appear [əˈpɪə]
auftreten (Künstler/in) perform [pəˈfɔːm]
aufwachen wake up [ˌweɪk_ˈʌp]
aufwachsen grow up [ˌgrəʊ_ˈʌp]
aufwecken: jn. aufwecken wake sb. up [ˌweɪk_ˈʌp]
aufzeichnen (Musik, Daten) record [rɪˈkɔːd]
Aufzug lift [lɪft]
Auge eye [aɪ]
Augenblick moment [ˈməʊmənt]
August August [ˈɔːgəst]
aus from [frɒm], [frəm] **aus … heraus / aus … hinaus** out of … [ˈaʊt_əv] **aus etwas (gemacht) sein** be made of sth.
ausblasen: etwas ausblasen blow sth. out [ˌbləʊ_ˈaʊt]
ausbrechen: in Tränen ausbrechen burst into tears [bɜːst]
ausbreiten; sich ausbreiten spread [spred]
ausdenken: sich etwas ausdenken think of sth. [θɪŋk]; (erfinden) make sth. up
Ausdruck expression [ɪkˈspreʃn]; phrase [freɪz]
Auseinandersetzung argument [ˈɑːgjumənt]
Ausflug trip [trɪp]
Ausfuhr export [ˈekspɔːt]
ausführen: den Hund ausführen walk the dog
ausgeben: Geld ausgeben (für) spend money (on) [spend]
Ausgehverbot: jm. Ausgehverbot erteilen ground sb. [graʊnd]
auskennen: sich mit etwas auskennen know about sth.
auslachen: jn. auslachen laugh at sb.
auspacken unpack [ˌʌnˈpæk]
ausprobieren try [traɪ]; check out [ˌtʃek_ˈaʊt] (infml)
auspusten: etwas auspusten blow sth. out [ˌbləʊ_ˈaʊt]
Ausritt ride [raɪd]
Ausrufezeichen exclamation mark [ˌekskləˈmeɪʃn mɑːk]
ausruhen: sich ausruhen rest [rest]; (entspannen) relax [rɪˈlæks]
Ausrüstung equipment [ɪˈkwɪpmənt]; kit
Aussage (Botschaft) message [ˈmesɪdʒ]
ausschalten: etwas ausschalten turn sth. off [ˌtɜːn_ˈɒf]
▶ S. 177 off
aussehen: glücklich/wütend/… aussehen look happy/angry/…
Außen- (im Freien) outdoor [ˈaʊtdɔː]
Außenseite: die Außenseite the outside [ˌaʊtˈsaɪd]
außer (bis auf) except [ɪkˈsept]
Äußere: das Äußere the outside [ˌaʊtˈsaɪd]
außergewöhnlich extraordinary [ɪkˈstrɔːdnri]
außerhalb von … outside … [ˌaʊtˈsaɪd]
Aussicht, Blick (auf) view (of) [vjuː]
Aussprache pronunciation [prəˌnʌnsiˈeɪʃn]
aussteigen get off [ˌget_ˈɒf] **aus einem Bus/Boot aussteigen** get off a

German – English

bus/boat **aus einem Auto aussteigen** get out of a car ▶ S. 177 off
ausstrecken: die Hand ausstrecken reach over [ˌriːtʃ ˈəʊvə]
aussuchen: (sich) etwas aussuchen choose sth. [tʃuːz]
auswählen: etwas auswählen choose sth. [tʃuːz]
auswandern emigrate [ˈemɪɡreɪt]
ausziehen: etwas ausziehen (Kleidung) take sth. off [ˌteɪk ˈɒf] ▶ S. 177 off
Auto car [kɑː] **mit dem Auto fahren** go by car
Autor/in author [ˈɔːθə]

B

Bach stream [striːm]
Bad bath [bɑːθ]
Badezimmer bathroom [ˈbɑːθruːm]
Bahnhof station [ˈsteɪʃn]
Bahnsteig platform [ˈplætfɔːm]
bald soon [suːn] **Bis bald.** See you. **schon bald** before long
Ball ball [bɔːl]
Banane banana [bəˈnɑːnə]
Band (Musikgruppe) band [bænd]
Bank (Geldinstitut) bank [bæŋk]
Bär bear [beə]
Barkeeper barman, pl barmen [ˈbɑːmən]
Bart beard [bɪəd]
Basketball basketball [ˈbɑːskɪtbɔːl]
bauen build [bɪld]
Bauer/Bäuerin farmer [ˈfɑːmə]
Bauernhaus farmhouse [ˈfɑːmhaʊs]
Bauernhof farm [fɑːm]
Baum tree [triː]
Beamte(r), Beamtin official [əˈfɪʃl]
beantworten answer [ˈɑːnsə]
bearbeiten (Texte, Videos) edit [ˈedɪt]
Becher mug [mʌɡ] **ein Becher …** a mug of …
bedecken (zudecken) cover [ˈkʌvə]
bedeuten mean [miːn]
Bedeutung meaning [ˈmiːnɪŋ]
bedienen: Bedien dich! (Greif zu!) Help yourself.
Bedingungen (Verhältnisse) conditions [kənˈdɪʃnz]
beeilen: sich beeilen hurry (up) [ˌhʌriˈʌp]
beenden: etwas beenden finish sth. [ˈfɪnɪʃ]; end sth.
beerdigen bury [ˈberi]
befördern carry [ˈkæri]
befragen: jn. befragen interview sb. [ˈɪntəvjuː]
begabt talented [ˈtæləntɪd]
Beginn beginning [bɪˈɡɪnɪŋ]
beginnen start [stɑːt]; begin [bɪˈɡɪn]
begraben (beerdigen) bury [ˈberi]
Begründung reason [ˈriːzn]

begrüßen: jn. begrüßen (in) (willkommen heißen) welcome sb. (to) [ˈwelkəm]
beheimaten: etwas beheimaten be home to sth.
behutsam (sanft) gently [ˈdʒentli]
bei (in Ortsangaben) at [æt], [ət] **bei den Blackwells zu Hause** at the Blackwells' house **bei Oma** at Grandma's **bei jm. sein** be with sb.
beibringen: jm. beibringen, etwas zu tun teach sb. to do sth. [tiːtʃ]
beide both [bəʊθ] **eins beide** (Ergebnis im Sport) one all [ˌwʌnˈɔːl]
Bein leg [leɡ]
beinahe almost [ˈɔːlməʊst]; nearly [ˈnɪəli]
Beispiel example [ɪɡˈzɑːmpl] **zum Beispiel (z.B.)** for example (e.g.) [ˌiːˈdʒiː] (from Latin exempli gratia)
beißen bite [baɪt]
bekämpfen: jn. bekämpfen fight sb. [faɪt]
bekannt well-known [ˌwelˈnəʊn], [ˈwelˌnəʊn]
bekommen get [ɡet] **etwas bekommen** (Krankheit) come down with sth. ▶ S. 180 (to) come across/down/over/…
belebt (Straße, Viertel) busy [ˈbɪzi]
bellen bark [bɑːk]
Bellen bark [bɑːk]
beliebt (bei) popular (with) [ˈpɒpjələ]
bemalt painted [ˈpeɪntɪd]
benehmen: sich benehmen behave [bɪˈheɪv]
benennen name [neɪm]
benötigen need [niːd]
benutzen use [juːz]
beobachten watch [wɒtʃ]; (untersuchen, studieren) study [ˈstʌdi]
Bereich area [ˈeəriə]
bereit ready [ˈredi]
bereits already [ɔːlˈredi]
Berg mountain [ˈmaʊntən]
bergab downhill [ˌdaʊnˈhɪl]
bergauf uphill [ˌʌpˈhɪl]
Bergwerk mine [maɪn]
Bericht report [rɪˈpɔːt]
berichten: jm. etwas berichten tell sb. about sth. [tel]
beruhigen: sich beruhigen calm down [ˌkɑːmˈdaʊn] **jn. beruhigen** calm sb. down
berühmt (für, wegen) famous (for) [ˈfeɪməs]
berühren touch [tʌtʃ]
beschäftigt sein (viel zu tun haben) be busy [ˈbɪzi]
Bescheid: über etwas Bescheid wissen know about sth.
beschließen decide [dɪˈsaɪd]
beschreiben: (jm.) etwas beschreiben describe sth. (to sb.) [dɪˈskraɪb] **jm. den Weg (nach …) beschreiben** tell sb. the way (to …)
Beschreibung description [dɪˈskrɪpʃn]
beschriften (etikettieren) label [ˈleɪbl]

Beschriftung (Etikett) label [ˈleɪbl]
beschützen: jn./etwas beschützen (vor jm./etwas) protect sb./sth. (from sb./sth.) [prəˈtekt]
Besetzung (Theaterstück) cast [kɑːst]
besiegen beat [biːt]
besitzen own [əʊn]
besondere(r, s) special [ˈspeʃl]
besonders (vor allem) especially [ɪˈspeʃli]
besorgen: (sich) etwas besorgen get sth.
besorgt worried [ˈwʌrid]
besser better [ˈbetə]
beste(r, s) best [best] **das Beste an …** the best thing about …
bestellen order [ˈɔːdə]
Bestrafung punishment [ˈpʌnɪʃmənt]
Besuch visit [ˈvɪzɪt]
besuchen: jn. besuchen visit sb. [ˈvɪzɪt]; see sb. [siː]
Besucher/in visitor [ˈvɪzɪtə]
Betonung stress [stres]
Betonungszeichen stress mark [ˈstres mɑːk]
betreten (hineingehen) enter [ˈentə]
Bett bed [bed]
beunruhigt worried [ˈwʌrid]
Beutel bag [bæɡ]
Bevölkerung population [ˌpɒpjuˈleɪʃn]
bevor before [bɪˈfɔː]
bewachen guard [ɡɑːd]
bewegen; sich bewegen move [muːv]
Bewegung movement [ˈmuːvmənt]
bewölkt cloudy [ˈklaʊdi]
bezahlen pay [peɪ] **etwas bezahlen** pay for sth. [peɪ] **bezahlt werden** get paid
Bibliothek library [ˈlaɪbrəri]
Bild picture [ˈpɪktʃə] **auf dem Bild** in the picture
bilden (formen) form [fɔːm]
Bildschirm screen [skriːn] **geteilter Bildschirm** split screen [splɪt ˈskriːn]
Bildschirm(auf)teilung split screen [splɪt ˈskriːn]
Bildung education [ˌedʒuˈkeɪʃn]
Bildunterschrift caption [ˈkæpʃn]
billig cheap [tʃiːp]
Bindestrich hyphen [ˈhaɪfən]
Bindewort linking word [ˈlɪŋkɪŋ wɜːd]
bis 1. till [tɪl]; until [ənˈtɪl] **bis zwölf Uhr** till/until twelve o'clock **bis spätestens 20 Uhr** by 8 pm [baɪ] **bis jetzt** so far **Bis gleich. / Bis bald.** See you. **bis zehn zählen** count to ten **bis (zu)** up to **von … bis …** from … to …
2. **bis auf** (außer) except [ɪkˈsept]
Biss bite [baɪt]
bisschen: ein bisschen a bit [ə ˈbɪt]
Bissen bite [baɪt]
bitte 1. (in Fragen und Aufforderungen) please [pliːz]
2. **Bitte sehr. / Hier bitte.** Here you are.

Dictionary

bitten: jemanden bitten, etwas zu tun ask sb. to do sth. [ɑːsk] **um etwas bitten** ask for sth.
blau blue [bluː]
bleiben stay [steɪ] **(mit jm.) in Verbindung bleiben** stay in touch (with sb.) [tʌtʃ] **Bleib/Bleiben Sie am Apparat.** Hold on a minute. [ˌhəʊld ˈɒn], *(oft auch kurz:)* Hold on.
Bleistift pencil [ˈpensl]
Blick (auf) view (of) [vjuː] **einen Blick auf etwas werfen** have a look at sth.
Blitz(e) lightning *(no pl)* [ˈlaɪtnɪŋ] **ein Blitz** a flash of lightning
Blockflöte recorder [rɪˈkɔːdə]
blöd *(albern)* silly [ˈsɪli]; *(dumm)* stupid [ˈstjuːpɪd]
Blog *(Weblog, digitales Tagebuch)* blog [blɒɡ]
Blogger/in blogger [ˈblɒɡə]
blond blond *(bei Frauen oft:* blonde) [blɒnd]
bloß 1. only [ˈəʊnli]; *(einfach nur)* just [dʒʌst]
2. *(Hände, Arme, Füße)* bare [beə]
Blume flower [ˈflaʊə]
Blut blood [blʌd]
Blüte flower [ˈflaʊə]
Boden ground [ɡraʊnd]
Boot boat [bəʊt]
Bootsfahrt cruise [kruːz]
Bord: an Bord on board [bɔːd]
böse auf jn. angry with sb. [ˈæŋɡri]
Botschaft *(Aussage)* message [ˈmesɪdʒ]
brauchen need [niːd]; *(Zeit)* take [teɪk] **du brauchst es nicht zu tun** you needn't do it [ˈniːdnt]
braun brown [braʊn]
brav good
brechen *(kaputt gehen)* break [breɪk]
breit wide [waɪd]
brennen burn [bɜːn]
Brief letter [ˈletə]
Brille glasses *(pl)* [ˈɡlɑːsɪz]
bringen *(mit-, herbringen)* bring [brɪŋ]; *(weg-, hinbringen)* take [teɪk] **etwas zustande bringen** *(schaffen)* manage sth. [ˈmænɪdʒ]
Brise breeze [briːz]
britisch British [ˈbrɪtɪʃ]
Broschüre brochure [ˈbrəʊʃə]
Brot bread [bred]
Brücke bridge [brɪdʒ]
Bruder brother [ˈbrʌðə]
brüllen roar [rɔː]
Brust(korb) chest [tʃest]
Buch book [bʊk]
buchen *(reservieren)* reserve [rɪˈzɜːv]
Bücherei library [ˈlaɪbrəri]
Buchhandlung bookshop [ˈbʊkʃɒp]
Buchstabe letter [ˈletə]
buchstabieren spell [spel]
bücken: sich bücken bend down [bend]
Bühne stage [steɪdʒ] **hinter der Bühne** backstage [ˌbækˈsteɪdʒ]
Burg castle [ˈkɑːsl]
Bürgermeister/in mayor [meə]
Bürgersteig pavement [ˈpeɪvmənt]
Büro office [ˈɒfɪs]
Bus bus **mit dem Bus fahren** go by bus

C

Café café [ˈkæfeɪ]
Camping camping [ˈkæmpɪŋ]
Cent cent [sent]
▶ S. 189 Pounds and euros
Champion champion [ˈtʃæmpiən]
Chance chance [tʃɑːns]
Chaos chaos [ˈkeɪɒs]
Chat chat [tʃæt]
chatten chat [tʃæt]
Checkliste checklist [ˈtʃeklɪst]
Chor choir [ˈkwaɪə]
Clown clown [klaʊn]
Cola cola [ˈkəʊlə]
Comedyshow comedy [ˈkɒmədi]
Computer computer [kəmˈpjuːtə]
cool cool [kuːl]
Cornflakes cornflakes [ˈkɔːnfleɪks]
Cottage cottage [ˈkɒtɪdʒ]
Cousin, Cousine cousin [ˈkʌzn]
Curry(gericht) curry [ˈkʌri]

D

da, dahin *(dort, dorthin)* there [ðeə]
da sein *(zu Hause sein)* be in **nicht da sein** *(nicht zu Hause sein)* be out **nicht (mehr) da sein** be gone [ɡɒn]
Dach roof [ruːf]
Dachboden attic [ˈætɪk] **auf dem Dachboden** in the attic
dagegen: etwas dagegen haben mind [maɪnd]
▶ S. 178 (to) mind
daheim at home [ət ˈhəʊm]
daher *(deshalb)* so [səʊ]
damit so that, *(oft auch kurz:)* so
danach after that
dankbar *(froh)* glad [ɡlæd]
Danke. Thank you. [ˈθæŋk juː]; Thanks. [θæŋks] **dank Maya** thanks to Maya **Danke, gut.** Fine, thanks. **Danke, dass ihr zugehört habt.** Thank you for listening.
danken: jm. danken thank sb. [θæŋk]
dann then [ðen]
darstellende Kunst drama [ˈdrɑːmə]
darum that's why
das *(Artikel)* the [ðə]
das *(Relativpronomen)* 1. *(für Dinge)* which; that
2. *(für Personen)* who; that
das (dort) *(Singular)* that [ðæt]; *(Plural)* those [ðəʊz] **das Auto dort** that car
dass that [ðæt], [ðət] **es zeigt, dass …** it shows that …
dasselbe wie … the same as … [seɪm]
dauern *(Zeit brauchen)* take [teɪk]
davor *(zeitlich)* before that
Deck deck [dek]
dein(e) … your … [jɔː], [jə]
deiner, deine, deins yours [jɔːz]
Delfin dolphin [ˈdɒlfɪn]
Demonstration demonstration [ˌdemənˈstreɪʃn]
denken think [θɪŋk] **an etwas denken** think of sth.; *(sich merken, nicht vergessen)* remember sth. [rɪˈmembə]
Denkmal memorial [məˈmɔːriəl]; monument [ˈmɒnjumənt]
denn: Was ist denn? What's the matter? [ˈmætə]
dennoch still [stɪl]
der *(Artikel)* the [ðə]
der *(Relativpronomen)* 1. *(für Personen)* who; that
2. *(für Dinge)* which; that
der … (dort) *(Singular)* that … [ðæt]; *(Plural)* those … [ðəʊz] **der … (hier)** *(Singular)* this … [ðɪs]; *(Plural)* these … [ðiːz]
derselbe wie … the same as … [seɪm]
deshalb so [səʊ]; that's why
Design design [dɪˈzaɪn]
Designer/in designer [dɪˈzaɪnə]
Detail detail [ˈdiːteɪl]
deuten: auf etwas deuten *(zeigen)* point to sth. [pɔɪnt]
deutlich clear(ly) [klɪə], [ˈklɪəli]
Deutsch; deutsch German [ˈdʒɜːmən]
Dezember December [dɪˈsembə]
Dialog dialogue [ˈdaɪəlɒɡ]
dich you [juː]; *(Reflexivpronomen)* yourself [jɔːˈself]
dick fat [fæt]
die *(Artikel)* the [ðə]
die *(Relativpronomen)* 1. *(für Personen)* who; that
2. *(für Dinge)* which; that
die … (dort) *(Singular)* that … [ðæt]; *(Plural)* those … [ðəʊz] **die … (hier)** *(Singular)* this … [ðɪs]; *(Plural)* these … [ðiːz]
Dieb/in thief [θiːf], pl thieves [θiːvz]
Dienstag Tuesday [ˈtjuːzdeɪ, ˈtjuːzdi]
dies (hier) *(Singular)* this [ðɪs]; *(Plural)* these [ðiːz]
diese(r, s): dieser Ort / diese Pause / dieses Fach this place/break/subject **diese Leute** these people **Diese(r, s) hier.** This one.
dieselbe(n) wie … the same as … [seɪm]
diesjährige(r, s): das diesjährige Musical/Theaterstück/… this year's musical/play/…
Ding thing [θɪŋ]
dir you [juː]; *(Reflexivpronomen)* yourself [jɔːˈself]
direkt direct [dəˈrekt], [daɪˈrekt]

German – English

Disko disco [ˈdɪskəʊ]
Diskussion discussion [dɪˈskʌʃn]
dokumentieren *(Daten festhalten)* record [rɪˈkɔːd]
Dom cathedral [kəˈθiːdrəl]
Donner thunder [ˈθʌndə]
Donnerstag Thursday [ˈθɜːzdeɪ, -di]
Doppel- double [ˈdʌbl]
Doppelpunkt colon [ˈkəʊlən]
Dorf village [ˈvɪlɪdʒ]
dort(hin) there [ðeə]   **dort entlang** that way   **dort unten** down there
Dose tin [tɪn]
dran: Ich bin dran. (It's) my turn. [tɜːn]
draußen outside [ˌaʊtˈsaɪd]   **nach draußen** out(side)
drehen: sich im Kreis drehen spin around [ˌspɪn_əˈraʊnd]
drei three [θriː]
Dreieck triangle [ˈtraɪæŋgl]
drinnen inside [ˌɪnˈsaɪd]   **nach drinnen** inside
dritte(r, s) third [θɜːd]
drittgrößte(r, s) third biggest
drüben: da/dort drüben over there
drücken press [pres]; *(schieben, stoßen)* push [pʊʃ]
du you [juː]
Dudelsack bagpipes *(pl)* [ˈbægpaɪps]
dumm stupid [ˈstjuːpɪd]
Dummerchen silly [ˈsɪli]
dunkel dark [dɑːk]
Dunkelheit dark [dɑːk]; darkness [ˈdɑːknəs]
Dunst(schleier) mist [mɪst]
durch through [θruː]
Durchsage announcement [əˈnaʊnsmənt]
dürfen can [kæn], [kən]; may [meɪ]; be allowed to [əˈlaʊd]   **du darfst es nicht tun** you mustn't do it [ˈmʌsnt]
Durst haben be thirsty [ˈθɜːsti]
durstig sein be thirsty [ˈθɜːsti]
Dusche shower [ˈʃaʊə]
duschen; sich duschen have a shower [ˈʃaʊə]
DVD DVD [ˌdiːviːˈdiː]

E

eben: gerade eben just [dʒʌst]
ebenso as well [əz ˈwel]
echt *(wirklich)* real [ˈriːəl]
Ecke corner [ˈkɔːnə]   **Church Road, Ecke London Road** on the corner of Church Road and London Road   **Laden an der Ecke** *("Tante-Emma-Laden")* corner shop [ˈkɔːnə ʃɒp]
egal: Geld ist mir egal. I don't care about money.   **Aber egal, ...** *(Wie dem auch sei)* Anyway, ... [ˈeniweɪ]   **egal, wann** whenever [ˌwenˈevə]
▶ S. 191 (to) care
▶ S. 195 whenever, wherever, whatever, whoever

Ehre honour [ˈɒnə]
Ehrenamtliche(r) volunteer [ˌvɒlənˈtɪə]
Ei egg [eg]
Eierkuchen pancake [ˈpænkeɪk]
eifersüchtig (auf) jealous (of) [ˈdʒeləs]
eigene(r, s): mein eigener Film / mein eigenes Zimmer / ... my own film/room/... [əʊn]
eigentlich in fact [ɪn ˈfækt]; actually [ˈæktʃuəli]
▶ S. 184 actually
Eiland *(kleine Insel)* isle [aɪl]
eilen; sich beeilen hurry (up) [ˈhʌri]
Eimer bucket [ˈbʌkɪt]
ein(e) *(Artikel)* a, an [ə], [ən]   **ein anderer .../eine andere .../ein anderes ...** another ... [əˈnʌðə]   **einer nach dem anderen** one by one   **eines Nachts/Tages** one night/day   **ein paar** a few [ə ˈfjuː]; some [sʌm], [səm]
einander *(sich gegenseitig)* each other [iːtʃ_ˈʌðə]
einbringen *(Heu)* bring in
Eindruck impression [ɪmˈpreʃn]
einfach   1. *(nicht schwierig)* easy [ˈiːzi]   2. **einfach nur** just [dʒʌst]
Einführung *(Einleitung)* introduction [ˌɪntrəˈdʌkʃn]
eingeschaltet sein *(Radio, Licht usw.)* be on
einhundert a hundred, one hundred [ˈhʌndrəd]
einige a few [ə ˈfjuː]; some [sʌm], [səm]
einigen: sich auf etwas einigen agree on sth. [əˈgriː]
Einkäufe erledigen do the/some shopping [ˈʃɒpɪŋ]
einkaufen shop [ʃɒp]   **einkaufen gehen** go shopping [ˈʃɒpɪŋ]; do the shopping / do some shopping
Einkaufszentrum shopping centre [ˈʃɒpɪŋ sentə]; shopping mall [ˈʃɒpɪŋ mɔːl], *(kurz auch:)* mall
einladen: jn. einladen (zu) invite sb. (to) [ɪnˈvaɪt]
Einladung (zu, nach) invitation (to) [ˌɪnvɪˈteɪʃn]
einlegen: eine Pause einlegen pause [pɔːz]
Einleitung introduction [ˌɪntrəˈdʌkʃn]
einmal   1. once [wʌns]   **noch einmal** again [əˈgen]   2. **auf einmal** *(plötzlich)* suddenly [ˈsʌdnli]   3. **(noch) nicht einmal** not even
einmarschieren: in ein Land einmarschieren invade a country [ɪnˈveɪd]
einreichen: etwas einreichen hand sth. in [ˌhænd_ˈɪn]
eins one [wʌn]   **eins zu eins/eins beide** *(Ergebnis im Sport)* one all [ˌwʌn_ˈɔːl]
einsam lonely [ˈləʊnli]
einschalten: etwas einschalten turn sth. on [ˌtɜːn_ˈɒn]
einschlafen fall asleep [ˌfɔːl_əˈsliːp]

einsilbig *(aus einer Silbe bestehend)* one-syllable [ˈsɪləbl]
einsteigen: in ein Auto/Taxi einsteigen get in(to) a car/taxi   **in einen Bus/einen Zug/ein Flugzeug einsteigen** get on a bus/train/plane
Eintrag, Eintragung *(im Tagebuch, Wörterbuch)* entry [ˈentri]
eintreffen arrive [əˈraɪv]
eintreten *(in Raum)* enter   **in einen Klub eintreten** join a club [dʒɔɪn]
Eintritt entry [ˈentri]
Eintrittskarte ticket [ˈtɪkɪt]
Einwohner(zahl) population [ˌpɒpjuˈleɪʃn]
Einzelheit detail [ˈdiːteɪl]
einziehen move in   **in ein Haus einziehen** move into a house
einzige(r, s): der/die/das einzige ...; die einzigen ... the only ... [ˈəʊnli]
Eis ice [aɪs]; *(Speiseeis)* ice cream [ˌaɪs ˈkriːm]
Eistee iced tea
Elefant elephant [ˈelɪfənt]
elektronisch electronic [ɪˌlekˈtrɒnɪk]
Element element [ˈelɪmənt]
elf eleven [ɪˈlevn]
Eltern parents [ˈpeərənts]
E-Mail email [ˈiːmeɪl]; mail
emigrieren *(auswandern)* emigrate [ˈemɪgreɪt]
emporragen *(Berge, Säulen, Türme, ...)* rise up [ˌraɪz_ˈʌp]
Ende end [end]; *(Abschluss)* ending   **am oberen Ende (von)** at the top (of)   **am unteren Ende (von)** at the bottom (of) [ˈbɒtəm]   **zu Ende sein** be over
enden finish [ˈfɪnɪʃ]; end
endlich *(schließlich)* at last [ət ˈlɑːst]; finally [ˈfaɪnəli]
Endspiel final [ˈfaɪnl]
Energie energy [ˈenədʒi]
eng *(schmal)* narrow [ˈnærəʊ]
Engel angel [ˈeɪndʒl]
Englisch; englisch English [ˈɪŋglɪʃ]
entgegnen reply (to) [rɪˈplaɪ]
entlang: die Straße/den Fluss/... entlang along the street/the river/... [əˈlɒŋ]   **dort entlang** that way
entscheiden: sich entscheiden decide [dɪˈsaɪd]
Entscheidung decision [dɪˈsɪʒn]
Entschuldigung.   1. *(Tut mir leid.)* (I'm) sorry. [ˈsɒri]   2. **Entschuldigung, ... / Entschuldigen Sie, ...** *(Darf ich mal stören?)* Excuse me, ... [ɪkˈskjuːz miː]
entsetzt shocked [ʃɒkt]; in horror [ˈhɒrə]
entspannen: sich entspannen relax [rɪˈlæks]
entwerfen *(konstruieren, entwickeln)* design [dɪˈzaɪn]
entwickeln *(entwerfen, konstruieren)* design [dɪˈzaɪn]
Entwurf draft [drɑːft]

Dictionary

er 1. *(männliche Person)* he [hiː] 2. *(Ding; Tier)* it [ɪt]
Erdbeere strawberry [ˈstrɔːbəri]
Erdboden ground [graʊnd]
Erde *(der Planet)* earth [ɜːθ] *(oft auch:* Earth*)* **auf der Erde** on earth **unter der Erde** underground [ˌʌndəˈgraʊnd]
Ereignis event [ɪˈvent]
Erfahrung(en) experience *(no pl)* [ɪkˈspɪəriəns]
erfinden invent [ɪnˈvent]
Erfolg success [səkˈses]
erforschen explore [ɪkˈsplɔː]
Ergebnis result [rɪˈzʌlt]
erhältlich available [əˈveɪləbl]
erhellen *(aufleuchten lassen)* light up [ˌlaɪt ˈʌp]
erinnern: sich an etwas erinnern remember sth. [rɪˈmembə]
Erinnerung memory [ˈmeməri]
erkältet sein have a cold [kəʊld]
Erkältung: eine Erkältung haben have a cold [kəʊld]
erklären: jm. etwas erklären explain sth. to sb. [ɪkˈspleɪn]
erkranken: an etwas erkranken come down with sth.
▶ S. 180 *(to) come across/down/over/…*
erkunden explore [ɪkˈsplɔː]
erlauben allow [əˈlaʊ]
erläutern: jm. etwas erläutern explain sth. to sb. [ɪkˈspleɪn]
erraten guess [ges]
erreichbar *(Telefon)* available [əˈveɪləbl]
erreichen reach [riːtʃ]
erröten go red
erscheinen *(auftauchen)* appear [əˈpɪə]
erschrecken: jn. erschrecken scare sb. [skeə]
erst only [ˈəʊnli] **erst um drei** *(nicht vor drei)* not till three; not until three
erstaunlich amazing [əˈmeɪzɪŋ]
erste(r, s) first [fɜːst] **als Erstes** first **der erste Tag** the first day **zum ersten Mal** for the first time
ertrinken drown [draʊn]
erwachsen werden grow up [ˌgrəʊ_ˈʌp]
Erwachsene(r) adult [ˈædʌlt]
erwarten: etwas erwarten expect sth. [ɪkˈspekt] **Ich kann es kaum erwarten, … zu sehen.** I can't wait to see …
erwidern reply (to) [rɪˈplaɪ]
erzählen (von) tell (about) [tel]
Erzählung story [ˈstɔːri]
Erziehung education [ˌedʒuˈkeɪʃn]
erzielen: einen Treffer erzielen score [skɔː]
es it [ɪt] **es ist … / es gibt …** there's … **es sind … / es gibt …** there are … **Ach, du bist es.** Oh, it's you. **Bist du es?** Is that you?
essen eat [iːt] **zu Abend/Mittag essen** have dinner/lunch
Essen *(Lebensmittel)* food [fuːd]; *(Mahlzeit)* meal [miːl]
Esszimmer dining room [ˈdaɪnɪŋ ruːm]

Etikett label [ˈleɪbl]
etikettieren label [ˈleɪbl]
etwas 1. something [ˈsʌmθɪŋ]; *(in Fragen)* anything [ˈeniθɪŋ] **sonst noch etwas** anything else
▶ S. 195 *… else*
2. *(ein bisschen)* some [sʌm], [səm]; a bit [ə ˈbɪt]
euch you [juː]; *(Reflexivpronomen)* yourselves [jɔːˈselvz]
euer …/eure … your … [jɔː], [jə]
eurer, eure, eures yours [jɔːz]
Euro euro (€) [ˈjʊərəʊ]
▶ S. 189 Pounds and euros
Europa Europe [ˈjʊərəp]
europäisch: die Europäische Union the EU [ˌiː ˈjuː] (the European Union [ˌjʊərəpiːən ˈjuːniən])
Eurozone eurozone [ˈjʊərəʊzəʊn]
ewig *(für immer)* for ever [fər ˈevə]
Exemplar copy [ˈkɒpi]
Export export [ˈekspɔːt]

F

Fackel torch [tɔːtʃ]
fähig sein, etwas zu tun be able to do sth. [ˈeɪbl]
Fahne *(Flagge)* flag [flæg]
Fähre ferry [ˈferi]
fahren go [gəʊ]; *(ein Auto/mit dem Auto)* drive [draɪv] **in Urlaub fahren** go on holiday **mit dem Bus/Auto/Zug fahren** go by bus/car/train **Rad fahren** ride a bike
Fahrkarte ticket [ˈtɪkɪt]
Fahrkartenschalter ticket office [ˈtɪkɪt ˌɒfɪs]
Fahrplan timetable [ˈtaɪmteɪbl]
Fahrrad bike [baɪk]
Fahrstuhl lift [lɪft]
Fahrt journey [ˈdʒɜːni]; ride [raɪd]
fair fair [feə]
Fakt fact [fækt]
Fall: Auf keinen Fall! No way! [ˌnəʊ ˈweɪ]
fallen fall [fɔːl]; drop [drɒp] **etwas fallen lassen** drop sth. [drɒp]
falls if [ɪf]
falsch wrong [rɒŋ]; false [fɔːls] **Nein, das ist falsch.** No, that's wrong.
Familie family [ˈfæməli] **eine vierköpfige Familie** a family of four **Familie Blackwell** the Blackwell family
Fan fan [fæn]
fangen catch [kætʃ]
fantastisch fantastic [fænˈtæstɪk]
Farbe colour [ˈkʌlə]
Farm farm [fɑːm]
Fasching carnival [ˈkɑːnɪvl]
fast almost [ˈɔːlməʊst]; nearly [ˈnɪəli]
Februar February [ˈfebruəri]
Federmäppchen pencil case [ˈpensl keɪs]

fehlen be missing [ˈmɪsɪŋ] **die fehlenden Wörter** the missing words **Was fehlt dir?** What's wrong with you?
Fehler mistake [mɪˈsteɪk]; *(Schuld)* fault [fɔːlt] **einen Fehler machen** make a mistake
Feier celebration [ˌseliˈbreɪʃn]
feiern celebrate [ˈselibreɪt]
fein fine [faɪn]
Feind/in enemy [ˈenəmi]
Feld field [fiːld]
Fell coat [kəʊt]
Fels, Felsen rock [rɒk]
felsig rocky [ˈrɒki]
Fenster window [ˈwɪndəʊ]
Ferien holidays *(pl)* [ˈhɒlədeɪz]
Fernbedienung remote control [rɪˌməʊt kənˈtrəʊl] *(kurz auch:* remote)
fernsehen watch TV [ˌwɒtʃ tiːˈviː]
Fernsehen, Fernsehgerät TV [ˌtiːˈviː] **im Fernsehen** on TV
fertig 1. **mit etwas fertig werden/sein** finish sth. [ˈfɪnɪʃ] **Wir sind fertig.** *(Wir haben es erledigt.)* We're finished. [ˈfɪnɪʃt]
2. *(bereit)* ready [ˈredi] **Wir sind fertig.** *(Wir sind bereit.)* We're ready. **sich fertig machen (für)** get ready (for)
3. **jn. fertig machen** *(zurechtweisen)* give sb. a hard time *(infml)*
Fertigkeit skill [skɪl]
Fest *(Festival)* festival [ˈfestɪvl]
festhalten: sich an etwas festhalten hold onto sth. [həʊld]
Festival festival [ˈfestɪvl]
fett fat [fæt]
Feuer fire [ˈfaɪə]
Feuerwerk fireworks *(pl)* [ˈfaɪəwɜːks]
Feuerwerkskörper firework [ˈfaɪəwɜːk]
Fieber temperature [ˈtemprətʃə] **Fieber haben** have a temperature
Figur *(in Roman, Film, usw.)* character [ˈkærəktə]; *(Gestalt)* figure [ˈfɪgə]
Film film [fɪlm]; movie [ˈmuːvi]
filmen film [fɪlm]
Filzstift felt pen [ˌfelt ˈpen]
Finale final [ˈfaɪnl]
finden find [faɪnd] **Freunde finden** make friends **Wie findest du …?** How do you like …?
Finger finger [ˈfɪŋgə]
Finsternis darkness [ˈdɑːknəs]
Fisch fish [fɪʃ], *pl* fish
Fischerei fishing [ˈfɪʃɪŋ]
Flagge flag [flæg]
Flasche bottle [ˈbɒtl]
Fleck spot [spɒt]
Fleisch meat [miːt]
fliegen fly [flaɪ]
fliehen escape [ɪˈskeɪp]
Flosse fin [fɪn]
Flucht escape [ɪˈskeɪp]
Flügel wing [wɪŋ]
Flughafen airport [ˈeəpɔːt]
Flugzeug plane [pleɪn] **im Flugzeug** on the plane

German – English

Fluss river ['rɪvə]
flussabwärts downstream [ˌdaʊn'striːm]
flussaufwärts upstream [ˌʌp'striːm]
flüstern whisper ['wɪspə] **..., sagte er flüsternd.** ..., he said under his breath. [breθ]
folgen follow ['fɒləʊ]
Folie *(für Projektor)* transparency [træns'pærənsi]
Form form [fɔːm]; *(Gestalt)* shape [ʃeɪp]
formen form [fɔːm]
Forschung(en) research *(no pl)* ['riːsɜːtʃ]
fort away [ə'weɪ]
fortfahren *(weiterreden)* go on [ˌgəʊ 'ɒn]
fortsetzen: etwas fortsetzen continue sth. [kən'tɪnjuː] **sich fortsetzen** *(weitergehen)* continue
Foto photo ['fəʊtəʊ] **auf dem Foto** in the photo **Fotos machen** take photos
Fotoapparat camera ['kæmərə]
fotografieren take photos [ˌteɪk 'fəʊtəʊz]; photograph ['fəʊtəgrɑːf]
Foul foul [faʊl]
Frage question ['kwestʃn] **eine Frage stellen** ask a question **Kommt nicht in Frage!** No way! [ˌnəʊ 'weɪ]
fragen ask [ɑːsk] **jn. nach dem Weg fragen** ask sb. the way **sich fragen** *(gern wissen wollen)* wonder ['wʌndə]
Fragezeichen question mark ['kwestʃən mɑːk]
Französisch; französisch French [frentʃ]
Frau 1. woman ['wʊmən], *pl* women ['wɪmɪn]
  2. **Frau Schwarz** Mrs Schwarz ['mɪsɪz]
  3. *(übliche Anrede von Lehrerinnen)* **Frau Bell** Miss Bell [mɪs]
frei free [friː] **einen Tag frei bekommen/haben** get/have a day off [ɒf]
Freistoß free kick [ˌfriː 'kɪk]
Freitag Friday ['fraɪdeɪ], ['fraɪdi]
Freiwillige(r) volunteer [ˌvɒlən'tɪə]
Freizeit free time [ˌfriː 'taɪm]
Freizeitaktivitäten free-time activities [ˌfriːtaɪm æk'tɪvətiz]
Fremdenführer/in guide [gaɪd]
freuen: sich auf etwas freuen look forward to sth. ['fɔːwəd] **Freut mich, dich/euch/Sie kennenzulernen.** Nice to meet you.
Freund friend [frend]; *(Partner)* boyfriend ['bɔɪfrend] **Freunde finden** make friends
Freundin friend [frend]; *(Partnerin)* girlfriend ['gɜːlfrend]
freundlich friendly ['frendli]; kind [kaɪnd]
Friede, Frieden peace [piːs]
friedfertig peaceful ['piːsfl]
friedlich peaceful ['piːsfl]
frieren be cold [kəʊld]
frisch fresh [freʃ]
Friseur/in hairdresser ['heədresə]

froh *(glücklich)* happy ['hæpi]; *(dankbar)* glad [glæd]
Frosch frog [frɒg]
Frucht fruit [fruːt]
früh early ['ɜːli]
früher (einmal) in the old days
Frühling spring [sprɪŋ]
Frühstück breakfast ['brekfəst] **Zimmer mit Frühstück** bed & breakfast
frühstücken have breakfast
Frühstückspension bed & breakfast
fühlen; sich fühlen feel [fiːl] **Ich fühle mich nicht gut.** I don't feel well.
führen lead [liːd]
füllen fill [fɪl]
Füller pen [pen]
fünf five [faɪv]
funktionieren work
für for [fɔː], [fə]
furchtbar terrible ['terəbl]; awful ['ɔːfl]
fürchterlich terrible ['terəbl]; awful ['ɔːfl]
Fuß foot [fʊt], *pl* feet [fiːt] **zu Fuß gehen** walk [wɔːk] **jm. auf die Füße treten** *(auch im übertragenen Sinne)* tread on sb.'s toes [tred] *(infml)*
Fußabdruck footprint ['fʊtprɪnt]
Fußball football ['fʊtbɔːl]
Fußboden floor [flɔː]
Fußgänger/in pedestrian [pə'destriən]
Fußgängerzone pedestrian zone [pə'destriən zəʊn]
Futter food [fuːd]
füttern feed [fiːd]
Fütterungszeit feeding time ['fiːdɪŋ taɪm]

G

Gabel fork [fɔːk]
Galerie gallery ['gæləri]
Gang 1. *(Korridor)* corridor ['kɒrɪdɔː]
  2. **im Gang sein** *(andauern)* go on
ganz *(völlig)* quite [kwaɪt] **ganz allein** all alone **ganz Plymouth** all of Plymouth
ganze(r, s) whole [həʊl] **das ganze Plymouth** all of Plymouth **den ganzen Tag** all day **die ganze Zeit** all the time **ganzer Satz** full sentence
gar nichts nothing ['nʌθɪŋ]
Garage garage ['gærɑːʒ], ['gærɪdʒ]
Garten garden ['gɑːdn]
Gartenarbeit gardening ['gɑːdnɪŋ]
Gärtnern gardening ['gɑːdnɪŋ]
Gast guest [gest]
Gastfamilie host family ['həʊst fæməli]
Gatter gate [geɪt]
gebackene Kartoffeln *(im Backofen in Fett gebacken)* roast potatoes [rəʊst pə'teɪtəʊz]
Gebäude building ['bɪldɪŋ]
geben give [gɪv] **Es gibt ...** *(Singular)* There's ...; *(Plural)* There are ... **Gibt**

es (irgendwelche) ...? Are there any ...? ['eni] **Was gibt es zum Mittagessen?** What's for lunch? **Was gibt's?** *(Was ist los?)* What's up?
Gebiet area ['eəriə]
geboren sein/werden be born [bɔːn]
gebrochen broken ['brəʊkən]
Geburtstag birthday ['bɜːθdeɪ] **Ich habe am 5. Mai Geburtstag.** My birthday is on 5th May. **Ich habe im Mai Geburtstag.** My birthday is in May. **Wann hast du Geburtstag?** When's your birthday?
Gedanke thought [θɔːt] **jemandes Gedanken lesen** read sb.'s mind [maɪnd]
Gedenk- memorial [mə'mɔːriəl]
Gedicht poem ['pəʊɪm]
Gefahr danger ['deɪndʒə]
gefährlich dangerous ['deɪndʒərəs]
gefallen: Wie gefällt dir ...? How do you like ...?
Gefangene(r) captive ['kæptɪv]
Gefängnis prison ['prɪzn]
Gefäß pot [pɒt]
Gefühl feeling ['fiːlɪŋ]
gegen 1. against [ə'genst]
  2. **gegen 18 Uhr** around 6 pm [ə'raʊnd]
Gegend area ['eəriə]; *(Landschaft)* countryside ['kʌntrisaɪd] **hier in der Gegend** round here [ˌraʊnd 'hɪə]
gegenüber (von) opposite ['ɒpəzɪt]
Gegenwart present ['preznt]
gehen go [gəʊ]; *(zu Fuß gehen)* walk [wɔːk]; *(weggehen, verlassen)* leave [liːv] **an Land gehen** land **ans Telefon gehen** answer the phone **einkaufen gehen** go shopping **Los geht's. / Jetzt geht's los.** Here we go. **nach Hause gehen** go home **segeln gehen** go sailing ['seɪlɪŋ] **spazieren gehen** go for a walk [wɔːk] **Wie geht's? / Wie geht es dir/euch/Ihnen?** How are you? **Mir geht's nicht gut.** I don't feel well. **Worum geht es in der Geschichte?** What is the story about? **Es geht um eine Möwe.** It's about a seagull.
gehören: zu etwas gehören *(zu etwas passen)* go with sth.
Gehweg *(Bürgersteig)* pavement ['peɪvmənt]
Geist ghost [gəʊst]
Gel gel [dʒel]
Gelächter laughter ['lɑːftə]
gelangen *(hinkommen)* get [get]
gelangweilt sein be/feel bored [bɔːd]
gelb yellow ['jeləʊ]
Geld money ['mʌni] **Geld ausgeben (für)** spend money (on) [spend] **Geld sammeln (für)** raise money (for) [reɪz]
Gelegenheit *(Chance)* chance [tʃɑːns]
gemacht: aus etwas gemacht sein be made of sth.
Gemeinde community [kə'mjuːnəti]

Dictionary

Gemeinschaft community [kəˈmjuːnəti]
Gemüse vegetables (pl) [ˈvedʒtəblz]
genannt werden (heißen) be called [kɔːld]
genau 1. (Adjektiv) exact [ɪgˈzækt] 2. (Adverb) exactly [ɪgˈzæktli] **genau hinschauen** look closely [ˈkləʊsli]
genau in dem Moment just then
genau wie … just like … [ˈdʒʌst laɪk]
genial brilliant [ˈbrɪliənt]
genießen enjoy [ɪnˈdʒɔɪ]
genug enough [ɪˈnʌf] **genug von etwas haben** (etwas satt haben, einer Sache überdrüssig sein) be tired of sth. [ˈtaɪəd]
geöffnet open [ˈəʊpən]
Geografie geography [dʒiˈɒgrəfi]
gerade (im Moment) at the moment [ˈməʊmənt] **gerade dann** just then
gerade eben just [dʒʌst] **jetzt gerade** (in diesem Moment) right now
geradeaus weiter straight on [streɪt ˈɒn]
Geräusch sound [saʊnd]; noise [nɔɪz]
gern: Ich tanze/singe/… gern. I like dancing/singing/… **Ich hätte gern …** I'd like … [ˌaɪd ˈlaɪk] (= I would like …) **Ich würde gern gehen.** I'd like to go. **Ich würde sehr gern bleiben.** I'd love to stay. **Was hättest du gern?** What would you like? [wʊd]
gernhaben like [laɪk]
gesamte(r, s) whole [həʊl]
Gesamtsumme: eine Gesamtsumme von … a total of … [ˈtəʊtl]
Geschäft (Laden) shop [ʃɒp]
geschäftig (belebt) busy [ˈbɪzi]
geschehen (mit) happen (to) [ˈhæpən]
Geschenk present [ˈpreznt]
Geschichte 1. (vergangene Zeiten) history [ˈhɪstri] 2. (Erzählung) story [ˈstɔːri]
geschieden divorced [dɪˈvɔːst]
Geschirr: das Geschirr abwaschen, spülen wash the dishes (pl) [ˈdɪʃɪz]
Geschwindigkeit speed [spiːd]
Gesicht face [feɪs]
Gesichtsausdruck facial expression [ˌfeɪʃl ɪkˈspreʃn]
gespannt (aufgeregt) excited [ɪkˈsaɪtɪd]
Gespenst ghost [gəʊst]
Gespräch talk; (Unterhaltung) conversation [ˌkɒnvəˈseɪʃn]
Gestalt (Figur) figure [ˈfɪgə]; (Form) shape [ʃeɪp]
Gestaltung (Design) design [dɪˈzaɪn]; (Layout) layout [ˈleɪaʊt]
gestern yesterday [ˈjestədeɪ], [-di]
gesund well [wel] **Ich bin wieder gesund.** I'm well again.
geteilter Bildschirm split screen [splɪt ˈskriːn]
Getränk drink [drɪŋk]
gewinnen win [wɪn]
Gewinn (Preis) prize [praɪz]
Gewinner/in winner [ˈwɪnə]
Gewitter storm [stɔːm]
gewöhnlich 1. (Adjektiv: üblich) usual [ˈjuːʒuəl] 2. (Adverb: normalerweise) usually [ˈjuːʒuli]
gießen pour [pɔː]
Giraffe giraffe [dʒəˈrɑːf]
Gipfel summit [ˈsʌmɪt]
Gitarre guitar [gɪˈtɑː] **Gitarre spielen** play the guitar
glänzend (großartig) brilliant [ˈbrɪliənt]
Glas glass [glɑːs] **ein Glas Wasser** a glass of water
glatt (rutschig) slippery [ˈslɪpəri]
glauben believe [bɪˈliːv]; think [θɪŋk]
gleich nachdem … just after …
gleichzeitig at one time
Gleis (Bahnsteig) platform [ˈplætfɔːm]
gliedern (strukturieren) structure [ˈstrʌktʃə]
Glocke bell [bel]
Glück: Glück haben be lucky **Viel Glück!** Good luck! [lʌk]
glücklich happy [ˈhæpi]
Glückspilz: Du Glückspilz. Lucky you. [ˈlʌki]
Gokart go-kart [ˈgəʊ kɑːt]
Gold gold [gəʊld]
golden, Gold- gold [gəʊld]
Gott God [gɒd]
Gottesdienst service [ˈsɜːvɪs]
Grab grave [greɪv]
Graben ditch [dɪtʃ]
Grabstein gravestone [ˈgreɪvstəʊn]
Grafschaft (in Großbritannien) county [ˈkaʊnti]
Gramm gram [græm]
Gras grass [grɑːs]
grau grey [greɪ]
grausam cruel [ˈkruːl]
Grenze border [ˈbɔːdə]
groß big [bɪg]; large [lɑːdʒ]; (Person) tall [tɔːl] **Wie groß soll der/dein Tee sein?** What size tea would you like?
großartig great [greɪt]; brilliant [ˈbrɪliənt]
Größe size [saɪz]
Großeltern grandparents [ˈgrænpeərənts]
Großmutter grandmother [ˈgrænmʌðə]
Großstadt city [ˈsɪti]
Großvater grandfather [ˈgrænfɑːðə]
grün green [griːn]
Grund (Begründung) reason [ˈriːzn]
gründen found [faʊnd]
Gruppe group (of) [gruːp]; (Band) band [bænd]
gruselig scary [ˈskeəri]
Gruß: Liebe Grüße, … (Briefschluss) Love, …
grüßen: Grüß … von mir. Say hello to … for me.
gucken look [lʊk]
▶ S. 180 (to) look after/around/for/…
gut good [gʊd]; (gesundheitlich) well; (Adverb) well [wel] **gut sein in Kung-Fu / gut Kung-Fu können** be good at kung fu **Danke, gut.** Fine, thanks. **Guten Morgen.** Good morning. [gʊd ˈmɔːnɪŋ] **Guten Tag.** Hello. [həˈləʊ] **Mir geht's nicht gut. / Ich fühle mich nicht gut.** I don't feel well.
gutaussehend good-looking [ˌgʊdˈlʊkɪŋ]
Güter goods (pl) [gʊdz]
Gymnastik gymnastics [dʒɪmˈnæstɪks]

H

Haar, Haare hair [heə]
haben have [hæv], [həv]; have got; (Idee, Vorschlag auch:) come up with **Durst haben** be thirsty [ˈθɜːsti] **genug von etwas haben** (etwas satt haben) be tired of sth. [ˈtaɪəd] **Glück haben** be lucky **Hunger haben** be hungry [ˈhʌŋgri] **Ich habe im Mai Geburtstag.** My birthday is in May. **jemand hat Recht/Unrecht** someone is right/wrong **viel zu tun haben** (beschäftigt sein) be busy [ˈbɪzi] **Wann hast du Geburtstag?** When's your birthday?
Hafen harbour [ˈhɑːbə]
Hai shark [ʃɑːk]
halb elf (10.30 / 22.30) half past ten [ˈhɑːf pɑːst]
Halbzeit half [hɑːf], pl halves [hɑːvz] **zur Halbzeit** at half time
Hallo. Hello. [həˈləʊ]
Hals neck [nek]; (Kehle) throat [θrəʊt]
Halsschmerzen haben have a sore throat [ˌsɔː ˈθrəʊt]
Halt stop [stɒp]
halten hold [həʊld] **einen Vortrag/eine Rede halten (über)** give a talk (about) **(mit jm.) Kontakt halten** stay in touch (with sb.) [tʌtʃ]
Haltestelle stop [stɒp]
Hamburger hamburger [ˈhæmbɜːgə]; burger
Hammer hammer [ˈhæmə]
hämmern hammer
Hamster hamster [ˈhæmstə]
Hand hand [hænd] **die Hand ausstrecken** reach over [ˌriːtʃ ˈəʊvə]
Handel trade [treɪd]
handeln: Es handelt von einer Möwe. It's about a seagull. **Wovon handelt die Geschichte?** What is the story about?
Handout handout [ˈhændaʊt]
Handpuppe puppet [ˈpʌpɪt]
Handschuh glove [ˈglʌv]
Handy mobile phone [ˌməʊbaɪl ˈfəʊn], (kurz auch:) mobile
Handzettel handout [ˈhændaʊt]
hängen hang [hæŋ]
hart hard [hɑːd]; (knallhart; schwierig) tough [tʌf] **hart werden** go hard

German – English

hassen hate [heɪt]
Haupt- main [meɪn]
Hauptsatz main clause ['meɪn klɔːz]
Hauptteil (eines Textes) body ['bɒdi]
Haus house [haʊs]   **nach Hause gehen** go home   **nach Hause kommen** come home   **zu Hause** at home   **zu Hause sein** be in   **nicht zu Hause sein** be out
Hausarrest: jm. Hausarrest erteilen ground sb. [graʊnd]
Hausaufgabe(n) homework ['haʊmwɜːk]   **Hausaufgaben machen** do my / your / ... homework   **Was haben wir als Hausaufgabe auf?** What's for homework?
Häuschen (Cottage) cottage ['kɒtɪdʒ]
Haustier pet [pet]
heftig: heftiger Regen heavy rain ['hevi]
Heftpflaster plaster ['plɑːstə]
Heide(kraut) heather ['heðə]
Heim (Zuhause) home [həʊm]
Heimat sein für etwas be home to sth.
Heimatstadt hometown ['həʊmtaʊn]
heiraten: jn. heiraten marry sb. ['mæri]
heiß hot [hɒt]
heißen (genannt werden) be called [kɔːld]   **Ich heiße ...** My name is ...   **Wie heißt du?** What's your name?   **jn. willkommen heißen (in)** welcome sb. (to) ['welkəm]
hektisch (geschäftig) busy ['bɪzi]
Held/in hero ['hɪərəʊ], pl heroes
helfen help [help]
Helfer/in helper ['helpə]
hell bright [braɪt]
Hemd shirt [ʃɜːt]
herauf up [ʌp]
heraus out [aʊt]   **aus ... heraus** out of ... ['aʊt ̮ əv]
herausfinden find out
herausfischen fish out
herausfordern: jn. herausfordern (zu etwas) challenge sb. (to sth.) ['tʃælɪndʒ]
Herausforderung challenge ['tʃælɪndʒ]
Herausgeber/in editor ['edɪtə]
herausnehmen take out
herausziehen pull out
Herberge hostel ['hɒstl]
Herbst autumn ['ɔːtəm]
hereinkommen come in [ˌkʌm ̮ 'ɪn]
Herr Schwarz Mr Schwarz ['mɪstə]
herrennen: hinter jm. herrennen run after sb. [ˌrʌn ̮ 'ɑːftə]
herrlich lovely ['lʌvli]
herüberkommen (zu/nach) come over (to)
▶ S. 180 (to) come across/down/over/...
herum: um ... herum around ... [ə'raʊnd]   **überall um sie herum** all around her   **um 18 Uhr herum** (gegen 18 Uhr) around 6 pm
herumgeben pass around [ˌpɑːs ̮ ə'raʊnd]

herumhacken: auf jm. herumhacken pick on sb. [pɪk] (infml)
herumirren wander ['wɒndə]
herumlaufen walk around; wander
herumreichen pass around
herumrennen run around
herumwirbeln (sich im Kreis drehen) spin around [ˌspɪn ̮ ə'raʊnd]
herunter down [daʊn]   **von ... herunter** off [ɒf]
▶ S. 177 off
hervorheben (mit Textmarker) highlight ['haɪlaɪt]
Herz heart [hɑːt]   **Tiere liegen mir am Herzen.** I care about animals.
▶ S. 191 (to) care
Heu hay [heɪ]
heute today [tə'deɪ]   **heute Nachmittag/Abend/...** this afternoon/evening/...   **heute Nacht, heute Abend** tonight [tə'naɪt]
hier here [hɪə]   **Hier bitte.** (Bitte sehr.) Here you are.   **hier in der Gegend** round here [ˌraʊnd 'hɪə]   **hier in der Nähe** near here   **hier herüber** over here   **hier oben** up here
hierher here [hɪə]   **bis hierher** (bis jetzt) so far
Hilfe help [help]
Himmel sky [skaɪ]; (im religiösen Sinn) heaven ['hevn]
hinauf up [ʌp]   **auf das Boot hinauf** onto the boat ['ɒntʊ]
hinaufklettern (auf) climb [klaɪm]
hinaus out [aʊt]   **aus ... hinaus** out of ... ['aʊt ̮ əv]
hinbringen take [teɪk]
hinein: in die Küche hinein into the kitchen ['ɪntʊ]
hineingehen go in; (eintreten) enter ['entə]
hineinspringen dive in [daɪv ̮ 'ɪn]
hinfallen fall [fɔːl]
hinkommen (gelangen) get [get]
hinlegen: etwas hinlegen put sth. down   **sich hinlegen** lie down [ˌlaɪ 'daʊn]
hinsetzen: sich hinsetzen sit down [ˌsɪt 'daʊn]
Hinsicht: in mancher Hinsicht in some ways   **in vielerlei Hinsicht** in many ways
hinstellen: sich hinstellen stand [stænd]
hinten: von hinten from behind [bɪ'haɪnd]
hinter behind [bɪ'haɪnd]   **hinter jm. herrennen** run after sb. [ˌrʌn ̮ 'ɑːftə]   **aus dem hinteren Teil des Buses** from the back of the bus   **hinter der Bühne** backstage [ˌbæk'steɪdʒ]
Hintergrund background ['bækgraʊnd]
hinterlassen: eine Nachricht hinterlassen leave a message [ˌliːv ̮ ə 'mesɪdʒ]

hinüberrennen (zu/nach ...) run over (to) ['əʊvə]
hinunter down [daʊn]
hinunterbeugen: sich hinunterbeugen bend down [bend]
Hinweis (Anhaltspunkt) clue [kluː]
hinweisen: (jn.) auf etwas hinweisen point sth. out (to sb.) [ˌpɔɪnt ̮ 'aʊt]
hinzufügen (zu) add (to) [æd]
Hirsch deer, pl deer [dɪə]
Hobby hobby ['hɒbi]
hoch high [haɪ]; (Gebäude, Baum) tall [tɔːl]
Hochland: das schottische Hochland the Highlands (pl) ['haɪləndz]
Hochmoor moor [mɔː], [mʊə]
hochsehen (aufschauen) look up [lʊk ̮ 'ʌp]
hochspringen jump up
hoffen hope [həʊp]
höflich polite [pə'laɪt]
Höhle cave [keɪv]
holen: (sich) etwas holen get sth.
Hölle hell [hel]
Holz wood [wʊd]
hölzern wooden ['wʊdn]
horchen listen ['lɪsn]
hören hear [hɪə]
Horn horn [hɔːn]
Hose trousers (pl) ['traʊzəz]
Hotel hotel [həʊ'tel]
hübsch pretty ['prɪti]; (schön, wunderbar) lovely ['lʌvli]
Hüfte hip [hɪp]
Hügel hill [hɪl]
Hund dog [dɒg]
Hunger haben be hungry ['hʌŋgri]
Hungersnot famine ['fæmɪn]
hungrig sein be hungry ['hʌŋgri]
Husten haben have a cough [kɒf]
Hut hat [hæt]
Hütehund sheepdog ['ʃiːpdɒg]

I

ich I [aɪ]   **Ich auch.** Me too.
ideal (perfekt) perfect ['pɜːfɪkt]
Idee idea [aɪ'dɪə]
identifizieren: jn./etwas identifizieren (anhand von etwas) identify sb./sth. (by sth.) [aɪ'dentɪfaɪ]
ihm him [hɪm]; (bei Dingen, Tieren) it
ihn him [hɪm]; (bei Dingen, Tieren) it
ihnen them [ðem], [ðəm]
Ihnen (höfliche Anredeform) you [juː]
ihr (Plural von „du") you [juː]
ihr: Hilf ihr. Help her. [hɜː]
ihr(e) ... (vor Nomen; besitzanzeigend)
1. (zu „she") her ... [hɜː, hə]
2. (zu „it") its ... [ɪts]
3. (zu „they") their ... [ðeə]
Ihr(e) ... (vor Nomen; besitzanzeigend) (zur höflichen Anredeform „you") your ... [jɔː, jə]

Dictionary

ihrer, ihre, ihrs *(zu „she")* hers [hɜːz]; *(zu „they")* theirs [ðeəz]
Ihrer, Ihre, Ihrs *(höfliche Anredeform)* yours [jɔːz]
im: im Jahr 1580 in 1580 **im Flugzeug** on the plane **im Radio** on the radio
Imbiss snack [snæk]
immer always [ˈɔːlweɪz] **für immer** for ever [fər ˈevə] **immer noch** still [stɪl] **immer wieder** again and again **etwas immer wieder / immer weiter tun** keep doing sth. [kiːp] **wann (auch) immer** whenever [ˌwenˈevə] **was (auch) immer** whatever [wɒtˈevə] **wer (auch) immer** whoever [huːˈevə] **wo (auch) immer** wherever [weərˈevə]
▶ S. 195 whenever, wherever, whatever, whoever
in in [ɪn]; *(in Ortsangaben auch oft:)* at [æt], [ət] **in der Beach Road** in Beach Road **in der Beach Road 8** at 8 Beach Road **in der Dean Street** in Dean Street **in der Dean Street 14** at 14 Dean Street **in der Nacht** at night **in der Nähe von** near **in der Schule** at school **in die Küche (hinein)** into the kitchen **in England** in England **in Ordnung** all right **in Schwierigkeiten sein** be in trouble [ˈtrʌbl]
Inder/in Indian [ˈɪndiən]
indirekt indirect [ˌɪndəˈrekt], [ˌɪndaɪˈrekt]
indisch Indian [ˈɪndiən]
Infinitiv infinitive [ɪnˈfɪnətɪv]
Information(en) (über) information (about) *(no pl)* [ˌɪnfəˈmeɪʃn]
Informations- und Kommunikationstechnologie ICT [ˌaɪ siː ˈtiː] (Information and Communication Technology)
Ingenieur/in engineer [ˌendʒɪˈnɪə]
Inhalt content [ˈkɒntent]
Inlineskaten skating [ˈskeɪtɪŋ]
Inlineskates skates [skeɪts]
innehalten pause [pɔːz]
Innenhof courtyard [ˈkɔːtjɑːd]
Innenseite: die Innenseite the inside [ˌɪnˈsaɪd]
Innere(r, s): im Innern von … inside … [ˌɪnˈsaɪd] **das Innere** the inside
innerhalb von … inside … [ˌɪnˈsaɪd]
Insel island [ˈaɪlənd]; *(Eiland)* isle [aɪl]
Inserat *(Anzeige)* advert [ˈædvɜːt]
insgesamt *(alles in allem)* altogether [ˌɔːltəˈgeðə]
Instrument instrument [ˈɪnstrəmənt]
Interaktion interaction [ˌɪntərˈækʃn]
interessant interesting [ˈɪntrəstɪŋ]
interessieren: sich interessieren (für) be interested (in) [ˈɪntrəstɪd] **jn. interessieren** interest sb. [ˈɪntrəst] **Wen interessiert das?** Who cares?
interessiert sein (an) be interested (in) [ˈɪntrəstɪd]
Internat boarding school [ˈbɔːdɪŋ skuːl]

international international [ˌɪntəˈnæʃnəl]
Interview interview [ˈɪntəvjuː]
interviewen: jn. interviewen interview sb. [ˈɪntəvjuː]
irgendetwas? anything? [ˈeniθɪŋ]
irgendjemand? anybody? / anyone? [ˈenibɒdi, ˈeniwʌn]
irgendwelche: Gibt es irgendwelche …? Are there any …? [ˈeni]
irren: jemand irrt sich *(jemand hat Unrecht)* someone is wrong [rɒŋ]

J

ja yes [jes] **Ja, das ist richtig. / Ja, das stimmt.** Yes, that's right.
Jacht yacht [jɒt]
Jacke, Jackett jacket [ˈdʒækɪt]
Jahr year [jɪə]
Jahrgang, Jahrgangsstufe year [jɪə]
Jahrhundert century [ˈsentʃəri]
Januar January [ˈdʒænjuəri]
je: besser als je zuvor better than ever
Jeans jeans *(pl)* [dʒiːnz]
jede(r, s) … every … [ˈevri]; *(jede(r, s) einzelne)* each … [iːtʃ]
Jedenfalls, … *(Wie dem auch sei)* Anyway, … [ˈeniweɪ]
jeder *(alle)* everyone [ˈevriwʌn], everybody [ˈevribɒdi] **sonst jeder** everybody else
▶ S. 195 … else
Jeep jeep [dʒiːp]
jemals ever [ˈevə] **Bist du jemals in … gewesen?** Have you ever been to …?
jemand somebody / someone [ˈsʌmbədi, ˈsʌmwʌn]; *(in Fragen)* anybody? / anyone? [ˈenibɒdi, ˈeniwʌn] **jemand anders** someone else **Finde jemanden, der …** Find someone who …
▶ S. 195 … else
jene(r, s): jener Ort / jene Fähre / jenes Kleid that place/ferry/dress **jene Leute** those people
jetzt now [naʊ] **jetzt gerade** right now **bis jetzt** so far **Jetzt, wo du …** Now that you …
Job job [dʒɒb]
Joghurt yoghurt [ˈjɒgət]
Jongleur/in juggler [ˈdʒʌglə]
jonglieren: mit etwas jonglieren juggle sth. [ˈdʒʌgl]
jubeln cheer [tʃɪə]
Judo judo [ˈdʒuːdəʊ]
Jugendliche(r) kid [kɪd] *(infml)*
Juli July [dʒuˈlaɪ]
jung young [jʌŋ]
Junge boy [bɔɪ]
Juni June [dʒuːn]
Juwelen jewels *(pl)* [ˈdʒuːəlz]

K

Kaffee coffee [ˈkɒfi]
Käfig cage [keɪdʒ]
Kajak kayak [ˈkaɪæk]
Kakao cocoa [ˈkəʊkəʊ]
Kalender diary [ˈdaɪəri]
kalt cold [kəʊld]
Kamera camera [ˈkæmərə]
Kameramann cameraman, *pl* -men
Kamin fireplace [ˈfaɪəpleɪs]
Kampf *(Schlägerei)* fight; *(Schlacht)* battle [ˈbætl]
kämpfen fight [faɪt] **gegen jn. kämpfen** fight sb.
Kämpfer/in fighter [ˈfaɪtə]
Kanal canal [kəˈnæl]
Kaninchen rabbit [ˈræbɪt]
Kante edge [edʒ]
Kantine canteen [kænˈtiːn]
Kapitän/in captain [ˈkæptɪn]
Kappe cap [kæp]
kaputt broken [ˈbrəʊkən] **kaputt gehen** break [breɪk] **etwas kaputt machen** break sth.
Karneval carnival [ˈkɑːnɪvl]
Karotte carrot [ˈkært]
Karren cart [kɑːt]
Karriere career [kəˈrɪə]
Karte (an) card (to) [kɑːd]
Kartoffel potato [pəˈteɪtəʊ], *pl* potatoes
Käse cheese [tʃiːz]
Kasse *(in Geschäften)* cash desk [ˈkæʃ desk]; *(für den Verkauf von Eintrittskarten)* ticket office [ˈtɪkɪt ˌɒfɪs]
Kästchen box [bɒks]
Kasten box [bɒks]
Kathedrale cathedral [kəˈθiːdrəl]
Katze cat [kæt]
kaufen buy [baɪ]
Käufer/in shopper [ˈʃɒpə]
kaum: Ich kann es kaum erwarten, … zu sehen I can't wait to see …
Kehle throat [θrəʊt]
kein(e) no [nəʊ] **keine(r, s) von …** none of … [nʌn] **Es gibt/sind keine …** There aren't any … [ˈeni] **Ich bin kein Junge.** I'm not a boy. **Ich mag kein Grün.** I don't like green. **er hat keine Zeit** he doesn't have time
Keks biscuit [ˈbɪskɪt]
kennen know [nəʊ] **Woher kennst du …?** How do you know …?
kennenlernen meet [miːt] **Freut mich, dich/euch/Sie kennenzulernen.** Nice to meet you.
kennzeichnen: etwas kennzeichnen mark sth. up [ˌmɑːk ˈʌp]
Kerze candle [ˈkændl]
Kette chain [tʃeɪn]
Kilogramm, Kilo (kg) kilogram [ˈkɪləgræm], kilo [ˈkiːləʊ] (kg)
Kilometer (km) kilometre [ˈkɪləmiːtə], [kɪˈlɒmɪtə] (km)

German – English

Kind child [tʃaɪld], *pl* children [ˈtʃɪldrən]; *(infml auch:)* kid [kɪd]
Kino cinema [ˈsɪnəmə]
Kirche church [tʃɜːtʃ]
Kiste box [bɒks]
Klang sound [saʊnd]
klar *(deutlich)* clear [klɪə]
Klasse class [klɑːs]
Klassenkamerad/in classmate [ˈklɑːsmeɪt]
Klassenzimmer classroom [ˈklɑːsruːm]
klatschen *(Beifall)* clap [klæp] **Klatscht in die Hände.** Clap your hands.
Klavier piano [piˈænəʊ] **Klavier spielen** play the piano
Klebestift glue stick [ˈgluː stɪk]
klebrig sticky [ˈstɪki]
Klebstoff glue [gluː]
Kleid dress [dres]
Kleidung, Kleidungsstücke clothes *(pl)* [kləʊðz]
klein little [ˈlɪtl]; small [smɔːl]; *(bes. Scottish English, infml:)* wee [wiː]
klettern climb [klaɪm]
Klingel bell [bel]
klingeln ring [rɪŋ]
klingen sound [saʊnd]
Klippe cliff [klɪf]
klopfen knock [nɒk]; *(tippen)* tap [tæp]
Klopfen tap [tæp]
Klub club [klʌb] **in einen Klub eintreten / sich einem Klub anschließen** join a club [dʒɔɪn]
klug clever [ˈklevə]
Knall bang [bæŋ]
knallhart tough [tʌf]
Kneipe pub [pʌb]
Knie knee [niː]
knien kneel [niːl]
kochen cook [kʊk]
Kohle coal [kəʊl]
Kohlebergwerk coal mine [ˈkəʊl maɪn]
Komiker/in comedian [kəˈmiːdiən]
komisch 1. *(lustig)* funny [ˈfʌni] 2. *(seltsam, merkwürdig)* funny; strange [streɪndʒ]; weird [wɪəd]
Komma comma [ˈkɒmə] **1,6 (eins Komma sechs)** 1.6 (one point six) [pɔɪnt]
▶ S. 181 Numbers
kommen come [kʌm]; *(gelangen, hinkommen)* get [get] **Ich komme aus Plymouth.** I'm from Plymouth. **Komm, Dad!** *(Na los, Dad!)* Come on, Dad. **nach Hause kommen** come home **auf etwas kommen** *(Idee, Vorschlag)* come up with sth. **Kommt nicht in Frage!** No way! [ˌnəʊ ˈweɪ]
▶ S. 180 (to) come across/down/over/...
Komödiant/in comedian [kəˈmiːdiən]
Komödie comedy [ˈkɒmədi]
König king [kɪŋ]
Königin queen [kwiːn]
königlich royal [ˈrɔɪəl]
Königreich kingdom [ˈkɪŋdəm]

können can [kæn], [kən]; be able to [ˈeɪbl] **ich kann nicht ... / du kannst nicht ...** *usw.* I can't ... / you can't ... *etc.* [kɑːnt] **gut Kung-Fu können** be good at kung fu
konnte(n): ich konnte ... I could ... [kʊd]; I was able to ... [ˈeɪbl] **ich konnte nicht ...** I couldn't ... [kʊdnt]; I wasn't able to ...
könnte(n): Was könnte besser sein? What could be better? [kʊd], [kəd] / What might be better? [maɪt]
▶ S. 188 möglich – wahrscheinlich – sicherlich
Konsonant consonant [ˈkɒnsənənt]
konstruieren *(entwerfen)* design [dɪˈzaɪn]
Kontakt: (mit jm.) Kontakt aufnehmen get in touch (with sb.) [tʌtʃ] **(mit jm.) Kontakt halten** stay in touch (with sb.)
Kontext *(Text-, Satzzusammenhang)* context [ˈkɒntekst]
Kontrolle *(Überprüfung)* check [tʃek]
kontrollieren *(überprüfen)* check [tʃek]
konzentrieren: sich konzentrieren (auf etwas) concentrate (on sth.) [ˈkɒnsntreɪt]
Konzert concert [ˈkɒnsət]
Koordinator/in coordinator [kəʊˈɔːdɪneɪtə]
Kopf head [hed]
Kopfschmerzen haben have a headache [ˈhedeɪk]
Kopie copy [ˈkɒpi]
kopieren copy [ˈkɒpi]
Korb basket [ˈbɑːskɪt]
Körper body [ˈbɒdi]
Körperteil part of the body
korrekt correct [kəˈrekt]
Korridor corridor [ˈkɒrɪdɔː]
korrigieren correct [kəˈrekt]
kosten cost [kɒst] **Die Kamera kostet ...** The camera is ... **Die DVDs kosten ...** The DVDs are ... **Was/Wie viel kostet ...?** How much is ...? **Was/Wie viel kosten ...?** How much are ...?
kostenlos free
köstlich delicious [dɪˈlɪʃəs]
Kostüm costume [ˈkɒstjuːm]
Kraft *(Energie)* energy [ˈenədʒi]
kräftig strong [strɒŋ]
Kram stuff [stʌf] *(infml)*
krank sick [sɪk]; ill [ɪl]
Krankenhaus hospital [ˈhɒspɪtl]
Krankheit illness [ˈɪlnəs]; *(ernsthaft; ansteckend)* disease [dɪˈziːz]
Krebs *(Tier)* crab [kræb]
Kreis circle [ˈsɜːkl]
Kreisverkehr roundabout [ˈraʊndəbaʊt]
kreuzen; sich kreuzen cross [krɒs]
Kreuzfahrt cruise [kruːz]
Kreuzotter adder [ˈædə]
Kreuzung *(Straßenkreuzung)* junction [ˈdʒʌŋkʃn]
Kreuzworträtsel crossword [ˈkrɒswɜːd]

Kricket cricket [ˈkrɪkɪt]
Krieg war [wɔː]
kriegen: Ärger kriegen get into trouble
Krone crown [kraʊn]
Küche kitchen [ˈkɪtʃɪn]
Kuchen cake [keɪk]
Kugelschreiber pen [pen]
Kuh cow [kaʊ]
kühl cool [kuːl]
kümmern: sich um jn. kümmern look after sb.
Kultur culture [ˈkʌltʃə]
Kunst art [ɑːt]
Künstler/in artist [ˈɑːtɪst]; performer [pəˈfɔːmə]
Kunststoff plastic [ˈplæstɪk]
Kunststück trick [trɪk]
kurz short [ʃɔːt] **kurz nachdem ...** just after ... **Kann ich Sie kurz sprechen?** May I have a word with you?
küssen; sich küssen kiss [kɪs]
Küste coast [kəʊst]

L

lächeln smile [smaɪl]
Lächeln smile [smaɪl]
lachen laugh [lɑːf] **über jn./etwas lachen** laugh at sb./sth.
Laden shop [ʃɒp] **Laden an der Ecke** *(„Tante-Emma-Laden")* corner shop [ˈkɔːnə ʃɒp]
Lage: in der Lage sein, etwas zu tun be able to do sth. [ˈeɪbl]
Lamm lamb [læm]
Lampe lamp [læmp]
Land *(auch als Gegensatz zur Stadt)* country [ˈkʌntri]; *(Grund und Boden)* land [lænd] **an Land gehen** land
landen land [lænd]
Landkarte map [mæp] **auf der Landkarte** on the map
Landschaft *(ländliche Gegend)* countryside [ˈkʌntrɪsaɪd]
Landwirt/in farmer [ˈfɑːmə]
lang long [lɒŋ] **eine Zeit lang** for a while **lange aufbleiben** stay up late
langsam slow [sləʊ] **er schüttelte langsam den Kopf** he shook his head slowly [ˈsləʊli]
langweilen: sich langweilen be/feel bored [bɔːd]
langweilig boring [ˈbɔːrɪŋ]
Laptop laptop [ˈlæptɒp]
Lärm noise [nɔɪz] **voller Lärm** noisy [ˈnɔɪzi]
lärmend noisy [ˈnɔɪzi]
lassen 1. let **Lass mich dir ... zeigen.** Let me show you ... **Lass(t) uns ...** Let's ...
2. leave [liːv] **Lass bitte das Fenster offen.** Leave the window open, please. **etwas übrig lassen (für jn.)** leave sth. (for sb.) **etwas fallen lassen** drop

Dictionary

sth. [drɒp]
3. Lass das! *(Hör auf damit)* Stop it! *(infml)*
laufen run [rʌn]; *(im Fernsehen, Radio)* be on
Läufer/in runner [ˈrʌnə]
laut loud [laʊd]; *(unangenehm laut)* noisy [ˈnɔɪzi] **laut (vor)lesen** read aloud [əˈlaʊd] **mit lauter Stimme** in a loud voice **etwas lauter stellen** turn sth. up [tɜːn]
läuten ring [rɪŋ]
lautlos silently [ˈsaɪləntli]
Lautsprecher loudspeaker [ˌlaʊdˈspiːkə]
Layout layout [ˈleɪaʊt]
Leben life [laɪf], *pl* lives [laɪvz] **am Leben sein** be alive [əˈlaɪv]
leben **1.** *(wohnen)* live [lɪv]
2. *(am Leben sein)* be alive [əˈlaɪv]
Lebensraum habitat [ˈhæbɪtæt]
lecker delicious [dɪˈlɪʃəs]; tasty [ˈteɪsti]; yummy [ˈjʌmi] *(infml)*
ledig *(alleinstehend)* single [ˈsɪŋgl]
leer empty [ˈempti]
legen *(hinlegen, ablegen)* put [pʊt]
Legende legend [ˈledʒənd]
Lehm clay [kleɪ]
lehren *(unterrichten)* teach [tiːtʃ]
Lehrer/in teacher [ˈtiːtʃə]
Lehrgang workshop [ˈwɜːkʃɒp]
Leiche body [ˈbɒdi]
leicht *(einfach)* easy [ˈiːzi]
leid: Es tut mir leid (wegen …) I'm sorry (about …)
leiden: nicht leiden können dislike [dɪsˈlaɪk]
leise quiet [ˈkwaɪət]; silent [ˈsaɪlənt] **sie sang leise** she sang softly [ˈsɒftli] **etwas leiser stellen** turn sth. down
leiten lead [liːd]
Leiter/in leader [ˈliːdə]; *(Orchester, Theater)* director [dəˈrektə]
lenken steer [stɪə]
lernen learn [lɜːn]; *(studieren)* study [ˈstʌdi]
Lernposter study poster [ˈstʌdi pəʊstə]
lesen read [riːd] **jemandes Gedanken lesen** read sb.'s mind [maɪnd]
Leser/in reader [ˈriːdə]
letzte(r, s) last [lɑːst]; *(Final-, End-)* final [ˈfaɪnl] **letztes Wochenende / letzten Freitag** last weekend/Friday **das Musical/Theaterstück vom letzten Jahr** last year's musical/play
leuchtend bright [braɪt]
Leute people [ˈpiːpl]; folk *(pl)* [fəʊk] *(infml)*
Licht light [laɪt]
Lichtblitz flash [flæʃ]
Liebe: Alles Liebe, … / Liebe Grüße, … *(Briefschluss)* Love, …
liebe(r, s) dear [dɪə]
lieben love [lʌv]
Liebling *(Schatz)* darling [ˈdɑːlɪŋ]
Lieblings-: mein Lieblingstier my favourite animal [ˈfeɪvərɪt]

Lied song [sɒŋ]
Lieferwagen van [væn]
liegen lie [laɪ] **Tiere liegen mir sehr am Herzen.** I really care about animals.
▶ S. 191 (to) care
lila purple [ˈpɜːpl]
Lineal ruler [ˈruːlə]
Linie *(U-Bahn)* line [laɪn]
linke(r, s) left [left] **auf der linken Seite** on the left **nach links** left **(nach) links abbiegen** turn left
Lippe lip [lɪp]
Liste list [lɪst]
Loch hole [həʊl]
Löffel spoon [spuːn]
Lokal *(Kneipe)* pub [pʌb]
Lokal- *(am/vom Ort)* local [ˈləʊkl]
los: Los geht's. / Jetzt geht's los. Here we go. **Los mit euch jetzt!** Off you go now. **Was ist los?** What's the matter? [ˈmætə]; What's up? **Was ist los mit Justin/dir?** *(Was fehlt Justin/dir?)* What's wrong with Justin/you?
lösen solve [sɒlv]
Löwe lion [ˈlaɪən]
Luchs lynx [lɪŋks], *pl* lynx *or* lynxes
Luft air [eə]
lustig: sich über jn./etwas lustig machen make fun of sb./sth.

M

machen *(tun)* do [duː]; *(herstellen)* make [meɪk] **aus etwas gemacht sein** be made of sth. **einen Fehler machen** make a mistake **einen Spaziergang machen** go for a walk [wɔːk] **Fotos machen** take photos **Hat es Spaß gemacht?** Was it fun? **jn. zu etwas machen** make sb. sth. **sich fertig machen (für)** get ready (for) [ˈredi]
Mädchen girl [gɜːl]
Magen stomach [ˈstʌmək]
magisch magic [ˈmædʒɪk]; magical [ˈmædʒɪkl]
Mahlzeit meal [miːl]
Mai May [meɪ]
Make-up make-up [ˈmeɪk_ʌp]
mal: (vorher) schon mal before [bɪˈfɔː] **Warst du schon mal hier?** Have you been here before?
Mal time [taɪm] **dieses Mal** this time **zum ersten Mal** for the first time
Malaria malaria [məˈleəriə]
malen paint [peɪnt]
Maler/in painter [ˈpeɪntə]
Mama mum [mʌm]
man you
manchmal sometimes [ˈsʌmtaɪmz]
Mann man [mæn], *pl* men [men]
Mannschaft team [tiːm]
Mantel coat [kəʊt]
Marine navy [ˈneɪvi]
Marionette puppet [ˈpʌpɪt]

markieren mark (up) [mɑːk]; *(mit Textmarker)* highlight [ˈhaɪlaɪt]
Markt market [ˈmɑːkɪt]
Marmelade jam [dʒæm]
März March [mɑːtʃ]
Maske mask [mɑːsk]
Material material [məˈtɪəriəl]
Mathematik maths [mæθs]
Matrose sailor [ˈseɪlə]
Matsch mud [mʌd]
Mauer wall [wɔːl]
Maul mouth [maʊθ]
Medien: soziale Medien social media *(pl)* [ˌsəʊʃl ˈmiːdiə]
Meer sea [siː] **am Meer** by the sea
Meerschweinchen guinea pig [ˈgɪni pɪg]
Megaphon loudspeaker [ˌlaʊdˈspiːkə]
mehr more [mɔː] **nicht mehr** not … any more **nicht mehr da sein** be gone [gɒn]
mehrere *(verschiedene)* several [ˈsevrəl]
Meile *(ca. 1,6 km)* mile [maɪl]
meilenweit for miles [maɪlz]
mein(e) … my … [maɪ]
meinen *(sagen wollen)* mean [miːn]
meiner, meine, meins mine [maɪn]
Meinung opinion [əˈpɪnjən] **meiner Meinung nach** in my opinion
meisten: die meisten Menschen most people [məʊst] **die meisten von ihnen** most of them
meistens usually [ˈjuːʒuəli]
Meister/in master [ˈmɑːstə]; *(Champion)* champion [ˈtʃæmpiən]
melden: sich melden put your hand up
Menge *(Menschenmenge)* crowd [kraʊd]
Mensa *(Kantine)* canteen [kænˈtiːn]
Menschen people [ˈpiːpl]
merken: sich etwas merken remember sth. [rɪˈmembə]
Merkzettel crib sheet [ˈkrɪb ʃiːt] *(infml)*
Messer knife [naɪf], *pl* knives [naɪvz]
Meter metre [ˈmiːtə]
mich me [miː]; *(Reflexivpronomen)* myself [maɪˈself]
Milch milk [mɪlk]
Million million [ˈmɪljən]
Mimik *(Gesichtsausdruck)* facial expression [ˌfeɪʃl_ɪkˈspreʃn]
Mine **1.** *(Bergwerk)* mine [maɪn]
2. *(Militär)* mine [maɪn]
Minute minute [ˈmɪnɪt]
mir me [miː]; *(Reflexivpronomen)* myself [maɪˈself]
mit with [wɪð] **mit dem Bus/Auto fahren** go by bus/car
Mitfahrgelegenheit lift [lɪft]
Mitglied member [ˈmembə]
Mitlaut *(Konsonant)* consonant [ˈkɒnsənənt]
mitmachen: (bei etwas) mitmachen join in (sth.) [dʒɔɪn]
Mitschüler/in classmate [ˈklɑːsmeɪt]
mitsingen: (mit jm.) mitsingen sing along (with sb.)

German – English

Mittag: zu Mittag essen have lunch [lʌntʃ]
Mittagessen lunch [lʌntʃ]
mittags at lunchtime [ˈlʌntʃtaɪm]
Mittagszeit lunchtime [ˈlʌntʃtaɪm]
Mitte middle [ˈmɪdl]; *(Zentrum)* centre [ˈsentə]
Mitternacht midnight [ˈmɪdnaɪt]
Mittwoch Wednesday [ˈwenzdeɪ, -di]
Mitwirkende *(Besetzung in Theaterstück, Film)* cast [kɑːst]
Möbel furniture *(no pl)* [ˈfɜːnɪtʃə] **Die Möbel sind neu.** The furniture is new. **ein Möbel(stück)** a piece of furniture [piːs]
Mobiltelefon mobile phone [ˌməʊbaɪl ˈfəʊn], *(kurz auch:)* mobile
möchte: Ich möchte ... (haben) I'd like ... [ˌaɪd ˈlaɪk] (= I would like ...) **Ich möchte gehen.** I'd like to go. **Was möchtest du (haben)?** What would you like? [wʊd] **Was möchtest du essen?** What would you like to eat?
Mode fashion [ˈfæʃn]
Model model [ˈmɒdl]
Modell model [ˈmɒdl]
modern modern [ˈmɒdən]
mögen like [laɪk]; *(auf etwas stehen)* be into *(infml)* **nicht mögen** dislike [dɪsˈlaɪk] **Ich mag Grün nicht. / Ich mag kein Grün.** I don't like green.
Möglichkeit *(Chance)* chance [tʃɑːns]
Möhre carrot [ˈkært]
Moment moment [ˈməʊmənt] **im Moment** at the moment **Warte einen Moment. / Moment mal.** Wait a minute.
Monat month [mʌnθ]
Mond moon [muːn]
Mondlicht moonlight [ˈmuːnlaɪt]
Monster monster [ˈmɒnstə]
Montag Monday [ˈmʌndeɪ, ˈmʌndi]
Monument (für/zum Gedenken an) monument (to) [ˈmɒnjumənt]
morgen tomorrow [təˈmɒrəʊ] **morgen früh, morgen Vormittag** tomorrow morning
Morgen *(Vormittag)* morning [ˈmɔːnɪŋ] **am Morgen** in the morning
morgens in the morning [ˈmɔːnɪŋ]
Moschee mosque [mɒsk]
Motorrad motorbike [ˈməʊtəbaɪk]
Möwe seagull [ˈsiːɡʌl]
MP3-Player, MP3-Spieler MP3 player [ˌempiːˈθriː ˌpleɪə]
müde tired [ˈtaɪəd]
Müll rubbish [ˈrʌbɪʃ]
Mund mouth [maʊθ]
Münze coin [kɔɪn]
murmeln: ..., murmelte er. ..., he said under his breath. [breθ]
Museum museum [mjuːˈzɪəm]
Musical musical [ˈmjuːzɪkl]
Musik music [ˈmjuːzɪk]
Musiker/in musician [mjuːˈzɪʃn]
müssen have to [ˈhæv tə]; need to [ˈniːd tə]; must [mʌst] **du musst es nicht tun** you don't have to do it; you don't need to do it; you needn't do it [ˈniːdnt]
▶ S. 188 möglich – wahrscheinlich – sicherlich
Mutter mother [ˈmʌðə]
Mutti mum [mʌm]

N

Na: Na ja, ... Well, ... [wel] **Na los, Dad!** *(Komm, Dad!)* Come on, Dad. **Na und?** So? [səʊ]; Who cares?
nach 1. *(örtlich)* to [tu], [tə] **nach draußen** outside [ˌaʊtˈsaɪd] **nach drinnen** inside [ˌɪnˈsaɪd] **nach Hause gehen/kommen** go/come home **nach oben** up; *(im Haus)* upstairs [ˌʌpˈsteəz] **nach unten** down; *(im Haus)* downstairs [ˌdaʊnˈsteəz] **nach vorn** to the front **einer nach dem anderen** one by one
2. *(zeitlich)* after [ˈɑːftə] **nach dem Frühstück** after breakfast **Viertel nach zehn (10.15 / 22.15)** quarter past ten [ˈkwɔːtə pɑːst]
Nachbar/in neighbour [ˈneɪbə]
nachdem after [ˈɑːftə] **gleich nachdem / kurz nachdem ...** just after ...
nachgehen *(Uhr)* be slow
Nachmittag afternoon [ˌɑːftəˈnuːn] **am Nachmittag** in the afternoon
nachmittags in the afternoon [ˌɑːftəˈnuːn]
Nachricht message [ˈmesɪdʒ] **eine Nachricht hinterlassen** leave a message [ˌliːv ə ˈmesɪdʒ]
Nachrichten news *(no pl)* [njuːz]
nachschauen have a look
nachschlagen look up
Nachspeise dessert [dɪˈzɜːt]
nächste(r, s) next [nekst] **das nächste Bild / die nächste Frage** the next picture/question **das Musical/Theaterstück/... vom nächsten Jahr** next year's musical/play/... **als Nächstes** next [nekst]
Nacht night [naɪt] **heute Nacht** tonight [təˈnaɪt] **in der Nacht** at night
Nachtisch dessert [dɪˈzɜːt]
nachts at night [ət ˈnaɪt]
nachverfolgen *(überwachen)* monitor [ˈmɒnɪtə]
nackt *(Hände, Arme, Füße)* bare [beə]
Nähe: in der Nähe von near [nɪə] **hier in der Nähe** near here
nahe (bei) near [nɪə]
nahegelegen: eine nahegelegene Stadt a nearby town [ˈnɪəbaɪ]
Name name [neɪm] **Mein Name ist Silky.** My name is Silky.
Nase nose [nəʊz]
nass wet [wet] **jn. nass spritzen** splash sb. [splæʃ]

Nation nation [ˈneɪʃn]
national, National- national [ˈnæʃnəl]
Naturkunde natural history [ˌnætʃrəl ˈhɪstri]
natürlich natural [ˈnætʃrəl]; *(selbstverständlich)* of course [əv ˈkɔːs]
Naturwissenschaft science [ˈsaɪəns]
Naturwissenschaftler/in scientist [ˈsaɪəntɪst]
neben next to [ˈnekst tʊ]
Nebensatz sub-clause [ˈsʌbklɔːz] **Nebensatz mit if** if-clause [ˈɪfklɔːz]
nehmen take [teɪk] **jn. am Arm nehmen** take sb. by the arm **etwas wichtig nehmen** care about sth. [keə]
▶ S. 191 (to) care
neidisch (auf) jealous (of) [ˈdʒeləs]
nein no [nəʊ] **Nein, das ist falsch. / Nein, das stimmt nicht.** No, that's wrong.
nennen name [neɪm]; *(rufen, bezeichnen)* call [kɔːl]
nervös nervous [ˈnɜːvəs]
nett nice [naɪs]; kind [kaɪnd]
Netz net [net]
neu new [njuː]
neugierig curious [ˈkjʊərɪəs]
Neuigkeiten news [njuːz]
neun nine [naɪn]
nicht not [nɒt] **auch nicht** not ... either [ˈaɪðə, ˈiːðə] **Ich auch nicht. Me neither.** [ˈnaɪðə, ˈniːðə] **Geh nicht.** Don't go. [dəʊnt] **Ich mag Grün nicht.** I don't like green. **Ich weiß (es) nicht.** I don't know. **nicht mehr** not ... any more **nicht vor drei** not till three; not until three **..., nicht wahr?** ..., right? **noch nicht** not ... yet [jet] **(noch) nicht einmal** not even
nichts not ... anything [ˈenɪθɪŋ]
nicken nod [nɒd]
nie never [ˈnevə] **(vorher) noch nie** not ... before, never ... before
niemals never [ˈnevə]
niemand no one [ˌnəʊ ˈwʌn], nobody [ˈnəʊbədi]; not ... anybody/anyone [ˈenibɒdi, ˈeniwʌn] **niemand anders / niemand sonst** no one else [els]
▶ S. 195 ... else
niesen sneeze [sniːz]
nirgendwo(hin) nowhere [ˈnəʊweə]
noch: noch ein Foto one more photo [mɔː]; another photo [əˈnʌðə] **noch einmal** again [əˈɡen] **noch nicht** not ... yet [jet] **noch nicht einmal** not even **immer noch** still [stɪl] **(vorher) noch nie** not/never before **sonst noch etwas?** anything else? **was (sonst) noch?** what else? **wer (sonst) noch?** who else?
▶ S. 195 ... else
Nomen noun [naʊn]
Norden north [nɔːθ] **nach Norden** north **Richtung Norden** northbound [ˈnɔːθbaʊnd]

two hundred and thirty-three **233**

Dictionary

nördlich north [nɔːθ]; northern [ˈnɔːðən]
Nordosten north-east [ˌnɔːθˈiːst] **nach Nordosten** north-east
nordöstlich north-east [ˌnɔːθˈiːst]
Nordwesten north-west [ˌnɔːθˈwest]
nach Nordwesten north-west
nordwestlich north-west [ˌnɔːθˈwest]
normal normal [ˈnɔːməl]
normalerweise usually [ˈjuːʒuəli]
Note (Musik) note [nəʊt]
nötig necessary [ˈnesəsəri]
Notiz note [nəʊt] **(sich) Notizen machen** (beim Lesen oder Zuhören) take notes **(sich) Notizen machen (über/zu etwas)** (zur Vorbereitung) make notes (on sth.)
notwendig necessary [ˈnesəsəri]
November November [nəʊˈvembə]
null, Null nil [nɪl]; (in Telefonnummern) o [əʊ]
Nummer number [ˈnʌmbə]
nun now [naʊ] **Nun, …** Well, … [wel] **Nun, da du …** Now that you …
nur only [ˈəʊnli]; (einfach nur) just [dʒʌst]

O

ob if **als ob** as if; like (infml)
oben (an der Spitze, am oberen Ende) at the top (of); (darüber) above [əˈbʌv]; (im Haus) upstairs [ˌʌpˈsteəz] **hier oben** up here **nach oben** up; (im Haus) upstairs
Oberfläche surface [ˈsɜːfɪs]
oberhalb (von) above [əˈbʌv]
Objekt object [ˈɒbdʒekt]
Obst fruit [fruːt]
Obstsalat fruit salad [ˌfruːt ˈsæləd]
oder or [ɔː]
offen open [ˈəʊpən]
öffnen; sich öffnen open [ˈəʊpən]
Öffnungszeiten opening times (pl)
oft often [ˈɒfn], [ˈɒftən]
ohne without [wɪˈðaʊt]
Ohr ear [ɪə]
Ohrhörer earphones (pl) [ˈɪəfəʊnz]
Oje! Oh dear! [dɪə]
okay OK [ˌəʊˈkeɪ]; all right [ɔːl ˈraɪt]
Oktober October [ɒkˈtəʊbə]
Öl oil [ɔɪl]
Oma grandma [ˈgrænmɑː]
Onkel uncle [ˈʌŋkl]
online online [ˌɒnˈlaɪn]
Opa grandpa [ˈgrænpɑː]
Orange orange [ˈɒrɪndʒ]
orange(farben) orange [ˈɒrɪndʒ]
ordnen order [ˈɔːdə]
Ordnung: in Ordnung (okay) all right [ɔːl ˈraɪt]; OK [ˌəʊˈkeɪ]
organisieren organize [ˈɔːgənaɪz]
Ort place [pleɪs] **am/vom Ort** local [ˈləʊkl]

örtlich local [ˈləʊkl]
Osten east [iːst] **nach Osten** east
Ostern Easter [ˈiːstə]
östlich east [iːst]; eastern [ˈiːstən]
Otter otter [ˈɒtə]
Ozean ocean [ˈəʊʃn]

P

paar: ein paar a few [əˈfjuː]; some [sʌm], [səm]; a couple [ˈkʌpl]
Paar: ein Paar a pair (of) [peə]; a couple [ˈkʌpl]
Päckchen packet [ˈpækɪt]
packen pack [pæk]; (sich greifen) grab [græb]
Packung packet [ˈpækɪt]
Palast palace [ˈpæləs]
Panik: in Panik geraten panic [ˈpænɪk]
Papa dad [dæd]
Papier paper [ˈpeɪpə]
Parade parade [pəˈreɪd]
Park park [pɑːk]
parken park [pɑːk]
Parlament parliament [ˈpɑːləmənt]
Partner/in partner [ˈpɑːtnə]
Party party [ˈpɑːti]
Pass (Reisepass) passport [ˈpɑːspɔːt]
Pass auf! (Vorsicht!) Watch out! [ˌwɒtʃ ˈaʊt]
passen: zu etwas passen (zu etwas gehören) go with sth. **zueinander passen** go together
passieren (mit) happen (to) [ˈhæpən]
Pause break [breɪk] **eine Pause einlegen** pause [pɔːz]
pausieren pause [pɔːz]
Pence pence [pens]
▶ S. 188 Pounds and euros
perfekt perfect [ˈpɜːfɪkt]
Person person [ˈpɜːsn]; (in Roman, Film, Theaterstück usw.) character [ˈkærəktə]
Personalausweis ID card [ˌaɪ ˈdiː kɑːd]
Pfad path [pɑːθ]; trail [treɪl]
Pfannkuchen pancake [ˈpænkeɪk]
Pfeffer pepper [ˈpepə]
Pfeife 1. (Trillerpfeife) whistle [ˈwɪsl] 2. (Tabakspfeife) pipe [paɪp]
pfeifen whistle [ˈwɪsl]; blow the whistle [bləʊ]
Pferd horse [hɔːs]
Pfiff whistle [ˈwɪsl]
Pflanze plant [plɑːnt]
pflanzen plant [plɑːnt]
Pflaster (Heftpflaster) plaster [ˈplɑːstə]
Pforte (Gatter) gate [geɪt]
Pfote paw [pɔː]
Pfund (britische Währung) pound (£) [paʊnd]
▶ S. 189 Pounds and euros
Piano piano [piˈænəʊ]
Picknick picnic [ˈpɪknɪk]
piepen beep [biːp]
pink pink [pɪŋk]

Pizza pizza [ˈpiːtsə]
Plan plan [plæn]; (Zeitplan, Programm) schedule [ˈʃedjuːl]
planen plan [plæn]
Planet planet [ˈplænɪt]
Plantage plantation [plɑːnˈteɪʃn]
Plastik plastic [ˈplæstɪk]
Plattform platform [ˈplætfɔːm]
Platz place [pleɪs]; (Position) position [pəˈzɪʃn]; (freier Raum) room [ruːm]; (Sportplatz, Spielfeld) pitch [pɪtʃ] **auf dem zweiten Platz** in second place
Plätzchen (Keks) biscuit [ˈbɪskɪt]
plaudern chat [tʃæt]
plötzlich suddenly [ˈsʌdnli]
Pokal (Trophäe) trophy [ˈtrəʊfi]
Polizei police (pl) [pəˈliːs]
Polizeiwache, -revier police station [pəˈliːs steɪʃn]
Polizist police officer [pəˈliːs ˌɒfɪsə]; policeman [pəˈliːsmən]
Polizistin police officer [pəˈliːs ˌɒfɪsə]; policewoman [pəˈliːswʊmən]
Pommes frites chips (pl) [tʃɪps]; (American English) fries (pl) [fraɪz]
Pony pony [ˈpəʊni]
populär (bei) popular (with) [ˈpɒpjələ]
Porträt (Personenbeschreibung) profile [ˈprəʊfaɪl]
Position position [pəˈzɪʃn]; (Standort) location [ləʊˈkeɪʃn]
Postamt post office [ˈpəʊst ˌɒfɪs]
Poster poster [ˈpəʊstə]
Posting (auf Blog) post [pəʊst]
Postkarte postcard [ˈpəʊstkɑːd]
praktisch practical [ˈpræktɪkl]
Praline chocolate [ˈtʃɒklət]
prallen: gegen etwas prallen hit sth. [hɪt]
Präsentation presentation [ˌpreznˈteɪʃn]
präsentieren: (jm.) etwas präsentieren present sth. (to sb.) [prɪˈzent]
Präsident/in president [ˈprezɪdənt]
Preis 1. (Kaufpreis) price [praɪs] 2. (Gewinn) prize [praɪz]
preiswert (billig) cheap [tʃiːp]
Prinz prince [prɪns]
Prinzessin princess [ˌprɪnˈses], [ˈprɪnses]
pro: einmal/zweimal pro Woche/Jahr once/twice a week/year
Probe (Theater) rehearsal [rɪˈhɜːsl]
probieren try [traɪ]
Problem problem [ˈprɒbləm]
Profil (Personenbeschreibung, Porträt) profile [ˈprəʊfaɪl]
Programm programme [ˈprəʊgræm]; (Zeitplan) schedule [ˈʃedjuːl]
Projekt project [ˈprɒdʒekt]
Prospekt (Broschüre) brochure [ˈbrəʊʃə]
Protest protest [ˈprəʊtest]
protestieren protest [prəˈtest]
prüfen (testen) test [test]; (überprüfen) check [tʃek]; (untersuchen) look into
Publikum audience [ˈɔːdiəns]
Pullover pullover [ˈpʊləʊvə]

German – English

Punkt point [pɔɪnt]; *(Satzzeichen)* full stop [ˌfʊl ˈstɒp]; *(Fleck)* spot [spɒt]
▶ S. 181 Numbers
Punktestand *(Spielstand)* score [skɔː]
putzen clean [kliːn]
Puzzle jigsaw [ˈdʒɪgsɔː]

Q

Quadratkilometer (km²) square kilometre (sq km) [ˌskweə kɪˈlɒmɪtə]
Quiz quiz [kwɪz]

R

Rabe raven [ˈreɪvn]
Rad *(Fahrrad)* bike [baɪk]   **Rad fahren** ride a bike [ˌraɪd ə ˈbaɪk]
Radiergummi rubber [ˈrʌbə]
Radio radio [ˈreɪdiəʊ]   **im Radio** on the radio
Rallye rally [ˈræli]
Rand edge [edʒ]
rasen race [reɪs]
Rasen grass [grɑːs]
raten guess [ges]
Rathaus town hall [ˌtaʊn ˈhɔːl]
Ratte rat [ræt]
rau *(See)* rough [rʌf]
Raubtier predator [ˈpredətə]
rauchen smoke [sməʊk]
rauf und runter up and down [ˌʌp ən ˈdaʊn]
räumen *(frei machen)* clear [klɪə]
rausgehen: mit dem Hund rausgehen walk the dog
reagieren (auf) react (to) [riˈækt]
Recherche research *(no pl)* [ˈriːsɜːtʃ]
Recht: jemand hat Recht someone is right
rechte(r, s) right [raɪt]   **auf der rechten Seite** on the right   **nach rechts** right   **(nach) rechts abbiegen** turn right
Rechtschreibung spelling [ˈspelɪŋ]
Redakteur/in editor [ˈedɪtə]
Rede talk [tɔːk]; *(offiziell)* speech [spiːtʃ]   **eine Rede halten (über)** give a talk (about)
reden talk [tɔːk]; speak [spiːk]
Redner/in speaker [ˈspiːkə]
Referat talk [tɔːk]   **ein Referat halten (über)** give a talk (about)
Refrain chorus [ˈkɔːrəs]
Regal shelf [ʃelf], *pl* shelves [ʃelvz]
Regel rule [ruːl]
regelmäßig regular [ˈregjələ]
Regen rain [reɪn]
Regenbogen rainbow [ˈreɪnbəʊ]
Regenmantel raincoat [ˈreɪnkəʊt]
Regenschirm umbrella [ʌmˈbrelə]
Regenwald rainforest [ˈreɪnfɒrɪst]

Regierung government [ˈgʌvənmənt]
regional regional [ˈriːdʒənl]
Regisseur/in director [dəˈrektə]
regnen rain [reɪn]
regnerisch rainy [ˈreɪni]
Reh deer, *pl* deer [dɪə]
reich rich [rɪtʃ]
Reihe   **1.** line [laɪn]
2. *(wartende Menschen)* queue [kjuː]
3. Ich bin an der Reihe. (It's) my turn. [tɜːn]
Reihenfolge order [ˈɔːdə]
Reim rhyme [raɪm]
Reise trip [trɪp]; journey [ˈdʒɜːni]
Reiseführer guidebook [ˈgaɪdbʊk]
Reiseleiter/in guide [gaɪd]
reisen travel [ˈtrævl]
Reisende(r) traveller [ˈtrævələ]
Reisepass passport [ˈpɑːspɔːt]
reiten ride [raɪd]
Reiten riding [ˈraɪdɪŋ]
Religion religion [rɪˈlɪdʒən]
rennen run [rʌn]
Rennen race [reɪs]
Reportage report [rɪˈpɔːt]
Republik republic [rɪˈpʌblɪk]
reservieren reserve [rɪˈzɜːv]
Respekt respect [rɪˈspekt]
Rest rest [rest]
Restaurant restaurant [ˈrestrɒnt]
Resultat result [rɪˈzʌlt]
retten save [seɪv]; *(in Sicherheit bringen)* rescue [ˈreskjuː]
Revier *(Territorium)* territory [ˈterətri]
Rezept *(Kochrezept)* recipe [ˈresəpi]
Rhythmus rhythm [ˈrɪðəm]
richten: etwas auf jn. richten point sth. at sb. [pɔɪnt]
richtig right [raɪt]; correct [kəˈrekt]   **Ja, das ist richtig.** Yes, that's right.
Richtung: in die Richtung that way   **in Richtung Bahnhof/Mr Bell** towards the station/Mr Bell [təˈwɔːdz]   **Richtung Norden** northbound [ˈnɔːθbaʊnd]
riechen smell [smel]   **an etwas riechen** smell sth.   **gut riechen** smell good
Riegel *(Schokolade, Müsli)* bar [bɑː]
Riese giant [ˈdʒaɪənt]
Riesenhunger: einen Riesenhunger haben be starving [ˈstɑːvɪŋ]
Riesenrad big wheel [bɪg ˈwiːl]
riesig huge [hjuːdʒ]
Rinderbraten roast beef [ˌrəʊst ˈbiːf]
Ring ring [rɪŋ]
Ritt ride [raɪd]
Ritter knight [naɪt]
Robbe seal [siːl]
Rock skirt [skɜːt]
Rockmusik rock (music) [rɒk]
Rolle *(in einem Theaterstück, Film)* role [rəʊl]
rollen roll [rəʊl]
rosa pink [pɪŋk]
rot red [red]   **rot werden** go red

Route route [ruːt]
Rücken back [bæk]
Rückenflosse dorsal fin [ˌdɔːsl ˈfɪn]
Rückmeldung feedback [ˈfiːdbæk]
Rucksack rucksack [ˈrʌksæk]
rufen call [kɔːl]; shout [ʃaʊt]
ruhen *(sich ausruhen)* rest [rest]
ruhig calm [kɑːm]; *(leise)* quiet [ˈkwaɪət]
Ruine ruin [ˈruːɪn]
Rundgang, Rundfahrt (durch) tour (of) [ˈtʊər_əv]
runter: rauf und runter up and down [ˌʌp ən ˈdaʊn]
runzeln: die Stirn runzeln frown [fraʊn]
rutschig slippery [ˈslɪpəri]

S

Sache thing [θɪŋ]
Saft juice [djuːs]
Sage *(Legende)* legend [ˈledʒənd]
sagen say [seɪ]   **jm. sagen, dass er/sie etwas (nicht) tun soll** tell sb. (not) to do sth.
Sahne cream [kriːm]
Salat *(Gericht, Beilage)* salad [ˈsæləd]
Samba samba [ˈsæmbə]
sammeln collect [kəˈlekt]   **Geld sammeln (für etwas)** raise money (for sth.) [reɪz]
Samstag Saturday [ˈsætədeɪ, ˈsætədi]
Sand sand [sænd]
Sandwich sandwich [ˈsænwɪtʃ], [-wɪdʒ]
sanft softly [ˈsɒftli]; *(behutsam)* gently [ˈdʒentli]   **mit sanfter Stimme** in a soft voice
Sänger/in singer [ˈsɪŋə]
satt: etwas satt haben be tired of sth. [taɪəd]
Satz sentence [ˈsentəns]   **Satz, der in das Thema eines Absatzes einführt** topic sentence [ˌtɒpɪk ˈsentəns]
sauber clean [cliːn]   **sauber machen** clean [kliːn]
Säugetier mammal [ˈmæml]
Säule column [ˈkɒləm]
Schach chess [tʃes]
schade: Es war schade, dass ... It was a pity that ... [ˈpɪti]
Schaf sheep, *pl* sheep [ʃiːp]
Schäfer/in shepherd [ˈʃepəd]
schaffen: etwas schaffen *(zustande bringen)* manage sth. [ˈmænɪdʒ]
Schafhirte/-hirtin shepherd [ˈʃepəd]
Schal scarf [skɑːf], *pl* scarves [skɑːvz]
Schatten *(einer Person, eines Gegenstandes)* shadow [ˈʃædəʊ]
Schatz *(Liebling)* darling [ˈdɑːlɪŋ]
schauen look [lʊk]
▶ S. 180 (to) look after/around/for/…
Schauspiel *(darstellende Kunst)* drama [ˈdrɑːmə]

Dictionary

Schauspieler/in actor [ˈæktə]
schauspielern act [ækt]
scheinen 1. *(Sonne)* shine [ʃaɪn]
2. *(zu sein/zu tun)* **scheinen** seem (to be/do) [siːm]
scheu shy [ʃaɪ]
Scheune barn [bɑːn]
schick: sich schick anziehen dress up [ˌdresˈʌp]
schicken: jm. etwas schicken send sth. to sb. [send]   **einem Freund/einer Freundin eine SMS schicken** text a friend [tekst]
schieben push [pʊʃ]
Schiedsrichter/in referee [ˌrefəˈriː]
schießen: ein Tor schießen score [skɔː]
Schiff ship [ʃɪp]
Schiffsreise cruise [kruːz]
Schild sign [saɪn]; *(Etikett)* label
Schildkröte tortoise [ˈtɔːtəs]
Schinkenspeck bacon [ˈbeɪkən]
Schirm umbrella [ʌmˈbrelə]
Schlacht battle [ˈbætl]
Schlaf sleep [sliːp]
schlafen sleep [sliːp]; *(nicht wach sein)* be asleep [əˈsliːp]
Schlafparty sleepover [ˈsliːpəʊvə]
Schlafzimmer bedroom [ˈbedruːm]
schlagen hit [hɪt]; *(besiegen)* beat [biːt]
Schlägerei fight
Schlagzeug drums *(pl)* [drʌmz]   **Schlagzeug spielen** play the drums
Schlagzeuger/in drummer [ˈdrʌmə]
Schlamm mud [mʌd]
Schlange 1. snake [sneɪk]
2. *(wartende Menschen)* queue [kjuː]   **Schlange stehen** queue [kjuː]
schlau clever [ˈklevə]
schlecht bad [bæd]   **schlechter** worse [wɜːs]   **der/die/das schlechteste …; am schlechtesten** worst [wɜːst]   **schlecht werden** *(Lebensmittel)* go bad   **Mir ist schlecht.** I feel sick.
schließen *(zumachen)* close [kləʊz]
schließlich at last [ət ˈlɑːst]; finally [ˈfaɪnəli]
schlimm bad [bæd]   **schlimmer** worse [wɜːs]   **der/die/das schlimmste …; am schlimmsten** worst [wɜːst]
Schloss castle [ˈkɑːsl]
Schluss end [end]; *(Abschluss)* ending [ˈendɪŋ]
Schlussfolgerung conclusion [kənˈkluːʒn]
Schlüssel key [kiː]
Schlüsselwort keyword [ˈkiːwɜːd]
schmal narrow [ˈnærəʊ]
schmecken taste [teɪst]
schmelzen melt [melt]
schmerzen hurt [hɜːt]
Schmetterling butterfly [ˈbʌtəflaɪ]
Schmuggel; das Schmuggeln smuggling [ˈsmʌglɪŋ]
schmuggeln smuggle [ˈsmʌgl]
Schmuggler/in smuggler [ˈsmʌglə]
schmutzig dirty [ˈdɜːti]

schnappen *(sich greifen)* grab [græb]
Schnee snow [snəʊ]
schneiden cut [kʌt]; *(Film, Video bearbeiten)* edit [ˈedɪt]
schnell fast [fɑːst]; quick [kwɪk]
Schnitt! *(beim Filmen)* Cut! [kʌt]
schockiert shocked [ʃɒkt]
Schokolade chocolate [ˈtʃɒklət]
schön beautiful [ˈbjuːtɪfl]; *(nett)* nice [naɪs]; *(herrlich, wunderbar)* lovely [ˈlʌvli]
schon already [ɔːlˈredi]   **schon bald** before long   **Hast du schon …?** Have you … yet? [jet]   **(vorher) schon mal** before
schottisch: das schottische Hochland the Highlands *(pl)* [ˈhaɪləndz]
Schrank cupboard [ˈkʌbəd]
schrecklich terrible [ˈterəbl]; awful [ˈɔːfl]
Schrei scream [skriːm]
schreiben write [raɪt]
Schreiber/in writer [ˈraɪtə]
Schreibtisch desk [desk]
Schreibweise spelling [ˈspelɪŋ]
schreien shout [ʃaʊt] or cry [kraɪ]; scream [skriːm]
Schriftsteller/in writer [ˈraɪtə]
Schritt step [step]
schüchtern shy [ʃaɪ]
Schuh shoe [ʃuː]
Schuld *(Fehler)* fault [fɔːlt]
Schule school [skuːl]   **in der Schule** at school
Schüler/in student [ˈstjuːdənt]
Schulfach (school) subject [ˈsʌbdʒɪkt]
Schulheft *(Übungsheft)* exercise book [ˈeksəsaɪz bʊk]
Schulleiter/in head teacher [ˌhed ˈtiːtʃə]
Schultasche school bag [ˈskuːl bæg]
Schulter shoulder [ˈʃəʊldə]
Schultyrann bully [ˈbʊli]
Schüssel bowl [bəʊl]
schütteln shake [ʃeɪk]   **er schüttelte den Kopf** he shook his head
schützen: jn./etwas schützen (vor jm./etwas) protect sb./sth. (from sb./sth.) [prəˈtekt]
schwarz black [blæk]
schweigend silently [ˈsaɪləntli]
Schwein pig [pɪg]
schwer 1. *(von Gewicht)* heavy [ˈhevi]
2. *(schwierig)* difficult [ˈdɪfɪkəlt]; hard [hɑːd]   **jm. das Leben schwer machen** give sb. a hard time *(infml)*
Schwert sword [sɔːd]
Schwester sister [ˈsɪstə]
schwierig difficult [ˈdɪfɪkəlt]; hard [hɑːd]; tough [tʌf]
Schwierigkeit: in Schwierigkeiten geraten get into trouble
Schwimmbad, Schwimmbecken (swimming) pool [puːl]
schwimmen swim [swɪm]
Schwimmer/in swimmer [ˈswɪmə]
Schwimmweste life jacket [ˈlaɪf dʒækɪt]

schwindlig dizzy [ˈdɪzi]
sechs six [sɪks]
See 1. *(Binnensee)* lake [leɪk]
2. *(die See, das Meer)* sea [siː]
seekrank seasick [ˈsiːsɪk]
Seemann sailor [ˈseɪlə]
Segelboot sailing boat [ˈseɪlɪŋ bəʊt]
segeln sail [seɪl]   **segeln gehen** go sailing [ˈseɪlɪŋ]
sehen see [siː]
Sehenswürdigkeiten sights *(pl)* [saɪts]
sehr very [ˈveri]   **Das hat uns sehr geholfen.** That helped us a lot.
seidig silky [ˈsɪlki]
Seil rope [rəʊp]
sein *(Verb)* be [biː]
sein(e) … *(vor Nomen; besitzanzeigend)*
1. *(zu „he")* his … [hɪz]
2. *(zu „it")* its … [ɪts]
seiner, seine, seins his [hɪz]
seit 1. seit 10 Uhr/letzter Woche/2012/… since 10 o'clock/last week/2012/… [sɪns]
2. seit Stunden/Wochen/Jahren/… for hours/weeks/years/…
Seite 1. side [saɪd]   **auf der linken Seite** on the left   **auf der rechten Seite** on the right
2. *(Buchseite)* page [peɪdʒ]   **Auf welcher Seite sind wir?** What page are we on?
Sekunde second [ˈsekənd]
selbst wenn even if [ˈiːvn ɪf]
Selbstlaut *(Vokal)* vowel [ˈvaʊəl]
selbstverständlich of course [əv ˈkɔːs]
seltsam strange [streɪndʒ]; weird [wɪəd]
senden: jm. etwas senden send sth. to sb. [send]
Sendung *(im Radio, Fernsehen)* programme [ˈprəʊgræm]
September September [sepˈtembə]
Sessel armchair [ˈɑːmtʃeə]
Set set [set]
setzen: sich setzen sit [sɪt]   **sich (mit jm.) in Verbindung setzen** get in touch (with sb.) [tʌtʃ]
seufzen sigh [saɪ]
Shorts *(kurze Hose)* shorts *(pl)* [ʃɔːts]
Show show [ʃəʊ]
sich 1. *(Reflexivpronomen)* herself [hɜːˈself]; himself [hɪmˈself]; itself [ɪtˈself]; themselves [ðəmˈselvz]; *(zur höflichen Anrede „Sie")* yourself [jɔːˈself]; yourselves [jɔːˈselvz]
2. sich (gegenseitig) *(einander)* each other [iːtʃ ˈʌðə]
sicher sure [ʃʊə], [ʃɔː]
Sicht: aus meiner Sicht from my point of view [ˌpɔɪnt əv ˈvjuː]
Sichtung sighting [ˈsaɪtɪŋ]
sie 1. *(Einzahl; weibliche Person)* she [ʃiː]   **Frag sie.** Ask her. [hɜː]
2. *(Einzahl; Ding, Tier)* it [ɪt]
3. *(Mehrzahl)* they [ðeɪ]   **Frag sie.** Ask them. [ðəm, ðɒm]
Sie *(höfliche Anredeform)* you [juː, jʊ]

German – English

sieben seven [ˈsevn]
Sieger/in winner [ˈwɪnə]
Signal (Stichwort, am Theater) cue [kjuː]
Silbe syllable [ˈsɪləbl]
Silvester New Year's Eve [ˌnjuː jɪəzˌˈiːv]
singen sing [sɪŋ]
Sirene siren [ˈsaɪrən]
Situation situation [ˌsɪtʃuˈeɪʃn]
Sitz seat [siːt]
sitzen sit [sɪt]
Sklave, Sklavin slave [sleɪv]
Sklaverei slavery [ˈsleɪvəri]
Skyline skyline [ˈskaɪlaɪn]
Smalltalk (spontan geführtes Gespräch in umgangssprachlichem Ton) small talk
SMS text message [ˈtekst mesɪdʒ], (kurz auch:) text **einem Freund/einer Freundin eine SMS schicken** text a friend
Snack snack [snæk]
so 1. (auf diese Weise) like that / like this **Und er so: „Stop ..."** He was like: "Stop ..." (infml)
2. **(nicht) so groß wie** (not) as big as [æz], [əz]
3. **so cool/nett/leise/...** so cool/nice/quiet/... [səʊ] **so ein/e ...** such a ... [sʌtʃ]
▶ S. 182 such a + noun / so + adjective
4. **so tun, als ob** pretend [prɪˈtend]
sobald as soon as [əz ˈsuːn_əz]
Socke sock [sɒk]
sodass so that, (oft auch kurz:) so
soeben just [dʒʌst]
Sofa sofa [ˈsəʊfə]
sofort immediately [ɪˈmiːdiətli]
sogar even [ˈiːvn]
Sohn son [sʌn]
Soldat/in soldier [ˈsəʊldʒə]
sollen: Soll ich ...? Shall I ... ? [ʃæl] **Du solltest ... / Ihr solltet ...** You should ... [ʃʊd], [ʃəd]
▶ S. 188 möglich – wahrscheinlich – sicherlich
Solo- solo [ˈsəʊləʊ]
Sommer summer [ˈsʌmə]
Sonnabend Saturday [ˈsætədeɪ, -di]
Sonne sun [sʌn]
Sonnenbrille sunglasses (pl) [ˈsʌŋglɑːsɪz]
Sonnenschein sunshine [ˈsʌnʃaɪn]
sonnig sunny [ˈsʌni]
Sonntag Sunday [ˈsʌndeɪ, ˈsʌndi]
sonst: sonst noch etwas? anything else? [els] **sonst jeder** everybody else **niemand sonst** no one else **was sonst noch?** what else? **wer sonst noch?** who else?
▶ S. 195 ... else
Sorge: sich Sorgen machen (wegen, um) worry (about) [ˈwʌri]
sorgen: dafür sorgen, dass ... make sure that ...
Souvenir souvenir [ˌsuːvəˈnɪə]
sowie (sobald) as soon as [əz ˈsuːn_əz]
soziale Medien social media (pl) [ˌsəʊʃl ˈmiːdiə]

Spagetti spaghetti [spəˈgeti]
spanisch Spanish [ˈspænɪʃ]
spannend (aufregend) exciting [ɪkˈsaɪtɪŋ]
Spannung (Anspannung) tension [ˈtenʃn]
Spaß fun [fʌn] **Spaß haben** have fun [fʌn] **Hat es Spaß gemacht?** Was it fun? **Viel Spaß!** Enjoy yourself.
spät late [leɪt] **Du bist spät dran. / Du bist zu spät.** You're late. **Wie spät ist es?** What time is it?
später later [ˈleɪtə]
spazieren gehen go for a walk [wɔːk]
Spaziergang walk [wɔːk] **einen Spaziergang machen** go for a walk
Spickzettel crib sheet [ˈkrɪb ʃiːt] (infml)
Spiegel mirror [ˈmɪrə]
Spiel game [geɪm]; (Wettkampf, Match) match [mætʃ]
spielen play [pleɪ] **Gitarre spielen** play the guitar **Klavier spielen** play the piano **Schlagzeug spielen** play the drums
Spieler/in player [ˈpleɪə]
Spielfeld pitch [pɪtʃ]
Spielstand (Punktestand) score [skɔː]
Spielzeug toy [tɔɪ]
Spitze top [tɒp] **an der Spitze (von)** at the top (of)
Sport; Sportart sport [spɔːt] **Sport treiben** do sport
Sportler/in sportsperson [ˈspɔːtspɜːsn]
Sportunterricht PE [ˌpiːˈiː] (Physical Education)
Sprache language [ˈlæŋgwɪdʒ]
sprechen (mit jm.) speak (to sb.) [spiːk] **Kann ich Sie kurz sprechen?** May I have a word with you?
Sprecher/in speaker [ˈspiːkə]
springen jump [dʒʌmp]
spritzen: jn. nass spritzen splash sb. [splæʃ]
Sprung jump [dʒʌmp]
spülen: das Geschirr spülen wash the dishes (pl) [ˌwɒʃ ðə ˈdɪʃɪz]
Spur: keine Spur von ... no sign of ... [saɪn]
Staat state [steɪt]
Stadion stadium [ˈsteɪdiəm]
Stadt town [taʊn]; (Großstadt) city [ˈsɪti]
Stadtplan map [mæp] **auf dem Stadtplan** on the map
Stammbaum family tree [ˈfæməli triː]
Stand (Marktstand) stall [stɔːl]
Standard; Standard- standard [ˈstændəd]
ständig: etwas ständig tun (immer wieder) keep doing sth. [kiːp]
Standort location [ləʊˈkeɪʃn]
Standpunkt point of view [ˌpɔɪnt_əv ˈvjuː]
Star star [stɑː]
stark strong [strɒŋ] **starker Regen** heavy rain [ˈhevi]

starren stare [steə]
Station (Haltestelle) stop [stɒp]
statt (anstelle von) instead of [ɪnˈsted_əv]
stattdessen instead [ɪnˈsted]
stattfinden take place [teɪk ˈpleɪs]
stechen: etwas in etwas stechen stick sth. into sth. [stɪk]
stecken: etwas in etwas stecken stick sth. into sth. [stɪk]
stehen stand [stænd] **auf etwas stehen** be into sth. (infml) **Schlange stehen** queue [kjuː] **Wie steht es?** (Sport) What's the score? [skɔː]
stehlen steal [stiːl]
steil steep [stiːp]
Stein stone [stəʊn]
steinig rocky [ˈrɒki]
Stelle place [pleɪs]; (Job, Arbeitsstelle) job [dʒɒb] **an zweiter Stelle** in second place
stellen (hinstellen, abstellen) put [pʊt] **eine Frage stellen** ask a question **etwas lauter/leiser stellen** turn sth. up/down [tɜːn]
Stempel stamp [stæmp]
sterben die [daɪ]
Stern star [stɑː]
steuern steer [stɪə]
Stichwort (im Wörterbuch) headword [ˈhedwɜːd]; (am Theater) cue [kjuː]
Stiefel boot [buːt]
Stift (zum Schreiben) pen [pen]
still quiet [ˈkwaɪət]; silent [ˈsaɪlənt]
Stimme voice [vɔɪs] **mit lauter Stimme** in a loud voice
stimmen: Ja, das stimmt. Yes, that's right. [raɪt] **Nein, das stimmt nicht.** No, that's wrong. [rɒŋ]
Stirn: die Stirn runzeln frown [fraʊn]
Stock stick [stɪk]
Stock(werk) floor [flɔː]
stöhnen groan [grəʊn]
Stöhnen groan [grəʊn]
stolz (auf) proud (of) [praʊd]
stoppen stop [stɒp]
stoßen push [pʊʃ] **gegen etwas stoßen** hit sth. [hɪt] **auf etwas stoßen** (zufällig) come across sth.
▶ S. 180 (to) come across/down/over/...
Strafe punishment [ˈpʌnɪʃmənt]
strahlend (leuchtend hell) bright [braɪt]
Strand beach [biːtʃ]
Straße street [striːt]; road [rəʊd]
Straßenkreuzung junction [ˈdʒʌŋkʃn]
Straßenkünstler/in street artist
Strecke (Route) route [ruːt]
Streit argument [ˈɑːgjumənt]
streiten; sich streiten argue [ˈɑːgjuː]
Strophe verse [vɜːs]
strukturieren structure [ˈstrʌktʃə]
Stück: ein Stück ... a piece of ... [piːs]
Student/in student [ˈstjuːdənt]
studieren study [ˈstʌdi]
Studio studio [ˈstjuːdiəʊ]
Stufe step [step]

Dictionary

Stuhl chair [tʃeə]
Stunde hour [ˈaʊə]; *(Unterrichtsstunde)* lesson [ˈlesn]   **ein einstündiges Konzert** a one-hour concert
Stundenplan timetable [ˈtaɪmteɪbl]
Sturm storm [stɔːm]
stürmisch *(rau, See)* rough [rʌf]
stürzen fall [fɔːl]
Subjekt subject [ˈsʌbdʒekt]
Substantiv noun [naʊn]
suchen: etwas suchen look for sth. [ˈlʊk fɔː]
Süden south [saʊθ]   **nach Süden** south
südlich south [saʊθ]; southern [ˈsʌðən]
Südosten south-east [ˌsaʊθˈiːst]   **nach Südosten** south-east
südöstlich south-east [ˌsaʊθˈiːst]
Südwesten south-west [ˌsaʊθˈwest]   **nach Südwesten** south-west
südwestlich south-west [ˌsaʊθˈwest]
Suppe soup [suːp]
süß sweet [swiːt]
Süßigkeiten sweets *(pl)* [swiːts]
Symbol symbol [ˈsɪmbl]
Szene scene [siːn]

T

Tabelle table [ˈteɪbl]
Tafel 1. *(Schultafel)* board [bɔːd]   2. *(Schokolade)* bar [bɑː]
Tag day [deɪ]
Tagebuch diary [ˈdaɪəri]
Tagesausflüge machen go on day trips [trɪps]
Taille waist [weɪst]
Tal valley [ˈvæli]
talentiert talented [ˈtæləntɪd]
Tante aunt [ɑːnt]
Tante-Emma-Laden corner shop [ˈkɔːnə ʃɒp]
Tanz dance [dɑːns]
tanzen dance [dɑːns]
Tänzer/in dancer [ˈdɑːnsə]
Tanzfläche dance floor [ˈdɑːns flɔː]
Tasche bag [bæg]; *(Manteltasche, Hosentasche usw.)* pocket [ˈpɒkɪt]
Taschenlampe torch [tɔːtʃ]
Tasse: eine Tasse ... a cup of ... [kʌp]
Tatsache fact [fækt]
tatsächlich actually [ˈæktʃuəli]
▶ S. 184 actually
Tatze paw [pɔː]
Team team [tiːm]
Technik, Technologie technology [tekˈnɒlədʒi]
Tee tea [tiː]
Teelöffel teaspoon [ˈtiːspuːn]
Teil part [pɑːt]   **aus dem hinteren Teil des Buses** from the back of the bus
teilnehmen: an etwas teilnehmen take part in sth. [ˌteɪk ˈpɑːt]; *(Wettkampf)* compete in sth. [kəmˈpiːt]

Telefon telephone [ˈtelɪfəʊn], *(kurz auch:)* phone   **am Telefon** on the phone   **ans Telefon gehen** answer the phone
Telefonat call [kɔːl]
Telefongespräch *(Anruf)* phone call [ˈfəʊn kɔːl], *(kurz auch:)* call
Telefonzelle telephone box
Teller: ein Teller ... a plate of ... [pleɪt]
Temperatur temperature [ˈtemprətʃə]
Tempus *(grammatische Zeit)* tense [tens]
Tennis tennis [ˈtenɪs]
Termin appointment [əˈpɔɪntmənt]
Territorium territory [ˈterətri]
Test test [test]
testen test [test]
teuer expensive [ɪkˈspensɪv]
Text text [tekst]   **einen Text schnell nach bestimmten Wörtern/Informationen absuchen** scan a text [skæn]
Theater theatre [ˈθɪətə]
Theaterstück play [pleɪ]
Thema theme [θiːm]; topic [ˈtɒpɪk]
Thermometer thermometer [θəˈmɒmɪtə]
tief deep [diːp]
Tier animal [ˈænɪml]
Tipp tip [tɪp]
tippen *(vorsichtig klopfen)* tap [tæp]
Tisch table [ˈteɪbl]
Tischler/in carpenter [ˈkɑːpəntə]
Tischtennis table tennis
Titel title [ˈtaɪtl]
Toast(brot) toast [təʊst]
Tochter daughter [ˈdɔːtə]
Tod death [deθ]
Toilette toilet [ˈtɔɪlət]
Tomate tomato [təˈmɑːtəʊ], *pl* tomatoes
Ton *(Lehm)* clay [kleɪ]
Top *(Oberteil)* top [tɒp]
Topf pot [pɒt]
Tor 1. *(Pforte, Gatter)* gate [geɪt]   2. *(Sport)* goal [gəʊl]   **ein Tor schießen** score (a goal) [skɔː]
Torfrau goalkeeper [ˈgəʊlkiːpə]
Tornetz goal net [ˈgəʊl net]
Torwart goalkeeper [ˈgəʊlkiːpə]
tot dead [ded]
töten kill [kɪl]
Tourist/in tourist [ˈtʊərɪst]
traditionell traditional [trəˈdɪʃənl]
tragen 1. carry [ˈkæri]   2. *(Kleidung)* wear [weə]
Trainer/in *(von Sportmannschaften)* manager [ˈmænɪdʒə]
trainieren practise [ˈpræktɪs]; train [treɪn]
Training training [ˈtreɪnɪŋ]
Traktor tractor [ˈtræktə]
Träne tear [tɪə]   **in Tränen ausbrechen** burst into tears [bɜːst]
Transporter *(Lieferwagen)* van [væn]
Trauerfeier funeral [ˈfjuːnərəl]
Traum dream [driːm]
traurig sad [sæd]

treffen; sich treffen meet [miːt]   **etwas treffen** hit sth.   **jn. treffen** *(zufällig)* come across sb.
▶ S. 180 (to) come across/down/over/...
Treffer: einen Treffer erzielen score [skɔː]
Treppe; Treppenstufen stairs *(pl)* [steəz]
treten kick [kɪk]   **jm. auf die Füße/Zehen treten** *(auch im übertragenen Sinne)* tread on sb.'s toes [tred] *(infml)*
Trick trick [trɪk]
Trimester term [tɜːm]
trinken drink [drɪŋk]
trocken dry [draɪ]
Trommel drum [drʌm]
Trommler/in drummer [ˈdrʌmə]
Trophäe trophy [ˈtrəʊfi]
trotzdem still [stɪl]
Tschüs. Bye. [baɪ]
T-Shirt T-shirt [ˈtiːʃɜːt]
Tulpe tulip [ˈtjuːlɪp]
tun do [duː]   **etwas tun müssen** have to do sth.; need to do sth.   **etwas tun wollen** want to do sth. [wɒnt]   **Tut mir leid.** (I'm) sorry.   **viel zu tun haben** be busy [ˈbɪzi]
Tunnel tunnel [ˈtʌnl]
Tür door [dɔː]
Türklingel doorbell [ˈdɔːbel]
Turm tower [ˈtaʊə]
Turnen gymnastics [dʒɪmˈnæstɪks]; *(Sportunterricht)* PE [ˌpiːˈiː] (Physical Education)
Turnhalle gym [dʒɪm]
Turnier *(Wettkampf)* trials *(pl)* [ˈtraɪəlz]
Turnschuh trainer [ˈtreɪnə]
Tyrann *(in der Schule)* bully [ˈbʊli]

U

U-Bahn: die U-Bahn the underground *(no pl)* [ˈʌndəgraʊnd]; *(in London)* the Tube *(no pl)* [tjuːb]
üben practise [ˈpræktɪs]
über 1. *(räumlich)* over [ˈəʊvə]; *(oberhalb von)* above [əˈbʌv]   **(quer) über das Moor/die Straße** across the moor/the street [əˈkrɒs]   2. *(mehr als)* over [ˈəʊvə]   **über 400 Jahre** over 400 years   3. **über mich/dich/...** about me/you/... [əˈbaʊt]   **über dich selbst** about yourself [jɔːˈself]
überall everywhere [ˈevriweə]   **überall um sie herum** all around her
überarbeiten *(Text u.Ä.)* revise [rɪˈvaɪz]
übereinander *(aufeinander)* on top of each other [iːtʃ ˈʌðə]
überfüllt *(voller Menschen)* crowded [ˈkraʊdɪd]
übergeben: Ich muss mich übergeben. I'm going to be sick.

German – English

überhaupt: Und überhaupt, ... And anyway, ... ['enɪweɪ]
überleben survive [sə'vaɪv]
übernachten (in/bei) (vorübergehend wohnen) stay (at/with) [steɪ]
überprüfen check [tʃek]
Überprüfung check [tʃek]
überqueren cross [krɒs]
überrascht surprised [sə'praɪzd]
Überraschung surprise [sə'praɪz]
Überschrift title ['taɪtl]
übersetzen translate [træns'leɪt]
Übersetzung translation [træns'leɪʃn]
übertragen werden (Programm, Sendung) be on
überwachen (nachverfolgen) monitor ['mɒnɪtə]
üblich usual ['juːʒuəl]
übrig: übrig sein be left [left] **etwas übrig lassen (für jn.)** leave sth. (for sb.) [liːv]
übrigens by the way [ˌbaɪ ðə 'weɪ]; actually ['æktʃuəli]
▶ S. 184 actually
Übung exercise ['eksəsaɪz]
Übungsheft exercise book ['eksəsaɪz bʊk]
Ufer (eines Sees) shore [ʃɔː]
Uhr 1. (Armbanduhr) watch [wɒtʃ]; (Wand-, Stand-, Turmuhr) clock [klɒk]
2. **4 Uhr morgens** 4 am [ˌeɪ ˈem] **4 Uhr nachmittags / 16 Uhr** 4 pm [ˌpiː ˈem], **um 1 Uhr / 13 Uhr** at 1 o'clock [ə'klɒk]
Uhrzeit time [taɪm]
um 1. (örtlich) **um ... (herum)** around ... [ə'raʊnd] **um die Welt** round the world [raʊnd]
2. (zeitlich) **um 1 Uhr / 13 Uhr** at 1 o'clock [ə'klɒk] **um 18 Uhr herum** (gegen 18 Uhr) around 6 pm
3. **um zu** to [tu], [tə]
umarmen: jn. umarmen hug sb. [hʌɡ]; give sb. a hug [hʌɡ]
umdrehen (wenden) turn around [ˌtɜːn_ə'raʊnd] **sich umdrehen** turn (around/round)
▶ S. 177 (to) turn
umher: in der Bücherei / auf dem Strand umher around the library/the beach [ə'raʊnd]
umher-: umherrennen run around [ˌrʌn_ə'raʊnd] **umherspazieren** walk around
umsehen: sich (auf der Farm) umsehen look around (the farm)
umsteigen change [tʃeɪndʒ]
umtauschen (Geld wechseln) change [tʃeɪndʒ]
Umweltverschmutzung pollution [pə'luːʃn]
umziehen (nach) move (to) [muːv]
Umzug (Parade) parade [pə'reɪd]
und and [ænd], [ənd] **Und du? / Und was ist mit dir?** What about you? **Und? / Na und?** So? [səʊ] **Und er**

so: „Stop ..." He was like: "Stop ..." (infml)
unfair unfair [ʌn'feə]
Unfall: einen Unfall haben crash [kræʃ]
ungefähr about [ə'baʊt]
ungerecht unfair [ʌn'feə]
ungewöhnlich unusual [ʌn'juːʒuəl]
unglaublich (erstaunlich) amazing [ə'meɪzɪŋ]
unglücklich unhappy [ʌn'hæpi]
unheimlich scary ['skeəri]
unhöflich impolite [ˌɪmpə'laɪt]
Uniform uniform ['juːnɪfɔːm]
Union: die Europäische Union the EU [ˌi: 'juː] (the European Union [ˌjʊərəpiːən 'juːnɪən])
unmöglich impossible [ɪm'pɒsəbl]
Unrecht: jemand hat Unrecht someone is wrong [rɒŋ]
unregelmäßig irregular [ɪ'reɡjələ]
uns us [ʌs], [əs]; (Reflexivpronomen) ourselves [ɑː'selvz], [aʊə'selvz]
unser(e) ... our ... ['aʊə]
unserer, unsere, unseres ours ['aʊəz]
unten (am unteren Ende) at the bottom (of) ['bɒtəm]; (darunter) below [bɪ'ləʊ]; (im Haus) downstairs [ˌdaʊn'steəz]
dort unten down there **nach unten** down; (im Haus) downstairs
unter under ['ʌndə]; (unterhalb von) below [bɪ'ləʊ] **unter der Erde** underground [ˌʌndə'ɡraʊnd]
unterbrechen interrupt [ˌɪntə'rʌpt]
untergehen (Sonne) go down [daʊn]
unterhalb (von) below [bɪ'ləʊ]
unterhalten: sich unterhalten (mit) talk (to) [tɔːk]
Unterhaltung 1. (Gespräch) conversation [ˌkɒnvə'seɪʃn]
2. (Vergnügen) entertainment [ˌentə'teɪnmənt]
unterirdisch underground [ˌʌndə'ɡraʊnd]
unterrichten teach [tiːtʃ]
unterstreichen underline [ˌʌndə'laɪn]
untersuchen (prüfen) look into; (studieren) study ['stʌdi]
Untertitel subtitle ['sʌbtaɪtl]
unterwegs out and about
Unwetter storm [stɔːm]
Urlaub holiday ['hɒlədeɪ] **in Urlaub fahren** go on holiday **in Urlaub sein** be on holiday
usw. (und so weiter) etc. (et cetera) [et'setərə]

V

Vater father ['fɑːðə]
Vati dad [dæd]
Vegetarier/in vegetarian [ˌvedʒə'teəriən]
vegetarisch vegetarian [ˌvedʒə'teəriən]

Verabredung appointment [ə'pɔɪntmənt]
verändern; sich verändern change [tʃeɪndʒ]
verängstigt scared [skeəd]
verantwortlich responsible [rɪ'spɒnsəbl]
Verb verb [vɜːb]
verbessern; sich verbessern improve [ɪm'pruːv] **etwas verbessern** (korrigieren) correct sth. [kə'rekt]
verbeugen: sich verbeugen bow [baʊ]
verbinden connect [kə'nekt]; link [lɪŋk]
Verbindung: sich (mit jm.) in Verbindung setzen get in touch (with sb.) [tʌtʃ] **(mit jm.) in Verbindung bleiben** stay in touch (with sb.)
verbreiten; sich verbreiten spread [spred]
verbrennen burn [bɜːn]
verbringen: Zeit verbringen (mit) spend time (on) [spend]
verbunden sein be connected [kə'nektɪd]
verdienen (Geld) earn [ɜːn]
vereinigt: das Vereinigte Königreich the UK (the United Kingdom) [ˌjuː 'keɪ], [juˌnaɪtɪd 'kɪŋdəm]
verfügbar available [ə'veɪləbl]
Vergangenheit past [pɑːst]
vergehen (Zeit) go by; pass [pɑːs]
vergessen forget [fə'ɡet]
vergewissern: sich vergewissern, dass ... make sure that ...
Vergnügungspark fun park
verhalten: sich verhalten behave [bɪ'heɪv]
Verhältnisse (Bedingungen) conditions (pl) [kən'dɪʃnz]
verheiratet (mit) married (to) ['mærɪd]
verkaufen sell [sel]
Verkäufer/in shop assistant ['ʃɒp_əˌsɪstənt], (kurz auch:) assistant
Verkehr traffic ['træfɪk]
Verkehrsampel traffic light ['træfɪk laɪt] (oft auch Plural:) traffic lights
verkehrt wrong [rɒŋ]
verkleiden: sich verkleiden dress up [ˌdres_'ʌp]
Verkleidung costume ['kɒstjuːm]
verknüpfen connect [kə'nekt]; link [lɪŋk]
verlassen leave [liːv]
verletzen hurt [hɜːt]
verletzt hurt [hɜːt]
verlieren lose [luːz]
vermissen miss [mɪs]
vermisst (verschollen) missing ['mɪsɪŋ]
verneigen: sich verneigen bow [baʊ]
verpassen miss [mɪs]
verrückt mad [mæd] **verrückt werden** go mad
Vers (Reim) rhyme [raɪm]; (Strophe) verse [vɜːs]
verschieden different ['dɪfrənt]
verschiedene (mehrere) several ['sevrəl]

Dictionary

Verschmutzung (der Umwelt) pollution [pəˈluːʃn]
verschollen missing [ˈmɪsɪŋ]
verschwinden disappear [ˌdɪsəˈpɪə]
versprechen promise [ˈprɒmɪs]
verstecken; sich verstecken hide [haɪd]
verstehen understand [ˌʌndəˈstænd] **Hast du es verstanden?** Did you get it? (infml) **Verstehe.** I see.
Versuch try [traɪ]
versuchen try [traɪ] **Versuch's mal.** Have a go.
verteidigen: jn./etwas verteidigen (gegen) defend sb./sth. (against) [dɪˈfend]
verwenden use [juːz]
Video video [ˈvɪdiəʊ]
Videokamera video camera [ˈvɪdiəʊ kæmrə]
viel a lot (of); lots (of); much [mʌtʃ] **Viel Glück!** Good luck! [lʌk] **viel zu tun haben** be busy [ˈbɪzi] **Wie viel kosten …?** How much are …? **Wie viel kostet …?** How much is …?
viele a lot (of); lots (of); many [ˈmeni]
vielleicht maybe [ˈmeɪbi] **sie sind vielleicht zu Hause** they may be at home [meɪ]
▶ S. 188 möglich – wahrscheinlich – sicherlich
vier four [fɔː]
Viertel: Viertel nach zehn (10.15/22.15) quarter past ten [ˈkwɔːtə pɑːst] **Viertel vor elf (10.45/22.45)** quarter to eleven [ˈkwɔːtə tʊ]
violett purple [ˈpɜːpl]
Visum visa [ˈviːzə]
Vogel bird [bɜːd]
Vokal vowel [ˈvaʊəl]
Volk people [ˈpiːpl]; nation [ˈneɪʃn]
voll full (of) [fʊl] **voller Menschen** crowded [ˈkraʊdɪd]
Volleyball volleyball [ˈvɒlibɔːl]
völlig quite [kwaɪt]
Vollmond full moon [fʊl ˈmuːn]
von of [ɒv], [əv]; from [frɒm], [frəm] **ein Lied von …** a song by … [baɪ] **von … bis …** from … to … **von … herunter** off [ɒf]
▶ S. 177 off
vor 1. (örtlich) in front of [ɪn ˈfrʌnt əv] **vor der Schule** (vorm Gebäude) in front of the school; (außerhalb der Schule) outside the school [ˌaʊtˈsaɪd] 2. (zeitlich) before [bɪˈfɔː] **vor der Schule** (vor Schulbeginn) before school **vorm Unterricht** before lessons **vor zwei Tagen** two days ago [əˈɡəʊ] **Viertel vor elf (10.45/22.45)** quarter to eleven [ˈkwɔːtə tʊ] **nicht vor drei** not till three; not until three
vorankommen (zurechtkommen) get on [ˌɡetˈɒn]
vorbei (an) past [pɑːst]
vorbei sein (zu Ende sein) be over

vorbei-: an etwas/jm. vorbeigehen/ vorbeifahren pass sth./sb. [pɑːs]
vorbeikommen (bei) (besuchen) come over (to)
▶ S. 180 (to) come across/down/over/…
vorbereiten: etwas vorbereiten prepare sth. [prɪˈpeə] **sich vorbereiten (auf)** get ready (for) [ˈredi]
Vordergrund foreground [ˈfɔːɡraʊnd]
Vorderseite front [frʌnt]
Vorfahr/in ancestor [ˈænsestə]
Vorführung (Demonstration) demonstration [ˌdemənˈstreɪʃn]
vorgehen (Uhr) be fast
vorhaben: Ich habe vor ein Lied zu singen. I'm going to sing a song.
vorher: vorher schon mal before **vorher noch nie** not … before, never … before
Vorlieben und Abneigungen likes and dislikes (pl) [ˌlaɪks ən ˈdɪslaɪks]
Vormittag morning [ˈmɔːnɪŋ]
vorn: nach vorn to the front [frʌnt]
vorschlagen: (jm.) etwas vorschlagen suggest sth. (to sb.) [səˈdʒest]
Vorschrift (Regel) rule [ruːl]
Vorsicht! Watch out! [ˌwɒtʃ ˈaʊt]
vorsichtig careful [ˈkeəfl]
vorspielen: etwas vorspielen act sth. out [ˌæktˈaʊt]
Vorspielen (Theater) audition [ɔːˈdɪʃn]
Vorsprechen (Theater) audition
vorstellen 1. (jm.) etwas vorstellen (präsentieren) present sth. (to sb.) [prɪˈzent] 2. jn. (jm.) vorstellen introduce sb. (to sb.) [ˌɪntrəˈdjuːs] 3. sich etwas vorstellen imagine sth. [ɪˈmædʒɪn] **Stell dir vor, Dad …** Guess what, Dad …
Vorstellung 1. (Idee) idea [aɪˈdɪə] 2. (Präsentation) presentation [ˌpreznˈteɪʃn] 3. (Show) show [ʃəʊ]
Vortrag talk [tɔːk] **einen Vortrag halten (über)** give a talk (about)
vorüber: vorbei (an), vorüber (an) past [pɑːst]
vorübergehen (Zeit) go by; pass [pɑːs]

W

wach awake [əˈweɪk]
Wache, Wachposten guard [ɡɑːd]
wachsen grow [ɡrəʊ]
wählen (aussuchen) choose [tʃuːz]
wahr true [truː] **…, nicht wahr?** …, right?
während 1. **während des Spiels** during the match [ˈdjʊərɪŋ] 2. **während wir spielten** while we were playing [waɪl]; as we were playing
▶ S. 175 German "während"
Wahrheit truth [truːθ]

wahrscheinlich probably [ˈprɒbəbli]
Währung currency [ˈkʌrənsi]
Wal whale [weɪl]
Wald forest [ˈfɒrɪst]
Walisisch; walisisch Welsh [welʃ]
Wand wall [wɔːl]
wann? when? [wen] **Wann hast du Geburtstag?** When's your birthday. **wann (auch) immer / egal, wann** whenever [ˌwenˈevə]
▶ S. 195 whenever, wherever, whatever, whoever
Waren (Güter) goods (pl) [ɡʊdz]
warm warm [wɔːm]
Warnung warning [ˈwɔːnɪŋ]
warten (auf) wait (for) [weɪt] **Warte einen Moment.** Wait a minute.
warum? why? [waɪ]
was what [wɒt] **Was gibt es zum Mittagessen?** What's for lunch? **Was haben wir als Hausaufgabe auf?** What's for homework? **Was hättest du gern? / Was möchtest du?** What would you like? **Was ist denn? / Was ist los?** What's the matter? / What's up? **Und was ist mit dir?** What about you? **was (auch) immer** whatever [wɒtˈevə] **was (sonst) noch?** what else?
▶ S. 195 whenever, wherever, whatever, whoever
▶ S. 195 … else
waschen wash [wɒʃ]
Wasser water [ˈwɔːtə]
Wasserfall waterfall [ˈwɔːtəfɔːl]
Website website [ˈwebsaɪt]
Wechselgeld change [tʃeɪndʒ]
wechseln (Geld) change [tʃeɪndʒ]
wecken: jn. wecken wake sb. up [ˌweɪkˈʌp]
weg away [əˈweɪ] **weg sein** (nicht mehr da sein) be gone [ɡɒn]
Weg way [weɪ]; (Pfad) path [pɑːθ]; trail [treɪl] **auf dem Weg zu/nach …** on the way to … **jm. den Weg (nach …) beschreiben** tell sb. the way (to …) **jn. nach dem Weg fragen** ask sb. the way
wegen: Es tut mir leid wegen … I'm sorry about …
weggehen leave [liːv]
wehtun hurt [hɜːt]
weich soft [sɒft]
Weide field [fiːld]
Weihnachten Christmas [ˈkrɪsməs] **1. Weihnachtstag** (25. Dezember) Christmas Day
weil because [bɪˈkɒz]
Weile: eine Weile (for) a while [waɪl]
weinen cry [kraɪ]
weise wise [waɪz]
Weise: auf diese Weise in this way
weiß white [waɪt]
Weißwandtafel whiteboard [ˈwaɪtbɔːd]
weit 1. (breit) wide [waɪd] 2. **weit (entfernt)** far [fɑː] **weiter** further [ˈfɜːðə] **am weitesten** furthest [ˈfɜːðɪst]

German – English

weiter 1. *geradeaus weiter* straight on [streɪt ˈɒn]
2. *etwas immer weiter tun* keep doing sth. [kiːp]
weiter-: weitergehen *(sich fortsetzen)* continue **weitergehen/-laufen/-segeln/…** walk/run/sail/… on **weitermachen** go on **weiterreden** go on
welche(r, s) 1. *Auf welcher Seite sind wir?* What page are we on? *Welche Farbe …?* What colour …?
2. *(aus einer begrenzten Anzahl)* which [wɪtʃ] *Welche Klubs …?* (= *Welche von diesen Klubs …?*) Which clubs …?
Welle wave [weɪv]
Welt world [wɜːld] *auf der Welt* in the world *Welt der Natur* natural world
Weltmeisterschaft World Cup [ˌwɜːld ˈkʌp]
wem? who? *Wem hast du es erzählt?* Who did you tell?
wen? who? *Wen kennt Sam?* Who does Sam know?
wenden 1. *(umkehren)* turn around [ˌtɜːn əˈraʊnd]
2. *sich an jn. wenden* turn to sb.
▶ S. 177 (to) turn
weniger (als) less (than) [les]
wenigstens at least [ət ˈliːst]
wenn 1. *(zeitlich)* when [wen]
2. *(falls)* if [ɪf] *selbst wenn* even if [ˈiːvn̩ ˌɪf]
wer? who? [huː] *Wer kennt Sam?* Who knows Sam? **wer (auch) immer** whoever [huːˈevə] **wer (sonst) noch?** who else?
▶ S. 195 whenever, wherever, whatever, whoever
▶ S. 195 … else
Werbespot advert [ˈædvɜːt]
Werbung *(Werbespot)* advert [ˈædvɜːt] *Werbung machen für etwas* promote sth. [prəˈməʊt]
werden become [bɪˈkʌm] *rot werden* go red / turn red **wütend/kalt werden** get angry/cold **hart/schlecht/verrückt werden** go hard/bad/mad
werfen throw [θrəʊ] **einen Blick auf etwas werfen** have a look (at sth.)
Werkstatt workshop [ˈwɜːkʃɒp]
wert worth [wɜːθ]
wessen? whose? [huːz]
Westen west [west] *nach Westen* west
westlich west [west]; western [ˈwestən]
Wettbewerb competition [ˌkɒmpəˈtɪʃn]; contest [ˈkɒntest]
Wetter weather [ˈweðə]
Wettkampf *(Match)* match [mætʃ]; *(Turnier)* trials *(pl)* [ˈtraɪəlz]
wichtig important [ɪmˈpɔːtnt] *etwas wichtig nehmen* care about sth. [keə] *Tiere sind mir sehr wichtig.* I really care about animals.
▶ S. 191 (to) care

wie 1. *(Fragewort)* how [haʊ] *Wie alt bist du?* How old are you? *Wie findest du …? / Wie gefällt dir …?* How do you like …? *Wie geht's? / Wie geht es dir/euch?* How are you? *Wie heißt du?* What's your name? *Wie ist sie (so)?* What's she like? *Wie spät ist es?* What time is it? *Wie viel kosten …?* How much are …? *Wie viel kostet …?* How much is …? *Wie war es?* What was it like? *Wie wäre es mit …?* What about …? *Wie dem auch sei, …* Anyway, … [ˈeniweɪ]
2. *wie Jungen* like boys [laɪk] *genau wie …* just like …
3. *der-/die-/dasselbe wie …* the same as … [æz], [əz] **(nicht) so groß wie** (not) as big as
4. *Wie John Lennon (einmal) sagte …* As John Lennon said …
wieder again [əˈgen] **immer wieder** again and again *etwas immer wieder tun* keep doing sth. [kiːp]
wiederholen 1. repeat [rɪˈpiːt]
2. *(Lernstoff)* revise [rɪˈvaɪz]
Wiederholung *(des Lernstoffs)* revision [rɪˈvɪʒn]
wiegen weigh [weɪ]
wild wild [waɪld]
willkommen: jn. willkommen heißen (in) welcome sb. (to) [ˈwelkəm] **Willkommen in Plymouth.** Welcome to Plymouth. [ˈwelkəm]
Wind wind [wɪnd]
windig windy [ˈwɪndi]
Winter winter [ˈwɪntə]
wir we [wiː]
wirklich really [ˈrɪəli]
Wirklichkeit: in Wirklichkeit *(eigentlich)* in fact [ɪn ˈfækt]
wischen *(Fußboden)* mop [mɒp]
Wischmopp mop [mɒp]
wissbegierig *(neugierig)* curious [ˈkjʊəriəs]
wissen know [nəʊ] *…, weißt du. / …, wissen Sie.* …, you know. [nəʊ]; …, you see. **über etwas Bescheid wissen** know about sth. **gern wissen wollen** wonder [ˈwʌndə] *Woher weißt du …?* How do you know …? *Weißt du was, Dad …* Guess what, Dad …
Witz joke [dʒəʊk]
witzig funny [ˈfʌni]
wo where [weə] **wo (auch) immer** wherever [weərˈevə]
▶ S. 195 whenever, wherever, whatever, whoever
Woche week [wiːk]
Wochenende weekend [ˌwiːkˈend] *am Wochenende* at the weekend
Wochentag day of the week
Woher kommst du? Where are you from? *Woher weißt/kennst du …?* How do you know …?
wohin? where? [weə]

wohlbekannt well-known [ˌwelˈnəʊn], [ˈwelˌnəʊn]
Wohlfahrtsorganisation charity [ˈtʃærəti]
Wohltätigkeit, wohltätige Zwecke charity [ˈtʃærəti]
wohnen *(leben)* live [lɪv]; *(vorübergehend)* stay [steɪ]
Wohnheim hostel [ˈhɒstl]
Wohnung flat [flæt]; apartment [əˈpɑːtmənt]
Wohnwagen caravan [ˈkærəvæn]
Wohnzimmer living room [ˈlɪvɪŋ ruːm]
Wolke cloud [klaʊd]
wollen: etwas haben wollen want sth. [wɒnt] **etwas tun wollen** want to do sth.
Workshop workshop [ˈwɜːkʃɒp]
Wort word [wɜːd]
Wortart part of speech [ˌpɑːt əv ˈspiːtʃ]
Wortstellung word order [ˈwɜːd ˌɔːdə]
Wovon handelt die Geschichte? What is the story about?
wund sore [sɔː]
wundervoll magical [ˈmædʒɪkl]
Wunsch wish [wɪʃ]
wünschen wish [wɪʃ] *Ich wünschte, ich wäre da.* I wish I was there. **sich etwas wünschen** make a wish
würde: Ich würde gern … I'd like to … **Ich würde sehr gern …** I'd love to …
Wurm worm [wɜːm]
wütend *(auf jn.)* angry (with sb.) [ˈæŋgri]

Y

Yoga yoga [ˈjəʊgə]

Z

Zahl number [ˈnʌmbə]; figure [ˈfɪgə]
zählen count [kaʊnt] **bis zehn zählen** count to ten
zauberhaft magical [ˈmædʒɪkl]
z.B. (zum Beispiel) e.g. [ˌiː ˈdʒiː] *(from Latin* exempli gratia*)*
Zahn tooth [tuːθ], *pl* teeth [tiːθ]
Zahnarzt/-ärztin dentist [ˈdentɪst]
Zahnschmerzen haben have a toothache [ˈtuːθeɪk]
Zauber- magic [ˈmædʒɪk]
Zaun fence [fens]
Zeh toe [təʊ] *jm. auf die Zehen treten (auch im übertragenen Sinne)* tread on sb.'s toes [tred] *(infml)*
zehn ten [ten]
Zeichen sign [saɪn]
Zeichensetzung punctuation [ˌpʌŋktʃuˈeɪʃn]
zeichnen draw [drɔː]
Zeichnung drawing [ˈdrɔːɪŋ]

Dictionary · English sounds

zeigen show [ʃəʊ] **auf etwas zeigen** point to sth. [pɔɪnt] **es zeigt, dass …** it shows that …
Zeile line [laɪn]
Zeit time [taɪm]; *(Tempus, grammatische Zeit)* tense [tens] **die ganze Zeit** all the time **eine Zeit lang** (for) a while **Zeit verbringen (mit)** spend time (on) [spend]
Zeitlupe slow motion [ˌsləʊ ˈməʊʃn]
Zeitschrift magazine [ˌmæɡəˈziːn]
Zeitung paper [ˈpeɪpə]
Zelt tent [tent]
zelten gehen go camping [ˈkæmpɪŋ]
Zeltplatz campsite [ˈkæmpsaɪt]
Zentrum centre [ˈsentə]
zerbrechen break [breɪk]
zerbrochen broken [ˈbrəʊkən]
zerstören destroy [dɪˈstrɔɪ]
Zeug *(Kram)* stuff [stʌf] *(infml)*
Ziege goat [ɡəʊt]
ziehen pull [pʊl]
ziemlich quite [kwaɪt]
Ziffer number [ˈnʌmbə]; figure [ˈfɪɡə]
Zimmer mit Frühstück bed & breakfast
Zimmerer/Zimmerin carpenter [ˈkɑːpəntə]
zischen hiss [hɪs]
Zoo zoo [zuː]
zu 1. *(örtlich)* to [tu], [tə] **auf den Bahnhof zu** towards the station [təˈwɔːdz] **auf Mr Bell zu** towards Mr Bell
2. **zu spät/kalt/groß/…** too late/cold/big/… [tuː]
3. **Es ist Zeit zu gehen.** It's time to go. **Nice to meet you.** Freut mich, dich/euch/Sie kennenzulernen.
zubereiten *(kochen)* cook [kʊk]
zudecken cover [ˈkʌvə]
zuerst first [fɜːst]; *(anfangs)* at first [ət ˈfɜːst]
Zug train [treɪn]
Zugabe encore [ˈɒŋkɔː]
zugehen: auf etwas zugehen head for sth. [hed]
zugreifen: Greif zu! *(Bedien dich!)* Help yourself.
Zuhause home [həʊm]
zuhören listen [ˈlɪsn] **Hör(t) mir zu.** Listen to me.
Zuhörer/in listener [ˈlɪsənə]
Zukunft future [ˈfjuːtʃə]
zukünftige(r, s) future [ˈfjuːtʃə]
zum Beispiel for example [fərˌɪɡˈzɑːmpl]
zulassen *(erlauben)* allow [əˈlaʊ]
zumachen close [kləʊz]
zumindest at least [ət ˈliːst]
Zunge tongue [tʌŋ]
Zungenbrecher tongue-twister [ˈtʌŋˌtwɪstə]
zurechtkommen get on [ˌɡet ˈɒn]
zurück back [bæk]
zurücklassen leave [liːv]
zusammen together [təˈɡeðə]
Zusammenhang *(Text-, Satzzusammenhang)* context [ˈkɒntekst]
zusammenpassen *(zueinander passen)* go together
Zuschauer/innen *(Publikum)* audience [ˈɔːdiəns]
zustande: etwas zustande bringen manage sth. [ˈmænɪdʒ]
zusteuern: auf etwas zusteuern head for sth. [hed]
zustimmen: jm. zustimmen agree with sb. [əˈɡriː]
Zutritt entry [ˈentri]
zuvor: besser als je zuvor better than ever
zuwenden: sich jm. zuwenden turn to sb. [ˈtɜːn]
zwei two [tuː]
zweimal twice [twaɪs]
zweisilbig two-syllable [ˈsɪləbl]
zweite(r, s) second [ˈsekənd] **auf dem zweiten Platz / an zweiter Stelle** in second place
zweitgrößte(r, s) second biggest
Zwillinge twins *(pl)* [twɪnz]
zwischen between [bɪˈtwiːn]
zwölf twelve [twelv]

English sounds

[iː]	gr**ee**n, h**e**, s**ea**
[i]	happ**y**, monk**ey**
[ɪ]	b**i**g, **i**n, **e**xpensive
[e]	r**e**d, y**e**s, **a**gain, br**ea**kfast
[æ]	c**a**t, **a**nimal, **a**pple, bl**a**ck
[ɑː]	cl**a**ss, **a**sk, c**a**r, p**a**rk
[ɒ]	s**o**ng, **o**n, d**o**g, wh**a**t
[ɔː]	d**oo**r, **o**r, b**a**ll, f**ou**r, m**o**rning
[uː]	bl**ue**, r**u**ler, t**oo**, t**w**o, y**ou**
[ʊ]	b**oo**k, g**oo**d, p**u**llover
[ʌ]	m**u**m, b**u**s, c**o**lour
[ɜː]	g**ir**l, **ear**ly, h**er**, w**or**k, T-sh**ir**t
[ə]	**a** partner, **a**gain, tod**a**y
[eɪ]	n**a**me, **eigh**t, pl**ay**, gr**ea**t
[aɪ]	t**i**me, r**igh**t, m**y**, **I**
[ɔɪ]	b**oy**, t**oi**let, n**oi**se
[əʊ]	**o**ld, n**o**, r**oa**d, y**e**ll**ow**
[aʊ]	t**ow**n, n**ow**, h**ou**se
[ɪə]	h**ere**, **yea**r, **i**dea
[eə]	wh**ere**, p**air**, sh**are**, th**eir**
[ʊə]	t**our**
[b]	**b**oat, ta**b**le, ver**b**
[p]	**p**ool, **p**aper, sho**p**
[d]	**d**ad, win**d**ow, goo**d**
[t]	**t**en, le**tt**er, a**t**
[ɡ]	**g**ood, a**g**ain, ba**g**
[k]	**c**at, **k**itchen, ba**ck**
[m]	**m**um, **m**an, re**m**ember
[n]	**n**o, o**n**e, te**n**
[ŋ]	so**ng**, you**ng**, u**n**cle, tha**n**ks
[l]	he**ll**o, **l**ike, o**l**d, sma**ll**
[r]	**r**ed, **r**uler, f**r**iend, so**rr**y
[w]	**w**e, **wh**ere, **o**ne
[j]	**y**ou, **y**es, **u**niform
[f]	**f**amily, a**f**ter, lau**gh**
[v]	ri**v**er, **v**ery, se**v**en, ha**v**e
[s]	**s**ister, po**s**ter, ye**s**
[z]	plea**s**e, **z**oo, qui**z**, hi**s**, mu**s**ic
[ʃ]	**sh**op, **s**tation, Engli**sh**
[ʒ]	televi**s**ion, u**s**ually
[tʃ]	tea**ch**er, **ch**ild, wa**tch**
[dʒ]	**G**ermany, **j**ob, pro**j**ect, oran**ge**
[θ]	**th**anks, **th**ree, ba**th**room
[ð]	**th**e, **th**is, fa**th**er, wi**th**
[h]	**h**ere, **wh**o, be**h**ind
[x]	lo**ch**

Am besten kannst du dir die Aussprache der einzelnen Lautzeichen einprägen, wenn du dir zu jedem Zeichen ein einfaches Wort merkst – das [iː] ist der **green**-Laut, das [eɪ] ist der **name**-Laut usw.

List of names

First names
(Vornamen)

Adam [ˈædəm]
Adrian [ˈeidriən]
Albert [ˈælbət]
Amelia [əˈmiːliə]
Angus [ˈæŋɡəs]
Ashling [ˈæʃlɪŋ]
Benandonner [ˌbenənˈdɒnə]
Beth [beθ]
Beyoncé [bɪˈjɒnseɪ]
Brian [ˈbraɪən]
Callum [ˈkæləm]
Cate [keɪt]
Charles [tʃɑːlz]
Charlie [ˈtʃɑːli]
Chloe [ˈkləʊi]
Clementine [ˈkleməntaɪn]
Dylan [ˈdɪlən]
Edward [ˈedwəd]
Emily [ˈeməli]
Finn [fɪn]
Frank [fræŋk]
Gareth [ˈɡærəθ]
Gemima [dʒəˈmeɪmə]
George [dʒɔːdʒ]
Giles [dʒaɪlz]
Gordon [ˈɡɔːdn]
Grace [ɡreɪs]
Gwen [ɡwen]
Hadrian [ˈheɪdriən]
Harry [ˈhæri]
Iain [ˈiːən]
Jack [dʒæk]
James [dʒeɪmz]
Jerry [ˈdʒeri]
Jimmy [ˈdʒɪmi]
John [dʒɒn]
Katie [ˈkeɪti]
Khan [kɑːn]
Knuckles [ˈnʌkəlz]
Lauren [ˈlɒrən]
Lewis [ˈluːɪs]
Luke [luːk]
Mary [ˈmeəri]
Maxine [mækˈsiːn]
Mishal [ˈmɪʃəl]
Mo [məʊ]
Morgan [ˈmɔːɡən]
Norman [ˈnɔːmən]
Oliver [ˈɒlɪvə]
Oonagh [ˈuːnə]
Paige [peɪdʒ]
Paul [pɔːl]
Philip [ˈfɪlɪp]
Ray [reɪ]
Ringo [ˈrɪŋɡəʊ]
Robert [ˈrɒbət]
Roger [ˈrɒdʒə]
Ronald [ˈrɒnəld]
Ross [rɒs]
Ruscaire [ˈrʌskərə]
Sandra [ˈsændrə], [ˈsɑːndrə]
Sandy [ˈsændi]
Sherlock [ˈʃɜːlɒk]
Skye [skaɪ]
Tom [tɒm]
Willy [ˈwɪli]

Family names / Surnames
(Familiennamen)

Abrams [ˈeibrəmz]
Baden-Powell [ˌbeɪdnˈpəʊəl]
Barnes [bɑːnz]
Bates [beɪts]
Beedle [ˈbiːdl]
Blanchett [ˈblɑːntʃət]
Bond [bɒnd]
Boyd [bɔɪd]
Carr [kɑː]
Clarke [klɑːk]
Dickens [ˈdɪkɪnz]
Edwards [ˈedwədz]
Evans [ˈevənz]
Ferguson [ˈfɜːɡəsən]
Foster [ˈfɒstə]
Fraser [ˈfreɪzə]
Grant [ɡrɑːnt]
Grimble [ˈɡrɪmbl]
Hammerstein [ˈhæməstaɪn]
Harrison [ˈhærɪsən]
Henri [ˈhenri]
Hill [hɪl]
Holmes [həʊmz]
Hunter [ˈhʌntə]
Jezzard [ˈdʒezɑːd]
Kirk [kɜːk]
Lennon [ˈlenən]
Macdonald [məkˈdɒnəld]
MacLeod [məˈklaʊd]
MacNeil [məkˈniːl]
McCartney [məˈkɑːtni]
McCool [məˈkuːl]
McCray [məˈkreɪ]
McGough [məˈɡɒf]
Nash [næʃ]
Nobel [nəʊˈbel]
Oscar [ˈɒskə]
Patten [ˈpætən]
Potter [ˈpɒtə]
Reid [riːd]
Rogers [ˈrɒdʒəz]
Ross [rɒs]
Scott [skɒt]
Seeger [ˈsiːɡə]
Skeefe [skiːf]
Smart [smɑːt]
Smith [smɪθ]
Starr [stɑː]
Twist [twɪst]

Place names
(Ortsnamen)

Bangor [ˈbæŋɡə]
Bannockburn [ˈbænəkbɜːn]
the Beat Museum [ˈbiːt]
Belfast [ˌbelˈfɑːst, ˈbelfɑːst]
Birkenhead [ˌbɜːkənˈhed]
Blackfriars [ˌblækˈfraɪəz]
Brandenburg [ˈbrændnbɜːɡ]
Buckingham Palace [ˌbʌkɪŋəm ˈpæləs]
the Burren [ˈbʌrən]
Caerdydd [kaɪəˈdiːð]
Caernarfon [kəˈnɑːvən]
Cardiff [ˈkɑːdɪf]
Carlingford [ˈkɑːlɪŋfəd]
Castlebay [ˌkɑːslˈbeɪ]
the Cavern Club [ˈkævən]
Chelsea [ˈtʃelsi]
Chinatown [ˈtʃaɪnətaʊn]
Dublin [ˈdʌblɪn]
Edinburgh [ˈedɪnbərə]
Euston [ˈjuːstən]
Everton [ˈevətən]
Fulham [ˈfʊləm]
Georgetown [ˈdʒɔːdʒtaʊn]
the Giant's Causeway [ˌdʒaɪənts ˈkɔːzweɪ]
Glasgow [ˈɡlɑːzɡəʊ]
Great Homer Street [ˌɡreɪt ˈhəʊmə striːt]
Hamburg [ˈhæmbɜːɡ]
Hammersmith [ˈhæməsmɪθ]
Hampstead Heath [ˌhæmpstɪd ˈhiːθ]
Hyde Park [ˌhaɪd ˈpɑːk]
Isle of Barra [ˌaɪl əv ˈbærə]
King's Cross [ˌkɪŋz ˈkrɒs]
Lambeth [ˈlæmbəθ]
Leeds [liːdz]
Liverpool [ˈlɪvəpuːl]
Loch Ness [ˌlɒx ˈnes]
London [ˈlʌndən]
Marble Arch [ˌmɑːbl ˈɑːtʃ]
Mathew Street [ˈmæθjuː]
Merseyside [ˈmɜːzisaɪd]
Moscow [ˈmɒskəʊ]
Notting Hill [ˌnɒtɪŋ ˈhɪl]
One New Change [ˌwʌn njuː ˈtʃeɪndʒ]
Oxford Street [ˈɒksfəd striːt]
Richmond [ˈrɪtʃmənd]
the River Clyde [klaɪd]
the River Mersey [ˈmɜːzi]
the River Thames [ˈtemz]
Russell Square [ˌrʌsl ˈskweə]
Saint Patrick's Cathedral [sənt ˌpætrɪks kəˈθiːdrəl]
Saint Paul's Cathedral [sənt ˌpɔːlz kəˈθiːdrəl]
the Shard [ʃɑːd]
Snowdon [ˈsnəʊdn]
Snowdonia [snəʊˈdəʊniə]
Southampton [ˌsaʊθˈhæmptən]
Temple Bar [ˌtempl ˈbɑː]
Urquhart Castle [ˈɜːkət]
Vauxhall [ˈvɒksɔːl]
the Watkin Path [ˈwɒtkɪn]
Wavertree [ˈweɪvətriː]
Westbourne Grove [ˌwestbɔːn ˈɡrəʊv]
Westminster [ˈwestmɪnstə]
Wimbledon [ˈwɪmbldən]

Other names

Bamana [bæˈmɑːnə]
Beatle [ˈbiːtl]
Big Ben [ˌbɪɡ ˈben]
djembe [ˈdʒembeɪ]
Doctor Who [ˌdɒktə ˈhuː]
Dracula [ˈdrækjʊlə]
Eisteddfod [əˈstedvɒd]
Google [ˈɡuːɡl]
Greaty [ˈɡreɪti]
Hobbit [ˈhɒbɪt]
Igbo [ˈiːbəʊ]
the Jubilee line [ˈdʒuːbəli]
leprechaun [ˈleprəkɔːn]
Ogoni [əʊˈɡəʊni]
Raven [ˈreɪvn]
the Rosetta Stone [rəʊˈzetə]
Shadow [ˈʃædəʊ]
the Titanic [taɪˈtænɪk]
udu [ˈuːduː]
UNESCO [juːˈneskəʊ]

Countries and continents

Country/Continent	Adjective	Person	People
*Marco is from **Italy**.*	*Pizza is **Italian**.*	*Marco is **an Italian**.*	***The Italians** invented pizza.*
Africa [ˈæfrɪkə] *Afrika*	African [ˈæfrɪkən]	an African	the Africans
Albania [ælˈbeɪniə] *Albanien*	Albanian [ælˈbeɪniən]	an Albanian	the Albanians
Asia [ˈeɪʒə, ˈeɪʃə] *Asien*	Asian [ˈeɪʃn, ˈeɪʒn]	an Asian	the Asians
Australia [ɒˈstreɪliə] *Australien*	Australian [ɒˈstreɪliən]	an Australian	the Australians
Austria [ˈɒstriə] *Österreich*	Austrian [ˈɒstriən]	an Austrian	the Austrians
Belarus [ˌbelˈruːs] *Weißrussland*	Belarusian [ˌbelˈruːsiən]	a Belarusian	the Belarusians
Belgium [ˈbeldʒəm] *Belgien*	Belgian [ˈbeldʒn]	a Belgian	the Belgians
Bosnia and Herzegovina [ˈbɒzniə ən ˌhɜːtsəgəˈviːnə] *Bosnien und Herzegowina*	Bosnian [ˈbɒzniən]; Herzegovinian [ˌhɜːtsəgəˈvɪniən]	a Bosnian; a Herzegovinian	the Bosnians; the Herzegovinians
Bulgaria [bʌlˈgeəriə] *Bulgarien*	Bulgarian [bʌlˈgeəriən]	a Bulgarian	the Bulgarians
China [ˈtʃaɪnə] *China*	Chinese [ˌtʃaɪˈniːz]	a Chinese	the Chinese
Croatia [krəʊˈeɪʃə] *Kroatien*	Croatian [krəʊˈeɪʃn]	a Croatian	the Croatians
Cyprus [ˈsaɪprəs] *Zypern*	Cypriot [ˈsɪpriət]	a Cypriot	the Cypriots
the **Czech Republic** [ˌtʃek rɪˈpʌblɪk] *Tschechien, die Tschechische Republik*	Czech [tʃek]	a Czech	the Czechs
Denmark [ˈdenmɑːk] *Dänemark*	Danish [ˈdeɪnɪʃ]	a Dane [deɪn]	the Danes
England [ˈɪŋglənd] *England*	English [ˈɪŋglɪʃ]	an Englishman / an Englishwoman	the English
Estonia [eˈstəʊniə] *Estland*	Estonian [eˈstəʊniən]	an Estonian	the Estonians
Europe [ˈjʊərəp] *Europa*	European [ˌjʊərəˈpiːən]	a European	the Europeans
Finland [ˈfɪnlənd] *Finnland*	Finnish [ˈfɪnɪʃ]	a Finn [fɪn]	the Finns
France [frɑːns] *Frankreich*	French [frentʃ]	a Frenchman / a Frenchwoman	the French
Germany [ˈdʒɜːməni] *Deutschland*	German [ˈdʒɜːmən]	a German	the Germans
(Great) Britain [ˈbrɪtn] *Großbritannien*	British [ˈbrɪtɪʃ]	a Briton [ˈbrɪtn]	the British
Greece [griːs] *Griechenland*	Greek [griːk]	a Greek	the Greeks
Greenland [ˈgriːnlənd]	Greenlandic [griːnˈlændɪk]	a Greenlander [ˈgriːnləndə]	the Greenlanders
Guyana [gaɪˈænə] *Guyana (früher: British Guyana)*	Guyanese [gaɪəˈniːz]	a Guyanese	the Guyanese
Hungary [ˈhʌŋgəri] *Ungarn*	Hungarian [hʌŋˈgeəriən]	a Hungarian	the Hungarians
Iceland [ˈaɪslənd] *Island*	Icelandic [aɪsˈlændɪk]	an Icelander [ˈaɪsləndə]	the Icelanders
India [ˈɪndiə] *Indien*	Indian [ˈɪndiən]	an Indian	the Indians
Ireland [ˈaɪələnd] *Irland*	Irish [ˈaɪrɪʃ]	an Irishman / an Irishwoman	the Irish
Italy [ˈɪtəli] *Italien*	Italian [ɪˈtæliən]	an Italian	the Italians
Kosovo [ˈkɒsəvəʊ] *Kosovo*	Kosovan [ˈkɒsəvən]	a Kosovan	the Kosovans

Countries and continents

Country/Continent	Adjective	Person	People
Marco is from Italy.	*Pizza is Italian.*	*Marco is an Italian.*	*The Italians invented pizza.*
Latvia [ˈlætvɪə] *Lettland*	Latvian [ˈlætvɪən]	a Latvian	the Latvians
Lithuania [ˌlɪθjuˈeɪnɪə] *Litauen*	Lithuanian [ˌlɪθjuˈeɪnɪən]	a Lithuanian	the Lithuanians
Luxembourg [ˈlʌksəmbɜːg] *Luxemburg*	Luxembourg	a Luxembourger [ˈlʌksəmbɜːgə]	the Luxembourgers
Macedonia [ˌmæsəˈdəʊnɪə] *Mazedonien*	Macedonian [ˌmæsəˈdəʊnɪən]	a Macedonian	the Macedonians
Malta [ˈmɔːltə] *Malta*	Maltese [mɔːlˈtiːz]	a Maltese	the Maltese
Moldova [mɒlˈdəʊvə] *Moldawien*	Moldovan [mɒlˈdəʊvən]	a Moldovan	the Moldovans
Montenegro [ˌmɒntɪˈniːgrəʊ] *Montenegro*	Montenegrin [ˌmɒntɪˈniːgrɪn]	a Montenegrin	the Montenegrins
the **Netherlands** [ˈneðələndz] *die Niederlande*	Dutch [dʌtʃ]	a Dutchman / a Dutchwoman	the Dutch
Nigeria [naɪˈdʒɪərɪə] *Nigeria*	Nigerian [naɪˈdʒɪərɪən]	a Nigerian	the Nigerians
North America [ˌnɔːθ_əˈmerɪkə] *Nordamerika*	North American [ˌnɔːθ_əˈmerɪkən]	a North American	the North Americans
Northern Ireland [ˌnɔːðən_ˈaɪələnd] *Nordirland*	Northern Irish [ˌnɔːðən_ˈaɪrɪʃ]	a Northern Irishman / a Northern Irishwoman	the Northern Irish
Norway [ˈnɔːweɪ] *Norwegen*	Norwegian [nɔːˈwiːdʒən]	a Norwegian	the Norwegians
Poland [ˈpəʊlənd] *Polen*	Polish [ˈpəʊlɪʃ]	a Pole [pəʊl]	the Poles
Portugal [ˈpɔːtʃʊgl] *Portugal*	Portuguese [ˌpɔːtʃuˈgiːz]	a Portuguese	the Portuguese
Romania [ruˈmeɪnɪə] *Rumänien*	Romanian [ruˈmeɪnɪən]	a Romanian	the Romanians
Russia [ˈrʌʃə] *Russland*	Russian [ˈrʌʃn]	a Russian	the Russians
Scotland [ˈskɒtlənd] *Schottland*	Scottish [ˈskɒtɪʃ]	a Scot [skɒt]; a Scotsman / a Scotswoman	the Scots, the Scottish
Serbia [ˈsɜːbɪə] *Serbien*	Serbian [ˈsɜːbɪən]	a Serbian	the Serbians
Slovakia [sləʊˈvækɪə] *die Slowakei*	Slovak [ˈsləʊvæk]	a Slovak	the Slovaks
Slovenia [sləʊˈviːnɪə] *Slowenien*	Slovenian [sləʊˈviːnɪən]	a Slovenian	the Slovenians
South America [ˌsaʊθ_əˈmerɪkə] *Südamerika*	South American [ˌsaʊθ_əˈmerɪkən]	a South American	the South Americans
Spain [speɪn] *Spanien*	Spanish [ˈspænɪʃ]	a Spaniard [ˈspænɪəd]	the Spanish
Sweden [ˈswiːdn] *Schweden*	Swedish [ˈswiːdɪʃ]	a Swede [swiːd]	the Swedes
Switzerland [ˈswɪtsələnd] *die Schweiz*	Swiss [swɪs]	a Swiss	the Swiss
Turkey [ˈtɜːki] *die Türkei*	Turkish [ˈtɜːkɪʃ]	a Turk [tɜːk]	the Turks
Ukraine [juːˈkreɪn] *die Ukraine*	Ukrainian [juːˈkreɪnɪən]	a Ukrainian	the Ukrainians
the **United Kingdom** [juːˌnaɪtɪd ˈkɪŋdəm] *das Vereinigte Königreich*	British [ˈbrɪtɪʃ]	a Briton [ˈbrɪtn]	the British
the **United States of America** [juːˌnaɪtɪd ˌsteɪts_əv_əˈmerɪkə] *die Vereinigten Staaten von Amerika*	American [əˈmerɪkən]	an American	the Americans
Wales [weɪlz] *Wales*	Welsh [welʃ]	a Welshman/-woman	the Welsh

Irregular verbs

infinitive	simple past	past participle	
(to) be	I/he/she/it **was**; you/we/you/they **were**	been	sein
(to) beat	beat	beaten	schlagen; besiegen
(to) become	became	become	werden
(to) begin	began	begun	beginnen, anfangen
(to) bend	bent	bent	sich bücken, sich beugen
(to) bite [aɪ]	bit [ɪ]	bitten [ɪ]	beißen
(to) blow sth. **out**	blew	blown	etwas auspusten, ausblasen
(to) break [eɪ]	broke	broken	brechen; zerbrechen
(to) bring	brought	brought	(mit-, her)bringen
(to) build	built	built	bauen
(to) burst into tears	burst	burst	in Tränen ausbrechen
(to) buy	bought	bought	kaufen
(to) catch	caught	caught	fangen
(to) choose [uː]	chose [əʊ]	chosen [əʊ]	aussuchen, (aus)wählen; sich aussuchen
(to) come	came	come	kommen
(to) cost	cost	cost	kosten
(to) cut	cut	cut	schneiden
(to) do	did	done [ʌ]	tun, machen
(to) draw	drew	drawn	zeichnen
(to) drive [aɪ]	drove [əʊ]	driven [ɪ]	(mit dem Auto) fahren
(to) drink	drank	drunk	trinken
(to) eat	ate [et, eɪt]	eaten	essen
(to) fall	fell	fallen	fallen, stürzen; hinfallen
(to) feed	fed	fed	füttern
(to) feel	felt	felt	fühlen; sich fühlen
(to) fight	fought	fought	(be)kämpfen
(to) find	found	found	finden
(to) fly	flew	flown	fliegen
(to) forget	forgot	forgotten	vergessen
(to) get	got	got	bekommen; holen, besorgen; werden; gelangen, (hin)kommen
(to) give	gave	given	geben
(to) go	went	gone [ɒ]	gehen
(to) grow	grew	grown	wachsen; anbauen, anpflanzen
(to) hang	hung	hung	hängen
(to) have	had	had	haben
(to) hear [ɪə]	heard [ɜː]	heard [ɜː]	hören
(to) hide [aɪ]	hid [ɪ]	hidden [ɪ]	verstecken; sich verstecken
(to) hit	hit	hit	schlagen
(to) hold	held	held	halten
(to) hurt	hurt	hurt	schmerzen, wehtun; verletzen
(to) keep	kept	kept	aufheben, aufsparen; aufbewahren
(to) kneel [niː]	knelt [nelt]	knelt [nelt]	knien
(to) know [nəʊ]	knew [njuː]	known [nəʊn]	wissen; kennen

Irregular verbs

infinitive	simple past	past participle	
(to) lead [iː]	led	led	führen, leiten
(to) leave [iː]	left	left	(weg)gehen; abfahren; (zurück)lassen; verlassen
(to) let	let	let	lassen
(to) lie	lay	lain	liegen
(to) light [aɪ]	lit [ɪ]	lit [ɪ]	anzünden
(to) lose [uː]	lost [ɒ]	lost [ɒ]	verlieren
(to) make	made	made	machen; herstellen
(to) mean [iː]	meant [e]	meant [e]	bedeuten; meinen
(to) meet [iː]	met [e]	met	treffen; sich treffen; kennenlernen
(to) pay	paid	paid	bezahlen
(to) put	put	put	(etwas wohin) tun, legen, stellen
(to) read [iː]	read [e]	read [e]	lesen
(to) ride [aɪ]	rode	ridden [ɪ]	reiten; (Rad) fahren
(to) ring	rang	rung	klingeln, läuten
(to) rise up [aɪ]	rose	risen [ɪ]	aufragen, emporragen
(to) run	ran	run	rennen, laufen
(to) say [eɪ]	said [e]	said [e]	sagen
(to) see	saw	seen	sehen
(to) sell	sold	sold	verkaufen
(to) send	sent	sent	schicken, senden
(to) shake	shook	shaken	schütteln
(to) shine	shone [ɒ]	shone [ɒ]	scheinen (Sonne)
(to) sing	sang	sung	singen
(to) sit	sat	sat	sitzen; sich setzen
(to) sleep	slept	slept	schlafen
(to) speak [iː]	spoke	spoken	sprechen
(to) spend	spent	spent	(Zeit) verbringen; (Geld) ausgeben
(to) spin around	spun	spun	sich (im Kreis) drehen; herumwirbeln
(to) spread [e]	spread [e]	spread [e]	ausbreiten, verbreiten; sich ausbreiten, verbreiten
(to) stand	stood	stood	setzen; sich (hin)stellen
(to) steal	stole	stolen	stehlen
(to) stick	stuck	stuck	stechen, stecken
(to) swim	swam	swum	schwimmen
(to) take	took	taken	nehmen, mitnehmen; (weg-, hin)bringen; dauern, (Zeit) brauchen
(to) teach	taught	taught	unterrichten, lehren
(to) tell	told	told	erzählen, berichten
(to) think	thought	thought	denken, glauben
(to) throw	threw	thrown	werfen
(to) tread [e]	trod	trodden	treten
(to) understand	understood	understood	verstehen
(to) wake up	woke up	woken up	aufwachen; (auf)wecken
(to) wear [eə]	wore [ɔː]	worn [ɔː]	tragen (Kleidung)
(to) win	won [ʌ]	won [ʌ]	gewinnen
(to) write	wrote	written	schreiben

True and false friends

True friends (Wahre Freunde)

Es gibt viele Wörter, die im Englischen und im Deutschen sehr ähnlich sind – das sind die „wahren Freunde". Manchmal gibt es allerdings Unterschiede in der Schreibung oder der Aussprache, die man beachten muss.

action [ˈækʃn] Aktion
activity [ækˈtɪvəti] Aktivität
address [əˈdres] Adresse
April [ˈeɪprəl] April
aquarium [əˈkweəriəm] Aquarium
arm [ɑːm] Arm
article [ˈɑːtɪkl] Artikel
August [ˈɔːɡəst] August
ball [bɔːl] Ball
band [bænd] Band, Musikgruppe
basketball [ˈbɑːskɪtbɔːl] Basketball
before [bɪˈfɔː] bevor
begin [bɪˈɡɪn] beginnen
blond [blɒnd] blond
bring [brɪŋ] bringen
burger [ˈbɜːɡə] Hamburger
bus [bʌs] Bus
café [ˈkæfeɪ] Café
camera [ˈkæmərə] Kamera
camping [ˈkæmpɪŋ] Camping, Zelten
clown [klaʊn] Clown
club [klʌb] Klub
cola [ˈkəʊlə] Cola
comedy [ˈkɒmədi] Comedyshow
comma [ˈkɒmə] Komma
computer [kəmˈpjuːtə] Computer
concert [ˈkɒnsət] Konzert
consonant [ˈkɒnsənənt] Konsonant
context [ˈkɒntekst] Kontext
cool [kuːl] cool
copy [ˈkɒpi] Kopie
cornflakes [ˈkɔːnfleɪks] Cornflakes
correct [kəˈrekt] korrekt
cost [kɒst] kosten
costume [ˈkɒstjuːm] Kostüm
cousin [ˈkʌzn] Cousin, Cousine

crash [kræʃ] crashen
cricket [ˈkrɪkɪt] Cricket
deck [dek] Deck (eines Schiffes)
demonstration [ˌdemənˈstreɪʃn] Demonstration
designer [dɪˈzaɪnə] Designer/in
dialogue [ˈdaɪəlɒɡ] Dialog
disco [ˈdɪskəʊ] Disko
doctor [ˈdɒktə] Doktor
DVD [diːviːˈdiː] DVD
elephant [ˈelɪfənt] Elefant
email [ˈiːmeɪl] E-Mail
end [end] Ende
fair [feə] fair, gerecht
fall [fɔːl] fallen
family [ˈfæməli] Familie
fan [fæn] Fan, Anhänger/in
farm [fɑːm] Farm, Bauernhof
film [fɪlm] Film
final [ˈfaɪnl] Finale
find [faɪnd] finden
fine [faɪn] fein
finger [ˈfɪŋɡə] Finger
fish [fɪʃ] Fisch
flag [flæɡ] Flagge
form [fɔːm] Form
garage [ˈɡærɑːʒ, ˈɡærɪdʒ] Garage
garden [ˈɡɑːdn] Garten
gel [dʒel] Gel
giraffe [dʒəˈrɑːf] Giraffe
glass [ɡlɑːs] Glas
go-kart [ˈɡəʊ kɑːt] Gokart
gold [ɡəʊld] Gold
gram [ɡræm] Gramm
grass [ɡrɑːs] Gras
guitar [ɡɪˈtɑː] Gitarre

gymnastics [dʒɪmˈnæstɪks] Gymnastik
hamburger [ˈhæmbɜːɡə] Hamburger
hamster [ˈhæmstə] Hamster
hand [hænd] Hand
hobby [ˈhɒbi] Hobby
hotel [həʊˈtel] Hotel
house [haʊs] Haus
instrument [ˈɪnstrəmənt] Instrument
interview [ˈɪntəvjuː] Interview
jeans [dʒiːnz] Jeans
job [dʒɒb] Job, Arbeitsstelle
judo [ˈdʒuːdəʊ] Judo
kilogram [ˈkɪləɡræm] Kilogramm
kilometre [ˈkɪləmiːtə] Kilometer
kung fu [ˌkʌŋ ˈfuː] Kung Fu
lamp [læmp] Lampe
land [lænd] Land
legend [ˈledʒənd] Legende
lip [lɪp] Lippe
list [lɪst] Liste
make-up [ˈmeɪk ʌp] Make-up
man [mæn] Mann
mediation [ˌmiːdiˈeɪʃn] Mediation
metre [ˈmiːtə] Meter
million [ˈmɪljən] Million
minute [ˈmɪnɪt] Minute
model [ˈmɒdl] Model
moment [ˈməʊmənt] Moment
monster [ˈmɒnstə] Monster
museum [mjuˈziːəm] Museum
music [ˈmjuːzɪk] Musik
musical [ˈmjuːzɪkl] Musical
name [neɪm] Name
object [ˈɒbdʒekt] Objekt
ocean [ˈəʊʃn] Ozean

True and false friends

online [ˌɒnˈlaɪn] online
orange [ˈɒrɪndʒ] orange
otter [ˈɒtə] Otter
parade [pəˈreɪd] Parade
park [pɑːk] Park
partner [ˈpɑːtnə] Partner/in
party [ˈpɑːti] Party
perfect [ˈpɜːfɪkt] perfekt
person [ˈpɜːsn] Person
photo [ˈfəʊtəʊ] Foto
picnic [ˈpɪknɪk] Picknick
pink [pɪŋk] pink, rosa
pizza [ˈpiːtsə] Pizza
plan [plæn] Plan
planet [ˈplænɪt] Planet
pony [ˈpəʊni] Pony
poster [ˈpəʊstə] Poster
prince [prɪns] Prinz
problem [ˈprɒbləm] Problem
programme [ˈprəʊɡræm] Programm
project [ˈprɒdʒekt] Projekt
quiz [kwɪz] Quiz, Ratespiel
radio [ˈreɪdiəʊ] Radio
rally [ˈræli] Rallye
religion [rɪˈlɪdʒən] Religion
ring [rɪŋ] Ring
rock (music) [rɒk] Rockmusik
roll [rəʊl] rollen

rucksack [ˈrʌksæk] Rucksack
ruin [ˈruːɪn] Ruine
samba [ˈsæmbə] Samba
sand [sænd] Sand
sandwich [ˈsænwɪtʃ] Sandwich
scene [siːn] Szene
second [ˈsekənd] Sekunde
set [set] Set, Satz
shorts [ʃɔːts] Shorts, kurze Hose
show [ʃəʊ] Show, Vorstellung
sing [sɪŋ] singen
snack [snæk] Snack, Imbiss
sofa [ˈsəʊfə] Sofa
solo [ˈsəʊləʊ] Solo-
song [sɒŋ] Lied, Song
sport [spɔːt] Sport
star [stɑː] (Film-, Pop-)Star
stop [stɒp] anhalten, stoppen
student [ˈstjuːdənt] Student/in
studio [ˈstjuːdiəʊ] Studio
subject [ˈsʌbdʒekt] Subjekt
symbol [ˈsɪmbl] Symbol
tea [tiː] Tee
team [tiːm] Team, Mannschaft
telephone [ˈtelɪfəʊn] Telefon
tennis [ˈtenɪs] Tennis
theatre [ˈθɪətə] Theater
theme [θiːm] Thema

thermometer [θəˈmɒmɪtə] Thermometer
title [ˈtaɪtl] Titel
toilet [ˈtɔɪlət] Toilette
tomato [təˈmɑːtəʊ] Tomate
top [tɒp] Top, Oberteil
tourist [ˈtʊərɪst] Tourist/in
tractor [ˈtræktə] Traktor
traditional [trəˈdɪʃənl] traditionell
train [treɪn] trainieren
trick [trɪk] Trick, Kunststück
T-shirt [ˈtiːʃɜːt] T-Shirt
tunnel [ˈtʌnl] Tunnel
uniform [ˈjuːnɪfɔːm] Uniform
vegetarian [ˌvedʒəˈteərɪən] Vegetarier/in
video [ˈvɪdiəʊ] Video
volleyball [ˈvɒlibɔːl] Volleyball
warm [wɔːm] warm
website [ˈwebsaɪt] Website
wild [waɪld] wild
wind [wɪnd] Wind
winter [ˈwɪntə] Winter
workshop [ˈwɜːkʃɒp] Workshop
yoga [ˈjəʊɡə] Yoga
yoghurt [ˈjɒɡət] Joghurt
zoo [zuː] Zoo

Some words look the same, but they don't mean the same.

The English word *become* means **werden**, not **bekommen**.

False friends (Falsche Freunde)

❗ Leider gibt es auch einige Wörter, die im Englischen und Deutschen ähnlich klingen oder aussehen, aber eine ganz andere Bedeutung haben.
Hier sind einige Beispiele für *false friends*:

English	German	German	English	English	German	German	English
also	= auch	also	= so; Well …	snake	= Schlange	Schnecke	= snail
become	= werden	bekommen	= get	stay	= bleiben	stehen	= stand
boot	= Stiefel	Boot	= boat	where	= wo	wer	= who
build	= bauen	bilden	= make, form	while	= während	weil	= because
chips	= Pommes frites	Kartoffelchips	= crisps				
fire	= Feuer	Feier	= celebration				
kind	= freundlich	Kind	= child				
handy	= praktisch	Handy	= mobile				
listen	= zuhören	Listen	= lists				
map	= Landkarte	Mappe	= folder				
mist	= Nebel	Mist *(Unsinn)*	= rubbish				

TIP
Wenn du nicht sicher bist, ob du *true friends* oder *false friends* vor dir hast, dann schau in einem guten Wörterbuch nach.

Early finisher – answers

Unit 1

a)

	1	2	3	4	5
1	B	E	G	**A**	N
2	C	H	O	**S**	E
3	**D**	R	O	V	E
4	**H**	E	A	R	D
5	T	H	**R**	E	W

BEGAN
CHOSE
DROVE
HEARD
THREW

Famous London building

SHARD

b)

	1	2	3	4	5
1	A	G	R	**E**	E	D
2	B	E	C	O	**M**	E
3	C	H	**O**	S	E	N
4	D	**R**	I	V	E	N
5	J	U	**M**	P	E	D
6	P	L	A	**Y**	E	D

AGREED
BECOME
CHOSEN
DRIVEN
JUMPED
PLAYED

Game

MEMORY

1 a) False. Our neighbours have been living here since 2011.
  b) True.
  c) False. Our neighbours have been living here for xx years.
     (In 2015 xx = 4 years. In 2016 xx = 5 years, etc.)

2 a) False. It's been raining for just under 7 hours.
  b) False. It's been raining since just after 8 o'clock.
  c) True.

3 a) True.
  b) False. Mrs Bell has been waiting since 10:05.
  c) False. Mrs Crown has been waiting for 20 minutes.

Unit 2

a) 1 scientist   2 furniture   3 rock
    4 school   5 fly   6 painter
    7 dentist   8 autumn   9 glove

b) a, I
   an, in
   air, all, ill, lip, paw, ran, win
   fair, fall, fill, pair, plan, rain, will, wall

2	the walk through the forest in hours
2	the time the students reached the summit
6	the time they arrived at the hostel
10	the time they started the walk
13	the walk in kilometres
24	the number of students in the class
59	the number of chocolate bars they ate
1,085	the climb to the summit in metres

two hundred and fifty

Early finisher – answers

Unit 3

1 Gareth thinks Morgan said: "Who is your favourite teacher?"
2 Gareth thinks Gwen said: "Where are we meeting the others?"
3 Gareth thinks Gwen said: "Do you live here?"
4 Gareth thinks Morgan said: "I'm thirty."
5 Gareth thinks Gwen said: "(Please) don't shout."

1 E post office
2 D short
3 B phone
4 F age
5 A egg
6 C bottle

Unit 4

a) coast   cliff
   currency   pound
   mayor   city
   navy   ship
   queen   crown
   president republic
   travel   passport

b) … it's important to be polite and friendly.

1 a) 1 point, b) 2 points, c) 3 points
2 a) 3 points, b) 1 point,   c) 1 point
3 a) 0 points, b) 2 points, c) 3 points / a) 0 points, b) 3 points, c) 0 points
4 a) 1 point, b) 3 points, c) 0 points / a) 3 points, b) 0 points, c) 1 point
5 a) 0 points, b) 3 points, c) 0 points
6 a) 0 points, b) 2 points, c) 3 points

How many points did you get?
20–24 points: You are a very polite person. Well done!
14–19 points: You are normally polite, but sometimes you forget.
less than 14 points: You should think before you speak. Don't forget to say 'please' and 'thank you'.
And smile!

a) 1 listen, 2 take, 3 do, 4 carry, 5 ride, 6 take, 7 tell, 8 wash
b) N, T, O, C, D, A, L, S = Scotland

1 in, 2 in, 3 in, 4 on, 5 on, 6 at, 7 on, 8 on, 9 on, 10 at, 11 in, 12 at, 13 at, 14 in, 15 on
Tina's birthday is on the 6th June.

Unit 5

1 see, 2 remember, 3 speak, 4 phone … text, 5 buy … presents

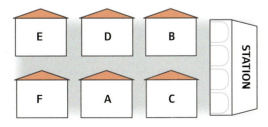

Classroom English

Zu Beginn und am Ende des Unterrichts

Guten Morgen, Frau …	Good morning, Mrs/Miss … *(bis 12 Uhr)*
Guten Tag, Herr …	Good afternoon, Mr … *(ab 12 Uhr)*
Entschuldigung, dass ich zu spät komme.	Sorry I'm late.
Auf Wiedersehen! / Bis morgen.	Goodbye. / See you tomorrow.

Du brauchst Hilfe

Können Sie/Kannst du mir bitte helfen?	Can you help me, please?
Auf welcher Seite sind wir, bitte?	What page are we on, please?
Was heißt … auf Englisch/Deutsch?	What's … in English/German?
Können Sie/Kannst du mir bitte … buchstabieren?	Can you spell …, please?
Können Sie es bitte an die Tafel schreiben?	Can you write it on the board, please?

Hausaufgaben und Übungen

Tut mir leid, ich habe mein Schulheft nicht dabei.	Sorry, I don't have my exercise book.
Kann ich bitte vorlesen?	Can I read, please?
Ich verstehe diese Übung nicht.	I don't understand this exercise.
Ich kann Nummer 3 nicht lösen.	I can't do number 3.
Entschuldigung, ich bin noch nicht fertig.	Sorry, I haven't finished.
Ich habe … Ist das auch richtig?	I have … Is that right too?
Tut mir leid, das weiß ich nicht.	Sorry, I don't know.
Was haben wir (als Hausaufgabe) auf?	What's for homework?

Wenn es Probleme gibt

Kann ich es auf Deutsch sagen?	Can I say it in German?
Können Sie/Kannst du bitte lauter sprechen?	Can you speak louder, please?
Können Sie/Kannst du das bitte noch einmal sagen?	Can you say that again, please?
Kann ich bitte das Fenster öffnen/zumachen?	Can I open/close the window, please?
Kann ich bitte zur Toilette gehen?	Can I go to the toilet, please?

Partnerarbeit

Kann ich mit Julian arbeiten?	Can I work with Julian?
Kann ich bitte dein Lineal/deinen Filzstift/… haben?	Can I have your ruler/felt tip/…, please?
Danke. / Vielen Dank.	Thank you. / Thanks a lot.
Du bist dran.	It's your turn.

Instructions

Diese Arbeitsanweisungen findest du häufig im Schülerbuch.

English	German
Act out the song.	Spiel das Lied vor.
Add more words to the table.	Füge weitere Wörter zur Tabelle hinzu.
Ask/Answer the questions.	Stelle/Beantworte die Fragen.
Check/Compare with a partner.	Prüfe/Vergleiche mit einem Partner/einer Partnerin.
Choose the correct/right words.	Wähle die richtigen Wörter.
Copy the words from the box.	Schreibe die Wörter aus dem Kästchen ab.
Correct the sentences.	Verbessere/Korrigiere die Sätze.
Find this information.	Finde/Suche diese Informationen.
Find out about cities in Britain.	Informiere dich über Großstädte in Großbritannien.
Finish/Complete the table below.	Vervollständige die Tabelle unten.
Get more words from page 44.	Hole zusätzliche Wörter von Seite 44.
Give reasons.	Gib Gründe an.
Give your text to another pair.	Gebt euren Text einem anderen Paar.
Go on with new ideas.	Mach weiter mit neuen Ideen.
Hang the poster up in your classroom.	Hänge das Poster im Klassenzimmer auf.
Hold up the card.	Halte die Karte hoch.
Imagine you're Silky.	Stell dir vor, du bist Silky.
Label your drawing.	Beschrifte deine Zeichnung.
Learn the rhyme.	Lerne den Reim/Vers auswendig.
Leave space for your answers.	Lass Platz für deine Antworten.
Listen to Morph.	Hör Morph zu.
Look at page 10.	Sieh auf Seite 10 nach. / Sieh dir Seite 10 an.
Look at the picture.	Schau dir das Bild an.
Look up the word if you don't understand it.	Schlag das Wort nach, wenn du es nicht verstehst.
Make appointments with three partners.	Verabrede dich mit drei Partnern/Partnerinnen.
Make groups of three.	Bildet Dreiergruppen.
Match the words to the pictures.	Ordne die Wörter den Bildern zu.
Practise the words.	Übe die Wörter.
Put all the verbs in the right place.	Setze alle Verben an der richtigen Stelle ein.
Put the card into your MyBook.	Lege die Karte in dein MyBook.
Put up your hand.	Melde dich.
Read the dialogue out loud to your group.	Lies deiner Gruppe den Dialog laut vor.
Rewrite the text.	Schreibe den Text neu.
Scan the text to find these words.	Überfliege den Text und versuche, diese Wörter zu finden.
Sing along with the chorus.	Sing den Refrain mit.
Start a profile for Sam.	Fang ein Profil für Sam an.
Swap cards with another team.	Tauscht Karten mit einem anderen Team.
Take turns.	Wechselt euch ab.
Talk to different partners about the photo.	Rede mit verschiedenen Partnern/Partnerinnen über das Foto.
Talk to your partner like this: …	Rede so mit deinem Partner/deiner Partnerin: …
Think of a sentence.	Denk dir einen Satz aus.
Use these words: …	Verwende diese Wörter: …
Walk around the classroom.	Geh im Klassenzimmer herum.
Write down the letters in the right order.	Schreibe die Buchstaben in der richtigen Reihenfolge auf.

Quellenverzeichnis

Titelbild
F1online digitale Bildagentur, Frankfurt/Main (The Shard (M); **mauritius images**, Mittenwald (Big Ben (M): ImageBROKER)

Illustrationen
Stefan Bachmann, Wiesbaden (S. 101; S 102); **Christian Bartz**, Berlin (S. 98; S. 99); **Roland Beier**, Berlin (S. 141; S. 142; S. 143; S. 144; S. 148; S. 149; S. 150; S. 157 unten li.; S. 158 Bild 1-3; S. 159 Bild 1-4; S. 168 Finn, Asif taking pictures, unten re. Bild 1-4; S. 173 oben; S. 174; S. 175; S. 177; S. 178; S. 179; S. 180; S. 181; S. 182; S. 183; S. 186; S. 187; S. 190; S. 192; S. 193; S. 194; S. 196); **Carlos Borrell**, Berlin (S. 8 oben United Kingdom inset (u. Hintergrund United Kingdom u. S. 4/5 u. 26/27); S. 8/9); S. 44 map; S. 64); S. 139; S. 140 oben u. unten); **Tobias Dahmen**, Utrecht/NL (S. 12; S. 19; S. 35; S. 36; S. 39; S. 43; S. 58 oben; S. 63; S. 68; S. 70; S. 75; S. 76; S. 81; S. 106-109; S. 112; S. 113; S. 114; S. 115; S. 116; S. 119; S. 123; S. 127; S. 130 oben; S. 154 unten; S. 155 unten; S. 157 oben, unten re.; S. 158 Morph; S. 159 Morph; S. 160 Morph; S. 161; S. 162 Morph; S. 163 Morph; S. 164; S. 165 Morph; S. 167; S. 168 unten li. Morph; S. 169 Morph; S. 248; S. 249); **Datavis Geografik**, **Thomas Klein**, Stegen (Umschlaginnenseite 2); **Jeongsook Lee**, Heidelberg (S. 110 unten; S. 111 Mitte Position of the Titanic; S. 172 unten); **M. B. Schulz** (S. 10 (M); S. 20 Pub (M); S. 24/25 (M); S. 30 (M); S. 34 (M); S. 41 (M); S. 56-57 Bild A-E (M); S. 60; S. 66 (M); S. 78 (M); S. 88 Bild 1-6 (M); S. 95 (M))

Bildquellen
A1PIX – YOUR PHOTO TODAY, Taufkirchen (S. 104 oben: YourPhotoToday/PM); **akg images**, Berlin (S. 111 Edward Smith: Universal Images Group; S. 132 (u. 135) Mona Lisa: IAM, Beethoven (u. 135): De Agostini Picture Lib.); **BBC** (S. 87 film stills); **Bridgeman Art Library**, Berlin (S. 67 Titanic: © BRIDGEMANART.COM; S. 134 unten: © BRIDGEMANART.COM; S. 111 oben: © BRIDGEMANART.COM/colour litho by Wong, Raymond; National Geographic Image Collection); **Clipdealer** (S. 33 Cardiff castle: Andres Rodriguez; S. 46 Bild 4 Liverpool Cathedral (M) (u. 132): ArTo; S. 80 yellow house: ArTo; S. 151: Robert Kneschke); **Colourbox.com** (S. 71 pot of gold); S. 110 oben ship, plane); **Corbis**, Düsseldorf (S. 6 oben li. (u. 66 (M)): Ric Ergenbright; S. 9 Bild B (u. 27): Rob Newell/ActionPlus, Bild C: Matt Gibson/LOOP IMAGES/Loop Images, Bild D: Rune Hellestad; S. 10 Hintergrund London (M): (c) Atlantide Phototravel; S. 14 unten re.: (c) English Heritage/Arcaid; S. 15 unten crown jewels: Jonathan Blair; S. 25 female dancer with eyes closed (M): Santino Pani/Demotix, group of dancers in the background (M): Olivia Harris/Reuters, S. 24/25 speactators: Eugenie Absalom/Demotix; S. 27 (u. 50): Bettmann; S. 30 workshop (M): (c) Jetta Productions/Blend Images; S. 46 Bild 1 Mathew Street (M): LOOP IMAGES; S. 47 Bild 3 Chinese Arch (M): (c) Atlantide Phototravel; S. 56/57 Hintergrund fans: RUSSELL CHEYNE/Reuters, S. 103: Robert Wallis; S. 111 unten: © The Mariners' Museum); **Cornelsen Schulverlage** (S. 22 film stills oben, Mitte, unten; S. 33 unten li. film still: Tellusvision; S. 70 Mitte; S. 85 unten; culture-images, Köln (S. 132 Tresure Island (u. 135) The digital file and its content are the property of **culture-images**/Lebrecht Music & Arts and protected by intellectual property); **Philip Devlin**, Berlin (S. 65 Bild H; S. 69 Dublin for kids poster stadium; S. 71 chocolate; S. 80 passports); **Dough Productions** (S. 73: Daniel Õ Hara) **dpa Picture-Alliance**, Frankfurt/Main (S. 9 Bild A: dpa; S. 13: dpa; S. 45 Käthe Kollwitz Schule (u. 62): dpa; S. 62 Werner-von-Siemens-Straße: dpa; S. 64 Bild D: C. Bämke/Ar; S. 80 girl looking at train schedule: dpa/Wolfgang Kumm; S. 86 Bannockburn celebration: empics; S. 91 unten: ZB); **F1online digitale Bildagentur**, Frankfurt/Main (S. 9 Bild E: RM Fotosearch; S. 33 Eisteddfod festival: Morris/AGE/F1online; S. 67 oben re.: Martin Siepmann; S. 105 oben: AGEFOTOSTOCK); **Fotolia** (S. 8 Bild F: zefart; S. 9 Bild M: metropolitana (copyright) cla' #1782447; S. 15 Mitte Tower of London: ian woolcock #55556662; S. 23 Bild 3: mohsinjamil #61003655; S. 55 re.: Claudio Divizia #49632794; S. 27 Bild 4 (u. 65): morrbyte; S. 67 map of Europe: Tanja Bagusat; S. 69 Irish writers brochure Oliver Goldsmith: Georgios Kollidas #55480724; S. 78 oben girls riding horses (M): aleksandrn #33490313; S. 80 timetable: drx #27961856; S. 83 Bild 4 sheep (M): Hugh Shaw; S. 84: Triple Jump; S. 85 oben: martin2014; S. 92 oben: lightpoet #67480800; S. 93 treasure chest (M): Cqinspiration); **Foundlight Productions** (S. 82 unten); **Stefanie Gira**, Berlin (S. 31 oben); **Glow Images**, München (S. 64 u. 65 Bild B oben Belfast, Dublin signs (M): Designpics; S. 64 Bild E: Irish Images Collection RM; S. 70 oben re.: Irish Images, S. 78 ruins (M): First Light; S. 80 ImageBROKER RM; S. 83 Bild 5: ImageBROKER RM; S. 85 Mitte bird: ScienceFaction; S. 104 Mitte: ImageZoo); **Stefan Höhne**, Berlin (S. 34 bottle (M)); **INTERFOTO**, München (S. 14 oben li.: Mary Evans/Natural History Museum, oben re.: Mary Evans/Natural History Museum; S. 48: Brown; S. 134: Mary Evans); **LAIF Agentur für Photos & Reportagen**, Köln (S. 9 Bild R: Gehard Westrich; S. 15 Bild C re. (M): Riachard Bowden/Loop Images; S. 23 Bild 5: Andrea Artz; S. 53 museum (M): MAISANT Ludovic/hemis.fr/laif; S. 57 Bild D stadium (M): Xavier DESMIER/RAPHO); **mauritius images**, Mittenwald (S. 4 Mitte li. (u. 28/29): Alamy/Alan Novelli, unten (u. 27 u. 44/45): Alamy/John Davidson Photos; S. 8 Bild I: Carlos Sánchez Pereyra; S. 9 Bild O: Alamy/Greg Balfour Evans, Bild P: United Archives; S. 15 unten li.: Alamy/Richard Green, unten re. signs: Alamy/Simon Montgomery; S. 23 Bild 1: Steve Vidler; S. 24 male dancer with red trousers and mask (M): Alamy/Renato Granieri; S. 27 Bild 3 (u. 65): Alamy/Rick Strange; S. 33 oben Mitte: Alamy/Jeff Morgan 01, oben re. signs: Alamy/Richard Naude; S. 41 oben sign (M): Alamy/Pat Shearman; S. 45 John Lennon Platz (u. 62), Martin-Gropius-Bau (u. 62): Josefine; S. 47 Bild 2 promenade (M) (PRÜFEN): Alamy/Bjanka Kadic, Bild 5 street (M): Alamy/Dave Ellison, Bild 6 bananas (M): Alamy/Jan Wlodarczyk, market (M): Alamy/Janine Wiedel Photolibrary; S. 51: Bildagentur Hamburg; S. 52 oben: © Sabena Jane Blackbird/Alamy; S. 54: Alamy/Sabena Jane Blackbird; S. 56 Bild A stadium (M): Alamy/Radharc Images;

Quellenverzeichnis

S. 64 Bild A: Alamy/Eye Ubiquitous; S. 65 Bild G: Alamy/Striking Images; S. 67 unten re.: Alamy/kp; S. 70 unten re.: Alamy/Kevin Foy; S. 71 museum: Alamy/Tim E White; S. 78 field (M): Alamy/Hon F. Lau; S. 80 Stadtinformation: Alamy/Premium Stock Photography GmbH, DJH logo: Steffen Beuthan; S. 82/83 tartan: Alamy/Victor Watts; S. 82 Bild 1 Fringe Festival (M): Alamy/Colin Woodbridge, Bild 2: Alamy/ROBIN MCKELVIE; S. 86 Urquhart Castle: Alamy/John McKenna, National Gallery: Alamy/malcolm sewell; S. 95 police officers (M): Alamy/ RTimages, path (M): Alamy/Peter Paterson; S. 96 Hintergrund field (M): Alamy/ simon evans; S. 104 unten: Alamy/ Rafael Ben-Ari; S. 105 unten: Alamy/Jeff Morgan 09; S. 132 Oliver Twist (u. 135): Alamy/DWD-Media; S. 136 oben: Alamy/VIEW Pictures Ltd) **Tony Morrissey** (S. 61 oben re.); **Nigel Wilson Photography**, Bristol (S. 4 Mo, Emily; S. 5 Dylan, Gwen, Morgan, Gareth; S. 6 Lewis (u. 70 u. 71 chat icon u. 74 chat icon); S. 7; S. 10 teenagers (M); S. 11 oben li. Mo; S. 20 people (M); S. 21; S. 24 girl running away (M); S. 30 girl, man (M); S. 34 boy, girl (M); S. 41 teenagers; S. 42; S. 46 teenagers looking at book, Bild 1 teenagers (M), Bild 4 teenagers (M); S. 47 Bild 2 teenagers (M), Bild 3 teenagers (M), Bild 5 teenagers (M), Bild 6 teenagers (M); S. 49 oben, unten; S. 53 teenagers (M); S. 56 Bild A, B, C teenagers (M); S. 57 Bild D, E teenagers (M); S. 64 boy (u. 124); S. 66 boy (M); S. 74 unten (u. 124); S. 78 teenagers (M); S. 82 oben li. Lewis and Skye (M); S. 83 Bild 4 Lauren (M); S. 88 Bild 1 boy (M), Bild 2 woman (2), Bild 3 boy and girl (M) Bild 4 woman and girl (M), Bild 5 boy and girl (M), Bild 6 boy and girl and woman (M); S. 90 Skye (u. 125), Sandra (u. 125); S. 94 girl (M); S. 95 girl li. (M); S. 96 girl (M); S. 117; S. 128); **Paramount Pictures Corp** (S. 11 London skyline: STAR TREK INTO DARKNESS © Paramount Pictures Corp. All Rights Reserved.); **Pathé** (S. 59 oben li., re., Mitte, unten: Stills and Footage from „There's Only One Jimmy Grimble" courtesy of Pathe); **Photoshot**, Hamburg (S. 23 Bild 4: Alpha-Jeff Spicer; S. 55 li.; S. 65 Bild C: Imagesbroker.net; S. 67 unten li.; S. 86 shop window); **Sapna Richter**, Berlin (S. 17 oben, unten; S. 37 oben li., re.; S. 39 two teenagers talking; S. 44 choir; S. 69 Bild 1, 2, 3, 4; S. 71 unten li. u. re.; S. 91 oben li., Mitte, re.; S. 92 unten; S. 93 folder (M); S. 97 Step 1 three teenagers talking; S. 150; S. 152; S. 153; Umschlaginnenseite 3); **Adam Roach**, Blaneau Gwent (S. 39 oben); **Shutterstock** (S. 4 oben li.: pisaphotography; S. 6 unten li.: Jane Rix; S. 8 Bild J: Bikeworldtravel; S. 9 Bild G: Monkey Business Images, Bild H: Kiev. Victor, Bild K: AdStock RF, Bild L: Cedric Weber, Bild N: Chris Jenner, Bild Q (u. 27): Peter Nadolski; S. 11 unten: DavidYoung; S. 14 unten li: lullabi; S. 15 Bild C li. London Eye (M): Anshar, unten raven: Anna Kucherova; S. 23 Bild 2: Nick Hawkes; S. 24 smiling female dancer behind male dancer (M): Gold Stock Images; S. 27 Bild 7: Joe Gough, Bild 8: chrisdorney; S. 33 oben li.: image4stock; S. 34 Vordergrund waterfall (M), Hintergrund waterfall (M): DJTaylor; S. 37 unten: Luminis; S. 52 Mitte: Bethan Collins, unten: Nikuwka; S. 58 umbrella: Tatiana Popova; S. 64 coins: Asaf Eliason; S. 65 coins: Claudio Divizia; S. 69 Dublin for kids brochure flag of Dublin: e X p o s e, Dublin at night: Bartkowski, Irish writers brochure Bernhard Shaw: Sergey Goryachev, William Yeates: Brendan Howard, Oscar Wilde statue: M Reel; S. 70 Chloe (u. 71 u. 74): BestPhotoPlus, Jack (u. 71): Aschindl; S. 71 Luke: Arina P Habich; S. 74 oben re.: frescomovie; S. 78 sky (M): S.Borisov; S. 80 money (M): Pelfophoto; S. 83 Bild 4 dog (M): Eric Isselee; S. 86 Cycle Arc Bridge: Targn Pleiades, street piper: Gyvafoto; S. 90 Mr. McCray (u. 125): ostill; S. 93 paper (M): DuH; S. 94 rock (M): Martin M303, dog (M): Mackland, bed (M): hxdbzxy; S. 95 beach (M): Spumador, S. 96 dog (M): Eric Isselee; S. 97 Step 4 li.: Anneka, Step 4 re.: Alexander Trinitatov; S. 132 (u. 135) Berlin Underground: PHOTOCREO Michal Bednarek, lift: Carsten Reisinger, Cologne Cathedral (u. 135): Taras Vyshnya, London Underground (u. 132): Stephen Bures, escalator (u. 135): Ekkachai; S. 133 oben: RAEVSKY; S. 136 Mitte re. boys playing basketball: Alexander Raths, unten li.: James Peragine, unten re.: Kenneth Sponsler; S. 137 oben: dotshock, unten: Kruglov_Orda; S. 172 oben (u. 173: Yulia Glam); S. 175: Anna Kucherova; S. 178: optimarc); **Transport for London** (S. 18 Tube map: used by permission of Pulse Creative Limited)

Textquellen

S. 32 u. S. 141 u. S. 142 Wörterbucheintrag, Schulwörterbuch English G 21, Cornelsen Verlag, Berlin 2011; S. 104 *When you are called names, remember, Mr Ifonly, The Panther's Heart* und. S. 105 *My Neighbour's Rabbit* taken from Brian Patten: „Juggling with gerbils". Puffin Books, London 2002; S. 112-115 The Off-side Trap by Mary Colson: in: „Scripts and Sketches". Heinemann Educational Publishers, Oxford 2001, S. 89 ff.

Liedquellen

S. 36 *If I had a hammer*. Text: Lee Hayes und Pete Seeger/Copyright by Ludlow Music, Inc. D/A/CH: Essex Musikvertrieb GmbH, Hamburg; S. 57 *You'll never walk alone*, Text: Oscar Hammerstein/WILLIAMSON-MUSIC-INC/Boosey & HawkeS. Bote & Bock, Berlin
S. 103 *Penny Lane*, Text: John Lennon, Paul McCartney/Sony-ATV Tunes LLC/Sony/ATV Music Publishing (Germany GmbH), Berlin

Giving feedback to your classmates

✓ Choose criteria[1] for your feedback.

✎ Add other criteria you need, e.g. for feedback on a story.

CONTENT

✓	You covered the important points in the task.
✓	The information was interesting/new.
✓	You gave examples/details.
✓	You gave your opinion.
✓	You gave arguments for your opinion.
✎	Your story had a plot.[2]
	You described the characters.
	…

STRUCTURE

✓	Your introduction said what the text is about.
✓	You used paragraphs.
✓	Each paragraph had a new idea.
✓	You had a conclusion.
✎	…

STRUCTURE

✓	You introduced the topic.
✓	Your presentation had a clear structure.
✓	You showed your main points on a poster/…
✓	You summed up at the end.
✓	You invited us to ask questions.
✎	…

LANGUAGE

✓	You used different adjectives and adverbs.
✓	You joined sentences with linking words.
✓	You used special vocabulary for the topic.
✓	Your spelling was correct.
✓	Your grammar was correct.
✎	…

COMMUNICATION

✓	You seemed relaxed.
✓	You made eye contact.
✓	You used notes.
✓	You spoke clearly.
✓	You explained your pictures.
✎	…

TIPS

1. Use the criteria you chose to assess[3] your classmate's work.

2. Give details when you say what a classmate did/didn't do well. Always start with something positive.

Where	What
In the first paragraph you	wrote a good introduction ….
At the end of your presentation you	didn't ask if we had questions /…

3. Suggest how the classmate could do better.
   You could try to use more linking words like **and** or **because** /use more pictures / …

---

[1] **criteria** (pl) [kraɪˈtɪərɪə] Kriterien   [2] **plot** [plɒt] Handlung   [3] (to) **assess** [əˈses] einschätzen